ALL ■ IN ■ ONE

PMP®

Project Management Professional

EXAM GUIDE

ABOUT THE AUTHOR

Joseph Phillips, PMP, PMI-ACP, ITIL, PSM, Project+, CTT+, is the Director of Education for Instructing.com, LLC. He has managed and consulted on projects for industries including technical, pharmaceutical, manufacturing, and architectural, among others. Joseph has served as a project management consultant for organizations creating project offices, maturity models, and best-practice standardization.

As a leader in adult education, Joseph has taught organizations how to successfully implement project management methodologies, adaptive project management, information technology project management, risk management, and other courses. He has taught at Columbia College, University of Chicago, and Ball State University, and for corporate clients such as IU Health, the State of Indiana, and Lawrence Berkeley National Laboratories. A Certified Technical Trainer, Joseph has taught more than 500,000 professionals and has contributed as an author or editor to more than 35 books on technology, careers, and project management.

Joseph is a member of the Project Management Institute (PMI) and is active in local project management chapters. He has spoken on project management, project management certifications, and project methodologies at numerous trade shows, PMI chapter meetings, and employee conferences in the United States and in Europe. When not writing, teaching, or consulting, Joseph can be found behind a camera or on the golf course. You can contact him through www.instructing.com.

About the Technical Editor

Karilena M. Harwitz, MS, PMP, PMI-ACP, holds 26 years of experience in the information technology (IT) industry. She began her career in IT consulting sales where she found that she could combine her love of working with people with her passion for learning, technology, and problem-solving. Karilena has held positions as a software developer, technical lead, project manager, program manager, and IT manager.

She has a bachelor of arts degree in anthropology and psychology from Indiana University and a master of science in educational psychology from Indiana University. She is currently pursuing her PhD in leadership studies at the University of the Cumberlands in Williamsburg, Kentucky.

In her spare time, Karilena volunteers her time to write grants to help support animal rescue organizations in south Atlanta. Most recently, she assisted two humane societies to win grants to help support spay/neuter programs. She is passionate about animal rescue. Karilena has a love of running and fitness. She has taught fitness classes, trained and participated in many running races, and led small fitness groups. She loves traveling and live music. Karilena lives with her husband, daughter, and three rescue dogs in Georgia.

ALL·IN·ONE

PMP®
Project Management Professional
EXAM GUIDE

Joseph Phillips

New York   Chicago   San Francisco
Athens   London   Madrid   Mexico City
Milan   New Delhi   Singapore   Sydney   Toronto

McGraw Hill books are available at special quantity discounts to use as premiums and sales promotions, or for use in corporate training programs. To contact a representative, please visit the Contact Us pages at www.mhprofessional.com.

PMP® Project Management Professional All-in-One Exam Guide

1 2 3 4 5 6 7 8 9   LCR   25 24 23 22 21

Library of Congress Control Number: 2021941849

ISBN: Book p/n 978-1-260-46745-1 and insert p/n 978-1-260-46746-8
of set 978-1-260-46747-5

MHID: Book p/n 1-260-46745-7 and insert p/n 1-260-46746-5
of set 1-260-46747-3

Sponsoring Editor	**Technical Editor**	**Production Supervisor**
Wendy Rinaldi	Karilena M. Harwitz	Thomas Somers
Editorial Supervisor	**Copy Editors**	**Composition**
Janet Walden	Kim Wimpsett and Lisa Theobald	KnowledgeWorks Global Ltd.
Project Editor	**Proofreader**	**Illustration**
Rachel Fogelberg	Tricia Lawrence	KnowledgeWorks Global Ltd.
Acquisitions Coordinator	**Indexer**	**Art Director, Cover**
Emily Walters	Ted Laux	Jeff Weeks

In memory of my father, Donald Phillips:
an example of hard work and entrepreneurship.
I miss him dearly.

CONTENTS AT A GLANCE

CONTENTS

Part IV   PMP Exam Considerations

ACKNOWLEDGMENTS

More than once, I've said that I'm the luckiest guy in the room. I get to write and talk for a living—what could be better than that? I'm so grateful for the opportunity to write, and I must thank the wonderful group of people at McGraw Hill Education for their belief in me to write yet another book on project management. Thank you to Wendy Rinaldi for all your help, great conversations, and guidance on this book and others. Thank you, Emily Walters, for your management and organization of this book—you are fantastic. Thank you to Rachel Fogelberg for your keen eye, attention to detail, and all your hours and help. Kim Wimpsett and Lisa Theobald, thank you both for helping me be a better writer. Thank you to production supervisor Tom Somers for your work on this book. Thanks also to the production teams at McGraw Hill and KnowledgeWorks Global Ltd. for your hard work in making this book a success.

Thank you to my lovely wife and best friend, Natalie. A big thank-you to my friends Greg and Mary Huebner, Brett and Julie Barnett, Don "Just Publish It Already" Kuhnle, Bill Tribble, Cathy Armbruster, Monica Morgan, and all my clients. If I wasn't writing, I was golfing thanks to my good friends Mark Kudlacik, Collin Kearns, Scott Jaffe and Levi Root. Finally, thanks to my parents, Don and Virginia Phillips, and my brothers, Steve, Mark, Sam, and Ben.

INTRODUCTION

This book is divided into five logical sections. Part I, which consists of Chapters 1–3, discusses the broad overview of project management and how it pertains to the Project Management Professional (PMP) exam. Part II contains Chapters 4–13, which details each of the ten knowledge areas your exam will focus on. The PMP exam will test your agile project management knowledge, so I've created Part III to isolate the agile concepts in Chapters 14–17. Agile and hybrid project management topics are roughly 50 percent on the PMP exam. Part IV of this book includes coverage of the PMP Code of Ethics and a final chapter of PMP prep. The last part of this book, Part V, contains two appendixes and a glossary. The first appendix covers the various types of project management documents. The second appendix provides information on how to access the digital resources I've created for you.

If you are just beginning your PMP quest, you should read the first section immediately, as it will help you build a strong foundation for your exam. If you already have a strong foundation in project management and need specific information on the knowledge areas, then move on to the second section. You'll find this section specific to the project management knowledge areas that will help you—gulp—pass the PMI examination.

The book is designed so that you can read the chapters in any order you like. However, I've written this book to follow a logical approach to project management beginning with the broadest concepts and ending with the new exam details focusing only on agile project management. It won't hurt you if you hop from topic to topic, but it might make more sense to read the book in the chronological order presented.

PMP Exam Objectives Map

PMI updated the PMP Exam Content Outline to focus on just three exam domains: People, Process, and Business Environment. Within these three domains you'll have tasks to do as a project manager. The domains and tasks do not reflect the same ordering as the *PMBOK Guide*, so don't expect a direct correlation; however, all the domains and tasks are covered in this book. In the following table, I've included all the tasks and the related chapter numbers for where you can find those tasks covered in this book. Be forewarned, most of these tasks are broad, so they'll likely touch on many different project management topics.

Domain I	People	42% 76 questions	Chapters
Task 1	**Manage conflict**		
	Interpret the source and stage of the conflict		10, 13, 15
	Analyze the context for the conflict		10, 13, 15
	Evaluate/recommend/reconcile the appropriate conflict resolution solution		10, 13, 15, 17
Task 2	**Lead a team**		
	Set a clear vision and mission		2, 3, 4, 10, 13, 14
	Support diversity and inclusion (e.g., behavior types, thought process)		9, 13, 15
	Value servant leadership (e.g., relate the tenets of servant leadership to the team)		14, 15
	Determine an appropriate leadership style (e.g., directive, collaborative)		3, 13, 15
	Inspire, motivate, and influence team members/stakeholders (e.g., team contract, social contract, reward system)		9, 14, 15
	Analyze team members and stakeholders' influence		9, 10, 14, 15, 16
	Distinguish various options to lead various team members and stakeholders		9, 10, 14, 15, 16
Task 3	**Support team performance**		
	Appraise team member performance against key performance indicators		7, 9, 14
	Support and recognize team member growth and development		9, 10, 14, 15, 18
	Determine appropriate feedback approach		10, 15
	Verify performance improvements		7, 8, 10, 16
Task 4	**Empower team members and stakeholders**		
	Organize around team strengths		9, 13
	Support team task accountability		9, 13, 16
	Evaluate demonstration of task accountability		9, 10, 16
	Determine and bestow level(s) of decision-making authority		4, 9, 10, 14, 16
Task 5	**Ensure team members/stakeholders are adequately trained**		
	Determine required competencies and elements of training		9, 11, 16
	Determine training options based on training needs		9, 11, 16

	Allocate resources for training	7, 9, 16
	Measure training outcomes	7, 9, 16
Task 6	**Build a team**	
	Appraise stakeholder skills	8, 9, 13, 17, 16
	Deduce project resource requirements	4, 5, 9, 14
	Continuously assess and refresh team skills to meet project needs	9, 14
	Maintain team and knowledge transfer	9, 15
Task 7	**Address and remove impediments, obstacles, and blockers for the team**	
	Determine critical impediments, obstacles, and blockers for the team	14, 16, 17
	Prioritize critical impediments, obstacles, and blockers for the team	14, 16, 17
	Use network to implement solutions to remove impediments, obstacles, and blockers for the team	9, 14, 15, 16, 17
	Re-assess continually to ensure impediments, obstacles, and blockers for the team are being addressed	9, 14, 15, 16, 17
Task 8	**Negotiate project agreements**	
	Analyze the bounds of the negotiations for agreement	12, 16
	Assess priorities and determine ultimate objective(s)	4, 5, 10, 14
	Verify objective(s) of the project agreement is met	4, 5, 10, 13, 15
	Participate in agreement negotiations	4, 5, 10, 13, 15
	Determine a negotiation strategy	4, 5, 10, 13, 15
Task 9	**Collaborate with stakeholders**	
	Evaluate engagement needs for stakeholders	9, 13, 15
	Optimize alignment between stakeholder needs, expectations, and project objectives	2, 13, 15
	Build trust and influence stakeholders to accomplish project objectives	10, 13, 15
Task 10	**Build shared understanding**	
	Break down situation to identify the root cause of a misunderstanding	10, 13, 15
	Survey all necessary parties to reach consensus	10, 13, 15
	Support outcome of parties' agreement	9, 10, 13, 15
	Investigate potential misunderstandings	9, 10, 13, 15

Task 11	**Engage and support virtual teams**	
	Examine virtual team member needs (e.g., environment, geography, culture, global, etc.)	2, 3, 9, 10, 13, 15
	Investigate alternatives (e.g., communication tools, colocation) for virtual team member engagement	2, 3, 9, 10, 13, 15
	Implement options for virtual team member engagement	13, 15
	Continually evaluate effectiveness of virtual team member engagement	13, 15
Task 12	**Define team ground rules**	
	Communicate organizational principles with team and external stakeholders	2, 3, 9, 10, 14, 15
	Establish an environment that fosters adherence to the ground rules	9, 14, 15
	Manage and rectify ground rule violations	9, 14, 10, 15
Task 13	**Mentor relevant stakeholders**	
	Allocate the time to mentoring	9, 14
	Recognize and act on mentoring opportunities	9, 14
Task 14	**Promote team performance through the application of emotional intelligence**	
	Assess behavior through the use of personality indicators	9, 10, 14
	Analyze personality indicators and adjust to the emotional needs of key project stakeholders	9, 10, 14
Domain II	**Process**	**50% 90 questions**
Task 1	**Execute project with the urgency required to deliver business value**	
	Assess opportunities to deliver value incrementally	8, 14
	Examine the business value throughout the project	4, 5, 7, 8, 14, 16
	Support the team to subdivide project tasks as necessary to find the minimum viable product	5, 8, 14
Task 2	**Manage communications**	
	Analyze communication needs of all stakeholders	9, 10
	Determine communication methods, channels, frequency, and level of detail for all stakeholders	9, 10

	Communicate project information and updates effectively	9, 10, 14
	Confirm communication is understood and feedback is received	9, 10, 14
Task 3	**Assess and manage risks**	
	Determine risk management options	11, 17
	Iteratively assess and prioritize risks	11, 17
Task 4	**Engage stakeholders**	
	Analyze stakeholders (e.g., power interest grid, influence, impact)	9, 15
	Categorize stakeholders	9, 15
	Engage stakeholders by category	9, 15
	Develop, execute, and validate a strategy for stakeholder engagement	9, 15
Task 5	**Plan and manage budget and resources**	
	Estimate budgetary needs based on the scope of the project and lessons learned from past projects	7, 14
	Anticipate future budget challenges	7, 14
	Monitor budget variations and work with governance process to adjust as necessary	7, 8, 14
	Plan and manage resources	7, 9, 14
Task 6	**Plan and manage schedule**	
	Estimate project tasks (milestones, dependencies, story points)	5, 14, 16
	Utilize benchmarks and historical data	5, 14, 16
	Prepare schedule based on methodology	5, 6, 14, 16
	Measure ongoing progress based on methodology	8, 14, 16
	Modify schedule, as needed, based on methodology	6, 14
	Coordinate with other projects and other operations	2, 3, 4, 5, 6, 14, 16, 17
Task 7	**Plan and manage quality of products/ deliverables**	
	Determine quality standard required for project deliverables	8, 16

	Recommend options for improvement based on quality gaps	4, 5, 8, 16
	Continually survey project deliverable quality	4, 8, 16
Task 8	**Plan and manage scope**	
	Determine and prioritize requirements	4, 5, 14, 16
	Break down scope (e.g., WBS, backlog)	5, 14
	Monitor and validate scope	5, 8, 14
Task 9	**Integrate project planning activities**	
	Consolidate the project/phase plans	3, 4, 14
	Assess consolidated project plans for dependencies, gaps, and continued business value	3, 4, 11, 14, 16, 17
	Analyze the data collected	3, 4, 11, 14, 16, 17
	Collect and analyze data to make informed project decisions	3, 4, 11, 14, 16, 17
	Determine critical information requirements	3, 4, 6, 7, 11, 14, 16, 17
Task 10	**Manage project changes**	
	Anticipate and embrace the need for change (e.g., follow change management practices)	4, 5, 6, 7, 11, 14, 17
	Determine strategy to handle change	4, 14
	Execute change management strategy according to the methodology	4, 5, 6, 7, 11, 14, 17
	Determine a change response to move the project forward	4, 5, 6, 7, 11, 14, 17
Task 11	**Plan and manage procurement**	
	Define resource requirements and needs	2, 3, 4, 5, 9, 12, 14
	Communicate resource requirements	9, 10, 14, 15
	Manage suppliers/contracts	4, 5, 6, 7, 11, 12, 14, 17
	Plan and manage procurement strategy	11
	Develop a delivery solution	3, 4, 5,14
Task 12	**Manage project artifacts**	
	Determine the requirements (what, when, where, who, etc.) for managing the project artifacts	2, 3, 4, 10, 14
	Validate that the project information is kept up to date (i.e., version control) and accessible to all stakeholders	2, 3, 4, 10, 14
	Continually assess the effectiveness of the management of the project artifacts	2, 3, 4, 10, 14

Task 13	**Determine appropriate project methodology/methods and practices**	
	Assess project needs, complexity, and magnitude	4, 5, 6, 7, 8, 11, 14, 16, 17
	Recommend project execution strategy (e.g., contracting, finance)	4, 7, 12, 14
	Recommend a project methodology/approach (i.e., predictive, agile, hybrid)	4, 10, 12, 17
	Use iterative, incremental practices throughout the project life cycle (e.g., lessons learned, stakeholder engagement, risk)	14, 15, 16, 17
Task 14	**Establish project governance structure**	
	Determine appropriate governance for a project (e.g., replicate organizational governance)	2, 3, 4, 14
	Define escalation paths and thresholds	4, 10, 11, 17
Task 15	**Manage project issues**	
	Recognize when a risk becomes an issue	11, 17
	Attack the issue with the optimal action to achieve project success	11, 17
	Collaborate with relevant stakeholders on the approach to resolve the issues	9, 10, 11, 16, 17
Task 16	**Ensure knowledge transfer for project continuity**	
	Discuss project responsibilities within team	4, 9, 10, 14, 15
	Outline expectations for working environment	4, 9, 10, 14, 15
	Confirm approach for knowledge transfers	4, 9, 10, 14, 15
Task 17	**Plan and manage project/phase closure or transitions**	
	Determine criteria to successfully close the project or phase	4, 14
	Validate readiness for transition (e.g., to operations team or next phase)	4, 10, 14
	Conclude activities to close out project or phase (e.g., final lessons learned, retrospective, procurement, financials, resources)	4, 10, 12, 14
Domain III	**Business environment**	**8% 14 questions**
Task 1	**Plan and manage project compliance**	
	Confirm project compliance requirements (e.g., security, health and safety, regulatory compliance)	2, 3, 4, 8, 11, 12, 14
	Classify compliance categories	5, 8, 14

PART I

Project Management Foundation

Preparing for the Exam

In this chapter, you will

- Learn to qualify for the PMP certification
- Learn PMP exam details
- Create a strategy to pass your project management certification exam
- Learn all about the *PMBOK Guide*, Sixth Edition
- Understand details on projects, project management, and operations
- Know how to be a successful project manager
- Work with programs and project management offices
- Qualify for your exam

This is a book on how to pass the Project Management Professional (PMP) exam.

If you're looking for a book on how to do project management, look elsewhere. If you're looking for a book on how projects—good projects—should operate, this book isn't for you. If you're looking for a primer on project management, move along. Plenty of excellent books are available that can help you reach those goals.

But if you're looking for a definitive book on how to pass the Project Management Professional certification examination, this is the book for you. It will clearly, quickly, and fully explain how to pass the certification exam the first time. And then you can get back to your life. After all, the exams aren't fun, and I'm certain you have more important things to do than spend more time than necessary to pass an exam.

 VIDEO For a more detailed explanation, watch the *Passing Your Project Management Certification Exam* video now.

The following describes what this book will do for you:

- Help you see the PMP exam objectives in detail.
- Enable you to watch me field various questions and subjects. Throughout this book, I'll reference videos that I've created to help with the more in-depth topics. Watch 'em and learn!

- Help you focus your efforts only on exam objectives.
- Tell you how to pass the PMP exam—not just take the exam.
- Offer you "roadmaps" for each chapter's content.
- Give you more than 900 practice questions (fun!).
- Make your life more exciting(!).

This first chapter covers many things that will help you prepare for and pass your PMP certification exam.

Not everyone can take the PMP exam—you must qualify first. I think this is great. We, and soon you, don't need the market flooded with the "paper certifications" that other industries have experienced. This certification is special—it proves that the certified professional has documented project management experience and education and has passed a tough, rigorous exam. If it were easy, everyone would do it.

 NOTE This book covers the PMP exam, which means you'll need to know about all the exam topics. You may have experience in a *predictive* environment, such as construction, while others may come from an *adaptive* environment, such as software development. You don't need to know anything about construction or software, but you'll need to know the principles of project management that may be applied in either discipline. The PMP Exam will challenge your knowledge of predictive, adaptive, and a mashup of the two approaches in a hybrid project environment. Don't worry; I'll guide you on all approaches to project management throughout this book. You can do this.

All About the PMP Exam

To become a PMP, you need the following (check out Figure 1-1; it's pretty):

- A bachelor's degree or the global equivalent, and 36 non-overlapping months of project management experience totaling 4,500 hours of project management activities within the last eight years.

  Or

- A high school diploma, associate degree, or the global equivalent, and 60 non-overlapping months of project management experience totaling 7,500 hours of project management tasks within the last eight years.
- Regardless of your degree, you will need 35 contact hours of project management education. (Ahem—I teach project management classes for companies around the world, including an exam boot camp that satisfies this requirement.

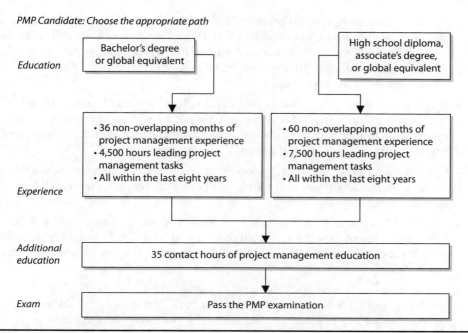

PMP Candidate: Choose the appropriate path

Figure 1-1   The PMP candidate must qualify to take the examination.

Check out the details on my web site, www.instructing.com.) Here are the PMI (Project Management Institute)-approved methods for accruing the project management education contact hours:

- University or college project management courses
- Courses offered by Authorized Training Partners
- Courses offered through your organization
- Distance learning education companies if they offer an end-of-course assessment
- Courses offered by training companies
- No, the PMI chapter meetings and self-study don't count (Darn! Just reading this book won't satisfy your project management education hours.)
- If you are a CAPM going for the PMP, the good news is that you won't need the 35 contact hours of training as part of your qualifications

- An extensive review of your application. Every application will pass through a review period. If your application needs an audit, you'll be notified via e-mail.

- An audit! Not every application is audited, but if your application is selected for an audit, you'll have to provide documentation of your experience and education, and verification of the projects you've worked on. It's fun, fun, fun. Oh, and the PMI can even audit you after you've "earned" your certification. (Yikes! Here's where honesty is the best policy.)

- Applicants must provide contact information on all projects listed on their PMP exam application. In the past, applicants did not have to provide project contact information unless their application was audited. Now each applicant has to provide project contact information as part of the exam process.

- Once the application has been approved, candidates have one year to pass the exam. If you procrastinate and wait a year before taking the exam, you'll have to start the process over.

- Be good. You will also agree to abide by the PMI Code of Ethics and Professional Conduct. You can get your very own copy through the PMI's web site: www.pmi .org. We'll cover this code in Chapter 18—something for you to look forward to (no peeking!).

- The PMI doesn't reveal what the actual passing score is for the PMP exam— you'll receive only a pass or fail score for the entire exam and a breakdown of your proficiency in each exam domain. The exam has 180 questions, five of which don't actually count toward your passing score. These five "seeded" questions are scattered throughout your exam and are used to collect stats on candidates' responses to see if these questions should be incorporated into future examinations. You won't know if you're answering a seeded question or a live question, so you have to answer all the exam questions with the same degree of focus and attention.

 CAUTION PMP candidates are limited to three exam attempts within one year. If you fail three times within one year, you'll have to wait one year after the third exam attempt before resubmitting your exam application again. Don't focus on this—focus on passing your exam the first time.

The PMP exam will test you on your experience and knowledge in three domains, as Table 1-1 shows. You'll have to provide specifics on tasks completed in each domain on your PMP examination application. Each domain task includes enablers; enablers are examples, not specific requirements, of how a project manager might accomplish the domain tasks. There's no need to memorize this stuff, but plan your study efforts accordingly. The following domain specifics and their related exam percentages are correct as of this writing. I strongly encourage you to double-check these specifics at www.pmi .org (look for the latest "Examination Content Outline" document). It's possible they've changed since this writing.

Domain I: People 42 percent of the exam 14 tasks	
Tasks	**Enablers**
Task 1: Manage conflict	Interpret the source and stage of the conflict Analyze the context for the conflict Evaluate/recommend/reconcile the appropriate conflict resolution solution
Task 2: Lead a team	Set a clear vision and mission Support diversity and inclusion (e.g., behavior types, thought process) Value servant leadership (e.g., relate the tenets of servant leadership to the team) Determine an appropriate leadership style (e.g., directive, collaborative) Inspire, motivate, and influence team members/stakeholders (e.g., team contract, social contract, reward system) Analyze team members and stakeholders' influence Distinguish various options to lead various team members and stakeholders
Task 3: Support team performance	Appraise team member performance against key performance indicators Support and recognize team member growth and development Determine appropriate feedback approach Verify performance improvements
Task 4: Empower team members and stakeholders	Organize around team strengths Support team task accountability Evaluate demonstration of task accountability Determine and bestow level(s) of decision-making authority
Task 5: Ensure team members/stakeholders are adequately trained	Determine required competencies and elements of training Determine training options based on training needs · Allocate resources for training Measure training outcomes
Task 6: Build a team	Appraise stakeholder skills Deduce project resource requirements Continuously assess and refresh team skills to meet project needs Maintain team and knowledge transfer
Task 7: Address and remove impediments, obstacles, and blockers for the team	Determine critical impediments, obstacles, and blockers for the team Prioritize critical impediments, obstacles, and blockers for the team Use network to implement solutions to remove impediments, obstacles, and blockers for the team Re-assess continually to ensure impediments, obstacles, and blockers for the team are being addressed

Table 1-1 Test Objectives for the PMP Examination

Domain I: People 42 percent of the exam 14 tasks	
Tasks	**Enablers**
Task 8: Negotiate project agreements	Analyze the bounds of the negotiations for agreement Assess priorities and determine ultimate objective(s) Verify objective(s) of the project agreement is met Participate in agreement negotiations Determine a negotiation strategy
Task 9: Collaborate with stakeholders	Evaluate engagement needs for stakeholders Optimize alignment between stakeholder needs, expectations, and project objectives Build trust and influence stakeholders to accomplish project objectives
Task 10: Build shared understanding	Break down situation to identify the root cause of a misunderstanding Survey all necessary parties to reach consensus Support outcome of parties' agreement Investigate potential misunderstandings
Task 11: Engage and support virtual teams	Examine virtual team member needs (e.g., environment, geography, culture, global, etc.) Investigate alternatives (e.g., communication tools, colocation) for virtual team member engagement Implement options for virtual team member engagement Continually evaluate effectiveness of virtual team member engagement
Task 12: Define team ground rules	Communicate organizational principles with team and external stakeholders Establish an environment that fosters adherence to the ground rules Manage and rectify ground rule violations
Task 13: Mentor relevant stakeholders	Allocate the time to mentoring Recognize and act on mentoring opportunities
Task 14: Promote team performance through the application of emotional intelligence	Assess behavior through the use of personality indicators Analyze personality indicators and adjust to the emotional needs of key project stakeholders
Domain II: Processes 50 percent of the exam 17 tasks	
Tasks	**Enablers**
Task 1: Execute project with the urgency required to deliver business value	Assess opportunities to deliver value incrementally Examine the business value throughout the project Support the team to subdivide project tasks as necessary to find the minimum viable product

Table 1-1   Test Objectives for the PMP Examination (*Continued*)

Domain II: Processes 50 percent of the exam 17 tasks	
Tasks	**Enablers**
Task 2: Manage communications	Analyze communication needs of all stakeholders Determine communication methods, channels, frequency, and level of detail for all stakeholders Communicate project information and updates effectively Confirm communication is understood and feedback is received
Task 3: Assess and manage risks	Determine risk management options Iteratively assess and prioritize risks
Task 4: Engage stakeholders	Analyze stakeholders (e.g., power interest grid, influence, impact) Categorize stakeholders Engage stakeholders by category Develop, execute, and validate a strategy for stakeholder engagement
Task 5: Plan and manage budget and resources	Estimate budgetary needs based on the scope of the project and lessons learned from past projects Anticipate future budget challenges Monitor budget variations and work with governance process to adjust as necessary Plan and manage resources
Task 6: Plan and manage schedule	Estimate project tasks (milestones, dependencies, story points) Utilize benchmarks and historical data Prepare schedule based on methodology Measure ongoing progress based on methodology Modify schedule, as needed, based on methodology Coordinate with other projects and other operations
Task 7: Plan and manage quality of products/deliverables	Determine quality standard required for project deliverables Recommend options for improvement based on quality gaps Continually survey project deliverable quality
Task 8: Plan and manage scope	Determine and prioritize requirements Break down scope (e.g., WBS, backlog) Monitor and validate scope
Task 9: Integrate project planning activities	Consolidate the project/phase plans Assess consolidated project plans for dependencies, gaps, and continued business value Analyze the data collected Collect and analyze data to make informed project decisions Determine critical information requirements
Task 10: Manage project changes	Anticipate and embrace the need for change (e.g., follow change management practices) Determine strategy to handle change Execute change management strategy according to the methodology Determine a change response to move the project forward

Table 1-1   Test Objectives for the PMP Examination (*Continued*)

Domain II: Processes	
50 percent of the exam	
17 tasks	
Tasks	**Enablers**
Task 11: Plan and manage procurement	Define resource requirements and needs Communicate resource requirements Manage suppliers/contracts Plan and manage procurement strategy Develop a delivery solution
Task 12: Manage project artifacts	Determine the requirements (what, when, where, who, etc.) for managing the project artifacts Validate that the project information is kept up to date (i.e., version control) and accessible to all stakeholders Continually assess the effectiveness of the management of the project artifacts
Task 13: Determine appropriate project methodology/methods and practices	Assess project needs, complexity, and magnitude Recommend project execution strategy (e.g., contracting, finance) Recommend a project methodology/approach (i.e., predictive, agile, hybrid) Use iterative, incremental practices throughout the project life cycle (e.g., lessons learned, stakeholder engagement, risk)
Task 14: Establish project governance structure	Determine appropriate governance for a project (e.g., replicate organizational governance) Define escalation paths and thresholds
Task 15: Manage project issues	Recognize when a risk becomes an issue Attack the issue with the optimal action to achieve project success Collaborate with relevant stakeholders on the approach to resolve the issues
Task 16: Ensure knowledge transfer for project continuity	Discuss project responsibilities within team Outline expectations for working environment Confirm approach for knowledge transfers
Task 17: Plan and manage project/phase closure or transitions	Determine criteria to successfully close the project or phase Validate readiness for transition (e.g., to operations team or next phase) Conclude activities to close out project or phase (e.g., final lessons learned, retrospective, procurement, financials, resources)

Table 1-1 Test Objectives for the PMP Examination (*Continued*)

Domain III: Business Environment 8 percent of the exam 4 tasks	
Tasks	**Enablers**
Task 1: Plan and manage project compliance	Confirm project compliance requirements (e.g., security, health and safety, regulatory compliance) Classify compliance categories Determine potential threats to compliance Use methods to support compliance Analyze the consequences of noncompliance Determine necessary approach and action to address compliance needs (e.g., risk, legal) Measure the extent to which the project is in compliance
Task 2: Evaluate and deliver project benefits and value	Investigate that benefits are identified Document agreement on ownership for ongoing benefit realization Verify measurement system is in place to track benefits Evaluate delivery options to demonstrate value Appraise stakeholders of value gain progress
Task 3: Evaluate and address external business environment changes for impact on scope	Survey changes to external business environment (e.g., regulations, technology, geopolitical, market) Assess and prioritize impact on project scope/backlog based on changes in external business environment Recommend options for scope/backlog changes (e.g., schedule, cost changes) Continually review external business environment for impacts on project scope/backlog
Task 4: Support organizational change	Assess organizational culture Evaluate impact of organizational change to project and determine required actions Evaluate impact of the project to the organization and determine required actions

Table 1-1   Test Objectives for the PMP Examination (*Continued*)

Money and Your Exam

This exam isn't free, and you don't want to waste your hard-earned cash by failing. Focus on passing the exam on your first shot. But just in case some of your colleagues ask, I've included the retake fees. You can, and should, confirm the costs I've listed here with the PMI through their web site. They've changed fees in the past, and you don't want your exam fees to dig into your beer and pizza cash:

- Join the PMI: $119 (join the PMI first because it lowers your exam fee by a few bucks; if you join your local PMI chapter, as you should, there will be an additional chapter fee, usually around $25)
- PMP exam for a PMI member: $405
- PMP exam for a non-PMI member: $555

- PMP re-exam for a PMI member: $275
- PMP re-exam for a non-PMI member: $375

 EXAM TIP If you join PMI you get an electronic copy of the *PMBOK Guide* as part of your membership.

Passing the Exam

Let's face the facts: This isn't much fun. Learning is hard work. The PMI's book, *A Guide to the Project Management Body of Knowledge*, Sixth Edition (which I'll just call the *PMBOK Guide* from now on, thank you), reads like the literary equivalent of a sleeping pill. PMI reports that the PMBOK Guide is just one of several books used as reference for the PMP exam questions. You don't want this process to last any longer than necessary, and your goal should be—it better be—to pass your certification exam on your first attempt. So don't simply think of "taking the exam." Instead, focus on "passing your exam," so you can get back to your real life.

Just as your projects have plans, you need a plan for how to study, how to prepare, and then how to pass the exam. You can relax on this part—I've done most of the work for you.

 EXAM COACH I'm not knocking the *PMBOK Guide*—really! It's a fine reference book and it's what your PMI exam is partly based on. The book is written, edited, and reviewed by hundreds of volunteer project managers. These are good people who've invested their time and experience into the book. Thank you to them for their hard work and contribution to the project management community. Having said that, know that it's a tough book to read. Use it as a reference point for your exam prep.

Creating Your Study Strategy

I'll be your study buddy. You need a realistic timeline and a realistic expectation for studying to pass your exam. You can create whatever strategy you like, but here's my recommended approach to passing your exam. This book has 19 chapters and two appendixes. Chapter 18 deals with the PMI's Code of Ethics and Professional Conduct. Chapter 19 is a detailed walkthrough of all the exam tasks and enablers—a bit of a cram session. Appendix A explains every project management document mentioned directly in the *PMBOK Guide*. The Glossary is a glossary—all the terms I use in this book (yeah, all of them).

 DIGITAL CONTENT Throughout this book, you'll see an icon that looks like this one. It means that you should download the digital content or use your e-reader and watch a video of me discussing the key concepts for that chapter.

Sometimes I'll include more than one video per chapter, depending on the topic. I recommend that you watch the chapter video before moving on to the next chapter. The videos are usually short, and I'm providing some good stuff. These are packed with information, I promise. I've also included for you a free, one-hour class on Agile as part of this book. Seriously. If you're new to Agile, complete this class as part of your exam prep: www.instructing.com/agileclass.

At the end of each chapter are key terms. Get a stack of index cards and make flashcards of the key terms. It's not that tricky to make yourself a set of flashcards: write the term on one side of the index card in big, fat letters. On the other side of the card, write the definition. The idea is that you'll "flash" through these every day as you plow through this beast of a book—it'll help you keep the early chapters fresh in your mind as you happily move toward the end of this fine piece of literature. Look at the name of the term and define the term aloud; flip the card over and make certain you're correct.

At the end of each chapter, you'll also find 20 practice exam questions. These questions test your comprehension of the chapter. I've written these questions to be as tough as what you'll likely encounter on the live exam. My logic is that if you can answer my questions, you can answer the PMI's questions, too. In the digital content, you'll find a Microsoft Excel spreadsheet titled "Exam Scores"—you can see an example of it in Figure 1-2. Enter your chapter scores in the spreadsheet, and you can track which chapters you need more work in and focus your study time accordingly.

 DIGITAL CONTENT For a more detailed explanation, check out the "Exam Scores" spreadsheet to track how you are performing on a chapter-by-chapter basis.

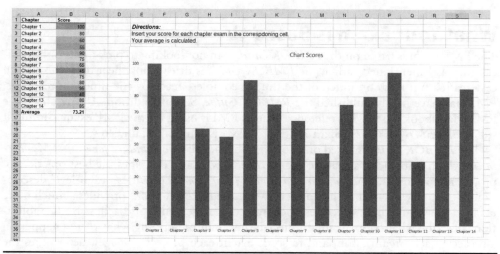

Figure 1-2 You can track your chapter scores to focus your studying accordingly.

The Total Tester Premium test engine that comes with this book contains 360 total PMP practice exam questions. You can customize your practice exams by domain or by chapter, and you can even select how many questions you want included in each exam and how much time you have to complete it. Check out Appendix B for more information about how the Total Tester Premium test engine works.

- **PMP Practice Exam Questions**   There are 360 practice exam questions in this pool that emulate those you'll find on the actual PMP exam. If you choose to take a PMP practice exam, it will pull 180 questions from the pool, weighted with the same balance you'll find on the actual PMP exam, and you'll have four hours to complete it.

I recommend you complete these exams after you've completed reading and taking the end-of-chapter exams in this book. Keep taking each exam over and over until you can answer every question correctly. (I'm assuming that you won't get 100 percent on the first attempt on this exam. My apologies if you do.) I love to say in my PMP Boot Camp that repetition is the mother of learning. Repetition is the mother of learning. I've outlined quick references for how you should study and then pass your exam. You may be slightly ahead of other readers in your exam preparations, so I've intentionally left dates and timelines to your discretion. I think a couple of chapters a week is realistic—but I wouldn't do more than five chapters a week. Take some time and create a schedule of when you'll study, and then take measures to make certain you can keep the schedule you create.

Table 1-2 provides a sample strategy that you can modify as you see fit. Many people have told me that they read a chapter in my book and then a chapter from the *PMBOK Guide*, which is a fine strategy. Your schedule may take more or less time—this is just a sample strategy.

What Your Exam Is Based On

The PMP exam is based on the *PMBOK Guide*. I'm not looking to pick fights or be critical, but, as I mentioned earlier, the *PMBOK Guide* is drier than wheat toast. It's not an easy read, a fun read, or, much of the time, a complete read. By the time you read this, PMI may have finally published the *PMBOK Guide*, Seventh Edition. Always check the PMP Handbook to see what reference sources PMI is using for the PMP exam—it might still be the *PMBOK Guide,* Sixth Edition… PMI is sometimes, uh, slow.

The *PMBOK Guide* is based on another publication: *The Standard for Project Management*, which is included as part of the *PMBOK Guide* and describes the best practices of project management. *The Standard for Project Management* provides a high-level description of the processes utilized in a project, while the *PMBOK Guide* provides a much more detailed view into these processes and project management approaches. Both publications describe what happens in a project rather than prescribing what *should* happen in a project. Each organization, and to some extent each project manager, determines the most appropriate processes and approach for the given project scenario.

Day	Chapter	Activities
Day 1	1	Complete chapter exam. Create and review flashcards.
Day 2	2	Complete chapter exam. Create and review flashcards.
Day 3	3	Complete chapter exam. Create and review flashcards.
Day 4		Review first three chapter exams. Memorize flashcards.
Day 5		Watch chapter videos again. Review flashcards.
Day 6	4	Complete chapter exam. Create and review flashcards.
Day 7	5	Complete chapter exam. Create and review flashcards.
Day 8	6	Complete chapter exam. Create and review flashcards.
Day 9		Review Chapters 4, 5, and 6. Review chapter exams to date. Review flashcards. Watch videos from Chapters 4, 5, and 6.
Day 10	7	Complete chapter exam. Create and review flashcards.
Day 11		Review chapter exams to date. Review flashcards. Watch videos from Chapter 7. Practice formulas from Chapters 6 and 7.
Day 12	8	Complete chapter exam. Create and review flashcards.
Day 13	9	Complete chapter exam. Create and review flashcards.
Day 14	10	Complete chapter exam. Create and review flashcards.
Day 15		Review chapter exams to date. Review flashcards. Watch videos from Chapters 8, 9, and 10.
Day 16	11	Complete chapter exam. Create and review flashcards.
Day 17	12	Complete chapter exam. Create and review flashcards.
Day 18	13	Complete chapter exam. Create and review flashcards. Watch videos from Chapters 11, 12, and 13.

Table 1-2   A Sample Study Strategy

Day	Chapter	Activities
Day 19	14	Complete chapter exam. Create and review flashcards.
Day 20	15	Complete chapter exam. Create and review flashcards.
Day 21	16	Complete chapter exam. Create and review flashcards.
Day 22	17	Complete chapter exam. Create and review flashcards.
Day 23	18	Compile agile flashcards from Chapters 14, 15, 16, and 17 Watch agile videos from Chapters 14, 15, 16, and 17
Day 24	19	Complete Chapter 18 and Chapter 19.
Day 25		Buzz through all the exam objectives and confirm your complete understanding. Review the appropriate objectives where needed.
Day 26		Complete a PMP Practice Exam. Keep taking PMP Practice Exams until you get a perfect score.
Day 27		Review key terms. Watch chapter videos.
Day 28	Appendix A	Confirm familiarity with project management documents.
Day 29		Confirm knowledge of key project management topics. Review flashcards.
Day 30		Review flashcards. Review chapter exams.
Day 31		Pass project management exam. Gloat to peers. Send e-mail to cs@instructing.com with comments on this book and how it helped you pass your exam.

Table 1-2   A Sample Study Strategy (*Continued*)

The *PMBOK Guide* doesn't aim to define all of the avenues of project management in great detail. Rather, it tries to provide a general overview of the good practices of project management. The *PMBOK Guide* defines the generally accepted project management practices that are most widely utilized. The funny thing about the *PMBOK Guide* is that it's not the project management body of knowledge; it's a *guide* to the project management body of knowledge. Everything you need to know about project management isn't in that book—but most of the things are. You'll need experience and other sources of exam preparation (like this book), along with constant effort to pass the PMP exam.

Another PMI tome to be familiar with is the Agile Practice Guide, since approximately half of the PMP exam will be agile or hybrid questions. The Agile Practice Guide paints the big picture of agile projects, recommendations for implementing agile projects, and organizational considerations for agile. I'll dive into these topics throughout this book—and into greater details in the last few chapters. It's an interesting thing that PMI is doing with the PMP and agile projects, considering they have a certification, the PMI-Agile Certified Practitioner, dedicated solely to agile topics.

One of my favorite lines from the *PMBOK Guide* is, "Good practice does not mean that the knowledge described should always be applied uniformly on all projects." I love this quote, because it's a fancy way of saying, "Calm down. You don't have to do every freaking process, activity, and system within this book—just determine the processes that are best for your project and then do them correctly."

EXAM TIP   Your exam will quiz you on all of the processes, systems, and documents identified by the *PMBOK Guide*, because although all of these characteristics are appropriate for projects, they are probably not appropriate for every project you'll manage.

When you join the PMI, you'll get an electronic version of the *PMBOK Guide* as part of your membership, or you can plunk down a few bucks at your favorite bookstore (or through the PMI's web site) and get a printed version of the book today. I recommend you have a copy of the *PMBOK Guide* for several reasons:

- Your exam is largely based on the *PMBOK Guide*. As much as I'd like for your exam to be based on just my writings, it isn't. You should always reference that book along with the one you're reading now.

- This book is based on the *PMBOK Guide*. Okay, I gave myself an out in the preceding paragraph, but, truthfully, I've worked very hard for my book to be in sync with the *PMBOK Guide* and the exam objectives. I'll occasionally reference the *PMBOK Guide* as we move through the chapters, but you can always double-check my facts, questions, and figures with the *PMBOK Guide* if you really want to.

- The *PMBOK Guide*, as dry as it may be, is an excellent book to have in your project management arsenal. It defines processes, systems, and documents that you'll likely encounter in your project management endeavors.

- Having a copy of the *PMBOK Guide* on your desk strikes fear and awe into your uncertified colleagues. Well, maybe just the ones from Petoskey, Michigan.

EXAM COACH   Throughout this book, I'll pop into my coaching mode. Like right now. Do you really need to read the *PMBOK Guide* to pass the exam? That's a tough question and I get it a bunch. For some people, no, they don't need to. For others, yes, they do. I've made a genuine effort to write for the exam objectives so you can study this book instead of the *PMBOK Guide*. I do believe, however, that you should have a copy of the *PMBOK Guide* as a handy reference for your exam prep. The *PMBOK Guide* is not an easy or fun read, but it can help support your exam efforts.

What Is a Project?

You're a project manager, so you've probably got a good idea of what a project is already. I'm hoping. The *PMBOK Guide* defines a project as "a temporary endeavor undertaken to create a unique product, service, or result." Projects, like good stories, have a definite beginning and a definite ending. A project is over when the product, service, or result is created; the scope is fulfilled; and the customer has accepted the end result. Or, in not-so-pleasant times, it's over when it becomes evident that the project won't be able to create the desired product, service, or result for whatever reason (skills, cost, time, and so on).

Projects can be launched, managed, and executed by an organization, by a collection of organizations, or even by a single person. A project to update your company's computer software, for example, could be launched and managed through the IT department. Or this project could be initiated by the sales department, managed by a project manager in the IT department, and led to completion by a group of people from a vendor, the IT department, and the sales department on the project team. There are so many different combinations of people, organizations, contractors, and vendors that can contribute to a project—and that contributes both to the challenges and opportunities of project management.

Temping a Project

Some project managers get hung up on the idea of a project being temporary. After all, some projects can last for years or decades—but they don't last forever. Projects are *temporary* in that they have a definite ending sometime in the future. Projects—at least, most projects—create something that will last for some time, usually longer than the project team or longer than the time it took to complete the project itself. Consider a project to build a house, create a park, or develop a software application—these deliverables will be utilized for some time. In other words, the project ends, but the benefits and deliverables of the project continue.

Notice that I said that project deliverables usually last longer than the project itself. For some special projects, this isn't true—such as for a project to host a trade show, an event, or a fantastic party. Once the event is over, the project is also over.

"Temporary" can also refer to the market window status. Remember the Internet dot-com boom? It was definitely temporary. I'm sure in your business you can identify examples of market windows that were temporary. Project teams are also examples of temporary structures: the team comes together, does the work of the project, and then, once the project is over, so is the project team.

Defining a Project's Uniqueness

Ready for a horrible joke? How do you catch a unique rabbit? Unique up on him. (As in, "You sneak up on him." My son loved this joke when he was eight—not so much anymore.) The point of the joke, in the context of project management, is that a project should be unique from the rest of your organization's operations. Consider the creation of a new car. The designing, drafting, modeling, and the process of creating a new car could be a project. The manufacturing of the automobile, however, typically isn't a project—that's operations. Here are a few unique things that a project can create:

- Products such as software
- Products that are components for other projects, such as the blueprints for a new warehouse
- A new service that will be integrated into your organization's functions, such as a help desk or an Internet application
- A feasibility study, research and development outcomes, or trend analysis

Changing the Organization

Projects are really about changing the organization by achieving a measurable outcome. From a business perspective, projects are initiated to move the organization from its current state to the desired future state. Think of a project to create new software; the current state is missing the benefits the app will bring, and the future state has the app in production, and it benefits the organization. Projects drive change by undertaking the work to achieve the specific goals of the project. If you achieve the goals of the project, specifically the scope of the project, then the goal becomes a reality for the organization and the business will achieve the desired future state.

Creating Business Value

When a project takes place in a business organization, one of the primary goals is to achieve a return on the investment of money, time, and energy for the project. Business value is a quantifiable return on that investment. Yes, it may be a financial benefit, but it can also be time, goods created, or even intangible benefits such as brand recognition. Basically, business value from a project describes the specific positive returns on the project's work.

Tangible benefits include the following:

- Money
- Stockholder equity
- Equipment
- Fixtures
- Market share

Intangible benefits include the following:

- Brand recognition
- Goodwill from clients and the public
- Trademarks
- Reputation

Progressively Elaborating a Project

Progressive elaboration is a process that all projects move through. The project manager and the project team start very broadly—typically with a project's concepts—and then the concepts are refined with details, studies, and discussion until a project *scope statement* is formed. The scope statement may pass through additional steps to continue to refine the project's objectives. Completing an entire project is an example of progressive elaboration: you begin with a concept, plan the project, do the work, and close the project with a completed deliverable.

Did you ever read any of the Sherlock Holmes stories? Holmes would create a very broad theory of the mystery's solution and then, through a scientific approach and deductive reasoning, narrow his theory more and more until he finally solved the case. He started very broad and then narrowed his hypothesis. This is one example of progressive elaboration (although Sir Arthur Conan Doyle never called it that). Basically, progressive elaboration means that you start with a very broad concept, and then, through steady progressions, you gather more detail to clarify the concept your project centers on. Figure 1-3 shows a simple example of progressive elaboration with a project to create a new home.

Why Do Projects?

Projects are typically endeavors that aren't part of an organization's normal operations. Basically, projects are chunks of work that need to be completed, but the work doesn't necessarily fit into any predefined function of an organization, such as accounting or sales.

Projects can also be managed by external organizations that complete projects for other organizations. Consider an IT consulting company that swoops into company after company to install and configure new networks, servers, or computer software. Or consider an architectural firm that designs buildings for other companies. Or think of practically any service-based business, and you'll find a performing organization that completes projects for other entities.

Figure 1-3
Progressive
elaboration
means
progressing
through steady,
incremental
steps.

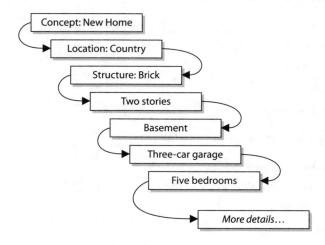

Organizations that treat practically every undertaking as a project are likely participating in management by projects. This means they operate by relying heavily on project management principles to complete their work. This isn't unusual in consulting agencies, construction firms, or IT shops—they exist through management by projects.

Projects are most likely undertaken for any of the following reasons:

- **Opportunity**   The market demand may call for a project to create a new product, service, or solution.

- **Organizational needs**   I bet you can identify some needs within your company that would make dandy projects: upgrading computers, training your staff, changing the menu in the company cafeteria. Usually, organizational needs focus on reducing costs or increasing revenue, and sometimes both (bonus!).

- **Customer needs**   Your customer wants you to create something that they need. Sometimes these requests develop into projects. Stakeholders can request that the project be initiated to achieve a goal.

- **Technology**   Technology seems to change and advance daily, and this often spurs new projects to keep up with or ahead of competitors. Know any IT gurus out there managing technical projects?

- **Legal requirements**   Laws and regulations can give rise to new projects. Publicly traded companies have been required to secure their IT data in compliance with the Sarbanes-Oxley Act. Healthcare organizations must adhere to HIPAA (Health Insurance Portability and Accountability Act of 1996) requirements. And U.S. companies have been working with Occupational Safety and Health Administration (OSHA) requirements for years and years. Initial conformance to these requirements often creates new projects. And, for our friends working in Europe, you'll need to address the General Data Protection Regulation (GDPR).

Creating Project Management Business Documents

You should be familiar with two important business documents: the project business case and the project benefits management plan.

Project Business Case

The project business case is created and maintained by the project sponsor and shows the financial validity of chartering and launching the project within the organization. Typically, the project business case is created before the launch of the project and may be used as a go/no-go decision point. The project business case defines the following:

- Why the project is needed
- What the project will accomplish
- High-level scope description
- Stakeholders affected by the project

- Root cause of the problem or opportunity
- Known risks the project will likely encounter
- Critical success factors the project must achieve

The project business case may also use criteria categories for different objectives the project aims to accomplish. Common criteria categories are required, desired, and optional. Each goal of the project would be tagged as either a required goal, a desired goal, or an optional goal to determine tradeoffs, return on investment, and risk and reward. These goals will ultimately be pared down to include what the project should and should not accomplish. This paring down of what the project should, or should not, accomplish can be grouped into three options:

- **Do nothing**   Don't do the project; it's not worth the risk, investment, or outcome.
- **Do the minimum**   Initiate a project that will do only the minimum work and incur the minimum cost and risk exposure to address the problem or opportunity.
- **Do more than the minimum**   Initiate a project that will fully address the minimum requirements and go beyond the minimum requirements for the problem or opportunity with an expectation of a better reward for the investment and risks.

Based on the project business case, the goals of the project are established; the project business case clearly defines why the project is being created and what the expected return on investment for the project will be. At the end of the project, the project business case will be compared to the actual results of the project to determine how successful the project was in relation to what the project aimed to accomplish.

Project Benefits Management Plan

The project benefits management plan is created and maintained by the project sponsor and the project manager. This plan defines what benefits the project will create, when the benefits will be realized, and how the benefits will be measured. The plan typically includes these elements:

- **Target benefits**   The benefits the project aims to achieve
- **Strategic alignments**   How the benefits the project creates support the business strategies
- **Timeframe**   When the benefits will be available; some projects may have intermittent benefits as opposed to all benefits being realized only at the conclusion of the project
- **Benefits owner**   An individual who will monitor, track, and measure the benefits of the project

- **Metrics**   How the benefits will be measured
- **Assumptions**   Things believed about the project and benefits that can affect the benefits realization if the assumptions prove otherwise than what is believed
- **Risks**   Uncertain conditions that can affect the realization of the benefits

The maintenance of the benefits management plan is an ongoing activity throughout the project's life cycle.

What Is Project Management?

You know what projects are, so what's project management? I can hear you sighing and saying, "It's just the management of a project." And I'd concur, but your exam will likely need a more robust definition. The *PMBOK Guide* defines "project management" as "the application of knowledge, skills, tools, and techniques to project activities to meet project requirements."

Managing a project centers on four things:

- Identifying your project's requirements
- Establishing clearly defined project objectives
- Managing project stakeholders by adapting your plans and approaches to keep those folks happy and the project moving along
- Keeping scope, schedule, costs, risk, resources, and quality all in balance

This last point really defines the Iron Triangle of Project Management. Sometimes this is also called the Triple Constraints of Project Management. Figure 1-4 demonstrates the Iron Triangle's concept: All three sides must remain in balance, or the project's quality or other facets will suffer. It's not rocket science. If your scope is enormous but your budget and/or schedule is puny, your project will likely suffer or even fail. Chapters 5, 6, and 7 in this book (and in the *PMBOK Guide*) focus on these three constraints of scope, time, and cost, so you'll see the Iron Triangle at least three more times.

Figure 1-4
The Iron Triangle of Project Management comprises scope, time, and cost.

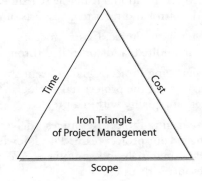

Time

Cost

Iron Triangle
of Project Management

Scope

Project management aims to accomplish the project objectives. Projects that are not well-planned or that do not operate within a defined framework will suffer from missed deadlines, cost overages, poor quality in the project and the project deliverables, rework, frustration among the project team and stakeholders, and a host of other problems. It's the complete management of the project that's needed to ensure project success. Complete chaos isn't typical in most projects, but most projects experience success in some areas and failure in others.

Back to the *PMBOK Guide*

I follow the *PMBOK Guide* section-by-section throughout this book. Of course, I expound on the *PMBOK Guide* just a bit—I hope you like it. You won't be tested on my explanations specifically, but they can be helpful to know as you organize your thoughts and study strategy. So here's the scoop on the *PMBOK Guide* contents and how this book treats them:

- Chapter 1, "Preparing for the Exam," sets the tone and paints the big picture of what the *PMBOK Guide* can do for you. It's breezy and gets you moving into the book.

- Chapter 2, "Managing a Project in a Different Environment," discusses the environment where projects happen. The project life cycle describes the phases a project moves through from start to completion.

- Chapter 3, "Working as a Project Manager," discusses the complete role of the project manager and how the project manager leads and manages the project team and stakeholders. It's a meaty chapter.

- Chapter 4, "Managing Project Integration," defines how each knowledge area is affected by the control and outcome of the other knowledge areas. Project integration management provides the gears of project management.

- Chapter 5, "Managing Project Scope," defines how a project manager should create, monitor, control, and complete the project scope.

- Chapter 6, "Managing Project Schedule," defines how the project manager should estimate the project duration, create the schedule, do some fancy math problems with time, and control and react to all aspects of managing the project schedule.

- Chapter 7, "Managing Project Costs," focuses on the project budget and how it is estimated, spent, audited, and controlled through the project. Cha-ching!

- Chapter 8, "Managing Project Quality," centers on defining and adhering to the quality expectations of the project stakeholders. We'll examine a whole bunch of charts that measure quality within a project.

- Chapter 9, "Managing Project Resources," delves into the methods to organize, lead, and manage your project team. This knowledge area also covers physical resources, such as materials and equipment. We'll also discuss some philosophies and human resources theories.

- Chapter 10, "Managing Project Communications," is all about how a project manager should gather, create, and disperse project information. The basic theme for this chapter is who needs what information, when they need it, and in what modality.

- Chapter 11, "Managing Project Risks," describes how the project manager, the project team, and other experts will identify, analyze, and plan responses to risks within your project. We'll cover risk matrixes, contingency reserves, and ways to track risks within your project.

- Chapter 12, "Managing Project Procurement," is all about buying the products and services your project may need to be successful. Procurement management includes obtaining acquisitions, selecting sellers, and creating contracts. Get your wallet ready.

- Chapter 13, "Managing Project Stakeholders," defines the stakeholder management planning, executing, and controlling processes. Once you've identified the stakeholders, in project initiation, you'll create a plan to keep the stakeholders in control throughout the project.

- Chapter 14, "Leading an Agile Project" is where things slide away from the *PMBOK Guide* directly. In this chapter, I'll discuss the fundamentals of Agile project management and how organizations are using hybrid approaches for the best of both of both management worlds. You'll need this chapter as a good primer for the agile portions of the PMP exam.

- Chapter 15, " Engaging Agile Stakeholders" fits nicely in to the PMP domain of People. In agile projects you'll have specific roles in the project—and you absolutely must know these for the PMP exam. I'll also discuss how you manage, or more likely, engage, the customers and end users of agile projects differently than in a predictive project.

- Chapter 16, "Measuring Agile Project Performance" is all about value and benefits realization. Much of the performance tracking and goal setting you do in a predictive project can be applied in an Agile project, but the terminology is slightly different. In any project, the point is to create business value, but the PMP exam you'll have to know the terminology to discuss value.

- Chapter 17, "Managing Risks in Agile Projects" risks are conditions that can threaten your project and issues are risk events that have occurred in the project. You'll need to know how to manage both of these things for your PMP exam. How you manage risks and issues in agile projects is a little bit different than in a predictive project, so your exam is sure to challenge you on these approaches. Don't worry—you'll do fine.

- Chapter 18, "Understanding the Code of Ethics and Professional Conduct," doesn't correspond directly to the *PMBOK Guide*, but it correlates to the PMI Code of Ethics and Professional Conduct. I'll explain how you can answer these questions directly and accurately for your exam. Keep in mind that agreement to abide by the Code of Ethics and Professional Conduct is required for PMP candidates, and you'll see several exam questions on ethics and on adhering to the PMI's professional code. I'm certain you'll do fine.

- Chapter 19, "Passing the PMP Exam" does not correlate the *PMBOK Guide* at all—which is a good thing. This final chapter is all the juicy stuff you absolutely must know in order to pass the PMP. It's the icing on the PMP Exam Prep cake—delicious.

Being a Project Expert

You can take a project management class and not be an expert in project management. You can even be a PMP and not be a good project manager. Sorry, but it's true. To be an expert in project management, you need to rely on more than just the tools, techniques, and other mechanics of project management. You'll need five things:

- Knowledge of the *PMBOK Guide*
- Expertise in your application area and an understanding of the relevant standards and regulations
- An understanding of the predictive, agile, and hybrid environment in which a project takes place
- General management knowledge and skills
- The ability to deal with people (good interpersonal skills)

These five attributes and how they interact with one another are depicted in Figure 1-5. The goal of this book is to help you pass your certification exam, but I'm certain your goal in passing the exam is to help you advance your career and become a better, more valuable project manager. With that thought process, it's easy to see how these skills are interdependent. Let's take a quick look at each of these project management attributes.

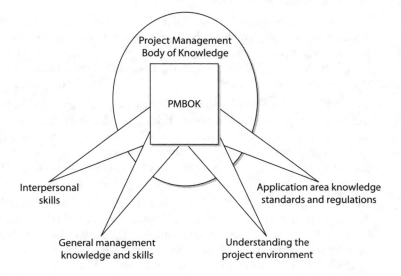

Figure 1-5
The project management areas of expertise overlap one another.

Project Management Body of Knowledge

PMBOK

Interpersonal skills

Application area knowledge standards and regulations

General management knowledge and skills

Understanding the project environment

Using the Project Management Body of Knowledge

Yep, back to the *PMBOK Guide* (technically, *A Guide to the Project Management Body of Knowledge*), which provides a wealth of information that is available to the project management community. As far as your exam is concerned, the *PMBOK Guide* is what's important.

Working with Your Application Area

An *application area* is your area of expertise—whether it be construction, manufacturing, sales, technology, or something else. And an application can get even more specific if we break down an organization into more detail: functional departments, technical domains, management arenas, and even industry groups such as automotive, healthcare, and so on. An application area is simply the area of expertise with which the project interacts.

Most, if not all, application areas have specific standards and regulations that the project management team must consider as they plan their work and implement their project plan. A *standard* is a generally accepted guideline for your industry, whereas a *regulation* is a rule that your industry must follow or risk fines and penalties. I like to say that standards are optional and regulations are not. No one ever went to jail because they didn't follow a standard. Plenty of people have visited the big house for not following regulations. On your PMP exam, you'll be tested on how you remain in compliance with requirements.

 EXAM TIP   You probably won't see questions on specific application areas, because the PMP exam will focus on project management, not on the arenas in which projects take place. Just know that application areas are industries and technologies that can host projects.

Examining the Project Management Context

Projects typically fall under some umbrella within an organization: project portfolio management, project offices, or programs. The project management context describes all the different scenarios where a project may reside. A project can be a stand-alone project, a project within a program, or a project within a portfolio. I'll discuss all of these scenarios in this section.

Your real-life organization may have one, all, or even none of these descriptions—don't sweat it. For your exam, however, you'll need to be familiar with these different organizational situations and how each one affects the project and the project manager.

Opening Your Portfolio

Project portfolio management is the selection, management, and collection of projects within an organization. Unlike a program, the projects may not be directly related, but they contribute to the organization's overall strategic plan. For example, a construction company may have a collection of projects, some of which are high-profile projects that could change a city skyline, while other projects are minor, such as the construction of a small garage or home.

The project portfolio defines the rules for selecting, maintaining, and even funding the projects within an organization. We all know that a company usually has only so much money to invest in the projects it selects. Project portfolio management defines the projects that should be selected based on need, risk and reward, return on investment, and practically any other issues an organization identifies. Portfolio management focuses on the selection and initiation of the best programs and projects that the organization should invest in. Portfolio management is not overly concerned with how the programs and projects should be managed—that's project and program management.

Unfortunately—or fortunately, depending on how you look at it—project managers aren't usually directly involved in project portfolio management. This activity is generally reserved for senior management because they decide which projects best propel an organization's mission, purpose, and strategy. Portfolio managers are in charge of the portfolio management processes—selecting projects, distributing risk exposure, and ensuring that the projects and programs are aligned with the organization's strategies and business objectives. Program managers and project managers inherit upper management's vision and then manage the programs and projects they've been assigned.

Working with Programs

A *program* is a collection of related projects organized to gain benefits from the projects that wouldn't be realized if the projects were managed independently. A program is a not just a large project; it's a collection of projects. Consider a program of building a skyscraper. There could be lots of projects within the skyscraper program: structure, elevators, electrical, plumbing, and tons more.

If each project were managed independently, a lot of work would have to be duplicated within the construction of the new skyscraper. But by creating a program, you can save time and effort by managing projects collectively. For example, the electrician, the telephone installer, and the network engineer can pool their resources to pull the electrical cables, telephone cables, and network cables all at once.

The point to take away from this discussion on programs is that projects are usually contributing one major deliverable and can work together to save time, effort, and dollars. Program managers manage programs. And yes, there are project managers within each project within the program.

Working with Subprojects

A *subproject* is a smaller project that's been lopped off from a larger project. For example, a project to build a new house may create a subproject for all of the home automation, home theater, and home network installation. The subproject is managed as its own project but has constraints and requirements within the confines of the larger project to create the new home. Here are some other examples of subprojects:

- **A single phase within a project life cycle** Consider, for example, the phases of construction on a new home: permits, excavation, foundation, framing, and so on. Each phase could be a subproject.

- **Human resource skill sets** Consider all of the work that plumbers, electricians, carpenters, and other skilled workers can do. The related work of each professional could form a subproject.

- **Specialized technology, materials, or activities** The installation of a new type of siding for a home construction project could be considered a subproject, in which a team of specialists would manage and complete the subproject.

Working with Project Management Offices

A *project management office*, often just called a PMO, oversees all of the projects and supports all of the project managers within an organization. PMOs can be organized to manage all projects within an organization, within departments, or even by the nature of the project work, such as IT versus marketing. Sometimes a project management office might be called a project office or program office.

Most PMOs support the project manager and the project team through software, training, templates, standardized policies, and procedures. PMOs often coordinate communications across projects, offer mentoring to project managers, and help resolve issues between project team members, project managers, and stakeholders. Project managers working with a PMO typically report to a chief project officer or program officer, depending on the organizational structure.

Considering Projects and Operations

Projects are temporary endeavors; operations are ongoing. Projects can be initiated to upgrade equipment and processes within operations, for example. Operations describe the ongoing overall activities of the business, such as manufacturing, constructing, consulting, and other application areas. Project resources, such as team members, on the project often have responsibilities in operations as well—the team members may have day-to-day work for operations and they'll have assignments for the project, too.

Projects and operations are two distinct things, but they usually interact in most organizations. Chances are you'll be interacting with operations throughout your project. One of the most common times you'll work directly with operations is at the end of a project, when you transfer the deliverables from the project ownership into operations. This is called *operational transfer* and usually is done as part of the project closure. Depending on what the project has created, resources from the project team may be required to support the solution, train the staff on the deliverables, or just be available as part of a service-level agreement (SLA) with the recipients of the thing your project has created.

Identifying the Project Life Cycle

Projects are born, they live, and then they die. Morbid, isn't it? But that simple metaphor of being born, living, and dying is exactly what the PMI calls the duration of a project: the project life cycle. A project life cycle is the project, from start to finish. Every project in the world has its own life cycle. Consider any project you've ever worked on, whether it was in construction, manufacturing, or information technology. Every project was born (initiated), lived (planned, executed, monitored, and controlled), and then died (closed). That's the project life cycle.

If we were to visit a technology guru and check out his projects, we'd see that they have life cycles different from those of a construction company's projects. Every project life cycle is unique to the nature of the work being completed.

 EXAM TIP Because every project has its own life cycle, regardless of the application area, it's tough for PMI to ask specific questions on this subject. You'll likely encounter questions about what a project life cycle is, but not on the activities that would take place in a project's life cycle.

Examining a Project Life Cycle

A project is an uncertain business, and the larger the project, the more uncertainty is involved. For this reason, among others, projects are broken down into smaller, more manageable phases. A project phase enables a project manager to see the project as a whole and yet still focus on completing the project one phase at a time.

Right now, I'm discussing predictive project life cycles—where you can predict the phases of a project. A predictive life cycle almost always comprises multiple phases. You can most often identify a project life cycle by the phases that exist within the project. A construction project may, for example, move through these predictable phases:

- Research
- Preconstruction
- Site work
- Foundation
- Framing
- Rough-in
- Interior finishes
- Exterior finishes
- Landscaping

The end result of a phase generally creates a project deliverable and enables the project to move toward its completion. Check out the preceding list. Just because a phase has been completed does not necessarily mean that the next phase can automatically begin. A *phase-end review* is needed to determine that the phase deliverable has met all its obligations, and then to authorize the initiation of the subsequent phase. A phase-end review is also known as a phase exit, phase gate, or a kill point.

 EXAM TIP Remember that the end of a project phase is also called a decision gate, stage gate, or kill point. A kill point is an ideal opportunity to "kill" a project at the end of a phase.

Imagine a construction project to build a new sports complex for your city. The foundation of the entire sports complex may not need to be 100 percent complete for the framing of the building to begin. The framing could begin as long as the risk associated with starting this phase of the project was acceptable. The practice of overlapping phases is called *fast tracking* (we'll see this again in Chapter 6 in a discussion on project schedule management). Though fast tracking does save project time, it can increase project risk.

 EXAM TIP Fast tracking is an example of schedule compression because it enables project phases to overlap. Fast tracking can, however, increase project risk. Fast tracking is not the same as lead time, which is the negative time between project activities—though some project managers do a type of fast tracking by adding lead time to activities on the critical path. Technically, fast tracking enables entire phases to overlap, whereas lead time enables activities within a phase to overlap.

In most organizations, regardless of the project manager's experience, management wants to see proof of progress, evidence of work completed, and good news about how well the project is moving. Phases are an ideal method of keeping management informed of the project progression. The following illustration depicts a project moving from conception to completion. At the end of each phase is some deliverable that the project manager can show to management and customers.

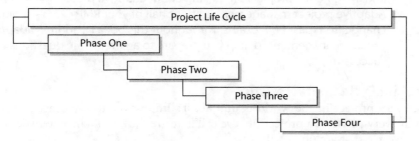

A *predictive life cycle*, more commonly called a plan-driven or waterfall approach, is a life cycle that "predicts" the work that will happen in each phase of the project. Through a series of waterfalls, where the outputs of one phase enable the next phase to begin, the project moves through a defined approach in each phase. Each phase in this approach usually requires different resources and skills, so the project team may be large, but team members may not necessarily all work on the project together other than on scope definition activities. Changes to the scope are more tightly controlled in this plan-driven approach than in other project management approaches.

An *iterative life cycle* starts with a vision of the project scope, but the schedule and cost estimates are still pretty rough. The project work is divided into chunks of time, called *iterations*, that enable the project team to tackle the top requirements first and also apply lessons learned to future iterations of project work. Iteration cycles have predefined types of work to create the project requirements, such as features defined, designed, developed, and tested. You might know iterations as time-boxed durations or sprints, but they are repeated cycles throughout the project.

The *incremental life cycle* is similar to the iterative life cycle, but the difference is that the project deliverables are created in increments. A few more features are added incrementally until the project is completed. An incremental life cycle is almost like an assembly line process: the features are added in predefined increments from the start until the final finished product.

The *adaptive life cycle* first creates a project scope for the project, which must be approved, and then the project may utilize an iterative or an incremental approach to create deliverables. Adaptive life cycles are commonly called change-driven life cycles as the project scope, though approved, is likely to change as the development team creates deliverables.

A *hybrid life cycle* is a combination of predictive and adaptive life cycles. Depending on the organization and the discipline, the components of the project that are established will follow a predictive life cycle, while the project components that are not fully defined may follow the adaptive life cycle approach.

 EXAM TIP   Here's a very basic way of identifying these different life cycles. Predictive life cycles predict everything. An iterative life cycle improves upon the project deliverable at each iteration. An incremental life cycle builds the project deliverable in increments. When I talk about iterative and incremental projects, I'm talking about adaptive project management. Adaptive project management is about half of your PMP exam—a big change from past PMP exams. Throughout this book I'll address adaptive project management to help you prepare to answer these questions successfully.

Project Life Cycle Characteristics

Because every project in the world is unique, it's impossible to say exactly what must happen in every phase of a project life cycle. There are, however, characteristics of every project life cycle that are universal:

- *Phases in a predictive life cycle are typically sequential, and the completion of a phase enables subsequent phases to begin.* Phases in an adaptive project are equal chunks of time throughout the project, usually two or four weeks, and are often called sprints.

- *Predictive phase durations describe the work to be done, such as foundation or framing.* Projects using adaptive approaches pull each phase's work from a list of prioritized requirements called a product backlog.

- *Project costs and staffing requirements are generally low at the project beginning phases, while costs and resources are highest in the project intermediate phases.* As the project moves toward completion, the cost and resource requirements generally wane.

- *The likelihood of the project's success is always lowest during the early phases of the project.* As the project moves toward completion, the likelihood of the project's success increases.

Every project moves through phases, and phases compose the project life cycle. Phases are logical approaches to segmenting the work, but they primarily allow management, an organization, or a project manager to have better control over the work done in each phase. Each phase within a project determines the following:

- The work that will happen in that phase
- The deliverables that will be created as a result of that phase
- How the phase deliverables will be reviewed, approved, and validated
- The needed resources for that phase
- How that phase will be approved to enable successor phases to launch

Comparing Project Life Cycles and Product Life Cycles

There must be some distinction between the project life cycle and the product life cycle. We've covered the project life cycle—the accumulation of phases from start to completion within a project—but what is a product life cycle?

A product life cycle is the whole life of the product the project has created. If your company had a brilliant idea to create a new piece of software, initiated and managed a project to create the software, and then implemented the software, that would be most of the product life cycle. The remainder of the product life cycle is the usage and support of the software until some day, sadly, when the software is determined to be out-of-date and retired from your organization. The product life cycle is the whole gosh-darn span of time, from concept to project to usage to retirement.

Working with Project Management Processes

Projects are chockablock with processes. A *process* is a set of actions and activities to achieve a product, result, or service. It's the work of project management to move the work of the project toward the deliverable the project aims to create. As you'll discover in this book, there are 49 project management processes that a project manager and the project team use to move a project along. The goal of these processes is to have a successful project, but a project's success is based on more than just leveraging these processes. A successful project depends on five main things:

- Using the *appropriate processes* at the *appropriate times*. A project manager must recognize situations within the project that call for different processes and then determine which process or combination of processes is most needed to meet the project objectives.

- Following a *defined project management approach* for execution and project control.

- Developing and implementing a solid *project management plan* that addresses all areas of the project.

- Conforming the project and the project management approach to the *customer requirements and expectations*.

- Balancing the project time, cost, scope, quality, resources, and risks while meeting the project objectives.

Sure, all of this sounds so easy on paper, doesn't it? But project management is not an easy task, and the goal of a certified project manager is to recognize the situations, react to the problems or opportunities, and move the project work toward achieving the customer's requirements. The 49 project management processes are the actions that help any project manager do just that.

This chapter covers the entire project management life cycle. We'll follow the activities that happen in each of the project management process groups and see the results of those actions.

Exploring the Project Management Processes

Before you get too deep into this book, learn this: *You do not have to do every single project management process on every single project.* The project manager and the project team must determine which project management processes are most appropriate for each project. Once the necessary processes have been identified, the project manager and project team must also determine to what extent the processes are needed. The processes are tailored to their project. Larger projects require more detail than smaller ones.

Tailoring is a common theme throughout the *PMBOK Guide* and in this book. It's an important concept for project managers because you'll need to tailor the project management process to every project you're managing. Every project is different, and not every project needs the same processes, to the same depth, and with the same approach. Tailoring is what project managers do on every project, though larger projects, as a rule, will require more detail and more processes than smaller projects. Of course, for your PMP, you need to know all of the processes and their characteristics, and how you might apply these processes in a given scenario.

The 49 project management processes have been recognized as good practices for most projects, but they are not a mandate for good practices on all projects. For your PMI examination, however, you'll be tested on all of the project management processes in detail. Yep. Although you might not use all of the project management processes in

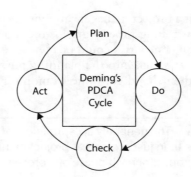

Figure 1-6
The standard
project model
is based on
Deming's
PDCA cycle.

the real world, the exam will test you on all of the processes. Why? Because there is, no doubt, more than one way to manage a project. The PMI isn't stubborn enough to say it's our way or no way—that'd be unreasonable.

The approach that the PMI does take, however, is based somewhat on W. Edwards Deming's plan-do-check-act (PDCA) cycle, as Figure 1-6 demonstrates. In Deming's model, adapted by the American Society for Quality (ASQ), the end of one process launches the start of another. For example, the end of the planning process enables the launch of the doing process. Once the work has been completed, you check it. This approach is called the Deming PDCA cycle. If the work checks out, you move right into the acting process.

The components of the model are called the *process groups*. Process groups are collections of the processes you'll be performing in different situations within your project. You've experienced, I'm sure, that projects are initiated, planned, executed, monitored and controlled, and then closed. Distinct actions fit nicely within each one of the process groups—that's the gist of this chapter.

Examining the Process Group Interactions

At first glance, the project management model seems simple. With more study, however, you'll see how complex the interactions between the groups can be. First, project managers realize that there is more than one way to manage a project. Second, these processes and their interactions are the generally accepted best approaches to project management. Having said that, there is no hard-and-fast rule as to the order in which processes should occur once the project is in motion. The nature of the project, the scenario, and the experienced conditions, along with the culture and maturity of the organization, will dictate which process is the best process at any given project moment.

The general consensus, not necessarily the order, of the process groups is as follows:

- Initiating
- Planning
- Executing
- Monitoring and controlling
- Closing

The caveat is that a project manager can move between the planning, executing, and monitoring and controlling process groups on an as-needed basis. For example, during project execution, a new risk could be identified. The project manager and project team would then move back into the planning phase to determine how to respond to the new risk, and then they'd continue to monitor and control the project for additional risks.

 EXAM TIP The generally accepted flow of the process groups can also apply to more than just projects. A project manager can use the processes within these groups for each phase of a project.

Choosing the Appropriate Processes

A moment of clarity: There's a bunch of processes in project management. Sure, we've already established that you won't need all these processes for every project you manage, but you can be darned certain you'll need all of the processes to pass your PMP exam. In this book, we'll dive in and check out these process groups and all their kids—the 49 project management processes.

In addition to project management processes, there are also product-oriented processes. These processes are unique to the organization that is creating the product of the project. Product processes are also unique to the type of work required to create the product. Let's put this in a real-world context: If you're creating a new software application, building a house, or designing a brochure, some processes are unique to that type of work. In addition, imagine all the different home construction companies in the world. Each company could be working on similar projects, but the internal product processes and terminology used could be unique to each company. The good news is that you won't have to know much about product processes for your PMP exam.

Working with Process Groups

Project management is more than just getting the project work done. It's the management, leadership, and execution of the work performed by the project team. (And, by "execution," I mean the project team executing the project plan, not you executing the team—although that can be tempting at times.) You'll move through some logical activities to get your project moving along. These are the process groups that are universal to project management. Let's take a more detailed look at these process groups and the type of work that will be happening in each:

- **Initiating**   Management and/or your customer is authorizing the project or a project phase to begin.
- **Planning**   You and the key stakeholders are defining and refining the project goals and objectives. Once the project objectives have been defined, you and the key stakeholders will plan on how to reach those objectives.

- **Executing**   Now that you have a project plan, it's time to put the plan into action. You've heard the saying, "Plan your work and now work your plan"? This is the "working your plan" part.

- **Monitoring and controlling**   Your project team is doing the work, but it's up to you to measure and monitor things to ensure that the project team is doing the work as it was planned. The results of your measurements—primarily in cost, time, scope, and quality—will show discrepancies between what was planned and what was experienced. These discrepancies are your project variances.

- **Closing**   Boy, howdy! There's nothing more fun, usually, than closing a project. This process group focuses on formal acceptance of the project's final deliverable. Note that technically the approval of the deliverable is the result of the verify scope process, a monitoring and controlling process. The close project process makes that acceptance formal with a project sign-off. The closing process group also focuses on bringing the project or project phase to a tidy ending.

Gathering Project Management Data and Information

Projects have a tendency to create lots of data and information. Even small projects can create loads of data: status of activities, activities performed, activities yet to start, actual costs, and lots more. It's important for the project manager to have a system in place to collect, sort, analyze, and communicate this data to the appropriate stakeholders. The project's communications management plan, which I'll discuss in Chapter 10, will guide you on who gets what information, when it's needed, and how you'll communicate the message, but there are some elements of data and information you should know now, because they'll be referenced throughout this book. Let's examine these three terms on data and information now.

Gathering Work Performance Data

Data is simply the raw observations, facts, and measurements about the project; activities in the project; quality; technical performance; and so on. Work performance data is simply the raw, unprocessed collection of data—it's not very useful because it's just plain old data that you've not sorted, analyzed, or pondered over. Work performance data is gathered and stored in your project management information system (PMIS), such as Microsoft Project, Smartsheet, or your favorite project management software.

Creating Work Performance Information

Once you have collected data, you can begin processing and analyzing it into useable information. Work performance information is the processed and analyzed data that will help you make project decisions. For example, you've collected data about the completion of project activities, the number of activities that are still being worked on, and the number of activities that are yet to start. Now you can begin pondering and analyzing the data into useable information. You can determine what resources are needed in the project, what activities are late and how their lateness may introduce risks, and how the project team's performance is trending.

Work performance information, unlike work performance data, is useable.

Communicating Through Work Performance Reports

One of the most important activities for a project manager to do is to communicate with stakeholders. Work performance reports, such as status reports and dashboards, are excellent methods to communicate what's happening within the project. Work performance reports are based on work performance information. You need the information to create the performance reports to communicate events and statuses in the project.

Work performance reports are used to make decisions, to help stakeholders become aware of what's happening in the project, and to keep stakeholders informed of the overall project health and status. All of this should be based on, of course, accurate work performance data, which is analyzed into work performance information, which enables you to create work performance reports.

EXAM TIP   You can keep the order of project management data and information straight by remembering that it's alphabetical. You gather *data*, and then process it into *information*, to create *reports*. Don't be tricked on the exam as to what's what when it comes to data and information.

Chapter Summary

You're done with Chapter 1. Congrats!

In this chapter, we talked about what it takes to be a Project Management Professional. Are you excited? Scared? Confident? It's okay to be a little of all three. With time and dedication your excitement will endure, your anxiety will diminish, and your confidence will increase. If thousands of other project managers can do this, you can too. The important thing right now is to create a plan and get to work. Get into the material and keep moving forward.

You'll need to know the 49 management processes and how these processes map to the ten knowledge areas of project management. This book discusses clearly and in detail these project management processes and knowledge areas you'll need to be familiar with to pass your certification exam. And don't forget that the Process Review Quiz will quiz you on all of the moving parts of project processes.

I also discussed what a project is—and is not. You now know that a project is a temporary endeavor to create a unique product or service. Projects are created for any number of reasons, from responding to marketplace demand, to solving a problem within an organization, to following laws and regulations.

Projects, regardless of why they were created, move through a progressive elaboration to provide accurate and complete descriptions of their goals and objectives. Recall that progressive elaboration typically starts with a broad synopsis of a project's goals, and through rounds of discussion, analysis, and brainstorming, the characteristics of a project become more detailed until, finally, the project vision is created.

The project life cycle is made up of the phases of the project. A project life cycle usually has multiple phases, and each phase describes the work that will happen within that phase of the project. At the end of a project phase, known as a stage gate or kill point, a decision is made at the phase-end review to determine whether the project is ready to move forward in the project life cycle, rework needs to be done in the phase, or the project should be terminated.

Predictive life cycles predict everything that should happen in the project. An iterative life cycle improves upon the project deliverables with each iteration in the project life cycle. An incremental life cycle builds the project deliverable in increments. Some organizations may use a hybrid approach to project management: some portions of the project are using predictive principles and other portions of the project are more adaptive. Nothing wrong with that, as long as everyone knows how to behave and things are getting done.

A project manager must understand the environment and circumstances in which the project will operate. The locale, culture, and conditions surrounding the project can affect the project success as much as the project manager's ability to lead and manage the facets of the project and the project team. If a project management office exists, it can provide training and support for the project manager to lead the project team to complete the project work effectively.

Questions

1. A series of activities to create a unique product or service by a specific date is best described as which one of the following?

    A. A program

    B. An operation

    C. A project

    D. A subproject

2. Ben is a new employee in your organization, and he's been assigned to your project team. Ben doesn't understand why he is on your project team because he thinks everything is part of the organization's day-to-day operations. Which of the following is likely to be part of an operation?

    A. Providing electricity to a community

    B. Designing an electrical grid for a new community

    C. Building a new dam as a source of electricity

    D. Informing the public about changes at the electrical company

3. You are the project manager of the HBH Project to install 40 new servers for your company network. You recommend, as part of your project planning, using progressive elaboration. Some of the project team members are confused about this concept. Of the following, which one is the best example of progressive elaboration?

   A. It is the process of decomposing the work into small, manageable tasks.

   B. It is the process of taking a project from concept to completion.

   C. It is the process of taking a project concept to a project budget.

   D. It is the process of identifying the business needs of a potential project.

4. Your organization would like to create a new product based on market research. This new product will be created in a project. This is an example of which one of the following reasons to launch a new project?

   A. Organizational need

   B. Customer request

   C. Market demand

   D. Legal requirement

5. Your organization utilizes projects, programs, and portfolios. Some of the project team members are confused about what a program is. A program is which one of the following?

   A. A very large, complex project

   B. A collection of small projects with a common goal

   C. A collection of projects with a common objective

   D. A collection of subprojects with a common customer

6. Sam and Sarah are in a heated discussion over a new program in the organization. They are trying to determine who will make the tactical decisions in the projects within the program. Who manages programs?

   A. Management

   B. Project sponsors

   C. Project managers

   D. Program managers

7. You have an excellent idea for a new project that can increase productivity by 20 percent in your organization. Management, however, declines to approve the proposed project because too many resources are already devoted to other projects. You have just experienced what?

   A. Parametric modeling

   B. Management by exception

   C. Project portfolio management

   D. Management reserve

8. Larger projects generally utilize more processes with more depth than smaller projects. What term is assigned to customization of processes within a project?

   A. Process mapping

   B. Process configuration

   C. Process tailoring

   D. Process selection

9. Holly is a new project manager and she's working toward her PMP certification. She is having some trouble understanding which processes she should implement in her new project based on the available processes in the *PMBOK Guide*. Of the following, which statement is correct?

   A. A project manager must use every process identified within the *PMBOK Guide* on every project.

   B. A project must use every tool and technique as identified within the *PMBOK Guide* on every project.

   C. A project manager must use the most appropriate processes on every project.

   D. A project manager must agree that she will use all of the project management tools and techniques on every project.

10. Projects are temporary endeavors to create a unique product, service, or result. Which one of the following does not relate to the concept of "temporary" in project management?

    A. The project team

    B. The market window status on which the project is capitalizing

    C. The project deliverable

    D. The project manager

11. Harold is the project manager of the JHG Project for his company and he's meeting with the key stakeholders to describe the deliverables of the project that will be implemented. Hanna, one of the stakeholders, is confused about why Harold talks about results of the project that aren't necessarily implemented. As an example, Harold says that a project creates a unique product, service, or result. Which one of the following is a result?

    A. A new piece of software

    B. A new airplane

    C. A feasibility study

    D. A call center

12. Which project management document can be utilized for a go/no-go decision in a project?

    A. Project business case

    B. Project charter

    C. Project benefits management plan

    D. Project management plan

13. Consider a project that is developing new software for an organization. Every eight weeks the project releases new features of the software. Initially, the software was very basic, but over a year, the software has become more and more robust with the new features added every eight weeks. What project management life cycle is being utilized in this scenario?

    A. Predictive

    B. Incremental

    C. Iterative

    D. Adaptive

14. Project managers must be aware of the political and social environments that the project operates within. These environments can affect the project's ability to operate, can limit working hours, or can cause embarrassment when the project manager assumes other cultures are the same as hers. Which one of the following is not a characteristic of a project's cultural and social environment?

    A. Economics

    B. Time zone differences

    C. Demographics

    D. Ethics

15. You are the project manager of the KHGT Project, which will span four countries around the world. You will need to consider all of the following characteristics of the international and political environment except for which one?

    A. International, national, regional, and local laws

    B. Customs

    C. Customers

    D. Holidays

16. Project managers need interpersonal skills, such as likeability, to help get the project work done. The project manager needs interpersonal skills to be effective in any organization and project. Which one of the following is not an example of an interpersonal skill?

   A. Financial management and accounting

   B. Influencing the organization

   C. Motivating people

   D. Problem solving

17. Jane is a senior project manager in your company. Wally is a new project manager who is working toward his PMP certification. Jane decides that Wally would be a good candidate to manage a subproject in the organization. Brenda, the project sponsor, isn't certain what Jane means by a subproject. What is a subproject?

   A. It is a smaller project that supports a parent project.

   B. It is a project that is performing below expectations.

   C. It is a project that has been experiencing project spin-off.

   D. It is the delegation of a project phase.

18. Erin is a new project manager who is working toward her PMP. She has been assigned a small project in her organization, but she feels that she could use some additional training, coaching, and mentoring. Where will a project manager most likely get project management mentoring?

   A. Project Management International

   B. The American Society for Quality

   C. The project management office

   D. Subject matter experts

19. Project managers and functional managers need to be able to recognize a condition that is best suited for a project and a condition that is an operation within an entity. Which one of the following is an example of operations?

   A. Creating a new community park

   B. Designing a new car

   C. Sending monthly invoices to an organization's 25,000 customers

   D. Removing an old server and replacing it with a newer one

20. When considering the selection of projects to be initiated, project portfolio management considers all of the following except for which one?

   A. Risk/reward categories

   B. Lines of business

   C. The project manager's experience

   D. General types of projects

Answers

1. **C.** A project is a temporary endeavor to create a unique product, service, or result. Deadlines and cost constraints are tied to the project. A is incorrect because programs are a collection of projects working toward a common cause. B is incorrect because operations are ongoing activities of an organization. D, a subproject, describes a project that is part of and supports a larger project, so it is also incorrect.

2. **A.** Providing electricity to a community is the best example of operations because it is an ongoing activity. B, C, and D are all examples of projects, as they are temporary and create a unique product, service, or result.

3. **B.** According to the *PMBOK Guide*, progressive elaboration means developing in steps and then continuing by increments. In this instance, you're starting broad with the project concept and then moving from the project life cycle to project completion. A describes the process of breaking down the project scope into the task list. C is not a valid choice for this question. D is part of determining whether a project should be chartered.

4. **C.** Projects can be created for a number of reasons, and this example supports the market demand choice. A, an organizational need project, is created to satisfy an internal need. B is incorrect because no specific customer asked for this new product. D is incorrect because there is no legal requirement to create the new product.

5. **C.** A program is a collection of projects that are completed together to gain benefits by managing the projects as a group rather than on an individual basis. A, B, and D are not attributes of programs because projects within a program neither are necessarily small nor are they subprojects.

6. **D.** Programs are managed by program managers. A, B, and C are incorrect choices.

7. **C.** Project portfolio management is the management, selection, and assignment of projects that support an organization's business objectives. A, B, and D are not valid answers.

8. **C.** Process tailoring enables the project manager to tailor the processes selected and the depth of their execution to what's most appropriate for the project. Not all projects need all processes. A, B, and D are not valid answers because they don't describe process tailoring.

9. **C.** A project manager does not have to use all of the processes within the *PMBOK Guide*—only the most appropriate ones. A, B, and D are incorrect statements because the project manager does not use every process or tool and technique within the *PMBOK Guide* for every project.

10. **C.** Most projects create a deliverable that will outlive the project itself. A, B, and D are incorrect because these attributes are temporary in nature.

11. **C.** The *PMBOK Guide* classifies the concept of creating a feasibility study as a result. A, B, and D describe products and services.

12. A. This is the best choice because the project business case is created before the project is launched and helps management and key stakeholders make a go/no-go decision based on the financial aspects, return on investment, and other factors for the project. B, C, and D are incorrect as these documents are not used for project selection.

13. B. This is an example of an incremental project life cycle. The software is released in increments of new features throughout the life cycle. At first, the project was very basic in its ability, but with each new increment, new features were added to the software. A, the predictive life cycle, predicts the entire project and usually has a just one final release for the project customers. C, iterative, isn't the best choice for the scenario presented; technically, an iterative project life cycle could also release the product in the same fashion, but iterative projects usually have much fewer releases than an incremental project. D, adaptive, also isn't the best choice because an adaptive project first defines the project scope and then may be incremental or iterative life cycles.

14. B. Time zone differences are not part of the cultural and social environment, but they are part of the international and political environment. A, C, and D are part of the cultural and social environment.

15. C. Customers are not part of the international and political environment. A, B, and D are part of this environment.

16. A. Financial management and accounting is not an interpersonal skill. B, C, and D are examples of interpersonal skills, so these choices are incorrect.

17. A. A subproject is a project that is typically smaller than and that supports an original parent project. B, C, and D do not accurately describe a subproject.

18. C. Project managers will most likely receive mentoring from the project management office. A is not a valid choice because Project Management International is not the same entity as the Project Management Institute (PMI). B is not a valid choice because ASQ does not provide mentoring for project managers. D is not the best choice for the question because the *PMBOK Guide* specifically identifies the PMO as a source for mentoring.

19. C. This is the best example of operations because the answer implies that this work is done every month. A, B, and D are all unique endeavors that may be done once or just occasionally, but they are not part of ongoing operations.

20. C. While the experience of the project manager is likely considered during the assignment of projects, it is not considered during project portfolio management. A, the risk and reward of the project, is considered. B and D, the lines of business and the general types of projects, are also considered as part of project portfolio management.

Managing a Project in Different Environments

In this chapter, you will

- Explore Agile methodologies for project management
- Learn how a project utilizes enterprise environmental factors
- Discover how to work with organizational process assets
- Understand how different organizations operate
- Learn the types of organizational structures and their characteristics

You've got lots of work to do as a project manager: meetings, planning, coordination, leading the project team, and ensuring that the project work is done according to the project plan. You're with the project all the way, from the get-go to the final closure report. You work with project stakeholders to gather requirements, keep them posted on the progress, and manage their influence over the project as much as possible. It's an ongoing job that ends just after the project work does.

Within your organization, several factors affect how you manage the project. You and the project team must follow organizational rules for managing and doing the project work. In your role as a project manager, you're expected to complete forms, specific software, templates, and other requirements that are unique to your organization. Regulations and laws may also affect how you and your team do the work. If you're using an Agile approach to project management, you must enforce and follow specific rules. In addition to these items, you may leverage and adapt past project files, records, and information databases to make the current project management experience more successful.

These *enterprise environmental factors, organizational process assets,* and *organizational systems* all affect your success as a project manager. For your PMP exam, you will need to be able to recognize these organization-specific factors that affect projects. Enterprise environmental factors and organizational process assets are referenced over and over in the *PMBOK Guide* (and in this book) because they have a direct influence on the processes you'll utilize in your projects.

 VIDEO   For a more detailed explanation, watch the *Project Environments* video now.

Exploring Agile Project Management

Adaptive, Agile, Scrum: you've likely heard Agile project management go by lots of different names. Agile project management, regardless of the specific approach, has one central theme: change is expected and welcome. The truth is, there are lots of different types of Agile project management and it's a growing philosophy to project management that's now a big part of your PMP exam. That's right; you'll need to know a good deal about Agile project management for your PMP exam. This is a big shift from PMP exams in the past, but don't worry if you're not experienced in Agile. In this section, I'll walk through the big picture of Agile project management, and I'll continue to address Agile concerns throughout the rest of this book.

Let's nail down the two big camps of project management right away: *predictive* and *Agile*. Predictive is the traditional project management approach, where everything is predicted up front in the project. The project team and stakeholders work together to define the requirements and create a plan, and then changes to the project scope are resisted, because any change in scope can skew the entire project. Agile project management is flexible: changes are welcome in the project. Agile projects prioritize requirements throughout the project, and changes can enter the project but have to be prioritized, so some initial items may get bumped down the requirements list to make room for more important stuff that the stakeholders decide they really want.

When you begin a project to build a house, you can define everything that's going to happen in the construction project. You can define everything all the way down to a single cabinet in the kitchen. When developing software, however, you don't always know exactly what's needed in that software. You and your customers may have a lot of the requirements identified, but those may change over time. In a predictive project, such as a construction project, it's difficult to change after the project is in motion. Agile welcomes change and expects change.

As of this writing, about half of your PMP exam will be on Agile project management. That's nearly 90 questions. Although that seems like a huge slice of the exam, consider that many of the topics are obvious to either predictive or Agile projects. You'll need to know some general rules of Agile, recognize the different Agile flavors, and always choose the best answer for business value. In that mix of 100 Agile questions, you'll also be tested on hybrid approaches to Agile—something that's really tough to define clearly because hybrid means an organization uses both predictive and Agile methodologies in one project.

Embracing the Agile Manifesto

One of the first things to grasp when looking at Agile projects is the idea that you're *being* Agile, not *doing* Agile: Doing Agile means you're trying to follow a recipe to do an Agile project. Being Agile means you're following the Agile values and principles. Being Agile means you're limber, you're focusing on getting things done rather than documenting work, and you're not getting in the way of the development team as they complete the project work.

The idea of the Agile mindset is founded upon the Agile Manifesto, a document created in February 2001 by a group of software developers who aimed to define common values for software development projects. The group of developers named themselves the Agile Alliance, and their initial set of values is what all Agile project managers, and Agile organizations, aim to achieve in each project. The Agile Manifesto is straightforward to learn, but difficult to always implement. Here are the four points of the manifesto:

Individuals and interactions	over	Processes and tools
Working software	over	Comprehensive documentation
Customer collaboration	over	Contract negotiation
Responding to change	over	Following a plan

The items on the left side are valued more than the items on the right side. This isn't to say that the items on the right side aren't valuable; they just aren't *as* valuable. For example, it's not unusual for a predictive project manager to say that she feels like she's spending more time completing forms and reports than she spends working on the project. I've worked on projects in which our team's technical writer created a 500-page manual to document the software, but it was never actually read—a complete waste of his time! Agile projects focus on people, working software, collaboration, and inevitable change, rather than on paperwork.

The Agile Alliance defined 12 principles to support and clarify these four values of the Agile Manifesto. You won't need to memorize these for your exam, but understanding these principles will help you correctly answer test questions:

1. Our highest priority is to satisfy the customer through early and continuous delivery of valuable software.

2. Welcome changing requirements, even late in development. Agile processes harness change for the customer's competitive advantage.

3. Deliver working software frequently, from a couple of weeks to a couple of months, with a preference to the shorter timescale.

4. Business people and developers must work together daily throughout the project.

5. Build projects around motivated individuals. Give them the environment and support they need and trust them to get the job done.

6. The most efficient and effective method of conveying information to and within a development team is face-to-face conversation.

7. Working software is the primary measure of progress.

8. Agile processes promote sustainable development. The sponsors, developers, and users should be able to maintain a constant pace indefinitely.

9. Continuous attention to technical excellence and good design enhances agility.

10. Simplicity—the art of maximizing the amount of work not done—is essential.

11. The best architectures, requirements, and designs emerge from self-organizing teams.

12. At regular intervals, the team reflects on how to become more effective, and then tunes and adjusts its behavior accordingly.

Obviously, these principles and values originated in the software development industry, but Agile practices have been adapted in all industries, not just technology. These 12 principles support the Agile mindset and will help you on your exam and in your Agile projects.

 EXAM TIP You'll likely encounter questions on your exam that offer scenarios in conflict with these Agile Manifesto principles, and you'll need to react accordingly. Always refer to the first principle: satisfy the customer through early and continuous delivery of valuable software. In Chapter 14 I'll get more into the details and common approaches of Agile, but for now, just think about getting value to the customer as soon as possible.

Comparing Predictive and Agile Projects

For the exam, you'll need to know the characteristics of a predictive project versus an Agile project.

Predictive projects have a clearly defined scope that provides a clear description of the product that the project aims to create. Predictive projects often use historical information from similar projects. For example, if a homebuilder will know the history of the types of homes the organization has completed in the past. Predictive projects must have a well-defined, up-front set of requirements. Predictive projects generally don't really expect a lot of changes, and are, in fact, even averse to changes. Predictive projects also have well-defined activities and phases: plumbing, electrical, framing, and foundation. Predictive projects generally have reliable estimating, too, because everyone agrees exactly what the project will create.

Predictive projects move through logical phases to get to the project closure. Your KPIs, or key performance indicators, equate to success. KPIs are things like time, cost, scope, quality, and requirements. The whole, completed project scope is generally needed for value; if you're only 90 percent complete with the home construction, that doesn't offer much value for the homeowners. Predictive projects are definable work projects, whereas Agile projects are usually found in high-uncertainty work projects. High-uncertainty work is exploratory, has frequent changes, is complex, and is often risky.

Agile projects are knowledge work projects. In knowledge work, the work happens in your brain more than in your brawn. And knowledge work expects change. You can look over at a developer and he's slamming away at some code, while another developer is pondering what to do next. Which developer is doing knowledge work? Both. Knowledge work is invisible; you don't really see it until you get to a result, or until you reach an increment. In predictive projects such as construction, if you go to a construction site and see a guy stacking cinder blocks, you can see the work that he's doing. You see the progress being made. Stacking cinder blocks is a labor-driven project, while software development is knowledge-driven and takes brain power.

Agile projects, or knowledge-based projects, often begin with a scope that isn't defined in detail at the project's launch. The product will emerge along with the work being done in the project. Agile project managers expect requirements to change, and they expect requirements to emerge over time. Specific project work activities can be vague up front.

Cost and time estimates are challenging. Processes are iterative, and you'll see that the work involves doing the same activities over and over and over. New work is often dependent on previous work. Customer satisfaction is how you find success.

 VIDEO You'll need to know about the many flavors of Agile for your PMP exam. For a detailed look, watch the *Agile Approaches* video now. With this book you also receive a free one-hour class from Instructing.com on Agile Project Management.

Identifying Different Agile Approaches

Agile projects, *Agile methodologies*, and *Agile approaches* are all generic names that describe different Agile project management approaches. The *PMBOK Guide* and the Agile Practice Guide, which is included in the *PMBOK Guide*, shy away from embracing specific Agile approaches, but they do acknowledge the most common approaches. You'll likely see these different Agile approaches on your PMP exam, and you'll need to know the main characteristics of each. Let's dive in.

Scrum

When people think of Agile projects, they almost always default to the most popular approach: Scrum. I'll admit that I'm biased toward Scrum, I'm certified in Scrum, and I love the Scrum approach to project management. Scrum has evolved since the 1990s, and the Agile Manifesto created a framework, a general structure, of how a Scrum project should operate. Scrum offers characteristics of product management—not just project management—because your goal is to create working software, or, for your exam, creating value for the customer.

The theory of Scrum is based on the *empirical process control theory*, or empiricism, which tells us that knowledge work comes from experience, whether the work is in development projects, in writing projects, or even in graphic design projects. Good code, good art, and good products generally are created based on what we've done in the past. Agile is all about making good decisions based on what we already know through *triangulation*. Basically, triangulation uses at least two points to predict how to get to the third point. For example, you know a tree is 120 yards from where you're standing, so a statue a bit to the left and behind the tree could be approximately 150 yards. You, the tree, and the statue form a little triangle. In Agile, there's the goal to be achieved and you can compare it to two other similar, completed goals to predict how to complete the work.

Scrum works through iterations of time periods called *sprints*. A sprint is an iteration of effort that repeats over and over until the project is complete. Sprints are predetermined in duration at the launch of the project, usually ranging from one to four weeks in duration. At the end of a sprint, the team will have reached an *increment*, which is a product in usable form that can be released (but doesn't have to be) to the customer or to the organization. Sprints help the development team optimize the predictability of what's coming, but they're also used to control risk. By delivering these small increments, you can ensure that the team has created good code and a good testable and well-tested deliverable. After the increment is released, the customer provides feedback.

What you don't want, of course, are *escaped defects*—any problems that go out to the customer along with the increment. But when a defect is found, it goes back into the product backlog of what needs to be fixed so you can create a new increment in a new sprint. This process helps keep risk to a minimum.

Scrum projects involve three key roles on the scrum team: scrum master, product owner, and the development team. There is no project manager in Scrum; instead, each role takes responsibility for managing a portion of the project. The scrum master serves the team by removing roadblocks, protecting the team from distractors, and helping to ensure that everyone is following the Scrum rules. The product owner is responsible for maintaining the list of requirements, known as user stories, in the prioritized backlog. The development team includes the cross-functional group of people who are building the product.

The easiest way to learn about Scrum is to walk through the flow of events, shown in Figure 2-1. Beginning at the left side, the *product backlog* is a list of requirements that the product owner, an ambassador for the business people, will prioritize with the development team. The prioritized product backlog includes everything that the project could create, from most important down to least important. The backlog is basically a big list, or queue, of everything the project could include, depending on how much time and money are available.

Within the product backlog are all of the requirements, called *user stories*. User stories show the roles, actions, and value of each requirement. Also in the backlog, you'll include *functional* and *nonfunctional* requirements. Nonfunctional requirements are things like stability, uptime, and security—things that you can't see and touch. It also includes the architecture. Sometimes the nonfunctional requirements have to be prioritized first, and that's why the developers need to be involved with the product owner, although the product owner isn't necessarily a developer.

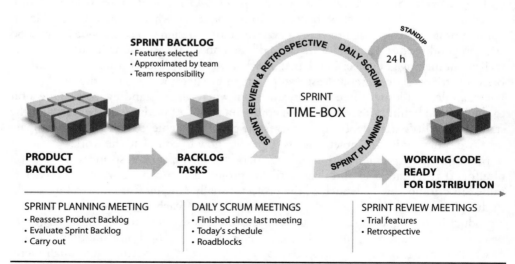

Figure 2-1   Scrum follows a predefined flow of activities.

The development team, product owner, and scrum master will then get together in a sprint planning meeting and decide how many of the items from the prioritized product backlog they can take on in the next sprint. Because the items in the backlog are prioritized, with items at the top having the most value, that's where the team will pull from first. These are not necessarily the easiest items, but they're the items that offer the most value to the customers. This is the Agile version of eating your dessert first—we go right to the good stuff.

The development team and the product owner determine how much work can be accomplished in the next sprint, and they assign *sizing points* to the stories in the backlog. The sizing points are a representation of the size of the individual requirements that are used to provide a sense of how many requirements can be accomplished in the next sprint. For example, requirements may be sized as extra-large, large, medium, and small. I've worked on Scrum projects where the organization used a cardinal scale for sizing, with ratings between one and nine. The selected user stories are then fed into the sprint. The team looks at the user stories to define and assign the tasks among themselves.

Every day during the sprint is the *daily scrum*, a 15-minute meeting in which each team member describes what they have accomplished since yesterday, what they are working on today, and whether they've encountered any impediments. The team usually stands up during the meeting, so sometimes it's called the *daily standup*.

At the end of the sprint, the team has created a *product increment*—the culmination of the work that the team has completed in the past four weeks (or another chosen duration) of the sprint. The team, the scrum master, the product owner, and sometimes key project stakeholders will attend a *sprint review*, where the team demonstrates their accomplishments from the past four weeks. The participants of the sprint review determine whether the "definition of done" has been met—this definition was agreed to by the participants at the beginning of the process. Any incomplete items return to the product backlog for possible selection for the next sprint.

The final meeting before starting the whole cycle over is the *sprint retrospective*. This meeting is attended by the development team and the scrum master to identify opportunities to improve performance in the next sprint of the project. It's not an opportunity to place blame but is intended as a forum to discuss what did and didn't work in the project so far, and how the team can improve on any issues. It's also where the team can discuss the product owner's feedback from the last iteration and make plans to incorporate those comments and suggestions into the next iteration of the project.

Kanban Method

The Kanban Method is an evolution of the Japanese lean-manufacturing approach used in knowledge work projects in the early 2000s. Kanban is pretty easy to get started, because its main idea is to start where you are. The primary characteristic of Kanban is the Kanban board, shown in Figure 2-2; that's where its name comes from—*Kanban* means visual signal. The Kanban board shows the flow of work through the system so that you can visualize where the team is in the process, how the team delivers work, what work exists, and any limits to the work in progress (WIP).

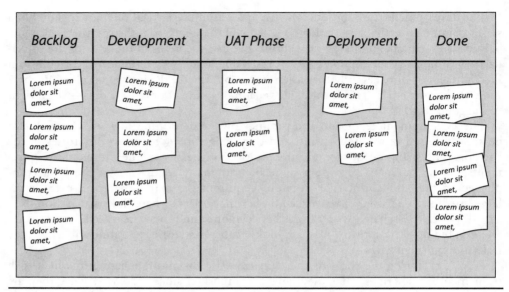

Figure 2-2   A Kanban board helps the team visualize the status of work items.

An organization using Kanban must establish and clearly communicate policies regarding how the work may enter and exit each stage of a project, and how much work—the WIP—a team can take on at any given time. Too much WIP can congest the workflow and prevent the team from delivering iterations frequently enough to the customers. Kanban focuses on managing the work and then allowing people to self-organize to complete the work in the project queue.

Kanban pulls the work through the flow, and in the Kanban board, from left to right. As new work items appear, they are added to the to-do list, or the Backlog column, on the board. Any team member who's available and competent can take on a work item and start working on the task to get it into the system. At each stage of the action, work items are moved to the appropriate columns on the Kanban board so that everyone can see the progress of items in the process; then they can anticipate the project workload.

Like Scrum, Kanban has some specific rules that need to be communicated and agreed upon at the beginning. The first rule you've already seen (pun intended): *Visualize the work.* The Kanban board visualizes the work and shows when the work is being launched—this is called the *commitment point.* The workflow illustrates the requirements needed before the work item can be released to the customer; these are called *delivery points.*

Kanban has nine basic principles, and you should know these for the PMP exam:

- **Transparency**   Share information clearly and openly, and use plain language.
- **Balance**   Aspects of the project, stakeholders' viewpoints, capabilities of the development team, and the requirements of the work must be balanced in order for the project to be effective.

- **Collaboration**   Communication, understanding of policies, and a clear vision of what needs to be done help people work together throughout the project.

- **Customer focus**   The focus of all project team members is to think of the project customer and how the efficiency of the workflow, the quality of the deliverables, and the timing of the product releases affect the customers of the project.

- **Flow**   This is a main theme of Kanban, that work flows through a defined system or defined project stages, and the work being completed is actually the flow of value.

- **Leadership**   Anyone can lead regardless of their project title. Leadership is needed throughout the project to align, motivate, and deliver value.

- **Understanding**   Team members, customers, and the organization need an understanding of the workflows through the project and the policies of the Kanban project.

- **Agreement**   All stakeholders agree to follow the rules, to look for opportunities to improve value, and to respect one another and the approaches taken within the workflow.

- **Respect**   All stakeholders must show consideration of others' opinions and must try to understand other points of view and approaches to the work.

In summary, you can think of Kanban as a way to visualize the work in small pieces that flow through a system. Kanban boards help the team members and stakeholders visualize the project work, how the work moves through the project, and where specific items are in the project timeline; they also identify the WIP. You'll see the concept of WIP and Kanban boards in many different Agile approaches; many organizations are creating hybrid examples of Agile project management using Kanban principles.

Exploring Lean Practices

You'll likely see a few questions on your PMP exam that address Lean, an approach that was developed by Japanese engineer Taiichi Ohno and originally called the Toyota Production System (TPS). Toyota developed this approach, which was all about reducing loss and creating a manufacturing environment for sustainable production.

Lean uses the Kanban board to help teams quickly see when inventory level goals are met. You may know this as *just-in-time production,* which created only enough inventory to balance time, cost, and demand.

From manufacturing, Lean principles have been adapted into Agile software production environments. IT teams work in a three-phase cycle of building, measuring, and learning. This approach creates a partnership mentality between the development team and the customers to ensure that the work being done is in constant alignment with the business value goals of the customers. Like all Agile approaches, Lean prioritizes work based on feedback from the customer, but it adds the principles of reducing waste and keeping things simple. Simple, of course, doesn't mean that it's easy; it means that it's the *minimum viable produc*t (MVP). MVP asserts that what's created is just enough to satisfy the project customers, while enabling the customers to offer feedback for improvements.

A key component of Lean that you should know about is *Kaizen*. Kaizen uses small, incremental changes to improve the product, the workflow, and how the team operates in each change. Kaizen is a whole philosophy not just in project management, but in life: it asserts that small changes over time add up to big results. There are volumes written about Kaizen, but for the exam, just know that Kaizen is utilized in Lean to implement small changes for consistent improvement and reducing waste.

There is no singular, uniform approach to Lean. In fact, there are lots of different flavors and approaches to Lean, which is why exam questions will be pretty direct when asking about it. Generally, Lean frameworks follow three guiding principles:

- The project teams are empowered to do the work, and team members are cross-functional (which means people take on more than one role on the project).
- Lean projects always look to implement approaches to continuous improvement.
- The managers in the organization serve as mentors or teachers to the project team and the customers.

There are seven principles you'll likely see on your exam that address Lean:

- **Eliminate waste** Remove anything that doesn't add value to the project customer.
- **Build quality in** Quality must first be defined, and then the team aims to accomplish quality. It also applies to the approach: remove excessive testing, automate tasks, and be transparent.
- **Create knowledge** Teams must document just enough to share and retain knowledge, openly share successes and failures, and train one another.
- **Defer commitment** This principle doesn't mean that the team avoids commitment; instead, the team commits to decisions when they've gathered enough information. There's no need to plan months in advance; plan only for imminence and based on solid data.
- **Deliver fast** Getting value to the project customers quickly, without over-engineering solutions, is a cornerstone of Lean. This doesn't mean overworking the team, but it means that the team should design an elegant, simple solution; get it to the customer quickly; and then incrementally improve upon the solution for business value.
- **Respect people** This principle applies to all aspects of teamwork. Consider communications among the team: encouraging one another to do good work, bringing new team members on board, empowering the team to do the work, and addressing issues throughout the project.
- **Optimize the whole** This is first about balancing the need for speed and the need for quality. Rushing through development results in sloppy code, which sets the project schedule back. Next, the testing process must not overload the testing folks; this creates delays in the project, creates a burden on the testers, and may enable defects to escape detection. Optimizing the whole is about balancing the quality, the schedule, and the workflow to create business value.

The Lean approach is deceptively simple. For Lean to be successful, the team and stakeholders need open communication, defined processes, and transparency throughout the project. Lean means constant improvement, constant growth, and the willingness to realize that increments of improvements—even small improvements—over time will result in increased business value.

Extreme Programming

Extreme Programming, or XP, is another Agile framework you'll likely encounter on the PMP exam. XP aims for quality software and a quality of life for the development team. When you think of XP, think of *pair programming*, in which all code is developed by a pair of programmers—two people, sitting together at the same machine. In pair programming, one person writes code while the other person does continuous code review. The pair will switch roles from time to time.

In addition to pair programming, you should know the five principles of XP:

- **Communication**   Because software development is knowledge work, communication is paramount in XP. The team has to work to transfer knowledge from person to person, and face-to-face communication is the preferred approach. You'll often use a white board to communicate and illustrate what's happening in the project.

- **Simplicity**   Like many of the Agile approaches, simplicity in XP aims to avoid waste and unnecessary work. It means that you will aspire to create the simplest thing that will work to satisfy the business value for the customer. Simplicity in XP also means you're working on only what's known, rather than trying to guess what the customer *might* want.

- **Feedback**   Feedback is paramount for XP teams. Based on what's been created and the feedback from others on the team and the customer, the team can adapt, improve, and move on with project work to create value.

- **Courage**   Courage is needed for the team to take action, but the team also needs to know they are empowered to act without fear of retribution should their actions fail. The team needs the courage to act to get things done, to experiment, and to speak up when things aren't working and a different approach is needed.

- **Respect**   Team members need to respect one another to bolster transparency and communication, and they need to be willing to listen to feedback that may not always be pleasant to receive.

XP embraces my personal favorite concept of testing: *test-first programming*, in which developers create an automated test of the code, which will initially fail because all the code has not been created yet. Because the programmers know what is needed to pass the test, they can work to develop test-successful code, run and pass the test, and then move on with their work.

Some challenges of XP are unique to software development. XP needs flexible teams that can quickly adapt to software requirements that are likely to change over the project.

XP teams can also face the challenge of organizations that still use waterfall approaches and that will try to impose fixed-time projects, so setting expectations early in the project is needed. You'll also find that XP works best with small teams that are colocated rather than virtual teams. Finally, XP really needs automated testing for unit and functional components.

Hybrid Agile Approaches

Agile project management approaches are evolving all the time. No laws dictate what approach an organization must use or how an organization chooses to utilize Agile. You're free to choose the best parts of several different approaches and meld together a new homegrown version of Agile that works for you. These homegrown approaches, called *hybrid* approaches, enable an organization to build a customized approach to project management. Hybrid can include waterfall methodologies, such as planning in detail up front, and can then implement Scrum practices thereafter.

 EXAM TIP   PMI promises that you'll see some questions about hybrid on your exam—nothing to be worried about. Recognize the main themes of these Agile approaches and the predictive approach used in waterfall environments.

Working with Enterprise Environmental Factors

Enterprise environmental factors (EEFs) are conditions that the project manager must live with—they are outside the project manager's control. Even if you don't like existing EEFs, there's not much you can do about them; you've simply got to deal with them. These factors will affect your project, influence your decisions, and even direct how you're allowed to do the project work. They can come from within your organization, such as a policy, or they can come from outside of the organization, such as a law or regulation.

Many project managers like to say that EEFs are negative because they constrain the project manager's choices, but that's not always the case. Though some EEFs can limit the project manager's options, some can make the project manager's job easier and help the project be more successful. For example, one EEF in an organization could require that all the scheduling be managed by a person in a scheduler role. That's a fantastic constraint that frees the project manager's time from the tedium of scheduling tasks.

Working with Internal Enterprise Environmental Factors

Internal EEFs are conditions that your organization has created for the project manager. You don't always know why these factors exist—they may result from a policy, a department requirement, or a tradition. It's not always necessary that you understand why you're required to do something; often it's just easier to accept it, do the work as requested, and move on. Sometimes, however, an EEF can be outdated, and it doesn't hurt to understand why it's required, especially if the factor is getting in the way of progress.

For your exam, you'll probably be required to accept any existing internal EEFs and work accordingly to answer exam questions.

Internal EEFs include the following:

- **Organizational culture, structure, and governance**   Your organization's mission, belief, culture, leadership, organizational hierarchy, and authority relationships are all examples of internal EEFs that are part of your organization.

- **Geographic distribution of facilities and resources**   Where your resources are located will affect how you manage the project, access resources, and schedule work. Resources are more than just people and also include physical resources. These factors can also address virtual teams and cloud computing—certainly elements that are now common and will affect the project.

- **Infrastructure**   The facilities, equipment, IT hardware and software, and capabilities of the infrastructure can limit, or propel, a project. You could reason that your project management methodology, Agile or waterfall, will also affect your infrastructure and how the people in the project operate.

- **Resource availability**   The time at which resources are available for your project will affect when your project can be completed. Resources include people, equipment, facilities, and materials.

- **Employee capability**   Consider the expertise of your project team members. Their skills and knowledge can directly affect the project work. If the project centers on a new technology, team members' learning curves or skills gaps can affect the project duration and approach to the work.

Considering External Enterprise Environmental Factors

While internal EEFs are created by the organization, external EEFs exist outside of the organization. External factors, like internal factors, can affect the project for better or worse. Here are some of the most common external EEFs you should be able to recognize:

- **Marketplace conditions**   The marketplace describes the climate your business operates within. Consider your organization's competitors, market share, brand recognition, and other factors that can affect how you manage your project.

- **Social and cultural influences**   The political climate, ethics, and perceptions about your business or trade can affect how you manage the project.

- **Legal restrictions**   Some of the most common EEFs are laws and regulations that directly affect your project, how you conduct business, and how you protect data.

- **Commercial databases**   Many industries, such as manufacturing and construction, utilize commercial databases to help predict duration of tasks, costs, risks, and what-if scenarios. If your organization uses such database types, it's using an external EEF.

- **Academic research** Publications, benchmarking, and industry studies that affect project decisions are EEFs to consider. This information doesn't have to come from a university but could include information from trade associations or groups to which your organization belongs.

- **Government or industry standards** Your organization may be required to adhere to government or industry standards regarding your project's production, quality of work, or products your organization creates.

- **Financial considerations** These external EEFs include international projects and currency exchange rates, interest rates, inflation rates for long-term projects, and other financial considerations that can influence project decisions.

- **Physical environmental elements** Where the project work will take place introduces external EEFs that can affect project decisions. The weather, access to job sites, and other constraints are all external EEFs.

Leveraging Organizational Process Assets

Unlike EEFs, *organizational process assets* (OPAs) are always internal to the organization. Organizational process assets include organizational processes, policies, procedures, and items from a corporate knowledge base. These assets are things that can be utilized to help the project manager do her job better. A common example of OPAs are documents from completed similar projects that can be adapted to the current project work to save time. Rather than create a project management plan from scratch with each project, the project manager can adapt a previous project to the current project and be on her way—that's one benefit of an OPA.

Of course, OPAs are much broader than that example, but that's one of the most common examples. Organizational process assets include anything from within the organization that you can use to manage the current project better, including artifacts, organizational knowledge bases, risk data, earned value management outcomes, and even lessons learned from past projects.

Organizational process assets are grouped into two categories:

- **Processes, policies, and procedures** These are created outside of the project, such as from a project management office, and aren't updated or changed by the project. Should a project manager want to change or deviate from a process, policy, or procedure, he'd need good reason to do so and would need to follow the organization's approach to changing the policy.

- **Organizational knowledge bases** My favorite type of OPA is updated throughout the project. As you add information, such as cost and time, actual experiences, lessons learned, and performance metrics, you'll update the associated OPA forms accordingly. Agile environments, particularly Scrum, don't document for the sake of documentation. In Agile, if the documentation isn't adding value, then it's generally not done.

NOTE See the difference? If it's a policy or process, you abide by it. If it's a form or template, you update, edit, and store it.

Adhering to Processes, Policies, and Procedures

Let's examine some OPAs that your organization may have in place that affect how you manage a project. Remember that these OPAs are unique to your organization; they are not universal to all organizations. Processes, policies, and procedures are not part of the 49 project management processes, but are unique organizational processes that determine how you get things done in your organization. The rules of your project management methodology will help dictate who's required to do what in the project, how the team interacts, and what the expectations of the stakeholders are.

Utilizing Initiating and Planning Processes, Policies, and Procedures

When a project is first launched, the project manager and possibly other stakeholders may pause to examine the big picture of the project. This examination takes place early in the project to determine the project's overall magnitude. The size and scope of the project can determine what OPAs are needed: Are you building a skyscraper, developing software, or replacing laptops? What processes are needed to complete the project, based on the size and scope of the project?

If you aren't going to be purchasing anything for your current project, there's no need to deal with the procurement processes. And if you are purchasing items, you may be required to use a preapproved vendor list to obtain these items, which is an OPA. Your organization may have created such process assets to help you select which project management processes are needed and which are not, based on the project's goals.

Other OPAs to consider at the launch of the project are human resource policies, management approaches, estimating techniques, checklists, and improvement goals for your project. Your organization may also require that templates be used for project plans and forms be used for resource assignments, and other assets may have been created for you to help assist the launch and planning of your project. Of course, all of these project management processes can be tailored to what works in your organization. The project management processes are not prescriptions, and not all processes are needed to the same depth on all projects.

Recognizing Executing, Monitoring, and Controlling Processes, Policies, and Procedures

As your project moves into executing the project plan, you'll also be working with monitoring and controlling activities. In both of these project management process groups, OPAs may have been created by your organization to use within portions of your project. One of the most common OPAs for any company is a process for how changes to the project are managed. Your organization can utilize forms, a web site, or special software to enter, track, and control changes—these are OPAs.

Tracking activities, requirements, costs, issues, and defects are also part of OPAs Though tracking such items is a typical requirement of project management, how you do this within your organization may be unique to your organization and entirely different from how a project manager tracks these items in another organization. The concept is the same, but the application of the OPAs is specific to each organization.

Several other OPAs are utilized in executing, monitoring, and controlling processes, policies, and procedures:

- Communications requirements and approaches to communicating
- Prioritizing, approving, and tracking work authorization
- Templates and forms (consider the change log, risk register, and issue log)
- Organizational standards for work, proposal evaluation for vendors, and performance measurement

Reviewing Closing Processes, Policies, and Procedures

Closing is a project management activity that can happen at the end of each project phase and at the end of the project. Your organization may have a particular approach to how you'll close a project or phase. Consider final project audits, evaluations, signoffs for deliverable acceptance, contract closure, release of project resources, and knowledge transfer. The final activities prescribed by your organization for a project are all part of its OPAs.

 EXAM TIP Remember that in Scrum, you close out each sprint with a retrospective to improve upon the next sprint of the project.

Leveraging Organizational Knowledge Repositories

Organizational knowledge repositories include the databases, files, and historical information that you can use to help plan and manage your projects. These OPAs are created internally in your organization through the ongoing work of operations and other projects. A knowledge repository should be organized, searchable, easy to access, and part of all project managers' go-to resources—though that may not be the case in every organization. (After working as a consultant with big and small companies, I have seen organizational knowledge repositories stuffed in a hallway closet, including reports and project plans—basically a jumbled mess, and hardly an ideal situation.)

For your exam, go with the idea that an organizational knowledge repository is an electronic set of databases that you can access quickly to find the information you need. Here are some examples of organizational knowledge repositories:

- Project files from past projects
- Metrics on data, processes, projects, and products
- Issue and defect databases

- Lessons learned knowledge repositories
- Financial databases from past projects
- Configuration management databases for versioning hardware and software, standards, policies, procedures, and project documentation

Working Within an Organizational System

Of course, where you manage a project will be entirely different from where I manage a project. The environment in which we both work, the expectations of our organizations, the reporting structures, and the rules we follow are unique to each organization. The structure of the organization and the governance framework create constraints that affect how the project manager makes decisions within the project. The organizational system directly affects how the project manager utilizes her power, influence, leadership, and even political capital, to get things done in the environment.

For your PMI exam, you'll need to recognize that the organizational system can be a type of constraint, because the organizational system will affect how the project manager acts within that system. Stakeholders with more power, influence, and political capabilities than the project manager can also directly affect how the project is managed, the goals of the project, and other stakeholder interests in the project. Though you won't need to know all the characteristics of organizational development, you will need to know some key facts about how projects may operate in different organizations.

Working in a System

Organizations are, to some extent, a system. A system uses multiple components to create things that the individual components could not create if they worked alone. For example, consider the system involved when purchasing something on the Internet: web client, service provider, web host, payment gateway, payment processor, credit card company, and likely more components, depending on the transaction and individuals involved. These different components are all needed to make the purchase happen. It's a system that creates a result for the customer and the retailer.

Regarding project management, *systems* describe the components your organization deals with to reach the desired result. Systems are dynamic and can be optimized for better performance. The individual components within a system can also be optimized independently of the system. Project managers typically don't manage a system—that's the responsibility of an organization's management—but the project manager may see opportunities for improvement within the system and may make recommendations accordingly. Projects operate within the system that the organization has created, and just because a system exists doesn't mean that the system was planned or that it is effective.

Operating Within a Governance Framework

The governance framework includes the rules, policies, and procedures that people within an organization agree to abide by. It's the structure that everyone agrees to operate within as part of the organization. Governance frameworks operate within systems, but frameworks are more about creating boundaries, providing directions, and establishing the roles and responsibilities of the people and groups within the organization. Governance frameworks define how the objectives of the organization are created, how risks are assessed and tracked, and how organizational performance can be optimized.

Organizations trying to adopt Agile often face challenges of how Agile works versus how things have been done in the past. The fluent nature of Agile requirements can conflict with the defined scope and detailed structure of predictive projects. The scrum master, or project manager in some organizations, must serve as an educator and coach to the organization to set expectations for the Agile environment. Over time, and with project success, the organization can see the benefits of Agile but still may have a challenge embracing the approach.

For your PMI exam, you'll need to recognize that the *governance framework* addresses the organization, but it also addresses portfolios, programs, and projects. Regarding portfolios, programs, and projects, the governance framework needs to address four key factors:

- Alignment with organizational mission
- Risk management and distribution of positive and negative risks
- Performance on time, costs, and technical objectives
- Communications with the correct stakeholders at the correct time

Governance framework is a top-down approach to control within the organization. Though the leadership and management of the organization may have created a governance framework, the governance of each project and program will be more specific to the particular program and project.

For your exam, know that *project governance* describes the rules and procedures that the project manager and the project team are expected to abide by. The project governance can be created by the project manager, or the governance framework can be established by the project management office, the department the project is operating within, or the organization itself.

Identifying the Organizational Influences

Projects happen within organizations, and in most instances, the organization is larger than the project. This means that you, as a project manager, must answer to someone, some department, or even a customer of the organization. As much as I'd like to call all the shots on all the projects I manage, and I'm sure you wish the same, we both know we must answer to someone within our organization. The people that project managers answer to are the *organizational influences*.

How a project is influenced is largely based on the type of organization that the project is occurring within. Project-centric organizations fall under two big umbrellas:

- **Organizations that exist primarily to perform projects for others** Think of architects, IT consulting firms, engineering firms, design consultants, and just about any other agency that completes work for others on a contract basis. (This is what I do as a writer and corporate educator, for example.)

- **Organizations that use management by projects to manage their business**   These organizations manage their work through their project management system. An IT department, for example, may treat an upgrade of all their network servers as a project. A manufacturer may treat the creation of a customer's product as a project. In the traditional sense, these activities are part of the organization's operations, but because there's a definite beginning and ending to that specific work, the organizations are taking advantage of project management systems they've adapted or created.

You also must consider the maturity of the organization in which the project is being hosted. A large internal organization that's been established for years will likely have a more detailed project management system than a startup entrepreneurial company. Organizational standards, regulations, culture, and procedures influence how the project should be managed, how the project manager will lead and discipline the project team, the reporting relationships, and the flow of communications that will take place.

It's also important for the project manager to know the organization's *cultural norms* and to operate accordingly. Consider the following cultural components within an organization:

- Defined values, beliefs, and expectations of the project work
- Policies and procedures, both within the organization and external to the organization (consider the policies that govern the banking industry, for example)
- Defined authority for the project manager and over the project manager
- Defined working hours and work ethics of the project team, project manager, and management

EXAM TIP   Remember that *cultural norms* describe the culture and the styles of an organization. Cultural norms such as work ethic, work hours, views of authority, and shared values can affect how a project is managed. Cultural norms can affect organizations that are experimenting with Agile approaches.

Completing Projects in Different Organizational Structures

In addition to the organizational system and the governance framework, project managers must also consider the organizational structure they are operating within. The organization structure is more than just the hierarchy of the organization, reporting structures, and authority over resources; it also defines how the authority, resources, roles, and functions are distributed throughout the organization. For example, a company could divide the organization according to departments, and departments "hire" teams from other departments to complete assignments. Or the organization could be structured by roles and responsibilities, where resources are freely used among the different departments and lines of business. Or there could hundreds of other structures, rules, and configurations regarding how an organization structures its lines of business, departments, and resources.

For your exam, you'll need to recognize the most common types of organizational structures and how each structure will influence the project manager's power over project decisions, the budget, and project team members. Which structure you're operating within will determine how much authority you have in the organization and in the project. For your exam, you'll need to recognize the organizational structure and then answer questions based on the structure presented in the question. You may see the same question more than once, and the only thing that changes in the question is the organizational structure—which would, of course, change the answer entirely. Knowing these structures will help you tremendously on the exam.

 VIDEO   Organizational structures can also affect the project life cycle. For a detailed look, watch the *Project Life Cycles* video now.

Recognizing Organizational Structures

Organizations are structured into one of several models that will affect some aspect(s) of the project. The organizational structure will set the level of authority, the level of autonomy, and the reporting structure that the project manager can expect to have within the project.

Organizational structures include the following:

- Organic or simple
- Functional (centralized)
- Multidivisional
- Weak matrix
- Balanced matrix
- Strong matrix
- Project-oriented
- Virtual
- Hybrid
- Project management office (PMO)

 NOTE   Understanding the type of organizational structure you're working in will help you be a better project manager. PMOs are a bit odd as far as organizational structures go, because you technically can have a PMO even within these other structure types. For your exam, just know that a PMO can be considered an organizational structure that supports, controls, or directs the project manager and the project. I'll talk a bit more about PMO types later in this chapter.

Organic or Simple Structure

An organic or simple organizational structure describes a loosely organized business or organization. There likely are no formal departments, and people work alongside one another regardless of their role or title in the organization. The project manager likely has little control over the project resources and may not be called a "project manager" at all. As you might expect, the project manager has little to no authority in the project. This kind of structure often exists in a small business environment or a startup company. In an organic or simple structure, the owner/operator of the organization will oversee the project budget, and you probably won't find administrative staff helping the project manager perform any administrative tasks.

Functional Structure

Functional organizations, sometimes called centralized organizations, are entities that have clear divisions regarding business units and their associated responsibilities. For example, a functional organization may have an accounting department, a manufacturing department, a research and development department, a marketing department, and so on. Each department works as a separate entity within the organization, and each employee works within a department unique to her area of expertise. In these centralized organizations, there is a clear relationship between an employee and a specific functional manager.

Functional organizations do complete projects, but these projects are specific to the function of the department that the project falls into. For example, the IT department could implement new software for the finance department. The role of the IT department is separate from that of the finance department, but the need for coordination between the two would be evident. Communications between departments flow through functional managers down to the project team.

Project managers in functional organizations have the following attributes:

- Little power
- Little autonomy
- Report directly to a functional manager
- May be known as a project coordinator, project expeditor, project administrator, or team leader (or project scapegoat)
- Project role is part-time
- Project team is part-time
- Little or no administrative staff to expedite the project management activities

Multidivisional Structure

Multidivisional structures describe organizations with a duplication of efforts within the organization, but not within each department or division of the organization. For example, the sales and marketing department could have a separate IT staff just for technology projects and support within the department. Meanwhile, the manufacturing department could also have its own IT staff for manufacturing projects and support. Each department is like its own organization within the company. Multidivisional structures are often like a functional structure from the project manager's perspective, because the project manager isn't likely to be a full-time role, the functional manager manages the project budget, and there's probably no administrative staff for the project manager.

Matrix Structure

Matrix structures are organizations that blend departmental duties and employees together on a common project. These structures allow for project team members from multiple departments to work together toward the project completion. In these instances, the project team members have more than one boss. Depending on the number of projects a team member is participating in, she may have to report to multiple project managers as well as to her functional manager.

Weak Matrix Structure

Weak matrix structures map closely to functional structures. The project team may come from different departments, but the project manager reports directly to a specific functional manager.

Project managers in weak matrix organizations have the following attributes:

- Limited authority
- Management of a part-time project team
- Part-time project role
- May be known as a project coordinator, project expeditor, project administrator, or team leader
- May have part-time administrative staff to help expedite the project

Balanced Matrix Structure

A balanced matrix structure has many of the same attributes as a weak matrix, but the project manager has more time requirements and power regarding the project. A balanced matrix structure includes time-accountability issues for all the project team members, because their functional managers will want reports on their time spent within the project.

Project managers in a balanced matrix have the following attributes:

- Reasonable authority over the project team and decisions
- May manage a part-time project team
- Have a full-time role as a project manager
- May have part-time administrative staff to help expedite the project

Strong Matrix Structure

A strong matrix equates to a strong project manager. In this type of organization, many of the same attributes for the project team exist, but the project manager gains power when it comes to project work. The project team may also have more time available for the project, even though the members may come from multiple departments within the organization.

Project managers in a strong matrix have the following attributes:

- A higher level of authority
- Management of a part-time to nearly full-time project team
- Have a full-time role as a project manager
- Have a full-time administrative staff to help expedite the project

Project-Oriented Structure

The project-oriented structure is at the pinnacle of project management structures. This organizational type groups employees, colocated or not, by activities on a project. The project manager in a project-oriented structure may have complete, or very close to complete, power over the project team. Project managers enjoy a high level of autonomy over their projects, but they also have higher levels of responsibility regarding the project's success.

Project managers in a project-oriented structure have the following attributes:

- High to complete level of authority over the project team
- Work full-time on the project with a team (though there may be some slight variation)
- Have a full-time administrative staff to help expedite the project
- Manage the budget

Virtual Structure

A virtual organization uses a network structure to communicate and interact with other groups and departments. A point of contact exists for each department, and these people receive and send all messages for the department. As you might assume, communications can sometimes be challenging in this structure because all messages are filtered through the department's point of contact.

Virtual organizations can be structured based on departments, but also on groups of stakeholders in a larger project. The project manager in a virtual organization has low authority over the project team and shares authority over the project budget with the functional manager. Depending on the project size, the project manager could be full-time, but the project team is likely part-time. In this structure, the project manager could have part-time or even full-time administrative staff to help with the project management.

Hybrid Structure

On paper, this organizational structure looks great. Truth is, few companies map to only one of these structures all the time. For example, a company using the functional model may create a special project consisting of talent from many different departments.

	Project Manager Authority	Project Manager Role	Resources on Project	Budget Control	Project Administrative Staff
Organic or simple	Low	Part-time	Little	Owner/operator	Little to none
Functional (centralized)	Low	Part-time	Little	Functional manager	Part-time
Multidivisional	Little	Part-time	Little	Functional manager	Part-time
Strong matrix	Moderate to high	Full-time	Moderate to high	Project manager	Full-time
Weak matrix	Low	Part-time	Low	Functional manager	Part-time
Balanced matrix	Low to moderate	Part-time	Low to moderate	Project manager and functional manager	Part-time
Project-oriented	High to almost total	Full-time	High to total	Project manager	Full-time
Virtual	Low to moderate	Full- or part-time	Low to moderate	Mixed	Part- or full-time
Hybrid	Mixed	Mixed	Mixed	Mixed	Mixed
PMO	High to total	Full-time	High to total	Project manager	Full-time

Table 2-1 Organizational Structures and Their Influence on Project Managers

Such project teams report directly to a project manager and will work on a high-priority project for its duration. These entities are sometimes called *composite* organizations, because they may be a blend of multiple organizational types.

Table 2-1 summarizes the most common organizational structures and their attributes.

Managing Project Teams

The type of organizational structure you're operating within will also determine the type of project team you're managing. As you might guess, in a project-oriented structure, you'll have a full-time project team, sometimes called a *dedicated* project team. In a functional or matrix environment, you'll likely have a part-time team. When you're working with project team members that float from project to project, as in a matrix environment, you'll have to coordinate with other project managers, functional managers, and the project team members about your project plans and need for resources.

Project teams in a functional, matrix, or project-oriented organizational structure often utilize contract-based workers to help achieve the project scope. These contractors are individuals who are represented by third parties or consulting agencies. When you're working with companies that have been hired to help and become part of the project team, you've created a partnership between your company and the vendor's company.

This partnership is ruled by the contract and may conflict with the project manager's approach, style, and project governance. You can alleviate much of the strain in a partnership by clearly communicating expectations of the entire project team and determining as early as possible whether the contractors have issues with the way the project team will be managed.

In today's electronic-based world, it's more and more common to work with virtual teams. Virtual teams use web-collaboration software to enable employees to work remotely, to attend meetings, and to share electronic workspaces. This, of course, saves on travel expenses, enables utilization of talented workers from all areas of an organization, and permits easier communications than telephone conversations and e-mail. Virtual teams can face additional problems that need to be addressed, such as time zone differences, language barriers, technology reliability, and cultural differences.

Working with a PMO

Recall that a PMO is a fancy-schmancy club where all the project managers get together for cigars and martinis. Not really—I just wanted to see if you were paying attention. The PMO coordinates the activities of all the project managers. Its primary goal is to create a uniform approach on how projects operate within the organization. PMOs can exist in any structure, but most are used in matrix structures and in project-oriented environments.

The role of the PMO is typically to support the project manager in the form of providing templates, project management software, training, and leadership, and even granting authority for the project's existence. Often, the PMO provides the administrative support a project manager can expect in a project-oriented environment.

Here's the big caveat with PMOs: Project team members in a PMO-oriented environment are traditionally working on one project at a time. A PMO, however, may elect to share project team members among projects if this best serves the organization. So, basically, there's no hard-and-fast rule for the assignment of project team members to an individual project if they are reporting to the PMO rather than directly to the project manager.

 EXAM TIP For the PMP exam, remember that the project manager reports to the PMO, and the PMO may exercise its authority over the project manager's control of the project team.

Here are some common PMO types you should recognize for your exam:

- **Supportive** The PMO plays a consultative role, providing templates, training, historical information, and best practices.
- **Controlling** The PMO controls the project through specific project management methodologies the project manager is required to use, such as frameworks, tools, forms and templates, and governance frameworks.
- **Directive** The PMO manages the project directly. The project manager is part of the PMO and is assigned to projects through the PMO only.

Chapter Summary

Two of the most important concepts of your PMI exam were covered in this chapter: enterprise environmental factors and organizational process assets. Enterprise environmental factors (EEFs) describe the conditions that will affect your project, influence your decisions, and even direct how you're allowed to do the project work. Enterprise environmental factors can come from within your organization, such as a policy, or they can come from outside of the organization, such as a law or regulation. You're going to see EEFs mentioned often throughout the *PMBOK Guide* and in this book, so make sure you've a good understanding of the things that can affect your project.

Organizational process assets (OPAs) are created only internally to the organization. Organizational process assets include organizational processes, policies and procedures, and items from a corporate knowledge base. These are things that can be utilized to help the project manager. Organizational process assets are grouped into two categories to consider: processes, policies, and procedures; and organizational knowledge bases. Processes, policies, and procedures are created outside of the project, such as from a project management office, and aren't updated or changed by the project. An organizational knowledge base is the treasure trove of information collected from past projects, databases, and knowledge repositories that you can access to help manage your current project.

Agile project management will make up nearly half of your PMP exam, and you'll be tested on pure Agile terminology and hybrid approaches to project management. You'll need to recognize the attributes of the most common Agile approaches even if you personally don't work with Agile. All Agile approaches adhere to the Agile Manifesto, which shows the four values of Agile project management. Your exam will certainly test you on the popular approaches to Agile, which included Scrum, Kanban, Lean, and XP. Scrum is the most popular approach and uses the idea of a product backlog, typically four-week sprints, daily scrums, sprint reviews, and retrospectives. Kanban breaks down the work but moves items through the system and illustrates the WIP in the Kanban board. Lean aims to reduce waste, empower the team, and build quality into the project. XP relies on paired programming, continuous integration, and test-first programming.

In this chapter, I also discussed governance framework. Governance framework describes the rules, policies, and procedures that people within an organization abide by. It's the structure that everyone agrees to operate within as part of the organization. Governance frameworks operate within the organizational system, but frameworks are more about creating boundaries, providing directions, and establishing the roles and responsibilities of the people and groups within the organization. Governance frameworks define how the objectives of the organization are created, how risks are assessed and tracked, and how organizational performance can be optimized.

The organizational structure can help the project team identify the stakeholders, and it also identifies the project manager's authority. There are ten organizational structures you should recognize for your exam: organic or simple, functional (centralized), multidivisional, weak matrix, strong matrix, balanced matrix, project-oriented, virtual, hybrid, and PMO. The PMO can be supportive, controlling, or directive—you should recognize each of these types of structures and their characteristics.

Case Study

Managing Projects from Start to Completion

This case study examines the project process and the phases a predictive project moves through to reach its conclusion. The Riverside Community Park Project was an endeavor to create a 140-acre community recreation park alongside the White River. The project, led by Thomas Stanford and assisted by Jan Steinberg, offered many deliverables for the community, including the following:

- A walkway along the river, connecting restaurants and neighborhoods
- Hiking trails
- Baseball and soccer fields
- Water access points
- Picnic areas
- Children's playgrounds
- An indoor swimming facility
- Parking areas

Examining the Project Deliverables

The first phase of the project was in-depth planning and development. The project scope was broken down into four major categories:

- River-related deliverables, such as docks and fishing areas
- Structural-related deliverables, such as the indoor swimming facility
- Environment-related deliverables, such as the hiking trails
- Common areas, such as the picnic and parking areas

Each of these deliverables was broken down into components that could, in turn, be broken down into exact deliverables for the project. For example, the indoor swimming facility included the excavation of the grounds for the building, the construction of the building, and the construction of the indoor swimming pool.

Each deliverable was broken down to ensure that all the required components were included in the project plan. Each category of deliverables went through a similar process to ensure that all the deliverables were accounted for and that the project plans were complete. Stanford and Steinberg worked with a large project team that specialized in different disciplines within the project work.

For example, Holly Johnson of EQHN Engineering served as team lead for the river-related deliverables. Johnson had years of experience in construction projects dealing with lakes, rivers, and manufactured waterways. Her expert judgment contributed to the development of the plan and the work breakdown.

Don Streeping of RHD Architecture and Construction helped Stanford develop the requirements, features, and components of the indoor swimming facility. RHD architects designed the building and swimming facilities for the project and helped map out the timeline for a feasible completion and successful opening day.

Grey Jansen with the Department of Natural Resources and Marci Koening with the Department of Urban Planning worked with Stanford to create several different hiking trails and a pedway along the riverfront. The elaborate trail system offered trails ranging from challenging hikes to pleasant strolls. In addition, the pedway enabled visitors to walk through more than 50 acres along the river and to visit restaurants, shopping centers, and other commercial ventures within the park. Without Jansen's and Koening's expertise, the project would not have been a success.

Finally, John Anderson led the team responsible for the common areas. The children's playgrounds were topnotch, with ample parking and access to the park. In addition, Anderson's team created soccer fields and two Little League baseball diamonds.

Examining the Project Phases

When the project was launched, the 140-acre tract was a marshy, brush-filled plot of land that was mostly inaccessible to the public. For this undertaking to be successful, the project had to move through several phases. Many of the deliverables, such as the parking areas and maintenance roads, had to be created first to enable the equipment and workers to access the sites throughout the park.

Phase One

The first phase of the project was in-depth planning. Stanford and Steinberg worked with each of the team leaders and other experts to coordinate the activities to create the deliverables in a timely fashion. To maximize the return on investment, the project's plan called for immediate deliverables for the public.

The planning phase of the project resulted in the following:

- The project plan and subsidiary plans, such as cost, risk, and scope management plans
- Design specifications for each of the major deliverables
- A schedule that enabled the project team and stakeholders to work together to create the project deliverable
- The creation of a work authorization system
- Continued community buy-in for the project

Phase Two

Once the project's plan and coordination between teams was realized, Anderson's crew went to work on Phase Two of the project: creating accessibility. This phase of the project became known as the "rough-in" phase, because roads, parking, and preparation of the park were needed immediately. This phase resulted in the following:

- Access roads throughout the park

- Entry roads to the park at several points throughout the city

- Junction roads that provided easy access for construction equipment to be stored on site for the project's duration

Phase Three

In Phase Three of the project, each team began working independently, each with an eye toward common delivery dates. For example, Johnson and Jansen had expertise in separate deliverables: the water access points and the trails throughout the park. The project plan called for trails along the river and through the woods, which would be built by Johnson's crew. In tandem with creating the hiking trails, Johnson's team went to work on the river pedway. At several points along the river pedway, trails from the woods would connect to the paved surface. These two deliverables were timed so that both teams would work together on connecting the nature trails with the river pedway. In addition, preservation of the environment in the woods and in the water was an important consideration.

Streeping's primary responsibility was the creation of the indoor swimming facility. This deliverable required excavation, construction of the indoor swimming pool, and construction of the facility to house the indoor swimming pool. Streeping had to coordinate the construction with Anderson, as the swimming pool required the largest parking area in the compound. Stanford and Steinberg worked with each team leader to facilitate a common schedule for each of the deliverables.

This phase saw its first completed deliverable for the project: a children's playground was opened near the park entrance that the public could begin using immediately. The playground could host up to 75 children at once with parking for up to 50 cars. In addition, a picnic shelter was opened adjacent to the playground. Because of the proximity of the park and playground to nearby shops and restaurants, this deliverable was well received by the community, and the public began enjoying the facilities immediately.

Other deliverables in the phase included the following:

- Restroom facilities installed at several points throughout the park

- Excavation of several water access points

- Excavation for the swimming facility

- Clearing and leveling for the soccer and baseball fields

Phase Four

Phase Four of the project focused on creating more usable deliverables for the public. The focus was on the hiking trails throughout the park and on partial completion of the river pedway. The hiking trails required the removal of brush and some trees, and the land needed to be graded for passable hiking. The pedway was initially formed as a concrete path that would be blacktopped once it was connected throughout the park. Like the hiking trails, the pedway required the removal of brush and trees while considering the environmental preservation of the river.

Jansen's and Anderson's teams worked together to clear the pedway, remove the brush along the riverbank, and preserve the older trees to create a stunning walk along the river. To create maximum deliverables, the pedway was implemented at opposite ends of the 50-acre trail, with plans to be connected at acre 25. This enabled the public to enjoy the deliverables in increments from either end of the park.

This phase created these deliverables:

- Seven of the ten hiking trails in the system were cleared and opened for public usage.
- A total of 30 acres of the river pedway was completed (15 acres on both ends of the pedway).
- The swimming pool was excavated, and the concrete body of the pool was installed.

Phase Five

Phase Five of the project was perhaps the most exciting, as it completed several deliverables:

- The remaining three hiking trails were completed. These trails included bridges over small creeks that fed into the White River.
- The remaining 20 acres of the river pedway were excavated and completed with the concrete pour. People could then walk or ride their bikes the entire 50-acre length alongside the river.
- The soccer and baseball facilities were installed, which included restrooms, concession stands, bleachers, fences, and dugouts. The fields were also seeded and fertilized, with expectations to be officially open for public use the following spring when the grass was healthy.

Phase Six

Phase Six of the project was the longest, but most satisfying, phase. This phase focused on the completion of the indoor swimming facility. The structure included two Olympic-sized swimming pools, diving boards, locker rooms, sauna and steam facilities, and a restaurant. The building was situated on a hill that overlooked the river pedway—it was the crown jewel of the park. The facility was completed as planned and was opened to the public.

This phase also included the following:

- Completion of blacktopping the 50-acre pedway along the river
- Closing and sodding of the temporary construction equipment corral
- Installation of the remaining playgrounds and picnic areas throughout the park
- Opening of the water access points, including a commercial dock for fishers and boaters
- Official opening of the soccer and baseball fields

Controlling Project Changes

Throughout the project, the public had many requests for changes to the project scope. The project scope was quite large, and the project budget had limited room for additional changes without requiring additional funds.

When changes were proposed, such as the addition of tennis courts to the common areas, they were considered for validity, cost, risk, and the impact on the project scope. A change control board, which Stanford initiated, considered the proposed changes and then approved or declined the changes based on predetermined metrics such as time, cost, and overall change to the original project scope.

When the project was initiated, a public meeting was held to gather input from the community on the deliverables they would most like to see in the park. At this point of the project, the stakeholders—the community at large—had a great opportunity to voice their opinions on what the park should and should not include. Once a consensus was created for the park deliverables and a scope was created, it became challenging for anyone to add to it.

Some changes, however, proved valuable and were added to project deliverables. For example, the commercial fishing and boating dock within the park was a viable opportunity for a local businessperson to provide a service for boaters and the community at no cost to the project. Keening and Johnson worked with the business to ensure that the dock met the city codes and safety regulations and fit within the scheme and overall effect of the project.

Other changes, such as the tennis courts, were declined. Though there were many tennis players in the community, this request was denied for several reasons:

- The city already supported many tennis courts in the community.
- A private tennis club near the park protested the addition of the tennis courts, because this would be an economic blow to their business.
- No tennis players had requested the courts at any of the public meetings discussing the creation of the park.

Changes, especially in a project of this size, had to be tracked and documented. Any changes that were approved or declined were cataloged as part of the change log for reference against future change requests that may have entered the project.

Questions

1. You are working with your project team and stakeholders to plan out the project work. Some of the resources are in Chicago and other resources are in London, UK. The distribution of resources, such as in your project, are also known as what?

    A. Enterprise environmental factors

    B. Organizational process assets

    C. Virtual team

    D. Constraints

2. Understanding enterprise environmental factors is an important part of your role as a project manager and an important part of the PMI exam. Of the following choices, which one is not an enterprise environmental factor?

   A. Employee capability

   B. Infrastructure

   C. Templates

   D. Organizational culture

3. In your industry, your products must adhere to a government regulation. This government regulation will affect how you manage your project. The government regulation in this scenario is best described as which one of the following?

   A. Organizational process asset

   B. External enterprise environmental factor

   C. Constraint

   D. External constraint

4. As the project manager, you must work with your project team to identify the project phases within the project schedule. To help with this identification, you are using the project plan and project documents from a completed and similar project. These project files are commonly known as what term?

   A. Enterprise environmental factors

   B. Lessons learned

   C. Organizational process assets

   D. Supportive PMO

5. Governance framework is important for the success of the project, programs, and portfolios within an organization. Governance framework addresses all the following items except for which one?

   A. Alignment with the organizational mission

   B. Change control procedures

   C. Performance on time, cost, and scope

   D. Communications with stakeholders

6. Mark is the owner of a small manufacturing company. He's working with the assemblers, production crew, and even the administrative staff to complete an order for a new client. There's no formal project manager on this project, but everyone is working together to complete the project on time. What type of structure is Mark operating in?

   A. Simple

   B. Multidivisional

   C. Project-oriented

   D. Strong matrix

7. You are a project manager working as a scrum master. You, the product owner, and the development team are reviewing the user stories that are of highest priority that will be selected for the development team to take on during their next sprint. What meeting is taking place in this scenario?

   A. Sprint planning

   B. Product backlog prioritization

   C. Sprint review

   D. Sprint retrospective

8. Marcy is the project manager of the GQD Project for her organization. She is working with Stan, the project sponsor, and they are identifying the most likely phases for this type of project work. Why would an organization divide a project into phases?

   A. To provide better management and control of the project

   B. To identify the work that will likely happen within a phase of the project

   C. To identify the resources necessary to complete a phase of the project

   D. To define the cash-flow requirements within each phase of the project

9. You are the project manager for your organization. Gary, a new project team member, is working on multiple projects at once. He approaches you, worried about who he reports to. In addition, Gary has a functional manager who is assigning him work. What type of structure are you and Gary operating in?

   A. Functional

   B. Weak matrix

   C. Program office

   D. Project-oriented

10. You are the project manager of a new project. When is the likelihood of failing to achieve the objectives the highest within your project?

    A. There is not enough information provided to know for certain.

    B. At the start of the project.

    C. At the end of the project.

    D. During the intermediate phases of the project.

11. A stakeholder approaches you, the scrum master, with a needed change for the project you're working on. The change is significant and important to the stakeholder, and they want the team to get to work on the change right away. Currently the development team is in week three of a four-week sprint. What should you do next?

    A. Cancel the sprint so the team may start the change request.

    B. Document the change as a user story and give it to the development team.

    C. Meet with the product owner to write a user story and get the change into the product backlog.

    D. Do nothing. No changes can be entered into the product backlog during a sprint.

12. You are the project manager for your organization and you're working with your company's project management office. The PMO has provided you with forms, templates, software, and some advice on how best to manage the project. What type of project management does your company have?

   A. Consultative

   B. Supporting

   C. Controlling

   D. Directive

13. You are a project manager acting in a functional organization. You and the functional manager disagree about several deliverables the project will be creating. The functional manager insists that you begin the project work now. What must you do?

   A. Begin work.

   B. Resolve all the issues with the functional manager before you begin working.

   C. Continue planning because you are the project manager.

   D. Begin work if the issues don't affect the project deliverables.

14. You are a project manager working under a PMO. Your project resources are shared among several projects. To whom will the project team members report?

   A. The project manager of each project

   B. The functional managers

   C. The PMO

   D. The project manager of their primary project

15. An organization is implementing a new Agile project management approach for their software development projects. In this approach, they've decided that one person will program, and a second programmer will evaluate the code being written to ensure accuracy. Which Agile project management approach is being implemented?

   A. Scrum

   B. Kanban

   C. XP

   D. Lean

16. You are the project manager for your organization and you're working with the project team to explain the approach of the project life cycle and how you'll be managing proposed changes to the project scope. Your company is a weak matrix company; who will make decisions on change control?

   A. Project manager

   B. Project team

   C. Functional manager

   D. PMO

17. Nancy is a project manager for the NHG Corporation. She has identified several positive stakeholders for her construction project and a few negative stakeholders. Nancy and the project team have been meeting regularly with the positive stakeholders but have not met with the negative stakeholders. Mike, the chief project officer from the PMO, tells Nancy she needs to meet with the negative stakeholders as quickly as possible. What type of PMO is Nancy working with?

A. Consultative

B. Directive

C. Controlling

D. Supportive

18. Don is the project manager for his organization. In this project, his team will comprise local workers and workers from Scotland, India, and Belgium. Don knows that he needs to consider the working hours, culture, and expectations of this virtual team to manage it successfully. All of the following are cultural attributes of an organization except for which one?

A. Policies and procedures

B. Work ethics

C. View of authority relationships

D. Experience of the project management team

19. You are a new project manager for your organization. Management has asked you to begin creating a project management plan with your project team based on a recently initiated project. The project management plan defines which one of the following?

A. Who the project manager will be

B. How the project manager will use the project management system

C. When the project team will be assembled and released

D. How the deliverable will be shipped to the customer

20. You are the project manager in your organization. Unlike your last job, which used a functional structure, this organization is utilizing a weak matrix. Who has full authority over project funding in a weak matrix?

A. The project manager

B. The functional manager

C. The PMO

D. The project sponsor

Answers

1. **A.** The distribution of resources is an enterprise environmental factor. The location of the resources can affect how the project operates and communicates with resources and stakeholders. B is incorrect; the distribution of project resources is not an organizational process asset. Though resources located in different parts of the world could be a virtual team (answer C), the better choice is enterprise environmental factors. D, constraints, is a tempting choice because the project manager may see the distribution of resources as a constraint, but the question doesn't tell us if this is a positive or negative factor for the project.

2. **C.** Templates are not enterprise environmental factors, so this choice is correct. The other choices, employee capability, infrastructure, and organizational culture, are all enterprise environmental factors, so these choices are incorrect for this question.

3. **B.** A government regulation is an external enterprise environmental factor that has been created outside of your organization. You must adhere to the regulation, so it is an enterprise environmental factor. Choices A, C, and D are not valid choices because organizational process asset, constraint, and external constraint do not correctly describe the regulation for your project. Organizational process assets are created internally to help the project. While the regulation may be seen as a constraint, the best choice is that a regulation is an external enterprise environmental factor.

4. **C.** Project files and documents from past, similar projects are organizational process assets. A is incorrect because enterprise environmental factors direct how the work is to be completed, rather than serving as an input for planning and decisions such as historical information. B, lessons learned, is an organizational process asset, but it's not the best answer for this question. D, a supportive PMO, may be welcome, but there's no evidence in this question that a PMO is being used.

5. **B.** Governance framework does not address the change control procedures. A, C, and D are incorrect because governance frameworks does address alignment with mission, performance issues, and stakeholder communications.

6. **A.** This is an example of a simple or organic organizational structure. The workers are all working together and alongside one another regardless of title or role. B, C, and D are incorrect because this is not a multidivisional, project-oriented, or strong matrix.

7. **A.** This is sprint planning. Sprint planning is completed by the product owner, scrum master, and the development team to select from the prioritized backlog what items will be accomplished during the sprint. The selected items become the sprint backlog. B is incorrect because there is no product backlog prioritization meeting. C, the sprint review, is done at the end of a sprint and is hosted by the development team. The development team will demonstrate what they've completed in the sprint. D is also incorrect because the sprint retrospective is a lessons-learned type meeting to discuss what's worked, or hasn't worked, so the sprint team may improve upon their work in the next sprint of the project.

8. A. Organizations often divide projects into phases to make the management and control of the project easier and more productive. B and C are incorrect because these statements identify an attribute of a phase, not the reason to create all phases. D is incorrect because this statement is not true for all projects. In addition, cash-flow forecasting is part of planning and is not universal to all project phases.

9. B. The best choice is that you and Gary are operating in a weak matrix structure. Gary is working on multiple projects and he is also receiving work assignments from his functional manager—something that isn't likely to happen in a functional or project-oriented structure. C is incorrect because a program office isn't a specific organizational structure.

10. B. Projects are most likely to fail at the start of the project. As the project moves closer to completion, the odds of it finishing successfully increase. A is not an accurate statement. C is incorrect because the project is more likely to finish successfully at the end of the project. D is incorrect because the intermediate phases show progress toward project completion. The farther the project moves away from its start and the closer toward completion, the higher the odds of success.

11. C. The best choice is that the scrum master should meet with the product owner to document the change and get it into the product backlog. The product owner is responsible for documenting the user story and prioritizing the user stories. A is incorrect as only the product owner may cancel a sprint—and that is a rare event in Scrum. B is incorrect as the changes to the project scope will go to the product owner, who will document it, enter it into the product backlog, and prioritize the backlog entries in consideration of the additional requirement. D is incorrect; doing nothing is almost always the worst choice for a change request. Changes are welcome and expected during Agile projects. Changes are entered into the product backlog at any time the product owner determines they are ready to be written as a user story and prioritized.

12. B. A supporting PMO will provide support, such as forms, templates, software, and advice on the project. A, consultative, is incorrect because this isn't a valid PMO type. C, controlling, is incorrect because this type of PMO is more concerned with compliance than supporting the project manager role. D, directive, is incorrect because a directive PMO manages the project directly.

13. A. Because you are working within a functional organization, you have little to no power, and the functional manager has all the power. You must obey the functional manager and get to work. B, C, and D are all incorrect choices for the project manager in a functional structure.

14. A. When resources are shared and a PMO exists, the project resources report to the PMO for staff assignments, but they'll report to the project manager of each project they're assigned to. B is incorrect because resources are not shared among several projects in a functional structure. In addition, a functional structure does require the project manager to report to the functional manager. C is incorrect because the PMO may be responsible for staff alignment and assignment, but the project team does not report to the PMO. D is not a valid answer.

15. **C.** In this scenario, the organization is implementing XP, or Extreme Programming. XP readily uses pair programming, where one programmer is writing the code and a second programmer evaluates the code for quality control and accuracy. A, B, and D are incorrect because Scrum, Kanban, and Lean do not utilize pair programming as XP does.

16. **C.** In a weak matrix, the functional manager has more authority than the project manager and will make project decisions. A, B, and D are incorrect because the project manager, the project team, and the PMO will not likely have change control authority in a weak matrix.

17. **C.** Nancy cannot simply ignore the negative stakeholders. Their influence on the project may cause the project to fail. Because the PMO is a controlling PMO, Nancy must do as asked and work with the negative stakeholders quickly to squelch their protests or consider their demands to ensure compliance or agreement with their issues. A is incorrect because there is not a PMO structure called consultative. B and D are incorrect because Gary is giving Nancy an assignment, something that wouldn't happen with a supportive or directive PMO; this is likely a controlling PMO.

18. **D.** The experience of the project management team is not a cultural attribute of an organization. A, B, and C—the policies and procedures, the work ethics, and the view of authority relationships—are all classic examples of an organization's culture.

19. **B.** The project plan defines how the project management system will be used. A is incorrect. The project charter defines who the project manager will be. C is incorrect because the staffing management plan defines how the project team will be assembled and managed. Technically, the staffing management plan is part of the overall project management plan, but B is the best answer presented. D is incorrect because not every project will need to ship a deliverable to a customer.

20. **B.** In a weak matrix, the functional manager has the power over the project funding, not the project manager. The functional manager is likely to be the project sponsor. A, C, and D are all incorrect statements because these do not define the authority of the project manager in a weak matrix structure.

Working as a Project Manager

In this chapter, you will
- Explore the project manager role
- Understand the project manager's influence
- Learn the project management competencies
- Learn to lead and manage a successful project
- Study project integration

As a PMP candidate, you're likely already serving as a project manager in your organization. The PMP exam will test your knowledge of the typical roles and responsibilities of a project manager. You'll need to be familiar with the most common types of activities and characteristics of a project manager. Be aware that this means you'll need to recognize the roles and responsibilities for both predictive environments and adaptive environments, even if you don't work with an organization that uses one of those approaches. I'll address both environments in this chapter and what you can expect in either.

Where you work or will work as a project manager is likely different from where other readers of this book work or will work. Just as every project is unique, so, too, is the environment in which a project exists. Consider software development projects, construction projects, IT infrastructure projects, learning and development projects, and as many different types of projects as you can imagine. Each of these different projects operates in a distinct environment. The environment is a factor of influence in these projects and in your projects. Remember for your exam that there is no blanket approach that fits every scenario; how you best operate as a project manager in your organization depends on the environment.

Exploring the Project Manager Role

Project management is about getting things done. You already know that projects are temporary endeavors that don't last forever. Project management is about getting the project started as quickly and as effectively as possible, and then leading the project team to completion: getting it done. Projects, especially in a predictive environment, often have no business value until they are complete. Consider a construction project:

Generally, no one can use the new building until the construction project is done. The project has no value until the completed building begins to earn a return on investment. The longer a project takes to complete, the greater the exposure to risk, the more expensive the project is likely to be, and the more frustrated stakeholders will be because the project is still in progress. Project managers get it done.

Adaptive projects often have a series of releases, usually about every three to six months. Adaptive projects can realize and use benefits as soon as it makes good sense to do so. For example, a project may have multiple releases of software planned: Version 1, 1.1, 1.2, and so on. Each release, or increment, of the completed product enables the organization to realize business value—which is not something we can always do in a predictive project.

In either case, you can't just charge in and start firing off assignments and putting people to work. Project management requires a structured approach. For starters, project managers are often involved in the project design before the project is even initiated. A project manager may meet with the portfolio review board, customers, and management to offer input before a project is selected, funded, initiated, and staffed. Project managers may work with business analysts (or take on the role of a business analyst) to gather requirements, create high-level estimates, and develop business cases and feasibility studies—all work that precedes project initiation.

The project manager has roles and responsibilities, but so do people on the project team. Roles are assigned to determine who does what on the project: developer, app tester, plumber, or technical writer, for example. In many projects, project team members, like the project manager, play multiple roles in a project. While the project manager is responsible for leading and managing the project team, the project team is responsible for completing their work assignments. Scrum projects, for example, call for the development team to be self-organizing and to determine who'll complete what work in each iteration.

During planning, which is an *iterative* activity, the project manager and the project team will plan the work; next, they'll execute the project work. As the project manager leads and manages the project team, she will rely on the project team's expertise, experience, skills, and technical abilities to complete assignments. It's unrealistic for the project manager to have the skills and depth of knowledge of each project team member. The project manager should rely on the expertise of the project team when it comes to planning, and then the project team members must complete their assignments as promised.

Defining the Agile Project Manager

To define the project management role in an adaptive project is tricky, because there are so many different agile approaches available. The flavor of agile project management will directly influence the project manager's roles and responsibilities in the approach. You'll need to recognize the project management roles and responsibilities for the most common adaptive approaches. For the most part, however, the principles of project management are similar in either adaptive or predictive approaches: follow the rules and get stuff done.

Throughout this book, I'll reference the roles, principles, and attributes of project management as if they apply to all project management approaches, unless there's a significant difference between the project management role in a predictive versus adaptive environment.

Here are the project management definitions for the most common adaptive (agile) project management approaches:

- **Scrum**   There is no project manager. Instead, the project management role is divided among the three roles: the scrum master, the product owner, and the development team. The scrum master, the closest role to a predictive project manager role, serves as a coach, protects the development team from interruptions, gets the development team what they need, and makes certain all roles are following the Scrum rules.

- **Kanban**   This project manager has typical project management duties but also follows the rules of Kanban and ensures that everyone is following the basic rules of Kanban. This means he'll ensure that defects aren't moving through the Kanban system, make sure that requirements are being completed, manage the WIP, maintain the Kanban board, and help stabilize the processes in the project.

- **Lean**   The project manager in a Lean environment also has many of the traditional project management responsibilities, but he also must work with the team to promote efficiency, accuracy, and reduce waste. The Lean project manager will aim to identify bottlenecks, perform root cause analysis (RCA), and then take steps to improve bottleneck issues. Lean project management begins with defining the value the project creates and then planning with the team how to achieve that value by eliminating waste, improving the process, and serving the project team.

- **XP**   There is no project manager. XP has two project management roles, which are typically fulfilled by different people who take on project management activities. The manager role tracks performance, ensures that everyone is following the rules, and leads the continual planning processes. The coach role coaches the team on the XP rules, remains calm even when others are panicking, helps the team become self-reliant, and intervenes only when there's a problem that the team is overlooking.

Leading the Project Team

It's been said that project managers manage things, but lead people. Project management is about doing whatever it takes to achieve the desired results. Leadership is all about motivating and inspiring individuals to work toward those expected results. Management and leadership go together in project management, and you'll need both to be an effective project manager.

Most of us have worked for a project manager who hasn't been all that motivating. A good project manager, like you, motivates and inspires people to see the vision and helps the project team realize how their work contributes to business value for the organization. The project manager needs to inspire the project team to overcome obstacles to get the work done. Motivation is a constant process, and the project manager must be able to motivate the team to move toward completion—instilling passion and providing inspiration for completing the work. Finally, motivation and inspiration must be real; the project manager must have a personal relationship with the project team members to help them achieve their goals.

 EXAM TIP Remember that leadership can also come from project team members, not just from the project manager. A leader does not always have to be a single person; leadership can come from multiple sources. This is the concept of emergent leadership—anyone can emerge as a leader.

Communicating Project Information

Communication is all important in project management. You can summarize communication as who needs what information, when the information is needed, what's the best modality to deliver the message, and who should have access to the information. As a project manager, you may spend most of your time communicating: talking with the project team, meeting with stakeholders, e-mailing management, coordinating with vendors, and more and more. If you're a good communicator, you can be a great project manager.

Communication is a two-way street that requires a sender and a receiver. *Active listening* is needed in important conversations. Active listening happens when the receiver of the message paraphrases what the sender has said to clarify and confirm the message. For example, if a project team member tells you that an assignment will be done in seven days, you'd respond that the work package will be done a week from today. This gives the project team member the opportunity to clarify that the work package will actually be done nine days from today because of the upcoming weekend—they'll need seven working days to complete the assignment.

There are several communication avenues:

- Listening and speaking
- Written and oral
- Internal, such as project team member to team member
- External, such as the project manager to an external customer
- Formal, such as reports and presentations
- Informal, such as e-mails and impromptu hallway meetings
- Vertical, which follows the organizational flowchart
- Horizontal, such as manager to manager within the organizational flowchart

Communication management includes variables and elements unique to the flow of communication. Although I'll discuss communications in full in Chapter 10, here are some key facts to know for now:

- **Sender-receiver models**   Communication requires a sender and a receiver. Within the sender-receiver model may be multiple avenues to complete the flow of communication, but barriers to effective communication may be present as well. Other variables within this model include recipient feedback, surveys, checklists, and confirmation of the sent message.

- **Media selection**   There are multiple choices of media for conveying information. Which medium is appropriate? Based on the audience and the information being sent, the medium should be in alignment. In other words, an ad hoc hallway meeting is probably not the best communication avenue to explain a large variance in the project schedule.

- **Style**   The tone, structure, and formality of the message being sent should be in alignment with the audience and the content of the message.

- **Presentation**   When it comes to formal presentations, the presenter's oral and body language, visual aids, and handouts all influence the message being delivered.

- **Meeting management**   Meetings are forms of communication. How the meeting is led, managed, and controlled all influence the message being delivered. Agendas, minutes, time boundaries, and order are mandatory for effective communications within a meeting. Meetings in adaptive environments often have specific rules, such as the duration of the meeting, the cadence, and the participants allowed.

Negotiating Project Terms and Conditions

You don't always get what you want, and as a project manager, you'll really know that's true. Project managers must negotiate for the good of the project. In any project, the project manager, the project sponsor, and the project team will have to negotiate with stakeholders, vendors, and customers to reach a level of agreement acceptable to all parties involved in the negotiation process. Negotiation is about more than give-and-take and compromise; negotiating is about determining what's most fair for everyone, deciding what's best for the project, and respecting all parties in the process.

In some instances, typically in less-than-pleasant circumstances, negotiations may have to proceed with assistance. Specifically, mediation and arbitration are examples of assisted negotiations. Negotiation proceedings typically center on the following:

- Priorities
- Technical approach
- Project scope

- Schedule

- Cost

- Changes to the project scope, schedule, or budget

- Vendor terms and conditions

- Project team member assignments and schedules

- Resource constraints, such as facilities, travel issues, and team members with highly specialized skills

 EXAM TIP   For the exam, remember that the purpose of negotiations is to reach a fair agreement among all parties. Be respectful of all involved; you may have to work with them throughout the project and beyond.

Active Problem-Solving

Projects can be cumbersome and tedious, can have competing objectives, and can have constraints that seem to box in the project manager. Project management demands problem-solving. Problem-solving is the ability to understand the problem, identify a viable solution, and then implement a solution. Though you want to be accurate in your decision, you don't want to take too long to act. This is why many project managers will say it's better to fail fast—try your best option, and if it doesn't work, adapt. In any project, countless problems require viable solutions. And like any good puzzle, the solution to one portion of the problem may create more problems elsewhere.

Active problem-solving is what the development team does in adaptive projects. They'll examine the work, determine how much work they can feasibly complete in the next iteration, and then be self-organizing to determine who'll do what work. Knowledge work, such as software development, is full of problem-solving. The XP framework, for example, takes problem-solving head-on by using paired programming to code, check, and partner on developing solid, quality code that works and that passes predefined tests.

Problem-solving requires a clear understanding of what the problem is—this means first defining the problem. A viable solution focuses on more than just the problem. In defining the problem, you must discern between its causes and effects. This requires root-cause analysis to identify the effects, which include the problem plus all the possible causes and combinations of causes. If a project manager treats only the symptoms of a problem rather than the cause of the problem, the symptoms will perpetuate and continue throughout the project's life. Root-cause analysis looks beyond the immediate symptoms to the cause of the symptoms—which then affords opportunities for solutions.

Root-cause analysis doesn't solve the problem, however; you'll still need to implement your solution. Solutions can be presented from vendors, the project team, the project manager, or various stakeholders, which the *PMBOK Guide* refers to as "expert judgment." In addition, a timely decision is needed, or the window of opportunity may pass, and then a new decision will be needed to address the problem. As in most cases, the worst thing you can do is nothing.

Identifying the Project Manager Influence

Project managers have a wide sphere of influence. The projects we manage can affect end users, customers, vendors, and the public, and people can still be affected even long after the project manager has retired. Projects can also be influenced by many different groups of people: end users, managers, vendors, the project team, and more. The influence you have as a project manager will often depend on your experience, your maturity within the organization, and the size of the project you're managing.

Influence isn't something we often think about as project managers, but it's a factor that you should consider when planning and executing the project, and certainly when you're communicating with stakeholders. Not that you must play politics, but a project manager must consider the implications of the project's success, the communications between the project manager and project team, and the perceptions of the stakeholders regarding the project and its leadership. Over time and with experience in your organization, you'll find it easier to understand the undercurrent of politics and the hidden messages in questions and comments, and you'll have a broader, wiser view into what's happening in the organization and how your project (and you) affects the environment. Figure 3-1 shows the levels of influence between stakeholders and project managers.

Figure 3-1
Stakeholder and project manager influence are connected.

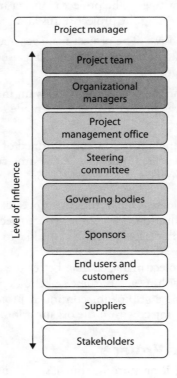

For your PMP exam, consider the different levels of influence the project manager has on the following stakeholders:

- **End users and customers**   The project manager is responsible to these people for what the project is creating, how the project may interfere with their lives as the project is in progress, and how the project will contribute to their lives once it is done.

- **Stakeholders**   All the people and groups that are affected by the project and can affect the project are stakeholders that the project manager can influence for the betterment of the project.

- **Project team**   The project manager leads and directs the team to reach the project's objectives.

- **Organizational managers**   The project manager will likely need to work with managers to have access to people, processes, and resources.

- **Project management office**   The project manager will work with the project management office, if one exists, to manage the project and provide assets, directions, and support.

- **Steering committee**   The project manager may have to report to the steering committee regarding the project status and progress.

- **Governing bodies**   The project manager may have to report to internal project governance or to government agencies regarding how the project is adhering to laws and regulations.

- **Sponsors**   The project sponsors will want information on the project status and decisions the project manager has made to keep the project moving forward toward its objectives.

- **Suppliers**   Suppliers need to be informed of when resources and services are needed, and they are influenced by the project manager's planning and the procurement policies of the organization.

These are stakeholders. One of the first processes you'll need to complete in a project is stakeholder identification. The sooner you correctly identify all the stakeholders, the better your project will perform. People don't like to be overlooked, especially when your endeavor is going to affect them. Stakeholders are linked to the project manager and influenced by the project manager. The better the project manager coordinates, plans, and communicates within each of these stakeholder spheres, the better the project manager can influence these groups for continued project support, improved synergy, and sustainability of the project within the organization.

Influencing the Project

No one sets out to fail on purpose, but it's not unusual for projects to fail, miss their key performance objectives, or scrape across the finish line with a blown budget and late delivery. The success, or failure, of a project is indicative of how well the project manager led the project team, balanced constraints, executed the project plan, and monitored the project progress. The person with the greatest influence over a project is the project manager, and the project's outcome is largely based on the project manager's ability to influence the project to reach its objectives. Sure, some projects are doomed from the start because of lack of finances and qualified resources, an unrealistic schedule, or other problems, but these are the exceptions, not the rule. Besides, a good project manager will address these issues and risks with management and stakeholders to find solutions.

Communication and a positive attitude can do wonders for the success of a project. Communication is paramount in project management; project managers must communicate with stakeholders through a variety of methods: verbal, written, and nonverbal. Messages must be direct and appropriate for the audience, and the communication style should be tailored based on what's being communicated to whom. Show me a project manager who doesn't communicate well and I'll show a project manager who's not great at leading projects.

Project managers must communicate good and bad news, project status, and other project information throughout the life of the project. Communication isn't one-way, however. The project manager will need to work with the team, customers, suppliers, and other stakeholders to get these individuals to contribute to the conversation. This means asking questions, listening to stakeholder concerns, following up on ideas and promises, and keeping the project stakeholders involved, excited, and motivated to continue the project.

A positive attitude is also a key component of project success. Although it's tough to quantify what constitutes a positive attitude, it's easy to agree that those with bad attitudes may be unhappy in their lives, in their jobs, and with their organization. Unhappiness is demonstrated in the way an unhappy person manages his projects; this attitude affects the project team and the stakeholders, and it can create a hostile work environment—or, at a minimum, a project that is no fun to work on. Negative project managers are incapable of inspiring others, leading the project team, and motivating people to do good work. A bad attitude or a good attitude is an infectious thing; how you behave as a project manager is a signal of how your team will also behave.

Influencing the Organization

You know that no two projects are alike, and this also holds true for organizations. Every organization is unique in its policies, modes of operations, and underlying culture. There are particular political alliances, differing motivations, conflicting interests, and unique power struggles within every organization. So where does project management fit into this rowdy scheme? Right smack in the middle. You need to know your organizational structure, the governance, the politics, and how things get done where you work.

Organizations that are new to adaptive project management often struggle with the rules and ceremonies of the project life cycle. The project management role, whether that be the coach in XP or the scrum master in Scrum, has an added responsibility of teaching others how the adaptive approach operates and informing everyone that they must follow the rules to give the project its best shot at being successful. Initially, the new adaptive approach may flounder, as support may be weak and stakeholders may be skeptical.

Over time, however, the successes of the development team and the constant support of the project management role can bolster efforts, and others in the organization will want to participate in or try the adaptive project management approach.

A project manager must understand the unspoken influences at work within an organization—as well as the formal channels that exist. An understanding of how to balance the implied and the explicit will enable the project manager to take the project from launch to completion. We all reference politics in organizations with disdain. However, politics aren't always a bad thing. Politics can be used as leverage to align and direct people to accomplish activities—with motivation and purpose.

 EXAM TIP Don't read too much into the questions, as far as political aspirations and influences go. Take each question at face value and assume that all the information given in the question is correct.

As a project manager, you'll also interact with other project managers within the organization. You'll discuss projects, competition for resources, priorities, project funding, and alignment of project goals with organizational goals. Such networking among project managers isn't gossip; the transfer of information helps each project manager see how his or her projects are faring and how decisions and events in the organization can affect projects and decisions, and it helps ensure their projects' viability and quality. This informal network of project managers can influence how things get done in the organization.

Considering Social, Economic, and Environmental Project Influences

Large projects have more influences than smaller projects. In a larger project, you'll likely have to deal with social, economic, and environmental influences—variables that can cause your project to falter, stall, or fail. You must take time to become aware of influences outside of traditional management practices. The acknowledgment of such influences, from internal or external sources, enables the project manager and the project team to plan how to react to these influences to help the project succeed.

Consider a construction project that will reduce traffic flow to one lane over a bridge. Obviously, stakeholders in this instance are the commuters who travel over the bridge. *Social influences* are the people who are frustrated by the construction project, the people who live near the project, and perhaps individuals or groups that believe their need for road repairs is more pressing than the need to repair the bridge. These issues must all be addressed, on some level, for the project team to complete the project work quickly and efficiently.

The *economic influences* in any organization are always present. The cost of a project must be weighed against the project's benefits and perceived worth. Projects may succumb to budget cuts, project priority, or their own failure based on the performance to date. Economic factors inside the organization may also hinder a project from moving forward. In other words, if the company sponsoring the project is not making money, projects may get axed to curb costs.

Finally, *environmental influence* on, and created by, the project must be considered. Let's revisit the construction project on the bridge. The project must consider the river under the bridge and how construction may affect the water and wildlife. You must consider not only the short-term effects that arise during the bridge's construction, but also long-term effects that the construction may have on the environment.

In most projects, the social, economic, and environmental concerns must be evaluated, documented, and addressed within the project plan. Project managers cannot have a come-what-may approach to these issues and expect to be successful.

Considering International Influences

For your PMP exam, consider the effects of a project that takes place in more than one country. In these types of projects, how will the project manager effectively manage and lead the project team? How will teams in Chicago communicate with teams in Antwerp? What about the language barriers, time zone differences, currency differences, regulations, laws, and social influences? These concerns, which can become risks, must be considered early in the project. Tools can include teleconferences, travel, face-to-face meetings, team leaders, and subprojects.

As companies and projects span the globe to offer goods and services, the completion of those projects will rely more and more on individuals from varying educational backgrounds, social influences, and values. The project manager must create a plan that takes these issues into account.

Considering Cultural and Industry Influences

When you apply for the PMP exam, you'll have the option of joining PMI, and I hope you take the opportunity! PMI will provide news and opportunities for learning, and it offers a great way to stay current on project management trends.

Good project managers stay abreast of what's happening in the project management community. They subscribe to newsgroups, read magazine articles, and take training to become more proficient in their role as a project manager. By staying current on what's happening in project management trends, you can identify opportunities, learn about new standards, and share best practices. In addition, you can monitor what's happening in your field: healthcare, construction, or information technology, for example. This will help you, as a project manager, identify trends, market conditions, and potential projects your organization may take on.

After you earn your PMP, you'll likely take continuing education to earn professional development units (PDUs) to maintain your PMP certification. A great opportunity, especially as you're learning more about agile approaches, is to add the PMI-Agile Certified Practitioner (PMI-ACP) credential to your arsenal. Not only will you already have a good foundation in the Agile framework, but you'll earn PDUs as you train to pass the PMI-ACP exam. Don't view this education as a chore, but as an opportunity to continue to advance your career and the project management profession.

Building Project Management Skills

It takes time and dedication to earn the PMP. By earning this credential, you're showing that you have both project management experience and project management knowledge. As I've mentioned, once you're a PMP, you'll need to maintain your certification with continuing education by earning PDUs. Your PMP certification is a three-year cycle, in which time you'll earn 60 PDUs to maintain your PMP. If you fail to earn the 60 PDUs, you'll lose your PMP status and must start the entire journey over—not a wise decision. I've met several people who've allowed their PMP to lapse and they've had to start the whole process over.

It's not terribly difficult to earn PDUs. You can earn them by serving as a project manager, by volunteering for PMI events, by writing books and articles, and by participating in many other activities. On PMI's web site (www.pmi.org), click the Certification link and look for the Continuing Certification Requirements System link to find complete rules and opportunities to earn PDUs. Not all your development can come through volunteering and events, however. As of this writing, PMPs will have to earn a minimum of 35 education PDUs and are allowed a maximum of 25 "giving back" PDUs for volunteering or contributing to the project management community.

Enhancing Skills and Competencies

Be smart about maintaining your PMP. If one of your goals with the PMP is to be marketable, then look for educational opportunities that'll give you PDUs and help you earn new certifications. To earn PDUs to maintain your certification, you'll attend online or in-person training. It's a good idea to take stock of what you know, or don't know, and choose your training accordingly. Consider your career goals, areas of your project management expertise that may be lacking, or what's interesting to you. Take training that will benefit you—don't just trudge through training because you must. Be smart! Choose training and education that will make you a better person and project manager, plus help you keep your PMP.

The *PMBOK Guide* walks through the five steps on the path for chosen competence (Figure 3-2) that we all move through as we learn new things:

1. **Unconsciously incompetent**   You're unaware of a skill that you don't have.

2. **Consciously incompetent**   You become aware that you don't have the skill.

3. **Consciously competent**   You learn and practice the skill to gain competence.

4. **Unconsciously competent**   You can do the skill without even thinking about it.

5. **Chosen conscious competence**   You practice and maintain the skill.

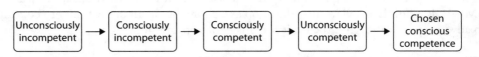

Figure 3-2   PMI path for chosen conscious competence

When we undertake a new endeavor, we begin by not being aware of a skill we don't have. Then we learn about the skill, practice the skill, and maintain the skill to become an expert. There are four steps to become skilled and remain skilled as an individual:

1. We gather data, such as observations and facts, about the skill.

2. We process that raw data into useable information.

3. We use that information to gain knowledge and find a deeper understanding and practice of the skill.

4. We gain wisdom and master the skill through practice and knowledge.

Introducing the PMI Talent Triangle

In recent years, PMI has established a Talent Triangle to illustrate the three domains of education required for PMPs, as shown in Figure 3-3. As a PMP, you'll need a total of 35 minimum PDUs. These hours are distributed across the three domains:

- Technical project management
- Leadership
- Strategic and business management

You must have at least 8 PDUs from each of the three domains, which equal 24 of your 35 PDUs. The remaining 11 PDUs can be distributed across any of the three domains—you pick. When you sign up for training, be sure to confirm which domain, or combination of domains, of the PMI Talent Triangle the training contributes to. These three domains correlate to the three domains of the exam: People, Processes, and the Business Environment.

Figure 3-3
The PMI Talent
Triangle requires
education in all
three domains.

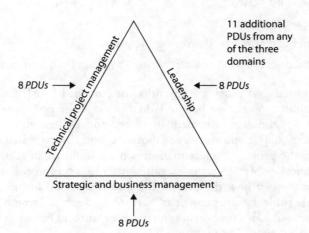

11 additional
PDUs from any
of the three
domains

Technical project management

Leadership

8 *PDUs* →

← 8 *PDUs*

Strategic and business management

8 *PDUs*

During your three-year certification cycle as a PMP, you must earn a total of 60 PDUs to maintain your certification. Of those PDUs, you'll need 8 PDUs from technical training, 8 PDUs from leadership training, and 8 PDUs from strategic training. You can earn all 60 PDUs through education by attending a few seminars or taking a few online courses and you're all set. Or you can volunteer at PMI events to earn up to 25 PDUs for your service, and attend educational activities for the remaining 35 PDUs to keep your certification. On PMI's web site you can download a PDU Handbook that explains all the different ways you can earn PDUs.

Technical project management skills are the core skills you apply in your role as a project manager. You'll focus on what it'll take to get the project done: planning the project work, executing the plan, monitoring and controlling the project, and closing out phases and eventually the entire project. Within these process groups, you'll choose and apply the necessary processes to keep the project moving toward its goals and objectives. You'll also communicate the project status, keep stakeholders involved and informed, track finances, control changes, and manage issues. We'll spend the bulk of our time in this book in the technical project management arena.

The PMI Talent Triangle also includes strategic and business management skills. In addition to managing the project, the project manager must examine the organization's bigger picture regarding why the project is important and why it has been initiated and funded by the organization. The goal is to understand and communicate the business strategy, effectively plan and deliver the project for the organization, and maximize the business value of the project. You'll need to understand how your project fits into the organization's strategy, mission, tactics, and overall prioritization of projects. You'll do this by managing the following:

- Risks and issues
- Project costs and budget
- Costs and benefits
- Business value
- Benefits realized by delivering the project
- Balance competing objectives, such as time, cost, and quality

Project managers provide leadership, the part of the PMI Talent Triangle that focuses on your ability to manage people. You'll manage the project team, work with vendors, and keep stakeholders informed, involved, and excited about the project. Leadership means that you'll be optimistic, collaborative, and able to manage conflicts that will creep up within the project. Project managers must build trust, address concerns with stakeholders, and be able to persuade, gain consensus, compromise, network, and provide a long-term view of how the project fits into the overall business strategy. A term you'll see in agile project management is "servant leadership," which means that while you're the leader, you're also supporting the project team and ensuring that they have what they need to do the work in the project.

Leadership requires the following qualities in a project manager:

- Respect for others
- Integrity and cultural sensitivity
- Problem-solving abilities
- Ability to give others credit
- Desire to learn and improve
- Ability to build and maintain relationships

Leadership in project management is about helping the team and business succeed. It's about doing what's right for the project, for the project team, and for the stakeholders. You'll work to focus on what's most important by prioritizing work, needs, and wants. Leaders act and make decisions, they are flexible and courageous, and they can deal directly with problems to rectify issues and keep the project moving forward.

Managing Politics in Projects

Yes, you'll have to deal with office politics in project management. Stakeholders almost always have a political agenda, and they can try to leverage the project manager to get their way. Unfortunately, project managers often get mired in stakeholders' competing objectives and succumb to office politics that can affect the project for the worse. Politics are really a way of describing how organizations operate—the undocumented, but present, undercurrent of how decisions are made within the organization. Project managers must understand how organizations work, who wields authority, and how to navigate through the politics, good or bad, to keep the project moving toward a successful conclusion.

Though the project manager may hope to avoid politics, it's nearly impossible to do so; politics can begin with the perception of the project manager and the power he has. Perception of power refers to how other people—from the project team, to management, to stakeholders—view not just the project, but also the project manager. The project manager does have some power over the project and the perceptions others have of him.

Although every scenario is different, you should be familiar with several types of power that affect your role as a project manager and for your PMP exam:

- **Positional power** The project manager's power is a result of the position she has as the project manager. This is also known as formal, authoritative, and legitimate power.
- **Informational power** The project manager has control over data gathering and distribution of information.
- **Referent power** The project manager is respected or admired because of the team's past experiences with her. This is about the project manager's credibility in the organization.

- **Situational power**   The project manager has power because of certain situations in the organization.

- **Personal or charismatic power**   The project manager has a warm personality that others like.

- **Avoiding power**   The project manager refuses to act, get involved, or make decisions.

- **Expert power**   The project manager has deep skills and experience in a discipline (for example, years of working in IT helps an IT project manager better manage IT projects).

- **Reward power**   The project manager can reward the project team.

- **Punitive or coercive power**   The project manager can punish the project team.

- **Ingratiating power**   The project manager aims to gain favor with the project team and stakeholders through flattery.

- **Pressure-based power**   The project manager can restrict choices to get the project team to perform the project work.

- **Guilt-based power**   The project manager can make the team and stakeholders feel guilty to gain compliance in the project.

Notice that I've framed these from the project manager's point of view, but the reality is that any stakeholder, from a customer to the project sponsor, can hold these powers. This is all part of the political side of organizations; being able to recognize the power being implemented can help you as project manager better manage a project and its outcomes.

 VIDEO   For a more detailed explanation, watch the Role of the Project Manager video now.

Serving as a Leader and Manager

Leadership and management are not the same things: Leadership is more about emotional intelligence and inspiring people to work together to achieve great things. Management is about getting things done. Management is concerned with the results and the work required to achieve those results. For the PMP exam, you'll need to discern between leadership and management. Understand that management focuses on getting the project done, while leadership is about inspiring and motivating people. There are opportunities to do both on every project.

As a successful project manager, you'll serve as both a leader and a manager. You'll lead the team by showing them opportunities that help them accomplish the project, create something new, and complete the project work with an eye toward how the project contributes to business value for the organization. As a manager, you'll keep the team organized and the work authorization moving, and you'll address the knowledge area of project management. You'll be accountable and hold the team accountable for the scope, costs, quality, risk management, and other facets of project management.

Learning Leadership Styles

Think about all of people you've worked for—specifically the managers you've admired. Think of how that individual led his team. Managers' characteristics, such as their temperaments and values, made you admire them. Employees often look to their managers to determine what is acceptable behavior—how they treat others, their energy about the project, and their ethics. A manager's characteristics, including project managers, inform how their team members behave. Leadership styles are the methods you and others employ to offer leadership within the project. That's an important concept, because it's not just the project manager who can offer leadership: the team, stakeholders, and even vendors can offer leadership at different times throughout the project.

Six leadership styles are utilized within organizations, and you should recognize these for your exam:

- **Servant leadership**   The leader puts others first and focuses on the needs of the people he serves. Servant leaders provide opportunity for growth, education, autonomy within the project, and the well-being of others. Adaptive project management relies heavily on servant leadership, and you should recognize this term for your exam. The primary focus of servant leadership is service to others.

- **Transactional leadership**   The leader emphasizes the goals of the project and offers rewards and disincentives for the project team. This is sometimes called management by exception, because it's the exception that is rewarded or punished.

- **Laissez-faire leadership**   The leader takes a hands-off approach to the project. This means the project team makes decisions, takes initiative in the actions, and creates goals. Although this approach can provide autonomy, it can make the leader appear absent when it comes to project decisions. Some newcomers to Agile feel that the scrum master is using laissez-faire leadership. Nope! The scrum master is involved, but she allows the team to be self-organizing and is available when problems erupt or the team needs help.

- **Transformational leadership**   The leader inspires and motivates the project team to achieve the project goals. Transformational leaders aim to empower the project team to act, be innovative in the project work, and accomplish through ambition.

- **Charismatic leadership**   The leader is motivating, has high energy, and inspires the team through strong convictions about what's possible and what the team can achieve. Positive thinking and a can-do mentality are characteristics of a charismatic leader.

- **Interactional leadership**   The leader is a hybrid of transactional, transformational, and charismatic leadership. The interactional leader wants the team to take action, is excited and inspired about the project work, yet still holds the team accountable for their results.

Creating a Leadership Persona

You need to define what it means to be a leader and how you'll improve upon those leadership qualities as a project manager. When you think of a leader, you'll likely think of a personality of someone who's excited, inspiring, and leads by doing. Or maybe you think of a football coach giving a great half-time speech about overcoming the odds and winning the game. Or perhaps it's some combination of leadership characteristics that motivate, inspire, and prove admirable. All of these traits are centered on the personality of a good leader.

For your PMP exam, you'll need to recognize some personality traits that directly affect your ability to serve as a leader for your project team. These personality traits stem from experience, maturity, patterns of thinking, feelings, and repeated behavior. Recognize these personality traits:

- **Authentic** Show concern for others and accept who they are.
- **Courteous** Be polite and behave respectfully toward others.
- **Creative** Create, think through problems, and seek solutions through creativity.
- **Cultural** Be sensitive to cultural norms and beliefs.
- **Emotional** Show empathy, understand others' emotions, and manage personal emotions.
- **Intellectual** Demonstrate intelligence and respect the intelligence of others.
- **Managerial** Use management aptitude in all aspects of the project.
- **Political** Understand the politics at play within an organization.
- **Service-oriented** Provide for others what they need to be successful.
- **Social** Be friendly and approachable, and understand the needs and wants of the project team and stakeholders.
- **Systemic** Understand existing frameworks and systems and build project systems to get things done in an orderly fashion.

Performing Project Integration

There's some unfortunate wording in the *PMBOK Guide* that may confuse some people. The *PMBOK Guide* uses the word "integration" in Chapter 4, but *integration*, in the context of our discussion here, is different from *project integration management*, discussed in the *PMBOK Guide*. Integration management in this chapter addresses how the project is integrated with the goals, tactics, and vision of the organization—not just the project scope and knowledge areas. Integration at this level means that you're working with the project sponsor to ensure that the goals and objectives of the project mesh with the goals and objectives of the organization. Projects must support the broader vision and purpose of the organization or the project likely isn't contributing to business value and may have challenges garnering support within the organization.

At the project level, the project manager continues integration by leading and managing the project team. The people who have the greatest effect on project success are the project team members. The project manager can't do everything, of course, and the project team will execute the project plan. When the project team executes the project plan, their work needs to support the goals of the project, which in turn must support the goals of the organization. If those two things are not in sync, the project will no doubt face challenges, issues, and unrest.

Integrating Processes

In Chapter 4 of this book and of the *PMBOK Guide*, you'll read that project integration management addresses the interrelationship among the project processes. *Processes* are the predefined actions, such as quality control, that bring about a specific result. *Process-level integration* means that each process affects other processes throughout the project. Some processes may occur only one time, such as creating the project charter, while other processes can happen over and over as needed in the project, such as risk identification. Still, some processes may not occur at all: Consider the procurement processes in a project that won't be purchasing anything from vendors. If you don't need the processes, they won't occur.

Don't miss this important point: do only the processes that are needed and always do the most appropriate process when it's needed. There is no blanket approach to project management, and processes can generally happen in any order that's needed once the project is initiated and the charter is created. Yes, you'll generally move into planning once the charter is created, but as the project is in motion, especially on larger projects, you'll move on to the needed process, not necessarily the next process described in the *PMBOK Guide*. Of course, what you do with one process has a direct effect on other processes in your project.

The larger and more complex the project, the more processes you are likely to use. The more processes that are introduced and needed in a project, however, means you'll need more project integration management. Project managers need not address only the processes of a project, but must also consider three other factors that contribute to the project's complexity:

- **Uncertainty in projects** Some projects aren't clear in requirements and what will happen throughout the project life cycle. Consider software development, long-term projects, and unknowns that are lurking in the work. Adaptive projects readily recognize the uncertainty and welcome change. Predictive projects see uncertainty as risk and are often risk-averse.

- **Human behavior** Perhaps the most complex aspect of project management is human behavior. People don't always get along, and this can cause problems within the project that stem from behavior outside of the project.

- **System behavior** How your organization works is entirely different from how other organizations work. You'll need to understand the business framework of what it takes to interact with employees, departments, and systems to manage the project.

Building Your Cognitive-Level Integration

When we first begin as project managers, we're often assigned projects that are low priority, with easily achievable objectives. As we become more mature in the role of a project manager and have gained experience and insight into project management, we're assigned more complex projects. It's the experience that gives us the wisdom to manage the more complex projects.

The idea of integration at the cognitive level means that we rely not only on our experience—an excellent teacher—but we also learn from others. We take classes, read books, attend PMI chapter meetings; we make a deliberate effort to learn more so that we can manage projects more effectively. Cognitive-level integration is the act of learning on purpose, not just by doing, to ensure that we're well-rounded in all knowledge areas of project management, even those areas we don't touch frequently. That's why your PMP exam will cover the whole breadth of project management, even if you have little experience in procurement, in risk management, or in any of the knowledge areas.

Examining Context-Level Integration

Context-level integration is the management of a project in consideration of how the project environment has changed, and is changing, in organizations today. Consider a project 20 or 30 years ago: social networking, texting, and virtual teams weren't a reality back then, but these variables are certainly in play in most organizations today. As project managers, we need insight into how our projects will take advantage of these and other evolving project landscapes and how these elements can create benefits, or disruptions, to the project.

Your organization may allow texting and virtual teams in a project, while another organization doesn't use those elements. This doesn't mean that one is better than the other; they're just different. Each facet of the context level brings benefits but also costs that can affect how a project moves forward. The project manager needs to understand what's allowed to be used, what's not allowed, what's being ignored, and why.

Chapter Summary

This chapter focused on the foundations of what it means to be a project manager. I wouldn't be surprised if you already recognize most of the information in this chapter if you're currently serving as a project manager and working toward your PMP certification. However, don't shrug off these elements, because you'll likely see the information on your exam.

One of the most important parts of this chapter is recognizing the difference between project management and leadership. Management is about getting things done. Leadership is about aligning, motivating, and inspiring people. Be familiar with both aspects of project management, not just the mechanics of getting things done.

Management utilizes positional power to do the following:

- Maintain the project.
- Administrate duties.

- Focus on project systems.
- Control the project work.
- Focus on the next project achievements.
- Question how and when things will happen.
- Control and administer finances.
- Keep the status quo.
- Do the right things at the right time.
- Address issues and problem-solve.

Leadership influences and inspires people to do the following:

- Develop personality and skills.
- Perform their work with innovation.
- Build relationships.
- Trust one another.
- Examine the long-range vision of the project.
- Question why and what will happen.
- Challenge the status quo.
- Do the right things at the right time.
- Align with the organization's vision with motivation and inspiration.

Some overlap exists between management and leadership, but the difference is in the attitude, the desire to do things well, and a positive mindset focused on serving others and serving in the best interest of the stakeholders, team, and organization.

The role of the project manager in any project management approach is to manage the project work, lead the project team, and get things done. While agile environments often don't have a project manager role, agile projects still use the principles of project management and leadership. The project manager works with the project team to achieve the project objectives, contribute to business value, and coordinate the activities, communications, and events that happen within a project. Project managers facilitate processes to reach predefined results and then usher the project through initiating, planning, execution, monitoring and controlling, and ultimately into project closing.

Through experience and training, the project manager's competency increases. The project manager should ascertain his level of skill in management and leadership areas; identify strengths, weaknesses, opportunities, and threats; and then decide to improve upon his management prowess. The PMI Talent Triangle aims to address the three common areas of education for project managers: technical project management, leadership, and strategic and business management.

The role of the project manager isn't just about managing project work and resources; it also includes leadership. Leadership is the ability to align, motivate, and inspire people to want to do the project work, succeed in their work lives, and focus on the long-range vision of the project. Leadership styles are the methods a project manager can utilize to help the project team members be inspired and motivated, and to perform well within the project.

Questions

1. You know that leadership and project management are not the same thing, but they are connected. Leaders and managers rely on communications within a project to help motivate, manage, and ensure that the project is moving forward toward its objectives. In communicating, the receiver restates what the sender has said to clarify the message and to enable the sender to offer more clarity if needed. What is this communication component called?

   A. Active listening

   B. Sender-receiver model

   C. Communications planning

   D. Leader listening

2. You are the project manager for your organization and you're working with a new client to start a project at the client's site. You and the client are negotiating the price, schedule, and other concerns for a contract for the new project. In the negotiating, you and the client should be negotiating for what result?

   A. Best price for the contracted work

   B. Fair agreement for both the client and the vendor

   C. Most profit for the contracted work

   D. Risk distribution between the two parties

3. You are the project manager of the Systems Upgrade Project for your organization. As a project manager, you want to influence the organization and the project team for the better. What two key aspects are most helpful in influencing your organization as a project manager?

   A. Management and leadership

   B. Communication skills and a positive attitude

   C. Experience and knowledge

   D. Experience and willingness to learn

4. Beth is a new project manager for her company and she's working with her project team utilizing the Scrum approach to project management. In the Scrum environment, all of the roles take on the project management activities except for which one?

   A. Product owner

   B. Scrum master

   C. Project team

   D. Development team

5. Teresa is the project manager for her department. She has been working with her manager to examine her skills and her career. Her manager believes that Teresa should take more training in a project management information system to make her a better project manager in her organization. Teresa agrees, though she feels that she doesn't know much about the project management information system her department uses. In the five steps of competence, where is Teresa with this realization?

   A. Unconsciously competent

   B. Consciously competent

   C. Consciously incompetent

   D. Unconsciously incompetent

6. As a PMP candidate in an environment utilizing XP, you understand that there is no project manager role in this framework. However, XP does utilize a role that is identified as a person who enforces the rules of XP, remains calm in times of trouble, and helps the team to become self-reliant. What is the name of this role in an XP environment?

   A. Manager

   B. Servant leader

   C. Coach

   D. Product owner

7. While management is about getting things done, leadership is said to be about motivating people. You know that leadership is a desirable trait for a project manager and is heavily referenced throughout the *PMBOK Guide*. Which one of the following characteristics is not an attribute of leadership?

   A. Fiscal responsibility

   B. Respect for others

   C. Problem-solving ability

   D. Desire to learn and improve

8. You are the project manager for your organization. Your current project has more than 100 stakeholders. Some of the stakeholders have competing objectives and are trying to leverage your project to meet their personal objectives. Influencing your organization requires which of the following?

   A. An understanding of the organizational budget

   B. Research and documentation of proven business cases

   C. An understanding of formal and informal organizational systems

   D. Positional power

9. Mark is a new project manager in his company. Before joining this company, Mark worked as a project manager for more than 20 years at an IT service provider. Mark has a deep understanding of electronics, software development, and data warehouse technology and is considered an expert in his field. His current project team, however, is pushing back on his recommendations and challenging his knowledge on the project. Since Mark is new, the project team reasons, he likely doesn't understand how things work in the organization. What type of power does Mark have in this scenario?

   A. Expert

   B. Positional

   C. Situational

   D. Informational

10. What type of power does a project manager have when the team admires the project manager because they've worked with her before the current project or they know of her reputation as a project manager?

   A. Situational

   B. Referent

   C. Personal

   D. Expert

11. Holly is the project manager for her company and her team likes working for her. Holly has a good attitude, is easy to work with, and is a good planner. The project team views Holly as a member of management who can give them a good review and possibly affect a bonus payment if the project is completed on time. What type of power does this project manager have?

   A. Punitive

   B. Situational

   C. Reward

   D. Guilt-based

12. You can adapt several different tactics and leadership styles in a project. Which one of the following is the best description of being a servant leader?

   A. The leader emphasizes the goals of the project and provides rewards and disincentives for the project team.

   B. The leader puts others first and focuses on the needs of the people he serves.

   C. The leader takes a hands-off approach to the project.

   D. The leader inspires and motivates the project team to achieve the project goals.

13. You are the project manager for your department. As a project manager, you will have to use some positional power to keep the project moving forward. You'll also need to develop leadership skills to align, motivate, and inspire people. Of the following choices, which one is most likely associated with management skills?

    A. Focus on the next project achievements

    B. Build relationships

    C. Support the project team

    D. Challenge status quo

14. You are the project manager for your organization. In your current project, you're coaching Mary on the project management knowledge areas. Mary has questions about project integration management at the process level. Which one of the following is the best example of project integration management at the process level?

    A. Poor quality management planning will likely affect the quality of the project deliverable.

    B. A robust communication management plan is dependent on the number of stakeholders involved in the project.

    C. Larger projects require more detail than smaller projects.

    D. Planning is an iterative activity that will happen throughout the project.

15. You are the project manager of a project. The project team is experiencing some trouble with a new material that the project will utilize. You gather the team to lead an active problem-solving session. Which one of the following is the best definition of active problem-solving?

    A. Define the problem and the desired solution.

    B. Discern the cause and the effect of the problem.

    C. Document the problem and its characteristics to see the whole effect.

    D. Test the materials to identify the solution.

16. Dwight was the project lead for the IT Upgrade Project, and Jim was serving as the project manager. Because of a family emergency, Jim stepped down from the project and took a leave of absence. Management then asked that Dwight serve as the project manager for the remainder of the project. What type of power does Dwight now have?

    A. Personal

    B. Expert

    C. Situational

    D. Reward

17. A project manager is meeting with his project team. In this meeting, the top 10 percent of project team members are openly praised for their hard work. The bottom 10 percent of the project team members are disciplined and somewhat berated in the meeting. The balance of the project team is not addressed. What type of leadership is happening in this scenario?

   A. Transactional leadership

   B. Laissez-faire leadership

   C. Interactional leadership

   D. Pressure-based power

18. Harrold is the project manager for his organization, and he has seven people on his project team. Who is responsible for executing the project plan and creating the project deliverables?

   A. Project lead

   B. Project manager and the project team

   C. Project manager

   D. Project team

19. As a project manager, you need both leadership and management skills. Which one of the following statements best describes the difference between leadership and management in a project?

   A. Management is the process of getting the results that are expected in the project. Leadership is the ability to motivate and inspire individuals.

   B. Management is the process of getting the results that are expected by the project stakeholders. Leadership is the ability to motivate and inspire individuals to work toward those expected results.

   C. Leadership is about creating excitement to be managed. Management is about managing the leadership.

   D. Leadership is the process of getting the project team excited to create results that are expected by project stakeholders. Management is the ability to keep track of the project results.

20. Communication is paramount in project management and can best be summarized as follows: who needs what information, when do they need it, and what's the best _____ to deliver the message? Choose the best answer:

   A. person

   B. resource

   C. format

   D. modality

Answers

1. **A.** Active listening is the participatory component of a conversation that confirms what was said and enables the sender to offer clarity, if needed. B is incorrect. The sender-receiver model shows how communication moves between two people. C is incorrect because communications planning is a project management process plan for who needs what information, when the information is needed, and in what modality. D, leader listening, is not a valid project management term so this choice is incorrect.

2. **B.** The purpose of negotiations is to reach a fair agreement for all parties involved. A and C are incorrect because these two choices are mutually exclusive and not concerned with the other party in the contract. D, risk distribution, is not a valid choice because the fair agreement among the parties would address the risk distribution.

3. **B.** The two key aspects that are most helpful in influencing an organization are communication skills and a positive attitude. A is incorrect because management and leadership are values for a project manager, but they aren't the most helpful aspects of influence. C is incorrect because experience and knowledge are self-contained skills and don't do much to influence, inspire, and motivate others. D is incorrect because experience and a willingness to learn are good attributes and are intrinsic for a good project manager, but they will not influence the organization.

4. **C.** In Scrum, project management is sliced across the three roles of the product owner, the scrum master, and the development team. There is no role called the project team. A, B, and D are incorrect because they represent three roles that take on the project management activities.

5. **C.** Teresa is consciously incompetent because she is aware that she needs more training to be competent in a new skill. A is incorrect because unconsciously competent happens when Teresa can do the skill without even thinking about it. B is incorrect because when Teresa learns and practices the skill to gain competence she is being consciously competent. D describes the state when Teresa is unaware of a skill she doesn't have.

6. **C.** XP doesn't have a project manager role, but instead utilizes the role of coach. A coach in XP coaches the team on the XP rules, remains calm even when others are panicking, helps the team become self-reliant, and intervenes only when there's a problem that the team is overlooking. A, manager, is incorrect. The manager in XP tracks performance, ensures that everyone is following the rules, and leads the continual planning processes. B, servant leader, describes the leadership approach for serving the team, but it isn't a role in XP. D, product owner, is incorrect because this role is in Scrum projects and is responsible for maintaining the product backlog.

7. **A.** Fiscal responsibility is a desirable trait for project managers, but it's a management skill rather than a leadership skill. B, C, and D are incorrect choices because leadership skills include respect for others, problem-solving abilities, and a desire to learn and improve.

8. **C.** To influence an organization (to get things done), a project manager must understand the explicit and implied organizational system within an organization. A is incorrect, because the project manager may not even have access to an organizational budget. B is incorrect because a proven business case may not map to every scenario when influencing an organization. D is incorrect because positional power may relate only to a small portion of an organization, not to multiple facets of influence.

9. **B.** Mark has positional power in this scenario because he's new to the organization and the team doesn't recognize his expertise in the technology. Positional power is also known as formal, authoritative, and legitimate power. A is incorrect because expert power means the team would recognize his expertise in the technology and respect his decisions. C is incorrect because situational power emerges because the project manager has power as a result of certain situations in the organization. D is incorrect because informational power means the individual has control of data gathering and distribution of information.

10. **B.** Of all the choices presented, referent power is the best answer. The project manager is respected or admired because her team can refer to her ability as a project manager because they have knowledge of past experiences with her. This is about the project manager's credibility in the organization. A is incorrect because situational power means the project manager has power because of certain situations in the organization. C is incorrect because with personal power, the project manager is liked because of her personality rather than her experiences with the project team in the past. D is incorrect because expert power means the project manager has deep skills and experience in a discipline.

11. **C.** When the project team sees the project manager as someone who can reward them, the project manager has reward power. A, B, and D are not valid answers. Punitive power means the team thinks the project manager can punish them. Situational power is when the project manager has power based on unique situations within the organization. Guilt-based power describes a manager who makes the team feels guilty if they don't complete their project work according to plan.

12. **B.** A servant leader puts others first and focuses on the needs of the people he serves. Servant leaders provide opportunity for growth, education, autonomy within the project, and the well-being of others. The primary focus of servant leadership is service to others. A is incorrect because this answer describes transactional leadership. C is incorrect because this answer describes a laissez-faire leadership approach. D is incorrect because this answer describes the transformational leadership style.

13. A. Management focuses on the next project achievements. B, C, and D are incorrect because these three choices are attributes of leadership. Leaders do build relationships, support the project team, and challenge the status quo. This isn't to say that managers don't do these things, but it's the attribute of management versus the attribute of leadership in this question.

14. A. Of all the choices presented, this answer is the best example of project integration management. Project integration management at the process level means that what you do in one process can have a direct effect on other processes. It is true that poor quality management planning will likely affect the quality of the deliverables, which is linked to project integration management. B, C, and D are incorrect examples of project integration management at the process level. We'll discuss more about project integration management in the next chapter of this book.

15. A. Active problem-solving begins with defining the problem and ends with implementing the desired solution. B is incorrect because the ability to discern between the cause and effect of the problem is only part of problem-solving. C is incorrect because documenting the problems is also only part of problem-solving. D is incorrect because testing the materials would be part of the discernment process to determine the cause of the problem, not the solution.

16. C. Dwight now has situational power and will become project manager because of a particular situation in the organization. A, personal power, means the project manager has a warm personality that others like. B is incorrect because expert power means that the project manager has deep skills and experience in a discipline, but Dwight was made project manager only because of the situation with Jim having to leave the project. D is incorrect because reward power means the project manager can reward the project team.

17. A. Transactional leadership means the leader emphasizes the goals of the project and offers rewards and disincentives for the project team. This is sometimes called management by exception, because it's the exception that is rewarded or punished. B is incorrect because laissez-faire leadership means the leader takes a hands-off approach to the project. C is incorrect because the interactional leader wants the team to act, is excited and inspired about the project work, yet still holds the team accountable for their results. D is incorrect because pressure-based power is not a leadership type, but rather a type of power where the project manager can restrict choices to get the project team to perform the project work.

18. D. The project team members are responsible for executing the project plan and creating the project deliverables. A is incorrect because the project lead isn't the only role responsible for executing the plan. B is tempting, but it is incorrect, because the project team is responsible for executing the plan—that is, doing the work to create the project deliverables—not the project manager. C, the project manager, isn't the best answer because, although the project manager may be accountable for the project, it's the project team that builds the project deliverables.

19. **B.** Of all the choices, this is the best answer. Management is the process of getting the results that are expected by project stakeholders. Leadership is the ability to motivate and inspire individuals to work toward those expected results. A, C, and D are incorrect because these statements do not correctly reflect the difference between management and leadership in a project.

20. **D.** Project communication can be summed up as follows: who needs what information, when do they need it, and what's the best modality to deliver the message. A, B, and C are incorrect. Although these are tempting choices, none of them is the best answer to the question.

PART II

Project Management Professional Knowledge Areas

Managing Project Integration

In this chapter, you will

- Learn what project integration management does for the project manager
- Develop the project charter
- Create the project management plan
- Direct and manage the project work
- Manage project knowledge
- Monitor and control the project work
- Understand how integrated change control works
- Close a project or phase

What the heck is *project integration management*? This is the heart of project management and is made up of the day-to-day processes the project manager relies upon to ensure that all parts of the project work together. What you do in one area of the project directly affects all the other areas of the project. Project integration management is about the project manager making the best decisions for work, resources, project issues, and all the logistics of the project so it is completed as planned. Project integration management is undertaken specifically by the project manager.

Project integration management is also about making trade-offs between competing objectives and alternatives. I'm certain you, as a project manager, have worked with stakeholders who want something that would cancel out a characteristic another stakeholder wants: Bob says he wants the house painted green, and Nancy wants it painted red. Or your client wants your organization to design a reliable, fast network operating system for thousands of users as long as it doesn't cost more than a few thousand dollars. Competing objectives require negotiations, balance, and lots and lots of aspirin.

 VIDEO For a more detailed explanation, watch the *Working with Project Integration Management* video now.

In the first part of this book, I discussed the project management life cycle and the project management processes. These processes are not isolated elements, but they overlap, interact, and complement one another. Project integration management is the coordination and support of these project management processes. Project integration management considers the interrelationship of the ten knowledge areas and how actions in one knowledge area affect all the others. In the integration management knowledge area, you'll also address how the project manager and the project team manage knowledge within the project and record that knowledge so that it can be accessed by future projects and other project teams.

A theme you'll see throughout the *PMBOK Guide*, and in this book, is that processes can be tailored to fit your environment. Project integration management can be tailored for the project life cycle, the management approach, and knowledge management. You can also tailor the change management approach and governance within the project. Tailoring is also encouraged for lessons learned, which is part of knowledge management, and you can tailor benefits management and reporting throughout the project. Project integration management, like all processes, is not universal and can always be tailored to fit your organization, rather than changing your organization to fit a project management approach.

Agile project life cycles rely on the team members, including the project manager, to define how plans and components will integrate. In Agile, product planning and delivery are completed by the project team, while the project manager oversees the project and promotes collaboration for decisions and change management. Agile environments welcome change, with some rules, and change can happen throughout the project.

Project integration management is key to organizations using a hybrid approach to project management: some chunks of the project are predictive and others are adaptive. In a hybrid approach, the project manager integrates the two project management approaches, follows the rules of both approaches, and works with stakeholders to mesh the approaches together for benefits.

 EXAM TIP   You will be tested on the idea of hybrid approaches on your PMP exam. Pay close attention to the idea of helping the team and stakeholder transition between the predictive and agile project management approaches. Communication, planning, and engaging the stakeholders will be key activities to manage the transition between the life cycles.

Developing the Project Charter

All projects officially start with a *project charter*—a formal document that authorizes the project to go forward in the organization and gives the project manager authority over the project resources. What's so great about the charter? It's the document that gives you, the project manager, the authority to use resources to do the project work—and authority over resources such as equipment and facilities. It's a powerful document and needs to be signed by someone with power in the organization. The project manager is assigned to the project as early as possible, and ideally while the charter is still being developed. The project manager needs to be assigned, without a doubt, before the project moves into the project planning process group.

In many organizations, the project manager is the person writing the charter, and that's fine—really!—but the charter cannot be signed by the project manager. Though the project may be backed by the project customer, the project champion, or the organization's project management office, the charter is officially backed by a project initiator, typically called the *project sponsor*, a person with more responsibility within the organization who can allocate funding and resources for the project. In other words, the project manager can't sign the charter because he's not "powerful" enough within the organization to assign resources and funds to his own project.

 EXAM TIP   Remember that the project charter authorizes the project, names the project manager, and also defines the project manager's level of authority. Project charters are not contracts, because no payments are exchanged or detailed in the charter.

Charters are created by an enterprise, a government agency, a program manager, or a project steering committee (sometimes called the portfolio organization). Charters are written so that a project can answer or satisfy one of the following:

- Market demand
- Business need
- Customer request
- Technological advance
- Legal requirement
- Ecological impact
- Social need

Your organization might call these opportunities, problems, or business requirements. Once you're a project manager, you'll just call 'em your favorite project. (Your favorite project is always the one you're currently managing.) Why some projects within an organization get selected and others do not can be due to finances, the project owner, sponsor influence, legal requirements, or any number of reasons. The message to take away is that regardless of why a project gets selected, you, the project manager, must have a charter for the project to be officially authorized.

 EXAM TIP   Adaptive projects should also have a project charter. Remember that you need a charter to authorize the project and the project manager regardless of the project management life cycle approach. If you don't have a charter, you don't have a project.

Charters should always include the following project information:

- Requirements for satisfaction of project stakeholder needs, wants, and expectations
- Business needs, a description of the project's product, or a mile-high view of the project's purpose
- Success criteria and who signs off on the project at completion
- The project manager and her level of autonomy
- Summary milestone schedule
- Key stakeholders
- Functional organizations and how they'll be involved with the project
- Project constraints and assumptions (environment, external, and organizational)
- Business case for the project and the project return on investment
- Summary project budget
- High-level risks, such as pending laws or dangerous work
- Project approval requirements
- Exit criteria (conditions required to close or cancel the project)
- Name and authority level of the project sponsor

Believe it or not, the project charter may be updated. For example, the summary project budget may be based on simple, rough order-of-magnitude estimates. As the project moves deeper into planning, the estimates become clearer and more precise. The more accurate estimates may cause the budget to change, requiring the project charter to be modified to reflect the new information.

Preparing to Create the Project Charter

The project charter is often written by the project manager and then signed by the project sponsor, so you'll need to know how to create it, what goes into it, and then what you can do with your charter—especially for the PMP exam. When preparing to create the project charter, you'll need four things: business case documents, agreements, enterprise environmental factors, and organizational process assets.

Business Case Documents

The business case defines why the project is worthy of the organization investing money in it. It explains why the project is needed and what type of return the organization can expect for its investment. A cost-benefit analysis is usually included in the business case to support the project's purpose in the organization. The business case may be written by the project manager, a business analyst, or even by a customer if the project is sponsored by someone external to your organization. In a Scrum project, a product owner role could write the business case, because this role is closest to managing the product for the customer.

Business cases can evolve from feasibility studies, because some of the information may overlap. The business case will define the market demand for the project's creation, the organizational need, ecological impacts, legal requirements, social need, or technological advance that the project will bring to the organization. In some instances, the business case could be based on a customer's request for additional services or on products that can provide opportunities for the organization to grow. Business cases define the economic viability and financial return on investment.

Agreements

Okay, I confess that you won't always need a contract, or an agreement, in order to create a project charter, but agreements are listed as inputs in the *PMBOK Guide*, so work with me for a moment. If you're working in an organization that performs projects for other entities, such as a consulting firm, an architectural firm, or an event planning company, you'll need a contract to make the project official: contracts are typically used when you're doing a project for a customer. Chapter 12 explores contracting, but for now you should know that you may need a contract if it's appropriate for your project. Agreements can also be memorandums of understanding, service-level agreements, letters of intent, verbal agreements, e-mail agreements, or other written agreements.

Enterprise Environmental Factors

The project charter also considers the organization where the project will take place and its culture, standards, regulations, and environment. You'll see these enterprise environmental factors discussed throughout the remainder of this book. Just so you understand these things once and for all, here are the enterprise environmental factors you'll need to be familiar with:

- Organization's culture and structure
- Industry standards and regulations
- Organization's facilities and equipment (the general infrastructure of the company)
- Human resources and their talents, skills, and availability
- Human resources administration
- Work authorization system
- Policies for the selected project management approach
- Marketplace conditions
- Stakeholders' tolerance for risk (also known as the utility function)
- Commercial databases for the organization's industry (such as cost-estimating databases for a builder or manufacturer)
- Project management information system (PMIS) (Think of—yes, I'll say it— Microsoft Project. Don't worry; you won't have to know any software vendors or their goods for the PMI exam. All of your favorite, or least favorite, project management software is just lumped into the generic term "project management information system.")

Organizational Process Assets

Anything that your organization has in its possession that can help your current project succeed is part of the organizational process assets. This means that the policies, procedures, plans, and documentation of past projects are part of the organizational process assets. The PMI breaks down the organizational process assets into two big categories. Let's explore them in detail.

Processes and Procedures for Project Work   These include the following:

- Standard processes and procedures for getting project work done, such as purchase requests, team member acquisitions, quality programs your projects subscribe to, checklists, and generally the way your company requires your projects to operate

- Guidelines on how your project team is to complete their work and proposal evaluations, and how you measure your project for performance

- Framework for predictive or adaptive projects and the rules for the project management life cycle your project will utilize

- Templates for project management

- How the project manager is allowed to tailor the project management processes to fit any given project

Communication, Archival, and Security Requirements, and Allowed Modalities for Communication   These include the following:

- How a project manager is to close a project

- Financial controls and procedures

- Issue and product defect management

- Change control procedures

- Risk management procedures

- Work authorization system processes

- Processes and procedures for contributing to and accessing a corporate knowledge base

- Process measurements

- Project files

- Historical information and lessons learned documentation

- Issue and defect records of past projects and products

- Configuration management for versioning, baselines, company standards, procedures, and prior project documents (for example, the versions of software, blueprints, and manuals)

- Financial databases

EXAM TIP Many of the adaptive approaches, such as Scrum and XP, don't include the specific role of project manager. For your exam, however, remember that the project management principles still apply. You'll need to recognize the characteristics of the adaptive approach and how you'll get things done as a project manager in that life cycle.

Choosing a Project to Charter

Once the organization and the project manager and team are armed with these inputs, you're ready to go about creating the project charter. Preparing to create the charter is often trickier than actually writing it. However, before the project management team can actually create a charter, there needs to be a project. This means the organization, the project steering committee, or the project portfolio management team needs to choose a project to initiate.

Unless you work for an incredible organization and/or are extremely lucky, you've probably discovered that not every good project ends up being authorized through a charter. After all, most companies have only a limited amount of funds to invest in new projects. There are two approaches an organization takes to choose new projects—and, no, flipping a coin is not one of them.

The first method uses a mathematical model such as the following to determine the likelihood of a project's success:

- Linear programming
- Nonlinear programming
- Dynamic programming
- Integer programming
- Multiobjective programming

Sounds like fun, doesn't it? Don't worry. You do not need to know how to perform any of these math tricks for your PMP exam. Just be topically aware of them, and know that they are examples of geeky mathematical models.

 EXAM TIP Remember that mathematical models are also known as "constrained optimization."

The second method, however, you will want to be a bit more familiar with. This project selection uses a benefits-comparison model to determine project success. Let's look at some models in more detail in the following sections.

Murder Boards

Murder boards are committees of folks who ask every conceivable negative question about the proposed project. Their goals are to expose strengths and weakness of the project—and to kill the project if it's deemed unworthy for the organization to commit

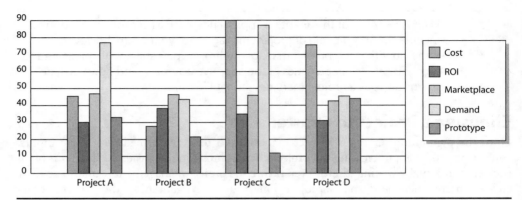

Figure 4-1   A scoring model bases project selection on predefined values.

to. Not a pleasant decision-making process. You might also know murder boards by slightly friendlier names: project steering committees or project selection committees.

Scoring Models

Scoring models (sometimes called weighted scoring models) use a common set of values for all of the projects up for selection. For example, values can be based on profitability, complexity, customer demand, and so on. Each of these values has an assigned weight. Values of high importance have higher weights, while values of lower importance have lower weights. The projects are measured against these values and assigned scores by how well they match the predefined values. The projects with higher scores take priority over projects with lower scores. Figure 4-1 demonstrates the scoring model.

Benefit/Cost Ratios

Just like they sound, benefit/cost ratio (BCR) models examine the benefit-to-cost ratio. A typical measure is the cost to complete the project and the cost of ongoing operations of the project product compared against the expected benefits of the project. For example, consider a project that will cost $575,000 to create a new product, market the product, and provide ongoing support for the product for one year. The expected gross return on the product, however, is $980,000 in year one. In this case, the benefit of completing the project is greater than the cost to create the product.

EXAM TIP   BCR statements may be written as ratios. For example, a BCR of 3:2 has three benefits to two costs—a good choice. A BCR of 1:3, however, is not a good choice. On the exam, pay special attention to which side of the ratio represents the cost (right side). It should not exceed the benefit (left side) if you want it to be selected.

Payback Period

How long does it take the project to "pay back" the associated costs? For example, the AXZ Project will cost the organization $500,000 to create over five years. The expected cash inflow (income) on the project deliverable, however, is $40,000 per quarter. From here, it's simple math: $500,000 divided by $40,000 is 12.5 quarters, or a little over three years to recoup the expenses.

This selection method, while one of the simplest, is also the weakest. Why? The cash inflows are not discounted against the time to begin creating the cash. This is the time value of money. The $40,000 per quarter five years from now is worth less than $40,000 in your pocket today. For example, in the late 1950s, sodas cost a nickel. The soda hasn't gotten better since then; the nickel is just worth a *lot* less today than it was way back then.

VIDEO For a more detailed explanation, watch the *Time Value of Money* video now.

Considering the Discounted Cash Flow

Discounted cash flow accounts for the time value of money. If you were to borrow $100,000 for five years from your uncle, you'd be paying interest on the money, yes? (If not, you've got a very nice uncle.) If the $100,000 were invested for five years and managed to earn a whopping 6 percent interest per year, compounded annually, it'd be worth $133,822.60 at the end of five years. This is the future value of the money in today's terms.

The magic formula for future value is $FV = PV(1 + I)^n$, where

- FV is future value
- PV is present value
- I is the interest rate
- n is the number of periods (years, quarters, and so on)

Here's the formula with the $100,000 in action:

$FV = 100,000(1 + 0.06)^5$

$FV = 100,000(1.338226)$

$FV = 133,822.60$

The future value of the $100,000 five years from now is $133,822.60. So how does that help? Now we've got to calculate the discounted cash flow across all of the projects up for selection. The discounted cash flow is really just the inverse of the preceding formula. We're looking for the present value of future cash flows: $PV = FV \div (1 + I)^n$.

In other words, if a project says it'll be earning the organization $160,000 in five years, that's great, but what's $160,000 five years from now really worth today? This puts the amount of the cash flow in perspective with what the projections are in today's money. Let's plug it into the formula and find out (assuming the interest rate is still 6 percent):

$PV = FV \div (1 + I)^n$

$PV = 160,000 \div (1.338226)$

$PV = \$119,561$

So, $160,000 in five years is worth only $119,561 today. If we had four different projects of varying time to completion, cost, and project cash inflows at completion, we'd calculate the present value and choose the project with the best present value, because it'll likely be the best investment for the organization.

 EXAM TIP You should be able to look at the present value of two proposed projects and make a decision as to which one should be green-lighted. The project with the highest present value is the best choice if that's the only factor you're presented with.

Calculating the Net Present Value

The net present value (NPV) formula is somewhat complicated, but it enables you to predict a project's value more precisely than the lump-sum approach found with the PV formula. NPV evaluates the monies returned on a project for each period the project lasts. In other words, a project may last five years, but there may be a return on investment (ROI) in each of the five years the project is in existence, not just at the end of the project.

For example, a retail company may be upgrading the facilities at each of its stores to make shopping and purchasing easier for its customers. The company has 1,000 stores. As each store makes the conversion to the new facility design, the project deliverables will begin, hopefully, generating cash flow. (Uh, we specifically want cash inflow from the new stores, not cash outflow. That's some nerdy accounting humor.) The project can begin earning money when the first store is completed with the conversion to the new facilities. The faster the project can be completed, the sooner the organization will see a complete ROI.

Here's how the NPV formula works:

1. Calculate the project's cash flow for time unit (typically quarters or years).

2. Calculate each time unit total into the present value.

3. Sum the present value of each time unit.

4. Subtract the investment for the project.

5. Take two aspirin.

6. Examine the NPV value. An NPV greater than zero is good, and the project should be approved. An NPV less than zero is bad, and the project should be rejected.

 DIGITAL CONTENT I bet you're wishing you could try some of these out for yourself, right? You're in luck. I've created for you a Microsoft Excel file called "Time Value of Money" that has a few exercises and all of the formulas to test your work. Enjoy!

Period	Cash Flow	Present Value
1	$15,000.00	$14,150.94
2	$25,000.00	$22,249.91
3	$17,000.00	$14,273.53
4	$25,000.00	$19,802.34
5	$18,000.00	$13,450.65
Totals	$100,000.00	$83,927.37
Investment		$78,000.00
NPV		$5,927.37

Table 4-1
Net Present Value
Calculation

When comparing two projects, the one with the greater NPV is typically better, although projects with high returns (PVs) early in the project are better than those with low returns early in the project. Table 4-1 provides an example of an NPV calculation.

EXAM TIP You likely will not have to calculate NPV on the PMP exam. I've included the whole scenario here to provide an understanding of the formula. Basically, better than zero is good, and less than zero means your project is losing money.

Considering the Internal Rate of Return

The last benefit measurement method is the internal rate of return (IRR). The IRR is a complex formula used to calculate when the present value of the cash inflow equals the original investment. Don't get too lost in this formula—it's a tricky business, and you won't need to know how to calculate the IRR for the exam. You will need to know, however, that when comparing IRRs of multiple projects, projects with high IRRs are better choices than projects with low IRRs. This makes sense. Would you like an investment with a high rate of return or a lower rate of return?

Organizations use the IRR to determine whether the organization should invest capital in the project. IRR is, technically, the yield on the funds invested into the project. You really know that you have a good, efficient investment when the IRR beats other rates of return for investing the capital in bonds or other projects, or even letting the cash stay in the bank. Organizations usually have a minimum acceptable rate of return (MARR) that the project needs to beat before it's even worth their time and cash to invest in the project. You might also know MARR as the hurdle rate—you've got to clear the hurdle before it's worth the risk of taking capital out of sure-thing investments and putting it into the chancy world of projects.

EXAM TIP The formulas on the time value of money are important for project selection and for the exam. You'll need to be familiar with the present value, future value, and net present value formulas; what they do; and why organizations use them to select projects. You should be topically familiar with the internal rate of return concepts, but I doubt you'll have to calculate any IRRs.

Knowing the Project Management Methodology

Before the project management team can dive in and create the project charter, they also need to understand how their organization approaches project management in general. When I teach my project management seminars, I find that some companies have a formal, highly structured, rigid project management approach. Other companies are, well, loosey-goosey. Their approach can vary from project manager to project manager, and they don't mind.

Roughly half of the PMP exam will test you on predictive approaches to project management and the other half will be on agile and hybrid approaches. Most project managers that I meet are well-versed in the predictive approach to project management; it's the idea of agile and hybrid that worry them. The good news is that these questions won't get too detailed about the nuances of agile project management but will likely focus more on the mechanics of agile project management.

 EXAM TIP Learn the rules and policies for agile and hybrid project management versus predictive. The general theme for agile and hybrid project management is that change is welcome and expected. The general theme for predictive is that change is generally opposed as everything has already been predicted in the project.

Whatever methodology an organization has adopted, the project management team must understand how it affects the level of detail they'll need to provide in their project charter. The great thing about this point, in light of your exam, is that every company in the world can use a different project management methodology, so it's tough to ask questions about what's proper or not.

Creating the Charter—Finally

After the project management team is armed with all the inputs, has considered the project selection methodology, and understands the project management methodology in place in their organization, they're ready to create the project charter. The project management team can use four tools to create the charter:

- **Expert judgment** Experts within the organization or external experts such as consultants, agencies, firms, or subject matter experts (SMEs) can help the project management team create all the needed elements for the charter.

- **Data gathering** Work with other people to get their insight, expertise, facts, and opinions about what needs to go into the project charter. There are three specific types of data gathering you'll want to know for your exam to create the project charter:

  - **Brainstorming** Led by a facilitator, the group creates as many ideas as possible and then the ideas are analyzed.

  - **Focus groups** A group of stakeholders and SMEs come together to discuss the project's merit, the potential risk, success criteria, and other aspects of the project.

- **Interviews**   The project manager and stakeholders meet, often in smaller groups or in one-on-one settings, and through conversation the project manager gathers input on the project's requirements, approval criteria, assumptions, constraints, and project details.

- **Interpersonal and team skills**   You'll see this tool and technique mentioned often throughout this book and in the *PMBOK Guide*. For creating the project charter, you should be familiar with three specific interpersonal and team skills:

  - **Conflict management**   The project manager works with stakeholders to find agreement and alignment of the project objectives, success criteria, requirements, and other aspects to be documented in the project charter.

  - **Facilitation techniques**   You'll use facilitation techniques often in your role as the project manager. These are approaches that involve brainstorming, problem-solving with stakeholders, conflict resolution, and group dynamics to reach a consensus for the project charter.

  - **Meeting management**   You'll most effectively manage meetings by creating and following an agenda, inviting the appropriate people to the meeting, ensuring that the time is used appropriately, keeping minutes, and sending the minutes and follow-up actions after the meeting.

- **Meetings**   Key stakeholders will meet to discuss the project objectives, the requirements, success criteria, assumptions, constraints, and all aspects of the project.

The project charter, as a final reminder for your exam, is endorsed by an entity or a person outside of the project boundaries. This person or entity has the power to authorize the project and grant the project manager the power to assign resources to the project work. The project charter should define the business needs and what the project aims to create in order to solve those business needs. The project charter typically defines the following:

- Metrics for the key project objectives (such as schedule, cost, and quality)
- High-level requirements for the project
- High-level description of the project's purpose
- Overall risk within the project
- Summary milestone schedule
- Preapproved financial resources
- Summary budget
- Key stakeholders in the project
- Stakeholders needed for approvals and sign-off on the project acceptance
- Project manager's name and level of authority
- Project sponsor or entity authorizing the project
- Who'll play what role in agile and hybrid projects

Many organizations create a standardized project charter as part of their organizational process assets and then adapt the project charter to each project. Whatever approach you take in your project—creating a charter from scratch or from a template—the most important thing is that the person who signs the project charter has the authority to back up the project manager for conflict resolution and issues in case there's a challenge to the project or the resources needed.

Creating the Assumptions Log

An *assumption* is something that you believe to be true, but that hasn't been proven to be true. Assumptions can include expected performance of a vendor, reliability of equipment, access to resources, the weather, and more. In projects, there are often some things that you have to assume to be true just to function; for example, you assume that the people the project team are going to be involved in the project for the duration of the project. Or some project managers may assume just the opposite—that some of the people on the project team will leave the project or organization before the project is done.

Whatever assumptions you have about the project—specifically at this stage of the project, dealing with the project charter and the requirements—you document in the assumptions log. Assumptions can also be examined a bit later for risk, but for now, as the project is getting started, you'll just jot down the assumptions in the assumptions log and keep moving forward. You can't worry about everything, but chances are some assumptions will hold true and some will not.

Developing the Project Management Plan

In a predictive project, you wouldn't go about building a house, creating a new piece of software, or launching any project without a project plan, right? The project management plan, however, is more than how the *work* will be done; it's how the *project* will be done. That's right, the project management plan defines how the project is executed, monitored and controlled, and then closed. It's a multifaceted plan on how to manage, coordinate, and integrate all the different knowledge areas and processes within a project.

Figure 4-2 shows the process necessary before the project management plan can be developed. Think of all the things a project manager and the project team will decide within the project plan that need to be documented:

- Which project management processes and their levels of implementation are appropriate for the project
- What tools and techniques will be used with which processes
- How the selected processes will be used to manage the project, including how the processes will interact as the project moves through its phases
- How the project work will be completed
- How change control will happen
- How configuration management will be performed

PART II

Figure 4-2
It's a logical approach to get to the project management planning phase.

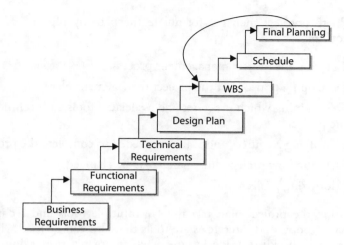

- The integrity of the project's baselines and how the measurements will be used to manage the project better
- Communication demand and techniques with the project stakeholders
- How the project phases will commence and proceed
- How stakeholder inclusion and management will occur
- When and how management will review the project performance

Agile projects don't have big, fat plans. Planning, and documentation, in agile is often seen as a waste. Well, waste may be a harsh description, but recall the Agile Manifesto: "We value working software over comprehensive documentation." Agile, by its very nature, doesn't really need plans to the same extent that a predictive project does. Agile projects have a sense of what the project will create, but they have a clear understanding that the project requirements, and therefore the project work, can change at any time and several times.

EXAM TIP   For your PMP exam you'll need to know the characteristics of the project management plan, because you'll be tested not just on the Agile approach, but on what to expect in projects that are predictive and hybrid.

Creating the Project Management Plan

A common tool and technique for project management processes is expert judgment. Expert judgment comes from SMEs, consultants, project team members, or other groups or individuals who can help you, the project manager, make the best decisions in the project. When it comes to creating the project management plan, expert judgment can help the project manager formulate the plan by offering advice and insight on the following:

- Tailoring the project management processes
- Developing portions of the project management plan
- Determining which processes and associated tools and techniques are needed for the project
- Identifying resources and skill sets needed to complete the project work
- Defining how project documents may be changed
- Prioritizing project work

Creating the project plan can involve multiple tools and techniques. Brainstorming, focus groups, and interviews are tools that also can be used with project planning. Another tool, checklists, is ideal to use when an organization is doing several of the same types of projects. The checklist can guide the project manager and project team to ensure that all of the required project management plan components have been addressed and included in the plan.

As the project completes project planning activities, the outputs will be assimilated into a collection of subsidiary project plans. The collection of these subsidiary project plans will address all of the previous points and help the project manager and the project team know where the project is going and how they will get there. Again, agile projects don't do this, but a hybrid project certainly can.

Let's take a moment and look at each of the minimum project management subsidiary plans the project management plan can include for a predictive project:

- **Scope management plan** This defines how the project scope will be planned, managed, and controlled. This plan is covered in detail in Chapter 5.
- **Requirements management plan** This plan defines how the project requirements will be defined, gathered, documented, and managed. This plan is covered in detail in Chapter 5.
- **Schedule management plan** This defines how the project schedule will be created and managed. The schedule management plan and its creation are covered in Chapter 6.
- **Cost management plan** This plan details how the project costs will be planned for, estimated, budgeted, and then monitored and controlled. Cost management is described in Chapter 7.
- **Quality management plan** Quality is expected on every project. This plan defines what quality means for the project, how the project will achieve quality, and how the project will map to organizational procedures pertaining to quality. Chapter 8 covers quality management in more detail.
- **Resource management plan** This plan defines how project team members will be brought onto the project team, managed, and released from the project team.

It also defines team training, safety issues, roles and responsibilities, and how the project's reward and recognition system will operate. Because resources aren't just people, this plan will also address physical resources, such as equipment, tools, and facilities. Chapter 9 defines the resource management plan in detail.

- **Communications management plan**   This plan defines who will get what information, how they will receive it, and in what modality the communication will take place. Chapter 10 explains communication in more detail.

- **Risk management plan**   Risk is an uncertain event or condition that may affect the project's outcome. The risk management plan defines how the project will manage risk. Chapter 11 includes a conversation on this plan.

- **Procurement management plan**   The procurement management plan, defined in Chapter 12, controls how the project will be allowed to contract goods and services.

- **Stakeholder engagement plan**   The stakeholder engagement plan, defined in Chapter 13, defines how stakeholders will be included, managed, and prioritized for the project.

These subsidiary plans are directly related to the project management knowledge areas. Each plan can be adapted from previous projects or templates within the company that the performing organization has created as part of its organizational process assets. While the project management is, for the most part, a compilation of project plans, additional plans and documents are included that you should know for your PMP certification:

- **Scope baseline**   This is a combination of three project documents: the project scope statement, the work breakdown structure (WBS), and the WBS dictionary. The creation of the project's deliverable will be measured against the scope baseline to show any variances from what was expected and what the project team has created.

- **Schedule baseline**   This is the planned start and finish of the project. The comparison of what was planned and what was experienced in the schedule is called the schedule variance.

- **Cost baseline**   This is the aggregated costs of all of the work packages within the WBS.

- **Performance measurement baseline**   This baseline combines scope, schedule, and cost to compare what's planned and what's being experienced in the project.

- **Change management plan**   This plan details the project procedures for entertaining change requests, and how change requests are managed, documented, approved, or declined. This plan is part of the control scope process.

- **Configuration management plan**   This plan is part of an input to the control scope process. It defines how changes to the features and functions of the project deliverable, the product scope, may enter the project.

- **Risk response plan**   This subsidiary plan defines the risk responses that are to be used in the project for both positive and negative risks.

- **Milestone list**   This list details the project milestones and their attributes. It is used for several areas of project planning but also helps determine how quickly the project may be achieving its objectives.

- **Resource calendar**   Resources are people and things, such as equipment, rooms, and other facilities. This calendar defines when the resources are available to contribute to the project.

Hosting the Project Kickoff Meeting

The project kickoff meeting usually occurs when the project is ready to begin executing. The kickoff meeting is all about communicating the project's intent, to explain the roles and responsibilities and the expectations for the project stakeholders, and to define how the project will be executed, monitored, and controlled. Some organizations may have a kickoff meeting right after project initiation, but usually it's a bit deeper into the project when the project manager and team have created a clear vision of where the project is going and who'll do what on the project.

On larger projects, there may be two different project teams: one that undertakes the planning processes and another that executes the plan. Construction is a great example of this approach: architects, structural engineers, and draftsmen do the planning, and then the professional builders create the structure based on the plan. In these types of environments, the kickoff is associated with the executing processes as the project execution is launching. Finally, if a project has multiple phases in its life cycle, there can be a kickoff meeting for each phase of the project. Agile projects do have a kickoff meeting to explain the goals of the project, the roles and responsibilities, and the goals of the agile project life cycle.

Directing and Managing the Project Work

So you've got a project plan—great! Now the work of executing the project plan begins. The *PMBOK Guide* process for this chunk of the project is to direct and manage the project work. This is where the project manager manages the project and the project team does the work. The project manager and the project team will go about completing the promises made in the plan to deliver, document, measure, and complete the project work. The project plan will communicate to the project team, the stakeholders, management, and even to the vendors what work happens next, how it begins, and how it will be measured for quality and performance.

 EXAM TIP   You'll likely be using a project management information system, such as Microsoft Project, Basecamp, or some other software to help you manage your project. For your exam, you won't be tested on these products, but you'll need to know that a project management information system helps the project manager make decisions and track project progress.

The product of the project is created during these execution processes. The largest percentage of the project budget will be spent now. The project manager and the project team must work together to orchestrate the timing and integration of all the project's moving parts. A flaw in one area of the execution can have ramifications in cost and additional risk and can cause additional flaws in other areas of the project.

 NOTE Execution in agile projects happens during the work iteration. During this time, the team doing the work is not to be interrupted, and it's up to the project manager to protect the team from interruptions, to ensure that the rules of the life cycle are being followed, and to remove impediments that are preventing the team from completing their assignments. The work in each phase is assigned and chosen by the project team members, not the project manager, as the team is self-organizing.

As the project work is implemented in predictive environments, the project manager refers to the project plan to ensure that the work is meeting the documented expectations, requirements, quality demands, target dates, and more. The completion of the work is measured and then compared against the cost, schedule, and scope baselines as documented in the project plan. Should there be—gasp!—discrepancies between the project work and the baselines, prompt and accurate reactions are needed to adjust the slipping components of the project.

The execution of the project includes many activities:

- Doing the work to reach the project objectives
- Spending the project budget to reach the objectives
- Building, training, and developing the project team
- Getting quotes, bids, and proposals for project vendors
- Selecting the project vendors
- Purchasing, managing, and using the resources, materials, equipment, and facilities the project needs to reach its objectives
- Implementing the organization's mandated methods and standards for the project
- Managing and verifying the project deliverables
- Completing risk assessment, monitoring, and response
- Managing those pesky vendors
- Dovetailing the approved changes into the project
- Communicating with and managing the project stakeholders
- Gathering project data on cost, schedule, quality, and status to forecast where the project will be in the future
- Collecting and creating the lessons learned documentation

Yes, agile and hybrid projects include these same activities, but not as distinctly as a predictive project. Agile projects, for example, welcome change, but not during a sprint or work iteration. Changes go into the product backlog, are prioritized for future work iterations, and are not entered directly into the current iteration. That's right, changes don't go right into production. Changes are prioritized and will go into future work iterations. In Scrum, for example, only the product owner may cancel a sprint, and that's an extremely rare event and there must overwhelming reason to do so.

 EXAM TIP Remember that hybrid project management approaches combine predictive and adaptive for what works best for the organization. There is no single hybrid approach that's universal; each is a custom approach to project management, so it's difficult to say what must happen, or even should happen, in a hybrid project.

Agile projects are also different from predictive when it comes to planning, in that the planning is from the most important items to the least important items (eating dessert first). Agile projects don't have the same overhead as predictive with all the upfront planning, but planning is done at the start of each iteration. In Scrum, for example, at a sprint planning meeting, the most important user stories are selected, and then the team will create a work breakout and determine who'll do what work in the sprint. Agile planning is for the next chunk of work, not the entire project, because things are likely to change anyway. Planning at a detailed level is for predictive and for some hybrid approaches, not pure agile approaches.

Creating the Project Deliverables

Execution is all about creating project deliverables; project deliverables are the products of the project, but they can also be components of the project management plan. Deliverables are anything that the project team creates or that the project acquires as a result of project execution. Though most deliverables are things that the customer or stakeholders receive from the project, not all deliverables are for the customer. For example, you might need to purchase some equipment for the project in order to complete the project work. The customer doesn't receive the equipment as a result of the project; your organization retains that equipment as an asset. The equipment, however, is considered a deliverable. Other deliverables can be data, lessons learned, new skills required, or project documents.

 EXAM TIP Remember these differences: In a predictive project, once a deliverable has been created, any change to the deliverable needs to follow the project's defined change control process. In Agile projects, changes are welcome at any time, but they are added to the product backlog for prioritization.

Creating an Issue Log

Issues are unexpected events that you must document and manage to prevent them from causing risks or other problems within the project. Issues are events that have happened, that reoccur, or that are going to happen that will likely disrupt the project. When an issue occurs, the project manager will document the issue in the issue log, assign an issue owner, and start tracking the issue through its resolution. Each issue identified in the issue log includes the following information:

- Date identified
- Person identifying the issue
- Details about the issue
- Summary of the issue
- Prioritization
- Issue owner
- Target resolution date
- Current status
- Final outcome

Responding to Project Conditions

Change requests, in predictive projects, are formal requests to change some aspect of the project. Change requests are needed to change project deliverables, make modifications to project documents and plans, or change project baselines. Change requests are managed through integrated change control, which is discussed in more detail later in this chapter. Change requests almost always stem from four aspects of a project: schedule, cost, scope, and contract. However, change requests can come from any area of the project, not just these four domains.

Directing and managing the project work also require the project management team to respond to conditions within the project. Risks, unlike issues, are events that may happen in the project that can have positive or, more often, negative results for the project. For example, consider a new immediate risk that demands a response. A new condition warrants that the project management team plan and then directly confront the problem. Four activities can also warrant a formal change request:

- Apply corrective actions to bring future project performance back into alignment with the project plan.
- Apply preventive actions to avoid negative risks within the project.
- Apply defect repairs to fix flaws and problems identified through quality control.
- Update the project management plan and execution as a result of change requests within the project.

Managing Project Knowledge

Ready for a new project management process? Well, it's new to the *PMBOK Guide*, Sixth Edition: *project knowledge management*. The idea is that when you manage a project, you'll rely on your existing knowledge, but you may also learn new things to manage the project better. Managing project knowledge isn't just about documenting information, but creating organized lessons learned to share openly in the current project, future projects, and in operations to support the solution the project creates.

There are two types of knowledge you'll need to know about:

- **Explicit knowledge**   Knowledge that can be quickly and easily expressed through conversations, documentation, figures, or numbers.

- **Tacit knowledge**   Knowledge that's more difficult to express, because it's personal beliefs, values, knowledge gained from experience, and "know-how" when doing a task.

Though it's tempting to lump this process into lessons learned, it involves more than just documenting what has been learned in the project. Yes, lessons learned is more explicit knowledge because it's easily codified, but lessons learned often lacks the deeper understanding that tacit (implied) knowledge provides. Tacit knowledge is more difficult to communicate through lessons learned, but it may be expressed by working alongside an experienced project team member or through in-depth training.

Preparing to Manage Knowledge

It's difficult to set start and end points for managing knowledge within a project because projects are ongoing, iterative activities. There are, however, several inputs that can help you manage knowledge within a project:

- **Project management plan**   All parts of the project management plan are inputs to managing knowledge and are documents based on the knowledge you've already collected in the project.

- **Lessons learned register**   The lessons learned register defines what's worked in the project (and other projects in the organization). Lessons learned documentation is updated throughout the project, not just at the end of the project. Scrum projects complete a sprint retrospective to implement lessons learned in the next sprint of the project.

- **Project team assignments**   Assignments identify the skills needed in the project and what skills might be missing in the project. Project team assignments give you insight into what type of knowledge the project team members have to contribute. Agile project teams are self-organizing and, as local domain experts, team members will determine who does what in the project.

- **Resource breakdown structure**   Visualize the utilization of resources, but also what knowledge may be collectively utilized based on the composition of project team resources.

- **Source selection criteria**   When choosing a vendor, this component can help you identify what knowledge you're obtaining from an outside resource.

Vendors may protect their knowledge, depending on the project, the discipline, and the time they have available to share information with you.

- **Stakeholder register** The stakeholder register will help you understand what knowledge stakeholders bring to the project. Stakeholders have insight into the project scope and requirements, and they can contribute to the project planning.

Understanding the project deliverables can help you ascertain knowledge. Project deliverables are the products, results, or capabilities created as a result of the project work. Deliverables take knowledge to create; therefore, understanding the nature of the deliverables, how the deliverables were created, and what it will take to support and maintain the deliverables will help you better manage the knowledge surrounding project deliverables. Although deliverables are usually things the customer of the project receives, they can also include other things, such as documents and items from the project management plan.

As with most process inputs, knowledge management can also rely on enterprise environmental factors (EEFs) and organizational process assets (OPAs). For EEFs, the culture of the customer, organization, and stakeholders can contribute to knowledge management. You'll also consider the geography of facilities and resources, rely on organization experts, and be in alignment with any legal and regulatory requirements. For OPAs, you'll consider policies, processes, and procedures. These assets also include personnel administration, communication requirements, and formal knowledge-sharing procedures (such as learning reviews throughout the project).

Reviewing Knowledge Management Tools and Techniques

One of the primary tools you'll use with knowledge management is expert judgment. You'll work with people who are skilled in knowledge and information management. This may be trainers and instructors, technical writers, or people who are skilled in knowledge management software. Whatever approach you take, the goal is the same: to capture, document, and share knowledge in the project. XP projects utilize local knowledge management through paired programming, where a pair of programmers work together to capture mistakes, develop better code, and write test-passing code based on predefined tests.

Knowledge management is also dependent on the size of the project and the number of stakeholders involved. Projects with a large number of stakeholders will likely need a more formal strategy to knowledge management than is required for smaller projects. Though expert judgment is an accessible tool for knowledge management, there are many other tools and techniques to consider, especially in a larger project:

- **Networking (live and web-based)** Informal conversations and open-based questions can provide knowledge.

- **Communities of practice** Sometimes called special interest groups, these can be live or web-based.

- **Meetings** Both live and web-based meetings can help inform and educate.

- **Work shadowing and reverse shadowing**   In *work shadowing*, you follow, or shadow, an expert in her work to learn about the job. In *reverse shadowing*, the expert follows you performing the skill to be learned; the expert can offer coaching or feedback at the end of the session.

- **Discussion forums and focus groups**   Like communities of practices, these can be live or online, and they help participants learn from others in an informal setting.

- **Training events**   Seminars, conferences, workshops, and training require participants to interact with one another.

- **Storytelling**   By using storytelling, team members and experts can help others better relate to tacit knowledge.

- **Creativity and ideas management techniques**   Blogs, journals, meeting scribes, and even software tools can help the project manager, team, and stakeholders capture their ideas from brainstorming and planning sessions.

- **Knowledge fairs and cafes**   Like a traditional fair, participants can move between "tents" or stations to learn from a trainer quick lessons about a topic. Knowledge fairs and cafes are a fun and quick way to learn lots of information, at a high-level, from a variety of speakers and on a variety of topics.

Another tool and technique in knowledge management is information management. Information management facilitates linking people to the information they need. These types of tools are useful for fast and direct access to document-explicit knowledge, such as creating lessons learned or accessing information in the lessons learned register. Depending on the size of your organization, you might also have library services for information. Of course, a robust PMIS can include document and information management.

Agile projects are a proponent of high-touch, low-tech tools. This can be sign boards, like the Kanban board, or a wall of information to share. Some fancy projects might use an electronic dashboard to update the work in progress (WIP), the burndown chart, and the items in queue for the work iteration. A centralized area in which to share information openly is called an *information radiator*, but it needs to be maintained by the project manager role in the project.

Information management is often driven by a tool, such as software, but knowledge management shouldn't be just data-driven. People have knowledge, not machines. Interacting with others and working process owners in the organization can often provide a richer, more meaningful way to learn and share information than a search engine. Face-to-face communication, active listening, facilitation, and leadership are all people skills. Coupled with this, people on both ends of the knowledge management equation will need political awareness of what's being asked and what information is being given.

Reviewing the Results of Knowledge Management

Knowledge management creates three outputs, which will be appended and updated throughout the project—they are not the final outputs of a simple process. As more knowledge becomes available, you'll need to revisit knowledge management and then update these three items accordingly:

- **Lessons learned register** The lessons learned register is an output of knowledge management, and it's something that you'll create early in the project, not at closing. Your lessons learned register can be a simple recording of what's been learned in the project, or, more likely, you can create categories of learning, the effects of what's been learned, and what recommendations you and the team have for different scenarios.

- **Project management plan updates** You'll see project management plan updates as an output of many processes, and knowledge management is no different. Note that when you need to change the project management plan, you'll follow the project's change management system. This is true for predictive and agile projects.

- **Organizational process assets updates** When a project creates new knowledge, that knowledge can be utilized not only in the current project, but in future projects and operations. New knowledge can be documented, shared, and implemented as a benefit of doing the current project.

Monitoring and Controlling the Project Work

As soon as a project begins, the project management monitoring and controlling processes also begin. These processes monitor all the other processes within the project to ensure that they are being done according to plan and according to the performing organization's practices, and to ensure that a limited number of defects enters the project. The monitoring and controlling process group includes several key activities:

- Comparing the project management plan against actual performance in the project
- Looking for situations where preventive or corrective actions are needed
- Identifying and tracking project risks events
- Documenting information about the product through the project
- Communicating the project status and progress, and forecasting schedule and cost issues
- Monitoring change requests and implementing approved changes into the project
- If part of a program, following the program rules and reporting on project status and performance to the program manager as required
- Aligning the project with the identified business needs

Monitoring the Project

Monitoring and controlling the project is not a one-time or random event. It's important for the project management team to continue to monitor the project and not to assume that all's well simply because the project work is being completed. By constantly monitoring the project, you confirm that the project work is being done properly and that if the work is flawed, you can prepare a response. Monitoring and controlling is also concerned with results. For example, a defect repair review follows a defect repair to ensure that the repair is accurate and that the project work may continue.

 NOTE Forecasting the project's performance on its cost and schedule is part of monitoring and controlling. In Chapter 7, we'll dive headfirst into earned value management and how it helps the project manager control the project and respond to cost and schedule variances and make forecasts about the likelihood of the project's success.

Analyzing Project Data

Depending on what's happening in the project and the overall size of the project, the project manager and team can use several different data analysis tools. First, recall that work performance data is gathered from the outputs of processes and activities within the project. Work performance data is raw data that's not useful until it's been analyzed. That's what's happening in this tool and technique of data analysis.

Raw data can be analyzed through one of several methods:

- **Alternatives analysis** The project manager and team examine all of the alternatives for selecting corrective, preventive, or a combination of corrective and preventive actions for the project.

- **Cost-benefit analysis** The project manager and team examine the costs of a solution and compare those to the benefits the solution may bring the project. This helps to determine the most cost-effective corrective action when there are likely to be cost deviations.

- **Earned value analysis** The project manager and team use a suite of formulas to show project performance and to forecast how the project is likely to perform in the future. (I'll discuss more on earned value management in Chapter 7.)

- **Root-cause analysis** The project manager and team look for the main causes of a problem. This is sometimes called cause-and-effect analysis.

- **Trend analysis** Based on what's already happened in the project, the project manager and team can identify trends in schedule and costs to predict what's likely to happen in the remainder of the project. Then you can respond to trends that may be hurting the project with a preventive action. In agile projects, you'll monitor trends like the WIP, the burndown chart, and team velocity. Velocity refers to how many user stories the team can complete per work iteration. The higher the velocity, the fewer iterations will be needed to complete the known product backlog.

- **Variance analysis** The project manager and team identify the difference between what was planned and what was experienced. The variance is the difference between the expectations and reality; variance can be positive or negative and can be used for cost, schedule, resource utilization, technical performance, and other metrics within the project.

Creating a Work Performance Report

Once data has been analyzed, it becomes work performance information—useable data that tells a story of how the project is performing. With performance information, you'll need to create a work performance report to format the information into useable communications for the project customers, management, and other stakeholders. Your organization may require that an organizational process asset, such as a form, be used for your work performance reports, or your organization may use an electronic work performance report to show performance on the project.

Work performance reports are sometimes called status reports or performance reports. They are typically a one-page summary of what's happening in the project, which may include some quick charts on performance, RAG ratings (Red-Amber-Green ratings) on project performance, and other metrics tied to key performance indicators (KPIs).

 EXAM TIP The PMP exam might try to trick you with questions on work performance facts. Here's the shortcut to remember: it's alphabetical. First you need the raw data: work performance *data*. Now the data is analyzed to make a decision, so you have work performance *information*. Finally, you'll communicate the information through work performance *reports*. So, it's data, information, and then reports—alphabetical.

Managing Integrated Change Control

Project managers must try to protect the project scope from changes in a predictive environment. Management, team members, customers, and other stakeholders are going to want changes to the project deliverables. Changes to the product often stem from the customer. Changes may also stem from suggestions of the stakeholders—such as small, innocent changes that bloom into additional time and costs. Finally, changes may come from the project team. It's important to note that change decisions may be verbally conveyed, but these should always be documented and entered into the project's change management system.

Agile projects welcome and expect change, of course. Bring on your changes! Changes, however, go into the product backlog, not the current work iteration. Changes are prioritized, so some user stories might be bumped down in the product backlog or even out of the project altogether. It's possible that a change in the product backlog may cause deliverables that have already been done to be reworked, so that must be considered as well. Changes are managed by the product owner in Scrum, though XP, Lean, and hybrid approaches may have the project manager role or coach role handle the change requests. Whatever approach an organization decides to take, the changes must be documented and tracked.

When it comes to integrated change control, the project manager must provide for the following:

- Identifying a change that is proposed or that has already occurred
- Influencing the stakeholders so that only approved changes are incorporated into the project work
- Reviewing and, when needed and applicable, approving change requests
- Managing changes by regulating the flow of change requests
- Reflecting the approved changes in the project baselines: schedule, cost, scope, and quality
- Reviewing and approving corrective and preventive actions
- Considering the impact of a change request on the rest of the project, as well as considering all of the knowledge areas and the impact of a change on each one
- Documenting the change request and the impact it may have on the project
- Communicating the change to the appropriate stakeholders
- Completing defect repair validation
- Continuing quality control

 EXAM TIP To help you remember this concept, think of integrated change control and the domino effect. Any proposed changes to the project can have serious impacts on other areas of the project. Because of this, all of the project management knowledge areas have to be evaluated with each project change.

When you're doing integrated change control, you might be working with a change control board. This is a committee of executives, project stakeholders, and other experts who'll examine and evaluate the change and make a determination on how the change should be managed. This management of the change includes approving, rejecting, or postponing the change. Not all projects utilize a change control board, but all projects should document the change control process and communicate how it'll work in the project.

Reacting to Change

Every project needs a change control system (CCS) to review, consider, track, and, if needed, approve the change requests. Rejected change requests should also be tracked and documented. Most often, projects rely on a change control board (CCB) to evaluate the worthiness of a proposed change before it is approved. Whatever approach a project management team elects or is required to take when dealing with changes, the approach should be documented. The key stakeholders must all agree to abide by the rules of the change control system before the project work begins. The project's change management plan provides the governance for all changes in the project, the role of the project manager and change requests, and how (and often when) the CCB will review proposed changes.

When changes are approved, the project manager must then update the project baselines, as changes will likely affect a combination of scope, cost, and schedule. The updated baselines enable the project to continue with the new changes fleshed in and provide for an accurate measurement of the project performance.

This is an important concept: *Update the project baselines.* Consider a project to which work has been added but for which the schedule baseline has not been updated. The project end date will be impossible to meet, because the project schedule baseline does not reflect the additional work that would extend that date. In addition, a failure to revise the project baseline could skew reporting, variances, future project decisions—and even future projects.

In agile projects, however, changes only affect the scope, and we work against a fixed budget and a fixed schedule. What this means is that some items in the product backlog may be pushed out of the project. We only have so much time and so much money to complete the prioritized user stories. The project team will work on the most important items first and then work down to the least important items. If we don't have enough money and enough time, in a pure agile project, then it's too darn bad for those lesser items. In reality, however, the project will likely need more time and/or more money to complete all of the user stories. Pure agile keeps the end date and the budget fixed with the communicated understanding that only low-level, lesser priority items will be pushed out of the project. It's possible that new projects can proceed after this one to complete the lower level items, but it's not guaranteed. This is the idea of the Inverted Iron Triangle, shown in Figure 4-3. Predictive project management has a fixed scope and allows time and cost adjustments. Agile projects have fixed time and costs but allow the scope to be freely adjusted.

NOTE Undocumented change requests should never be implemented in a project.

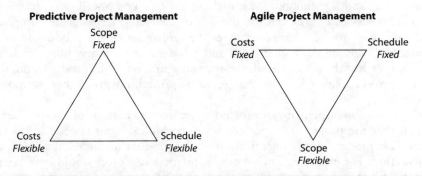

Figure 4-3   Agile projects use the Inverted Iron Triangle of Project Management.

Consider a project manager who does not update the project baselines after a change. The completion of the project goes into the archives and can serve as historical information for future projects. The historical information is skewed, however, because it does not accurately account for the added work and the projected end date or budget.

Note that change requests do include any corrective or preventive actions, but these actions do not justify changes to the project baselines. Basically, if you have an error in the project and need to employ corrective actions, you should also have a change request for that corrective action, but the error doesn't justify a change to the cost and schedule baseline. Only changes that are additions or reductions to the existing project scope can justify a change to the performance baselines. In some cases, such as with a really flawed schedule estimate, the change control board may allow a rebaselining of the schedule, but usually an error counts as a variance against the project performance.

Using the Project Management Information System

You already know that the PMIS is a software tool that helps the project management team plan, execute, monitor and control, and then close the project. The PMIS, contrary to what some managers want to believe, does not replace the project manager, however. Within the PMIS are two important systems that you will need to know for your PMP exam and for the remainder of this book. Let's get these down now and be happy for the next nine chapters.

The Configuration Management System

We all know that changes are likely to happen to the project scope. How these change requests are submitted, reviewed, approved, and tracked are part of the configuration management system. This system, established early in the project, defines how stakeholders are allowed to submit change requests, the conditions for approving a change request, and how approved change requests are validated in the project scope. When a change is proposed that will affect the features and functions of the product or the project scope, you need configuration management.

The configuration of the project's product or service must be accurately and completely defined. This includes the labeling of the components, how changes are made to the product, and accountability for making the changes. Specifically, accountability refers to the ownership of the change, the cost of the change, the schedule impacts, and the influence the product change has over the remainder of the product features and components. For example, a change to add a basement to a new home construction project would affect the project baselines, the configuration of the product, and, depending on the project status when the change was approved, possibly other components of the house.

Configuration management also includes the documentation of the product information so that the project management team can quickly and effectively manage the product. This process means organization of the product materials, details, and prior documentation. For example, a new home construction project would have blueprints, permits, field drawings, vendor and customer specifications, and more information that needs to be cataloged, managed, and quickly accessed throughout the project.

Configuration management is concerned with the performance and functional attributes of the product. In the new home construction project, the role of configuration management is to ensure that the new home is built according to the configuration documentation. Variances between what was completed and what was planned would have to be reviewed and responded to via defect repair or corrective actions.

Configuration management addresses several activities:

- **Configuration item identification**   Documents and controls changes to each configurable item of the product

- **Configuration item accounting**   Records and reports status, performance, and adherence of each configurable item of the product

- **Configuration item verification and audit**   Ensures that each configurable item of the product is accurate and that any approved changes to the product have been documented, tracked, and applied to the product as planned

- **Product documentation**   Documents the functional and physical characteristics of a product or component

- **Change control**   Controls changes to any of a product's physical characteristics

- **Change recording and documentation**   Documents changes to the product's physical characteristics and the conditions surrounding the changes

The Change Management System

You'll be hearing an awful lot about integrated change control throughout this book. It's essential for a predictive project to have an established change control system, or the project will be riddled with change requests. Integrated change control communicates the process for controlling changes to the project deliverables. This system works with the configuration management system and seeks to control and document proposals to the project's product. Figure 4-4 demonstrates an example of a change management system in a predictive project.

NOTE   I won't bash Microsoft Project—it's an excellent, excellent tool. However, some managers believe that if you have Microsoft Project installed on your PC, you should be able to manage a project without any flaws, questions, or issues. Ha! That's like saying that just because you have Microsoft Word installed, you should be able to write a novel. Project management is more than a piece of software.

Closing the Project or Phase

Every project manager that I know loves to close a project. There's something rewarding about completing a project and then transferring the deliverable to the customer or project user. I've also learned from participant feedback in my PMP Boot Camp seminars that closing the project is the category in which they missed the most questions on their way to their PMP certification. I imagine they're winded by the time their studying

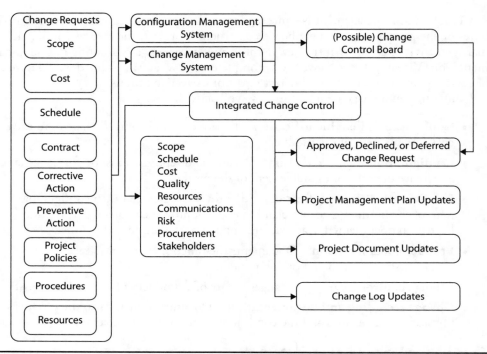

Figure 4-4 All change requests must be documented and must pass through a change management system.

efforts get to closing. With that in mind, give yourself a stretch, have another sip of coffee, and really home in on this closing discussion. I want you to pass your exam!

The closing process group may be applied to the end of a project or to the end of the project phase in a multiphased project. Closing the project or phase means that the project manager confirms that all of the needed activities within the other process groups have been completed and that the project deliverables have been handed over to the customer. If a project is terminated for any reason, the project manager should still close the project to account for the work that has been performed on the project and to learn why the project may have failed.

NOTE Projects can be moving along swimmingly and still get terminated. Consider an organization's cash flow or the project's priority, or perhaps the project deliverable may not be needed any longer. Just because a project was canceled doesn't always mean the project was a failure.

Documenting the Closing

You can close the entire project or, in larger projects, you can close just a phase of the project. The process of closing the project or phase is about finalizing everything in the project and ensuring that there are no loose ends, that everyone has the information they need, and that the project is officially done. The project manager documents everyone who is involved in the project closure: team members, vendors, management, the sponsor, and often the project customer. Part of this documentation defines each person's role and related responsibility to close out the project. Consider a large construction project. Lots of people are involved in the formal closing proceedings, so documentation explaining who'll be needed, what they'll be doing, and when they'll be doing it makes great sense for the project manager.

When the project manager prepares to close the project or phase, she'll need to gather eight specific items as process inputs:

- **Project charter**   The project charter defines what the project will accomplish, what constitutes project success, and who will sign off on the project completion.

- **Project management plan**   The project management plan includes the project scope, the project requirements, and expectations for the project objectives. When a project is being completed for another organization, the contract serves as a guide for how the project may be closed. The project plan may also reference the enterprise environmental factors to consider as part of project closing. Agile projects don't have a detailed project management plan.

- **Project documents**   You may rely on some (or all) of the project documents to close the project. This can include the assumptions log, basis of estimates, change log, issue log, lesson learned register, milestone list, communications, quality control measurement, quality reports, requirements documentation, risk register, and any risk reports.

- **Deliverables**   The project has to create something, so it's no surprise that the deliverables serve as input to the project closing processes.

- **Business documents**   The business case that justified the need for the project and the benefits management plan are referenced in closing.

- **Agreements**   Any contracts or similar documents that need to be closed are included as part of the closing project phase or project process. The terms of contract closure should be part of any contract.

- **Procurement documentation**   All procurement documentation is gathered and filed. This includes all vendor performance information, contract change information, payments, and inspection results. Your project may also have "as-built" or "as-developed" plans, drawings, and documentation that need to be archived.

- **Organizational process assets**   An organization may have procedures and processes that every project manager must follow to close a phase or project. These can include financial, reporting, and human resource obligations.

Project closure includes analyzing the success of the project through data analysis. One of the most common approaches is regression analysis. It's a mathematical model to examine the relationship among project variables, such as cost, time, labor, and other project metrics. For regression analysis, you can use a scatter diagram to help visualize the correlation between the dependent variables, such as the project's budget, against the independent variables, such as errors in the project, changes to the project, and any delays stakeholders may have caused to the project. This helps to identify trends, especially in phases, and helps you prepare for future projects and other phases yet to begin within the project.

The goal of project closure is to get formal acceptance of the project deliverables. *Formal acceptance* means that the project customer or sponsor agrees that the deliverable provided is in alignment with the project scope and that it is acceptable. A formal documentation of project acceptance, such as a project certificate of closure or a project closure sign-off, is needed to confirm that the project deliverable has been transferred from the project manager to the recipient of the project.

Creating the Final Project Report

When you've confirmed that the project deliverable has been transferred to the customer or organizational party, ensured that the project resources have been released from the project, and obtained project sign-off from the key stakeholders such as the project sponsor, you'll create the final project report. This final report is a summation of the entire project and the experience of the project manager and the project team. The final report is all about determining how well the project performed and how efficiently the project was managed to reach its objectives.

The final project report typically includes the following:

- Summation of the project
- Scope objectives and evidence of when the scope objectives were met or missed
- Quality performance of the project and its deliverables
- Schedule performance, milestone delivery dates, and overall schedule management
- Cost performance, actual costs, cost variances, and earned value management performance
- Final product, service, or result performance and ability to meet the scope objectives and business objectives of the organization
- Summation of project risk management and how risks were managed within the project
- Success or failure status of the project and reasons

Should the project be cancelled during its execution, the project manager should still follow the close project process and create the final project report. After creating the project report, the project manager will submit it to the project sponsor and any other key stakeholders who require the document. Typically, not all stakeholders receive the final project report, only the key stakeholders who are privy to the information, such as the project sponsor. Finally, all of the project documentation, support materials, and lessons learned information are entered into organizational process assets to help future projects.

Chapter Summary

Project integration management is an ongoing process completed by the project manager to ensure that the project moves from initiation to closure. It is the gears, guts, and grind of project management—the day-in, day-out business of completing the project work. Project integration management coordinates the activities, project resources, constraints, and assumptions of the project plans and massages them into a working model. Once the model exists, it's up to the project manager and project team to monitor and control the project from initiation to closure, and to ensure that everything goes according to plan—and if it doesn't, to fix it.

Of course, project integration management isn't an automatic process. It requires you, the project manager, to negotiate, finesse, and adapt to project circumstances. It relies on general business skills (such as leadership), organizational skills, and communication to get all the parts of the project working together.

Project integration management includes seven processes:

- **Developing the project charter** The project charter authorizes the project. It names the project manager and enables the project to commence. Projects are chartered for varying reasons: to satisfy market demand, to respond to customer requests, to solve a problem, or to address a social need. While the charter authorizes the project, it also defines the requirements for stakeholder satisfaction, the project purpose, and the project assumptions and constraints.

- **Developing the project management plan** Project management plan development is an iterative process that requires input from the project manager, the project team, the project customers, and other key stakeholders. It details how the project work will accomplish the project goals. The project management plan comprises 11 subsidiary plans and several other documents. Agile projects often don't have a project management plan because change is welcome and expected.

- **Directing and managing the project work** Once the project management plan has been created, the project manager and the project team can implement the plan. Directing and managing the project work creates the project deliverables for the project or phase. Corrective actions, preventive actions, and defect repair all happen through directing and managing the project work. Agile project teams are self-organizing, and the team will decide in each iteration who'll do what work.

- **Managing project knowledge** The project manager and the project team members come into the project with knowledge about the work, but that knowledge isn't always easily shared with one another. Explicit knowledge—knowledge that can be quickly and easily expressed through conversations, documentation, figures, or numbers—is easily communicated. However, tacit knowledge is more difficult to express, because it's about personal beliefs, values, knowledge gained from experience, and "know-how" when doing a task.

- **Monitoring and controlling the project work** This process starts with the project's conception and finishes with the project completion. Its goal is to make certain that the project stays on track and finishes according to the project plan. Measurements for project performance, schedule, cost, and quality are implemented. If there are variances, responses to these will happen through preventive, corrective, or defect repair actions.

- **Performing integrated change control** Changes can kill a project. Change requests must be documented and sent through a formal change control system to determine their worthiness for implementation. Integrated change control manages changes across the entire project. Change requests are evaluated and considered for impacts on risk, costs, schedule, and scope. Not all change requests are approved—but all change requests must be documented and reviewed.

- **Closing the project or phase** Projects and phases are closed. Administrative closure confirms that all of the needed processes for each process group have been completed. Administrative closure also gathers all project records for archival purposes, including documentation of the project's success or failure. Contracts and agreements, when used, must also be closed after inspection of the contract deliverables. Contracts are always closed according to the agreed-upon terms.

Questions

1. You are the project manager for a pharmaceutical company. You are currently working on a project for a new drug your company is creating. A recent change in a law governing drug testing will impact your project and change your project scope. What is the first thing you should do as project manager?

   A. Create a documented change request.

   B. Proceed as planned since the project will be grandfathered beyond the new change in the law.

   C. Consult with the project stakeholders.

   D. Stop all project work until the issue is resolved.

2. You are the project manager for the HALO Project. You and your project team are preparing the project plan. Of the following, which one is a project plan development constraint you and your team must consider?

   A. The budget as assigned by management

   B. Project plans from similar projects

   C. Project plans from similar projects that have failed

   D. Interviews with SMEs who have experience with the project work in your project plan

3. You are the project manager of a new project to develop a new software product. Management has not required a formal project management plan in the past, but they'd like you to develop a project management plan to serve as a model or template for all other projects in the organization. What is the primary purpose of your project management plan?

   A. To define the work to be completed to reach the project end date

   B. To define the work needed in each phase of the project life cycle

   C. To prevent any changes to the scope

   D. To provide accurate communication for the project team, project sponsor, and stakeholders regarding how the project will be executed, controlled, and closed

4. You are the project manager of a hybrid project incorporating the planning of a predictive project and the workflow of iterations of Agile. How will you likely manage changes to the project scope in this approach?

   A. Schedule and cost change control

   B. Process change control

   C. Product backlog prioritization

   D. No changes are allowed to the project scope once it has been baselined

5. Robert is the project manager of the HBQ Project. This project requires all of the telephones in the organization to be removed and replaced with Internet phones. He's learned that the removal of some of the phones has damaged the walls in the office building and they will need to be repaired. This project has a deadline and little time for repairing issues that weren't anticipated. Based on this information, which one of the following is the best example of defect repair review?

   A. Adding labor to a project to reduce issues during the installation of hardware

   B. Retraining the project team on how to install a new material so that all future work with the new materials is done correctly

   C. Repairing an incorrectly installed door in a new home construction project

   D. Inspecting work that has been corrected because it was done incorrectly the first time

6. Your organization utilizes Scrum for all software development projects. Susan is a project team member who has been developing software applications for years. She has knowledge about her routine, her approach to software development, and the processes she has developed over time that are complex to explain in planning meetings. What type of knowledge does Susan have?

   A. Tacit knowledge

   B. Explicit knowledge

   C. Factual knowledge

   D. Experiential knowledge

7. The project plan provides a baseline for several things. Which one of the following does the project plan NOT provide a baseline for?

   A. Scope

   B. Cost

   C. Schedule

   D. Control

8. You are the project manager for your organization. When it comes to integrated change control, you must ensure that which one of the following is present?

   A. Supporting detail for the change

   B. Approval of the change from the project team

   C. Approval of the change from a subject matter expert

   D. Risk assessment for each proposed change

9. Keisha is the project manager for her organization and she's working with her project team to develop the project management plan for a new project. The project team is confused about the change management plan and how it governs changes within the project. The project plan provides what with regard to project changes?

   A. A methodology to approve or decline changes

   B. A guide to all future project risk management decisions

   C. A vision of the project deliverables

   D. A fluid document that may be updated as needed based on the CCB

10. You are assisting the project manager for the DGF Project. This project is to design and implement a new application that will connect to a database server. Management has requested that you create a method to document technical direction on the project and any changes or enhancements to the technical attributes of the project deliverable. Which one of the following would satisfy management's request?

   A. The configuration management system

   B. Integrated change control

   C. Scope control

   D. The change management plan

11. You are a project manager of an agile project that is part of a program. There has been some conflict among the project team about who assigns activities and directs the project execution. In this scenario, who directs the performance of the planned project activities?

   A. The project manager and the project management team

   B. The project team

   C. The project sponsor

   D. The program manager

12. You have just informed your project team that each team member will be contributing to the lessons learned documentation. In Scrum, when will lessons learned activities take place?

    A. At the end of the project

    B. During the sprint review

    C. During the sprint retrospective

    D. Throughout each sprint through paired programming

13. Fred is the project manager of a bridge construction project. His organization and the city inspectors both have an interest in the success and overall performance of the project and have asked Fred to identify the approach he'll use to measure and report project performance. Which one of the following measures project performance?

    A. WBS

    B. The project plan

    C. The earned value technique

    D. The work authorization system

14. Configuration management is a process for applying technical and administrative direction and surveillance of the project implementation. Which activity is NOT included in configuration management?

    A. Controlling changes to the project deliverables

    B. Creating a method to communicate changes to stakeholders

    C. Creating automatic change request approvals

    D. Identifying the functional and physical attributes of the project deliverables

15. The project manager can help write the project charter but is not the person who signs the project charter. Regardless of who actually writes the charter, several elements should be included in the document. All of the following are addressed in the project charter, except for which one?

    A. Requirements to satisfy the project customer, project sponsor, and other stakeholders

    B. Assigned project management and level of authority

    C. Summary budget

    D. Risk responses

16. Terri's organization is moving through the process of selecting one of several projects. Her organization utilizes mathematical models to determine the projects that should be initiated. Which one of the following is an example of a mathematical model used to select projects for selection?

    A. Future value

    B. Linear programming

    C. Present value

    D. Benefit/cost ratio

17. May is the project manager for her organization. She realizes that some of the subsidiary plans in her project management plan have incorrect data now because of a change within the project scope. What should May do with the subsidiary project plans that have already been approved by her project sponsor?

    A. Create a risk response for the project plans that are now incorrect.

    B. Notate the project plan as being incorrect and why.

    C. Communicate with the project sponsor and stakeholders about the incorrect plan.

    D. Create a change request to correct the project plan.

18. The project management plan has several purposes, and all predictive projects should have a plan. What is the purpose of the project management plan?

    A. It defines the project manager and her level of authority on the project.

    B. It authorizes the project manager to assign resources to the project work.

    C. It defines how the project will be planned and executed.

    D. It defines how the project will be executed, monitored and controlled, and then closed.

19. The project steering committee is considering which project they should invest capital in. Mary's project promises to be worth $175,000 in four years. The project steering committee is interested in Mary's project, but they would like to know the present value of the return if the interest rate is 6 percent. What is the present value of Mary's project?

    A. $175,000

    B. $139,000

    C. $220,000

    D. $43,750

20. You are the project manager for your organization. A change has recently been approved by your organization's change control board. You need to update the scope baseline and what other document?

   A. The cost baseline

   B. The quality baseline

   C. The risk management plan

   D. The change log

Answers

1. A. Any change requests should be documented in the project's change control system. B is incorrect because the new law will require changes to the project. C is incorrect because it may be inappropriate to consult with the project stakeholders, especially on a large project. D is incorrect because we do not know the impact of the change, and it may not justify halting the project work.

2. A. A predetermined budget set by management is an example of a project constraint. B and C are examples of organizational process assets that the project manager will use as inputs to project management planning. D, interviews with subject matter experts, is an example of expert judgment and is a tool and technique used in project management plan development.

3. D. The primary purpose of the project management plan is to define how the project will be managed and to communicate that information to project stakeholders. A and B are incorrect because these address only the project work. C is incorrect because this answer addresses the project's change control system.

4. C. A hybrid project that will combine the planning processes of predictive and the work iterations of Agile will likely allow changes through the prioritized product backlog. Once the scope has been planned in the predictive fashion, the management of the project will likely change to the rules of the agile environment. Changes may enter the project, but they cannot interrupt the current work of the project. Changes will go into the prioritized product backlog, will be prioritized among the known requirements, and then the team will take on the work in future work iterations. A is incorrect because schedule and cost change control are more geared toward predictive project management. Schedule and cost change control can still take place as part of integrated change control, but this isn't the best answer for this question. B, process change control, isn't a valid project management term; in addition, the scope is being changed, not a project management process. D is incorrect because changes are allowed to the project scope even after a baseline has been created.

5. D. Defect repair review is a review of the defect repair. Even though the project may be on a deadline, Robert's project team will still need to repair the walls and confirm that the repair is acceptable. A is an example of a preventive action. B is an example of a corrective action. C is an example of defect repair.

6. A. Susan has tacit knowledge; this knowledge has been gained by experience and it's not easy to communicate or quickly explain to others. B, C, and D are incorrect. Explicit knowledge is factual knowledge and is easy to explain to others. Factual and experiential knowledge are not project management terms used to describe the knowledge management process.

7. D. The project management plan provides baselines for the schedule, cost, and scope. Control is a project activity and part of the monitoring and controlling process group. A, B, and C are incorrect answers, because scope, cost, and schedule do have associated baselines. Recall that a baseline is what's predicted and the actuals are the experiences of the project. The difference between the baseline and what actually happened reveals the variances of the project.

8. A. Integrated change control requires detailed reasons for implementing the change. Without evidence of the need for the change, there is no reason to implement it. B is incorrect because the project team does not approve change requests. C is incorrect because a subject matter expert is not always needed for a requested change. D is incorrect because risk assessment for a proposed change is not always needed. The change could be rejected or approved for reasons other than the potential of risk events.

9. A. The project management plan defines how changes will be approved or declined. B describes the risk management plan. C defines the project charter and project scope. D is incorrect because the change control board may be part of the change control process.

10. A. The configuration management system documents all functional physical characteristics of the project's product. It also controls changes to the project's product. B, C, and D are incorrect answers; integrated change control, scope control, and the change management plan do not address the management of the product.

11. B. In an agile project, the team is self-organizing, and they will determine who'll take on what activities during each work iteration. A is incorrect because the project manager and the project management team direct the performance of the project activities in a predictive project. In a program, the program manager assigns the project manager authority over the project resources and authorizes the project manager to direct the project work. C and D are incorrect because the project sponsor and program manager do not direct performance.

12. C. Lessons learned happens during the sprint retrospective, which is the final meeting of each sprint. This is a meeting to learn what did and didn't work well in the past iteration so the team can make adjustments for the next sprint of the project. A is incorrect because lessons learned happens in each sprint during the sprint retrospective. B is incorrect because the sprint review is a demonstration of what the development team has accomplished during the sprint. D is incorrect because lessons learned happens during the sprint retrospective; in addition, Scrum doesn't used paired programming; this is an attribute of XP.

13. **C.** The earned value technique, commonly called earned value management (EVM), measures project performance on several factors, including cost and schedule. A, the WBS, is a breakdown of the project scope. B, the project plan, defines how the project will be controlled, executed, and closed. D, the work authorization, enables work to progress within a project.

14. **C.** Change requests should not be automatically approved. All documented change requests should flow through the change control system, should be evaluated, and then a decision should be made. A, B, and D are all part of configuration management.

15. **D.** Risk responses are not addressed in the project charter. High-level risks may be identified, but the responses to those risks are not included in the project charter. These responses will be documented in the project's risk response plan. A, B, and C are incorrect because the requirements to satisfy the project customer, the project manager, and the summary budget are defined in the charter.

16. **B.** Linear programming is an example of a mathematical model that can be used for project selection. Recall that mathematical models are also known as constrained optimization. A, C, and D are incorrect because future value, present value, and the benefit/cost ratio are all examples of benefits comparison models.

17. **D.** Of all the choices presented, this is the best answer, because changes to project documents and plans do require change requests. A is incorrect because creating a risk response isn't the best answer. B, notating the project plan, isn't a viable choice because the plan has incorrect information that should be corrected. C is also incorrect because May can communicate the error to the project sponsor, but she is not likely to do so with the stakeholders. In addition, the communication doesn't update the error in the plan.

18. **D.** The project management plan communicates how the project will be executed, monitored and controlled, and then closed. A and B both describe components of the project charter. C does not answer the question as completely as D.

19. **B.** $139,000 is the present value of Mary's project. This is found through the following formula: $PV = FV \div (1 + I)^n$, which is future value divided by 1 plus the interest rate to the power of the periods the project will last. This formula would read ($175,000)/(1.26) because the interest rate provided was 6 percent. A, C, and D are all incorrect calculations.

20. **D.** When a change enters the project, the change log must be updated to reflect the change. A and C are incorrect because the question did not indicate that new costs or risks will be entering the project. B, the quality baseline, is not a valid answer because quality is a reflection of the completion of the project scope.

Managing Project Scope

In this chapter, you will

- Plan project scope management
- Collect project requirements
- Define the project and product scope
- Create the work breakdown structure
- Validate the project scope
- Control the project scope

You're the project manager of a large, complex project that's using a predictive approach. You've worked with the project team and the key stakeholders to define the project scope and the project is moving along. Everyone agrees that the project must be completed within one year, the budget is tight, and there's little room for error. One of your project team members, Tony, has taken it upon himself to incorporate "extras" into the project deliverable to make it snappier, better, and easier for the product customer to use. Though his project additions are clever, they aren't in the project scope.

Tony argues that his creative additions don't cost the project anything extra and the customer will love what he's come up with. The trouble for you, the customer, and Tony, however, is that the time he's spent changing the scope should have been spent doing the things that are *in* the scope. In addition, the extras weren't managed and reviewed as change requests, so they will likely be a surprise to the project customer—not to mention the added risks, potential for defects, and the contempt shown for an established change control system.

 VIDEO For a more detailed explanation, watch the *Working with Scope Changes* video now.

Managing the project scope is the project manager's job; it ensures that all the required work—and only the required work—is done to complete the project successfully. Project scope management doesn't permit Tony's, or anyone else's, additions without proper change management. Scope management involves agreeing on what's in the scope and then defending that agreement.

In managing scope, there is a difference between managing a project with a predictive life cycle versus a project with an adaptive life cycle. A *predictive life cycle*, as in the preceding example, predicts what the project will create and how the project will create it. A predictive cycle can also be known as a *waterfall* project management approach, in which the project is completed in distinct stages that flow linearly like a waterfall. An *adaptive life cycle*, as you'll find in an iterative or incremental environment, expects change to happen in the project. The scope in an adaptive life cycle is defined and decomposed into the product backlog. With each iteration of the life cycle, the project team will collect requirements, define the scope, and create the work breakdown structure (WBS) for that iteration of the project. Basically, you'll take the product backlog, prioritize the items, and then choose what items can feasibly be accomplished in the next iteration of the project.

These items from the product backlog are requirements, also called *user stories*. User stories are quick descriptions of the requirement from the users' perspective. Each user story receives story points from the project team. Story points represent how much effort is required to create the user story, and there are only so many points available for each iteration, called a *sprint* in a true agile project. The number of available story points is determined by the project team and will vary by project. Some requirements for adaptive projects can be so big that they can't fit into one iteration—these are called *epics*. Epics describe really big requirements that are broken down into user stories and can span multiple iterations of the project.

 VIDEO For a more detailed explanation, watch the *Writing User Stories* video now.

Adaptive life cycles keep the project sponsor and customer representative engaged and involved in the project. The product owner role works closely with the project team and the project management role to prioritize the product backlog and answer questions about the product. The validate scope and control scope processes happen with each iteration of the project; the project team creates the items from the product backlog, and they'll review the results with the project manager and the product owner at the end of each iteration.

In projects with predictive or adaptive life cycles, Tony can't just add changes to the project because he feels like it—regardless of how cool or great he thinks the changes might be. Bad Tony! Both predictive and adaptive approaches allow, or at least entertain, changes to the project scope. Tony's changes might be great, but it's not his role in the project to make that determination. In this chapter, I'll walk through how Tony, or any stakeholder, can get his or her changes documented and reviewed to be included in the project scope.

Planning the Project Scope Management

One of the first things you'll have to achieve in your role as the project manager of a new project is to define the project's scope management plan. Your organization may rely on organizational process assets in the form of a template for all projects, but it's possible that you'll be creating this scope management plan from scratch. In this section, you'll learn both approaches that you can apply to your projects and your PMI exam.

This process is all about creating the *scope management plan* and the *requirements management plan*. These are two subsidiary plans for the overall project management plan that you'll assemble and never touch again. Kidding! Because these are planning processes, chances are you'll be editing these plans over and over as you move through planning. The point is that these two plans shape your approach to how you'll define and control both the project's scope and the project's requirements.

In an adaptive project, there is no time spent creating a detailed scope management plan. That's because the scope is developed during the project through the product backlog. In Scrum, for example, the product owner will document and prioritize the user stories. The product backlog is consistently refined and prioritized throughout the project by the product owner. The product backlog welcomes changes without all the overhead we see in predictive projects. Changes are prioritized and then fed into the work iterations.

 EXAM TIP   Adaptive project management sounds really nice, and for many projects it is nice, but the truth is, adaptive projects won't work for every project. Some projects require a specific ordering of events, detailed planning, and a more rigid control over the scope items. That's why you see knowledge-based projects, such as software development, embracing Agile. It's easier to change some code than it is to rip up the foundation of a house to add a bedroom. This is where the hybrid approach to project management is gaining traction: combining the best of predictive and agile project management.

To begin this process, you'll need the information already gathered and included in the project charter. That's right—the project charter. You'll use the charter because it's the launching point of the project and already maps out the high-level requirements and vision for the project. The project charter sets the direction for the project, while the scope management plan and the requirements management plan define how the project will achieve those objectives.

Creating the Project Scope Management Plan

Once the project moves from the initiating processes into planning, one of the first plans to be created is the project scope management plan. This plan includes the following:

- How the project scope will be defined
- How the detailed project scope statement will be created
- How the work breakdown structure will be created
- How scope validation will be performed at the end of each phase and at the end of the project
- How the project scope will be controlled

The project scope management plan is based first on the details of the project charter. Recall that the project charter authorizes the project within an organization and defines the general project boundaries and goals. When the project management team is ready to begin creating the project scope management plan, they'll actually rely on four inputs to this project management process:

- Enterprise environmental factors
- Organizational process assets
- The project charter
- The project management plan

The project management team can use expert judgment to help them analyze these four inputs to create the best project scope management plan. Don't get too hyper over expert judgment—you'll see this term throughout the *PMBOK Guide* and this book. *Expert judgment* is just an approach that uses people such as experts and consultants (assuming they're truly experts—wink, wink) who have exceptional knowledge about the product the project will be creating. For example, in a skyscraper project, expert judgment could include world-renowned architects, city planners, union representatives, and more.

The project management team can also use templates, forms, and standards as part of the process to create the project scope management plan. If an organization is completing the same type of project over and over, there's no real benefit to starting from scratch each time. Instead, they'll logically use previous projects' plans, forms, WBSs, and more as part of the current planning. These are collectively referred to as organizational process assets.

You now know that the project scope management plan will be used to define, validate, manage, and control the project scope. There are four more juicy facts you need to know about this hefty plan:

- The project scope management plan defines how the official project scope statement will be defined based on the project charter.
- The plan defines how the WBS will be created, controlled, and approved. We'll talk about the WBS in more detail later in this chapter.
- The plan documents the process for scope validation. To clarify, scope validation is the inspection of the project deliverables by the project customer. The goal of scope validation is to validate that the deliverables are in alignment with the project goals so that they can be formally accepted.
- The plan documents and defines how changes to the project scope will be managed and controlled. This is linked to our conversation in Chapter 4 on integrated change control. As a refresher, integrated change control acknowledges that a change in one knowledge area can affect any of the other knowledge areas.

The project scope management plan is a subsidiary of the project management plan. This plan sets the tone for the remainder of the project. As you may have already guessed, the larger the project, the more important this plan. As a general rule, larger projects require more detail. For adaptive projects, the larger the project, the stricter the requirement that the team follow the rules, be transparent, and control the work in progress.

The scope management plan can rely heavily on OPAs and enterprise environmental factors (EEFs). From OPAs, you can call on the policies and procedures that you must follow as a project manager in your organization. From the EEFs, you'll enable the organization's culture, organizational structure, project team administration rules, and the overall marketplace conditions to influence your planning and development. The marketplace conditions are especially important if you're a vendor completing a project for someone else. When you're a vendor, the relationship between you and the customer differs from the relationship of a project manager completing a project inside her own organization.

The primary tool and technique for creating the scope management plan is planning—and this means meetings. Every project manager loves meetings, and you'll have lots of these in order to shape this plan. You'll call on the project sponsor, in some cases the project team (assuming they've been selected), key stakeholders that can help with the processes, and any other experts. "Any other experts" means that you might be calling on the program manager if this project takes place within a program, other project managers who can help with the drafting of the plan, and even consultants.

The primary meetings you'll use in Scrum are the sprint planning meetings, where the development team, the scrum master and the product owner will work together to estimate how much work it may take on for the next sprint. Other adaptive approaches have a similar approach to prioritizing and selecting how much work can reasonably accomplished in the next chunk of the project.

Creating the Requirements Management Plan

The second plan that comes out of this process is the requirements management plan. While similar in nature to the project scope management plan, this plan explains how the project will collect, analyze, record, and track the requirements throughout the project. Like the scope management plan, this plan doesn't list the actual requirements, but sets the rules for how the project manager, team, and stakeholders will interact with the project's requirements. This plan is also a subsidiary plan for the overall project management plan.

This plan can be based on a template, just like the scope management plan can be, but you can tailor it to your project as needed. The following elements can be included in this plan:

- The process for planning, tracking, and recording all of the project requirements
- Configuration management activities for the product (changing the product, specs for the product scope, and who can approve any changes to the product)
- The process for analyzing and prioritizing requirements
- Metrics for measuring the acceptability of the requirements
- How requirements will be managed if using hybrid or adaptive life cycle
- How the requirements will be tracked through the project (usually through a requirements tracing matrix)

Collecting the Project Requirements

It's great to have a project, but it's even greater to understand what the stakeholders want the project to create. The collect requirements process aims to identify and document what the stakeholders need from the project. The requirements you'll identify from the project sponsor, customer, and other stakeholders need to be quantifiable, measurable, and documented in order to confirm that the results of the project satisfy the needs of the stakeholder. You don't want requirements that use subjective terms to describe the project deliverables. What's "good" to you may not be "good" to someone else.

You'll rely on the project charter as one of the inputs to this process. Recall that the project charter identifies the project and defines the business need of the project. This should give you some direction for collecting the project requirements. The project charter will also contain high-level requirements that can be refined for details regarding the project stakeholder's expectations.

Other inputs for this process are project documents, including the stakeholder register. The stakeholder register is a directory of all the stakeholders, their contact information, and details about their relationship with the project. You'll need this document to contact the stakeholders so you can begin the process of collecting project requirements. When you're dealing with large groups of stakeholders—for example, all of the users of a particular software your project centers on—a smaller part of the group can represent the larger group in the project. The other two project documents needed are the assumptions log and the lessons learned register. The assumptions log will help you challenge and document any assumptions about the requirements. The lessons learned register contains information from lessons learned in the project already—and this is where you'll continue to document lessons.

You'll need to collect project requirements from seven inputs:

- **Project charter** Identifies the business needs of the project
- **Project management plan** Specifically, the scope management plan, the requirements management plan, and the stakeholder engagement plan
- **Project documents** Assumptions log, lessons learned register, and stakeholder register
- **Business documents** References the business case for the project
- **Agreements** Contracts or service-level agreements that you're utilizing in the project
- **Enterprise environmental factors** Information to ensure that you follow the rules and governance framework for your organization
- **Organizational process assets** Standards, guidelines, checklists, forms, or other assets you can rely upon to capture requirements

 EXAM COACH What are your requirements for your upcoming examination? Have you made your own list of requirements that you'll need to satisfy to achieve your PMP? You need to know what you must create in order to create it.

Working with Project Stakeholders

You'll have to work with the project stakeholders in order to identify the requirements your project needs. This is where the *stakeholder register* comes in handy, because you'll need to contact the stakeholders to schedule times to elicit their project requirements. One favorable approach is to categorize the types of users and stakeholders to streamline your requirements collection process.

In Agile, one of the key principles is that stakeholders are involved in requirements gathering. You and the team will need to talk with stakeholders to really understand the problem or goal the stakeholders want to achieve. If you don't have good insight and understanding with regard to what the stakeholders want, there'll be waste and frustration as the team tries to accomplish the stakeholders' goal. By grouping similar stakeholders together, you can save time and effort and keep the project moving along. You can use any of a variety of tools to collect requirements from the stakeholders, such as the following.

Expert Judgment

Rely upon individuals and groups to help you gather requirements. You'll often use expert judgment to help with business analysis, requirements elicitation and analysis, requirements documentation, and diagramming techniques. Depending on the size of your project, you might need an expert to facilitate meetings and perform conflict management.

Data Gathering

You can use many different data gathering tools and techniques to gather requirements. Here are a few of the most common you should be familiar with:

- **Brainstorming**   This approach encourages participants to generate as many ideas as possible about the project requirements. No idea is judged or dismissed during the brainstorming session.

- **Interviewing**   The interviewer must prepare questions to guide the interviewee to discussing the needs that the project will satisfy. Usually interviews are performed one-on-one, though it's not unusual for the project manager to interview several stakeholders at once. Open-ended questions are best for essay-type answers, while closed-ended questions (yes or no) can nail down the specifics of the requirements.

- **Focus groups**   This is a collection of stakeholders that interacts with a trained moderator who leads the group through a conversation, engages all of the participants, and remains neutral about the topic at hand. Focus groups can build trust, create new relationships, and help the group of stakeholders reach consensus on the project requirements. A scribe or recorder documents the conversation for analysis after the focus group is concluded.

- **Questionnaires and surveys**   When you have hundreds, or even thousands, of stakeholders to gather requirements from, a survey is an ideal tool and technique to rely on. The project manager can leverage web tools to disseminate the survey quickly, track responses, and organize the participants' responses.

- **Benchmarking** This technique compares two or more items to determine the best solution for the current project's requirements. For example, you could compare different software packages to make the best selection for your project. You could also compare projects or other organizations for performance goals and metrics.
- **Facilitated workshop** This meeting with all of the key stakeholders helps the group define the project requirements quickly. Facilitated workshops are interactive, often include stakeholders from different functional areas of the project, and can expose conflicting objectives and disagreements. Agile projects often used a facilitated workshop to write user stories. A good facilitator keeps the group focused on the project requirements and can help resolve conflicts and disagreements in requirements.

 EXAM TIP You may know about focus groups through a facilitated workshop called the Joint Application Design (JAD) session. These software development workshops enable designers and users to interact and discuss the software requirements. JAD, frankly, isn't used too much in Agile because the product owner is responsible for collecting requirements. For your exam, however, just recognize JAD—it may show up.

Data Analysis

The collected data needs to be analyzed to provide useful information. One of the most common approaches to data analysis is document analysis. In most projects, lots of documents contribute to the project scope and requirements: plans, brochures, blueprints, organizational process assets, proposals, and more. Document analysis requires that the project manager and the project team study these documents for anything that should be included in the requirements and referenced from the document. You'll keep all of the documentation that you reference as part of the project's supporting details. At the end of the project, these documents are included in the project archives and become part of the OPAs.

Group Decisions

Group decisions can help the project manager prioritize, classify, and even generate requirements. Multicriteria decision analysis is a technique that uses a decision matrix to help make the best decision. The matrix includes different factors such as risk, business value, schedule, costs, and other variables to rank and evaluate the ideas for requirements. Another decision-making technique is voting. The participants in the group determine the appropriate method for reaching a group decision, and there are four approaches:

- **Unanimity** Everyone must be in agreement.
- **Majority** More than 50 percent of the group must be in agreement.
- **Plurality** The largest block of voters makes the decision, even if they don't represent more than 50 percent of the group. (Consider three or four factions of stakeholders for three or more different choices, none of which receives more than 50 percent of the vote.)
- **Autocratic** Only one individual makes the decision for the group.

Data Representation

Data representation refers to techniques used to enable visualization of the data you've gathered. It takes some time to sort and format the data, but here are two common approaches you might see on your exam:

- **Affinity diagrams**   When stakeholders create a large number of ideas, you can use an affinity diagram to cluster similar ideas together for further analysis.
- **Mind mapping**   This approach maps ideas to show the relationship among the requirements and the differences between them. The map can be reviewed to identify new solutions or to rank the identified requirements.

Nominal Group Technique

This approach builds on brainstorming by adding a vote to each idea to rank the ideas for acceptance, for more brainstorming, or just to prioritize the identified requirements. Here's how it works:

1. The participants silently write down their ideas.
2. The participants share their ideas with the group and the moderator writes down the ideas on a whiteboard until all of the ideas have been captured.
3. Each idea is discussed for clarity.
4. Individuals vote privately on the ideas, with 1 being the lowest score and 5 being the highest possible score.
5. Voting and conversation can take place over many rounds to gain consensus on each item's score and prioritization.

Observations

One of the best requirements-gathering techniques is observation or job shadowing. The project manager goes into the field and observes the work being done to determine what requirements are appropriate for the project work. *Passive* observation, sometimes called invisible observation, requires the project manager to observe the work without asking questions or interrupting the workflow. In *active* observation, the project manager talks and interacts with the participant to help the project manager fully understand the work being done. In some instances, the project manager may actually work alongside the participant to understand the work that the project requirements may affect.

Prototypes

A prototype is a model of the finished deliverable that enables the stakeholders to see how the final project deliverable may operate. In software development, a *vertical* prototype approach details the interface, the functionality, and sometimes both. A *horizontal* prototype shows a very broad view of the deliverable, with very little operability at this point. Either prototype can be considered a throwaway prototype, or the model can be developed in more detail by the project team. Adaptive projects often create models to confirm that the developers and the stakeholders have the same requirements in mind.

Context Diagrams

Imagine a project to design a computer network: it would include servers, workstations, wireless access points, even the physical network. A context diagram would show how data moves around on the network, how people would interact with the network, what the network would provide, and how people would contribute information to and from the devices on the network. A context diagram shows all of these components, called *actors*, and how they will interact with the thing.

Examining the Outputs of Requirement Collection

Once you've gathered all of the project requirements, you'll need to do something with them. The first place to start is the requirements documentation—a listing of all of the project requirements and the supporting details for the identified requirements. Requirements need to be measurable and consistent and then they can be presented to the key stakeholders for their confirmation of what you've captured and what the stakeholders were expecting to receive from you. Here are some examples of requirement types:

- Business requirements
- Stakeholder requirements
- Project objectives
- Solution requirements
- Quality requirements
- Operational transfer requirements
- Training and support of the requirements for production

You should know two important terms attached to solution requirements: *Functional requirements* describe how the solution functions, including actions, processes, data, and interactions the product will have. When you describe what the product does, it's likely a functional requirement. *Nonfunctional requirements* describe the attributes of the product that are needed in order for it to be effective. For example, an IT solution may have uptime, redundancy, security, level of service, supportability, and other conditions that describe a nonfunctional requirement. Both functional and nonfunctional requirements are captured and documented as part of the project requirements. Functional and nonfunctional requirements can also be entered into the product backlog as user stories so they are prioritized and incorporated into the sprint planning sessions.

Because requirements can make for a long, long list, it's better to record them in a table called a *requirements traceability matrix*. This table documents and numbers each requirement and its status in the project, and shows how each requirement is linked to a specific deliverable that the project will create or has created. You'll also, usually, provide a little narrative about the requirement in the matrix as a point of reference, the current status of the requirement, the owner, and the status date. For more detail, you'll reference the actual requirements documentation. The traceability matrix helps the project manager and the project customer see the product of the project and compare it against the requirements to confirm that all of the requirements have been met and are in existence in the final deliverable for the customer.

PART II

Defining Project and Product Scopes

Building a skyscraper has to be one of the largest projects a project manager could manage. Think of all the different facets of the project: the design of the building, structural requirements, government building regulations, and the concern and interest of all the stakeholders within the project. The skyscraper would require months, if not years, of serious planning, tight change control, and incredible organization to complete. The scope of the skyscraper would be massive, and any change within the scope could have ramifications further down the blueprinted line.

Now imagine a project to build a barn. It would still require considerable planning, and the stakeholders of the barn might be concerned with its planning and construction, but probably not to the same depth as with the skyscraper project. The priority and impact of each project is important to the key stakeholders of each, but no doubt the skyscraper has a much broader impact than a barn. My point? Larger projects require more detail when it comes to scope creation and planning. Lots more.

Let's define scope—er, scopes—before moving forward. Project scope and product scope are different entities.

Project scope deals with the work required to create the project deliverables. For instance, our projects to create a new barn and the new skyscraper would focus only on the work required to complete the projects, with the specific attributes, features, and characteristics called for by the project plan. The scope of the project is specific to the work required to complete the project objectives. The project scope focuses on what must be done to create the deliverable.

Product scope, on the other hand, refers to the attributes and characteristics of the deliverables the project is creating. As in the preceding barn or skyscraper project, the product scope would define the features and attributes of the barn or skyscraper. In this instance, the project to create a barn would not include creating a flower garden, a wading pool, and the installation of a fence, just as the skyscraper project likely wouldn't include a neighboring park. There would be specific requirements regarding the features and characteristics of each project: the materials to be used, the dimensions of the space, the function of each building, and all the related details that make a skyscraper a skyscraper and a barn a barn. The product scope is what the customer of the project envisions.

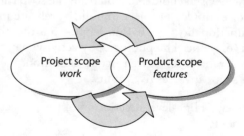

The project scope and the product scope are bound to each other. The product scope constitutes the characteristics and features of the product that the project creates. The end result of the project is measured against the requirements for the product. The project scope is the work required to deliver the product. Throughout the project execution, the work is measured against the project plan to validate that the project is on track to fulfill the product scope. The product scope is measured against requirements, while the project scope is measured against the project plan.

 EXAM TIP When it comes to *project* scope management, as is covered in the bulk of this chapter, focus on the work required to complete the project according to the project plan. The *product* scope, meanwhile, is specific to the deliverable of the project. Just remember that the exam will focus on *project scope management*. If you're stumped on any exam questions about project management processes, consider a huge project scope, like the skyscraper project.

Creating the Project Scope Statement

A project manager and the project team cannot plan how to complete the project until they know what it is and exactly what they are being asked to complete. That's where the project scope statement is needed. Before the project management team can get to the good stuff of deciding how the project work will be done, they must first create the project scope statement.

When a project is initiated, the focus is on what the project will deliver: the product scope. It's all dreamy and blue sky. After the project has moved into planning, things are tightened through the project scope statement, which is built on the foundations defined in the project's initiation: major deliverables, constraints, and assumptions. The scope statement is also built on the output of the collect requirements process. In planning, more information about the exactness of the project deliverables comes to light through planning, research, stakeholder analysis, and product analysis. The wants and needs of the stakeholders are considered, and eventually they evolve into the project requirements.

The project manager, the project team, and the key stakeholders need to work together to examine the project for additional constraints and assumptions so that the project can be planned completely. The key stakeholders are needed because their insight into the project's deliverables can help the project manager and the project team define all that the project is to deliver. The key stakeholders help create the scope and agree on what's out of the project scope. For example, a project to build a web site may include the layout, design, and database functionality—all within scope—but the photography needed for the web site may be out of scope. The photography activity may be in an entirely different project, so it's not relevant to the current scope definition.

Creating the project scope involves five inputs:

- **The project charter** High-level description of the project, product, and approval requirements

- **The project management plan** Mainly the scope management plan

- **Project documents** The assumptions log, requirements documents, and risk register

- **Enterprise environmental factors**   The organization's culture, infrastructure, personnel administration, and the marketplace conditions
- **Organizational process assets**   Historical information, templates, and lessons learned documentation

These five inputs help the project management team work together to define all of the contents of the project scope. This isn't a quick or necessarily easy process, but it's vital to prepare an accurate and complete project scope statement; otherwise, the project will be haunted by errors and omissions. You'll especially rely on the outputs of the collect requirements process as a foundation for what goes into the project scope.

TIP   Projects fail in the beginning, not at the end. Poor planning early in the project will lead to poor execution later in the project. A rushed scope definition will likely cause problems later on in the project. The project scope is the stakeholders' opportunity to define exactly what they want. Changes to the scope are easy early in the project, but they are much more difficult later in the project because of the work, time, and monies already invested.

Using Product Analysis

If you were the project manager for a company that wanted to create a new camera, you might choose several of your competitors' cameras to study, experiment with, and improve upon. You'd compare the features and functions of the other cameras in light of the requirements and goals of your current project. *Product analysis* is the study of how a thing was made and how it works. It's real easy in Agile to say everything related to the product goes to the product owner, but that's not true. The development team needs to be working with the product owner and stakeholders to identify the requirements fully and to understand what's needed in the project. While it's true that Agile welcomes change, it's wasteful not to take some time to create a good set of requirements to work from at the project launch.

Product analysis is an approach to creating the project scope statement. Product analysis, however, is more than just analyzing a product. It focuses on how the product works, the function of the product, and what's the most profitable approach to creating the product. There are six flavors of product analysis. Don't be consumed with memorizing these approaches for your PMP examination; just be topically aware of these product analysis methods.

Product Breakdown

This approach breaks down a product much as the project management team breaks down the project scope into a WBS. For example, a computer could be broken down into the physical components, such as the hard drive, processor, memory, network card, and so on. A product breakdown structure illustrates the hierarchical structure of the product.

Systems Analysis

This approach studies and analyzes a system, its components, and the relationship of the components within the system. For example, a manufacturing company's system for placing an order from a customer through delivery may have several steps, from sale to completion and interaction between departments on that journey. Systems analysis would study the relationship between each component and how the process could be improved or the time reduced, or how practically any variable within the system could be documented for additional study.

Systems Engineering

This project scope statement creation approach studies how a system should work, designs and creates a system model, and then enacts the working system based on the project goals and the customer's expectations. Systems engineering aims to balance the time and cost of the project in relation to the project scope. A successfully designed system can be profitable and productive, and it can create quality that is acceptable to the project sponsor and the project customer.

Value Engineering

This approach to project scope statement creation attempts to find the correct level of quality in relation to a reasonable budget for the project deliverable, while still achieving an acceptable level of performance of the product. Basically, this approach wants the biggest bang for the project's buck—as long as the bang and the buck create a deliverable that performs as expected. Consider a home remodeling project: The homeowners could choose silk drapes and gold doorknobs or wool drapes and brass doorknobs and get the same function. Their demand for quality, grade, and function is in relation to how much capital they'd like to invest in their home project.

Value Analysis

Like value engineering, this approach examines the functions of the project's product in relation to the cost of the features and functions. This is where, to some extent, the grade of the product relates to the cost of the product. Consider Microsoft Word's features and cost in relation to the features and cost of your computer's Notepad application. While the price range is broadly different between the applications, the functions associated with Word are far more powerful than those of Notepad.

Functional Analysis

This is the study of the functions within a system, project, or—what's more likely in the project scope statement—the product the project will be creating. Functional analysis studies the goals of the product, how the product will be used, and the expectations the customer has of the product once it leaves the project and moves into operations. Functional analysis may also consider the cost of the product in operations, which is known as life-cycle costing.

Using Alternatives Generation

Your customer wants you to install an e-mail system for their organization. They don't care which solution you and your project team come up with, as long as it is reliable, is easy to manage, and provides a central calendaring system. If you're from the IT world,

I imagine you immediately thought of several different approaches to solving this project for your customer. That's alternative identification at its root.

Alternatives generation is more than just coming up with different products that can solve the customer's problem. It also means examining what solution makes the most economical sense for the project and for the customer's ongoing support of the product once it's been created. In the e-mail system, the project manager, project team, and experts would need to examine how the customer will use all of the different aspects of the e-mail system, their long-term goals for the system, and what their budget for the project and any ongoing maintenance of the system would be.

To do alternatives generation, the project management team will do research, brainstorming, and lateral thinking. Their focus is to identify all of the feasible alternatives to the project's deliverable or even to components within the project. Alternatives generation also broaches a quality topic: grade. *Grade* is the ranking of materials or services, such as first class versus coach, or plywood versus oak. We'll see this again in Chapter 8.

Using Stakeholder Analysis

Stakeholder analysis is almost always involved when it comes to creating the project scope statement. It's all about the customer's demands, wants, and goals for the project. The project management team interviews the stakeholders and categorizes, prioritizes, and documents what the customer wants and needs. This is fundamental to project management: You and the key stakeholders must be in agreement on what the project will create, or the project scope statement cannot be created and approved. Without an agreement regarding the requirements for acceptance, the project is moving toward inevitable failure.

Here's another "gotcha" with stakeholder analysis: If you can't quantify it, and you can't measure it, then you can't create it. For example, a "fast" office network isn't quantified. "Customer satisfaction" isn't quantified. And "happy," "warm-fuzzy," and "good" aren't quantified. The project scope statement needs to define in exact terms the acceptable ranges for all of the project deliverables. All project requirements must be quantifiable. Here's a general rule: If you can measure it, you can quantify it.

 TIP   Failure to quantify the project objectives raises risks that the project won't achieve the customer's expectations. After all, what's fast and good to you may mean something entirely different to the project customer.

Examining the Project Scope Statement

The project scope statement identifies all of the project deliverables and defines the work required to create the deliverables. This document creates a common lexicon and understanding of what the project will deliver for all of the project stakeholders. The project scope statement clearly states the project objectives and communicates the goals of the project so that all of the project team members, the project sponsor, and the key stakeholders are in agreement as to what the project will accomplish. In adaptive environments, the scope statement is the prioritized product backlog, not a separate document. Hybrid environments might use both a product backlog and a scope statement.

The project scope statement also guides the remainder of the project planning processes. Should changes be proposed to the project, the project scope statement helps determine whether the proposed changes are within or outside the project's boundaries. A well-written scope can ward off change requests, while a loose, poorly written scope is often an invitation for change requests and additional work by the project team.

So what goes into a project scope statement? Glad you asked! There are a bunch of things, which the following sections explain.

Product Scope Description

This is a narrative of what the project is creating as deliverables for the project customer. Early in the project, the product scope may be somewhat vague, but as the project scope is progressively elaborated, the product scope description may be updated to reflect its evolution and clarifications.

EXAM TIP "Progressive elaboration" is a PMI term you should know for the exam. The term is used to describe an incremental process of redefining and clarifying any facet of a project. For example, a house project may start broad, as a three-bedroom, two-car garage home, and then, through progressive elaboration, all of the details down to the kitchen sink and doorknobs are defined.

Product Acceptance Criteria

The project scope statement components work with the project requirements but focus specifically on the product and on the conditions and processes required for formal acceptance of the product. This is a key point in Agile, called the *Definition of Done* (DoD). How you know when you are done working on a project or a requirement in an agile project is to define *done*: it's reality. The feature or requirement is done and potentially shippable, or it is not done. There is no value until a feature is done.

Project Deliverables

These are all the things that the project will create. Consider that the project deliverables are more than just the product and also include ancillary deliverables, such as project reports, communications, and lessons learned that the organization may use for future projects. The documentation and experience within the current project become part of the organizational process assets for future projects.

Project Exclusions

A project exclusion clearly states what is excluded from it (out of scope). Project exclusions are also called project boundaries. Creating this helps to eliminate assumptions between the project management team and the project customer. For example, a software programmer may create a new application for a customer as part of the project, but the distribution of the software to the customer's 10,000 computer workstations is a project exclusion that is defined as out of scope.

Planning a Sprint

You know that a *sprint* in Scrum is a time period of up to four weeks. The sprint planning meeting is part of the sprint, but it precedes the actual work that the team will do. In sprint planning, the team examines the items in the product backlog and then considers how much work they can take on during the next sprint. Recall that the items in the product backlog are prioritized by the product owner, so the team will always work on the most important items in the product backlog down to the least important items in the backlog.

The items in the product backlog, the user stories, are *sized* based on how much effort it may take to complete the item and in relation to the other user stories in the product backlog. *Story point sizing* enables the team to compare one story to another based on their respective sizes to help them determine how much work they can complete in an iteration. When sizing stories, the team considers several factors beyond just the effort needed: the risk, complexity, deployment concerns, interdependencies with other stories, and implementation.

You should know these three different approaches to sizing:

- **Fibonacci series sequence**   This sizing approach uses the numbers 1, 2, 3, 5, 8, 13, 21—a sequence in which two preceding numbers are added to produce the next number in the sequence. So, for example, in the sequence shown, $1 + 1 = 2$, $2 + 1 = 3$, $3 + 2 = 5$, $5 + 3 = 8$, and so on, up to 21. Each story is sized up to 21 points, which is the largest story, with 1 being the smallest story.

- **T-shirt sizing**   This approach is quick and easy. Each story is sized like a t-shirt—Extra Small, Small, Medium, Large, and Extra Large. The sizing of each story is comparable to the other stories.

- **Planning poker**   In this approach, the product owner reads the story to the team and the team will discuss the story and its complexity. Each person secretly decides on what the value of the story should be, usually using the Fibonacci series sequence, and everyone reveals their size at once. Some teams actually use a deck of cards or apps on their phones to vote. After everyone reveals their secret sizing, the conversation that ensues is centered on why the participants voted the way they did.

Once the user stories have been sized, the team determines how many story points they can take on during the next work iteration. For example, a team may decide that they can take up to 30 story points. The team chooses the top items in the product backlog with ratings that equate up to or close to 30 points. These selected items then become the sprint backlog for the next iteration of the project. Based on the sprint backlog, the team creates a task breakout of who does what in the sprint. This is an example of a self-organizing team, rather than a team with a project manager role that assigns tasks.

The *velocity* is the number of stories a team can complete in a sprint. For example, of the 30 user story points selected, if the team can complete only 20 of the user story points, then the velocity is 20. Over the first few sprints, the velocity may be wild and unpredictable, but over several sprints, the velocity will normalize, for example, as 25 story points. The velocity will also help the product owner and the scrum master predict how many sprints are needed. Consider a product backlog with 140 remaining user story points. Based on the velocity of 25 story points per sprint, there will be six sprints in the project. If each sprint is four weeks in duration, the project will take 24 weeks.

Creating the Work Breakdown Structure

The WBS is all about the project deliverables. It's a breakdown of the project scope into a hierarchy of deliverables. Each layer of the WBS breaks down the layer above it into smaller, manageable deliverables, until it arrives at the smallest item in the WBS, the *work package*.

NOTE The *work* in the WBS refers to the deliverables the project will create, not the effort your project team will have to put forth to create the deliverables.

Figure 5-1 shows an example of a simple WBS. In the figure, the house project has five major categories of deliverables: project management, paperwork, construction, interior

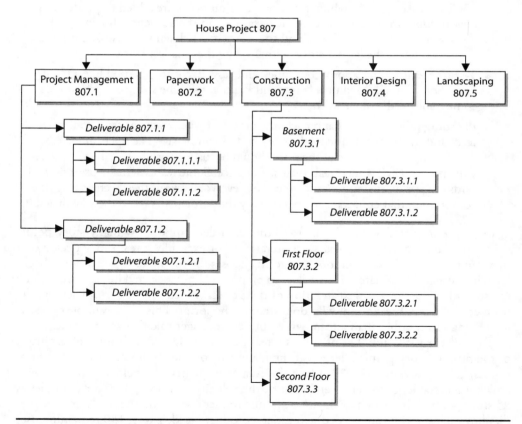

Figure 5-1   A WBS is the breakdown of a project scope.

design, and landscaping. Each of these first-tier deliverables can be broken down into smaller deliverables. In Figure 5-1, the construction deliverable has been broken down to several smaller deliverables: the basement, first floor, and second floor. Each of these deliverables could be broken down farther to another level, and so on. The smallest item in the WBS is called a *work package*, which can be used effectively to estimate cost and time and can be monitored and controlled within the project.

So how far must the project scope be broken down? There's no right answer that fits every project: each project scope should be broken down to the level of detail that's appropriate for the project priority, scope, and objectives. A guideline for WBS breakdown is the *8/80 rule*. This rule states that the labor to create a work package should equate to no more than 80 hours and no fewer than 8 hours of labor for the associated activities. Of course, this is just a guideline, not a regulation. Some projects may call for work packages that take far less time than 8 hours.

 EXAM TIP The WBS is primarily about things, not activities. The work package is just a label for the smallest deliverable within the WBS. For your PMP exam, know that the smallest element in the WBS is a work package and that it can be scheduled, estimated for costs, and then monitored and controlled. The PMI has lightened their stance on allowing appropriate activities, such as testing, into the WBS.

Usually, the WBS is a visual mapping of the subdivision of the project deliverables, though this approach isn't always the best technique to use. The WBS can also be created by using the project phases, by subcontractors that will complete parts of the project work, or even by the type of labor the WBS will require.

Using a WBS Template

If an organization does the same type of project work over and over, they likely won't need to start a WBS from scratch with every new project. Instead, they could use a previous, similar project as a template for the current one. This is ideal, since most projects within an organization have similar life cycles, deliverables, and milestones. A previous project's WBS makes an ideal template for the current project, provided the projects are similar enough. The project management team may still need to edit the template, but using a template is a huge timesaver in the long run.

Other organizations may use a template in the more traditional sense. Just as you may have a template for a newsletter, a report, or a memo, an organization can create a WBS template of prepopulated WBS deliverables. In Figure 5-1, for example, I included the project management deliverables as part of the WBS. Project management deliverables could be a common component of every WBS an organization creates, so it'd be ideal to include these items in a standard WBS template for all project managers to use.

Decomposing the Deliverables

Horrible joke warning: *What's Beethoven doing now? Decomposing.*

All right, so it's not the best joke in the world, but it's relevant. Like Beethoven, the project team will first compose and then decompose. In project management, the project scope statement is first composed, and then the scope is broken down, or decomposed, into the individual items that the project will create.

Some items in the WBS may not be available for decomposition because they're far off in the future. In these instances, the project team will break down those items as more information regarding the deliverables becomes available. This is an example of *rolling wave planning*. Some projects may elect to create their WBS based on the phases within the project, rather than on the total deliverables of the project. Either approach is fine.

The following activities are required to decompose the project scope into a WBS:

- Identify the project deliverables and related work.
- Form the WBS structure.
- Decompose the upper tier deliverables into lower tier deliverables.
- Create and assign WBS identification codes to the WBS packages. (This is called the *code of accounts* and is a numbering system that identifies each element within the WBS.)
- Confirm that the decomposition is appropriate for the type of project.

Creating the WBS Dictionary

Along with the WBS, a WBS dictionary defines all of the characteristics of each element within the WBS. The primary documentation of the WBS dictionary is on the work package, the smallest item in the WBS, but upper tier deliverables can also be documented. Each work package in the WBS is cross-referenced in this companion document and includes the following details where appropriate:

- Code of account identifier and charge number
- Work package description
- Statement of work
- Work package owner or responsible role
- Schedule milestones
- Contract information
- Quality requirements
- Technical references
- Associated activities and work packages
- Schedule
- Resources
- Cost

NOTE You'll use the scope baseline often in your PMP endeavors. The scope baseline is the combination of the project scope, the work breakdown structure, and the WBS dictionary.

Validating the Project Scope

Imagine a project to create a full-color, slick catalog for an electronics manufacturer. The project manager has completed the initiation processes, moved through planning, and is now executing the project work. The only trouble is that the project manager and the experts on the project team aren't sharing the work progress with the customer. And the work they are completing is not in alignment with the product description or the customer's requirements.

The project team has created a trendy 1950s-style catalog with funky green and orange colors, lots of beehive-hairdo models wearing horn-rimmed glasses, and tongue-in-cheek jokes about "the future" of electronics. The manufacturer, however, wants to demonstrate a professional, accessible, current look for its publications. What do you think will happen if the project manager presents the catalog with his spin rather than following the request of the customer?

Scope validation is the process of the project customer accepting the project deliverables. It happens either at the end of each project phase or as major deliverables are created. Scope validation ensures that the deliverables the project creates are in alignment with the project scope. It is concerned with the acceptance of the work. A related activity, *quality control* (QC), is concerned with the correctness of the work. Scope validation and QC can happen in tandem, because the quality of the work contributes to scope validation. Poor quality will typically result in scope validation failure.

Preparing for Project Inspection

You could just rush into scope validation, but that'd be a waste of time and not a very organized approach to confirming that the project deliverables are accurate. It's better to collect some inputs to help you prepare for the project inspection. You'll need the following:

- **Project management plan** Within the project management plan, you'll reference the scope management plan, because it defines the scope validation and approval process. You'll also reference the requirements management plan. This documentation of what the stakeholders expect from the project defines all of the technical requirements that must be present for the work to be accepted by the stakeholders. You'll also reference the scope baseline.

- **Project documents** From the project documents, you'll reference the lessons learned register, quality reports, requirements documentation, and the requirements traceability matrix.

- **Verified deliverables**   These are deliverables that your project team has completed that have passed your project's quality control process.
- **Work performance data**   This information defines how well the deliverables are in compliance with the project scope and records those requirements that are not in compliance.

These four things will help you and the project stakeholders inspect the project work to confirm that what you've created is what was promised to the customer. In Scrum, scope validation happens at the end of each sprint during the sprint review meeting. At this meeting, the development team reviews what they have accomplished in the sprint. This review is for the scrum master, the product owner, and often some key stakeholders. The Sprint review puts some pressure on the development team to create the user stories as promised, but it's also a chance for everyone to recognize the team's diligence and the results of their hard work.

Inspecting the Project Work

To complete scope validation, the deliverables must be inspected or voted upon for completeness. Inspection may require measuring, examining, and testing the product to prove that it meets the customer's requirements. Inspection usually requires that the project manager and the customer inspect the project deliverables for verification, which, if verified, results in acceptance. Depending on the industry, inspections may also be known as

- Reviews
- Product reviews
- Audits
- Walkthroughs
- Group decision-making techniques

Assuming the scope has been validated, the customer accepts the deliverable. This is a formal process that requires signed documentation of the acceptance by the sponsor or customer. Scope validation can also happen at the end of each project phase or when major deliverables within the project are achieved. In these instances, scope validation may be conditional, based on the work results. When the scope is not validated, the project may undergo one of several actions. It may be canceled and deemed a failure, sent through corrective actions, or put on hold while a decision is made based on the project or phase results.

In an agile project, once the sprint review is done, the approved work of the development team is called a potentially shippable product (PSP). This means the development team has met the DoD and the result of the sprint could be shippable. This doesn't mean the product owner is obligated to release the PSP, only that the team has created the target user stories and the final product of the sprint could be shipped, or released, if needed. The product owner's product roadmap determines when the product will be released, usually based on the compilation of several features.

Should a project get canceled before it has completed the scope, scope validation is measured against the deliverables to the point of the project cancellation. In other words, scope validation measures the completeness of the work up to the time of cancellation, not the work that was to be completed after project termination.

 EXAM TIP If a project scope has been completed, the project is complete. Resist the urge to do additional work once the project scope has been fulfilled. Also, be cautious of instances where the scope is fulfilled and the product description is exact, but the customer is not happy with the product. Technically, for the exam, the project is complete even if the customer is not happy.

Controlling the Project Scope

Scope control is about protecting the project scope and the product scope from change and, when changes do happen, managing those changes. Ideally, all requested changes follow the scope change control system, which means that change requests must be documented. Those changes that sneak into the project scope are lumped into that project poison category of *scope creep*. Scope creep is bad, bad news. Of course, if you're working in an adaptive environment, there is still change control to the product scope and project scope, but change is managed through refinements of the product backlog. Change in a predictive environment is anticipated, but change follows the integrated change control process.

Corrective actions—steps taken to move the project back into alignment with the project scope—do require formal change requests, because the project manager isn't changing the scope, but rather the work that's outside of the project scope. Corrective actions are a part of scope control because you're nudging, and sometimes shoving, work back into alignment with the project scope. The trouble with scope creep and corrective actions is that the project team is doing or fixing work that should never have entered the scope in the first place—and that means wasted time and dollars. That's one sure way for a project to be late and over budget.

 NOTE Corrective actions and preventive actions will require formal change requests.

The project manager must control the project team and the project stakeholders from doing anything—absolutely anything—that's outside of the project scope. This also means that the project management team should capture the customer's vision in planning before much of the project work begins. For example, it's much easier to make changes on a blueprint before construction begins than to make changes to an already-built structure. Gathering all requirements and creating an accurate project scope statement can ward off changes during execution.

You'll need four things as inputs to the control scope process:

- **Project management plan**   Within the project management plan, you'll reference the scope management plan, requirements management plan, change management plan, configuration management plan, scope baseline, and the project performance measurement baseline.

- **Project documents**   The most common project documents you'll reference are the lessons learned register, requirements documentation, and the requirements traceability matrix.

- **Work performance data**   This is the status of the deliverables—the work that's been started, finished, or has yet to begin. The data can also be facts on the number of change requests, change requests approved or declined, and what deliverables have been validated and completed.

- **Organizational process assets**   Your organization may have scope management policies, guidelines, and reporting methods that you must use as part of scope control.

Using a Change Control System

Though it's dreamy and ideal for requirements to be completely gathered before the work begins, change requests to the project work are still likely even in a predictive project. Every project demands a change control system that defines and controls how changes to the project and to the product can be approved. The scope management plan defines the change control system, its procedure, and how the change decisions can be made—often with a fee just to entertain the change request. The change control system should be reviewed during the project kickoff meeting so that all of the stakeholders are aware of the process. Change control is part of the project management information system to help control changes to the project scope. This helps automate the procedure, but it doesn't necessarily make approving or denying change requests any easier.

The change control system also considers integrated change control, which examines the proposed change and how it affects all of the project's knowledge areas. For example, integrated change control considers the following questions:

- How does this change affect the project scope?
- What is the cost of the change?
- How does this change affect the project schedule?
- How does this change affect quality?
- What resources are needed or affected by the change?
- How does this change affect communications?
- What risks does this change present?
- Will procurement be affected by this change?

The change control system should do several things for the project management team:

- Document all change requests.
- Track each change request.
- Document approval levels required for a scope change.
- Provide the status of each change request.

 TIP Agile projects welcome and expect change, sure, but even agile projects need to consider the effects of a proposed change. Changes to the product backlog undergo refinement and aren't automatically added to the top of the product backlog. Some changes may cause the team to have to undo things that have already been done to accommodate the new items added to the product backlog.

Planning for Project Scope Changes

When a change is presented, part of considering the change involves additional planning. The project manager and the project team must reconvene to examine the change and how it may affect the project work and the knowledge areas discussed earlier. Changes are sometimes rejected, such as when a project team member takes the initiative for a change and does not follow the change control procedures. In these instances, the project management team must consider the change and examine the variance to determine the response.

Consider a team member who moves the light fixtures in a kitchen construction project by 2 feet. The team member believes the kitchen would be better lit with the lights moved to their new position, but he didn't follow the change control process to make the change. Now there is a variance in the scope—a difference between what the specification documents called for and what the team member actually did. The project management team has to consider how to manage the variance. Should they redo the work or accept the change the team member has made? If they redo the work, they may lose time and money, but they'll be in scope. If they leave the change as is, then they're out of scope.

Another consideration for all changes is the configuration management system. Configuration management documents all of the features and functions of the project's product. When a change is requested, the impact on the features and functions of the product is documented with the change request before the change is allowed to move through the integrated change control process. For example, a change to add French doors to a home construction project would need all of the features and functions of those French doors so that the true impact on the project's knowledge areas could be examined fully. Failure to document the change accurately can lead to assumptions proving false, new risks, schedule slippage, and financial costs within the project.

NOTE Undocumented change requests should not be considered at all. Change requests must be documented according to the project scope management plan. When there is a difference between what was planned and what was created, variance analysis is needed to determine what corrective actions should be implemented. This is true for all projects regardless of their management approach.

Approving a Change

It's a safe bet that changes to the project scope will happen during a project. Why do change requests happen? And which ones are most likely to be approved? Most change requests are a result of the following:

- **Value-added changes** These changes will reduce costs (often resulting from technological advances made since the time the project scope was created).

- **External events** These could be such things as new laws or industry requirements.

- **Errors or omissions** Ever hear this one: "Oops! We forgot to include this feature in the product description and WBS!" Errors and omissions can happen both to the project scope, which includes the work to complete the project, and the product scope, which includes the features and functions of the deliverable, and they typically constitute an overlooked feature or requirement.

- **Risk response** A risk has been identified, and changes to scope are needed to mitigate the risk.

When a change request is approved, the effects of that change should be documented throughout the project. The Iron Triangle of Project Management is a good example: if the project scope increases, then the project schedule and the project costs will likely need to be changed to reflect these changes. Here are all of the project components that will most likely need to be updated to reflect any approved changes to the project:

- Requirements documentation
- Requirements traceability matrix (RTM)
- Project scope statement
- Work breakdown structure (WBS)
- WBS dictionary
- Scope baseline
- Additional requested changes
- Organizational process assets
- Risk register
- Project management plan

Change requests must always follow the change control system, or they are considered out of scope. As the project manager and the project team discover and report changes that are out of scope, the project management team must deal with the changes to remove them through corrective actions or incorporate them through the change control process. Those changes that are incorporated into the project must still be documented and then reflected in the preceding project components. No changes sneak by!

Chapter Summary

Project scope management is the ability to complete all of the project's required work—and only the required work. This means no extras, no favors, and no cutting corners. The project scope is the focus of the project—the necessary work to complete the project. Project scope management is a tool the project manager uses to determine what work is included in the project and what work is out of scope.

The project scope management plan will help the project management team determine how the project scope will be defined, how the WBS will be created, how the scope will be controlled throughout the remainder of the project, and how the scope will be verified by the project customer, both at the end of each project phase and at the end of the project. The project scope management plan makes the project team consider all of the knowledge areas and how they may be affected by changes to the project scope.

The scope in agile projects is the product backlog. Requirements, or user stories, are entered into the product backlog, prioritized, and estimated for size thorough story point sizing. The team will determine how many story points it can accomplish in the next work iteration. The actual number of stories created determines the velocity of the team. The velocity, over time, will help predict how long the project will take to complete.

To determine what the project scope actually is, you'll need plenty of scope planning. The project manager and the project team must have a clear vision of the project, the business need for the project, the requirements, and the stakeholder expectations for the project. The end result of the scope planning processes is the project scope statement, which says, in no uncertain terms, what is in the project and what is not in the project. This is a more detailed project scope statement than what's created during project initiation.

For your PMP exam, focus on protecting the project scope in predictive projects and welcoming change in adaptive projects. This includes finding the real purpose of the project so that the scope is in alignment with the identified need. Once the scope has been created in a predictive project, the project team, stakeholders, project sponsor, and project manager should not change it unless there is overwhelming evidence for a change. All changes should be documented and must follow the change control system as defined in the project scope management plan.

Questions

1. Henry is the project manager for his organization, and management has asked him to create a project management plan to define the scope statement. Which project management plan guides the creation of the detailed project scope statement?

   A. The charter

   B. The project management plan

   C. The project scope plan

   D. The project scope management plan

2. You are the project manager of the GYH Project. This project will create a walking bridge across the Tennessee River. You've been asked to start the process of creating the project scope statement and you need to gather the elements for this process. Which one of the following is not needed to define the project scope?

   A. A project charter

   B. Organizational process assets

   C. A risk management plan

   D. Requirements documentation

3. You are the project manager of the BHY Project. Your project customer has demanded that the project be completed by December 1. Currently, the product backlog has 225 user story points and the team's velocity is 30. If each sprint takes four weeks to complete, how long will this project take to complete??

   A. 7.5 weeks

   B. 6 weeks

   C. 32 weeks

   D. 15 weeks

4. Marty is the project manager of the Highway 41 Bridge Project and he's working with his project team members to create the WBS. Marty shows the team how to break down the project scope into the WBS components, but the team doesn't understand how far down the breakdown should occur. What is the lowest level item in a WBS?

   A. A deliverable

   B. A work package

   C. An activity

   D. A leaf object

5. You are working with the project team to create the WBS. Some elements in the WBS can't be broken down yet. You and the team elect to break down these items later in the project as more details become available. This approach to creating the WBS is also known as what?

   A. Decomposition

   B. The 8/80 rule

   C. Parkinson's Law

   D. Rolling wave planning

6. You are the project manager for your organization and you're creating the WBS for a new project. In your WBS, you're numbering each level of the components following a project sequenced numbering order. Your WBS is numbered in a hierarchical fashion for easy identification and reference. This numbering scheme is called what?

   A. Code of accounts

   B. Chart of accounts

   C. WBS template

   D. WBS dictionary

7. You'll use the scope management plan to define the project scope statement. You'll also use this plan to build the scope baseline. Which two items are parts of the scope baseline for the project?

   A. The project scope management plan and project charter

   B. The project scope management plan and the WBS

   C. The WBS and WBS dictionary

   D. Time and cost baselines

8. Throughout the project, you have milestones scheduled at the end of each phase. Tied to these milestones is a project management requirement of scope validation. Scope validation leads to what?

   A. Defect repair

   B. Formal acceptance of the complete project scope

   C. Rework

   D. Inspection

9. You've just reached the end of your project, and management has asked you and several key stakeholders to begin the scope validation process. How is scope validation accomplished during scope validation in an agile project?

   A. Sprint review meeting

   B. Sprint retrospective meeting

   C. Stakeholder analysis

   D. Definition of done review

10. David, one of your project team members, has been making changes to his work, which, as a result, changes the project scope. David's changes are also known as what?

A. Gold plating

B. Scope control defect

C. Scope creep

D. Improvised scope composition

11. As the project manager, you are averse to change once the scope statement has been approved. You do not want changes to enter the project because they can have a wide impact on the project as a whole. Which process defines how the project scope can be changed?

A. The integrated change control process

B. The project integrated management system

C. The project management information system

D. Change control

12. A scope change has been approved in Marcy's predictive project. All of the following must be updated to reflect the change except for which one?

A. The project scope statement

B. The WBS

C. The WBS dictionary

D. Defect repair review

13. A project team member has, on his own initiative, added extra vents to an attic to increase air circulation. The project plan did not call for these extra vents, but the team member decided they were needed based on the geographical location of the house. The project team's experts concur with this decision. This is an example of which of the following?

A. Cost control

B. Ineffective change control

C. Self-led teams

D. Value-added change

14. It's important for you, the project manager, to understand what each of the project management processes creates. One of the key processes you'll undertake is scope control throughout your project. Which of the following is an output of scope control?

A. Workarounds

B. Change request for a corrective action

C. Transference

D. Risk assessment

PART II

15. You are the project manager for the JHG Project, which will create a new product for your industry. You have recently learned that your competitor is also working on a similar project, but their offering will include a computer-aided program and web-based tools, which your project does not offer. You have implemented a change request to update your project accordingly. This is an example of which of the following?

    A. A change due to an error and omission in the initiation phase

    B. A change due to an external event

    C. A change due to an error or omission in the planning phase

    D. A change due to a legal issue

16. You are the project manager of a large project. Your project sponsor and management have approved your outsourcing portions of the project plan. What must be considered if a change request affects the procured work?

    A. The project sponsor

    B. The contractual agreement

    C. Vendor(s)

    D. The cause of the change request

17. A project team member has asked you what a scope statement is. Which of the following is a characteristic of a project scope statement?

    A. Defines the scope baseline for the project

    B. Defines the requirements for each project within the organization

    C. Defines the roles and responsibilities of each project team member

    D. Defines the project deliverables and the work needed to create those deliverables

18. One of the stakeholders of the project you are managing asks why you consider the project scope statement so important in your project management methodology. You answer her question with which of the following?

    A. It is mandatory to consult the plan before authorizing any change.

    B. Project managers must document any changes before approving or declining them.

    C. The project scope helps the project manager determine whether a change is within or outside of scope.

    D. The project plan and earned value management (EVM) work together to assess the risk involved with proposed changes.

19. You are the project manager for a large construction project using a hybrid approach. The architect has provided your project team with blueprints detailing the exact layout of the building your team will be creating. He insists that the team follow the blueprints as he's designed them. The blueprints are an example of which one of the following?

A. Project specifications

B. Approval requirements

C. Project constraints

D. Initially defined risks

20. Complete this sentence: Project scope management is primarily concerned with defining and controlling _____.

A. What is and is not included in the project

B. What is and is not included in the product

C. Changes to the project scope

D. Changes to the configuration management system

Answers

1. D. The project scope management plan defines the creation of the detailed project scope statement. A, the charter, does include the preliminary project scope statement, but not the detailed one defined by the project scope management plan. B, the project management plan, is a parent of the project scope management plan. C is not a valid plan, so this answer is incorrect.

2. C. At this point, you won't need, or likely have, the risk management plan to define the project scope. A, B, and D are incorrect because you'll need the project charter, organizational process assets, and the requirements documentation to define the project scope.

3. C. To determine the project duration, you'll first determine how many sprints the project will need with a velocity of 30 user story points by dividing the current product backlog of 225 by 30 for a result of 7.5 sprints. Each sprint will last 4 weeks, so you'll multiply 7.5 by 4 and choose the closest answer which is 32 weeks. A, B, and D are incorrect calculations.

4. B. The smallest item in the WBS is called the work package. A, deliverables, may be true to a degree, but B is a more precise answer. C is incorrect because activities are found in the activity list. D is an invalid WBS term.

5. D. This is a clear example of rolling wave planning. A is incorrect because decomposition describes the breakdown process of the project scope. B is incorrect because the 8/80 rule defines the guideline for the amount of labor that should be related to each work package in the WBS. C, Parkinson's Law, is not relevant to this question. Parkinson's Law states that work will expand to fill the amount of time allotted to it.

6. **A.** The WBS numbering scheme is called the code of accounts. B, chart of accounts, is a project management accounting system. C, a WBS template, can be a prepopulated WBS or a WBS from a previous project used to define the current project's WBS. D is incorrect because the WBS dictionary defines the attributes of each WBS element.

7. **C.** The WBS and WBS dictionary are two of the three components of the scope baseline. The approved detailed project scope statement is the third portion of the scope baseline. A, B, and D are all incorrect because they do not accurately define the scope baseline.

8. **B.** Scope validation leads to one thing: formal acceptance of the complete project scope. A, C, and D are incorrect because defect repair, rework, and inspection are not outputs of scope validation.

9. **A.** Scope validation is accomplished through a sprint review meeting. This meeting calls on the development team to demonstrate what they have accomplished during the past work iteration. B, a sprint retrospective meeting, is used to discuss what's worked or hasn't worked in the sprint and to enable the team to make adjustments for the next work iteration. C is incorrect because stakeholder analysis is done to determine stakeholder engagement and requirement needs. D is incorrect because the definition of done describes what constitutes a potentially shippable product in the project.

10. **C.** Undocumented changes are examples of scope creep. A, gold plating, is when the project team adds changes to consume the project budget. B and D, scope control defect and improvised scope composition, are not valid change management terms.

11. **A.** The only process that defines how project can be changed is the integrated change control process. B, the project integrated management system, is not a valid term. C, the project management information system, is the parent system of the project scope change control system. D, change control, is a system, not a process.

12. **D.** Defect repair review does not require a change request, so this choice is correct. A, B, and C, the project scope statement, the WBS, and the WBS dictionary, do require updates when change requests are approved.

13. **B.** Even though the change is agreed upon, this is an example of ineffective change control. The team member should have followed the change control process as defined in the project scope management plan. A, C, and D are incorrect choices because cost control, self-led teams, and value-added change aren't what's being reflected as an ineffective change control in this question.

14. **B.** Change requests for corrective actions are an output of scope control. This is because the project team may be doing work outside of the project scope. Corrective action would stop the extraneous work and bring the project team member's actions back into the work within the project scope. A, workarounds, aren't an output of scope control and are most often associated with risk management. C, transference, is a risk response that happens when you hire someone else to manage the risk. D, risk assessment, is the activity used to rank a risk's probability and impact.

15. **B.** This is a change due to an external event—the event being the product your competitor is creating in their project. A is incorrect because this is not an example of an error or omission in the initiation phase. C is incorrect because this is not an error or omission in the planning phase, but a response to a competitor. D is incorrect because this is not a legal issue.

16. **B.** If a change to the project scope affects the procured work, the project manager must consider the contract. This is because the change may affect the existing contract between the project manager and the vendor. A and C are incorrect. Although the sponsor and vendors are likely to be involved with the change, the contractual agreements override all other internal systems. D, the cause of the change request, is not as relevant as the contract.

17. **D.** The project scope statement defines the project deliverables and the associated work to create those deliverables. A is incorrect because the project scope statement, the WBS, and the WBS dictionary are considered to be the project scope baseline. B is incorrect because the project scope statement does define the requirements for every project, but it is project-specific. C is incorrect because the project scope statement does not define the roles and responsibilities of the project team.

18. **C.** The project scope statement can help the project management team determine whether a proposed change is within or outside of the project boundaries. A, B, and D are true statements, but they do not answer the question with regard to the importance of the project scope statement.

19. **A.** Blueprints are an example of the project specifications. B is incorrect because this is not an example of approval requirements. C is incorrect because this is not an example of a constraint. D is also incorrect because the blueprints are not examples of initially defined risks.

20. **A.** Project scope management is primarily concerned with defining and controlling what is and is not included in the project. B, C, and D are all incorrect statements.

Managing Project Schedule

In this chapter, you will

- Plan schedule management
- Define the project activities
- Sequence the project activities
- Estimate activity duration
- Develop the project schedule
- Control the project schedule

Time has a funny way of sneaking up on you—and then easing on by. As a project manager, you've got stakeholders, project team members, and management all worried about your project deliverables, how the project is moving forward, and when, oh when, the project will be done. You've also got vacations, sick days, demands from other project managers, and delays from vendors to deal with.

Management frets over how much a project will cost. Project customers fret over the deliverables the project will create. Everyone, as it turns out, frets over how long the project will take. Of course I'm talking about the Triple Constraints of Project Management: cost, scope, and schedule. If any one of these constraints is out of balance with the other two, the project is unlikely to succeed. The schedule, as it happens, is often the toughest of the three constraints to manage, because interruptions come from all sides of the project.

Your Project Management Institute (PMI) exam and this chapter will cover schedule management for predictive and agile projects. The processes within project schedule management, like much of project management, are interdependent on one another and on other processes in the project management life cycle. In a predictive project, you'll likely be using the critical path approach to project schedule management. In an agile project, you'll use time-boxed iterations or sprints to manage the project schedule and the project execution.

Adaptive environments use a product backlog, unlike a predictive environment. Recall that the product backlog is a list of prioritized requirements, or user stories. The project team assigns story points to the user stories as a way to estimate the amount of effort required to create these requirements, and there are only so many story points available per time-boxed iteration. In other words, the team defines how much they can feasibly get done in an iteration based on the complexity of the user stories. This agile approach helps ensure realistic expectations of what can be completed in an iteration and assures the product owner that the most important requirements are built first. This is my favorite idea of agile projects: eat your dessert first.

Let's get into project schedule management right now!

Planning Schedule Management

The project management planning processes are iterative, as you know, and will happen over and over throughout the project. You and the project team—and even some key stakeholders—will work together to define the project's schedule management plan. This will happen early in the project's planning processes, but you'll probably need to return to schedule management planning to adjust, replan, or focus on the schedule you've created for the project.

Planning schedule management is not the creation of the actual project schedule. That'd be too easy. Instead, the schedule management plan defines how the project's policies and procedures for managing the project schedule will take place. You'll define the procedures for completing schedule management.

Of course, agile projects don't include the overhead of detailed project schedule planning. You'll instead work with a fixed schedule and then create as many requirements as time allows and the team's velocity permits. With a fixed schedule, or deadline, you'll start with the most important requirements first so there's less risk of running out of time and not creating value—something we always fear in predictive environments.

 EXAM TIP For your exam, you'll need to know both the predictive and agile approaches to project scheduling management, even if you don't use both approaches on your projects. Just remember that agile projects have a fixed schedule, while predictive projects predict duration.

To do this planning, you'll gather your project team, key stakeholders, and subject matter experts such as people from management and consultants to help you plan what it is you're about to schedule. You'll need the project management plan, the project charter, enterprise environmental factors, and organizational process assets.

Creating the Schedule Management Plan

The actual process of creating the schedule management plan involves you, the project team, and other experts meeting to discuss and agree upon the policies and procedures the schedule management processes should have. You'll rely on organizational process assets for much of the discussion: historical information, past project information, and existing organizational processes.

This event of creating the schedule management plan may also include the identification and approval of the tools and techniques to be used for scheduling and controlling the project work. For example, an organization may not allow an employee to work more than a certain number of hours on the project. Or the organization could prevent certain activities from being done in tandem because of the associated risks. Every organization and its approach will be different, so you'll need to know if your company has any restrictions, scheduling rules, or policies on overtime, labor utilization, or coordination of resources. These will all affect the actual schedule of the project and should be documented in the project's schedule management plan.

During the creation of the plan, you'll also identify any software you'll utilize for scheduling the project work, tracking project performance, completing tasks, managing workflow, and reporting. This is the project management information system that will assist you in your project management duties.

Examining the Schedule Management Plan

The schedule management plan could be adapted from a previous project, or, if you need to, you could design the plan from scratch. For your PMP examination, you should be familiar with the information documented in the plan:

- **Project schedule model development**   This approved scheduling methodology and project management information system will help you develop the project schedule.

- **Project schedule model maintenance**   You'll use this component of the plan when you update the project progress.

- **Release and iteration length**   If you're working in an adaptive environment, you'll define how long the time-boxed iterations will last (for example, two or four weeks per iteration).

- **Level of accuracy**   You'll need to establish confidence in the provided project duration estimates (such as +/–48 hours, or 10 percent), any rounding of hours (for example, you could say the smallest task assignment is one workday), and how confident you are in your ability meet the project's deadline, if one exists.

- **Units of measure**   Your schedule management plan can define the schedule in hours, days, weeks, or even percentage of employee schedule.

- **Organizational procedure links**   The schedule management plan is part of the overall project management plan and is a project deliverable that will become part of historical information. The work breakdown structure (WBS) is linked to the schedule management plan as the duration estimates are linked to the activities and the WBS work packages.

- **Control thresholds**   Depending on the confidence in the activity duration estimates, a level of tolerance for the project schedule should be identified, such as +/–10 percent. This is considered the threshold or tolerance for error. Any value outside the 10 percent will be a cause for a corrective action in the project.

- **Rules of performance measurement**   The schedule management plan should define how the project will be measured for performance. The most common approach is a suite of formulas called earned value management. (I'll discuss these in detail in Chapter 7.)

- **Reporting formats**   Based on project performance, the project manager will need to report the schedule status to management, key stakeholders, and project customers.

Utilizing an On-Demand Scheduling Approach

On-demand scheduling also uses a backlog of requirements, but as resources become available in the project, the next requirement is launched. This pull-based approach to scheduling stems from lean manufacturing and is used with a Kanban system, which you learned about in Chapter 2. You'll remember that the Kanban board is used to show what's being worked on (the work-in-progress, or WIP), which requirements are completed, and which requirements still need to be worked on until each process reaches the "done" stage. You pull the requirements from left to right as the project moves through the stages of production, as shown in the example in Figure 6-1. Agile approaches use shorter increments of project work versus longer phases that you may enjoy in a predictive environment.

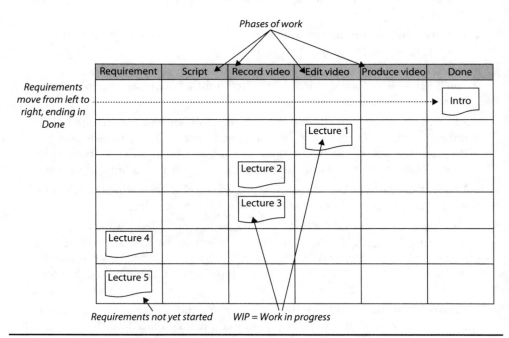

Figure 6-1   A Kanban board shows work in progress and completed phases of work.

Defining the Project Activities

When a project is first initiated, project managers often focus immediately on the labor and activities that will be required to complete the project work. But that focus ignores the scope. In Chapter 5, I discussed the project scope and the WBS as prerequisites to defining the project activities. For your PMI examination, know the following sequence of events for predictive projects that the project manager should have in place before getting to the work the project team will complete:

1. Project scope statement
2. Work breakdown structure
3. WBS dictionary
4. Work packages
5. Schedule activities

The work package, the smallest item in the WBS, is broken down into *schedule activities*, which include the labor to create the things defined in the WBS. The WBS, of course, reflects the project scope statement. The preceding list is the logical sequence of how the project management team will work together to create the activity list, but there are just three inputs to activity definition:

- Project management plan (specifically the schedule management plan and the scope baseline)
- Organizational process assets
- Enterprise environmental factors

These inputs and the order of precedence mentioned earlier will help the project team define the activities to create the components of the project scope. We're still in the planning process group, so this process is iterative. Any changes to the project scope will likely cause the project manager to revisit these processes throughout the project.

Making the Activity List

You and your project team are armed with the inputs I've listed previously and are ready to start defining the activities you'll need to create the project schedule in a predictive project. For agile projects, the activity list is built from the selected user stories from the product backlog in each sprint planning meeting. This iterative activity maps out the work the development team will tackle in the next sprint. The selected user stories become the sprint backlog, and then task definition occurs. The development team is self-organizing, so the team will decide who does what in the iteration.

Predictive projects have a bit more front-loaded overhead when it comes to scheduling. The activity list definition process and its complexity will be in proportion to the size of the project scope. In other words, larger projects require more detail and more planning time, while smaller projects, such as changing all the keyboards in your company, won't be all that complicated or too time-consuming to plan.

 EXAM COACH My advice to you—the Project Management Professional (PMP) candidate—for your exam is to think of the largest project you can imagine, such as creating a skyscraper, and then you'll understand why you need to use all or most of these project processes.

Let's look at the methods used to define the project activities, which the following sections explain in detail.

Decomposing the Work Packages

Yep, more decomposition. You know that the project scope is decomposed into deliverables, and then those deliverables are decomposed into work packages, the smallest item in the WBS. Now that you and your project team are focused on defining the project activities, you'll be breaking down the work packages into the labor needed to create each work package.

Some project managers follow a sequential pattern for this process. First, they decompose the project scope into first-tier deliverables, then they decompose those project deliverables into second-tier deliverables, and so on, until they've created the work packages. Armed with the work packages, they'll decompose those into the schedule activities we're discussing here. Other project managers will decompose the project scope, then the work packages, and then create the schedule activities in one swoop.

Either approach, in fact, is just fine—even with our pals at the PMI. Complete decomposition of the project scope down to the schedule activities is needed—how you get there doesn't matter. What matters is that all the work packages are decomposed and that the project management team follows the internal policies and procedures (if they exist) to create the schedule activities.

Relying on Templates

Who wants to start a project from scratch when you've got an older, similar project just waiting to be manipulated? That older, similar project is a template. Sometimes in the project management world, we think of a template as an empty shell with prepopulated fields and deliverables—and that's fine. A template can also be an older, similar project that can be used and updated for the current project.

A project manager can use a standard activity list if the project work is similar to past projects. There's no real advantage to starting from scratch. Templates can include not only the activity list, but also the resource skills, estimated hours of effort, risks, deliverables, and any relevant project work information.

 EXAM TIP If an organization is completing the same type of project work over and over they don't have to start from scratch. Even agile projects can begin the project with a predefined list of requirements and defined activities. For the exam, remember that templates are past project files that can be manipulated and used for the current project.

Using Rolling Wave Planning

Have you ever done "the wave" at a football game? You can see the wave moving toward you from across the stadium, then you're in it, and then it surges past. The *rolling wave* in project management planning includes the iterations of planning and then doing the project work. Progressive elaboration, which you use to create the WBS and the WBS dictionary, is an example of rolling wave planning.

Rolling wave planning considers the big picture of what the project scope will create but focuses on the short-term activities to move the project along. Figure 6-2 shows how a project to create a piece of software considers all the project requirements for the deliverable, but focuses on the immediate activities necessary to complete a portion of the deliverable. Once that work is done, the project management team convenes and plans how to create the next portion of the project. The team plans, does the work, and then reconvenes for more planning.

 EXAM TIP Remember that rolling wave planning focuses on the immediate while considering the big picture of the project. (Which is easier to plan and accomplish: what you must do this week, or what you must do during a week a year from now?)

Using Expert Judgment

Let's face facts. As a project manager, you aren't always the person who knows the most about the work that the project centers on. Using expert judgment is about working

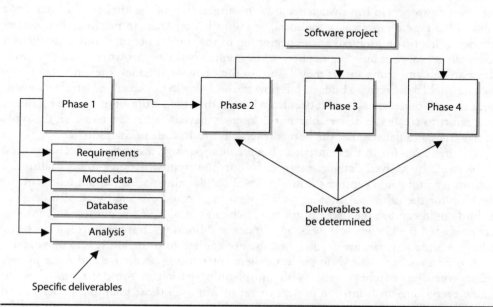

Figure 6-2 Rolling wave planning details the imminent work and keeps future work at the high level.

smart, not hard. The project manager relies on the project team, subject matter experts, and consultants to help determine the work that needs to be completed to create the project scope. You'll see expert judgment throughout this book and the *PMBOK Guide*. It's simply about leveraging other people's brainpower so that the project manager can make the best decisions regarding the project.

Creating Planning Components

A third element of the scope baseline is the WBS, which uses a component that has hooks into project time performance: a control account. A *control account* is a marker within the WBS that tracks the performance of the work packages associated with the control account. For example, a home construction project could create a control account for the basement, first floor, and second floor. The work packages associated with each floor of the house are tracked by the corresponding control account. Now you can see an overall performance of the project, or you can see how each control account is performing.

Of course, there's no predetermined rule about how you use control accounts, except that a work package can be associated with only one control account at a time. In the home construction project, you could create control accounts for framing, electrical, plumbing, even landscaping, and track the performance by these categories. The performance information you'll most likely use is earned value management (EVM)—something we'll get into in detail in Chapter 7. For now, know that control accounts enable you to track performance for separate chunks of the WBS by using EVM to track performance in time and cost.

Sometimes enough information just isn't available in the WBS to determine what activities are needed in the activity list. Let's go back to the new home construction project. Your customers in this instance knows the dimensions of the kitchen, but they don't know what type of appliances, cabinets, or even tile they want to put into their deluxe kitchen. This isn't a problem at the beginning of the project because your construction team can get to work building the home, but eventually the homeowners must decide on the materials and components they'll want in their fancy-schmancy kitchen.

The kitchen may have a budget, but how the budget will be consumed isn't yet known, because the homeowners haven't decided where in the kitchen they'll spend their monies. The effort to create the deliverables in the kitchen may also fluctuate based on the types of materials and deliverables the homeowners elect to include in their kitchen.

What you can use in these instances is a *planning package,* a signal that decisions need to be made by a given date or instance. In our home construction project example, a control account could capture the kitchen, while a planning package could represent the decision for the cabinets. Another planning package could capture the appliances, and a third could capture the decision for the kitchen flooring. We know these three things are needed in the kitchen (cabinets, appliances, and flooring), but we don't know exactly what schedule activities are needed, because not enough information is yet known.

A good example of a hybrid project, where you're using predictive and Agile project management approaches, is the WBS and planning packages. You don't really have to know everything up front in a project to get to work. So those planning packages and control account plans can be treated as Agile. You have a predetermined deadline and a budget for the kitchen. Create a product backlog for the elements in the kitchen, prioritize them, and work accordingly. The catch can be, of course, that some decisions are going to be difficult to undo, because, for example, the cabinet selection will affect where the appliances can go, but you can still prioritize and work accordingly.

Examining the Activity List

The primary output of decomposing the work is the *activity list,* a collection of all the work elements required to complete the project. The activity list is actually an extension of the WBS and will serve as a fundamental tool in creating the project schedule. The activity list is needed to ensure that all the deliverables of the WBS are accounted for and that the necessary work is mapped to each work package.

The activity list also ensures that no extra work is included in the project. Extra work costs time and money—and defeats the project scope. The WBS comprises all the components the project will create, while the activity list is made up of all the work required to create the components within the WBS. In addition, the work on the activity list includes attributes of each identified activity. This ensures three things:

- That the team members agree on what each activity accomplishes
- That the work supports and creates the WBS deliverables
- That the work is within the project scope

Documenting the Activity Attributes

Every activity in the activity list has attributes that must be documented. The documentation of each activity's characteristics will help with additional planning, risk identification, resource needs, and more. Of course, the activities and depth of the attributes will vary by project discipline. For your PMI exam, here are some attributes you should consider:

- Activity identifier
- Activity codes
- Activity description
- Predecessor and successor activities
- Logical relationships
- Leads and lags
- Resource requirements
- Imposed dates
- Constraints and assumptions
- Responsibility of the project team member(s) completing the work
- Location of the work
- Type and amount of effort needed to complete the work

These activity attributes are especially useful for generating reports. With this information, you could quickly filter the activities to identify the work where a particular vendor is involved. Or you could filter the events based on location, risk, and project team member. You could use the activity attributes in nearly endless ways to help you communicate information to management, to stakeholders, and to your project team.

 EXAM TIP You should know that *level of effort* (LOE) and *apportioned effort* (AE) can be part of the activity description. LOE activities are the project maintenance–type activities that have to be done over and over: budgeting, reporting, communicating. These activities almost always go to the project manager. AE activities can't be easily broken down into individual, traceable events. For example, quality assurance is part of every project activity, but it isn't just one activity in the project.

Building the Milestone List

Milestones are significant markers of progress in a project. If you're building a house, you could say the first milestone is the design of the house. The next milestone will be securing the permits from your city government. Then it's building the foundation. And you'll continue to identify the milestones that represent the big successes within the project. Milestones are often, but not always, created at the end of a phase in the project life cycle. The milestone list identifies all the milestones you've identified in the project, when you're expected to reach each milestone, and can, as things progress, show any variances between the planned date of the milestone and the actual realization of the milestone. To be clear, milestones are just markers—no duration is assigned to the milestone; duration is assigned to activities, not milestones.

Creating the Product Roadmap

In adaptive projects you'll work with a product roadmap in lieu of a milestone list. A product roadmap is a tool to show the major product deliverables, when they'll be available based on project conditions, and how the product can grow. A product roadmap also helps you, or the product owner, to secure project funding, because it'll show the business value the adaptive project will create. Product roadmaps aren't easy to create because adaptive projects change frequently; you don't want the product roadmap to be so tight that it doesn't allow changes, but you also don't want it to be so loose that there's little value in the document.

Product roadmaps don't get married to specific project deliverables, but rather embrace goals, visions, and business value. Product roadmaps identify the pain points of an organization, the business value of why the project is being undertaken, and loosely tie the forecasted deliverables to the overall goals and solutions of the project. This enables the project requirements to shift as expected in an agile project without conflicting with big promises in the product roadmap.

The product roadmap aims to describe what the project will accomplish more than what the project will create. It can be used to describe when releases from the project will happen, such as, "when this business value is realized, a release will go live in the organization." It's tricky business, but it needs to be created to communicate what the project will accomplish and to ensure stakeholders that the project will create value in ratio to the cost and time needed for the project to exist.

Updating the Work Breakdown Structure

When creating the activity list, the project team and the project manager may discover discrepancies or inadequacies in the existing WBS. Updates to the WBS enable the project manager to ensure that all the needed project deliverables are included in the WBS and then to map the discovered deliverables to the identified work in the activity list. When you add items to the WBS, remember that you'll need to provide a change request. The change request must flow through integrated change control.

In addition, the elements within the WBS may not be defined fully or correctly. During the decomposition of the work, elements of the WBS may need to be updated to reflect the proper description of the elements. The descriptions should be complete and full and leave no room for ambiguity or misinterpretation. Finally, updates to the WBS may also include cost estimates to the discovered deliverables.

 NOTE Updates to the WBS are called *refinements*. As the project moves toward completion, refinements ensure that all the deliverables are accounted for within the WBS. They may also call for, indirectly, updates to the activity list.

Sequencing the Project Activities

Now that the activity list has been created, the activities must be arranged in a logical sequence. This process calls on the project manager and the project team to identify the logical relationships between activities, as well as the preferred relationship between those activities. This can be accomplished in a few different ways:

- **Computer-driven** Many different scheduling and project management software packages are available. These programs can help the project manager and the project team determine which actions need to happen in what order and with what level of discretion.

- **Manual process** In smaller projects, and on larger projects in the early phases, manual sequencing may be preferred. An advantage of manual sequencing is that it's easier to move around dependencies and activities than it is in some programs.

- **Blended approach** A combination of manual and computer-driven scheduling methods is fine. It's important to determine the correctness of the activity sequence, however. Sometimes a blended approach can be more complex than relying on just one or the other.

Considering the Inputs to Activity Sequencing

There are many approaches to completing activity sequencing. Perhaps the best approach, however, is activity sequencing that involves the entire project team, rather than being a solo activity. The project manager must rely on the project team and these inputs to activity sequencing:

- **Project management plan**   The schedule management plan is needed because it will direct how the activity sequence is to occur. The scope baseline is also needed because the project scope statement, WBS, and WBS dictionary will help identify the activities you're about to sequence.

- **Project documents**   From the project documents, you'll need the activity list, the list of actions needed to complete the project deliverables. You'll need the activity attributes, because each scheduled activity has attributes that need to be documented. For example, the successor and predecessor of each activity, the lead and lag information, and the person responsible for completing the activity should all be documented. This information is important when it comes to schedule development and project control. You'll also reference the assumptions log for identified assumptions about the project activities, and you'll also need the milestone list you've created.

- **Organizational process assets**   If you've done this type of work in the past, you can rely on historical information to help you sequence the current work.

- **Enterprise environmental factors**   Any rules or regulations that you must follow in your project's activity sequencing must be documented and upheld.

Creating Network Diagrams

Network diagrams help you visualize the project work. A network diagram shows the relationships between the work activities and how they will progress from start to completion. These diagrams can be extremely complex or easy to create and configure. Most network diagrams in today's project management environment use an approach called "activity-on-node" to illustrate the activities and the relationships among those activities.

 EXAM TIP   Older network diagramming methods used "activity-on-arrows" to represent the activities and their relationships. In the exam, don't be tempted to choose activity-on-arrows, because this diagramming method is long gone from the PMBOK.

Using the Precedence Diagramming Method

The precedence diagramming method (PDM) is the most common method of arranging the project work visually. The PDM puts the activities in boxes or circles, called *nodes*, and connects the boxes with lines. The lines represent the relationships and dependencies of the work packages. The following illustration shows a simple network diagram using PDM:

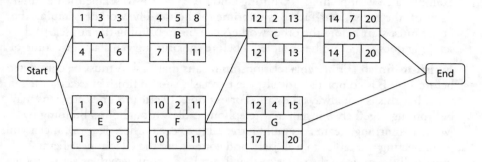

 NOTE PDM is the most common approach to network diagramming because it's used by most project management information systems. It can also be done manually, however.

Relationships between activities in a PDM constitute one of four different types (as shown in Figure 6-3):

- **Finish-to-start (FS)** This relationship means that Task A must be completed before Task B can begin. This is the most common relationship. For example, in a construction project, the foundation must be set before the framing can begin.

Figure 6-3
Task relationships can vary, but finish-to-start is the most common.

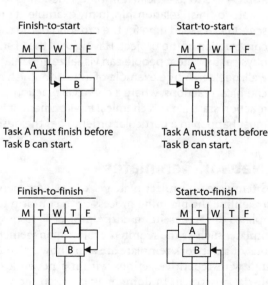

Finish-to-start

Task A must finish before Task B can start.

Start-to-start

Task A must start before Task B can start.

Finish-to-finish

Task A must finish before Task B can finish.

Start-to-finish

Task A must start before Task B can finish.

- **Start-to-start (SS)** This relationship means that Task A must start before Task B can start. This relationship enables both activities to happen in tandem. For example, a crew of painters is painting a house. Task A is to scrape the flecking paint off the house, and Task B is to prime the house. The workers scraping the house must start before the other workers can begin priming the house. All the scraping doesn't have to be completed before the priming can start, just some of it.

- **Finish-to-finish (FF)** This relationship means that Task A must be completed before Task B is completed. Ideally, the two tasks should finish at exactly the same time, but this is not always the case. For example, two teams of electricians may be working together to install new telephone cables throughout a building by Monday morning. Team A is pulling the cable to each office. Team B, meanwhile, is connecting the cables to wall jacks and connecting the telephones. Team A must pull the cable to the office so that Team B can complete their activity. The activities need to be completed at nearly the same time, by Monday morning, so that the new phones are functional.

- **Start-to-finish (SF)** This relationship is unusual and is rarely used. It requires that Task A start so that Task B may finish. Such relationships may be encountered in construction and manufacturing. It is also known as just-in-time (JIT) scheduling. An example is a construction of a shoe store. The end of the construction is soon, but an exact date is not known. The owner of the shoe store doesn't want to order the shoe inventory until the construction is nearly complete. The start of the construction tasks dictates when the inventory of the shoes is ordered.

NOTE I like to use the just-in-time scheduling as a practical way to describe a start-to-finish relationship. In my example, it's really some *soft logic* by the scheduler, as lead time for the ordering of the shoes could account for the construction of the project. Having said that, I still like to use something physical that most people can visualize and relate to. Now I'll get geeky—well, geekier. A true example of a start-to-finish relationship involves chemical reactions, where a chemical reaction cannot finish before another reaction starts. In this chemical environment, it is *hard logic*—the reaction must happen in a particular order to get the desired effect.

Utilizing Network Templates

As with WBS templates, a project manager can rely on network templates that may be available to streamline the planning process or to conform to a predetermined standard. Network templates can represent an entire project, if appropriate, although portions of a network template, such as the required project management activities, are common.

The portions of a network template are also known as *subnets* or *fragnets*. Subnets are often associated with repetitive actions within a network diagram. For example, each floor in a high-rise apartment building may undergo the same or similar actions during construction. Rather than complete the network diagram for each floor, a subnet can be implemented.

Determining the Activity Dependencies

The progression of the project is built on the sequence of activities. In other words, predecessor activities must be complete before successor activities can begin. The following are the dependencies you should know for your PMP exam:

- **Mandatory dependencies**   These dependencies are the natural order of activities. For example, you can't begin building your house until your foundation is in place. These relationships are called *hard logic*.

- **Discretionary dependencies**   These dependencies are the preferred order of activities. Project managers should use these relationships at their discretion and document the logic behind the decision. Discretionary dependencies enable activities to happen in a preferred order because of best practices or conditions unique to the project work, or because of external events. For example, a painting project typically allows the primer and the paint to be applied within hours of each other. Because of expected high humidity during the project, however, all of the building will be completely primed before the paint can be applied. These relationships are also known as *soft logic*, preferred logic, or preferential logic.

- **External dependencies**   As the name implies, these are dependencies outside of the project's control. Examples include the delivery of equipment from a vendor, the deliverable of another project, or the decision of a committee, a lawsuit, or an expected new law.

- **Internal dependencies**   Some relationships are internal to the project or the organization. For example, the project team must create the software as part of the project's deliverable before the software can be tested for quality control.

 EXAM COACH   You have dependencies for passing your PMI exam. It's mandatory that you apply for the exam. You've an external dependency with the PMI approving your application—it's somewhat out of your hands. You also have some discretionary dependencies, such as when you study, your mental attitude, and the order of the chapters you study. Take charge and keep pressing yourself toward passing the exam. You can do this!

Considering Leads and Lags

Leads and *lags* are values added to activities to alter the relationship slightly between two or more activities. For example, a finish-to-start relationship may exist between applying primer and applying the paint to a warehouse. The project manager in this scenario has decided to add one day of lead time to the activity of painting the warehouse. Now the painting can begin one day before the priming is scheduled to end. Lead time is considered a negative value, because time is subtracted from the downstream activity to bring it closer to the start of the project.

Lag time is waiting time. Imagine a project to install wood floors in an office building. Currently, there is a finish-to-start relationship between staining the floors and adding a layer of shellac to seal them. The project manager has elected, because of the humidity in the building, to add two days of lag time to the downstream activity of sealing the floors. Now the shellac cannot be applied immediately after the stain, but must wait two additional days. Lag time is considered a positive value, since time is added to the project schedule.

This illustration shows the difference between lead and lag times. Leads and lags must be considered in the project schedule, since an abundance of lag time can increase the project's duration. An abundance of lead time, while decreasing duration, may increase risks.

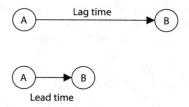

 EXAM TIP Remember that lead time is always "accelerated time" and is negative time, because the work is moving closer to the project start date. Lag time is always waiting time and is considered positive time, because the project manager is adding time to the project schedule.

Estimating Activity Durations

How many times have you heard management ask, "Now, how long will all of this take?" Countless times, right? And maybe right after that, "How much will all of this cost?" We'll talk about cost estimates in Chapter 7. For now, let's talk about time.

The answer to the question "How long will it take?" depends on the accuracy of the estimates, the consistency of the work, the project management life cycle approach, and other variables within the project. The best a project manager can do is to create honest estimates based on the information provided. Until the schedule is finalized, no one will know the duration of the project.

First, you identify the activities, then sequence the activities, then define the resources, and then estimate durations. These processes are needed to complete the project schedule and the project duration estimate. These four processes are iterated as more information becomes available. If the proposed schedule is acceptable, the project can move forward. If the proposed schedule is too long, the scheduler can use a few strategies to compress the project. We'll discuss the art of scheduling in the next section.

Activity duration estimates, like the activity list and the WBS, don't come from the project manager—they come from the people completing the work. The estimates may also undergo progressive elaboration. In this section, we'll examine the approach to completing activity duration estimates, the basis of these estimates, and how to allow for activity list updates.

Considering the Activity Duration Estimate Inputs

The importance of accurate estimates is paramount. The activity duration estimates will be used to create the project schedule and to predict when the project should end. Inaccurate estimates could cost the performing organization thousands of dollars in fines, missed opportunities, lost customers, or worse. To create accurate estimates, the project manager and the project team will rely on several inputs:

- **Project management plan** You'll need the schedule management plan and the scope baseline.

- **Activity lists** You know this, right? Activity lists are the work elements necessary to create the deliverables.

- **Activity attributes** *Effort* is the amount of labor applied to a task. *Duration*, on the other hand, is how long the task is expected to take with the given amount of labor. For example, a task to unload a freight truck may take eight hours with two people assigned to the task. If the effort is increased by adding more labor to the task (in this instance, more people), then the duration of the task is decreased. Some activities, however, have a fixed duration and are not affected by the amount of labor assigned to the task. For example, installing a piece of software on a computer will take the same amount of time if one computer administrator is completing the work or if two computer administrators are doing it.

- **Assumptions log** You'll need the assumptions log to reference any assumptions about the project work that may need to be challenged or studied at this portion of the project.

- **Lessons learned register** Activity duration information from past projects and past activities within a project may have lessons learned that you can reference for better planning in the current project.

- **Milestone list** The milestone list can help you identify and estimate activity durations for activities needed to reach the project milestones.

- **Project team assignments** The project team members who have been assigned to the project team are assigned roles to complete the project work.

- **Resource breakdown structure** This diagram shows a hierarchy of the resources, both physical resources and human resources, that are utilized on the project.

- **Resource requirements** Activity resource requirements define the resources (human or physical) needed to complete a particular activity. For example, a project to build a home will require lots of different resources: plumbers, electricians, architects, framers, and landscapers. The project manager would not, however, assign all the different resources to every task, but only to the tasks that the resource was qualified to complete. Remember that resources also include equipment and materials, so those are identified as part of the resource requirements as well.

- **Resource calendars** The project manager will need to know when resources are, or are not, available for utilization on the project.

- **Risk register** The risk register can help the project manager and the project team identify key activities and their associated risks. This information may influence the constraints and task relationships in the project. Should risks come true, there may also be consideration of the timing of risk responses. (I'll talk more about risk management in Chapter 11.)

- **Organizational process assets** Okay, the big one here is historical information. Historical information is always an excellent source of data on activity duration estimates. It can come from several sources, such as the following:

  - Historical information can come from project files on other projects within the organization.

  - Commercial duration-estimating databases can offer information on how long industry-specific activities should take. These databases should take into consideration the materials and the experience of the resources, and they should define the assumptions the predicted work duration is based upon.

  - Project team members may recollect information regarding the expected duration of activities. Though these inputs are valuable, they are generally less valuable than documented sources, such as other project files or the commercial databases.

- **Enterprise environmental factors** Your organization may require the project manager to use duration-estimating databases, productivity metrics based on your industry, or other commercially available information.

You'll need to consider the resource capabilities of your project team. Consider a task in an architectural firm. Reason says that a senior architect assigned to the task will complete it faster than a junior architect will. Material resources can also influence activity time. Consider predrilled cabinets versus cabinets that require the carpenter to drill into each cabinet as it's installed. The predrilled cabinets enable the job to be completed faster.

The project manager should also reference the project management plan. Specifically, the project manager and the project team must evaluate the risk register. Risks, good or bad, can influence the estimated duration of activities. The risks of each activity should be identified, analyzed, and then predicted as to their probability and impact. If risk mitigation tasks are added to the schedule, the mitigation activities will need their duration estimated and then sequenced into the schedule in the proper order. We'll discuss risk in detail in Chapter 11.

Using Analogous Estimating

Analogous estimating relies on historical information to predict current activity durations. Analogous estimating, also known as top-down estimating, is a form of expert judgment. To use analogous estimating, activities from the historical project that are similar in nature are used to predict similar activities in the current project.

A project manager must consider whether the work has been done before and, if so, what help the historical information provides. The project manager must consider the resources, project team members, and equipment that completed the activities in the previous project compared with the resources available for the current project. Ideally, the activities should be more than similar; they should be identical. And the resources that completed the work in the past should be the same resources used in completing the current work. When the only source of activity duration estimates is the project team members, instead of expert judgment and historical information, your estimates will be uncertain and inherently risky.

EXAM TIP   Remember that analogous estimating uses historical information and is more reliable than predictions from the project team members.

Applying Parametric Estimates

Quantitatively based durations use mathematical formulas to predict how long an activity will take based on the "quantities" of work to be completed. For example, a commercial printer needs to print 100,000 brochures. The workers include two press operators and two bindery experts to fold and package the brochures. The duration is how long the activity will take to complete, while the effort is the total number of hours (labor) invested because of the resources involved. The decomposed work, with quantitative factors, is shown in Table 6-1.

EXAM TIP   *Duration* is how long an activity takes, while *effort* is the billable time for the labor to complete the activity. You'll likely see questions dealing with these two terms on the exam, especially with regard to project costs. Consider, for example, an activity that is scheduled to last 40 hours. The project manager must consider the cost of the time of the person assigned to complete the project work. For example, a senior engineer may be able to complete the activity in 40 consecutive work hours, but the cost of this employee's time may be more than the value of the activity. A part-time employee may be able to complete the task in two segments of 20 hours, at a substantially lower rate.

Creating a Three-Point Estimate

How confident can a project manager be when it comes to estimating? If the project work has been done before in past projects, then the level of confidence in the duration estimate is probably high. But if the work has never been done before, there are lots of

Table 6-1 Decomposed Work with Quantitative Factors	Workers	Units per Hour	Duration for 100,000	Effort
	Press operators (two)	5000	20 hours	40 hours
	Bindery experts (two)	4000	25 hours	50 hours
	Totals		45 hours	90 hours

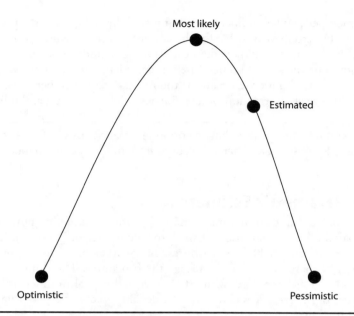

Figure 6-4 Three-point estimates use the formula (optimistic + most likely + pessimistic)/3 to estimate an activity's duration.

unknowns—and with them comes risk. To mitigate the risk, the project manager can use a *three-point estimate*. A three-point estimate requires that each activity have three estimates: optimistic, most likely, and pessimistic estimates. This is also known as simple averaging. Based on these three estimates, an average can be created to predict how long the activity should take (see Figure 6-4).

If you think this sounds familiar to the program evaluation and review technique (PERT), you're correct. The formula for PERT is similar to the three-point estimate. PERT is (Optimistic + (4 × Most Likely) + Pessimistic)/6. The denominator is 6 in PERT because you're using six factors. This is also known as weighted averaging. Triangular distribution is the average of the three factors. Beta distribution, which is PERT, uses a weight averaged for the most-likely time.

Estimating from the Bottom Up

If you were to start at a zero duration for your project and then began adding up the duration of each of the work packages, you'd be creating a bottom-up estimate. A bottom-up estimate is the most reliable type of duration estimate, because you are aggregating the predicted duration of each work package in the WBS. The challenge with a bottom-up estimate, however, is that you first need to create a WBS and the activity list in order to produce the estimate. That's right—before you can create a bottom-up estimate you must first have the WBS.

This creates challenges for project managers and stakeholders alike. The stakeholders, such as management, want you to tell them how long the project will take to complete—and they want that prediction right now. Project managers want to provide an accurate estimate, but to do so, they must first create the project scope statement, decompose that into the WBS, then break down the work packages into the activity list, and then begin adding up the duration—that's no quick and easy process.

The challenge is that, when there isn't much information, such as early in the planning stage, it's nearly impossible to provide an accurate duration estimate. Later in the planning stage, however, when the WBS is created, the project manager can provide a much more detailed duration estimate because there's more information available. In addition to this, you truly don't know how long (or really how much) a project will take (cost) until you've completed the project work—there's uncertainty in the endeavor. But, as you know, no stakeholder is going to take "I'll tell you how long the project takes to complete when I'm done" as an answer.

Factoring in Reserve Time

Parkinson's Law states that "Work expands so as to fill the time available for its completion." This little nugget of wisdom is oh-so-true. Consider a project team member who knows an activity should last 24 hours. The team member decides, in his own wisdom, to say that the activity will last 32 hours. These extra 8 hours, he figures, will allow plenty of time for the work to be completed should any unforeseen incidents pop up. The trouble is, however, that the task will magically expand to require the complete 32 hours. Why does this happen? Consider the following:

- **Hidden time**   Hidden time, the time factored in by the project team member, is secret. No one, especially the project manager, knows why the extra time has been factored into the activity. The team member can then "enjoy" the extra time to complete the task at his leisure.

- **Procrastination**   Most people put off starting a task until the last possible minute. The trouble with bloated, hidden time is that people may wait through the additional time they've secretly factored into the activity. Unfortunately, if something does go awry in completing the activity, the work result comes later than predicted.

- **Demands**   Project team members may be assigned to multiple projects with multiple demands. The requirement to move from project to project can shift focus, result in a loss of concentration, and require additional ramp-up time as workers shift from activity to activity. The demand for multitasking enables project team members to take advantage of hidden time.

- **On schedule**   Activities are typically completed on schedule or later, but rarely early. Workers who have bloated the activity duration estimates may finish their task ahead of when they promised, but they tend to hold onto those results until the activity's due date. This is because workers aren't usually rewarded for completing work early. In addition, workers don't want to reveal the inaccuracies in their time estimates. Workers may believe future estimates may be based on actual work durations rather than estimates, so they'll "sandbag" the results to protect themselves—and finish "on schedule."

So, what's a project manager to do? First off, the project manager should strive to incorporate historical information and expert judgment on which to predicate accurate estimates. Second, the project manager should stress a genuine need for accurate duration estimates. Finally, the project manager can incorporate a reserve time.

A *reserve time* is a percentage of the project duration or a preset number of work periods, and it is usually added to the end of the project schedule or just before project milestones. Reserve time may also be added to individual activity durations based on risk or uncertainty in the activity duration. When activities are completed late, the additional time for the activity is subtracted from the reserve time. As the project moves forward, the reserve time can be reduced or eliminated as the project manager sees fit. Reserve time decisions should be documented.

Evaluating the Estimates

Estimating activities provides three outputs:

- **Activity duration estimates**   Activity duration estimates reflect how long each activity will take to complete. Duration estimates should include an acknowledgment of the range of variance. For example, an activity whose duration is expected to be one week may have a range of variance of one week plus or minus three days. This means that the work can take up to eight days or as few as two days, assuming a five-day workweek.

- **Basis of estimates**   Any supporting detail and approach you utilized during the creation of the duration estimates should be documented. This includes not just the basis of your estimates, but any constraints or assumptions used, range of possible variations attached to your estimates, and your confidence level for the final duration estimate.

- **Project documents updates**   Activity attributes are updated with the duration estimates. The assumption log is updated to reflect any assumptions about the activities that may have been used to predict durations, such as resource availability. You might also need to update the lessons learned register with any effective methods you and your team have developed to improve duration predictions.

Predicting Duration in Agile Projects

Recall that agile projects use a fixed schedule and fixed budget. This means, for time, you've a deadline that's already been determined, likely by the business analyst, the product owner, or the customer. A deadline is just fine in adaptive projects—it's expected. Instead of all the upfront overhead of planning and analysis we see in predictive projects, the adaptive team gets to work creating value much quicker. The deadline simply means the team will create as much as it can from the most important items to the least important items in the project.

Well, customers may demand that all of the requirements need to be created by a given date, and that's not always realistic. Agile projects utilize user story sizing using the story points that rate the story size from extra small to extra large or by relative sizing using the Fibonacci sequence. The development team can take on only so much work in a sprint—the selected amount of story points they can feasibly accomplish. The amount of story points a team actually accomplishes is the velocity, and the higher the velocity, the quicker the team can finish the product backlog.

So if the product backlog has 645 user story points total and the team's velocity is 30 points per iteration, you can quickly calculate that it'll take 22 sprints to complete everything in the product backlog. If each sprint is four weeks, which is the typical case, you're looking at 88 weeks, not counting holidays and fluctuations in velocity. If the deadline is less than 88 weeks, either the lower prioritized items get lopped off from the product backlog, the deadline gets moved to a more realistic date, or the lower level items get shifted into a follow-up project.

 VIDEO   For a more detailed explanation, watch the *Agile Duration* video now.

Developing the Project Schedule

The project manager, the project team, and possibly even the key stakeholders will examine the inputs previously described and apply the techniques discussed in this section to create a feasible schedule for the project. The point of the project schedule is to complete the project scope in the shortest possible time without incurring exceptional costs or risks or a loss of quality.

Creating the project schedule is part of the planning process group. It is calendar-based and relies on both the project network diagram and the accuracy of time estimates. When the project manager creates the project schedule, she'll also reference the risk register. The identified risks and their associated responses can affect the sequence of the project work and when the project work can take place. In addition, if a risk comes to fruition, the risk event may affect the scheduling of the resources and the project completion date.

Applying Mathematical Analysis

Mathematical analysis is the process of factoring theoretical early and late start dates and theoretical early and late finish dates for each activity within the project network diagram (PND). The early and late dates are not the expected schedule, but rather a potential schedule based on the project constraints, the likelihood of success, the availability of resources, and other constraints.

The most common approach to calculating when a project may finish is by using the critical path method. It uses a "forward" and "backward" pass to reveal which activities are considered critical. Activities on the critical path may not be delayed; otherwise, the project end date will be delayed. The critical path is the path with the longest duration to completion. Activities not on the critical path have some float (also called slack) that allows some amount of delay without delaying the project end date.

EXAM TIP For the exam, remember that the critical path is used to determine which activities have no float. You can also use the critical path to determine the earliest date for when the project may be completed. There can be more than one critical path in a project, as two paths can have the same duration, and it's possible for the critical path to change. You should also understand the concepts of forward and backward passes and be able to find the critical path and float in a simple network diagram.

Calculating Float in a PND

Float, or slack, is the amount of time an activity can be delayed without postponing the project's completion. Technically, there are three different types of float:

- **Free float** This is the total time a single activity can be delayed without affecting the early start of any successor activities.
- **Total float** This is the total time an activity can be delayed without affecting project completion.
- **Project float** This is the total time the project can be delayed without passing the customer-expected completion date.
- **Negative total float** A constraint on an activity, such as the activity must start on a specific date, or a deadline for the project completion, can cause negative float. This means the activities on the critical path don't have enough time to meet the defined finish date for the project or the constrained activity.

NOTE There are a couple of different approaches to calculating float. I'm sharing the approach that I learned and that I think is the best approach. You may have learned a different method that you prefer. You won't hurt my feelings if you use your method to get the same result I get from my method.

Most project management software will automatically calculate float. On the PMP exam, however, candidates will be expected to calculate float manually. Don't worry—it's not too tough. The following describes the process.

You'll examine the PND and find the critical path. The critical path is typically the path with the longest duration and will always have zero float. The critical path is technically found once you complete the forward and backward passes. You start with the forward pass. After the backward pass, you can identify the critical and near-critical paths, as well as the float.

VIDEO For a more detailed explanation, watch the *Finding Float* video now.

1. The early start (ES) and early finish (EF) dates are calculated by first completing the forward pass. The ES of the first task is 1. The EF for the first task is its ES, plus the task duration, minus 1. Don't let the "minus 1 value" throw you. If Task A is scheduled to last three days, it would take only three days to complete the work, right? The ES is 1, the duration is 3, and the EF is 3, because the activity would finish within three days, not four days. The following illustration shows the start of the forward pass:

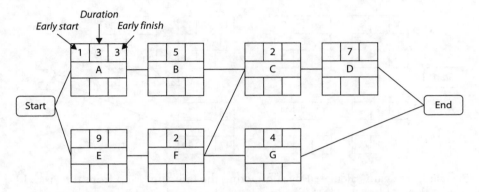

2. The ES of the next task(s) will be the EF for the previous activity, plus 1. In other words, if Task A finishes on day 3, Task B and Task C can begin on day 4.

3. The EF for the next task(s) equals its ES plus the task duration, minus 1. Sound familiar?

4. Now each task moves forward with the forward pass. Use caution when there are multiple predecessor activities; the EF with the largest value is carried forward. The following illustration shows the completed forward pass:

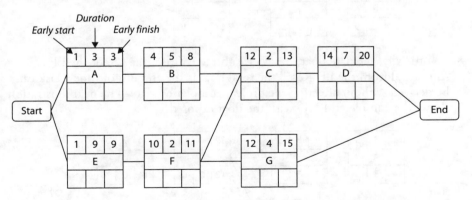

5. After the forward pass is completed, the backward pass starts at the end of the PND. The backward pass is concerned with the late finish (LF) and the late start (LS) of each activity. The LF for the last activity in the PND equals its EF value.

The LS is calculated by subtracting the duration of the activity from its LF and then adding 1. The 1 is added to accommodate the full day's work; it's just the opposite of subtracting the one day in the forward pass. Here's a tip: The last activity is on the critical path, so its LF will equal its EF.

6. The next predecessor activity's LF equals the LS of the successor activity, minus 1. In other words, if Task D has an LS of 14, Task C will have an LF of 13. The following illustration shows the process of the backward pass:

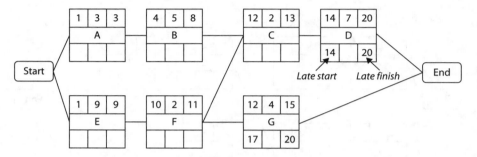

7. The LS is again calculated by subtracting the task's duration from the task's LF and then adding 1. The following shows the completed backward pass:

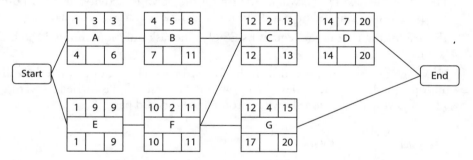

8. To officially calculate float, the ES is subtracted from the LS, or the EF is subtracted from the LF. Recall the total float is the amount of time a task can be delayed without affecting the project completion date. The next illustration shows the completed PND with the float exposed.

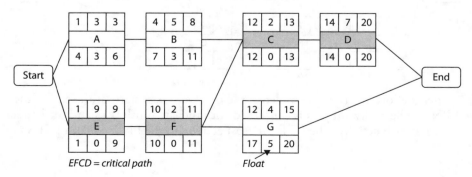

EFCD = critical path   Float

DIGITAL CONTENT I bet you're wishing you could try this one out for yourself, right? The Adobe PDF document titled "Chapter Six Float Exercise" includes a project network diagram that you can print and use to test your float-ability. You can also just create your own diagrams and practice finding float.

Encountering Scheduling on the PMP Exam

Out here in the real world, where you and I work every day, we likely aren't calculating float manually. On your PMI exam, however, you'll need to be able to calculate float. Why? You're proving that you understand the theory and application of managing project time. On your regular gig, you'll use your project management software to do this magic for you. You'll encounter float, scheduling, and critical path activities on the exam. You should count these questions as "gimmies" if you remember a few important rules:

- Always draw out the network diagram presented on your scratch paper. It may be used in several questions.

- Know how to calculate float. (The complete process was shown earlier in the "Calculating Float in a PND" section.)

- You may encounter questions that ask on what day of the week a project will end if no weekends or holidays are worked. No problem. Add up the critical path, divide by 5 (Monday through Friday), and then figure out on which day of the week the activity will end.

- You may see something like Figure 6-5 when it comes to scheduling. When three numbers are presented, think three-point estimate. Optimistic is the smallest number and pessimistic is the largest, so most likely, it's somewhere between the two. When a number is positioned directly over the tasks, it is the task duration. When a number is positioned to the upper-right of a task, this represents the EF date.

Figure 6-5
Scheduling follows many rules to arrive at a project completion date.

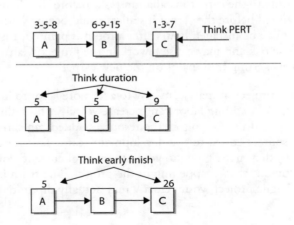

Applying Schedule Compression

Schedule compression is also a mathematical approach to scheduling. The trick with schedule compression, as its name implies, is calculating ways the project can get done sooner than expected. Consider a construction project slated to last eight months. Because of the expected cold and nasty weather typical of month seven, the project manager needs to rearrange activities, where possible, to end the project as soon as possible.

In some instances, the relationship between activities cannot be changed because of hard logic or external dependencies. The relationships are fixed and must remain as scheduled. Now consider the same construction company that is promised a bonus if they can complete the work by the end of month seven. Now there's incentive to complete the work, but there's also the fixed relationship between activities.

To apply duration compression, the performing organization can rely on two different methods. These methods can be used independently or together and are applied to activities or to the entire project based on need, risk, and cost:

- **Crashing** This approach adds more resources to activities on the critical path to complete the project earlier. In the crashing process, costs grow as resources are added. Crashing doesn't always work. Consider activities that have a fixed duration and won't finish faster with additional resources. The project manager must also consider the expenses in relation to the gains of completing on time. For example, a construction company may have been promised a bonus to complete the work by a preset date, but the cost incurred to hit the targeted date may be more than the bonus.

- **Fast tracking** This method changes the relationship of activities. With fast tracking, activities that would normally be done in sequence are done in parallel or with some overlap. Fast tracking can be accomplished by changing the relation of activities from FS (finish-to-start) to SS (start-to-start) or by adding lead time to downstream activities. For example, a construction company could change the relationship between painting the rooms and installing the carpet by adding lead time to the carpet installation task. Before the change, all the rooms had to be painted before the carpet installers could begin. With the added lead time, the carpet can be installed hours after a room is painted. Fast tracking can, however, increase risk and may cause rework in the project. Can't you just imagine those workers getting fresh paint on the new carpet?

In an agile project, it may seem easy to add more labor to increase velocity. Well, hold on, professor. Yes, adding labor can increase velocity and reduce the overall duration of the project if, and this is a big if, the resources added can actually contribute. You need the right resources added to the development team. This means the resources have the needed skills, they aren't going to get in the way of current work, and they can get up to speed quickly on what's happening in the project. The truth is, when you add labor to, or crash, an agile project, your velocity may actually dip initially, because it'll take some time for the new resources to overcome the learning curve. The new resources will need some coaching, they'll need to get acclimated to the project work, and they'll need to learn who's who and where stuff is. Crashing in Agile isn't as easy as adding painters to paint the wall.

 EXAM TIP For the exam, it's easy to remember the difference between these two actions. Crashing and cost both begin with C—we're adding resources, and too many people will "crash" into each other. Fast tracking is about speeding things up. However, haste can be risky.

Using a Project Simulation

Project simulations enable a project manager to examine the feasibility of the project schedule under different conditions, variables, and events. You can play "what-if" scenarios with your project. For example, the project manager can imagine the circumstances if activities were delayed, if vendors missed shipment dates, or if external events affected the project.

Simulations are often completed by use of *Monte Carlo analysis*. Named for the world-famous gambling district of Monaco, Monte Carlo analysis predicts how scenarios may work out, given any number of variables. The process doesn't actually churn out a specific answer, but a range of possible answers. When Monte Carlo is applied to a schedule, it can examine, for example, the optimistic completion date, the pessimistic completion date, and the most likely completion date for each activity in the project.

As you can imagine, in a typical network diagram, there are likely thousands, if not millions, of combinations of tasks that complete early, late, or as expected. Monte Carlo analysis shuffles these combinations, usually through computer software, and offers a range of possible end dates coupled with an expected probability for achieving each end date. In other words, Monte Carlo analysis is an odds-maker. The project manager chooses, or is at least influenced by, the end date with the highest odds of completion in ratio to the demands for completion by an expected time. The project manager can then predict with some certainty that, for example, the project has an 85 percent chance of completion by a specific date.

 NOTE Monte Carlo analysis can be applied to more than just scheduling. It can also be applied to cost, project variables, and, most often, to risk analysis.

Simulations also provide time to factor in "what-if" questions, worst-case scenarios, and potential disasters. The end result of simulations is to create responses to the feasible situations. Then, should the situations come into play, the project team is ready with a planned response.

Using Resource-Leveling Heuristics

First off, a *heuristic* is a fancy way of saying "rule of thumb." A resource-leveling heuristic is a method to flatten the schedule when resources are overallocated. Resource leveling can be applied using different methods to accomplish different goals. One of the most common methods is to ensure that workers are not overextended on activities.

Resource leveling usually limits the total amount of labor a resource can contribute in a given period. For example, you may have a constraint that limits your project team members to 25 hours per week on your project. If you've created a schedule that requires your project team members to work 40 hours per week on your project, then each team member is now overallocated on your project by 15 hours. So now you have to lop off 15 hours per week per resource, which increases the total duration of your project. There won't be more hours of labor, but it'll take longer on the calendar to do the same amount of work.

Another method for resource leveling is to take resources off noncritical path activities and apply them to critical path activities to ensure that the project end date is met. This method takes advantage of available slack and balances the expected duration of the noncritical path with the expected duration of the critical path. When you're doing resource leveling on noncritical path activities, it's also known as *resource smoothing*.

Finally, some resources may be scarce to the project. Consider a highly skilled technician or consultant who is available to contribute to the project on a particular date only. These resources are scheduled from the project end date, rather than from the start date. This is known as *reverse resource-allocation scheduling*.

Using Project Management Software

When it comes to project management software, take your pick: the market is full of choices. Project management applications are tools, not replacements, for the project management processes. Many of the software tools today automate the processes of scheduling, activity sequencing, work authorization, and other activities. The performing organization must weigh the cost of the PMIS (project management information system) against the benefits the project managers will actually see. In an agile environment, you'll also complete release planning. This is where you'll predict when the releases of the software or product of your project will be published. The release schedule will often be between three and six months, and this is decided early in the project.

Relying on a Project Coding Structure

The coding structure identifies the work packages within the WBS and is then applied to the PND. This enables the project manager, the project team, experts, and even key stakeholders to extract areas of the project to examine and evaluate. For example, a project to create a catalog for a parts distributor may follow multiple paths to completion. Each path to completion has its own "family" of numbers that relate to each activity on the path, as outlined in Table 6-2.

Table 6-2
Possible Paths
in Creating a
Catalog

Path	Coding for Path	Typical Activities
Artwork	4.2	Concept (4.2.1) Logos (4.2.2) Font design (4.2.3)
Photography	4.3	Product models (4.3.1) Airbrushing (4.3.2) Selection (4.3.3)
Content	4.4	Message (4.4.1) Copywriting (4.4.2) Editing (4.4.3) Rewrites (4.4.4)
Print	4.5	Signatures (4.5.1) Plates (4.5.2) Four-color printing (4.5.3)
Bind	4.6	Assembly (4.6.1) Bindery (4.6.2) Trimming (4.6.3) Shrink-wrap (4.6.4)
Distribution	4.7	Packaging (4.7.1) Labeling (4.7.2) Shipping (4.7.3)

Considering the Outputs of Schedule Development

After dealing with all the challenges of examining, sequencing, and calculating the project activities, you'll create a working schedule. Schedule development, like most project management planning processes, moves through progressive elaboration. As the project moves forward, discoveries, risk events, or other conditions may require the project schedule to be adjusted. In this section, we'll discuss the project schedule and how it is managed.

Reviewing the Schedule Baseline

Once the schedule model has been created and approved by the appropriate stakeholders, it becomes the *schedule baseline*. The baseline is what you believe will happen with the project's timeline. Once the schedule baseline is agreed upon and approved, it cannot be changed without passing through integrated change control. The actual duration and completion of activities are tracked throughout the project and compared to the schedule baseline for any variances. The schedule is part of the overall project management plan.

Examining the Project Schedule

The project schedule includes, at a minimum, a date when the project begins and a date when the project is expected to end. The project schedule is considered "proposed" until the resources needed to complete the project work are ascertained. In addition to the schedule, the project manager should include all the supporting details. Project schedules can be presented in many different formats, including the following:

- **Project network diagram (PND)**   This illustrates the flow of work, the relationships among activities, the critical path, and the expected project end date. PNDs, when used as the project schedule, should have dates associated with each project activity to show when the activity is expected to start and end.
- **Bar charts**   These show the start and end dates for the project and the activity duration against a calendar. They are easy to read. Scheduling bar charts are also called Gantt charts.
- **Milestone charts**   These plot the high-level deliverables and external interfaces, such as a customer walkthrough, against a calendar. Milestone charts are similar to Gantt charts, but with less detail regarding individual activities. The following is an example of a milestone chart:

Milestone	July	Aug	Sep	Oct	Nov	Dec
Customer sign-off	△ ▼					
Architect signature		△	▼			
Foundation			△			
Framing					△ ▼	
Roofing						△

Legend	△ Planned
	▼ Actual

Utilizing the Schedule Management Plan

The schedule management plan is a subsidiary plan of the overall project plan. It is used to control changes to the schedule. A formal schedule management plan has procedures that control how changes to the project plan can be proposed, accounted for, and then implemented. An informal schedule management plan may consider changes on an instance-by-instance basis. A change request is needed to update the schedule baseline, the schedule management plan, or any component of the project management plan.

I know we've not really talked about costs just yet—that's in the next chapter—but it's directly tied to scheduling in project management. You must consider several elements of the project's cost management plan when it comes to project scheduling. First, like the schedule baseline, you'll be creating a cost baseline. The cost baseline will reflect how much the project will cost, but also the cumulative totals of the costs as the project moves forward. You might also, depending on project duration, have to predict when capital expenses will occur for cash-flow planning for your organization. Things like expensive pieces of equipment, procurement planning, and vendor payments are all tied to scheduling. For now, know that the cost baseline, the cost management plan, and project scheduling are all related.

Updating the Resource Requirements

As a result of resource leveling, more resources may need to be added to the project. For example, a proposed leveling may extend the project beyond an acceptable completion date. To reach the project end date, the project manager elects to add resources to the critical path activities. The resources added by the project manager should be documented, the associated costs accounted for, and everything approved.

Controlling the Project Schedule

Schedule control is part of integrated change management, as discussed in Chapter 4. Throughout a typical project, events may require updates to the project schedule. Schedule control is concerned with three primary actions:

- The project manager works with the factors that can cause changes in the schedule in an effort to confirm that the changes are agreed upon. Factors can include project team members, stakeholders, management, customers, and project conditions.

- The project manager examines the work results and conditions to determine whether the schedule has changed.

- The project manager manages the actual change in the schedule.

Managing the Inputs to Schedule Control

Schedule control, the process of managing changes to the project schedule, is based on several inputs:

- Project management plan, specifically the schedule management plan, schedule baseline, scope baseline, and the performance measurement baseline
- Project documents, specifically the lessons learned register, project calendars, project schedule, resource calendars, and schedule data
- Work performance data
- Organizational process assets

Applying Schedule Control

Schedule control is a formal approach to managing changes to the project schedule. It considers the conditions, reasons, requests, costs, and risks of making changes. It includes methods of tracking changes, approval levels based on thresholds, and the documentation of approved or declined changes. The schedule change control activities are part of integrated change management.

Measuring Project Performance

Poor performance may result in schedule changes. Consider a project team that is completing its work on time, but all of the work results are unacceptable. The project team may be rushing through their assignments to meet their deadlines. To compensate for this, the project may be changed to allow for additional quality inspections and more time for activity completion. Project performance is often based on earned value management, which we'll discuss in Chapter 7.

Examining the Schedule Variance

The project manager must actively monitor the variances between when activities are scheduled to end and when they actually end. An accumulation of differences between scheduled and actual dates may result in a schedule variance.

The project manager must also pay attention to the completion of activities on paths with float, not just the critical path. Consider a project that has eight different paths to completion. The project manager should first identify the critical path, but she should also identify the float on each path. The paths should be arranged and monitored in a hierarchy from the path with the smallest float to the path with the largest float. As activities are completed, the float of each path should be monitored to identify any paths that may be slipping from the scheduled end dates.

Creating Burndown and Burnup Chart

Though burndown charts are typically used in agile projects, you can use them to illustrate the amount of work left to do in the project or iteration. Burndown charts, such as the one shown in Figure 6-6, start in the upper left corner and predict the amount

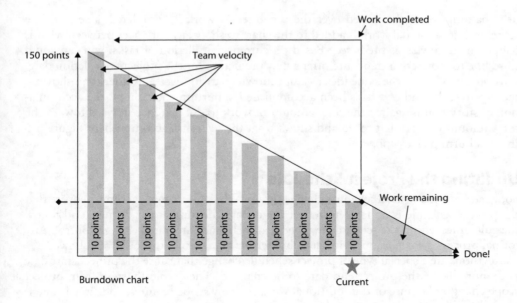

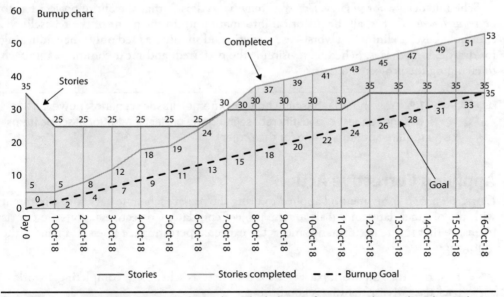

Figure 6-6 Burndown and burnup charts show the balance of activities, the predicted completion of activities, and the forecast for when activities are likely to be finished.

of remaining work distributed over the timeline. As work is completed, a second line representing the actual work is added to the chart to show any variances between what is happening and what is predicted. Based on current completion of tasks, you can add a third line to represent a trend and offer a new prediction for the project completion date.

A burnup chart is the same idea as a burndown chart in reverse. Rather than showing the downward trend of what's been accomplished, a burnup chart shows the accumulation of story points against the total amount of work to do. It trends upward toward the total amount of work left to do and shows what the team has accomplished. Figure 6-6 shows a burnup chart too.

Updating the Project Schedule

So, what happens when a schedule change occurs? The project manager must ensure that the project schedule is updated to reflect the change, document the change, and follow the guidelines within the schedule management plan and integrated change control. Any formal processes, such as notifying stakeholders or management, should be followed.

Revisions are a special type of project schedule change that cause the project start date and, more likely, the project end date to be changed. They typically stem from project scope changes. Because of the additional work the new scope requires, additional time is needed to complete the project.

Schedule delays, for whatever reason, may be so drastic that the entire project has to be *rebaselined*—that is, all the historical information up to the point of the rebaseline is eliminated. Rebaselining is a worst-case scenario and should be used only when adjusting for drastic, long delays. Schedule revision is the preferred, and most common, approach to changing the project end date.

 TIP You should rebaseline only in extreme, drastic scenarios; however, a change request can justify rebaselining the project if additional scope items require additional time for the project.

Applying Corrective Action

Corrective action is any method applied to bring the project schedule back into alignment with the original dates and goals for the project end date. Corrective actions are efforts to ensure that future performance meets the expected performance levels. It includes the following:

- Ensuring that the work packages are complete as scheduled; completing a work package early isn't always a good thing
- Extraordinary measures to ensure that work packages complete with as little delay as possible
- Root-cause analysis of schedule variances
- Measures to recover from schedule delays

Chapter Summary

All projects take time—time to plan the project, do the work, control the work, and confirm that the work has been done according to plan. Of course, there are many other things that eat into a project's schedule: change request reviews, corrective and preventive actions, defect repair, defect repair review, and scope verification. When a project manager first looks at planning the project work, she and her project team will consider all the activities that will need to be completed based on the project WBS.

Once all the project work has been identified and the activity list has been generated, it's time to put the activities into the order necessary to reach the project completion. This means the activity attributes are considered. Activities that must happen in a particular order use hard logic, whereas activities that don't have to happen sequentially can use soft logic. The sequencing of the project activities happens with the project management team.

Putting the activities in the order in which they'll happen leads to the creation of a project network diagram. It's pretty. The PND most likely will be using the precedence diagramming method—that's where you can clearly identify the predecessors and successors within the project. The relationships between the activities signal the conditions that must be true to allow the work to progress.

Adaptive projects work with a predefined end date. The velocity of the development team against the amount of user story points in the product backlog determine how quickly the project can reach business value. The better the velocity, which will normalize over time, the faster the team can create the items in the product backlog. Kanban boards are useful to show what's in the project queue and help the team control the work in progress. Because agile projects work from the most important items in the product backlog to the least important items, it's often okay if the team can't realistically get everything done. I say "often" because stakeholders may demand that everything be done, and that will mean more time, more money, and more realistic expectations.

Once the work has been organized and visualized, it's time to staff it. This is project resource estimating, which also contributes to the cost of the project. Resource utilization considers not only the people that your project will need, but also the materials and equipment. This activity considers the quantity of resources the project demands and when the resources are available. This is a tricky business in large projects, so rolling wave planning may be incorporated into the project.

Of course, management and the project stakeholders will want to know how long the project work will take to complete. After the network diagram has been created and the resources have been identified, the project management team can more accurately estimate the project duration. The project manager can use the identified labor, which is commonly done, or the project manager can rely on analogous estimating, which isn't as accurate as bottom-up estimating. In some instances, the project manager can also use parametric estimating to predict the project duration.

As the project manager examines the network diagram, he'll want to find opportunities to shift resources and determine where delays will affect the project end date. Of course, I'm talking about the critical path—the path with no float and with activities that cannot, better not, be delayed, or the project end date will go beyond what's been scheduled. Activities not on the critical path have float and can often be delayed if needed. You'll see a few questions on float on the exam, and I encourage you to watch the video referenced in this chapter to nail down the float process.

A project manager must control the project schedule. Sometimes this means compressing the project schedule. Recall that crashing adds resources to the project work, but crashing adds cost. The project manager can crash the project work only if the activities are effort-driven. Activities that are of fixed duration, such as printing a million booklets on a particular printing press, won't get done faster just because the project manager adds labor to the activities. The printing press can print only so many booklets per hour. Other activities can benefit from fast tracking; this approach enables phases to overlap but increases the project risk.

Questions

1. You are the project manager of the HGF Project. You would like to use a portion of the activity list from the HGB Project, which is similar to your current project. The portion of the activity list from the HGB Project is best described as which one of the following?

   A. Rolling wave planning

   B. Analogous estimating

   C. A template

   D. Expert judgment

2. You are the project manager of a large project for your organization. Much of the project will center on new software that you'll be installing on 4,500 laptops in stages. Because of the likelihood of change, you've recommended a rolling wave planning approach. Which one of the following is the best example of rolling wave planning?

   A. Using expert judgment for the current project

   B. Using a portion of the activity list from a previous project

   C. Breaking down the project scope

   D. Planning the immediate portions of the project in detail and the future project portions at a higher level

3. You are the project manager for your organization and you're serving as a scrum master in the project. You would like to create a chart that shows the balance of user story points in the product backlog against the number of iterations and velocity of the development team. What chart should you create?

   A. Pareto chart

   B. Burndown chart

    C. Kanban board

    D. Velocity tracking chart

4. You and the project team have created the work breakdown structure based on the project scope and requirements. Your next step is to create the project's activity list. Which one of the following will not be included in the activity list created with the project management team?

    A. Activities that are not part of the project scope

    B. Quality control activities

    C. Activities to create the work packages

    D. Physical terms, such as linear feet of pipe to be installed

5. Mary has created an activity list with her project team. She has included activity attributes for each of the activities in her project activity list. Of the following, which one is not an example of an activity attribute that Mary likely included?

    A. Scope validation

    B. Predecessor activities

    C. Leads and lags

    D. Geographic area where the work must take place

6. Why do adaptive projects create value much faster than predictive projects do?

    A. Because the development team gets into execution faster than predictive teams.

    B. Because the development teams have less administrative overhead than predictive teams.

    C. Because adaptive projects are generally used for projects with smaller scope.

    D. Because adaptive projects have no schedule and don't plan like predictive projects do.

7. You are working with your project team to schedule activities for your construction project. You have scheduled the painting activity to be completed before the carpet installation activity may begin. The relationship between the painting activity and carpet installation activity can best be described as which one of the following?

    A. Lag

    B. Lead

    C. Finish-to-start

    D. Start-to-finish

8. You are the project manager for your organization, and the following illustration represents your project. Based on the following illustration, how long will the project last?

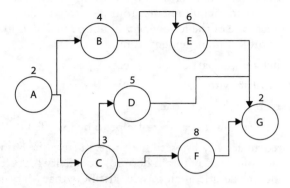

    A. 15 days

    B. 12 days

    C. 14 days

    D. 41 days

9. Beth is the project manager of her company and she's asked you to help her with project schedule network analysis. Examine the following illustration. If Activity B is delayed by two days, how late will the project be?

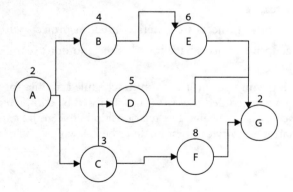

    A. The project will not be late because Activity B may use float.

    B. The project will be late by one day.

    C. The project will be late by two days.

    D. The project will be late by four days.

10. Ronald is the project manager for his company. He has created a project network diagram for the activities in the activity list and he's trying now to begin the process of float determination. He's asked for your help. Examine the following illustration. Which path is the critical path?

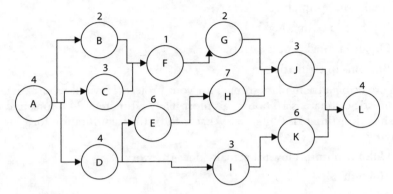

   A. ABFGJL

   B. ACFGJL

   C. ADEHJL

   D. ADIKL

11. Consider a project that has 420 user story points left in the product backlog. The team's velocity is 30. If each sprint of the Scrum project lasts four weeks, how much longer will this project likely last?

   A. 14 weeks

   B. 56 weeks

   C. 49 weeks

   D. It's impossible to predict as agile projects change frequently

12. Mike, a project manager in your company, is falling behind on the project schedule. He has elected to crash the project. What is crashing?

   A. Adding lag time between all project activities

   B. Adding lead time between all project activities

   C. Adding additional project resources to the project work

   D. Removing all unneeded project deliverables

13. You are the project manager of the PJG Project for your company. This project is similar to a project you completed a few months ago, and you'd like to reference the older project for information. Which estimating technique uses a similar project to predict how long the current project will take to complete?

   A. Analogous estimating

   B. Parametric estimating

   C. Organizational process assets

   D. Bottom-up estimating

14. You are using a triangular estimate for your project. Howard reports that his optimistic estimate is 16 hours, his most likely estimate is 24 hours, and the pessimistic estimate is 65 hours. What is the estimated duration for Howard's activity?

   A. Unknown until Howard actually does the work

   B. 105 hours

   C. 24 hours

   D. 35 hours

15. The framing activity cannot begin until the concrete has cured for 36 hours. The time between the concrete activity and the framing activity is best described as which one of the following?

   A. Hard logic

   B. Lag time

   C. Lead time

   D. Finish-to-start relationship

16. You are the project manager of the Data Warehouse Project. You've just recently created the project network diagram and you now want to identify the critical path. Which one of the following best describes the critical path?

   A. It is always one path with no float.

   B. It determines the earliest the project can finish.

   C. It has the most activities.

   D. It has the most important project activities.

17. Management has asked that you create the schedule management plan to identify the different processes and procedures your project will require. During the creation of the plan, you need to identify schedule change control and its components. Schedule change control is part of which project management process?

   A. Change control

   B. Cost control

   C. WBS refinements

   D. Integrated change control

18. Terry is the project manager of the network update project, and the project stakeholders have requested that four new servers be added to the project. This addition will cause changes in the project costs and schedule. Which process can manage changes to the project schedule?

   A. Change control system

   B. Schedule change control system

   C. Integrated change control

   D. Change control board

19. Which schedule development tool does not consider the availability of the project resources but instead considers when the work may take place in the project?

   A. The critical path method

   B. The critical chain method

   C. Schedule compression

   D. Arrow on the node method

20. You are working with your project team to respond to some delays in the project schedule. You have elected to crash the project schedule, and management wants to know what effect this will have on the project as a whole. What happens when a project manager elects to crash a project?

   A. The project will end early.

   B. The project will end on time.

   C. The project costs will increase.

   D. The project team morale will decrease.

Answers

   1. C. This is an example of using the previous project as a template. A is incorrect because rolling wave planning describes the detailed planning of the imminent project work, and the high-level planning of work that is further away in the project schedule. B is incorrect because analogous estimating describes the method of using a similar project to create the current project's time and/or cost estimate. D is incorrect because expert judgment is using an expert to provide needed information for the current project.

   2. D. Rolling wave planning is the planning of the immediate portions of the project in detail and the future work at a higher level. A is incorrect because expert judgment is using an expert to help the project manager make informed decisions within the project. B is incorrect because it describes using a template for the current project. C is incorrect because it describes the process of creating the WBS by breaking down the project scope.

3. **B.** You should create a burndown chart. A burndown chart shows the number of user story points in the product backlog and shows how many iterations the development team has completed. In each iteration, you'll track the velocity of the team against the planned velocity to show any variances. Over time, you'll see a downward trend signifying the diminishment of total user stories left in the product backlog. A is incorrect because a Pareto chart shows categories of failure from greatest to smallest. C is incorrect because a Kanban board shows the work in queue and the status of the work as it moves through the project phases until completion. D is incorrect because there is no such thing as a velocity tracking chart.

4. **A.** The activity list must not include any activities that are not part of the project scope. B, C, and D are incorrect because these activities and terms are included in the activity list.

5. **A.** Scope validation leads to acceptance decisions with the project customer, but it is not part of the activity attributes. B, C, and D are incorrect because they are all part of the activity attributes that Mary may include.

6. **A.** Adaptive projects do create value faster than predictive projects do because there is less upfront planning and overhead in an adaptive project. This enables the development team to get directly into execution on the most important items in the project scope based on the product backlog. B is incorrect because, although it may be true that adaptive teams have less administrative overhead than predictive projects, the best answer is that the development team can get right to work on the project scope. C is incorrect because adaptive projects do not have to be used for smaller scope projects. Adaptive projects can be large or small. D is incorrect because adaptive projects do follow a schedule, just not the same type of schedule as predictive projects follow. In addition, adaptive projects do complete planning, but they don't follow the same approach used in predictive projects.

7. **C.** The painting activity must finish first, and then the carpet installation activity can begin. A, lag, is incorrect because this describes the waiting time between project activities. B, lead, is incorrect because this describes a schedule compression technique to move project activities closer together. D, start-to-finish, is a relationship between activities, typically used in just-in-time scheduling, but that is not what is described in this example.

8. **A.** The project will last 15 days. The path ACFG is the critical path that will take 15 days to complete. B and C are incorrect because they are both representative of paths that are less than the critical path. D, 41 days, is incorrect because it is the sum of the number of days of labor if you added the duration of each project activity in the project. The total of 41 days, however, is not an accurate calculation of the total number of days to complete the project based on the critical path.

9. **B.** If Activity B is delayed by two days, the total duration of the project changes to 16 total days—one more day than the critical path will allow. A, C, and D are incorrect calculations for this project. For more information, see the *PMBOK Guide*, Section 6.5.2.2.

10. C. ADEHJL is the critical path because this one takes the longest to complete. A, B, and D are incorrect because these are examples of paths that have float, not the critical path.

11. B. The project will last 56 weeks. This is determined by taking the total number of user stories remaining in the product backlog, which is 420, and dividing by the velocity, which is 30. This number is the number of remaining sprints in the project, which is 14. If each sprint lasts four weeks, the project will last 56 weeks. A is incorrect because 14 represents the number of sprints remaining in the Scrum project. C is incorrect because this is not a valid calculation. D is incorrect because agile projects do change frequently, but based on current conditions, 56 weeks is the likely duration.

12. C. Crashing is when a project manager elects to add resources to the project work in an attempt to compress the project schedule. Crashing adds costs to the project. A is incorrect because adding lag time would cause the project duration to increase. B, adding lead time, is an example of fast tracking. D is not a valid choice.

13. A. Analogous estimating uses an analogy between similar projects to determine the current project's duration. B, parametric estimating, uses a parameter—such as 10 hours per unit installed—to predict the project duration. C is not a valid answer. D, bottom-up estimating, accounts for every work package in the WBS and the total amount of time for each deliverable. It is the most reliable time-estimating technique, but also takes the longest to create.

14. D. A triangular, or three-point, estimate takes the sum of the optimistic, pessimistic, and most likely estimates and divides it by 3: $(16 + 24 + 65)/3 = 35$. A, B, and C are incorrect answers for this three-point estimate.

15. B. The framing activity cannot begin immediately after the concrete activity; there is waiting time, which is commonly known as lag time. A, hard logic, describes the order in which activities must happen; it does not describe the time between activities. C, lead time, is incorrect because it would actually allow activities to overlap. D, finish-to-start, is incorrect because, although it does describe the relationship between the concrete and the framing activities, it does not answer the question.

16. B. The critical path reveals the earliest that a project may finish. This question tricks many project managers as they often think the critical path shows only the latest a project may finish. Remember that the forward pass shows the early finish and the late finish for a project. A is incorrect because the project may have more than one critical path if two or more paths have the same duration, so it's not always just one path. C is incorrect because the critical path may have fewer activities than other paths in the project, but may still take longer to complete. D is incorrect because the critical path does not reflect the importance of the path's activities, just their duration.

17. **D.** Schedule change control is part of the integrated change control process. A, B, and C are incorrect because they do not completely answer the question.

18. **C.** In the integrated change control process, all changes from any area of the project must flow through integrated change control. A, the change control system, isn't a valid system in a project. B, the schedule change control system, is also not a valid component of project management. D, the change control board, may be utilized, but it is not a process, so this choice is incorrect.

19. **A.** The critical path method considers only when the work may take place and not the availability of the resources. B, the critical chain method, is incorrect because it does consider when the resources are available. C and D are not valid choices for this question.

20. **C.** Crashing adds cost to the project because it adds labor, and labor costs money. A and B are incorrect because crashing a project does not necessarily ensure that the project will end early or on time. D is incorrect because there's not enough information in the question to determine whether the team morale will decrease if the project manager elects to crash the project.

Managing Project Costs

In this chapter, you will

- Plan for project cost management
- Estimate the project costs
- Administer the project budget
- Manage project cost control
- Work with earned value management

Money. Cash. Greenbacks. Dead presidents. They're all the same when you get down to it, and all are required to move projects from start to completion. It's often the project manager's job to estimate, control, and account for the finances a project demands. Projects consume the project budget during execution, when all those project management plans we've discussed are put into action. The project budget is monitored and controlled during, well, the monitoring and controlling processes. Project cost management is all about how much the resources—physical and human resources—will cost to complete the project.

What's that you say? You don't have any control over the monies your project requires? Management gives you a predetermined budget, and it's up to you to make it all work out? Yikes! Financing is always one of the scariest things I hear about with regard to project management. Or is it? If management's decision is based on previous projects, business analysts' research, or should-cost estimates from experts, then it's not so scary. I'll give you this much, however: a predetermined project budget is always a constraint, and it's rarely fun for the project manager.

And what about those projects that don't have any monies assigned to the project work? You know, the projects for which the project scope is completed just by the project team's work, and there really aren't any materials or items to purchase? Well, there are still costs associated with these projects, because someone, somewhere, is paying for the project team's time. Salaries can also be considered a project cost. After all, time is money.

Adaptive projects don't manage money the same way predictive projects do. For adaptive projects, generally speaking, a predetermined amount of funds (and time) is available to the project, and this amount is considered fixed. It's the total amount of monies available to complete the project work. So then the question isn't, "How much will this ice cream cost?" but rather, "How much ice cream can I get for this much money?" A fixed budget actually works out really nicely in adaptive projects, because it's one less thing that can cause an agile project manager to lose sleep over.

 VIDEO   For a more detailed explanation of project management costs, watch the *Cost Management for Adaptive Projects* video now.

Finally—and here's the big whammy—it doesn't really matter where your project monies come from, whether you actually control them, and what processes your organization uses to spend them. Your PMP exam requires that you understand all of the appropriate processes and procedures regarding how projects are estimated, budgeted, and then financially controlled. And that's what we'll discuss in this chapter.

There are four primary processes you'll be tested on when it comes to project cost management: planning cost management, cost estimating, cost budgeting, and cost controlling. Isn't that reassuring? Your PMI exam will, no doubt, have questions on costs, but so much of the content of this chapter refers to your *enterprise environmental factors*. (Remember that term? It's how your company does business.) Your cost management plan defines and outlines your organization's and project's procedures for cost management and control. I'll not pass the buck anymore. Let's go through this chapter like a wad of cash at an all-night flea market.

Planning for Project Cost Management

In a predictive project, you need a plan just for project costs. You need a plan that helps you define what policies you and the project team must adhere to regarding costs, what documents determine how you get to spend project money, and what inputs indicate how cost management will happen throughout your entire project. Well, you're in luck! This plan, a subsidiary plan of the project management plan, is the cost management plan.

As with most subsidiary plans, you can use a template from past projects, your project management office, or your program manager to build a plan that's specific to your project. Or, if you really must, you can create a cost management plan from scratch. It's not much fun, but I'll show you how to do it. You'll also need to know the business of preparing this cost management plan for your PMI examination—you'll certainly have some questions about what's included in the plan and how you and the project team work together to build the plan and execute it throughout the project.

Preparing the Cost Management Plan

To prepare to complete the process of cost management planning, you'll need four inputs:

- Project charter
- Project management plan, specifically the schedule management plan and the risk management plan

- Enterprise environmental factors
- Organizational process assets

Don't let the idea of the project management plan scare you. Remember that planning is an iterative activity. You'll have some elements of the project management plan already completed when you start this cost management planning—and some parts of the project management plan won't be completed yet. As more and more information becomes available, you can return to the cost management plan and adjust it as necessary. For example, you may not know the specific rules about how your company can purchase materials. You might need to speak with your project sponsor, the purchasing department, or your program manager to confirm these rules, and then you could return to the cost management plan and update the information accordingly.

The schedule management plan is needed because it helps you define when activities will happen and what resources you'll need for the activities. Resources include materials, equipment, supplies, and human resources. All these resource requirements will need to be estimated and their costs managed. The second subsidiary plan you'll reference is the risk management plan. Risks, something I've not really discussed yet, need to be considered because, should a risk event occur, it will likely have a financial impact, and you may have risk responses that require a financial commitment. I'll talk more about risks in Chapter 11—for now, just know that there is a financial consideration for risks when it comes to cost management planning.

NOTE You'll reference the project charter for the summary budget and the preapproved financial commitment to the project. Remember that the project charter includes a summary budget for the project, so you'll use that amount as a foundation for project cost management.

The actual creation of the cost management plan relies heavily on information you gather at meetings. Nothing like some meetings about the project budget, right? You'll need meetings specifically with your key stakeholders and subject matter experts. These people can help guide and direct you about the organization's environment, tell you about similar projects they've worked on or sponsored, and help with the enterprise environmental factors and organizational processes you'll have to adhere to in cost management.

These meetings will likely include the use of some techniques to analyze the anticipated cost of the project, the return on investment, and how the project should be funded. *Self-funding* means the organization pays for the project expenses from their cash flow. *Funding with equity* means the organization balances the project expenses with equity they have in their assets. *Funding with debt* means the company pays for the project through a line of credit or bank loan. There are pros and cons to each approach, and an analysis of the true cost of the project, the cost of the funding, and the risk associated with the project are examined as part of the decision.

NOTE The time value of money was covered in Chapter 4. Present value, future value, net present value, and the internal rate of return are all applicable here, too.

Examining the Project Cost Management Plan

Once you've created the cost management plan, you have a clear direction on how you'll estimate, budget, and manage the project costs. This plan defines, much like the schedule management plan, the level of precision identified for the project and the units of measurement. For example, you might round financial figures to the nearest $100 or keep track of costs to the exact penny. Your unit of measurement isn't just dollars, yen, or euros; it also includes things like a workday, hours, or even weeks for labor. Keep in mind that some organizations do not include the cost of labor in the project, while other companies do. Your estimates will also likely include a range of variance, such as +/–10 percent; this is your level of accuracy, which shows your degree of confidence in the estimate.

If you're using control accounts in your work breakdown structure (WBS), you'll reference those control accounts in your cost management plan. Recall that a control account is like a "mini-budget" for a chunk of the WBS. For example, a house project may have separate control accounts for the basement, the first floor, and the second floor. Or you could get more specific and have a separate control account for the kitchen in the house project. Whatever approach you're using, you'd reference that information in the cost management plan—the *PMBOK Guide* calls this an "organizational procedure link."

Just as you defined control thresholds for your schedule, you'll do the same for your project costs. Control thresholds, remember, are the limits of variance before a corrective action is needed in the project. For example, a project may have a control threshold of 10 percent off budget before a predefined action is taken. Or the control threshold could be that any cost variance greater than $5000 requires project management action. The action could be a corrective action but also may include an exceptions report or variance report to management.

Depending on your enterprise environmental factors, you may be required to define the rules for performance measurement. These can include such things as earned value management (EVM) or line-item reporting for each expense the project incurs. I'll talk more about EVM later in this chapter. Your cost management plan may also address what type of reports you must create to communicate cost status. Your communications management plan would also address these reporting requirements.

Preparing for Adaptive Cost Management

While it's true that budgets in adaptive projects are predetermined, there are still a few things to consider for your PMP exam when it comes to cost management in an adaptive project management approach. First, remember the Agile Manifesto and its highest priority: to deliver valuable software. The software, or the product of your project, is what the customer wants, needs, and values. The results of your project, both intermittent results and the final product, must provide value so that your organization can sell it to customers. This principle is why adaptive projects first focus on the prioritized product backlog and the development team begins creating the most important items first in the project. Value is provided when you create the items your customers value the most and then work down the list of requirements.

With a predefined budget, it's possible that all the stuff in the product backlog won't get created if budgeted funds are depleted. But with the adaptive approach, the stuff that might not get created holds lesser value than the items that do get created. And as your customer's needs change, your organization can refine the product backlog to prioritize the changes to reflect what the customer wants, not what the project manager or development team wants. The team always works toward creating software or a product that provides value to the organization's customers.

Adaptive projects are largely knowledge work projects—the work happens in the creators' brains, for the most part. Adaptive projects do not typically involve swinging a hammer and seeing results. Because of this characteristic, the biggest expense in adaptive projects is not materials and equipment, but labor. Your project's budget—its cost—is directly related to the hours of knowledge work the team puts into the project. So it's fair to say that the longer an adaptive project lasts, the more expensive the project will be. The longer the team takes to complete the valuable software, the more expensive the software will be to create and the longer it'll take the organization to recoup the costs of building the software.

Here's where things get interesting. If the team can create value early by building an app that customers want, and customers begin buying and using the solution, then the project (or parts of it) can be financed by the software being released and purchased. Imagine, for example, a project to create a new app used for a phone's camera and photos. In the first iteration, the team creates a working app that the organization can start selling to customers. The money your organization receives from selling the app can then be invested back into the project to pay for updates, future releases, and future iterations of the software. Those releases help the organization gain more sales, and the investment cycle continues. If sales aren't so hot, the organization has to pony up the funds to keep the project going or decide to stop working on the app and move onto the next endeavor. The concept in this scenario is pretty common: organizations can fund the project one release at a time, and based on the release's performance and value, the organization can determine whether or not to move forward.

Determining Project Costs

One of the first questions a project manager is likely to be asked when a project is launched is, "How much will this cost to finish?" That question can be answered only through progressive elaboration. To answer the question, the project manager, or the project estimator as the case may be, first needs to examine the costs of the resources needed to complete each activity in the project. Resources, of course, are people, but they are also things: equipment, material, training, and even pizza if the project demands it.

Figure 7-1
There are
three generally
accepted types
of cost estimates.

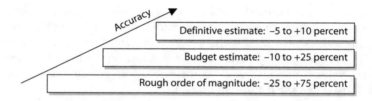

On top of the cost of the resources, all the variances must be considered: project risks, fluctuations in the cost of materials, the appropriate human resources for each activity, and oddball elements such as shipping, insurance, inflation, and monies for testing and evaluations.

Estimates, as Figure 7-1 depicts, usually come in one of three flavors through a series of refinements. As more details are acquired as the project progresses, the estimates are refined. Industry guidelines and organizational policies may define how the estimates are refined.

- **Rough order of magnitude (ROM)** This estimate is rough and is used during the initiating processes and in top-down estimates. The range of variance for this estimate can range from –25 percent to +75 percent.

- **Budget estimate** This estimate is also somewhat broad and is used early in the planning processes and also in top-down estimates. The range of variance for this estimate can range from –10 percent to +25 percent.

- **Definitive estimate** This estimate type is one of the most accurate. It's used late in the planning processes and is associated with bottom-up estimating. You need the WBS to create the definitive estimate. The range of variance for this estimate can range from –5 percent to +10 percent.

NOTE The ranges of variance percentages are pretty typical of these estimate types, but there's no steadfast rule that the estimates must follow these ranges. Your organization may use entirely different ranges of variance for each estimate type.

Though project managers typically think of project estimates as some unit of measure such as dollars, euros, or yen, it's possible and often feasible to estimate project costs based on labor. Consider the number of hours the project team must work on creating a new piece of software. You could even estimate based on the number of full-time employees assigned to the project for a given duration.

Estimating the Project Costs

Assuming that the project manager and the project team are working together to create the cost estimates, there are many inputs to the cost-estimating process. Let's have a look, shall we?

EXAM TIP For your PMI exam, it would behoove you to be familiar with these inputs. These are often the supporting details for the cost estimate the project management team creates.

Referencing the Cost Management Plan

You've created the cost management plan, so you might as well use it. Use the plan as an input for cost estimating, because it defines the level of detail you'll need in the cost estimates you're creating. You'll follow the cost management plan's requirements for cost estimating, rounding, and adherence to enterprise environmental factors.

Referencing the Quality Management Plan

Quality is basically met by satisfying the project scope; I'll talk more about quality in the next chapter. You'll use the quality management plan to address the financial requirements needed to ascertain the expectations of quality in your project. To satisfy the project scope, for example, you may have to train your project team, or purchase special equipment, or get permits from your local government—all of these things will involve a financial consideration.

Using the Project Scope Statement

You'll need the project scope statement often enough—first, because it is an input to the cost-estimating process. What a surprise! The project scope statement defines the business case for the project, the project justifications, and the project requirements—all things that'll cost cash to achieve. The project scope statement can help the project manager and stakeholders negotiate the funding for the project based on what's already been agreed upon. In other words, the size of the budget has to be in proportion to the demands of the project scope statement.

While the project scope statement defines constraints, it also defines assumptions. In Chapter 11, which discusses risk management, we'll discuss how assumptions can become risks. Basically, if the assumptions in the project scope statement prove false, the project manager needs to assess what the financial impact may be.

Consider all of the elements in the project scope statement that can contribute to the project cost estimate:

- Contractual agreements
- Insurance
- Safety and health issues
- Environment expenses
- Security concerns
- Cost of intellectual rights
- Licenses and permits

Perhaps one of the more important elements in the project scope statement is the requirements for acceptance. The cost estimate must reflect the monies needed to attain the project customer's expectations. If the monies are not available to create all of the elements within the project scope, then either the project scope must be trimmed to match the monies that are available or more cash needs to be dumped into the project.

Next, you'll need the second part of the scope baseline: the WBS. The WBS is needed to create a cost estimate, especially the definitive estimate, because it clearly defines all of the deliverables the project will create. Each of the work packages in the WBS will cost something in the way of materials, time, or often both. You'll see the WBS as a common theme in this chapter, because the monies you spend on a project are for the things you've promised in the WBS.

Finally, you'll need the WBS's pal, the WBS dictionary, because it includes all of the details and the associated work for each deliverable in the WBS. As a general rule, whenever you have the WBS involved, the WBS dictionary tags along.

Examining Resource Availability

The availability of resources is needed for cost estimating: when the resources will do the work, when capital expenses will be spent, and other schedule details. The schedule management plan can also consider contracts with collective bargaining agreements (unions) and their timelines, the seasonal cost of labor and materials, and any other time details that may affect the overall cost estimate. The project schedule can help you determine not only when resources are needed, but when you'll have to pay for those resources.

 EXAM TIP Adaptive projects may not consider the cost of labor as part of the project expenses, but may instead use a predetermined fixed cost for a worker's time—such as $175 per hour, per developer on the project. The more developers added, the more costs increase, but you can also create value faster, because more developers can complete more user stories (requirements) per iteration.

Examining the Project Schedule

The project schedule identifies the physical and human resources utilized on the project. The schedule will help you predict how much the resources will cost, when the resources will be needed, and what expenses will be incurred at what point of the project. Considerations are given for seasonal fluctuations in cost, availability of resources, and cash-flow forecasting that may affect operations and project decisions.

Referencing the Risk Register

A risk is an uncertain event that may cost the project time, money, or both. The risk register is a central repository of the project risks and the associated status of each risk event. The project team can spend funds to alleviate some risks, whereas other risks will cost the project if they are realized. We'll discuss risks in detail in Chapter 11, but for now, know that the risk register is needed because the cost of the risk exposure helps the project management team create an accurate cost estimate.

EXAM TIP Risks may not always cost monies directly, but they can affect the project schedule. Keep in mind, however, that this could in turn cause a rise in project costs because of vendor commitment, penalties for lateness, and added expenses for extra labor.

Relying on Enterprise Environmental Factors

Every time I have to say or write "enterprise environmental factors," I cringe. It's just a fancy-pants way of saying how your organization runs its shop. Within any organization, "factors" affect the cost-estimating process. Surprise, surprise. There are two major factors to know for your exam:

- **Marketplace conditions**   When you have to buy materials and other resources, the marketplace dictates their price, what resources are available, and from whom you will purchase them. We'll talk all about procurement in Chapter 12, but for now, know that there are three conditions that can affect the price of anything your project needs to purchase:

  - **Sole source**   Only one vendor can provide what your project needs to purchase. Examples include a specific consultant, a specialized service, or a unique type of material.

  - **Single source**   Many vendors can provide what your project needs to purchase, but you prefer to work with a specific vendor. Perhaps the vendor is your favorite.

  - **Oligopoly**   In this market condition, the market is so tight that the actions of one vendor affect the actions of all the others. Can you think of any examples? How about the airline industry, the oil industry, or even training centers and consultants?

- **Commercial databases**   One of my first consulting gigs was for a large commercial printer. We used a database—based on the type of materials the job was to be printed on, the number of inks and varnishes we wanted to use, and the printing press we'd use—to predict how much the job would cost. That's a commercial database. Another accessible example is any price list your vendors may provide so that you can estimate the costs accurately.

EXAM TIP   Here's a goofy way to remember all the market conditions for your PMI exam. For a sole source, think of James Brown, the Godfather of Soul. There's only one James Brown, just as there's only one vendor. For a single source, think of all the single people in the world and how you want to date only your sweetie instead of all the others. With a single source, you consider all the different available vendors, but you have your favorite. And for oligopoly? It sounds like "oil," which we know is a classic example of an oligopoly market. Hey, I warned you these were goofy!

Using Organizational Process Assets

Here's another term that makes my teeth hurt: "organizational process assets." These are things your organization has learned, created, or purchased that can help the project management team manage a project better.

When it comes to cost estimating, an organization can use many assets:

- **Cost-estimating policies**   An organization can, and often will, create a policy on how the project manager or the cost estimator is to create the project cost estimate. It's just their rule. Got any of those where you work?

- **Cost-estimating templates**   In case you've not picked up on this yet, the PMI and the Project Management Body of Knowledge (PMBOK) love templates. Templates in project management don't usually mean a shell in the way that Microsoft Word thinks of templates. We're talking about using past similar projects to serve as templates for the current project.

- **Historical information**   Beyond the specific costs of previous projects, historical information is just about anything that came before this project that can help the project manager and the project team create an accurate cost estimate.

- **Project files**   Project archives and files from past projects can help with the cost-estimating process. Specifically, the project manager is after the performance of past similar projects in areas of cost control, the cost of risks, and quality issues that could affect costs.

- **Project team knowledge**   Your project team usually consists of the experts closest to the project work, and they can provide valuable input to the project cost-estimating process. Be forewarned—for the real world and your PMI exam, project team recollections are great, but they aren't the most reliable source of input. In other words, Marty's war stories about how Project XYZ was $14 billion over budget don't compare with historical information that says Project XYZ was $14 over budget.

- **Lessons learned register**   It's always good to rely on lessons learned as an input during planning. After all, it's easy to learn from someone else's mistakes.

 EXAM TIP   Sometimes an organization has two projects, or opportunities, and they can choose only one of the projects to complete. For example, Project A is worth $75,000, and Project B is worth $250,000. The organization will likely choose Project B because it is worth more and let Project A go because it is worth considerably less. *Opportunity cost* is a term used to describe the total amount of the project that was let go in lieu of the project that was selected. In this instance, the opportunity cost is $75,000: the worth of Project A.

Creating the Cost Estimate

All of the cost inputs are needed so that the project cost estimator, likely the project management team, can create a reliable cost estimate. The estimates you'll want to know for the PMP exam, and for your career, reflect the accuracy of the information the estimate is based upon. The more accurate the information, the better the cost estimate will be. Basically, all cost estimates move through progressive elaboration: as more details become available, the more accurate the cost estimate is likely to be. Let's examine the most common approaches to determining how much a project is likely to cost.

 NOTE If your organization doesn't use a cost estimator, the project manager and the project team can work together to estimate the project costs. Historical information is a key component to predict cost duration in adaptive projects, for example.

Using Analogous Estimating

Analogous estimating relies on historical information to predict the cost of the current project. It is also known as "top-down estimating" and is the least reliable of all the cost-estimating approaches. The process of analogous estimating uses the actual cost of a historical project as a basis for the current project's cost. The cost of the historical project is applied to the cost of the current project, taking into account the scope and size of the current project as well as other known variables.

Analogous estimating is considered a form of expert judgment. This estimating approach takes less time to complete than other estimating models, but it is also less accurate. This top-down approach is good for fast estimates to get a general idea of what the project may cost. The trouble, or risk, with using an analogous estimate, however, is that the historical information the estimate is based upon must be accurate. For example, if I were to create a cost estimate for Project NBG based on a similar project Nancy did two years ago, I'd be assuming that Nancy kept accurate records and that her historical information is accurate. If Nancy didn't keep good records, however, my project costs are not going to be accurate, and I'm going to be really mad at Nancy.

Using Parametric Estimating

"That'll be $465 per metric ton."
"You can buy our software for $765 per license."
"How about $125 per network drop?"

These are all examples of parameters that can be integrated into a parametric estimate. *Parametric estimating* uses a mathematical model based on known parameters to predict the cost of a project. The parameters in the model can vary based on the type of work being completed and can be measured by cost per cubic yard, cost per unit, and so on. A complex parameter can be cost per unit, with adjustment factors based on the conditions of the project. The adjustment factors may have several modifying factors, depending on additional conditions.

There are two types of parametric estimating:

- **Regression analysis**   This statistical approach predicts future values based on historical values. Regression analysis creates quantitative predictions based on variables within one value to predict variables in another. This form of estimating relies solely on pure statistical math to reveal relationships between variables and to predict future values.

- **Learning curve**   This approach is simple: The more units workers complete, the less the per unit cost, because workers learn as they complete the required work (see Figure 7-2). Basically, the more an individual completes an activity, the easier it is to complete. The estimate is considered parametric, since the formula is based on repetitive activities, such as wiring telephone jacks, painting hotel rooms, or other activities that are completed over and over within a project. This is the case in adaptive projects, as the team's velocity early in the project may be wild and unpredictable, but after a few iterations the velocity begins to normalize.

 EXAM TIP   Don't worry too much about regression analysis for the exam. You're more likely to see questions about the learning curve.

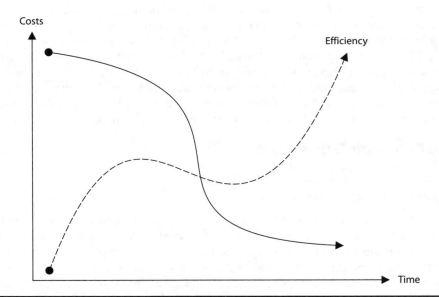

Figure 7-2   The learning curve affects the cost of efficiency.

Using Bottom-Up Estimating

Bottom-up estimating starts from zero, accounts for each component of the WBS, and arrives at a sum for the project. It is completed with the project team and can be one of the most time-consuming methods used to predict project costs. Although this method is more expensive because of the time invested to create the estimate, it is also one of the most accurate methods. A fringe benefit of completing a bottom-up estimate is that the project team may buy into the project work since they see the value of each cost within the project.

Implementing Three-Point Estimating

A *three-point estimate* uses three factors to predict a cost: pessimistic, optimistic, and most likely. A three-point estimate can use a simple average of the three factors, or it can use a weighted factor for the most likely factor. For example, suppose a project manager predicts the pessimistic cost to be $5600, the most likely cost to be $4800, and the optimistic cost to be $3500. With the simple average, you'd just add up the three amounts and divide by 3 for a value of $4633.

With the weighted average, you'll consider all of the same costs, but the most likely amount is multiplied by 4, and then you'll divide the sum of the three values by 6. Here's what this looks like with the same costs: ($5600 + (4 × $4800) + $3500)/6 = $4716. In this instance, the weight average leans more toward the most likely amount than does the simple average. Yes, this is the same approach we discussed back in schedule management. When you use the average, you're using triangular distribution. When you're using the weighted average of 6, you're using beta distribution.

Determining the Cost of Resources

Resources include more than just the people doing the project work. The cost estimate must also reflect all the equipment and materials that will be utilized to complete the work. In addition, the project manager must identify the quantity of the needed resources and when the resources are needed for the project. The identification of the resources, the needed quantity, and the schedule of the resources are directly linked to the expected cost of the project work.

There are four variations on project expenses to consider:

- **Direct costs** These costs are attributed directly to the project work and cannot be shared among projects (such as airfare, hotels, long-distance phone charges, and so on).

- **Indirect costs** These costs are representative of more than one project (such as utilities for the performing organization, access to a training room, project management software license, and so on).

- **Variable costs** These costs vary depending on the conditions applied in the project (such as the number of meeting participants, the supply and demand of materials, and so on).

- **Fixed costs** These costs remain constant throughout the life cycle of the project (such as the cost of a piece of rented equipment for the project, the cost of a consultant brought onto the project, and so on).

And, yes, you can mix and match these terms. For example, you could have a variable cost based on shipping expenses that is also a direct cost for your project.

EXAM TIP Don't get too hung up on these cost types—just be topically familiar with them for your PMI exam.

Creating a Reserve Analysis

Do you think it'll snow next December in Michigan? I do, too. But do we know the exact date of the snowfall? That's a quick and easy example of a *known unknown*. You know that something is likely to occur, but you don't know when or to what degree. Projects are full of known unknowns, and the most common unknown deals with costs. Based on experience, the nature of the work, or fear, you suspect that some activities in your project will cost more than expected—that's a known unknown.

Rather than combating known unknowns by padding costs with extra monies, the PMBOK suggests that we create "contingency allowances" to account for these over-runs in costs. The contingency allowances are used at the project manager's discretion to counteract cost overruns for scheduled activities. In Chapter 6, we discussed the concept of management reserve for time overruns. This is a related concept when it comes to the cost reserve for projects. This reserve is sometimes called a *contingency reserve* and is tradi-tionally set aside for cost overruns resulting from risks that have affected the project cost baseline. Contingency reserves can be managed in a number of ways. The most common is to set aside an allotment of funds for the identified risks within the project. Another approach is to create a slush fund for the entire project for identified risks and known unknowns. The final approach is an allotment of funds for categories of components based on the WBS and the project schedule.

Considering the Cost of Quality

The *cost of quality*, which we'll discuss in Chapter 8, defines the monies the project must spend to reach the expected level of quality within a project. For example, if your project will use a new material that no one on the project team has ever worked with, the project team will likely need training so they can use it. The training, as you can guess, costs something. That's an example of the cost of quality.

On the other side of the coin (cost pun intended, thank you), there's the cost of poor quality, sometimes called the *cost of nonconformance to quality*. These are the costs your project will pay if you don't adhere to quality the first time. In our example with the project team and the new materials, a failure to train the team on the new materials will mean that the team will likely not install the materials properly, will take longer to use the materials, and may even waste materials. All these negative conditions cost the project in time, money, team frustration, and even loss of sales.

Using Good Old Project Management Software

Who's creating estimates with their abacus? Most organizations rely on software to help the project management team create an accurate cost estimate. Although the PMP examination is vendor neutral, you'll need to have a general knowledge of how computer software can assist the project manager. Several different computer programs are available that can streamline project work estimates and increase their accuracy. These tools can include project management software, spreadsheet programs, and simulations.

Keeping Agile Simple

The Agile Manifesto includes this line: "Simplicity—the art of maximizing the amount of work not done—is essential." This doesn't mean the development team doesn't do their work, but rather they do only the work that adds value. Specifically, we're using a key principle of the Lean approach to reduce waste by not doing unnecessary work. We don't drive costs, take on busy work in the project, or create tons of unneeded documentation. We deliver value based on what our customers see as value. Things like regulatory compliance, safety, and uptime are all values we must include, and these are things customers are likely to expect in the project. But we don't need to create things that aren't in the value stream. So there's a new term: *value stream*. A value stream, a Lean principle, includes all of the actions needed to create value for the project customer from the very start. If the work isn't in the value stream, the work isn't needed and can be considered part of the work that's not done. Simple—especially for an organization that's just launching an adaptive initiative—isn't easy.

New adaptive teams may struggle with the old, predictive way of doing things. That's a disruption in the value stream. The leader in the project, be it the coach or scrum master, will have to work to keep the team focused on the rules of Agile and to break free of the predictive overhead that doesn't create value in adaptive projects. This also means that stakeholders will need to be coached and trained to follow the rules of Agile, which is something that's easy to understand but not always easy to follow.

Examining the Cost Estimate

Once all the inputs have been evaluated and the estimate creation process is completed, you get the cost estimate. The estimate is the likely cost of the project—it's not a guarantee, so there is usually a modifier, which is sometimes called an acceptable range of variance. That's the plus/minus qualifier on the estimate—for example, $450,000 or +$25,000 to –$13,000—based on whatever conditions are attached to the estimate. The cost estimate should, at the minimum, include the likely costs for all of the following:

- Labor
- Materials
- Equipment
- Services
- Facilities

- Information technology
- Special categories, such as inflation and contingency reserve

It's possible for a project to have other cost categories, such as consultants, outsourced solutions, and so on, but the preceding list is the most common. Consider this list when studying to pass your exam.

Along with the cost estimate, the project management team includes the *basis* of the estimate. This includes all the supporting details of how the estimate was created and why the confidence in the estimate exists at the level it does. Supporting details typically include all of the following:

- Description of the work to be completed in consideration of the cost estimate
- Explanation of how the estimate was created
- Assumptions used during the estimate creation
- Constraints the project management team considered when creating the cost estimate

A project's cost estimate may lead to some unpleasant news in the shape of change requests in predictive projects. I say "unpleasant," because changes are rarely enjoyable. Changes can affect the scope in two primary scenarios when it comes to cost:

- We don't have enough funds to match the cost estimate, so we'll need to trim the scope.
- We have more than enough funds to match the cost estimate, so let's add some stuff into the scope.

All change requests in a predictive environment must be documented and fed through the integrated change control system, as discussed in Chapter 4. In agile projects, however, changes go into the product backlog and are prioritized based on value to the customer. In either project management approach, the project manager wants to be leery of gold plating. *Gold plating* occurs when the project manager, the project sponsor, or even a stakeholder adds in project extras to consume the entire project budget. It's essentially adding unneeded features to the product to use up all the funds allocated to the project. Though this often happens in the final stages of a project, it can also begin during the project cost estimating. Gold plating delivers more than what's needed and can create new risks and work, and it can contribute to a decline in team morale.

If changes are approved, then integrated change control is enacted, the project scope is updated, the WBS and WBS dictionary are updated, and so on, through all of the project management plans as needed. The cost management plan needs to be updated as well to reflect the costs of the changes and their impact on the project cost estimate. Your estimate could cause the assumptions log, the lessons learned register, and the risk register to be updated too.

Budgeting the Project

After the project estimate has been created, it's time to determine the budget. Cost budgeting is really cost aggregation, which means the project manager will be assigning specific dollar amounts for each of the scheduled activities or, more likely, for each of the work packages in the WBS. The aggregation of the work package cost equates to the summary budget for the entire project. This process creates the cost baseline, as Figure 7-3 shows.

Cost budgeting and cost estimates may go hand in hand, but estimating is completed before a budget is created—or assigned. Cost budgeting applies the cost estimates over time. This results in a time-phased estimate for cost, which enables an organization to predict cash flow, to project return on investment, and to perform forecasting. The difference between cost estimates and cost budgeting is that cost *estimates* show costs by *category*, whereas a cost *budget* shows costs across *time*.

 NOTE Adaptive projects don't have the same approach to budgeting as predictive projects. Predictive projects try to predict what the project will cost, while adaptive projects work against a fixed budget. User stories at the bottom are of lesser value than those at the top of the product backlog. If there's not enough in the budget, the lesser valued items get squeezed out of the project.

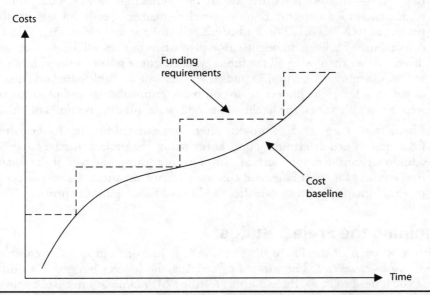

Figure 7-3   The cost baseline shows how much the project will cost, demonstrated on an S-curve.

Creating the Project Budget

Good news! Many of the tools and techniques used to create the project cost estimates are also used to create the project budget. The following is a quick listing of the tools you can expect to see on the PMP exam:

- **Cost aggregation** Costs are parallel to each WBS work package. The costs of each work package are aggregated to their corresponding control accounts. Each control account is then aggregated to the sum of the project costs.

- **Reserve analysis** Cost reserves are for unknown unknowns within a project. The contingency reserve is not part of the project cost baseline but is included as part of the project budget.

- **Historical relationships** This is kind of a weird concept. Historical relationships in cost estimating describe the history of costs in a given industry. For example, construction uses a cost per square foot, while software development can charge a fee per hour depending on the type of resource being used. This approach uses a parametric model to extrapolate what costs will be for a project (for example, cost per hour and cost per unit). It can include variables and the additional percentage of fee points based on conditions. The historical information review requires an accurate model to begin with, quantifiable parameters in the model, and a model that is scalable to different-sized projects.

- **Funding limit reconciliation** Organizations have only so much cash to allot to projects—and, no, you can't have all the monies right now. Funding limit reconciliation is an organization's approach to managing cash flow against the project deliverables based on a schedule, milestone accomplishment, or data constraints. This helps an organization plan when monies will be devoted to a project rather than using all the funds available at the start of a project. In other words, the monies for a project budget will become available based on dates and/ or deliverables. If the project doesn't hit predetermined dates and products that were set as milestones, the likelihood of additional funding becomes questionable.

- **Financing** Larger, longer projects often have external funding in the form of financing. When determining project financing, the project manager may have additional considerations such as cash-flow forecasting, the cost of the financing in the form of interest rates, and communications requirements on project progression and how they can affect additional funding for the project.

Examining the Project Budget

As with most parts of the PMBOK, you don't get just one output after completing a process—you get several. The process of creating the project budget is no different, because you'll need to know three outputs for the PMI examination: cost baseline, project funding requirements, and project documents. The following sections look at these in detail.

Working with the Cost Baseline

The *cost baseline* shown earlier in Figure 7-3 is actually a "time-lapse exposure" of when the project monies are to be spent in relation to cumulative values of the work completed in the project. Most baselines are shown as an S-curve, on which the project begins at the left and works its way to the upper-right corner. When the project begins, it's not worth much and usually not much has been spent. As the project moves toward completion, the monies for labor, materials, and other resources are consumed in relation to the work. In other words, the monies spent on the project over time will equate to the work the project is completing.

Some projects, especially high priority or large projects, may have multiple cost baselines to track cost of labor, cost of materials, or even the cost of internal resources compared with external resources. This is all fine and dandy, as long as the values in each of the baselines are maintained and consistent. It wouldn't do a project manager much good if the cost baseline for materials was updated regularly and the cost baseline for labor was politely ignored.

EXAM TIP   Monies that have already been spent on a project are considered sunk into the project. These funds are called *sunk costs*—they're gone.

Determining the Project Funding Requirements

Projects demand a budget, but when the monies in the project are made available depends on the organization, the size of the project, and just plain old common sense. For example, if you were building a skyscraper that costs $850 million, you wouldn't need all of the funds on the first day of the project, but you would forecast when those monies would be needed. That's cash-flow forecasting.

The funding of the project, based on the cost baseline and the expected project schedule, may happen incrementally or may be based on conditions within the project. Typically, the funding requirements have been incorporated into the cost baseline. The release of funds is treated like a step function, which is what it is. Each step of the project funding enables the project to move on to the next milestone, deliverable, or whatever step of the project the project manager and the stakeholders have agreed to.

Adaptive projects don't just get a pot of money to work from. Agile projects will often have to predict how much the project will cost—something that's really tricky when the scope is likely to change throughout the project. The key thing in predicting project costs in agile isn't to give a definite number, but to determine if the project can be realistically, feasibly, accomplished. Much of this work is on the product owner, but there may be some input from the development team in creating a cost estimate the project can work from. In adaptive projects, however, much of the cost will come down to labor and how effectively the team can work. The user story sizing and the velocity of the team are directly related to the final costs of the product the project creates.

Initially, if the team overestimates the amount of work they can accomplish in the iteration, they'll downsize the amount of work they'll predict they can accomplish in the iterations moving forward. This is the idea of how velocity, the amount of work a team can create in an iteration, may be wild in the first few sprints and then normalize over time. User story items that aren't completed in the sprint hold zero value—there is no value in the product if it's not finished. These items go back into the product backlog for prioritization and are taken back into the agile process. The longer a project lasts, the more it will likely cost or the fewer items will get accomplished to meet the original budget.

The project funding requirements also account for the amount of funds in the management contingency reserve, which is a pool of funds to cover cost overruns. Typically, the management contingency reserve is allotted to the project in each step, though some organizations may elect to disburse contingency funds on an as-needed basis only—that's just part of organizational process assets. Not all agile projects utilize a contingency reserve, though an organization may elect to do so depending on the priority of the project and the identified risks.

To be crystal clear, the *cost baseline* is what the project *should* cost in an ideal, perfect world. The *management contingency reserve* is the "filler" between the cost baseline and the maximum funding. In most cases, the management contingency reserve bridges the gap between the project cost baseline and the maximum funding to complete the project. Figure 7-4 demonstrates the management contingency reserve at project completion.

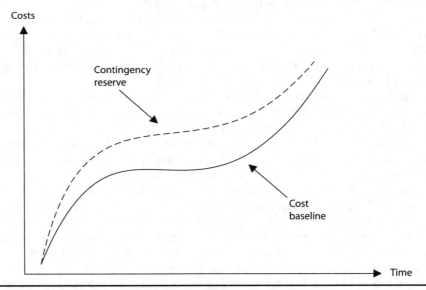

Figure 7-4 Contingency reserve provides funding for cost overruns.

The Usual Suspects

There are three more outputs of the cost-budgeting process:

- **Cost baseline**   This is the budget of the project—usually in ratio to when the funds are needed and how far along the project has progressed. In other words, in larger projects, you don't get all the budgeted project funds at the start; instead, the monies are spent throughout the project. This is where you might see an S-curve of how much the project is predicted to spend in relation to the progress the project is to make. Ideally, you'll run out of money just when the project reaches its conclusion.

- **Project funding requirements**   Part of the project's budget is a prediction of when you'll need the money: capital expenses, monthly labor burn rates, contractual obligations, and project liabilities. You will need to consider the total budget requirements as part of the funding requirements. This includes the cost baseline and any management reserves for risk events.

- **Project document updates**   You may need to update the risk register, cost estimates, and the project schedule.

Controlling Project Costs

Once a project has been funded, it's up to the project manager and the project team to work effectively and efficiently to control costs. This means doing the work right the first time. It also means—and this is tricky—avoiding scope creep and undocumented changes, as well as getting rid of any non–value-added activities. Basically, if the project team is adding components or features that aren't called for in the project, they're wasting time and money.

Cost control focuses on controlling the ability of costs to change and on how the project management team may allow or prevent cost changes from happening. When a change does occur, the project manager must document the change and the reason why it occurred, and then, if necessary, create a variance report. Cost control is concerned with understanding why the cost variances, both good and bad, have occurred. The "why" behind the variances enables the project manager to make appropriate decisions on future project actions.

 EXAM TIP   Variance reports are sometimes called exception reports.

Ignoring the project cost variances may cause the project to suffer from budget shortages, additional risks, or scheduling problems. When cost variances happen, they must be examined, recorded, and investigated. Cost control enables the project manager to confront the problem, find a solution, and then act accordingly. Specifically, cost control focuses on the following:

- Controlling causes of change to ensure that the changes are actually needed
- Controlling and documenting changes to the cost baseline as they happen
- Controlling changes in the project and their influence on cost
- Performing cost monitoring to recognize and understand cost variances
- Recording appropriate cost changes in the cost baseline
- Preventing unauthorized changes to the cost baseline
- Communicating the cost changes to the proper stakeholders
- Working to bring and maintain costs within an acceptable range

Managing the Project Costs

Controlling the project costs is more than a philosophy—it's the project manager working with the project team, the stakeholders, and often management to ensure that costs don't creep into the project, and then managing the cost increases if they do happen. To implement cost control, the project manager must rely on several documents and processes:

- **Project management plan** This cost management plan dictates how cost variances will be managed. A *variance* is the difference between what was expected and what was experienced. In some instances, the management contingency reserve allowance can "cover" the cost overruns. In other instances, depending on the reason why the overrun occurred, the funding may have to come from the project customer. Consider a customer who wanted the walls painted green, but after the work was completed, changes his mind and wants the walls to be orange. This cost overrun results from a change request and not from a defect repair, and the customer would pay the additional costs.

- **Cost baseline** The cost baseline, the technical part of the project management plan, is the expected costs the project will incur and when those expenses will happen. This time-phased budget reflects the amount that will be spent throughout the project. The cost baseline is a tool used to measure project performance.

- **Performance measurement baseline** The performance measurement baseline is used with earned value management, which I'll discuss in the next section, to expose variances and overall performance of the project. When variances occur, the project manager can determine whether a corrective action, preventive action, or another change request is needed.

- **Project funding requirements** The funds for a project are not allotted all at once but are delivered gradually in alignment with project deliverables. Thus, as the project moves toward completion, additional funding is allotted. This allows for cash-flow forecasting. In other words, an organization doesn't need to have the project's entire budget available at the start of the project. It can predict, based on expected income and predicted expenses, that the amount will be available in increments.

- **Work performance data**   This is raw data on the costs of the project. This data can include the costs that have been authorized in the project, the actual costs of the project, invoice information, what's been paid to vendors, hours of labor incurred, and other cost information.

Controlling Changes to Project Costs

Way, way back in Chapter 5, I discussed the change control system in regard to project scope in a predictive environment. Whenever some joker wants to add something to the project scope, or even take something out of our project scope, the scope change control is engaged. Similarly, the cost change control examines any changes associated with scope changes, the costs of materials, and the costs of any other resources you can imagine.

When a cost change enters the system, the project manager must complete the appropriate paperwork, use a tracking system, and follow established procedures to obtain approval on the proposed change. Figure 7-5 demonstrates a typical workflow for cost change approval. If a change gets approved, the cost baseline is updated to reflect the approved change. If a request gets denied, the denial must be documented for future potential reference. You don't want a stakeholder wondering at the end of the project why his change wasn't incorporated into the project scope without having some documentation describing why.

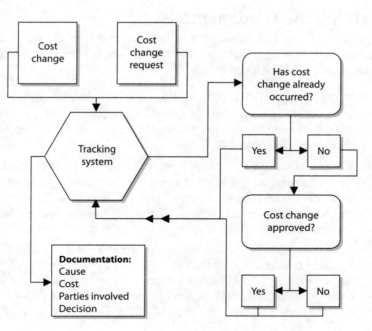

Figure 7-5
A cost change control examines all cost changes.

EXAM TIP For the exam, you'll need to remember and apply the four specific areas of change control in integrated change: scope, schedule, costs, and contract.

Using Earned Value Management

When I teach a PMP Boot Camp, attendees snap to attention when it comes to earned value management and their exam. This topic is foreign to many folks, and they understandably want an in-depth explanation of this suite of mysterious formulas. Maybe you find yourself in that same position, so here's some good news: It's not that big a deal. Relax—you can memorize these formulas, answer the exam questions correctly, and worry about tougher exam topics. I'll show you how.

Earned value management (EVM) is the process of measuring the performance of project work against what was planned to identify variances, to note opportunities to improve the project, or just to check the project's health. EVM can help predict future variances and the final costs at completion. It is a system of mathematical formulas that compares work performed against work planned, and it measures the actual cost of the work your project has performed. EVM is an important part of cost control because it enables a project manager to predict future variances from the expenses to date within the project.

 VIDEO For a more detailed explanation, watch the *Earned Value Management* video now.

Learning the Fundamentals

EVM, in regard to cost management, is concerned with the relationships among three formulas that reflect project performance. Figure 7-6 demonstrates the connection between the following EVM values:

- **Planned value (PV)** Planned value is the work scheduled and the budget authorized to accomplish that work. For example, if a project has a budget of $500,000 and month six represents 50 percent of the project work, the PV for that month is $250,000.

- **Earned value (EV)** Earned value is the physical work completed to date and the authorized budget for that work. For example, if your project has a budget of $500,000 and the work completed to date represents 45 percent of the entire project work, its earned value is $225,000. You can find EV by multiplying the percent complete times the project budget at completion (BAC).

- **Actual cost (AC)** Actual cost is the actual amount of monies the project has required to date. In your project, your BAC, for example, is $500,000 and your earned value is $225,000. As it turns out, your project team had some waste, and you spent $232,000 in actual monies to reach the 45-percent-complete milestone. Your actual cost is $232,000.

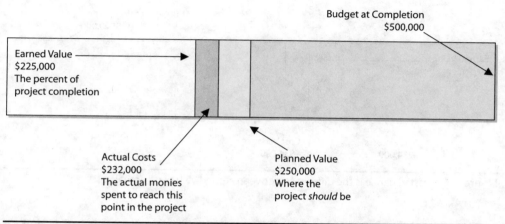

Budget at Completion
$500,000

Earned Value
$225,000
The percent of
project completion

Actual Costs
$232,000
The actual monies
spent to reach this
point in the project

Planned Value
$250,000
Where the
project *should* be

Figure 7-6   Earned value management shows project performance.

That's the fundamentals of EVM. All remaining formulas center on these simple formulas. Just remember that earned value is always the percent of work complete times the given budget at completion. On your PMI exam, you'll always be provided with the actual costs, which are the monies that have already been spent on the project. You'll have to do some math to find the planned value, which is the value your project should have by a given time. The formula for planned value is the percentage of project completion based on how complete the project should be at a given time. For example, let's say you're supposed to be 80 percent complete by December 15. If your budget is $100,000, in this instance your planned value is $80,000.

Finding the Project Variances

Out in the real world, I'm sure your projects are never late and never over budget (ha ha—pretty funny, right?). For your exam, you'll need to be able to find the cost and schedule variances for your project. I'll stay with the same $500,000 budget I've been working with in the previous examples and as demonstrated in Figure 7-7. Finding the variances helps the project manager and management determine a project's health, set goals for project improvement, and benchmark projects against each other based on the identified variances.

Finding the Cost Variance

Let's say your project has a BAC of $500,000 and you're 40 percent complete. You have spent, however, $234,000 in real monies. To find the cost variance, you'll find the earned value, which is 40 percent of the $500,000 budget. As Figure 7-7 shows, this is $200,000. In this example, you spent $234,000 in actual costs. The formula for finding the cost variance is earned value minus actual costs. In this instance, the cost variance is –$34,000.

PART II

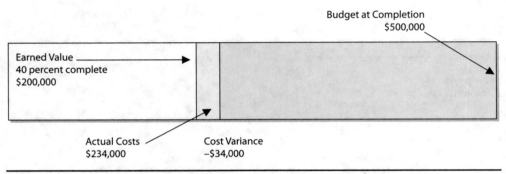

Figure 7-7   Cost variance is the difference between earned value and actual costs.

This means you've spent $34,000 dollars *more* than what the work you've done is worth. Of course, the $34,000 is in relation to the size of the project. On this project, that's a sizeable flaw, but on a billion-dollar project, $34,000 may not mean too much. On either project, a $34,000 cost variance would likely spur a cost variance report (sometimes called an exceptions report).

Finding the Schedule Variance

Can you guess how the schedule variance works? It's basically the same as cost variance, only this time, we're concerned with planned value instead of actual costs. Let's say your project with the $500,000 budget is supposed to be 45 percent complete by today, but we know that you're only 40 percent complete. We've already found the earned value as $200,000 for the planned value.

Recall that planned value, where you're supposed to be and what you're supposed to be worth, is planned completion times the BAC. In this example, it's 45 percent of the $500,000 BAC, which is $225,000. Uh-oh! You're behind schedule. The schedule variance formula, as Figure 7-8 demonstrates, is earned value minus the planned value. So, in this example, the schedule variance is –$25,000.

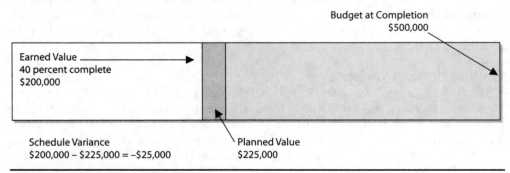

Figure 7-8   Schedule variance is the difference of earned value and planned value.

Finding the Indexes

In mathematical terms, an *index* is an expression showing a ratio—and that's what we're doing with these indexes. Basically, an index in EVM shows the health of the project's time and cost. The index, or ratio, is measured against 1: the closer to 1 the index is, the better the project is performing. As a rule, you definitely don't want to be less than 1, because that's a poorly performing project. And, believe it or not, you don't want to be too far from 1 in your index, as this shows estimates that were bloated or way, way too pessimistic. Really.

Finding the Cost Performance Index

The cost performance index (CPI) measures the project based on its financial performance. It's an easy formula: earned value divided by actual costs, as Figure 7-9 demonstrates. Your project, in this example, has a budget of $500,000, and you're 40 percent complete with the project work. This is an earned value of how much? Yep. It's 40 percent of the $500,000, for an earned value of $200,000.

Your actual costs for this project to date (the cumulative costs) total $234,000. Your PMI exam will always tell you your actual costs for each exam question. Let's finish the formula. To find the CPI, divide the earned value by the actual costs, or $200,000 divided by $234,000. The CPI for this project is .85, which means that you're 85 percent on track financially—not too healthy for any project, regardless of its budget.

Another fun way to look at the .85 value is that you're losing 15 cents on every dollar you spend on the project. Yikes! That means for every dollar you spend for labor, you actually only get 85 cents worth of value. Not a good deal for the project manager. As stated earlier, the closer to 1 the number is, the better the project is performing.

Finding the Schedule Performance Index

The schedule performance index (SPI) measures the project schedule's overall health. The formula, as Figure 7-10 demonstrates, is earned value divided by planned value. In other words, you're trying to determine how closely your project work is being completed in relation to the project schedule you created. Let's try this formula.

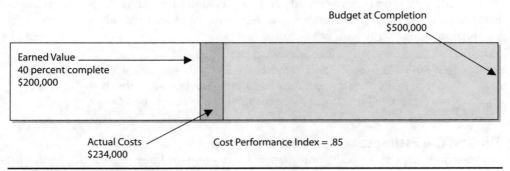

Figure 7-9 The CPI is found by dividing earned value by the actual costs.

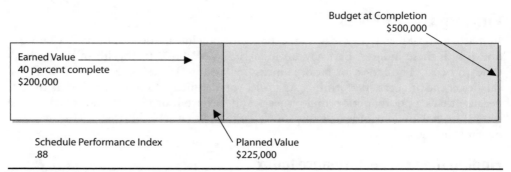

Figure 7-10   The SPI is found by dividing the earned value by the planned value.

Your project with the $500,000 budget is 40 percent complete, for an earned value of $200,000, but you're supposed to be 45 percent complete by today. That's a planned value of $225,000. The SPI for this project at this time is determined by dividing the earned value of $200,000 by the planned value of $225,000, for an SPI of .88. This tells me that this project is 88 percent on schedule—or, if you're a pessimist, the project is 12 percent off track.

 EXAM TIP   Adaptive projects don't typically use EVM because it's tough to say where a project should be at a certain point in time and what the work should be worth, and the estimate at completion is already determined as the project budget. A hybrid project, however, could use EVM because it will have a blend of adaptive and predictive approaches.

Predicting the Project's Future

Notice in the preceding paragraph I said, "at this time." That's because the project will, hopefully, continue to make progress, and the planned value and earned value numbers will change. Naturally, as the project moves toward completion, the earned value amounts will increase, and so will the planned value numbers. Typically, these indexes, both schedule and costs, are measured at milestones, and they enable the project management team to do some prognosticating as to where the project will likely end up by its completion. That's right—we can do some forecasting.

 NOTE   The forecasting formulas are swift and easy to calculate, but they're not really all that accurate. After all, you never really know how much a project will cost until you've completed all of the project work.

Finding the Estimate to Complete

So, your project is in a pickle, and management wants to know how much more this project is going to cost. They're after the estimate to complete (ETC) equation. There are three flavors of this formula, based on conditions within your project.

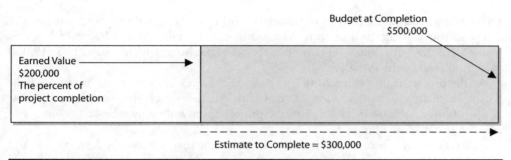

Figure 7-11 The estimate to complete can consider atypical variances.

ETC Based on a New Estimate Sometimes you just have to accept the fact that all the estimates up to this point are flawed, and you need a new estimate. Imagine a project where the project manager and the project team estimate that the work will cost $150,000 in labor, but once they get into the project, they realize it'll actually cost $275,000 in labor because the work is much more difficult than they anticipated. That's a reason for the ETC on a new estimate.

ETC Based on Atypical Variances This formula, shown in Figure 7-11, is used when the project has experienced some wacky fluctuation in costs and the project manager doesn't believe the anomalies will continue within the project. For example, the cost of plywood was estimated at $18 per sheet. Because of a hurricane in another part of the country, however, the cost of the plywood has changed to $25 per sheet. This fluctuation in the cost of materials has changed, but the project manager doesn't believe the cost change will affect the cost to deliver the other work packages in the WBS. Here's the formula for atypical variances: ETC = BAC − EV.

Let's say that this project has a BAC of $500,000 and is 40 percent complete. The earned value is $200,000, so our ETC formula would be ETC = $500,000 − $200,000, for an ETC of $300,000. Obviously, this formula is shallow and won't be the best forecasting formula for every scenario. If the cost of the materials has changed drastically, a whole new estimate would be more appropriate.

ETC Based on Typical Variances Sometimes in a project, a variance appears, and the project management team realizes that this is going to continue throughout the rest of the project. Figure 7-12 demonstrates the formula: ETC = (BAC − EV)/CPI.

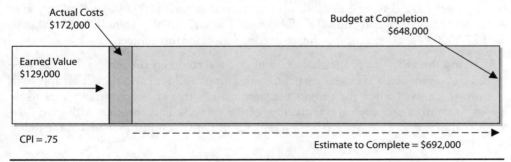

Figure 7-12 ETC may consider expected variances within a project.

For example, consider a project to install 10,000 light fixtures throughout a university campus. You and the project team have estimated it'll take 12,000 hours of labor to install all of the lights, and your cost estimate is $54 per hour, which equates to $648,000 to complete all of the installations.

As the project team begins work on the install, however, the time to install the light fixtures actually takes slightly longer than anticipated for each fixture. You realize that your duration estimate is flawed, and the project team will likely take 16,000 hours of labor to install all the lights.

The ETC in this formula requires that the project manager know the earned value and the cost performance index. Let's say that this project is 20 percent complete, so the EV is roughly $129,000. As the work is taking longer to complete, the actual cost to reach the 20 percent mark turns out to be $172,000. The CPI is determined by dividing the earned value, $129,000, by the actual costs of $172,000. The CPI for this project is .75.

Now let's try the ETC formula: (BAC – EV)/CPI, or ($648,000 – $129,000)/.75, which equates to $692,000. That's $692,000 more that this project will need in its budget to complete the remainder of the project work. Yikes!

Finding the Estimate at Completion

One of the most fundamental forecasting formulas is the estimate at completion (EAC). This formula accounts for all those pennies you're losing on every dollar if your CPI is less than 1. It's an opportunity for the project manager to say, "Hey! Based on our current project's health, this is where we're likely to be at the end of the project. I'd better work on my resume." Let's take a look at these formulas.

EAC Using a New Estimate   Just as with the estimate to complete formulas, sometimes it's best just to create a whole new estimate. This approach with the EAC is pretty straightforward—it's the actual costs plus the estimate to complete. Let's say your project has a budget of $500,000, and you've already spent $187,000 of it. For whatever reason, you've determined that your estimate is no longer valid, and your ETC for the remainder of the project is actually going to be $420,000—that's how much you're going to need to finish the project work. The EAC, in this instance, is the actual costs of $187,000 plus your ETC of $420,000, or $607,000.

EAC with Atypical Variances   Sometimes anomalies within a project can skew the project estimate at completion. The formula for this scenario, as Figure 7-13 demonstrates, is the actual costs plus the budget at completion minus the earned value. Let's try it. Your project has a BAC of $500,000, and the earned value is $100,000. However, you've spent $127,000 in actual costs. The EAC would be $127,000 + $500,000 – $100,000, or $527,000. That's your new estimate at completion for this project.

EAC Using the CPI   If a project has a CPI of .97, you could say the project is losing three pennies on every dollar. Those three pennies are going to add up over time. This approach is most often used when the project manager realizes that the cost variances are likely going to continue through the remainder of the project. This formula, as Figure 7-14 demonstrates, is EAC = AC + ((BAC – EV)/CPI). Don't you just love nested formulas? Let's try this one out.

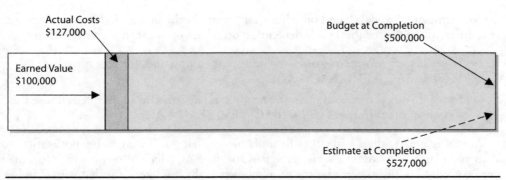

Figure 7-13   The EAC can also account for anomalies in project expenses.

Your project has a BAC of $500,000, and your earned value is $150,000. Your actual costs for this project are $162,000. Your CPI is calculated as .93. The EAC would be $162,000 + (($500,000 – $150,000)/.93), or $538,344. Wasn't that fun?

 EXAM TIP   There won't be as many questions on these EVM formulas as you might hope, but knowing these formulas can help you nail down the few questions you'll likely have.

Calculating the To-Complete Performance Index

Imagine a formula that would tell you if the project can meet the budget at completion based on current conditions. Or imagine a formula that can predict whether the project can even achieve your new estimate at completion. Forget your imagination and just use the *to-complete performance index* (TCPI). This formula can forecast the likelihood of a

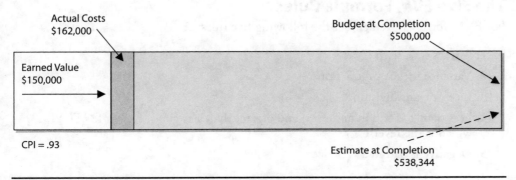

Figure 7-14   The EAC can also use the CPI as a modifier.

project achieving its goals based on what's happening in the project right now. There are two different flavors for the TCPI, depending on what you want to accomplish:

- To see if your project can meet the budget at completion, use this formula: TCPI = (BAC − EV)/(BAC − AC).

- To see if your project can meet the newly created estimate at completion, use this version of the formula: TCPI = (BAC − EV)/(EAC − AC).

Anything greater than 1 in either formula means that you'll have to be more efficient than you planned in order to achieve the BAC or the EAC, depending on which formula you've used. Basically, the greater the number over 1, the less likely it is that you'll be able to meet your BAC or the EAC, depending on which formula you've used. The lower the number under 1, the more likely you are to reach your BAC or EAC (again, depending on which formula you've used).

Finding Big Variances

Two variances relate to the entire project, and they're both easy to learn. The first variance you don't really know until the project is 100 percent complete. This is the project variance, and the formula is simply BAC − AC. If your project had a budget of $500,000 and you spent $734,000 to get it all done, then the project variance is $500,000 − $734,000, which equates, of course, to −$234,000.

The second variance is part of our forecasting model, and it predicts the likely project variance. It's called the variance at completion (VAC), and the formula is VAC = BAC − EAC. Let's say your project has a BAC of $500,000 and your EAC is predicted to be $538,344. The VAC is $500,000 − $538,344, for a predicted variance of −$38,344. Of course, this formula assumes that the rest of the project will run smoothly. In reality, where you and I hang out, the project VAC could swing in either direction based on the project's overall performance.

The Five EVM Formula Rules

For EVM formulas, remember the following five rules:

1. Always start with EV.

2. Variance means subtraction.

3. Index means division.

4. Less than 1 is bad in an index, and greater than 1 is good. Except for TCPI, which is the reverse.

5. Negative is bad in a variance.

The formulas for earned value analysis can be completed manually or through project management software. Table 7-1 shows a summary of all the formulas, as well as a sample, albeit goofy, mnemonic device.

Name	Formula	Mnemonic
Planned value	PV = percent complete of where the project should be	Please
Earned value	EV = percent complete × BAC	Eat
Cost variance	CV = EV – AC	Carl's
Schedule variance	SV = EV – PV	Sugar
Cost performance index	CPI = EV/AC	Candy
Schedule performance index	SPI = EV/PV	S (This and the following two spell "SEE")
Estimate at completion (typical variance)	EAC = BAC/CPI	E
Estimate at completion (atypical variance)	EAC = BAC + AC – EV	E
Estimate at completion	EAC = AC + ETC	Everyone
Estimate to complete	ETC = EAC – AC	Eat
To-complete performance index (BAC)	(BAC – EV)/(BAC – AC)	The
To-complete performance index (EAC)	(BAC – EV)/(EAC – AC)	Taffy
Variance at completion	VAC = BAC – EAC	Violin

Table 7-1   A Summary of EVM Formulas

EXAM TIP   For the exam, you'll want to memorize these formulas.

DIGITAL CONTENT   These aren't much fun to memorize, I know, but you should. Although you won't have an overwhelming number of EVM questions on your exam, these are free points if you know the formulas and can do the math. I have a present for you—it's an Excel spreadsheet called "EV Worksheet." It shows all these formulas in action. I recommend you make up some numbers to test your ability to complete these formulas and then plug in your values to Excel to confirm your math. Enjoy!

Chapter Summary

Projects require resources and time, both of which cost money. Project costs are estimated, or predicted, according to how much the project work will likely cost to complete. There are multiple flavors and approaches to project cost estimating. Project managers can use analogous estimating, parametric estimating, or, the most reliable, bottom-up estimating. Whatever cost estimating approach the project manager elects to use, the basis of the estimate should be documented in case the estimate should ever be called into question.

When a project manager creates the project cost estimate, he should also factor in a contingency reserve for project risks and cost overruns. Based on the enterprise environmental factors of an organization, and often the project priority, the process to create and receive the contingency reserve may fluctuate. The contingency reserve is not an allowance to be spent at the project manager's discretion but more of a safety net should the project go awry. Variances covered by the contingency reserve can't be swept under the rug but must be accounted for and hopefully learned from.

Cost budgeting is the aggregation of the costs to create the work packages in the WBS. Sometimes, cost budgeting refers to the cost aggregation as the "roll-up" of the costs associated with each work package. Cost budgeting effectively applies the cost estimates over time. Most project managers don't receive the entire project funding in one swoop, but rather in stepped increments over the life of the project.

Cost management in adaptive projects is pretty straightforward. An estimate of the work is created and then a budget is assigned. The major costs of an adaptive project are labor costs, though some projects may have physical resources to consider, such as equipment and software costs. The items in the product backlog equate the cost of the work. The most important items—the items of the highest value—are accomplished first, and the lower prioritized items are done last if the project schedule and budget allows. The velocity of the team affects the likelihood of all the project user stories being completed. If the velocity is lower than expected, there's a real possibility of items getting squeezed from the product backlog.

Adaptive projects also adhere to the principle of the value of work not done. This means keeping things simple by doing only the work that contributes to the value of the project. To create value in Agile requires working software and reaching the definition of done. There is zero value in mostly completed work. This idea also means the project doesn't have the same depth of documentation you'll find in Agile—the work should first focus on protecting the value stream of the project.

Once the project moves from planning into execution, it also moves into monitoring and control. The project manager and the project team work together to control the project costs and monitor the performance of the project work. The most accessible method to monitor the project cost is through earned value management (EVM), which demonstrates the performance of the project and enables the project manager to forecast where the project is likely to end up financially.

Questions

1. You are using a previous, similar project to predict the costs of the current project. Which of the following best describes analogous estimating?

   A. Regression analysis

   B. Bottom-up estimating

   C. Organizational process assets

   D. Enterprise environmental factors

2. You are the project manager for a new technology implementation project. Management has requested that your estimates be as exact as possible. Which one of the following methods of estimating will provide the most accurate estimate?

   A. Top-down estimating

   B. Top-down budgeting

   C. Bottom-up estimating

   D. Parametric estimating

3. Amira is the project manager for her company, and she's working with the project team to determine the effect of a proposed change on the project's budget. When Amira looks at the change, she tells the team that the change will pass through the project's cost change control system. What does the cost change control system do?

   A. It defines the methods to approve a change to the cost baseline.

   B. It defines the methods to create the cost baseline.

   C. It evaluates changes to the project costs based on changes to the project scope.

   D. This is not a valid change control system.

4. You have just started a project for a manufacturer. Project team members report they are 30 percent complete with the project. You have spent $25,000 of the project's $250,000 budget. What is the earned value for this project?

   A. 10 percent

   B. $75,000

   C. $25,000

   D. Not enough information to know

5. You and your project team are about to enter a meeting to determine project costs. You have elected to use bottom-up estimating and will base your estimate on the WBS. Which one of the following is not an attribute of bottom-up estimating?

   A. People doing the work create the estimates.

   B. It creates a more accurate estimate.

   C. It's more expensive to do than other methods.

   D. It's less expensive to do than other methods.

6. You are the project manager for a consulting company. Your company has two possible projects to manage, but they can choose only one. Project WQQ is worth $217,000, while Project LB is worth $229,000. Management elects to choose Project LB. The opportunity cost of this choice is which one of the following?

   A. $12,000

   B. $217,000

   C. $229,000

   D. Zero, because Project LB is worth more than Project WQQ

7. You are the project manager of an adaptive project and you're working with the stakeholders to explain the Agile approach to cost management. You explain that although the costs of the project are fixed, it's possible that some items may be removed from the product backlog. The customer is concerned because they think all of the items should be included in the project. What should you tell the customer?

   A. Adaptive projects don't work that way.

   B. They'll need more time and money to complete all the project work.

   C. If items are removed from the product backlog, they will be lower valued items.

   D. The removed items will be the most costly, so the project will meet the fixed budget.

8. You are the project manager of a construction project scheduled to last 24 months. You have elected to rent a piece of equipment for the project's duration, even though you will need the equipment only periodically throughout the project. The cost of the equipment rental per month is $890. This is an example of which of the following?

   A. Fixed cost

   B. Parametric cost

   C. Variable cost

   D. Indirect cost

9. You are the project manager of the BHG Project. Your BAC is $600,000. You have spent $270,000 of your budget. You are now 40 percent done with the project, though your plan called for you to be 45 percent done with the work by this time. What is your CPI?

   A. 100

   B. 89

   C. .89

   D. .79

10. Management has requested that you complete a definitive cost estimate for your current adaptive project. What should you do next?

   A. Create a project scope statement.

   B. Explain that definitive cost estimates are not possible because of the nature of adaptive projects.

   C. Work with the product owner and the development team to build out the product backlog and predict the costs.

   D. Ask management what they would like the cost estimate to be and then add 50 percent to their estimate.

11. You need to procure a highly specialized chemical for a research project. Only one vendor provides the materials you need. This scenario is an example of what market condition?

    A. Constraint

    B. Single source

    C. Sole source

    D. Oligopoly

12. You are the project manager of the Network Upgrade Project for your company. Management has asked that you create a cost estimate of the project so they can determine the project funding. You gather the inputs for the cost estimate and begin the process of cost estimating. Of the following cost estimating inputs, which one is the least reliable?

    A. Team member recollections

    B. Historical information

    C. Project files

    D. Cost estimating templates

13. You can purchase pea gravel for your project at $437 per metric ton. You need 4 tons of the pea gravel, so you predict your costs will be $1748. This is an example of which cost-estimating approach?

    A. Parametric

    B. Analogous

    C. Bottom-up

    D. Top-down

14. You are the project manager of an adaptive project to create new software for your marketplace. You need to create a cost estimate based on labor for the project even though your organization has not done this type of project before. Which one of the following is an example of resource cost rates that a project manager could use to predict the cost of the project?

    A. Analogous estimating

    B. Bottom-up estimating

    C. Commercial database

    D. Procurement bid analysis

15. You have created a cost estimate for a new project that you'll be managing in your organization. All of the following should be included in your cost estimate except for which one?

    A. Description of the schedule activity's project scope of work

    B. Assumptions made

    C. Constraints

    D. Team members the project will utilize

16. Lila is the project manager of a construction project. The budget for her project is $275,000. The project team made a mistake early in the project that cost $34,000 in added materials. Lila does not believe mistakes will likely happen again because the team is 30 percent complete with the project and things are once again going smoothly. Her sponsor wants to know how much more funding Lila will likely need on the project. What should Lila tell the sponsor?

A. $192,500

B. $241,000

C. $309,000

D. $275,000

17. A project had a budget of $750,000 and was completed on time. The project expenses, however, were 15 percent more than what the project called for. What is the earned value of this project?

A. Impossible to know—not enough information

B. $112,500

C. $637,500

D. $750,000

18. A project had a budget of $750,000 and was completed on time. The project expenses, however, were 15 percent more than what the project called for. What is the variance at the completion for this project?

A. Impossible to know—not enough information

B. $112,500

C. $637,500

D. $750,000

19. Marty is the project manager of a software development project. He has reviewed the project's costs and progress and realizes that he has a cost variance of $44,000. He needs to complete what type of report?

A. Status report

B. Exceptions report

C. Forecast report

D. Lessons learned

20. You are a construction manager for a construction project. The project will be using a new material that the project team has never worked with before. You allot $10,000 to train the project team on the new material so that the project will operate smoothly. The $10,000 for training is known as what?

A. Cost of quality

B. Cost of poor quality

C. Sunk costs

D. Contingency allowance

Answers

1. **C.** Analogous estimating is based on historical information, which is part of organizational process assets. A, regression analysis, is incorrect, because this choice describes the study of a project moving backward so that it may ultimately move forward. B is incorrect because this is the most reliable cost-estimating technique and is based on the current project's WBS. D, enterprise environmental factors, is a term that describes the internal policies and procedures a project manager must follow within the project.

2. **C.** Bottom-up estimating takes the longest to complete of all the estimating approaches, but it is also the most reliable approach. A, top-down estimating, is also known as analogous estimating, and it is not reliable. B, top-down budgeting, is not a valid term for this question. D, parametric estimating, is an approach that predicts the project costs based on a parameter, such as cost per hour, cost per unit, or cost per usage.

3. **A.** The cost change control system defines how changes to the cost baseline may be approved. B, C, and D are all invalid choices.

4. **B.** Earned value is found by multiplying the percentage of the project that is completed by the project's budget at completion. In this instance, the answer is $75,000. A, C, and D are all incorrect.

5. **D.** Bottom-up estimating is typically more expensive to do than other estimating approaches, because of the time required to create this type of estimate. A, B, and C are all accurate attributes of a bottom-up estimate.

6. **B.** The opportunity cost is the worth of the project that the organization cannot undertake; in this case, Project WQQ cannot be done and is worth $217,000. A is incorrect because the $12,000 represents the difference between the worth of two projects. C, $229,000, is incorrect because this is the worth of the LB project. D is incorrect because this is not an accurate statement.

7. **C.** The idea that all of their requirements may not be met can be challenging for customers new to adaptive projects. You'll need to explain how the project will first deliver the most valued items and then work its way to lower valued, lower priority items in the product backlog. Items can't be removed from the backlog by the project facilitator; only the product owner or customer rep can do this, and even then removal is based on customer requirement prioritization. You should also remind the customer that this is the worst-case scenario and you'll be more likely to predict the costs and likelihood of meeting all requirements as your team moves deeper into the project. A is incorrect; although it's true that adaptive projects don't work like predictive projects, you'll need to use more finesse than this explanation provides. B is incorrect; some project managers may demand more time and more money, but there's really no proof that this is needed. D is incorrect, because it's not the most costly items that are removed from the product backlog should the project funds be depleted, but the lower level, lower priority items.

8. A. This is an example of a fixed cost. The cost of the equipment will remain uniform, or fixed, throughout the duration of the project. B is incorrect because parametric costs can be identified as cost per unit. C is incorrect because the cost of the equipment does not fluctuate. D is incorrect because indirect costs are a way to describe costs that may be shared between projects.

9. C. The CPI is determined by dividing the earned value by the actual cost. The earned value is 40 percent of $600,000, which is $240,000. The actual cost is $270,000. CPI is $240,000 divided by $270,000, which equates to .88. A is incorrect because the project is not performing at 100 percent. B is incorrect because 89 is not the correct value, which is .89. D is an incorrect calculation of the CPI.

10. B. Adaptive projects do not utilize definitive cost estimates because of the nature of the project approach and the expected changes. You'll gently explain that adaptive projects can create a likely cost estimate, but because the items of the product backlog will likely change, the cost estimate will likely become flawed once the product backlog changes. A is incorrect, because there is no project scope statement in adaptive projects. C is incorrect; this approach would not be adding value to the project because of the expected changes in the product backlog. D is incorrect, because management can't predict the cost of the project and they're asking you to create the cost estimate.

11. C. Sole source is the best choice, because it describes the marketplace condition in which only one vendor can provide the goods or services your project requires. A, constraint, is not a valid market condition. B, single source, describes the marketplace condition in which multiple vendors can provide the goods or services your project demands, but you prefer to work with just one vendor in particular. D, an oligopoly, is a market condition in which the actions of one vendor affect the actions of the other vendors.

12. A. Team member recollections are the least reliable input to cost estimating. B, C, and D are all valid inputs to the cost-estimating process.

13. A. The cost of the pea gravel is a parametric estimate. B, analogous, is incorrect because no other project cost estimate is being referenced. C, bottom-up, is not described in this instance because the WBS and each work package is not being estimated for cost. D, top-down estimating, is another name for B, analogous estimating, so this choice is invalid.

14. C. Commercial databases often provide resource cost rates for project estimating, so this is the correct answer for this question. If you had done this type of project work before, A, analogous estimating, could be correct, because this is historical information you could apply to the costs of your project. B is incorrect because adaptive projects don't use bottom-up estimating because the product backlog is likely to change in the project. D is incorrect because this project work is being done internally, not outsourced to a vendor and requiring a bid.

15. **D.** The team members that the project manager will utilize are not included in the cost estimate. The project manager will include the project scope of work, the assumptions made, and the constraints considered when creating a cost estimate, so A, B, and C are incorrect.

16. **A.** The formula for this instance, because the conditions experienced were atypical, is ETC = BAC − EV. The formula for Lila's project would be ETC = \$275,000 − \$82,500 = \$192,500. B, C, and D are all incorrect calculations of the estimate-to-complete formula.

17. **D.** The earned value is simply the percent complete times the BAC. In this instance, the project's budget was \$750,000, and since the project is 100 percent complete, the answer is D. A, B, and C are all incorrect.

18. **B.** The formula for this problem is variance at completion minus the actual costs for the project. A, C, and D are all incorrect.

19. **B.** Because Marty has a variance, he needs to complete a variance report. A variance report is also known as an exceptions report, so B is the best answer. A, a status report, is used to communicate the status of the project, not the variances. C is not a valid report type. D, lessons learned, is an ongoing project document, not a report type.

20. **A.** Training for the project team is known as the cost of quality. B, the cost of poor quality, is incorrect, because this would be the costs the project would incur if it did not attain the expected level of quality. C, sunk costs, describes the monies that have been spent on a project already. D, contingency allowance, is an amount of funds allotted to cover cost overruns in a project.

Managing Project Quality

In this chapter, you will

- Plan for quality
- Work with the quality management process
- Control quality in projects
- Recognize the quality control charts

What good does it do if a project launches and the project execution consumes the monies and time, but the project deliverable is of unacceptable quality? Imagine, for example, a project to build a new house, and at the project completion, the house is tilting to one side, the windows all have cracks and holes in them, and the roof has obvious gaps for the rain and birds to enter. This is not, I'm sure, what the homeowners had in mind. Or consider an agile project to create new software. The product owner has worked with the stakeholders to identify the requirements, create a product roadmap, and prioritize the software requirements. The development team, however, has ignored the nonfunctional requirements of stability and security, they've taken shortcuts during the product work, and they've skimped on testing. Quality will obviously suffer, and the mistakes will be embarrassingly clear when the team demonstrates what they've created. That's a big letdown.

Fortunately, in project management—that is, *good* project management—mechanisms are in place to plan and implement quality throughout the project, and quality is not just an afterthought. Project quality management is all about the project manager, the project team, and the performing organization working together to ensure that the project performs according to the project plan, so that the project deliverable aligns with the project scope statement. Quality in a project is really all about getting the project done and creating a deliverable that satisfies the project requirements and that can actually be used effectively by the project customer. Quality in adaptive projects is about delivering value by creating working software for the project customer.

According to the American Society for Quality (ASQ), "Quality is the degree to which a set of inherent characteristics fulfills requirements." Well, isn't that interesting? Let's go back in time. A project is launched and a project charter is issued to the project manager. Then the project manager and the project team create what document?

The *project scope statement* defines all the requirements for the project, including what's in and what's out of scope. Quality, therefore, means satisfying everything that the project scope statement requires.

The project scope statement defines what the project will create, its requirements for acceptance, and the metrics used to measure project success. In project quality management, we plan quality into the project, inspect the project and deliverables for the existence of quality, and then move toward the scope validation process, which confirms that we've created what our customer expected. Quality is about delivering on promises.

In an agile project the approach is similar, with a few caveats: the product roadmap and product vision is created, and then the requirements are hashed out, prioritized, and sized with the development team. Everyone begins with the Definition of Done (DoD), which defines when the quality requirements are satisfied. A solid plan for requirements testing needs to be implemented along with strict rules for addressing issues that don't pass the tests. In theory, agile development uses the same approach used by any other style of development: know exactly what to create and then create it exactly. Mistakes aren't delivered to the customer before they are repaired. The customer gets what they've asked for, from most important, to least important.

No discussion on quality is complete without a nod to our pal W. Edwards Deming. You likely won't need to know much about Deming for the exam, but you should be familiar with his famed plan-do-check-act (PDCA) cycle. (I highly recommend Mary B. Walton's book, *The Deming Management Method* [Perigee Books, 1988], for the complete story of Deming—maybe after you pass your PMI examination.) You should also know that Deming's philosophy on quality management considers of paramount importance customer satisfaction, prevention over inspection, a call for management responsibility, and a desire to do the work correctly the first time.

 VIDEO   For a more detailed explanation, watch the *Quality Management Facts* video now.

The first step toward achieving quality is to define what constitutes quality in your project. To define quality, project stakeholders must be in agreement regarding the scope requirements, the tolerances for quality, and the stakeholders' expectations with regard to quality. In other words, quantifiable goals are required for quality to achieve quality in the project. Agile projects embrace this idea by establishing the DoD for each requirement, which provides a clear vision of what "done" looks like for the team.

Tailoring quality in project management means that you'll build a quality approach, or adapt a quality approach, for your organization that supports its vision of quality. Considerations for tailoring quality in any organization include the following:

- **Policy compliance and auditing**   You may be required to adhere to regulations and compliance concerns. Your organization may have a quality assurance department or group that sets internal policies for quality, and they may audit the project and project results to confirm adherence.

- **Continuous improvements** You'll need to define up front what the quality aspirations are and how you'll achieve them. You'll also define quality improvement for the project work, the processes, and the project management approach to be implemented throughout the project.

- **Stakeholder engagement** You want stakeholders to be engaged with the project work, to feel a sense of ownership in the project. The stakeholder management plan, which I'll discuss in Chapter 13, is key for improving stakeholder engagement.

Quality, even in agile projects, is about meeting the project requirements. Of course, the project requirements are defined in the iteration planning sessions and directly before the project team takes on the work for the current iteration. As the product owner and the development team review the number of user stories that can be completed within the current iteration, the team, product owner, and project manager seek clarification on what exactly is required to deliver on the selected user stories.

In agile and adaptive environments, quality reviews are conducted throughout the project rather than occurring only at the end of the project or iteration. *Sprint reviews* are opportunities for scope validation of what the team has created, and sometimes errors and defects become apparent in this meeting. At the end of each iteration, you'll also host a special *sprint retrospective* meeting to look back on what worked (or didn't work) in the last iteration. This enables the project manager and team to make changes to processes and adjustments to improve upon the project processes and the execution of the work to create the user stories.

This chapter is core to the PMI's idea of project integration management. If quality suffers, all of the knowledge areas are affected. You can also see the effect on integration management if any of the other knowledge areas suffers in performance. Quality is directly affected by all of the areas of project management, and all of the areas of project management are affected if quality is missing. It's a busy, two-way street.

Planning for Quality

Planning quality management is the process of first determining which quality standards are relevant to your project and then finding the best methods for adhering to those quality standards. Planning quality management involves the quality of how the project is managed and the quality of the project deliverables. The quality of how the project is managed is a great example of project integration management, which I mentioned earlier in the chapter. Quality planning is core to the planning process group, because each knowledge area has relevant standards that affect quality, and quality planning is integrated into each planning process.

In other words, if a project manager rushes through planning for each of the knowledge areas, quality is likely to suffer. When change requests are proposed, the impact of each change request on each of the knowledge areas is considered. You already know that a change request could have a financial impact, a schedule impact, and more. Quality management asks, "What impact does quality have on this proposed change, and what impact does this change have on the overall quality of the project?"

Although changes are welcome in adaptive projects, there must also be a process for integrated change control. Changes that pop into the product backlog early in the project are easy to incorporate and take on. Changes late in the project can be cumbersome to shoehorn into work that's already been done. In fact, some changes can even cause the project team to have to undo work to include the new changes in the project deliverable. Even if that's all acceptable, the size of the change can cause the sizing of the requirements to increase when the team considers how to get the change done, what will be the affect of the change on accomplished work, and what other risks the change may introduce into the project. The scrum master, or coach in Extreme Programming (XP), needs to work to keep morale high and to remind the team that change is expected and it's all part of the approach.

 EXAM TIP Although it's true that agile projects aren't planned to the extent of predictive projects, it's not fair to say they aren't planned at all. Agile projects will include plans on how to achieve quality in the project, in each sprint, and during the sprint retrospectives. Planning isn't as front-loaded in agile as it is in predictive projects.

Throughout the project planning process, the focus is on completing the project by satisfying the project requirements. Quality is enmeshed in all project planning. The foundation of quality planning states that quality is planned into the project, not inspected in. In other words, planning how to achieve the expected level of quality and then executing the project plan is easier, more cost-effective, and less stressful for everyone involved than catching and fixing mistakes as the project moves toward completion. Like my dad used to say, "Do it right the first time."

There are five approaches to quality management:

- *Let the customer find the defects.* This approach is the most expensive and most aggravating, and it can lead to loss of sales, reputation, warranty claims, and other costs. Defects that make it to production are called *escaped* defects. Not good.

- *Find the defects through quality control.* This approach uses quality control (QC) to inspect the deliverables to keep mistakes out of the customer's hands. This approach still has internal costs (called *internal failure costs*), because you must correct the defects and redo work. Agile projects utilize testing to catch defects before they escape to the project customers.

- *Prevent defects through quality assurance programs.* Quality assurance (QA) means inspecting and creating processes to try to ensure that the work is completed correctly the first time, resulting in good, quality work. Truly understanding what the customer wants and writing good user stories will help the team recognize the DoD and what is required to pass QA tests.

- *Plan and design quality from the beginning of the project.* By planning quality in the design of the product specifications, quality is more likely to be achieved in the execution. The product owner and team should work together to gain a full understanding of the value the customer expects from the project.

- *Establish quality in the organizational culture.* Quality in the organizational culture makes quality a priority and a way of doing business for all members of the organization. When an organization first embraces an adaptive approach, some customers may find it difficult to "follow the rules" of agile.

There are five inputs to planning for quality in a predictive or hybrid project:

- **Project charter**   The charter defines the high-level requirements, product characteristics, and project approval requirements. The project charter will also define what objectives are to be measured and achieved and what constitutes success in the project.

- **Project management plan**   The project management plan is needed for quality planning—specifically, the requirements management plan, the risk management plan, the stakeholder engagement plan, and the scope baseline. The requirements management plan defines the requirements that satisfy the project scope, and that in turn will satisfy project quality. The risk management plan addresses risks that may affect the project and the product. The stakeholder engagement plan, something we've not yet discussed, defines the stakeholders' needs and expectations for quality within the project. The scope baseline is needed because the scope statement, work breakdown structure (WBS), and WBS dictionary all define the quality standards and objectives, acceptance criteria, and specifics for what constitutes quality in the project work packages.

- **Project documents**   Five project documents are referenced as part of quality management planning:

  - **Assumptions log**   All assumptions and constraints are considered; these items can affect the quality of the project.

  - **Requirements documentation**   The requirements of the project should be documented to reflect the expectations of the project stakeholders. The project's work is to create all the requirements and fulfill the product scope.

  - **Requirements traceability matrix**   The RTM defines the connection between the defined product requirements and the project deliverables. It also includes a record of testing of the requirements to ensure compliance to quality standards.

  - **Risk register**   The risk register contains all the identified risks and information on how potential risks may affect the overall quality of the project.

  - **Stakeholder register**   You'll need to know which stakeholders have a specific interest in the quality objectives of the project and how to contact them. Some stakeholders may have concerns about specific deliverables, so you'll want to communicate with those folks when quality issues arise.

- **Enterprise environmental factors**   These are the policies and procedures your organization must adhere to. In particular, the enterprise environmental factors referenced here are the mandates that affect the application area your project is dealing with. In other words, for example, a construction project follows codes and regulations that differ from those of a project to bake a million cookies.

- **Organizational process assets** These are the methods of operation your organization uses and the guidelines that are specific to your organization. Historical information, lessons learned, and guidelines within your organization are there for the project managers to rely on. Within the organization, a quality policy may have been issued by senior management for all projects to adhere to—this is part of organizational process assets. And what if a quality policy doesn't exist? It's up to the project management team to create one for the project.

Using Quality Planning Tools

The project manager and the project team can use several tools to plan for quality in the project. *Expert judgment,* for example, is a common tool and technique for planning quality in the project. The goal of all these tools is to plan quality into the project rather than attempt to inspect quality into the project. (To repeat, do the work right the first time.) Let's take a look at quality planning tools and how the project manager and the project team can use them to their benefit.

Benchmarking Performance

Benchmarking involves comparing two similar things to measure which one performs best. For example, you could benchmark the same activities on two different computers, test drive several different cars, or even benchmark an organization before and after a project. Benchmarking, in regard to quality planning, examines project practices against other projects to measure performance, and then selects the best practices for performance in the current project.

 EXAM TIP Resist the temptation to benchmark two different agile project teams. The teams are working on different requirements and different skillsets, and each may be using a different sizing approach to user stories. You can benchmark internally to measure velocity from iteration to iteration.

Brainstorming and Interviews

Brainstorming is used in requirements gathering, but it can also be used for data gathering from your project team or group of stakeholders. Project team members, customers, vendors, and other stakeholders can be interviewed to get a sense of quality expectations, perceptions of quality, and concerns about quality within the project.

Agile uses at least three brainstorming techniques you should recognize:

- **Brain writing** The topic is introduced to the team and everyone writes down their ideas in private. This ensures that everyone's ideas are shared, prevents anchoring onto one idea, and lets everyone contribute rather than just the stronger personalities on the team.
- **Brain-netting** The topic is shared with a virtual team and people collaborate through online software to share ideas, explore topics, and contribute remotely rather than in a centralized location.

- **Round robin**   The team forms a circle and each person shares one idea in order around the circle. This helps ensure that everyone can contribute and gives everyone a chance to speak and to listen to other ideas.

Using a Cost-Benefits Analysis

Ever go shopping and compare prices? For example, you might consider the costs of two cars with regard to the features they provide. Or you might consider hiring a more experienced worker because she has some competencies that make the extra dollars worth the costs. Part of planning for quality is moving through this process of cost-benefits analysis.

Using cost-benefits analysis is more than just considering how much to spend for features and materials used in the project deliverable, although that is part of the process. Cost-benefits analysis also considers the cost of completing the project work and the best approach to achieving quality in the project in relation to the monies required to complete the work. For example, you could always use senior engineers to complete even the most menial tasks, but that wouldn't be a good use of their time or of the monies to pay for their time. Figure 8-1 shows an example of using a cost-benefits analysis.

A cost-benefits analysis is simply the study of the quality received in proportion to the cost to reach quality expectations. The project management team must understand how much money is appropriate to spend to satisfy the project customer. If the project spends too much to reach a level of quality that is far beyond what the customer expects or wants, that's considered waste. The same is true if the project team produces less than the level of quality the customer expects and rework is needed, because this also requires more monies to be spent.

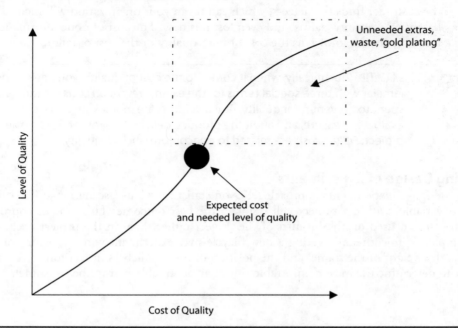

Figure 8-1   Quality should meet, but not exceed, the customer's expectations.

EXAM COACH Quality is achieved by satisfying exactly what the scope calls for. What's the scope for your exam? It's a pass or fail exam, so your scope is probably to pass, right? Don't aim for a 100 percent—aim for a passing grade. Put your efforts into the biggest exam objectives to get the biggest bang for your exam buck.

Considering the Cost of Quality

The cost of quality (COQ) considers how much must be spent to achieve the expected level of quality within the project. There are two types of costs directly tied to quality:

- **Cost of conformance to quality** This cost is associated with the monies spent to attain the expected level of quality, such as the cost of training, safety issues, and purchasing the appropriate equipment and materials, which all contribute to the expected levels of quality. The cost of conformance includes prevention costs for training, documenting processes, procuring the appropriate equipment, and having the time to do the work correctly. The cost of conformance is also where you'll determine appraisal costs to test the product, complete destructive testing loss, and perform inspections. These all require that money be spent to avoid failures.

- **Cost of nonconformance to quality** This cost is associated with not satisfying the quality expectations. The cost of nonconformance is evident when the project has to spend money because of failures within the project. Internal failure costs are in the form of rework and scrap. External failure costs happen when the customer finds the defects, which can mean your organization will incur liabilities, warranty claims, and even lost business. The cost of nonconformance to quality is also known as the cost of poor quality or the cost of failure.

 EXAM TIP Technically, when it comes to the cost of quality, you need to be familiar with three special terms for the exam. *Prevention costs* are monies spent to prevent poor quality. *Appraisal costs* are monies spent to test, evaluate, measure, and audit the product, deliverables, or services of the project. *Failure costs* are related to nonconformance to quality.

Using Design of Experiments

The design-of-experiments approach relies on statistical what-if scenarios to determine what variables within a project will result in the best outcome. This type of approach is most often used on the product of the project rather than on the project itself. For example, a project team creating a new bicycle may experiment with the width of the tires, the weight of the frame, and the position of the handlebars in relation to the bike seat to determine the most comfortable ride at an acceptable cost to the consumer.

Although design of experiments is most often associated with product design, it can be applied to project management activities. For example, a project manager may evaluate the activities within a project and determine the time and cost of activities, depending on which employees are assigned to complete the work. A more experienced worker may cost the project more money on an hourly basis, but this individual is expected to complete the work in a third of the time that a less experienced worker would. This is design of experiments: experimenting with different variables to find the best solution at the best cost.

Design of experiments is also used as a method to identify which variables within a project or product are causing failures or unacceptable results. The goal of design of experiments is to isolate the root cause of an effect and to adjust that cause to eliminate the unacceptable results.

Using Data Representation for Quality Management Planning

Data representation techniques can help the project manager and project team identify, document, and visualize the quality expectations and perceptions for the project. Although not every project will utilize these techniques, you should be familiar with them for your PMP and exam:

- **Flowcharts**   A flowchart shows the flow of steps, activities, and information through a system. Also called process maps, flowcharts can show branching, loopbacks, or multiple paths through the system. Use a Suppliers, Inputs, Processes, Outputs, and Customers (SIPOC) flowchart to show how vendors and customers may interact in a project.

- **Logical model data**   This data is used to visualize the organization's data in common business language. For example, data for each employee could include country, state or region, phone, e-mail, and other facts. Logical model data would simply illustrate all of the data that contributes to the information for an employee in generic terms.

- **Matrix diagrams**   These tables show the relationship among different factors— for example, roles and responsibilities, costs and risks, quality and scope.

- **Mind mapping**   This same technique is used in scope management. Mind mapping is an exercise to organize information around a specific topic. Mind mapping quality management planning can be used to gather quality requirements, dependencies among the quality objectives, and quality relationships through the project.

Creating the Quality Management Plan

The end result of the quality planning phase is to find a method to implement the quality policy. Because planning is iterative, the quality planning sessions often require several revisits to the quality planning processes. Longer projects may have scheduled quality planning sessions to compare the performance of the project in relation to the quality that was planned.

One of the major outputs of quality planning is the quality management plan. This document describes how the project manager and the project team will fulfill the quality policy. In an ISO 9000 environment, the quality management plan is referred to as the "project quality system."

The quality management plan addresses the following things about the project and the project work:

- Quality standards the project will utilize
- Quality objectives the project must achieve
- Quality roles and responsibilities among the project team and key stakeholders
- Deliverables and processes that will be reviewed for quality
- How quality process activities will be controlled
- Quality tools the project will utilize
- How the project will address nonconformance to quality issues, corrective activities, and continuous process improvement

Establishing Quality Metrics

You need some quality metrics: if you don't measure quality, your project cannot improve. Specifically, I'm talking about the quantifiable terms and values used to measure a process, activity, or work result. An example of quality metrics is an expected value for the required torque to tighten a bolt on a piece of equipment. By testing and measuring the torque, QA engineers can create an operational definition that will prove or disprove the quality of the product. Other examples of quality metrics include hours of labor to complete a work package, required safety measures, cost per unit, and so on.

Operational definitions are clear, concise measurements. Designating that 95 percent of all customer service calls should be answered by a live person within 30 seconds is a metric. A statement that all calls should be answered in a timely manner is not. Agile projects will create the DoD for each user story and for the project as a whole that may equate to the product owner's roadmap or release plan. When quality goals have been met at key milestones, for example, a release may be initiated to the customer.

Updating the Project Management Plan and Documents

The quality management plan is an iterative activity that may warrant updates to the project management plan and some project documents. The two components that are most likely to be updated as a result of quality management planning are the risk management plan and the scope baseline. Risks can threaten quality within the project, and the scope baseline may need to be updated to reflect the quality requirements. Recall that the scope baseline includes the project scope statement, the WBS, and the WBS dictionary.

In addition to these items, you may also have to update the lessons learned register, the requirements traceability matrix, the risk register, and the stakeholder register based on the outcome of quality management planning.

Managing Quality in the Project

Once you've created the quality management plan, it's time to implement the plan. This is all about implementing the quality policies of the organization and the quality goals you've identified in the quality management plan. Much of this conversation is related to quality assurance, though the *PMBOK Guide* doesn't necessarily identify this conversation as "quality assurance." The *PMBOK Guide* calls it the "Manage Quality process," which is, frankly, analogous to many principles of quality assurance.

Quality assurance (QA) is the sum of the creation and implementation of the plans by the project manager, the project team, and management to ensure that the project meets the demands of quality. QA is not something that is done only at the end of the project; it occurs before and during the project as well. Quality management is prevention-driven; this helps you and the team to do the work correctly the first time. Technically, quality assurance is much broader than the QA activities you'll do in a project, but the concepts are very similar.

In some organizations, the QA department or another entity will complete the QA activities. QA focuses on preventing defects and assuring that QC fixes any product problems.

There are many different approaches to QA, depending on the quality system adopted by the organization or project team. QA is, to some extent, a parent for continuous process improvement. Continuous process improvement aims to remove waste and non–value-added activities, so it works hand-in-hand with QA.

When it comes to QA in agile projects, think of two things: the product backlog and the sprint retrospective. The product backlog must have clear requirements and well-defined user stories with acceptance tests. If the team can't understand a user story, they shouldn't launch the work. Clarification of the user story is needed. In the retrospective, the team discusses how to improve the project approach, how to improve the product, and what specific actions they can take in the next sprint of the project.

Preparing to Manage Quality

The project manager and the project team will need several inputs to prepare to manage quality within a project:

- **Project management plan** For the project management plan, you'll rely on the quality management plan. This plan defines how the project team will implement and fulfill the quality policy of the performing organization.

- **Project documents** The project manager will reference the lessons learned register, QC measurements, quality metrics, and any relevant risk reports.

- **Organizational process assets** The project manager may reference organizational process assets, which may include the organization quality management system, quality templates such as check sheets and test plans, audit results, and lessons learned from similar projects.

Managing Quality Within a Project

The QA department, management, or, in some instances, even the project manager can complete the requirements for QA. QA can be accomplished using the following tools (many of the same tools are used during quality planning):

- **Data gathering**   One of the most common techniques for data gathering in the quality management process is to use a checklist. A checklist is a list of structured steps that a person or team must "check off" after each step is completed. For example, an electrician may have a checklist of tasks to complete when installing a new electrical fixture. The checklist of steps for the activity ensures safety and consistency, as well as providing some evidence that all steps have been followed by the team members doing the work.

- **Alternative analysis**   This technique helps the project manager and project team determine which quality approach is most appropriate to use within the project. Agile project teams are empowered to experiment, fail fast, and explore approaches to get results.

- **Document analysis**   Dig into the documents to identify what's working, what's not working, and what parts of the project may be suffering, all of which could affect quality objectives in the project. Documentation is light in adaptive projects, but it's the work performance data that can help the team overcome challenges.

- **Process analysis**   This technique examines the project management processes to see what processes need improvement, have constraints, or may be non–value-added activities for the project. If it doesn't add value, in agile, it shouldn't be done.

- **Root-cause analysis**   This determines the causal factors that are contributing to the effect, or problem, experienced in the project. By removing the root cause(s) of the problem, the problem will be resolved. If the problem still exists after root causes are removed, it means that not all of the root causes, or the correct root cause, has been identified.

- **Affinity diagrams**   These diagrams break down ideas, solutions, and project components and group them together with like-minded ideas. For example, an IT solution may group all of the ideas about hardware, then software, and then the network, and so on.

- **Cause-and-effect diagrams**   Cause-and-effect diagrams visualize the effect, which is the problem you're attempting to resolve, and the causes, which are the things likely causing the problem. Cause-and-effect diagrams are also known as Ishikawa diagrams, fishbone diagrams, and why-why diagrams. These are also used in the control quality process, which I'll discuss later in the chapter.

- **Flowcharts**   Yes, you can use flowcharts to help represent data and manage quality in your project. Flowcharts can help with managing quality by showing what's contributing to a quality breakdown or defect in the project.

- **Histograms** A histogram is a bar chart that can represent categories of defects, ranking of quality problems, and any other data you want to display regarding managing quality.

- **Scatter diagrams** A scatter diagram plots out the relationship between two variables. The closer the two variables trend in the diagram, the more likely the two variables are related and affect each other in the process or project.

 NOTE A cause-and-effect diagram is also called an Ishikawa diagram (named for its creator, Japanese theorist Kaoru Ishikawa). Ishikawa charts are more often used in predictive projects, but they can be used in adaptive projects as well.

Completing a Quality Audit

Quality audits are about learning. The idea of a quality audit is to identify the lessons learned on the current project to determine how to make things better for this project as well as for other projects within the organization. For example, quality audits can help project manager Susan to learn from the implementations of project manager Bob, and vice versa.

Quality audits are formal reviews of what's been completed within a project, what worked, and what didn't work. The end result of the audit is improved performance for the current project, other projects, or the entire organization.

Quality audits can be scheduled at key intervals within a project or—surprise!—they can come without warning. The audit process can vary, depending on who is completing the audit: internal auditors or hired third-party experts.

Designing for X

Design for X (DfX) is a philosophy in product design, where the "X" can mean excellence, or, more often, a specific characteristic of a solution. The X is usually a variable that the project is trying to address, such as cost, uptime, return on investment, or another facet the organization is pursuing. Design for X considers all components of the design and how the component affects the X variable for better or for worse. Common project goals for DfX include lowered costs, improved service, more reliability, improved safety, and better overall quality. DfX can be used in all project types.

Implementing Problem-Solving Techniques

When there's a problem in the project, it's the project manager and the project team's responsibility to attempt to resolve the problem to assure that the project can continue and overcome the setback or challenge. In the quality management process, problem-solving will address quality issues and concerns by following a six-step approach:

1. Define the problem.
2. Define the problem's root cause.

3. Generate solutions to the problem.

4. Select the best solution for the problem.

5. Implement the selected solution.

6. Test and verify the effectiveness of the selected solution.

Reviewing the Results of Managing Quality

The primary output of managing quality? Quality improvement. But it's not just about the quality of the project's deliverables, but also the quality of the process to complete the project work. This is process analysis, and it follows the guidelines of the process improvement plan. There are four outputs of the process:

- Quality reports
- Test and evaluation documentation
- Project management plan updates (which can include quality management plan, scope baseline, schedule baseline, and cost baseline)
- Project document updates (which can include issue log, lessons learned register, and risk register)

Quality improvement requires actions to improve the project's effectiveness. The actions to improve the effectiveness may have to be routed through the change control system, which means change requests, analysis of the costs and risks, and involvement from the change control board.

Controlling Quality in a Project

There is a subtle difference between controlling quality and performing QC. Quality control is technically broader than just project management, even though many project managers and organizations use the term quality control to refer to the activities performed in this portion of the project. PMI tells us that control quality is the official project management process, and that's what you should recognize and embrace for the exam's sake. Where you work, however, the controlling quality project management process may be referred to as quality control. I, too, call this quality control and see tiny differences between the concepts. However, for the exam, I'll acknowledge those tiny differences and call this process by its *PMBOK Guide* name of controlling quality.

This is the part of the project where the project manager and the project team have control and influence. QA, for the most part, is specific to your organization, and the project manager doesn't have much control over the QA processes—he just has to do them. Controlling quality, on the other hand, is specific to the project manager in a hybrid or predictive project, so the project manager has lots of activities to do.

 EXAM TIP Pay close attention to the QC mechanisms mentioned in exam scenarios, and remember that there are things the project manager has control over in every project.

Controlling quality requires that the project manager, or another qualified party, monitor and measure project results to determine whether they are up to the quality standards. If the results are unsatisfactory, root-cause analysis follows the control quality activities. Root-cause analysis enables the project manager to determine the cause and apply corrective actions. On the whole, controlling quality occurs throughout the life of a project, not just at its end.

Controlling quality is concerned not only with the product the project is creating, but also with the project management processes. Controlling quality measures performance, scheduling, and cost variances. The experience of the project should be of quality—not just the product the project creates. Consider a project manager who demands that the project team work extreme hours to meet an unrealistic deadline. Team morale suffers, and likely so does the project work the team is completing.

The project team should do the following to ensure competency in the controlling quality process:

- Conduct statistical QC measures, such as sampling and probability.
- Inspect the product to avoid errors.
- Perform attribute sampling to measure conformance to quality on a per-unit basis.
- Conduct variable sampling to measure the degree of conformance.
- Study special causes to determine anomalies.
- Research random causes to determine expected variances of quality.
- Check the tolerance range to determine whether the results are within or outside an acceptable level of quality.
- Observe control limits to determine whether the results are in or out of QC.

Preparing to Control Quality

The control quality process relies on several inputs, including the following:

- **The project management plan**   The project management plan contains the quality management plan as a subsidiary plan. This defines how the quality processes will be applied to the project, the expectations of quality, and the organization's approach to performing QC.

- **Project documents**   Project documents will help you determine what the specific levels of quality are to be as you measure the project deliverables. Quality metrics are operational definitions that define the metrics for the project, which are needed so that you can measure and react to the results of project performance. You'll also reference the test and evaluation documents that show the outcome of inspection and testing. The project manager can also reference the lessons learned register from past, similar projects for insight and expectations.

- **Approved change requests** Approved change requests affect how the project work is scheduled and performed, which may affect the project's overall quality. Controlling quality verifies that approved change requests are implemented properly. Agile projects welcome changes, of course, but there's still consideration for the effect the change may have on quality.

- **Deliverables** You need something to inspect. Deliverables are the results of the project work, and they will be inspected to confirm that they're great and full of quality as the customer (and you, the project manager) expects. Testing is the key activity for controlling quality in an agile project.

- **Work performance data** The results of the project work are needed to compare with the quality standards. The expected results of the product and the project can be measured from the project plan. In other words, the project must meet the expected quality metrics, or corrective action needs to be taken.

- **Enterprise environmental factors** Your PMIS can help track quality issues and defects. Your organization may follow governmental requirements that affect quality and testing, and there may be additional standards and guidelines in your discipline that affect your control quality activities.

- **Organizational process assets** This shouldn't be a surprise, because I'd bet dollars to donuts your organization has quality standards that you must adhere to. You may also have to utilize forms, check sheets, and communications policies.

Relying on the Seven Basic Quality Tools

You should be familiar with seven basic quality tools for your PMI examination. You can use these tools in quality planning, managing quality, and most likely with the control quality process:

- **Cause-and-effect diagrams** Also known as fishbone, Ishikawa, or why-why diagrams, these help you determine causal factors for a problem you'd like to solve.

- **Flowcharts** A flowchart shows the sequence of events with possible branching and loopbacks to reach an end result of a process or a series of processes.

- **Check sheets** These are used to tally up problems, effects, conditions, or other aspects about a project's product during inspection. The results of check sheets help project managers quickly ascertain problems within the project.

- **Pareto diagrams** These charts categorize problems from largest to smallest.

- **Histograms** This bar chart can be used to show frequency of problems, ranking of services, or any other distribution of data.

- **Control charts** These show trends over time and help a project manager determine the stability of a process, an improvement, or other analysis of the project work. These are ideal for repeatable processes as in manufacturing.

- **Scatter diagrams** These charts measure the relationship between a dependent project variable and an independent project variable. The closer the variables trend, the more likely there is a connection.

Inspecting Results

Although quality is planned, not inspected, into a project, inspections are needed to prove conformance to the requirements. An inspection can be done on the project as a whole, on a portion of the project work, on the project deliverable, or even on an individual activity. Inspections are also known as

- Reviews
- Product reviews
- Audits
- Walkthroughs

Testing Deliverables in Adaptive Projects

Agile embraces testing to prevent mistakes from entering the customers' hands. Agile begins with the idea that testing is continuous throughout the project, not just at the end. Recall the idea that tests are written first with the understanding the test will fail. Then the development team writes the code to pass the test. The test is written against the user story; this means that the test will be written to the behavior of the user story. Testers aren't a separate group of people, but they are part of the team, and they work with the developers and the product owner to understand what should be written based on the behavior the functional requirement will accomplish.

Adaptive projects also use exploratory testing. This is the fun stuff, as testers play with the software in a nonscripted approach. They act like they're users, trying all sorts of activities and what-if scenarios to see if they can break the software. (It's like my dad and a new laptop: he'll break things in the computer I never knew possible. If it can be broken, my Pops can do it.)

Creating a Flowchart

Technically, a flowchart is a diagram illustrating how components within a system are related. An organizational flowchart shows the bottom crew of operations up to the "little squirt" on top. Like a heating, ventilation, and air conditioning (HVAC) blueprint shows how the air flows through a building from the furnace to each room, flowcharts show the relationship between components from bottom to top and help the project team determine where quality issues may be present to plan accordingly.

You'll need to be concerned with two types of flowcharts for the exams:

- **Cause-and-effect diagrams** These diagrams show the relationship between the variables within a process and how those relationships may contribute to inadequate quality. They can help organize both the process and team opinions, as well as generate discussion on finding a solution to ensure quality. Figure 8-2 shows an example of a cause-and-effect diagram.

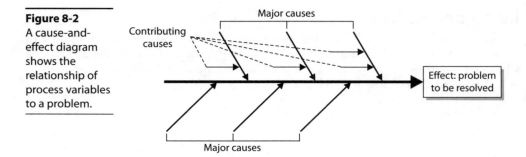

Figure 8-2
A cause-and-effect diagram shows the relationship of process variables to a problem.

- **System or process flowcharts** These flowcharts illustrate the flow of a process through a system, such as a project change request through the change control system or work authorization through the controlling quality process. A process flowchart does not have to be limited to the project management activities; it could instead demonstrate how a manufacturer creates, packages, and ships the product to the customer (as shown in Figure 8-3).

Creating a Control Chart

Ever feel like your project is out of control? A control chart can prove it.

Control charts illustrate the performance of a project over time. They map the results of inspections against a chart, as shown in Figure 8-4. Control charts are typically used in projects or operations that include repetitive activities—such as product manufacturing, a series of tests, or help desk issues.

The outer limits of a control chart are set by the customer requirements. Within the customer requirements are the upper control limits (UCLs) and the lower control limits (LCLs). The UCL is typically set at +3 or +6 sigma, while the LCL is set at −3 or −6 sigma.

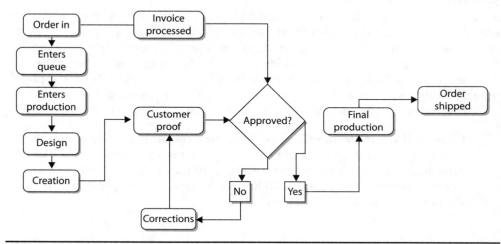

Figure 8-3   A flowchart demonstrates how processes within a system are related.

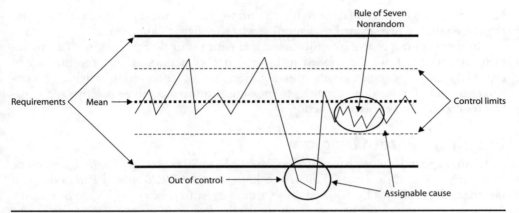

Figure 8-4   Control charts demonstrate the results of inspections.

Sigma results show the degree of correctness. Table 8-1 outlines the four sigma values representing normal distribution. You'll need to know these for the PMP exam.

So, what happened to 4 sigma and 5 sigma? Nothing. They're still there. It's just that the difference between 3 sigma at 99.73 percent and 6 sigma at 99.99 percent is so small that statisticians just jump to 6 sigma. The *mean* in a control chart represents the expected result, while the *sigma* values represent the expected spread of results based on the inspection. A true 6 sigma allows only two defects per million opportunities, and the percentage to represent that value is 99.99985 percent. For the exam, remember the 99.99 percent.

For example, if a manufacturer creates 1,000 units per hour and expects 50 units each hour to be defective, the mean would be 950 units. If the control limits were set at +/–3 sigma, the results of testing would actually expect as many as 953 correct units and as few as 947 correct units.

Over time, the results of testing are plotted in the control chart. Whenever a result of testing is plotted beyond the UCL or LCL values, it is considered to be "out of control." When a value is out of control, there is a reason why—it's called an *assignable cause*. Something caused the results to change for better or for worse, and the result must be investigated to understand the why behind the occurrence.

Another assignable cause is the *Rule of Seven*, which states that whenever seven consecutive results are all on one side of the mean, this is an assignable cause. Thus, there's

Table 8-1	Value	Percent Correct
The Four Sigma Values Representing Normal Distribution	+/– 1 sigma	68.26 percent
	+/– 2 sigma	95.46 percent
	+/– 3 sigma	99.73 percent
	+/– 6 sigma	99.99 percent

been some change that caused the results to shift to one side of the expected mean. Again, the cause must be investigated to determine why the change happened.

Although control charts are easily associated with recurring activities, such as manufacturing, they can also be applied to project management. Consider the number of expected change requests, delays within a project, and other recurring activities. A control chart can plot out these activities to measure performance, show positive and negative results, and track corrective actions.

Creating a Pareto Diagram

A Pareto diagram is somewhat related to Pareto's Law: 80 percent of the problems come from 20 percent of the issues. This is also known as the *80/20 rule*. A Pareto diagram illustrates the problems by assigned cause, from largest to smallest, as Figure 8-5 shows. The project team should first work on the larger problems and then move on to the smaller problems.

Creating a Histogram

A histogram is a bar chart showing the frequency of variables within a project. For example, a histogram could show which states have the most customers. Within project management, a common histogram is a resource histogram that shows the frequency of resources used on project work.

Creating a Run Chart

A run chart, as Figure 8-6 shows, is a line graph that shows the results of inspection in the order in which they've occurred. The goals of a run chart are first to demonstrate the results of a process over time and then to use trend analysis to predict when certain trends may reemerge. Based on this information, an organization can work to prevent the negative trend or work to capitalize on an identified opportunity.

Figure 8-5
A Pareto diagram is a histogram that ranks the issues from largest to smallest.

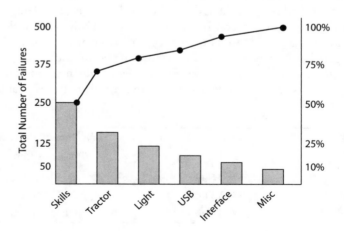

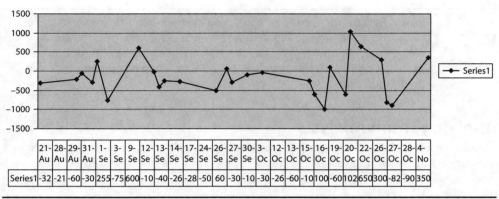

Figure 8-6 A run chart tracks the results of inspections over time.

Creating a Scatter Diagram

A scatter diagram tracks the relationship between two variables. The two variables are considered related the closer they track against a diagonal line. For example, a project manager could track the performance of two team members, the time and cost, or even the changes between functional managers and the project's schedule.

Completing a Statistical Sampling

Statistical sampling is the process of choosing a percentage of results at random. For example, a project creating a medical device may randomly select 20 percent of all units to check for quality. This process must be completed on a consistent basis throughout the project, rather than on a sporadic schedule.

Statistical sampling can reduce the costs of QC, but mixed results can follow if an adequate testing plan and schedule are not followed. The science of statistical sampling (and its requirements to be effective) is an involved process. Many books, seminars, and professionals are devoted to the process.

EXAM TIP For the PMP exams, know that statistical sampling uses a percentage of the results to test for quality. This process can reduce QC costs.

Revisiting Flowcharting

Flowcharting uses charts to illustrate how the different parts of a system operate. This is valuable in QC, because the process can be evaluated and tested to determine where in the process quality begins to break down. Corrective actions can then be applied to the system to ensure that quality continues as planned—and as expected.

NOTE Refactoring means that the development team cleans up its code throughout the project. Refactoring involves clarifying the code and cleaning up the shortcuts and quick fixes that can pile up throughout the project. Continuous refactoring is paramount when it comes to creating quality software in agile.

Applying Trend Analysis

Trend analysis is the science of using past results to predict future performance. Sports announcers use trend analysis all the time: "The Cubs have never won in St. Louis on a Tuesday night in the month of July when the temperature at the top of the third inning was above 80 degrees."

The results of trend analysis enable the project manager to apply corrective actions to intervene and prevent unacceptable outcomes. Trend analysis on a project requires adequate records to predict results and set current expectations. Trends, good or bad, are often displayed in an information radiator for everyone to see in an agile project. It can monitor the following:

- **Technical performance** Trend analysis can ask, "How many errors have been experienced up to this point in the project schedule, and how many additional errors were encountered?"
- **Cost and schedule performance** Trend analysis can ask, "How many activities were completed incorrectly, came in late, or had significant cost variances?"

Examining Control Quality Process Results

Controlling quality should, first and foremost, result in quality improvement. The project manager and project team, based on the results of the tools and techniques used to implement control quality, apply corrective actions to prevent unacceptable quality and to improve the overall quality of the project management processes.

The corrective actions and the defect repairs the project manager and the project team want to incorporate into the project may require change requests and management approval. The value and importance of a change should be evident so that the improvement to quality is approved and folded into the project.

In addition to quality improvement, there are other results of QC:

- **Quality control measurements** Based on the project's quality management plan, QC measurements need to be documented and kept as part of the project's documentation.
- **Verified deliverables** The goal of controlling quality in a project is to keep mistakes out of customers' hands. If you've inspected the deliverables and they're acceptable by the quality metrics, they should be acceptable for the project customer. Verified deliverables are an output of controlling quality and an input to scope validation.

- **Work performance information** The information created by the project's controlling processes is one of the outputs of controlling quality. This includes schedule control, scope control, cost control, and controlling quality. The integrated relationship of the project causes the control of other knowledge areas to affect the quality of the project's deliverables.

- **Change requests** Should the quality in the project be less than what was planned for, there may be change requests for corrective actions, preventive actions, or defect repair.

- **Project management plan updates** Based on the experiences of controlling quality, the project management plan could be updated. You should be concerned primarily with the possibility that the quality management plan and process improvement plan will require an update in the project.

- **Project document updates** Updates to the issue log, lessons learned register, risk register, and the test and evaluation documents may be made to control quality in the project.

Chapter Summary

What good is a project deliverable if it doesn't work, is unacceptable, or is faulty? Project quality management ensures that the deliverables that project teams create meet the expectations of the stakeholders. For your PMP examination, quality means delivering the project at the exact level of the design specifications and the project scope—no more, no less.

Grade and quality are two different things. Grade is the ranking assigned to different components that have the same functional purpose. For example, sheet metal may come in different grades based on what it is needed for. Another example is the grade of paper based on its thickness, ability to retain ink, and so on. Low quality is always a problem; low grade may not be.

Quality is built into agile by first establishing the Definition of Done (DoD) for each user story and each deliverable of the project. Tests are written against the desired behavior for the user story. Sprint reviews are used to demonstrate what has been created by the development team, and the product owner can approve or reject the work based on what's demonstrated. The sprint retrospective is an opportunity for the team to discuss what's working or not working and then create an approach for the next sprint to improve their processes and the product.

Quality planning happens before project work begins, but also as work is completed. Quality planning can confirm the preexistence of quality or the need for quality improvements. Quality is planned into a project, not inspected in. However, controlling quality requires inspections to prove the existence of quality within a project deliverable.

The cost of quality is concerned with the monies invested in the project to attain the expected level of quality. Examples include the costs of training, safety measures, and quality management activities. The cost of nonconformance centers on the monies lost by not completing the project work correctly the first time. In addition, this cost includes the loss of sales, loss of customers, and downtime within the project.

Managing quality is prevention-driven and is a management process. Controlling quality is inspection-driven and is a project process. On your PMI exam, keep those two thoughts separate and you'll be ahead of the game.

Questions

1. You are leading an agile project for your organization, and your manager has concerns regarding how you'll meet quality if you don't know all of the requirements at the launch of the project. What should you tell your manager to best alleviate her concerns?

   A. User stories and tests will be written to meet the Definition of Done.

   B. The product owner is responsible for quality assurance in agile.

   C. A separate quality assurance team will test the actual product.

   D. Quality is met when there is business value.

2. You are the project manager for the Photo Scanning Project. This project is similar to another project you have completed. This project will electronically store thousands of photos for your city's historical society, and quality is paramount. Management approaches you and asks why you have devoted so much of the project time to planning. Your response is which of the following?

   A. This is a first-time, first-use project, so more time is needed for planning.

   B. Planning for a high quality project of this size is mandatory.

   C. Quality is planned into a project, not inspected in.

   D. Quality audits are part of the planning time.

3. You are the project manager for a hybrid project called the Floor Installation Project. Today you will meet with your project team to discuss the product backlog and the strict project requirement that the project must be executed with no deviations or errors. This process is which of the following?

   A. Quality planning

   B. Quality management

   C. Quality control

   D. Quality assurance

4. You are the project manager for the ASE Project, which must map to industry standards to be accepted by the customer. You and your team have studied the requirements and have created a plan to implement the deliverables with the appropriate level of quality. What is this process called?

   A. Quality planning

   B. Quality management

   C. Quality control

   D. Quality assurance

5. Juan is the project manager for his organization and he's asked Beth, a project team member, to help him create a fishbone diagram. Beth doesn't know what this is and asks for your help. You tell her that a fishbone diagram is the same as a(n) _____ diagram.

    A. Ishikawa

    B. Pareto

    C. flow

    D. control

6. Management has asked you to define the correlation between quality and the project scope. Which of the following is the best answer?

    A. The project scope includes metrics for quality.

    B. Quality metrics are applied to the project scope.

    C. Quality is the process of completing the scope to meet stated or implied needs.

    D. Quality is the process of evaluating the project scope to ensure that quality exists.

7. You are the project manager of the Condo IV Construction project and you're working with your project team and the project sponsor to identify the quality metrics and develop the quality management plan for the project. In light of this planning event, which of the following is most true about quality?

    A. It will cost more money to build quality into the project.

    B. It will cost less money to build quality into the project process.

    C. Quality is inspection-driven.

    D. Quality is prevention-driven.

8. You are the project manager for the KOY Project, which requires quality that maps to federal guidelines. To ensure that you can meet these standards, you have elected to put the project team through training specific to the federal guidelines your project must adhere to. The costs of these classes can be assigned to which of the following?

    A. The cost of doing business

    B. Cost of quality

    C. Cost of adherence

    D. Cost of nonconformance

9. You are the project manager of an adaptive project to develop new software. Jon, a senior developer, urges everyone in the team to refactor their code often. Why is this needed in regard to quality?

    A. Refactoring keeps project costs down.

    B. Refactoring keeps build time to a minimum.

    C. Refactoring ensures that the code is clean and helps for future builds.

    D. Refactoring is quality control in software development projects in agile.

10. You are the project manager of the JKL Project, which currently has some production flaws. Which analysis tool will enable you to determine the cause and effect of the production faults?

   A. A flowchart

   B. A Pareto diagram

   C. An Ishikawa diagram

   D. A control chart

11. Brinda is the project manager of a manufacturing project. She and her project team are using design of experiments to look for ways to improve quality. Which of the following best describes design of experiments?

   A. It enables the project manager to move the relationship of activities to complete the project work with the best resources available.

   B. It enables the project manager to experiment with the project design to determine what variables are causing the flaws.

   C. It enables the project manager to experiment with variables to attempt to improve quality.

   D. It enables the project manager to experiment with the project design document to become more productive and to provide higher quality.

12. You are the project manager of the Global Upgrade Project. Your project team consists of 75 project team members around the world. Each team member will be upgrading a piece of equipment in many different facilities. Which of the following could you implement to ensure that project team members are completing all of the steps in the install procedure with quality?

   A. Checklists

   B. Work breakdown structure (WBS)

   C. Project network diagram (PND)

   D. The WBS dictionary

13. Denzel is the project manager of the PMH Project. Quality inspections of the deliverables show several problems. Management has asked Denzel to create a chart showing the distribution of problems and their frequencies. Given this, management wants which of the following?

   A. A control chart

   B. An Ishikawa diagram

   C. A Pareto diagram

   D. A flowchart

14. In the accompanying illustration, what does the circled area represent?

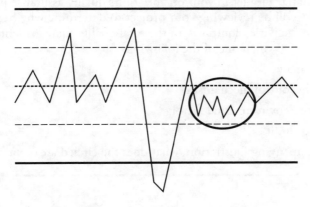

    A. Out-of-control data points

    B. In-control data points

    C. The Rule of Seven

    D. Standard deviation

15. You are an IT project manager and are working with the project team to determine the best computer system for the project. You and the project team decide to measure the performance of two systems to determine which one performs best. This is an example of which one of the following?

    A. Cost-benefits analysis

    B. Benchmarking

    C. Design of experiments

    D. Determining the cost of quality

16. A project manager has elected not to enforce safety measures on his construction project. One of the project team members has been injured because of this oversight, and the job site is closed until an investigation into the lack of safety measures is completed. The project will now likely be late, and your company will be fined for the error and will lose credibility with the customer. This is an example of which one of the following?

    A. Risk

    B. Trigger

    C. Cost of nonconformance to quality

    D. Cost of conformance to quality

17. Your organization uses total quality management as part of its quality assurance program. Maria, a leader in your organization's quality assurance program, informs you that she will be reviewing your project to determine whether your project management activities comply with the total quality management program. This is an example of which one of the following?

   A. Process analysis

   B. A quality control mechanism

   C. Enterprise environmental factors

   D. A quality audit

18. In the accompanying illustration, what does the circled area represent?

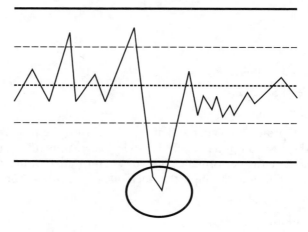

   A. Out-of-control data points

   B. In-control data points

   C. The Rule of Seven

   D. Standard deviation

19. You are the project manager for a plastics manufacturer. You would like to illustrate the categories of quality failure within your project so that you and your project team can attack the largest areas of failure first. This type of chart is known as which of the following?

   A. A control chart

   B. An Ishikawa diagram

   C. A Pareto diagram

   D. A flowchart

20. What is the type of chart in the illustration called?

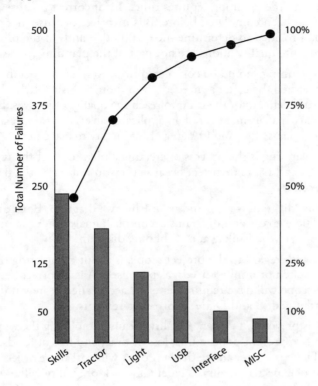

A. A Pareto diagram

B. A control chart

C. A fishbone diagram

D. An Ishikawa diagram

Answers

1. A. Each user story in the product backlog must be clearly written so that the DoD is understood by all team members and customers. Tests will be written toward the behavior that the user stories aim to accomplish. B is incorrect because quality assurance is owned by everyone on the team, not just the product owner. C is incorrect because adaptive projects don't utilize separate teams for quality assurance, which is part of the agile approach. D is incorrect; even though it's true that business value is needed, A is the best answer. By reaching the DoD, your project completely satisfies the requirements and met quality.

2. C. Of all the choices presented, C is the best answer. Quality is planned into the project, and the planning requires time. A is incorrect because a project of this nature has been completed before. B is incorrect because there isn't enough information provided to determine the quality demands of the project. D is incorrect because quality audits are not part of the planning processes.

3. A. Quality planning should be completed prior to the work beginning—and should be revisited thereafter as needed. Even though this is a hybrid project, quality must be clearly defined for the team to reach the quality objectives. B is incorrect because quality management is not an applicable answer to the scenario. C and D are incorrect because QC and QA are part of quality management.

4. A. Quality planning is the process of creating a plan to meet the requirements of quality. B, C, and D are incorrect because they do not name the process in the question's scenario.

5. A. A fishbone diagram is the same as an Ishikawa diagram. B, C, and D are incorrect. These charts and diagrams accomplish goals other than the cause-and-effect outcome of the Ishikawa, or fishbone, diagram.

6. C. Quality, with regard to the project scope, is about completing the work to provide the stated or implied needs, as promised. A is incorrect because, although the project scope will have requirements for acceptance, it may not have metrics for quality defined. B and D are incorrect statements.

7. D. Quality is prevention-driven. Quality means completing the work correctly the first time to prevent poor results, loss of time, and loss of funds. A and B are incorrect. There is no guarantee that a project will cost more or less depending on the amount of expected quality. Incidentally, lack of quality will likely cost more than quality planning because of the cost of nonconformance. C is incorrect because quality is planned into a project, not inspected in.

8. B. Training to meet the quality expectations is attributed to the cost of quality. A, C, and D are incorrect because these choices do not describe training as a cost of quality.

9. C. Refactoring involves cleaning the software code for consistency and future builds. This helps the software meet its quality objectives throughout the project. A and B are incorrect because refactoring doesn't necessarily keep costs or build time down in an agile project. D is incorrect because refactoring is not quality control in software development.

10. C. The key words "cause and effect" equate to the Ishikawa diagram, also called a cause-and-effect diagram. A is incorrect because a flowchart will show how a process moves through the system, not the causes and effects of the problems involved. B is incorrect because a Pareto diagram maps out the causes and frequency of problems. D is incorrect because a control chart plots the results of sampling, but it doesn't show the causes and effects of problems.

11. **C**. Design of experiments uses experiments and "what-if" scenarios to determine what variables are affecting quality. A is incorrect because design of experiments, with regard to quality, is not about changing the relationship of activities to complete project work. B and D are incorrect because design of experiments will not be changing project design to determine where flaws exist or to become more productive.

12. **A**. Checklists are simple but effective quality management tools that the project manager can use to ensure that the project team is completing the required work. B, C, and D are all incorrect. The WBS, PND, and WBS dictionary are not tools the project team can necessarily use to prove they've completed required work. Checklists are the best approach for this scenario.

13. **C**. Management wants Denzel to create a Pareto diagram. Recall that a Pareto diagram maps out the causes of defects and illustrates their frequency. A is incorrect because a control chart does not identify the problems, only the relation of the results to the expected mean. B is incorrect because a cause-and-effect diagram does not map out the frequency of problems. D is also incorrect. Flowcharts show how a process moves through a system and how the components are related.

14. **C**. The circled area shows seven consecutive sampling results, all on one side of the mean. This is known as the Rule of Seven and is an assignable cause. A is incorrect because these values are in control. B is correct, but it does not answer the question as fully as C does. D is incorrect because standard deviation is a predicted measure of the variance from the expected mean of a sampling.

15. **B**. This is an example of benchmarking, because the project team is comparing one system to another. A is incorrect because the cost-benefits analysis would compare the costs and associated benefits of each system, rather than just how the two systems compare against each other. C is incorrect because the design of experiments is a method that determines which factors influence the variables of the project's deliverable. D is incorrect because the cost of quality is the dollar amount the project must invest to achieve the expected level of quality.

16. **C**. This is an example of the cost of nonconformance to quality, also called the cost of poor quality. The project manager should have followed appropriate safety measures for the job site. Costs associated with the safety measures are considered part of D, the cost of conformance to quality. A is incorrect because risk is inherent to application work, while the ramifications of not enforcing the safety measures is an example of the cost of poor quality. B is incorrect because trigger is a risk management term that references a condition or warning sign that a risk is coming into the project.

17. **D**. This is an example of a quality audit to confirm that your project is adhering to the quality assurance program established within your organization. A and B are incorrect. C is incorrect because, although enterprise environmental factors may be a valid characteristic of the total quality management program, this is not the best answer for the question, which centers on the audit process rather than on how the audit will be performed.

18. **A.** The circled area shows out-of-control data points. B is incorrect because these are not in-control data points. C is incorrect because the Rule of Seven refers to seven consecutive measurements, all on one side of the mean. D is incorrect because standard deviation is a predicted measure of the variance from the expected mean of a sampling.

19. **C.** You want to create a Pareto diagram. A is incorrect because a control chart does not identify the problems, only the relationship of the results to the expected mean. B is incorrect because an Ishikawa diagram aims to find the root cause of a defect or issue, rather than categorize and rank the identified defects. D is also incorrect. Flowcharts show how a process moves through a system and how the components are related.

20. **A.** This is a Pareto diagram. B is incorrect because a control chart shows the results of measurements over time. C and D are both incorrect; a fishbone diagram and an Ishikawa diagram are the same type of chart.

CHAPTER 9

Managing Project Resources

In this chapter, you will

- Plan for resource management
- Estimate activity resources
- Acquire the project resources
- Develop the project team
- Manage the project team
- Control project resources

Your project relies on people doing the work, but these people need the correct tools, equipment, software, materials, and other necessary resources to complete the project work. You cannot install meters and meters of electrical wiring without the correct people, tools, and equipment. This chapter on resource management addresses both the human resources and the physical resources needed in project management.

First, people—specifically those on your project team—look to you, the project manager, to provide leadership, direction, and motivation. Your job is to help them know what their project assignments are, get their work done, and resolve issues and dilemmas within the project. It's a blast! Okay, that's a bit of sarcasm. In reality—and you should know this for your PMI exam—the people involved with the project will know what is expected of them by the project manager, management, and the stakeholders, and they'll attempt to meet or exceed those expectations. And if they don't? Then it's up to the project manager, the functional managers, and even the other project team members to enforce the project's ground rules so that all team members work toward the requirements stated in the project scope statement.

 VIDEO For a more detailed explanation, watch the *Human Resource Theories* video now.

Next, physical resources are needed for the project team to do their work. It's frustrating for everyone involved when the project team is ready to do the work, but the equipment, tools, or materials aren't available. It means wasted time and money for the project—and it's not helping the project be successful. The project manager must make certain that she understands what physical resources are needed and then deliver those resources to ensure that the project moves forward as expected. In addition, it's critical to get the correct physical resources—the resources that are actually needed, that meet the quality expected, and that are available on time. Availability, with regard to materials, can often mean inventory: too much inventory and your funds are tied up in resources; too little inventory and you're waiting for resources to be replenished. Having the right resources available at the right time is often more difficult than it may seem.

The type of organizational structure—from functional to projectized—will influence how the project manager may discipline, motivate, and manage the project team. In a functional environment, the project manager won't have much autonomy to discipline or offer rewards beyond what management has deemed appropriate. In a projectized structure, the project manager has much more autonomy both to discipline and to reward. The project management approach, whether adaptive or predictive, will also affect how you manage the project.

You must also consider the culture of the organization in which the agile project is being implemented. The culture may see the speed of agile projects as a deterrent to effective quality management. Or the culture may see the change-friendly approach to agile as a threat to the team actually hitting a deadline. The culture of the organization will affect the rigidity of the project approach, the flexibility of the product requirements, and how you, as the project manager, oversee the agile project. Culture isn't just about resource management; it affects all areas of the project. And an organization's culture is driven by the people within the organization.

Your project team may be assigned to you, or you may have to build the team one person at a time. Chances are, you'll have a core project team at the beginning of the project and then more and more team members will join as the project scope is defined and the activities are identified. Adding people to the project team can influence how you do the work and can introduce new risks and opportunities—based on their interest in the project, experience levels, and, frankly, their competency regarding the project work. An analysis of the project team can help you plan your team development approach.

As the project manager, you'll need to manage and lead the project—yes, there is a difference between management and leadership. Management is about getting things done. Leadership is about aligning, motivating, and directing people. I believe that people will work harder, smarter, and better for someone they want to work for than they will for someone they are required to work for. As you lead and manage your team, you must maintain a professional and ethical demeanor. Avoid playing favorites, balance the tasks among the project team, and get involved in the work when the team needs your help.

For your PMI examination, you'll need to know some vital facts about managing the project team and controlling the project resources. We'll cover these vital facts in this chapter.

Planning for Resource Management

Here we go again. Have you noticed that every knowledge area for your PMI examination starts with a planning process? Hmmm, I hope so. Planning is an iterative process that begins early in the project and continues throughout the project management life cycle. Planning for project resources is vital to a successful project. After all, you've got to plan how the project work will be completed and which resources will complete that work.

NOTE   Don't get overwhelmed with all the planning activities you'll read about in this chapter. Every project requires some planning, but not every project needs an in-depth plan. You'll learn about the differences between planning for adaptive projects and planning for predictive projects in this chapter.

When it comes to planning resources, the project manager should consider several facets of the project. Specifically, the planning process answers the following questions:

- What project roles and physical resources are needed on the project?
- What is the responsibility of each role on the project?
- To whom does each role report?
- Will resources on the project come from inside or outside the organization?
- How will project team members and physical resources be acquired?
- How will project team members and physical resources be released from the project?
- What training needs to be completed for the project team?
- What rewards and recognition systems may the project utilize?
- What compliance and safety issues must be addressed?
- How will the use of the resources affect the operations of the organization?

Phew! That's a bunch of questions the project management team must answer during this portion of planning. The good news is that you can answer some of these questions when you're doing other project management planning exercises, such as time and cost estimating. All of the answers to these questions are documented in the resource management plan. The resource management plan is the primary output of the human resources planning process.

Identifying Organizational Approach for Managing Resources

Project management is becoming more and more about empowering the project team members to make decisions rather than the project manager making all the project decisions. This collaborative approach fosters trust, shared ownership, and a reliance on experts on the project team. You'll need to know which approach your organization prefers, and for your PMP exam, you should be familiar with these trends in managing resources:

- **Just-in-time (JIT) manufacturing**   Resources are in place only as they are needed. This approach reduces waste, keeps inventory at a minimum, and helps the project manager forecast resource utilization more accurately.

- **Kaizen**   Small changes to the organization and project team over time result in large changes overall. Kaizen posits that small changes in processes are easier to accept and incorporate than large, sweeping changes for the organization or project.

- **Total productive maintenance**   Continuous maintenance on equipment and quality systems keeps equipment working well and efficiently. This approach aims to reduce downtime by avoiding equipment failure.

- **Theory of constraints**   A management system is limited by its weakest components—the constraints—and works to remove those constraints. It's an adaption of the phrase "a chain is only as strong as its weakest link." This idea is most often seen in environments that use the Lean approach.

- **Emotional intelligence**   A person is aware of his inbound and outbound emotions; by becoming emotionally competent, the person can better control his emotions and understand the emotions of others.

- **Self-organizing teams**   In agile environments, the project manager may be called a scrum master, coach, or servant leader. The project team takes charge of deciding who'll do what tasks to accomplish the project objectives. Agile teams are self-organizing and self-led.

- **Virtual teams/distributed teams**   These teams are non-collocated, can be dispersed around the globe, and rely on technology to interact, communicate, and contribute to the project. Communication becomes a central focal point in virtual teams.

The resource management process can be tailored to fit your project and organization. The project manager will consider the diversity of the project team and the strengths, weaknesses, opportunities, and threats (SWOT) that the diverse group may bring to the project. When work is completed by virtual teams, the physical location of each team member is also evaluated for how best to manage the resources.

Your industry may require special resource considerations, such as unions or inspectors. All project managers, regardless of the industry, will have to follow the organization's policies for acquiring and managing the project team. Finally, the project life cycle can affect how you manage project team members. Specifically, you'll consider the peaks and valleys of team utilization depending on the type of work that's taking place in the project at any given time.

Relying on Enterprise Environmental Factors

You've seen "enterprise environmental factors" mentioned over and over throughout this book. When it comes to relying on the good ol' enterprise environmental factors for resource planning, the focus is on how the organization identifies and utilizes roles and responsibilities and how the organization interacts with the project management team. When planning resources, the project manager needs to identify which departments will be involved in the project. The team considers how the project will interact with these different departments, as well as what relationships exist among the departments, the project team, and management.

Have you ever worked with project team members who were located around the world? What about project team members who were all within footsteps of other team members? The logistical interface considers just that—the logistics of the project team and the stakeholders—and how they affect your ability to manage the project. You'll also consider any physical resources that need to be located close to where the project is happening. Think of materials that must be shipped, equipment that is being utilized on other projects, and other physical resources that will affect the timing, cost, and planning of your project. The project manager must consider geographical locales, time zones, countries, and any other logistical concerns that may affect the project.

Here are three common constraints that may affect your resource planning:

- **Organizational structure** The structure of the organization has a direct correlation to the project manager's power over the project. Figure 9-1 provides a refresher on the types of organizational structures. For a more in-depth refresher, see Chapter 2.

Figure 9-1
The organizational structure affects the project manager's power.

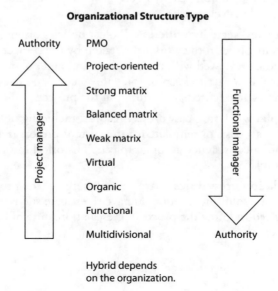

Organizational Structure Type

- **Collective bargaining agreements**   Contracts and agreements with unions or other employee groups may serve as constraints for the project.

- **Marketplace conditions**   Your organization may experience a hiring freeze, reductions in the training budget, or a reduction of most travel expenses. The marketplace conditions can also affect the price and availability of the physical resources your project needs.

NOTE   Contracts and grievances with unions are constraints. The unions themselves, however, are stakeholders.

Using the Organizational Process Assets

In many organizations, new projects may be similar to past projects. For example, an architecture firm designs buildings, an IT consultancy designs software or networks, and a manufacturer assembles products. For projects in these types of organizations, past project records, lessons learned, and even past resource management plans can be adapted for a current project.

Organizational process assets provide for resource planning—you should know these for your PMI exam:

- **Organization standards**   Understand the human resources policies, procedures, expectations, and role descriptions, and the rules and policies for physical resources to which you, the project manager, will need to adhere. Adaptive projects may require that you coach some project stakeholders about how the adaptive life cycle works.

- **Safety and security policies**   Project policies often need to address any safety issues involved in the work undertaken by the project team. Safety policies should be reviewed with the project team, and safety measures must be followed; the goal is always to keep people safe. Security policies address how the physical resources are secured and utilized in the project.

- **Templates**   Using past project records, including older staffing management plans, as a basis or template for the current project is a great way to save time and maintain consistency among projects. Historical information can serve as a type of template.

- **Escalation procedures**   Are you in charge of the project team when it comes to issue resolution? Or do you have to escalate such concerns to management? You need to know the process for escalation and your level of authority over the project team.

- **Checklists**   When it comes to planning for human resources, checklists, which are part of the organizational process assets, attempt to identify common elements within similar projects. A checklist can help the project management team identify the following:

  - Roles and responsibilities
  - Competencies for the project work
  - Training programs
  - Team ground rules
  - Safety issues
  - Compliancy
  - Rewards and recognition considerations

Referencing the Project Management Plan

The project management plan must include several considerations regarding staffing the project and utilizing physical resources for the project. Let's take a quick peek at each subsidiary plan, elements within the project management plan, and how they may affect what resources the project manager will require for the project team.

Here are the elements of the project management plan for a predictive project:

- **Project scope management plan**   This defines how the project scope will be planned, managed, and controlled. This plan is included because the project team will be doing the work to create the product that the scope promises, and physical resources are likely needed to satisfy the scope.

- **Schedule management plan**   This plan defines how the project schedule will be created and managed. The availability of, and demand for, the project team and physical resources are influenced by the schedule management plan—and vice versa.

- **Cost management plan**   This plan details how the project costs will be planned for, estimated, budgeted, and then monitored and controlled. In most projects, the project manager will need to account for the cost of the project team and their contributions to the project work. The cost management plan will also address the cost of the physical resources.

- **Change management plan**   Changes are likely to happen on the project, so you'll need to communicate the change management process to the project team. Explain how all changes will be captured, analyzed, and then, if approved, implemented into the project. Changes can affect what the project will create and how it is created, and you don't want this to be a surprise to the project team.

- **Configuration management plan**   Documentation, control, and confirmation of the features and functions of the project's product are needed. Tied to scope management, the configuration management plan communicates how changes to the product may be permitted.

- **Quality management plan**   Quality is expected on every project. This plan defines what quality means for the project, how the project will achieve quality, and how the project will map to organizational procedures pertaining to quality. The project team members will need to adhere to quality expectations, which may include training, team development, peer reviews, and inspections.

- **Resource management plan**   This plan defines project roles, responsibilities, and the reporting structure. It includes both physical and human resources.

- **Communications management plan**   This plan defines who will get what information, how they will receive it, and what communications modality will be used. The project team will need to communicate with the project manager, sponsor, stakeholders, vendors, and one another.

- **Risk management plan**   Risk is an uncertain event or condition that may affect the project's outcome. Project team members will need to know what risks are within the project, which risk owners are identified, and how risk responses will be planned and communicated.

- **Procurement management plan**   The project may need to procure goods and services. The project team may need to interact with vendors, consultants, and even internal stakeholders such as a procurement office or purchasing department. This plan may also address how procured consultants will serve as project team members.

- **Schedule baseline**   This is the planned start and finish of the project. The comparison of what was planned and what was experienced is the schedule variance.

- **Cost baseline**   This is the aggregated costs of all the work packages within the work breakdown structure (WBS).

- **Quality baseline**   This documents the quality objectives for the project, including the metrics for stakeholder acceptance of the project deliverable.

- **Stakeholder register**   This document identifies all the project stakeholders, their interests in the project, and their roles. The stakeholder register can help identify who has control over physical and human resources in the project.

- **Risk register**   This centralized database consists of the outcome of all the other risk management processes. Consider the outcome of risk identification, qualitative analysis, and quantitative analysis.

 EXAM TIP   Remember the differences between project types. Predictive projects plan in-depth. Adaptive projects plan throughout the project but don't create tons of documentation. Hybrid projects can combine the documented plans of predictive life cycles and the iterative approaches in adaptive life cycles. Hybrid projects are a mishmash of what works for an organization, so hybrid project team members can do pretty much whatever they want, if it works.

Charting the Human Resources

Lots of charts can help the project manager and the project management team determine required resources, existing responsibilities, reporting relationships, accountability concerns, and plenty more within a project. The PMP examination will quiz you on these "schmancy" charts and how they're used. Don't worry—they're not difficult. Let's have a look.

Using a Hierarchical Chart

A hierarchical chart shows the relationships among superior and subordinate employees, groups, disciplines, and even departments. You've already seen one hierarchical chart: the WBS.

When it comes to human resource planning, consider the following five types of charts:

- **Organization chart**   This traditional chart shows how the organization is structured by departments and disciplines. It is sometimes called the organizational breakdown structure (OBS) and is arranged by departments, units, or teams. With regard to project management, an OBS can be used to show which project responsibilities are linked with which departments.

- **Resource breakdown structure (RBS)**   This hierarchical chart can decompose the project by the types of resources it contains. For example, your project may be using mechanical engineers, specialized equipment, and materials in several different deliverables throughout the project. The RBS would organize all of the usage of the mechanical engineers, as well as the physical resources, by their disciplines and types rather than by where they are being utilized. An RBS is an excellent tool for tracking resource utilization and costs.

- **Responsibility assignment matrix (RAM)**   A RAM chart shows the correlation between project team members and the work they've been assigned to complete. A RAM chart doesn't necessarily have to be specific to individual team members; it can also be decomposed to project groups or units. Most often, however, RAM charts depict activities and individual workers.

- **RACI chart**   A RACI chart is another matrix chart. It represents the assignments of responsibilities to people who are responsible, accountable, consulted, or informed (hence, the acronym RACI). Technically, a RACI chart is a form of the responsibility assignment matrix, but I include it here as a separate entry. This chart, depicted in Figure 9-2, has gained some popularity in recent years, so I'd wager you'll see it on your PMI examination. Notice how the different roles have only one of four responsibilities—responsible, accountable, consulted, or informed—for each assignment, but only one person is accountable per activity.

- **Text-oriented chart**   A text-oriented chart is really more of a shopping list of what a team member is responsible for within the project. It defines project responsibilities, reporting relationships, project authority, competencies, and qualifications. You may also know these as position descriptions or role-responsibility-authority forms.

	Project Team Member				
Activity	Steve	Martha	Sam	Liza	Mike
Foundation	A	R	C	I	C
Framing	R	A	C	I	C
Wiring	A	C	C	R	C
Testing	R	I	A	C	C

Figure 9-2   A RACI chart shows the relationships among activities and project team members.

Networking Human Resources

My buddy Rick and I do an exaggerated used-car salesman thumbs-up whenever one of us mentions networking. We know networking works—it's a great way to meet new people, find new business, and make friends. Attending networking events—such as your PMI chapter meetings and luncheons, where you can work the room—can help you move your project forward by furthering your understanding of how your organization deals with political and interpersonal relationships.

Basically, networking supports the old adage that people like to do business with people they like. If people don't know you, they won't get a chance to like you. Networking functions, especially those internal to your organization, are great places to meet and greet others and share news about your projects. Attending networking events on an ongoing basis is effective. Some project managers fall into the trap of networking only at the launch of a project; however, steady networking builds relationships.

Networking means more than selling things. If you work in a large company, the organization may schedule internal networking events, where you can meet colleagues and share what you're doing in the organization. This is a great way to meet others, learn about opportunities, and, if your organization is trending toward agile projects, discuss agile and how it works.

Identifying Roles and Responsibilities

Human resource planning accomplishes wonderful things. It communicates information about the resources the project will need, the project team's roles and responsibilities, the structure of the project team, and more. One of the fundamental things that human resource planning does for the project is to identify the attributes of the project team. You'll need to know these four attributes for your PMI examination:

- **Role**   This denotes what a person is specifically responsible for in a project. Roles are usually tied to job titles, such as network engineer, mechanical engineer, and electrician. It's what a person does at work.

- **Authority**   Project team members may have authority over other project team members, may have the ability to make decisions, and may even sign approvals for project work and purchases. Authority levels define which project team members have what levels of authority within the project.

- **Responsibility**   A responsibility is the work that a role performs. More precisely, it's the work that a project team member is responsible for within the project.

- **Competency**   This attribute defines what talents, skills, and capacities are needed to complete the project work. A skill gap can result in training, development, hiring, and even schedule and scope changes.

Creating a Project Organization Chart

Another output of the human resource planning process for your project is a project organization chart. This chart, as its name implies, illustrates the organization of the project, the project team members, and all the associated reporting relationships. The level of detail of the project organization chart is relative to the size of the project team and the priority of the project. In other words, organizing a massive international project with 3,000 project team members around the globe will likely require a higher level of detail than organizing a 20-person project team to create a new piece of software.

Creating a Team Charter

A team charter document is typically created by the project team to define the values, agreements, and ground rules for the project. In some organizations, the team charter may be developed for the project team, though the charter works best when the project team creates its own document—or at least has a part in creating it. Agile projects typically have a team charter rather than a project charter. The team charter includes the following:

- Vision and mission
- Team values
- Communication guidelines
- Decision-making process
- Conflict resolution process
- Meeting guidelines
- Team agreements
- Definition of Done or Success

When ground rules are created and agreed upon, it's up to all project team members to enforce them. The team charter helps to establish the values and agreement as to how the project team will operate and abide by the ground rules. We can see this in agile projects as the team is self-led and self-organizing, and team members hold one another accountable through pair programming, retrospectives, and transparency.

Estimating the Activity Resources

Resources include materials, equipment, and people. After the project manager and the project team have worked together to determine the sequence of the activities, they must determine which resources are needed for each activity, as well as how much of each resource is needed. As you can guess, resource estimating goes hand in hand with cost estimating. After all, if you need a metric ton of pea gravel, that's a resource estimate, but someone's got to pay for that gravel.

To estimate the demand for the project resources, you'll need several inputs:

- Project management plan, specifically the resource management plan and the scope baseline
- Activity list
- Attributes of each activity
- Assumptions log
- Cost estimates
- Availability of the resources you'll need, in the form of two calendars:
  - **Resource calendars** These let you know when individual resources are available. A resource calendar tells you when Bob has scheduled a vacation, when a piece of equipment that your project needs is already scheduled for use, and even when facilities such as meeting rooms are available.
  - **Project calendars** These communicate when the project work may take place. For example, your project may allow work to happen between 6 A.M. and 6 P.M., Monday through Friday. Your project calendar will also identify any holidays when the project work won't happen.
- Risk register
- Enterprise environmental factors
- Organizational process assets

Using Expert Judgment

The project manager and the project team have worked together to create the WBS, the activity list, and the sequence of activities, so it makes sense that they'll continue to work together to create the resource estimates. And they do. According to the *PMBOK Guide*, the project management team may work with experts to help make the best decisions. This is using the old standby "expert judgment," when the project manager relies on someone more knowledgeable to help make the best decision.

Using Bottom-Up Estimating

Every time I mention bottom-up estimating in one of my seminars, someone snickers and pantomimes drinking a shot of booze. Ha-ha.

Bottom-up estimating is the most accurate time-and-cost estimating approach a project manager can use. This estimating approach starts at "the bottom" of the project and considers every activity, its predecessor and successor activities, and the exact amount of resources needed to complete each activity. Bottom-up estimating accounts for all of the resources needed to complete all of the project work. Although it is the most accurate estimating approach, it is also the most time consuming.

 EXAM TIP To complete bottom-up estimating, especially for costs, a WBS must be present. Bottom-up estimating for costs is also known as "creating the definitive estimate."

Relying on Analogous Estimating

Recall that analogous estimating relies on historical information from similar projects to predict duration and cost in the current project. With estimating activity resources, an analogous estimate will consider a past project to examine the types of resources utilized, the amount of resources, the cost of resources, and even the duration of the activities for which the resources were utilized. This is a quick estimating approach, and its accuracy is dependent on the accuracy of the historical information the estimate is based upon. Analogous estimating is sometimes called a top-down estimate.

Utilizing Parametric Estimating

Parametric estimating uses a parameter, such as cost per square foot or eight hours of labor per fixture, to predict resource utilization and cost. The parameter must be well established and agreed upon, such as the eight hours of labor per fixture. If the parameter isn't well established, the estimate is likely going to be flawed. For example, if your project team has 2,500 fixtures to install, and your team estimates that it'll take four hours to install each fixture, but they've never installed even one of these fixtures before, that's a risky estimate. The better the data the estimate is based upon, the more reliable the estimate will be.

Identifying Alternatives

As the project management team determines what resources are needed, there will be plenty of opportunities to determine which solution is the best solution for the project. Whenever more than one solution is presented, this is called *alternative analysis*. Alternative analysis is a type of data analysis and comes in many different flavors. Here are some examples:

- **Resources**   Employees or consultants, junior or senior engineers
- **Tools and equipment**   Power tools or handheld tools, newer versus older machinery

- **Types of materials**   Oak versus plywood
- **Make-or-buy decisions**   Build-your-own software or buy a solution from a vendor

 EXAM TIP   The term "alternative analysis" is used throughout the *PMBOK Guide*, so you'll likely see this term on the PMP exam. Whenever you have two feasible choices for a component in your project, you're working with alternative analysis.

Relying on Published Estimating Data

If you are a project manager in construction, you know that the cost of the labor you use, the materials you routinely work with, and seasonal factors you consider for each project typically vary, depending on what part of the country, or even the world, your project is operating within. Many companies provide estimating data on the resources your project can purchase based on the project's geographic locale, resource supply and demand, and the season of your purchases. Published estimating data helps the project management team determine the exact cost of the resources the project will utilize.

Building an Agile Project Team

Members of agile project teams, like all teams, need the right knowledge and skillsets to get the work done. Agile teams are ideally collocated, and team members work on one project all the time rather than hopping from project to project. Agile project teams shouldn't be too big—just three to nine members is the recommended maximum—because a smaller team makes it easier to see who's doing what and enables the team to self-manage its approach and decisions, while also controlling the work in progress. Agile teams follow the rules of the approach, be it Scrum, XP, Lean, or some other flavor, and they want servant leaders to support their decisions and remove impediments.

Agile project teams begin with dedicated people working on a single project. Agile teams are often described as a group of *generalizing specialists* who specialize in one or more technologies, are knowledgeable about software development and the business domain in which they work, and actively seek new skills in a variety of areas. Specialists have specific expertise and generalists are flexible in taking on different assignments and roles.

Regardless of the agile methodology an organization embraces, you should recognize the following three basic roles for your exam:

- **Cross-functional team members**   These generalizing specialists are getting the work done and serving in more than one role. These workers include designers, developers, testers, and other roles who contribute to the final product of the project. The goal is to remove the silo mentality, in which a person performs one task only.

- **Product owner**   This individual is responsible for the tasks in the product backlog. The product owner works with the team but is responsible for prioritizing the backlog, managing changes to the product, and communicating directly with the team.

- **Team facilitator**   This is the scrum master, coach, team lead, facilitator, or other title that acts as a servant leader to the team, ensures that everyone is following the rules, and teaches others the agile approach.

Specialists in agile communities are often categorized into two kinds of people: I-shaped people and T-shaped people. I-shaped people have depth in a specific subject matter, but not much cross-functionality. T-shaped people have depth, too, but they can also collaborate and contribute in more than one area. Agile projects want T-shaped people who can do more than one role and who can contribute throughout the project. I-shaped people can become bottlenecks if they're the only person on the team who can perform a specific role.

Examining the Activity Resource Estimates

So what do you get when the project manager, the project team, and experts estimate the required activity resources? This is not a trick question! You get the requirements for all the project resources. The activity resource estimation process enables the project manager, the project team, management, and your key stakeholders to determine the resources needed to complete each work package in the WBS. Specifically, at the end of this process, you'll have the following:

- **Resource requirements for each activity**   You'll know what resources are needed, the assumption your project management team used to create the resource requirements, and the basis for each estimate.

- **Basis of estimates**   Your supporting details for creating the resource estimates should be documented. You'll document how the estimate was created, what resources you used to create the estimate, any assumptions and constraints, and a range of estimates. You should also include how confident you are in the estimate and document the risks associated with the estimate.

- **Resource breakdown structure**   On some projects, especially larger projects, you may create an RBS. The RBS visualizes the resources needed throughout the project. It can follow the same structure used for the WBS, or you can arrange the breakdown by types of resources, such as roles, equipment, facilities, and materials. The RBS can help you define what resources you need to acquire or procure, and what roles are needed in the project work.

- **Activity attribute updates**   The activities will be updated to reflect the resource requirements you've identified with this process.

- **Assumptions log**   Any assumptions about the resource type, quantity, constraints, and other related information is recorded.

- **Lessons learned register**   If any lessons were learned during the process, such as the effectiveness of how the estimates were created, they should be documented.

Acquiring the Project Team

Have you ever managed a project in which the resources you wanted were not available? Or a project in which the resources you were assigned weren't the best resources to complete the project work? To complete the project work successfully, you must acquire the appropriate resources, and you need to be familiar with the policies and procedures of the performing organization to obtain these resources by using negotiation, communication, and political savvy.

Examining the Staffing Pool

Sometimes the project manager doesn't have any say over which project team members are assigned to the project team. In other instances, the project manager can influence the decision-makers to acquire the best team members. Your project team may also include contractors that you'll have to manage. These are all part of the enterprise environmental factors—how an organization operates.

To put together a team, the project manager should always ask about the following things:

- **Availability**   Will the project team members desired for the project be available? Project managers should confer with functional managers on the availability of potential team members.

- **Cost**   Can the organization afford the desired resource?

- **Capability**   Is this the correct resource for the project work?

- **Experience**   What is the experience of the project team member? Has he done similar work in the past? Has he done it well?

- **Knowledge**   What is the competency and proficiency of the available project team members?

- **Competency**   Does the team member have the knowledge and skills to complete the project work?

- **Attitude**   Does the team member have a good attitude, and can she work with others?

- **International factors**   Where is the team member located, and will communication be an issue?

If the project manager cannot acquire the correct or most appropriate resources for the project, the schedule, costs, and quality of the project can be affected. A failure to secure the correct resources can introduce risks and even delays for the project—and in a worst-case scenario, not having the correct resources can cause the project to be cancelled altogether.

An alternative resource can be used, however, when a resource you need (or want) isn't available. For example, you may prefer to work with a specific piece of equipment, but if it's already assigned to another project, you'll have to work with a less efficient piece of equipment. That logic works with people, too: you'd like the senior engineer to be on your project, but she's already booked, so you'll bring on the junior engineer instead.

Negotiating for Resources

Most projects require that the project manager negotiate with functional managers to obtain the needed resources to complete the project work. The functional managers and the project manager may struggle over an employee's time because of demands from ongoing operations, other projects, and desires to use resources effectively. In other instances, functional managers may want to assign underutilized resources on projects to consume their otherwise idle employees' time.

Project managers may also have to negotiate with other project managers to share needed resources among projects. Scheduling the needed resources between the project teams will need to be coordinated so that both projects may complete successfully.

Working with Preassigned Staff

Project team members are often preassigned to a project for a number of reasons:

- Availability of the individual
- Promised as part of a competitive contract
- Required as part of the project charter for an internal project
- Opportunity for the staff member to complete on-the-job training

Whatever the reasoning behind the assignment of the staff to the project, the project manager should evaluate the project team for skill gaps, availability to complete the project work, and expectations of the project team members. The project manager must address any discrepancies between the requirements of the project work and the project team's ability to complete the work.

Procuring Staff

In some instances, the project manager may have no alternative but to look outside the organization to procure the project team or individuals to complete the project work. (I'll talk all about procurement in Chapter 12.) The project manager may use this alternative for reasons such as the following:

- The performing organization lacks the internal resources with the needed skills to complete the project work.
- The work is more cost-effective to procure.
- The project team members are present within the organization, but they are not available to work on the current project because of the organizational structure, such as a functional or projectized structure.
- The project team members are present within the organization, but they cannot complete the needed work because of their other project assignments.

Managing a Virtual Team

Placing all of the project team members in one geographical location is ideal for many project managers. In theory, having all of the project team members in one location enables the team members to communicate quickly, work together, and generally work better as a team. In reality, however, colocation is not always possible: Team members may be working around the globe, space may not be available in one locale, and other logistics can prevent bringing all of the project team together in a project war room. (And, yes, there's no fighting in the war room.)

Virtual teams are likely in today's world. Collaboration software, Internet tools, phone calls, and e-mails can help increase communications and the sense of a colocated team without the expense and improbability of a colocated team. Virtual teams enable the organization to do the following:

- Create a project team that comprises experts from around the globe
- Enable people to work from home offices
- Enable people to work different shifts and hours
- Include people on the project team who may have mobility limitations
- Save money by not incurring travel expenses and office expenses

The negative side to virtual teams is that communication can be more difficult, and costs can be incurred from coordinating and managing the needed communication among the virtual team members.

 EXAM TIP Remember that *colocated* teams are located in the same physical area. Colocated teams are also known as a *tight matrix*. Virtual teams working in separate locations are sometimes called *non-colocated*.

Utilizing a Multicriteria Decision Analysis Process

A "multicriteria decision analysis" process may sound very formal, scientific, and scary, but it's simply a method to rank a potential project team member on several factors to determine whether the person should be included on the project team. To use this approach, you'd identify several factors, assign scores to the different factors, and then measure each team member by those factors. Here's a quick example I made up with scoring:

- **Skills, 5 points**   What skills does the person have that the project needs?
- **Knowledge, 3 points**   Does this person have specialized knowledge about the processes, the customer, or the project life cycle?
- **Costs, 6 points**   How much is this person going to cost the project?
- **Availability, 3 points**   Will this person be available for the duration of the project?
- **Experience, 4 points**   Does this person have experience with the technology the project will be implementing?

Using such simple factors, you could measure and compare each potential team member and make a determination of each of their scored values to the project. You can add as many factors as needed and perhaps create a minimum threshold of points that the person must have to be invited onto your project team.

Assembling the Project Team

With the project team assembled, the project manager can continue planning, assigning activities, and managing the project progression. Project team members can be assigned to the project on a full- or part-time basis, depending on the project conditions. Once the project team is built, a project team directory should be assembled. The project team directory should include the following information about each team member:

- Name
- Phone number
- E-mail address
- Mailing address, if the team is geographically dispersed

It should also include the following:

- Contact information for key stakeholders
- Additional relevant contact information for team members, such as photos, web addresses, and so on

Creating Agile Team Workspaces

Ideally, as mentioned, agile teams work in one physical location so that they can communicate better, collaborate, and easily access information. In most collaborative workspaces, teams aren't tucked away in offices or cubes, but are all working together in one open space. However, people often need time to focus or work on problems alone, so there may be quiet nooks or offices for people to sequester themselves for a time period. Sometimes this open space and quiet nook mentality is called caves and commons—*commons* are the common spaces and nooks are the *caves*.

When colocation isn't a reality, virtual teams are the norm. The team can leverage technology using web collaboration software, webcams, and apps to work together. Virtual teams can do their daily standup meetings online, but attendees will need to consider time zones and possibly language differences. It's always a good idea to get all the team members together for face-to-face, in-person meetings throughout the project if that's possible.

 TIP For large projects with multiple teams working together across multiple time zones, a "follow-the-sun" approach can be implemented. This means the work is passed onto the next team each day, from one location to the next, east to west, across the globe. The work days in times zones overlap, so that as the work day ends at one site, the work day at the next site begins. Both teams may attend a meeting at the transfer point to discuss progress, daily plans, and roadblocks.

Fishbowl windows can also be used when workers are not colocated. At the beginning of the day, the team starts a video conference that's shared with all the virtual team members. Each team member has a "window" into the other team members as they work. The idea is that all team members are working "together," can view other team members, and can communicate quickly, no matter where the other workers are located. This approach prevents the lag time that virtual teams sometimes experience when trying to communicate with other remote workers through more conventional means.

For agile projects using the paired programming approach, such as XP, remote pairing can be used among programmers in different locations. In this approach, two programmers at different locations can work together via web collaboration to share screens, make edits, and communicate as if they were working in the same physical location.

 VIDEO   For a more detailed explanation, watch the *Agile Team Space* video now.

Developing the Project Team

The project manager develops the project team by enhancing the competencies of the individual project team members and promoting the interaction of all the team members. Throughout the project, the project manager must strive to involve and develop the team members as individuals completing project work, and as team members completing the project objectives together.

In matrix organizations, the project team members are accountable to the project manager and to their functional managers. Developing such a project team can prove challenging, because team members may feel pulled between multiple bosses.

Being a Servant Leader

Another major aspect of team development in an agile project is your role as a servant leader. Servant leadership means that you serve the project to make certain the team has everything it needs to create a successful product. Sometimes, this is described as "carrying food and water," though you're not literally carrying food and water—you're doing whatever it takes to get the team the right information, to protect the team from interruptions, and to remove impediments for the team by removing waste, freeing bottlenecks, and doing whatever you can to support the team.

Servant leadership also means having and promoting self-awareness and emotional intelligence. You're helping the team grow, coaching the team and stakeholders, and promoting safety, respect, and trust. Your goal is to empower the team to make decisions without fear of retribution, to be self-organized, and to be self-led. As a servant leader, you're doing much more coaching and a lot less controlling than a project manager may do in a predictive environment. The focus is on collaboration, getting the team to work together to solve problems, and facilitating interaction over processes and tools.

Preparing for Team Development

Team development is a natural process, but it's also a process that the project manager can usher along. If you're the project manager and you want team members to work together, get along, and focus on completing the project rather than focusing on who's really in charge of the project, you'll need these inputs:

- **Project management plan**   Recall that the project management plan, and specifically the resource management plan, details how project team members will be brought onto the project, managed, and released from the project team.

- **Project documents**   Five project documents will serve as inputs to team development: lessons learned register, project schedule, project team assignments, resource calendars, and the team charter.

- **Enterprise environmental factors**   Your organization's human resource policies for hiring and firing people, reviews, training and development records and procedures, and any rewards and recognitions systems are needed. Other enterprise environmental factors you'll likely reference include team members competencies, skills, and location information.

- **Organizational process assets**   Any historical information that you can use, such as the lessons learned repository or past project archives, will be beneficial.

Relying on Interpersonal Management Skills

As a project manager, you need interpersonal skills to lead the project team. You may know these as *soft skills* or *emotional intelligence*—it's about understanding what motivates people, determining how you can lead people, and knowing how to listen to people on your project team. Though the bottom line in project management is about getting things done, you're dealing with people who have issues, concerns, stresses, anxieties, and lives beyond your project. You need to listen to team members' concerns, empathize with them as needed, and help them manage their project work and assignments. An experienced project manager can shift from the manager role to see the project from the perspectives of the team members.

Specifically, the project manager relies on the following:

- **Conflict management**   Project managers cannot allow conflicts to hinder progress. Sure, some conflicts are serious, but the goal of management is to get things done. Although a project manager isn't a counselor, you'll need to balance the emotional intelligence of leadership with the desire to get things done.

- **Influencing**   Project managers use their influence to help team members achieve results by maintaining a high morale, teamwork, and courage.

- **Motivation**   Good project managers master the art of establishing direction, aligning people, and motivating the project team to complete the project work.

- **Negotiating**   Project managers will likely negotiate for scope, cost, terms, assignment, and resources.

- **Team building**   Project managers facilitate team building, including hosting activities to bring people together, build trust and relationships, and communicate with one another. Team-building exercises can be quick five-minute activities or daylong events. Team building often happens at the beginning of the project, but it should be an ongoing activity throughout the project as well.

 EXAM TIP   Although agile teams are self-led, they still need leadership from their coach or scrum master. The central role of project management in adaptive projects is to help the team, especially in the early stages of the project, to make decisions and get organized, and to walk the team through the rules of the agile approach. As the team becomes more and more experienced, they'll work more independently of the scrum master or coach.

Creating Team-Building Activities

Team-building activities encourage cooperation and trust among the team members through facilitated events. The goal of team-building exercises is to enable the project team to learn about one another, rely on one another, and work cohesively together. Activities can include the following:

- Involving the team during planning processes
- Backlog prioritization and user story sizing
- Sprint planning sessions, reviews, and retrospectives
- Defining rules for handling team disagreements
- Holding off-site activities
- Facilitating quick team-involvement activities
- Facilitating activities to improve interpersonal skills and form relationships

A theory of team development that was created by Dr. Bruce Tuckman in 1965 posits that a project team goes through its own natural development process. This process can shift, linger, and even stall, based on the dynamics of the project team. Here are the five phases of team development, called the Tuckman ladder, from bottom to top:

- **Forming**   The project team meets to learn about their roles and responsibilities on the project. Little interaction among the project team happens in this stage, as the team is learning about the project and project manager. The project manager guides the project team through this stage of team development by introducing members and helping them learn about one another.

- **Storming**   The project team struggles for project positions, leadership, and project direction. Project team members can become hostile toward the project leader, challenge ideas, and try to establish and claim positions about the project work.

The amount of debate and fury can vary depending on whether the project team members are willing to work together, the nature of the project, and the control of the project manager. The project manager's role in this stage is to mediate disagreement and squelch unproductive behavior.

- **Norming** Project team members go about getting the project work, begin to rely on one another, and generally complete their project assignments. In this stage of team development, the project manager allows the project team to manage themselves.

- **Performing** If a project team can reach the performing stage of team development, team members trust one another and work well together, and issues and problems are resolved quickly and effectively. The project manager stays out of the project team's way but is available to help the team get their work done.

- **Adjourning** Once the project is done, either the team moves on to other assignments as a unit or the project team is disbanded and individual team members go on to other work. The project manager uses the staffing management plan as a guide for how project team members are released from the project team.

NOTE Tuckman originally used only the first four stages of team development, but he added adjourning to the model in the 1970s. If a team has worked together in the past, they may skip a stage. Some teams may get stuck in a stage or even move down the ladder instead of advancing.

Establishing Project Ground Rules

Creating ground rules for the project team is part of the team charter. Ground rules establish the project expectations for the project team and define what is and is not acceptable behavior by all of the project team members, including the project manager. When all of the project team members agree to abide by the defined ground rules, misunderstandings diminish while productivity increases. Once ground rules are defined in the team charter, it's the responsibility of all the project team members to enforce them.

EXAM TIP Remember that ground rules are enforced by the project team, not just the project manager.

Rewarding the Project Team

When discussing human resource planning, I mentioned that you, the project manager, should create a rewards and recognition system. This system is part of team development and encourages the behavior you want from your project team—that is, the behavior that promotes the project to completion and meets the project scope statement. Performance appraisals tell the project manager, and sometimes functional management, which team members should be rewarded based on the confines of the reward system.

Obviously, positive behavior should be rewarded. If a project team member willingly agrees to work overtime to ensure that the project will hit its schedule objective, that should be rewarded or recognized by the project manager. However, if a project team member has to work overtime because he has wasted time or resources, a reward is not in order.

Win-lose awards, sometimes called zero-sum awards, should be avoided, because they can hurt the project team's cohesiveness. Any award for which only some project team members qualify shouldn't be given. For instance, I once worked on a project where the project manager awarded a bonus to the software developer who created the most code every month. Well, since I wasn't a software developer, I could never qualify for that bonus. (Thanks a lot, Ron! Ron was my boss then, and oh what sweet printed vengeance this is. Just kidding.... He dropped the bonus program when he realized the trouble with his plan.)

 TIP Your rewards and recognition system should also consider cultural differences. Creating team rewards in a culture that encourages individualism can be difficult. In other words, the reward system must mesh with the culture within which the project manager is operating.

Assessing the Project Team

You want your project team to be the best unit of people possible. You want them to rely on one another, help one another, and communicate without fear of retribution. You also want the project team to be competent in the project work and execution of the project management plan. Personnel assessment tools, such as exams and surveys, can help you gain some insight into the project team and determine where each person's strengths and weaknesses lie. This can help you determine the best ways to manage the project team, improve performance, and gain insight into what motivates team members.

The assessments of the project team can measure all sorts of factors, but there are some common measurements that can result from an assessment program:

- Technical success of the project execution
- Project schedule adherence
- Cost baseline management
- Improvement in competencies
- Reduction in staff turnover
- Team functionality in communications and problem-solving

Project team members' performance is reviewed and tied to their overall performance on the project team. Performance appraisals can be in the form of a 360-degree appraisal, where a project team member is reviewed in all directions by the project team, the project manager, stakeholders, and even vendors, where appropriate.

Managing the Project Team

Once the project manager has planned for the human resources and developed the project team, she can focus on managing the project team. This process involves tracking each team member's performance, offering feedback, taking care of project issues, and managing those pesky change requests that can affect the project team and its work. The staffing management plan may be updated based on lessons learned and changes within the team management process.

In a matrix environment, where the project team members are accountable both to the project manager and a functional manager, team management is a tricky business. The project manager and the functional managers need to work together to communicate the utilization of the project team member in both operations and on the project. The project team's demand for dual reporting to the project manager and the functional manager also has to be considered—and is often the responsibility of the project manager rather than the functional manager or project team member.

In an agile project, the project manager role isn't as clearly defined as the role in a predictive project. This is because the different types of adaptive project management use different titles for the role of the project manager. You may be called a coach, a facilitator, scrum master, team lead, or another title. It's not the title that's important; instead, it's the actions you take to ensure that the team has what they need to be successful, that you're communicating with stakeholders on how the agile approach works, and protecting the team from interruptions. You want to create a safe environment for the team to be successful and then trust them to do their work without hovering or interfering with team decisions.

 CAUTION Beware multitasking! Multitasking is task switching, and that's considered wasteful in an adaptive project. Singularity of purpose, the ability to focus and do deep work, is valued and promoted in agile project work.

Preparing for Team Management

Managing the project team is based on many conditions and scenarios within the project. Management of the project team is really about one thing: getting the project work done as promised in the project scope statement. There are many inputs to project team management:

- **Project management plan**   The resource management plan, part of the project management plan, defines when project team members will complete their project work, the training needs for the project, certification requirements, and any labor compliance issues.

- **Project documents**   You'll need to prepare four project documents to manage the project team: issue log, lessons learned register, project team assignments, and team charter.

- **Work performance reports**   The project management team observes and records the work that each project team member performs. This doesn't necessarily mean the project management team micromanages the project team members; instead, it observes the team members' participation in team activities, delivery on action items, and thoroughness in communications.

- **Team performance assessments**   You'll know if your project team is doing a good job or not, but you'll want to quantify their performance so that you can make recommendations where needed. Assessments include information on the project team's skills, competencies, turnover rate, and cohesion.

- **Enterprise environment factors**   You must follow the human resource policies for managing the project team and any organizational rules for reviews, resource utilization, and reporting on team performance.

- **Organizational process assets**   Consider the organization's approach to rewarding employees for their work in a project. Organizational process assets in team management rely on rewards such as certificates of appreciation, shirts and mugs with the company logo, newsletters, and other methods to recognize a project team's hard work on a project.

All of these inputs feed directly into the actual process of managing the project team. The project manager and the project management team will use these inputs to manage the team better and move the project toward successful completion.

Dealing with Team Disagreements

In most projects, the project team, management, and other stakeholders may disagree on the progress, decisions, and proposed solutions within the project. It's essential for the project manager to keep calm, lead, and direct the parties to a sensible solution that's best for the project. Here are seven reasons for conflict, listed from most common to least common:

- Schedules
- Priorities
- Resources
- Technical beliefs
- Administrative policies and procedures
- Project costs
- Personalities

 EXAM TIP   You can expect questions on these areas of conflict on the exam. Don't be duped into thinking personality conflicts are the biggest problem with conflict resolution. They are the least important. Agile teams may look more to the project management role to help make decisions and resolve conflicts early in the project, then as the team becomes more interdependent, they'll make their decisions and take actions without relying so much on the project management role.

So what's a project manager to do with all the potential for strife in a project? Of course, not all conflicts are important. Some are petty, childish, and part of the nonsense that project managers have to deal with. Other conflicts, however, are more serious and require some thought and a delicate approach. Here are five considerations for conflict management before acting on the conflict:

- Importance of the conflict and how disruptive the conflict is
- Possibility of the conflict disrupting the project progress immediately
- Power of the people in the conflict and how they can influence the project
- Need for the project manager to maintain relationships with the people involved
- Need for a long-term resolution or a short-term fix for the project's sake

Once you've a good grasp on the conflict, the people involved, and how it'll affect the project, you'll consider these five different approaches to conflict resolution:

- **Collaborate/problem-solve**   This approach utilizes multiple viewpoints and perspectives to find a resolution. To use this method, the participants need a collaborative attitude to confront the problem rather than each other.
- **Force/direct**   The person with the power makes the decision. The decision made may not be the best decision for the project, but it's fast. As expected, this autocratic approach does little for team development and is a win–lose solution. It should be used when the stakes are high and time is of the essence, or if maintaining relationships is not important.
- **Compromise/reconcile**   This approach requires that both parties give up something. The decision made is a blend of both sides of the argument. Because neither party really wins, it is considered a lose–lose solution. The project manager can use this approach when the relationships are equal and no one can truly "win." This approach can also be used to avoid a fight.
- **Smoothing/accommodating**   This approach smooths out the conflict by minimizing the perceived size of the problem. It is a temporary solution that can calm team relations and boisterous discussions. Smoothing may be acceptable when time is of the essence or when any of the proposed solutions will not currently settle the problem. This can be considered a lose–lose situation as well, since no one really wins in the long run. The project manager can use smoothing to emphasize areas of agreement between disagreeing stakeholders and thus minimize areas of conflict.
- **Withdrawal/avoidance**   This conflict resolution has one side of the argument walking away from the problem, usually in disgust. The conflict is not resolved, and it is considered a yield–lose solution. The approach can be used, however, during a cooling-off period or when the issue is not critical.

Creating an Issue Log

It's okay to have issues within a project as long as the issues are recorded in the issue log. An *issue,* technically, is something that may be preventing the project team from reaching the project objectives. Typically, issues are identified and recorded in the issue log.

Each issue is assigned an owner who needs to find a method that will resolve the issue by a given date. Each issue should also be identified as to its status and possible resolution. Common issues include the following:

- Differences of opinion
- Situations to be investigated
- Unanticipated responsibilities that need to be assigned to someone on the project team

---

 EXAM TIP Be familiar with the concept of *emotional intelligence,* which is the ability to recognize and manage your emotions, other people's emotions, and the emotions of groups involved in the project. Emotional intelligence recognizes that emotions are real, can affect the project success, and can affect relationships with the project team, stakeholders, and the project manager.

Examining the Outputs of Team Management

Team management begins as soon as the project team comes together, and it ends as soon as the project is closed. Throughout the project, different conditions and scenarios will affect how the project manager and the project management team will manage the project and the resources within it.

There are four outputs of managing the project team:

- **Requested changes** Seems like just about everything can result in a change request, doesn't it? Changes to the project team can have ripple effects on project scheduling, project cost, and even the project scope statement, so a change request is needed when certain conditions are present. Corrective actions can include moving people to different assignments, outsourcing some of the project work, and replacing project team members who may have left the organization or project. Preventive actions can include cross-training, role clarification, and even additional labor through hiring or procurement to ensure that all of the project work is completed as planned.

- **Project management plan updates** As with any other area of project management, if the project management plan needs to be updated, it should be. Project management plan updates could include updates to the resource management plan, schedule baseline, and the cost baseline.

- **Project document updates** Updates to the issue log, lessons learned register, and team assignments should be reflected in the project documents as needed. You may need to update the roles and responsibility charts, such as your RACI chart, to reflect the changes within the project and/or project team.

- **Enterprise environmental factor updates**   It is possible that your management approach could affect the enterprise environmental factors within your organization. You may need to update the process for performance appraisals and any information about project team members' new skills as a result of the project training.

Relating to Organizational Theories

You can expect to see some of these topics on your exam, so let's have a look at these theories in more detail.

Maslow's Hierarchy of Needs

According to American psychologist Abraham Maslow, people work to take care of a *hierarchy of needs*. The pinnacle of their needs is self-actualization. People want to contribute, prove their worth, and use their skills and abilities. Figure 9-3 shows the pyramid of needs that all people try to ascend by fulfilling each layer, one at a time.

Maslow's five layers of needs, from lowest to highest, are

- **Physiological**   People require these necessities to live: air, water, food, clothing, and shelter.
- **Safety**   People need safety and security. This can include stability in life, work, and culture.
- **Social**   People are social creatures and need love, approval, and friends.
- **Esteem**   People strive for the respect, appreciation, and approval of others.
- **Self-actualization**   At the pinnacle of needs, people seek personal growth, knowledge, and fulfillment.

Figure 9-3
Maslow's theory states that people ultimately work for self-actualization.

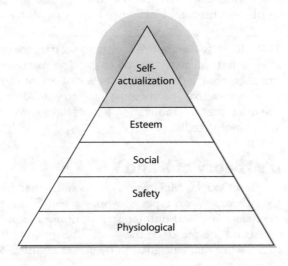

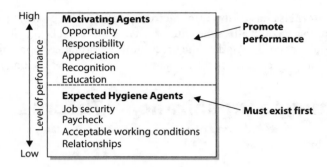

Figure 9-4
Hygiene agents
do nothing to
motivate, but
their absence
will cause
performance
and morale
to decline.

Herzberg's Theory of Motivation

According to Frederick Herzberg, a psychologist and authority on the motivation of work, there are two catalysts that affect workers' motivation:

- **Hygiene agents**   These elements are the expectations all workers have. They include job security, a paycheck, clean and safe working conditions, a sense of belonging, civil working relationships, and other basic attributes associated with employment.

- **Motivating agents**   These elements motivate people to excel. They include responsibility, appreciation of work, public recognition for a job well done, the chance to excel, education, and other opportunities associated with work aside from financial rewards.

Herzberg's Theory posits that the presence of hygiene factors will not motivate people to perform because these are expected attributes. However, the absence of these elements will demotivate performance. For people to excel, the presence of motivating factors must exist. Figure 9-4 illustrates Herzberg's Theory of Motivation.

 EXAM TIP   Use Herzberg's Theory to prepare for your exam. Find some things that will motivate you to excel so you can pass your exam: a career advancement, a day off work, new clothes, or some other reward. Create an incentive that means something to you. After all, part of Herzberg's Theory is that the motivating agents have to interest the person who's being motivated.

McGregor's Theory of X and Y

Professor and author Douglas McGregor's theory states that, from their perspective, management believes there are two types of workers, bad (X people) and good (Y people). Theory X workers are lazy and uninterested in doing the project work, and they must be micromanaged and coerced to do the work. Theory Y workers are good, self-directed, and able to do the work that's assigned to them, see Figure 9-5.

Figure 9-5
In this theory, management believes that X people are bad and Y people are good.

X People

Micromanagement
No trust
Lazy
Avoid work

Y People

Self-led
Motivated
Capable

- *X is bad.* These people need to be watched all the time, micromanaged, and cannot be trusted. X people avoid work, shun responsibility, and lack the aptitude to achieve.

- *Y is good.* These people are self-led, motivated, and can accomplish new tasks proactively.

Ouchi's Theory Z

American author and professor William Ouchi's theory is based on the Japanese participative management style. This theory suggests that workers are motivated by a sense of commitment, opportunity, and advancement. Workers in an organization subscribing to Theory Z learn the business by moving up through the ranks of the company.

EXAM TIP   If you need a way to keep McGregor's X and Y and Ouchi's Z theories separate in your mind, think of this: X is bad, Y is good, Z is the best.

Ouchi's theory also credits the idea of *lifetime employment.* Workers will stay with one company until they retire because they are dedicated to the company, which is in turn dedicated to them.

NOTE   Mary is a good software developer, so she would be a good project manager of software development projects, right? Not necessarily. This is the *halo effect*—when you make a judgment about a person based on seemingly related characteristics. Just because Mary is skilled in one area doesn't mean she'll also be skilled in another, somewhat related, area.

Vroom's Expectancy Theory

Business professor Victor Vroom's Expectancy Theory posits that people will behave based on what they expect as a result of their behavior. In other words, people will work in relation to the expected reward of the work. If the attractiveness of the reward is desirable to the worker, she will work to receive it. In other words, workers expect to be rewarded for their efforts.

PART II

McClelland's Theory of Needs

American psychologist David McClelland developed his acquired-needs theory based on his belief that a person's needs are acquired and develop over time. These needs are shaped by circumstance, conditions, and life experiences for each individual. McClelland's Theory of Needs is also known as the Three Needs Theory, because each individual has three main needs; depending on the person's experiences, the order and magnitude of each need shifts:

- **Need for achievement**   These people need to achieve, so they avoid both low-risk and high-risk situations. Achievers like to work alone or with other high achievers, and they need regular feedback to gauge their achievement and progress.

- **Need for affiliation**   People who have a driving need for affiliation look for harmonious relationships, want to feel accepted by people, and conform to the norms of the project team.

- **Need for power**   People who have a need for power are usually seeking either personal or institutional power. Personal power generally is the ability to control and direct other people. Institutional power is the ability to direct the efforts of others for the betterment of the organization.

McClelland developed the Thematic Apperception Test to determine what needs are driving individuals. The test is a series of pictures that the test-taker must create a story about. Through the storytelling, the test-taker will reveal which need is driving his or her life at that time.

Controlling Resources

Controlling resources is about monitoring and controlling resource allocation for the project, tracking the cost and utilization of resources, communicating any problems with resources, and managing changes when they occur in the project. Changes to resources can result from vendor issues; conflicts with other people utilizing the resource, such as equipment or facilities; and issues that happen because of defects in the project work. When defects happen, you'll likely need to submit a change request to order more materials, and this means the cost of the project increases.

Of course, in adaptive projects, controlling resources is not as confined. Early in the project, the team will likely need more coaching and direction, but as the project moves forward, the team should become more independent. The team will learn to determine who does what work for the iteration, and team members will learn how to keep one another accountable for getting the work done. The sprint retrospective, for example, is an opportunity for the team to discuss what's worked well in the project and what hasn't worked. It's not an opportunity to place blame; comments should be respectful, but also open and transparent. Then the team should make adjustments for the next iteration to work better as a team.

Preparing to Control Resources

To control resources, you'll rely on five inputs to this straightforward process:

- **Project management plan**   In particular, the subsidiary resource management plan
- **Project documents**   The issue log, lessons learned register, physical resource assignments, schedule, resource breakdown structure, resource requirements, and the risk register
- **Work performance data**   Raw data gathered on project status and resource utilization
- **Agreements**   Contracts and agreements with vendors and groups regarding the project resources
- **Organizational process assets**   Policies for resource control, resource assignment, escalation processes, and lessons learned from similar projects

Reviewing the Tools and Techniques to Control Resources

Data analysis is used with controlling resources to examine alternatives analysis. When a resource is not available—perhaps a vendor can't deliver the physical resource as promised—alternatives analysis is used to determine whether another resource could work or a different vendor could deliver the solution. Analysis can also involve an examination of what the late delivery would mean to the project schedule and whether the project team can work on other tasks while waiting for the delivery of the resource from the vendor.

Performance reviews are also part of controlling resources. The project manager can compare the actual performance of physical resources to the planned performance of the resources. If the performance of a planned resource is not meeting expectations, the project manager can use cost-benefits analysis to determine whether changing vendors, materials, or both is cost efficient.

The final data analysis technique you can use to control resources is trend analysis. Trend analysis will enable you to examine how well physical resources have performed and to identify trend lines in the analysis to plan for future work. For some materials or equipment, the trend line may reflect the learning curve of using the resource. If the project team members have never used a material before, for example, it will likely take some time for the team to learn the best application of the material, develop an approach to doing the work, and master the use of the material. A trend line can track this progress over time.

Project managers in adaptive projects want to promote the idea that a team is working full time on a project, rather than switching between tasks among multiple projects. Agile project teams focus on one project, ideally, and communicate face-to-face daily. The project manager role also wants to break down the idea of silos in projects and have team members that are cross-functional and serve as generalizing specialists.

Problems with materials are common issues for the project manager or experts on the project team. When materials aren't performing as expected, you'll need to create a solution to keep the project moving forward. Problems can come from inside the organization, such as equipment damaged by a team member, or from outside the organization, such as a vendor that can't deliver, bad weather, or other external issues. When problem-solving, use methodical, logical steps to find a solution:

- Identify the problem, not the evidence of the problem.
- Break the problem down into manageable chunks.
- Investigate the problem, collect data, and experience the problem.
- Analyze the problem to discover the root causes.
- Find a solution that's time and cost efficient.
- Confirm that the solution is working.

Reviewing the Results of Controlling Resources

Controlling resources is an ongoing need throughout the project. The first output of the process, work performance information, provides useable data about the performance of the physical resources in the project. This information can help the project manager determine whether a change request is needed for the materials. Change requests are the second output of this process; all change requests must be submitted to the project's integrated change control process.

The project management plan could need to be updated as a result of controlling resources. When the project management plan is updated, a change request should be submitted as well. Changes can occur to the project management plan as a result of controlling resources such as the following:

- **Resource management plan**   Results of resources should be compared to what was planned for the resources.
- **Schedule baseline**   Any changes to the project schedule resulting from controlling resources should be reflected in the schedule baseline.
- **Cost baseline**   Defects, changes in the price of materials, and other changes to the costs of the resources must be updated and reflected in the cost baseline.

The process of controlling resources can also require that several project documents be updated:

- **Assumptions log**   Any assumptions about the physical resources that could affect the project should be logged.
- **Issue log**   Issues are risks that have be realized; issues with physical resources must be documented, tracked, and monitored.
- **Lessons learned register**   What was learned about the physical resources is documented.
- **Physical resource assignments**   Should the assignments for the physical resources change, the change needs to be documented and updated.

- **Resource breakdown structure**   Where the resources are utilized in the project can be reflected in the resource breakdown structure.

- **Risk register**   Any risks that are introduced or changed as a result of physical resources must be updated in the risk register.

Chapter Summary

The project manager has to plan for the human resources needed to complete the project work and for the physical resources the project will need. In addition, the project manager plans for how the human resources will be managed, trained, motivated, and led throughout the duration of the project. The project team works to identify their roles and responsibilities within the project, including the activities needed to complete the project work. The key output of planning for human resources is the resource management plan, which defines how the project team will be acquired, managed, trained, rewarded for the work, and then released from the project team. The resource management plan also identifies the physical resources needed in the project, along with the acquisition process and management of resources.

The project team is acquired as specified in the resource management plan. The team, however, isn't always selected—it's often preassigned to the project. Sometimes, the project manager can negotiate with the functional managers and other project managers to get the best possible resources for the project. When the resources aren't available inside the organization, the project manager may deal with contracted help, which means procurement.

Adaptive project teams are self-organizing and self-led. This means that the team members will determine who'll do what work in the sprint backlog, will hold one another accountable, and will work transparently, with trust and with confidence to experiment and sometimes fail. Early in the project, the team may need more coaching from the scrum master, coach, or project manager in a hybrid approach, but with experience, the team will become more independent and able to work together to get things done.

In some teams, team members all work together at one locale and may periodically huddle in the project's war room. The idea of a colocated team supports ad hoc conversations, team cohesiveness, and project performance. However, in many cases, the project team is not colocated and a virtual team is created. Virtual teams enable people with mobility handicaps or travel issues, as well as home office workers, to be actively involved in the project—and they save expenses for travel and office space. Adaptive projects utilize caves and commons; commons are the public work area and caves are isolated nooks to use when focused work is needed.

Whatever conditions affect the project team, the project manager must work to develop the team. Team development centers on building team cohesiveness through team-building exercises, training, and team involvement. One team development tool and technique is the creation of ground rules. Ground rules are created and agreed upon by the project team to promote performance within the project. Once ground rules are created, it's up to the project team to enforce them.

Through conversations, observations, performance appraisals, conflict management, and the issue log, the project manager will manage the project team. The goal of team management is getting the project done—which is all about results. The project manager needs interpersonal skills, sometimes called the soft skills of project management, to communicate and effectively manage the project team. Controlling the project resources, which also involves using interpersonal skills, focuses on controlling human resources and physical resources.

Human resource theories, such as Maslow's Hierarchy of Needs, McGregor's Theory of X and Y, Ouchi's Theory Z, and Vroom's Expectancy Theory, all seek to determine what motivates an employee to complete project tasks. Project managers can use these theories to determine the best approach to motivate or inspire a project team member to elicit the behavior the project manager expects.

Questions

1. You are the project manager for the JHG Project. This project requires coordination with the director of manufacturing, HR, the IT department, and the CIO. The director of manufacturing wants to ensure that materials are delivered to the job site only as they are needed because of space limitations. What approach to resource management is this?

   A. Just-in-time manufacturing

   B. Kaizen

   C. Total productive maintenance

   D. Human resource coordination

2. You are the project manager of the Newton Construction Project. Your team for this project will include internal and external employees. Your project requires an electrician at month eight. This is an example of which of the following?

   A. Organizational interfaces

   B. Staffing requirements

   C. Contractor requirements

   D. Resource constraints

3. You are the project manager of the PUY Project. This project requires a chemical engineer for seven months of the project, although there are no available chemical engineers within your department. This is an example of which of the following?

   A. Organizational interfaces

   B. Staffing requirements

   C. Contractor requirements

   D. Resource constraints

4. You are the project manager in an organization with a weak matrix. Your project team members will come from three different lines of business within the organization, and they are also working on at least two other projects. Who will have the authority in your project?

A. The project manager

B. The customer

C. Functional management

D. The team leader

5. You are the project manager for the LMG Project. Your project will have several human resource issues that must be coordinated and approved by the union. Which of the following statements is correct about this scenario?

A. The union is considered a resource constraint.

B. The union is considered a management constraint.

C. The union is considered a project stakeholder.

D. The union is considered a project team member.

6. You are the project manager of the PLY Project. This project is similar to the ACT Project you have completed. What method can you use to expedite the process of organizational planning?

A. Use the project plan of the ACT Project on the PLY Project.

B. Use the roles and responsibilities defined in the ACT Project on the PLY Project.

C. Use the project team structure of the ACT Project on the PLY Project.

D. Use the project team of the ACT Project on the PLY Project.

7. You are the project manager in your organization. Your project is part of a larger program led by Nancy Whitting. Nancy is a believer of McGregor's Theory of X and Y. Which of the following is an example of Theory X?

A. Self-led project teams

B. Micromanagement

C. Team members able to work on their own accord

D. Earned value management

8. You are the project manager of the PLN Project. You are using a RACI chart to organize roles and responsibilities for project assignments. In a RACI chart, what is the maximum number of people that can be accountable for an assignment?

A. One

B. Two

C. Two, if one of the two people is also responsible

D. As many people that are on the project team

9. You are the coach for a software development project using an agile approach. Your team is physically located in one place, but some of team members report they need some quiet time to focus on their work. What should you do next?

A. Remove those team members from the common workplace to cubicles.

B. Install cubicles for quiet workspaces.

C. Implement caves and commons for the project team.

D. Purchase headphones for the team members that need quiet time.

10. Management has approached Ming, one of your project team members. Ming is a database administrator and developer whose work is always on time, accurate, and of quality. He also has a reputation of being a "good guy" and is well liked. Because of this, management has decided to move Ming into the role of a project manager for a new database administration project. This is an example of which of the following?

A. Management by exception

B. The halo effect

C. Management by objectives

D. McGregor's Theory of X and Y

11. You are the project manager of the Holson Implementation Project for your company. It's come to your attention that three of your project team members are in a disagreement about the direction the project work should take. This disagreement is stalling the project schedule and causing the other project team members to become uncomfortable. You need to resolve this situation quickly and professionally. Which problem-solving technique is the best for most project management situations?

A. Collaborating/problem-solving

B. Compromising

C. Forcing

D. Avoiding

12. Aaliyah is an outspoken project team member. All of the project team members respect her for her experience with the technology, but often things have to go in Aaliyah's favor; otherwise the team's in for a bumpy ride. During a discussion on a solution, a project team member waves her arms and says, "Fine, Aaliyah, do it your way." This is an example of which of the following?

A. A win–win solution

B. A leave–lose solution

C. A lose–lose solution

D. A yield–lose solution

13. You are the project manager for the GBK Project. This project affects a line of business, and the customer is anxious about the success of the project. Which of the following is likely not a top concern for the customer?

    A. Project priorities

    B. Schedule

    C. Cost

    D. Personality conflicts

14. You should understand several management theories for your PMI exam and for your role as a project manager. Which theory posits that workers need to be involved with the management process?

    A. McGregor's Theory of X and Y

    B. Ouchi's Theory Z

    C. Herzberg's Theory of Motivation

    D. Vroom's Expectancy Theory

15. You need a method to keep workers motivated and inspired on your project. This project has many conditions that the project team sees as unfavorable, but they do like you as a project manager. Which of the following theories states that as long as workers are rewarded, they will remain productive?

    A. McGregor's Theory of X and Y

    B. Ouchi's Theory Z

    C. Herzberg's Theory of Motivation

    D. Vroom's Expectancy Theory

16. You are the project manager for Industrial Lights Project. Your project team can have access to the job site only between 8 P.M. and 7 A.M. Which project document would document this information for your project?

    A. Project charter

    B. Project calendar

    C. Project schedule

    D. Resource management plan

17. You are the project manager for GHB Project. You have served as a project manager for your organization for the past ten years. Most of your projects come in on time and on budget. Part of your planning is to consider when project team members are available for doing the project work. Which one of the following will detail team members' availability for your project?

    A. Resource management plan

    B. Project calendar

    C. Resource calendar

    D. Gantt chart

18. You are the project manager for your organization's first agile project and it's come to your attention that some of the project team members are in disagreement with the senior network engineer about the installation of some equipment. What should you do next in this scenario?

    A. Meet with the senior network engineer about the issue.

    B. Meet with the project team members about the issue

    C. Determine the best solution for the project to keep things moving.

    D. Encourage the team to collectively come to a decision for the project's value.

19. Miguel is the project manager for a hybrid project with a very tight schedule. The project is running late, and Miguel believes that he does not have time to consider all the possible solutions that two team members are in disagreement over. He quickly decides to go with the team member with the largest amount of seniority. This is an example of which of the following?

    A. Problem-solving

    B. Compromising

    C. Forcing

    D. Withdrawal

20. You are a project manager in a projectized organization. Your job as a project manager can be described best by which of the following?

    A. Full-time

    B. Part-time

    C. Expeditor

    D. Coordinator

Answers

1. **A.** With just-in-time manufacturing, resources are in place only as they are needed. This approach reduces waste, keeps inventory at a minimum, and helps the project manager forecast resource utilization more accurately. B is incorrect because Kaizen utilizes changes to the organization and project team over time, resulting in large changes overall. C is incorrect because continuous maintenance on equipment and quality systems keeps equipment working well and efficiently. This approach aims to reduce downtime by avoiding equipment failure. D is incorrect because human resource coordination is not a valid project management term.

2. **B.** Because the project requires an electrician, a project role, this is a staffing requirement. A is incorrect because it does not accurately describe the situation. C is incorrect because contractor requirements would specify the procurement issues, the minimum qualifications for the electrician, and so on. D is incorrect because a resource constraint, while a tempting choice, deals more with the availability of the resource or the requirement to use the resource.

3. B. The project needs the resource of the chemical engineer to be successful. When the project needs a resource, it is a staffing requirement. A and C are incorrect because this is not a situation describing an organizational interface or contractor requirements. D is incorrect because resource constraints may include a requirement to use a particular resource or that a resource must be available when certain project activities are happening.

4. C. In a weak matrix structure, functional management will have more authority than the project manager. A, B, and D are all incorrect. These roles do not have as much authority on a project in a weak matrix environment as functional management will have.

5. C. In this instance, the union is considered a project stakeholder because it has a vested interest in the project's outcome. The union is not a constraint, the rules of the union may constraint options, but the union itself is not a constraint. A is incorrect because the union is not a resource constraint; it is interested in the project management methodology and the project human resource management. B is incorrect because the union is not a constraint, though their rules may be. D is incorrect because the union is not a project team member.

6. B. When projects are similar in nature, the project manager can use the roles and responsibilities defined in the historical project to guide the current project. A is incorrect because the entire project plan of the ACT Project is not needed. Even the roles and responsibilities matrix of the historical project may not be an exact fit for the current project. C is incorrect because copying the project team structure is not the best choice of all the answers presented. D is incorrect because using the same project team may not be feasible at all.

7. B. Theory X states that workers have an inherent dislike of work and will avoid it if possible. With regard to this theory, micromanagement is a method used to make certain workers complete their work. A and C are incorrect. These are examples of McGregor's Theory Y. D is incorrect because EVM is not directly related to McGregor's Theory of X and Y.

8. A. In a RACI chart, which stands for responsible, accountable, consulted, and informed, only one person is accountable. B, C, and D are incorrect. These choices enable more than one person to be accountable.

9. C. The best answer is to use a caves and commons approach. Commons are the public workspace the team is currently using, but caves would be quiet, isolated areas for the team members to focus on their work as needed. A is incorrect because the team shouldn't be removed entirely from the common workspace. B is incorrect because although cubicles may be isolated, they aren't likely to be quiet if installed in the common workplace environment. D is incorrect because purchasing headphones doesn't provide the same value as utilizing as the caves and commons approach.

10. B. The halo effect is the assumption that because the person is good at a technology, he would also be good at managing a project dealing with that said technology. A, C, and D are all incorrect because these do not describe the halo effect.

11. **A.** Collaborating/problem-solving is the best problem-solving technique because it meets the problem directly. B is incorrect because compromising requires both sides of an argument to give up something. C is incorrect because forcing requires the project manager to force a decision based on external inputs, such as seniority, experience, and so on. D is incorrect because avoiding ignores the problem and does not solve it.

12. **D.** Aaliyah always has to win an argument and team members begin to give in to her demands simply to avoid an argument rather than finding an accurate solution. This describes a yield–lose situation. A is incorrect because both parties do not win. B is incorrect because the project team member did not leave the conversation, but instead ended it. C is incorrect because a lose–lose is a compromise in which both parties give up something.

13. **D.** Personality conflicts may be a concern for the customer, but they are not as important or as likely to be of concern as project priorities, schedule, and cost. The customer hired your company to solve the technical issues. A, B, and C are all incorrect. These are most likely the top issues for a customer in a project of this magnitude.

14. **B.** Ouchi's Theory Z states that workers need to be involved with the management process. A is incorrect because McGregor's Theory of X and Y posits that X workers don't want to work and need constant supervision, while Z workers will work if the work is challenging, satisfying, and rewarding. C is incorrect because Herzberg's Theory of Motivation describes types of people and what excites them to work. D is incorrect because the Expectancy Theory describes how people will work based on what they expect in return.

15. **D.** Vroom's Expectancy Theory describes how people will work based on what they expect in return. If people are rewarded because of the work they complete, and they like the reward (payment), they will continue to work. A, B, and C are all incorrect. These theories do not accurately describe the scenario presented.

16. **B.** The project calendar defines when the project work can be done, so this is the best answer. A is incorrect because the project charter will not typically define when the project team may access the job site. C is incorrect because the project schedule may define this information, but not necessarily. The project schedule typically defines actual start and finish dates for tasks, not access times to the job site. D is incorrect because the resource management plan provides information on the identification of resources, how to acquire the resources, and specific roles and responsibilities of the resources.

17. **C.** The resource calendar defines when resources, both people and physical resources, are available for utilization in the project. A is incorrect as the resource management plan defines how resources will be managed, not when resources are available. B is incorrect as the project calendar defines when the project work may take place. D is incorrect as the Gantt chart is a scheduling tool of when activities will take place in the project.

18. **D.** The best solution is to encourage the team to work together and make a collective decision on what's best for the project's value. Agile teams are to be self-led and self-organizing, rather than the command-and-control approach of predictive projects. As this is the team's first agile project, the project manager serves more as a coach and makes certain everyone is following the rules of the project. A and B is incorrect as this approach interjects the project manager into the solution and may create a divide among the team. The project manager should not interfere with the team's self-led decision-making. C is incorrect as this is the project manager making the decision for the team and is not a value of agile project management.

19. **C.** Forcing happens when the project manager makes a decision based on factors that are not relevant to the problem. Just because a team member has more seniority does not mean this individual is correct. A is incorrect because problem-solving is not described in the scenario. B is incorrect because compromising happens when both parties agree to give up something. D is incorrect because withdrawal happens when a party leaves the argument.

20. **A.** Project managers are typically assigned to a project on a full-time basis in a projectized organization. B, C, and D are incorrect. They do not accurately describe the work schedule of a project manager in a projectized environment.

Managing Project Communications

In this chapter, you will
- Plan for project communications
- Manage project communications
- Monitor project communications

In the movie *Cool Hand Luke*, Captain, the prison warden, says, "What we've got here is failure to communicate." It's a famous line that has been repeated by musicians and politicians, and even muttered by project managers. Ideally, when you, the project manager, quote this line, you aren't viewed as the prison warden by your project team.

The point is, many projects experience a breakdown in communications. It's been said that 90 percent of a project manager's time is spent communicating. If you think about it, this certainly makes sense. Your project plans all communicate what you're going to do. Your project reports and forms communicate what you are doing or have done. All of your status meetings, ad hoc meetings, and presentations are examples of communicating.

 VIDEO For a more detailed explanation, watch the *Communications Model* video now.

Managing project communications is all about the creation, collection, distribution, storage, and handy retrieval of project information. It's what the project manager does day in and day out. The project manager is at the hub of communications and works with the project team, the project stakeholders, the sponsor, the vendors, and often the public to send and receive communications about the project. It can be exhausting, because somebody always needs to tell you something or you need to tell somebody else something. The key, of course, is to plan how to communicate and then to share that plan and those expectations at the launch of the project.

For adaptive projects, all that we need to do is refer to the Agile Manifesto and its first point: "We value individuals and interactions over processes and tools." In project management, it's always better to sit down and have a face-to-face chat with someone than to shove forms at them. Talking with stakeholders is the real way to understand what stakeholders want from the project, not reading a form for a project request. Speaking with the project team helps the project facilitator understand what's happening in their work. Far too often I see managers attempt to shortcut the communication process by creating forms and web templates to gather information. That's not communication—it's data collection. Communication is what's needed, what's valued, in all projects, but it's even more evident for adaptive projects.

This chapter discusses the three processes that project communication centers on. Of course, you'll also need to know these processes to pass your Project Management Institute (PMI) exam.

Examining the Communications Foundation

Communications are central to project management in predictive, adaptive, and hybrid project approaches, and as part of communications management, they work with and through all of the other knowledge areas. A poor job of communicating ensures that the other knowledge areas will likely suffer. Integration management, which I discussed in Chapter 4, makes an appearance in this chapter since communication is the monitor of the other knowledge areas and serves as the vehicle for reporting information on these other facets of project management.

When communicating in a project, you will encounter many variables that affect how you communicate. How you speak to a colleague or a project team member may be much more casual and relaxed than how you would speak to the chief executive officer (CEO) or a customer. The audience, message, and other factors all affect project communications. In addition, you'll follow different communication approaches depending on the project management approach you're using. Factors that affect communications begin with the following:

- **Internal** Communicating inside the organization, with project stakeholders within the organization
- **External** Communicating with stakeholders outside the organization, such as customers, vendors, media, government agencies, and the public
- **Formal** Communicating through reports, meetings, minutes, and project presentations
- **Informal** Communicating through relaxed conversations, e-mails, ad hoc meetings, and even social media

PART II

- **Hierarchical focus**   Communicating upward, downward, and horizontally through the organization, where upward represents senior management, downward represents the project team and other project contributors, and horizontally represents your peers

- **Official**   Communicating with official documents, such as annual reports or communications to government agencies and the media

- **Unofficial**   Communicating with the project team, customers, and other stakeholders to represent the project through more relaxed and informal communications

- **Written and oral**   Communicating through both verbal and nonverbal methods and understanding that the message is affected by the words chosen and how the words are conveyed

Communications are, obviously, an important factor in every project's success. Projects that are failing can often blame poor communications for part of the failure. If you want to improve the project, you don't necessarily need to communicate more, but communicate more effectively.

The following are some trends that you should be familiar with in communication practices:

- **Involving stakeholders in project reviews**   Through regular reviews of the project, stakeholders or stakeholder representatives can be invited to review the project work, deliverables, and objectives. This ensures continued support of the project and confirmation that the project is meeting the stakeholders' objectives and project goals.

- **Inviting stakeholders to project meetings**   Although project meetings are often viewed as private, this approach reverses that mindset and invites stakeholders or stakeholder representatives to meetings to hear what's happening in the project. In an agile project, the team meets for short standup meetings to which stakeholders are regularly invited, but they don't necessarily speak in the meeting.

- **Leveraging social computing in project management**   Social media, texting, video chats, and no doubt other new technologies will enter the project management landscape that will affect how communication happens. Where appropriate, and allowed, social media and these technologies can contribute to the overall effectiveness of project communications.

- **Creating a communications strategy**   An organization or a project manager can create a strategy for how best to communicate. The project manager can choose from all of the available technologies and craft an approach for concise and appropriate communications that works for the project team and the stakeholders. The project manager must, however, consider the technology, the preferences of the project team, the comfort and availability of using the technology, and the established cultural norms of the project team when it comes to communications.

Communication Factors

The *PMBOK Guide* introduction to Chapter 10 includes some interesting tips and terms that you'll likely see on your PMI examination. The first foundational factors you need to know with regard to project communications are some of the skills a project manager uses to communicate. Consider the following:

- **Sender–receiver models**   These are feedback loops and barriers to communications. Your project status meeting is a great example of a feedback loop, because all of your project team members hear what the other team members say, offer feedback to the speaker, hear the speaker respond, and so on. Basically, a feedback loop is a conversation between one or more speakers centering on one specific topic. A barrier to communication is anything that prevents communication from occurring at optimum levels. For example, if you and I are on the same project team but we're mad at each other, we're not going to communicate effectively—if at all.

- **Choice of media**   The best modality to use when communicating is the one that is relevant to the information that's being communicated. Some communications demand a formal report, whereas others warrant only a phone call, a face-to-face meeting, or a few sentences in a text message or on a sticky note. The appropriate medium is dictated by what needs to be communicated.

- **Writing style**   You don't have to be E.B. White to write effectively (look at me!). You should, however, be conscious of the message you want to communicate and choose the appropriate writing style.

- **Presentation techniques**   Some people cannot stand to be in front of an audience, but as a project manager, they often find themselves having to present project news and statuses. The presentation techniques, such as confidence, body language, and visual aids, promote or distract from the message the presenter is offering to the audience.

- **Meeting management techniques**   Ever attend a WOT meeting? That's a "waste of time" meeting. Meetings should have an agenda and order, and someone needs to keep the meeting minutes for the project. Adaptive meetings, such as the daily scrum, sprint review, and sprint retrospective, follow a cadence and a predefined agenda.

When communicating, the project manager needs to be an active listener; this means the project manager is engaged and involved in the conversation. In some instances, the project manager must be aware of cultural and personal differences that can affect the message meaning and understanding between the parties in the conversation. Project managers may also need to persuade, motivate, coach, and negotiate with the project team, vendors, management, and other stakeholders. The effectiveness of communication is also affected by the five C's of communication:

- **Correct grammar and spelling**   Poor spelling and grammar not only can change the message meaning but also can affect the credibility of the sender.

- **Concise messaging**   When it comes to writing a message, less is often more. Be concise. Get to the point. Don't ramble.

- **Clear purpose of the message**   As well as being concise, messages need to be clear and get to the point. Don't let stakeholders guess what you're trying to communicate.

- **Coherent flow**   Effective messages often follow a logical approach: introduction, body, and summary or closing.

- **Controlling flow of the message**   Controlling the flow of the message, especially in larger communications, can include summaries, bullet points, or graphics.

Understanding the Communications Model

The second foundation that is tucked into the introduction of Chapter 10 of the *PMBOK Guide* is the communications model. As you can see in Figure 10-1, the model demonstrates how communication moves from one person to another. I like to think of each portion of the model as a fax machine to visualize all the components. Take a look.

- **Sender**   This is the person who will send the message. Let's say I want to fax you a contract.

- **Encoder**   This is the device that encodes the message to be sent. My fax machine is the encoder.

- **Medium**   This is the device or technology that transports the message. The telephone line is the medium between our fax machines.

- **Decoder**   This is the device that decodes the message as it is being received. Your fax machine is the decoder.

Figure 10-1
The communications model demonstrates the flow of communication.

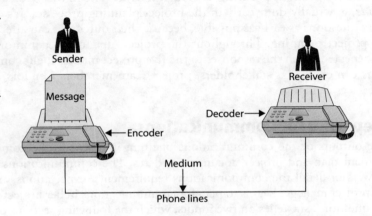

- **Receiver**   This is the person who receives the message.
- **Noise**   This can be anything that interferes with or disrupts the message. It's possible that static on the phone line may distort the fax message between the two fax machines.
- **Acknowledgment**   Some fax machines can print an acknowledgment of receipt. In a conversation, the receiver can offer nonverbal clues of acknowledgment. Acknowledgment means receipt of the message, but not necessarily agreement with the message.
- **Feedback/response**   You receive my fax, jot down a note to me, and then send it back through your fax machine to mine. When you send your message to me, the communications model is reversed.

You'll likely see some of this business on your PMI exam. However, throughout this chapter, this model affects how communication happens between people.

Planning for Communications

As expected, effective communications begin with effective planning. The point of planning for communications is to determine and answer five fundamental project management questions:

- Who needs what information?
- When do they need the information?
- In what modality is the information needed?
- Who will provide the information?
- Who should have access to the information?

Communications planning, although it comes late in this book and in the *PMBOK Guide*, is actually done early in the project planning processes. It's essential to answer these questions as early as possible, because their outcomes can affect the remainder of the project planning. Throughout the project, updates to communications planning are expected. Even the responses to the five project management communication questions can change as stakeholders, project team members, vendors, and other project interfaces change.

Preparing for Communications

The outputs of the communications planning process are the communications management plan and project document updates. The communications management plan answers in detail the communications requirements, expectations, and timings. When the project manager begins to plan for communications in her project and answers essential questions, she relies on five inputs, which the following sections describe.

Referencing the Project Charter

The first input to planning project communications is the project charter. Recall that the project charter names the key stakeholders, their concerns and objectives for the project, and their roles and responsibilities in the project. The project manager and the project sponsor are also named in the project charter, so that establishes one of the first communication channels and sets expectations for reporting from the start of the project.

Relying on the Project Management Plan

You'll need the project management plan because almost all areas in the project management plan affect communications. This is an example of project integration management—what you do in one area of the project affects all other areas of the project. You must also consider that this is an iterative activity, so in the early stages of project planning, the project management plan may be sparse, but as more details enter the project plan, more communications planning can happen.

In the project management plan, you'll reference the resource management plan and the stakeholder engagement plan. The resource management plan is needed to communicate effectively with the people involved with the resources, both human and physical, to schedule, coordinate, and discuss the need of the resources. You'll reference the stakeholder management plan, which is discussed in Chapter 13, to coordinate stakeholder communications and to meet stakeholder requirements for communications.

Relying on Project Documents

The stakeholder register defines whom you'll communicate with. Based on the stakeholder register and the stakeholder analysis you've completed, you'll know which stakeholders are most interested in your project and how much influence they have over your project. For each stakeholder, you should know the following:

- Their interest in the project
- Their influence over the project
- Strategies for gaining stakeholder support
- Strategies for removing obstacles

This information can be sensitive, so it's important for the project manager to guard this information and share it only with the people who need to know this information. In other words, you don't want to document how much of a pain the IT director is and then post it on your blog. Though it's important that you create a definitive strategy for managing stakeholders' fears, threats, concerns, and objections, it's just as important that you guard the strategy from reaching the wrong people in your organization.

 EXAM TIP The coach or scrum master may not be the person who is communicating as much with the project customers of stakeholders. In Scrum projects, the product owner takes on much of the stakeholder communication responsibility. The scrum master communicates with the product owner, the development team, and stakeholders about the rules and approach to the adaptive project.

The project requirements documentation is also needed, because this will help the project manager communicate about the requirements the project is fulfilling. You'll reference the requirements as the project is moving forward, and the requirements will help you communicate project status, address stakeholder concerns, and communicate how key performance indicators are being met, such as time, cost, and scope. The requirements documentation will also help you communicate with the project team and vendors about what the project should be creating and any concerns regarding the requirements, timing, costs, risks, or quality concerns.

Using Enterprise Environmental Factors

Many of the communications management processes are linked to the enterprise environmental factors. The following enterprise environmental factors affect project communications planning:

- Organizational culture and structure
- Standards and regulations the project must comply with
- Logistics and organizational infrastructure
- Human resources the project will rely on and interact with
- Policies and procedures for personnel administration
- Project's work authorization system
- Marketplace conditions
- Stakeholder risk tolerances
- Commercial databases that the project may use for estimating
- Project management information system

Using Organizational Process Assets

The organizational process assets affect how the project manager, the project team, and the stakeholders will communicate within a project. The following are the primary organizational process assets that affect communication:

- Standards and policies unique to the organization
- Organizational guidelines, work instructions, and performance measurement criteria
- Organizational communication requirements for all projects, required and approved technologies, security issues, archiving, and allowed communication media
- Project closure requirements
- Financial controls and procedures
- Issue and defect management procedures for all projects
- Change control procedures

- Risk control procedures
- Work authorization systems
- Process measurement databases
- Project file structure, organization, and retention
- Historical information and lessons learned requirements
- Issue and defect management databases
- Configuration management databases
- Project financial databases detailing labor hours, costs, budget issues, and cost overruns

EXAM COACH Most project managers are good communicators to begin with. You're probably going to do fine on this exam topic if you do fine in your role as project manager, but don't let your guard down. Pay attention to the terms and communications management plan in this chapter. These may be things you don't use in your day-to-day role as a project manager, but you'll find them on your exam. Keep positive communications with yourself. You can pass this exam!

Identifying Communication Requirements

The project manager and the project team work together to analyze and identify who needs what information and when the information is needed. In other words, the project management team needs to know the requirements for successful communications to plan how to meet those requirements.

Stakeholders will need different types of information, depending on their interest in the project and the priority of the project. The project manager will need to complete an analysis of the identified stakeholders to determine what information they actually need, as well as how often the information is needed. This includes examining the number of different communication channels, stakeholder relationships, and interdependencies among stakeholders.

There is no value in expending resources on generating information, reports, and analyses for stakeholders who have no interest in the information. Your accurate assessment of stakeholders' needs for information is required early in the project planning processes. As a rule of thumb, provide information when its presence contributes to success or when a lack of information can contribute to failure.

The project manager and the project team can identify the demand for communications using the following:

- Organization charts
- Project structure within the performing organization
- Stakeholder responsibility relationships

Figure 10-2
Communication channels can be calculated using a simple formula.

Step 1
Know the formula.

$$\frac{N(N-1)}{2}$$

Step 2
Enter the values.

$$\frac{10(9)}{2}$$

Step 3
Get your answer.

$$\frac{90}{2} = 45$$

- Departments and disciplines involved with the project work
- Number of individuals involved in the project and their locales
- Internal and external information needs
- Stakeholder information

On the PMP exam, and in the real world, the project manager will need to identify the number of communication channels within a project. Here's a magic formula to calculate the number of communication channels: $N(N-1)/2$, where N represents the number of identified stakeholders. For example, if a project has ten stakeholders, the formula would read $10(10-1)/2$, for a total of 45 communication channels. Figure 10-2 illustrates the formula.

EXAM TIP   Know this formula: $N(N-1)/2$, where N represents the number of stakeholders. It's easy, and you'll probably encounter it on the PMP exam.

Exploring Communication Technologies

Let's face it, a project manager and a project team can use many different avenues to communicate. Project teams can effectively communicate through hallway meetings or formal project status meetings. Information can be transferred from stakeholder to stakeholder through anything, from written notes to complex online databases and tracking systems.

As part of the communications planning, the project manager should identify all of the required and approved methods of communicating. Some projects may be highly sensitive and contain classified information that not all stakeholders are privy to, while other projects may contain information that's open for anyone to explore. Whatever the case, the project manager should identify what requirements exist, if any, for the communication modalities.

Communication modalities can also include meetings, reports, memos, e-mails, and so on. The project manager should identify the preferred methods of communicating based on the conditions of the message to be communicated. Because of the demands of the project, technology changes may be needed to fulfill the project request. For example, the project may require an internal web site that details project progress. If such a web site does not exist, time and monies will need to be invested into this communications requirement. Also consider that some technologies you're currently using on the project may be replaced by newer, better communication technologies. That's right—the length of the project can influence the project technology you use.

When you consider the technology you'll use to communicate, you have to consider the pros and cons of the technology and how it may affect the project success and abilities of all stakeholders to communicate with the chosen technologies. Consider the following, which may have an effect on the communications plan:

- **Urgency of the information**   *When* the information is communicated can often be as important as *what's* being communicated. For some projects, information should be readily available, while other projects are less demanding. The technology has to support the urgency: if everyone involved in the communication doesn't have the required technology, then communications are ineffective.

- **Reliability**   Is the technology tool reliable and available for everyone involved? Consider international concerns, phone signals, connectivity issues with the geographical locations of the work, and security concerns that may restrict use of communication devices.

- **Ease of use**   Any communication tools that are selected for the project should be easy to use, have training available if necessary, and be widely available for all of the project team to utilize. You can imagine the frustration if the project team is required to use a particular tool that is difficult to use.

- **Project environment**   How a team communicates often depends on its structure. Consider a colocated team versus a virtual team. Each type can be effective, but there will be differing communication demands for each type of team.

- **Protecting the information**   Some of the information that's available in the project will likely be sensitive and confidential. Pay grades, contracts, team member disciplinary actions, and even stakeholder management will be confidential, and not all stakeholders should see this information. You'll need to take steps to protect this information during and after the project. You'll also need to determine the most appropriate method to communicate this sensitive information.

There are loads of ways that communication can happen—e-mail, faxes, text messaging, web technologies—and new ways of communicating are being created all the time. Think of all the new technologies that can help your project team communicate that didn't exist just a few years ago. All these new methods of communicating are part of the basic communications model. When you consider all of the different ways to communicate, you'll find that all communication falls into one of three categories:

- **Interactive communication**   This is the most common and most effective approach to communication, in which two or more people exchange information. Consider status meetings, ad hoc meetings, phone calls, and videoconferences.

- **Push communication** This approach pushes the information from the sender to the receiver without any real acknowledgment that the information was actually received or understood. Consider letters, faxes, voicemail messages, e-mails, and other communication modalities in which the sender packages and sends information to the receivers through some intermediary network.

- **Pull communication** This approach pulls the information from a central repository, such as a database of information. Pull communications are good for large groups of stakeholders who want to access project information at their discretion. Consider a project web site where stakeholders can periodically visit for a quick update on the project status.

 EXAM TIP Adaptive projects often rely on Kanban boards, information radiators, or whiteboards to transparently share information. As a general rule, these communication centers are low-tech, high-touch. Low-tech, high-touch means they're not electronic, computer-driven, but are easy to use with notepads, markers, and sticky notes.

Creating the Communications Management Plan

Based on stakeholder analysis, the project manager and the project team can determine what communications are needed. There's no advantage to supplying stakeholders with information that isn't needed or desired, and the time spent creating and delivering such information is a waste of resources.

A communications management plan can organize and document the process, types, and expectations of communications. It provides the following:

- **Stakeholder communications requirements** These requirements include what is required to communicate the appropriate information as demanded by the stakeholders. The product owner will gather this information in Scrum projects. The facilitator or coach may have this responsibility in other adaptive approaches.

- **Information on what is to be communicated** This plan includes the expected format, content, and detail—think project reports versus quick e-mail updates.

- **Details on how needed information flows through the project to the correct individuals** The communication structure documents where the information will originate, to whom the information will be sent, and in what modality the information is acceptable.

- **Appropriate methods for communicating** This can include e-mails, memos, reports, and even press releases.

- **Schedules of when the various types of communication should occur** Some communications, such as status meetings, should happen on a regular schedule, while other communications may be prompted by conditions within the project.

- **Escalation processes and timeframes** These are required for moving issues upward in the organization when issues can't be solved at lower levels.

- **Instructions on how the communications management plan can be updated**   The plan can be updated as the project progresses.

- **A project glossary**   This describes any special terms, acronyms, or other details that project stakeholders may need to reference. This is not the same thing as the work breakdown structure (WBS) dictionary; rather, it is more general for the project.

- **Identification of the stakeholder responsibilities**   This may identify who will communicate specific project information or who is responsible for managing, controlling, and releasing confidential project information.

- **Schedule, budget, and resource allocation**   This is included for all communication activities.

- **Communication constraints**   These can include technology, regulations, political issues, cultural differences, policies, and other enterprise environmental factors.

The communications management plan may also include information, guidelines, agendas, and cadence for project status meetings, team meetings, daily standup meetings, e-meetings (that's electronic meetings, not meetings about the letter *e*), and even e-mail. Setting expectations for communications and meetings early in the project establishes guidelines for the project team and stakeholders.

Managing Project Communications

After the project's communications management plan has been created, it's time to execute it. Managing project communications is the process of ensuring that the proper stakeholders get the appropriate information when and how they need it. Essentially, it's the implementation of the communications management plan. This plan details how the information is to be created and dispersed and also how the dispersed information is archived.

Examining Communication Skills

Here's a newsflash: communication skills are used to send and receive information. Sounds easy, right? If communication is so easy, then why do so many problems on projects stem from misunderstandings, miscommunications, failures to communicate, and similar communication failings? Communication skills are part of the project manager's arsenal of general management skills—basically, they deliver on the promise that the right stakeholders will get the right information at the right time. General management skills, with regard to project communications, are also about managing stakeholder requirements.

In the communications model that your Project Management Institute (PMI) exam will quiz you on, it's the sender's responsibility to make the message clear, complete, and concise so that the recipient can receive it. The sender must also confirm that the recipient truly understands the information. Have you ever been in a project team meeting where a team member implied that he understood the message that was being sent but later proved that he really didn't understand what was being sent?

EXAM TIP   Face-to-face meetings, such as those in ad hoc meetings, are ideal for project communications.

Communication happens when information is transferred from one party to another. Transmission of a message is just like a radio signal—it's transmitting, but there's no evidence that anyone is actually picking up the signal. Along these same lines, the acknowledgment of a message means that the receiver has indeed received the message, but she may not necessarily agree with the message that has been sent.

Osmotic communication is information that is heard in the common workplace—not eavesdropping, but just overhearing what others are saying. For example, Hanna tells Jim that she'll be out next week for a little surgery, and you overhear that message. Next week, Julie comes looking for Hanna and can't find her. You can help Julie because of osmotic communications—you heard that Hanna will gone for a little surgery. It's like osmosis; you absorb the information because it's being communicated around you, not necessarily toward you.

 VIDEO   For a more detailed explanation, watch the *Agile Communications* video now.

Examining Communication Factors and Technologies

The most common type of communication between a sender and a receiver is verbal communication. When verbal communications are involved, the project manager should remember that half of communication involves listening. This means that the project manager must confirm that the receiver understands the message being sent. The confirmation of the sent message can be evident in the recipient's body language, feedback, and verbal confirmation of the sent message. Five terms are used to describe the process of communicating:

- **Paralingual**   The pitch, tone, and inflections in the sender's voice affect the message being sent.
- **Feedback**   The sender confirms that the receiver understands the message by directly asking for a response, questions for clarification, or other confirmation of the sent message.
- **Active listening**   The receiver confirms that the message is being received through feedback, questions, prompts for clarity, and other signs of confirmation.
- **Effective listening**   The receiver is involved in the listening experience by paying attention to visual cues from the speaker and paralingual characteristics and also by asking relevant questions.
- **Nonverbal**   It's been said that approximately 55 percent of communication is nonverbal. Facial expressions, hand gestures, and body language contribute to the message.

Figure 10-3
The words used in communication are only a small portion of a message.

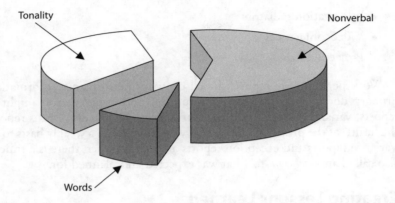

Tonality

Nonverbal

Words

As pictured in Figure 10-3, the words in an oral message actually account for only 7 percent of the message. The tonality of the message accounts for 38 percent of the message. The remaining 55 percent is body language. A classic example involves a person talking to a dog. If the person has a friendly voice and posture, the dog will likely be receptive. However, if the person has a mean voice and guarded posture, the dog may feel threatened and on guard. When project managers talk with stakeholders, they must be aware of their body language and posture—not just the words they are communicating.

The medium in communication can help or hinder the message. For example, when a project manager talks to a stakeholder in person, the stakeholder has the advantage not only of hearing the speaker's message and tone, but also of seeing his body language. Remove body language from a conversation, and the message is interpreted by just the words and tonality. Always be aware of the downsides of various nondirect communication modalities, such as e-mail, reports, memos, and letters.

Distributing Information

Throughout the project, the project manager, project sponsor, project team, and other stakeholders are going to need to supply information to one another. The methods for distributing information can vary, but the best modality is the one that's most appropriate to the information being conveyed. In other words, an e-mail may not be the correct format in which to share variance information regarding project costs.

Information can be distributed through some of the following methods, given project demands and available technology:

- Project meetings
- Hard-copy documentation
- Databases
- Faxes
- E-mail
- Telephone calls

- Information radiators
- Videoconferences
- Project web site

Work performance reports, based on work performance information, are often the primary documents used to report project performance. You might call these status reports, variance reports, or exception reports. Technically, status reports communicate the health of the project and are usually distributed on a weekly basis to key stakeholders. Variance reports and exception reports are created when there is a time or cost variance, also called an *exception*, to what was expected and planned for.

Creating Lessons Learned

Do you ever wish you could travel back in time? With lessons learned, you almost can. The whole point of lessons learned is to improve future projects by sharing what was learned during the current project.

A lessons learned session is completed by the project manager, the project team, and key stakeholders to identify lessons they've learned in the technical, managerial, and project processes. Think of it: you're helping other project managers in the future by documenting what works and what doesn't in your project. The sprint retrospective is an active lessons learned session that allows the development team to implement lessons learned in the next sprint of the project.

Lessons learned should happen throughout the project, not just at the project's conclusion. As a project moves through each phase, project managers can use a lessons learned session as a good team-building exercise. This means documenting and learning from what worked and what didn't within the project.

Examining the Results of Communications Management

Communications management results in the following:

- **Project communications** All project communications are also part of the organizational process assets. This includes e-mails, memos, letters, and faxes. In some instances, the project team can also contribute by keeping their records in a project notebook.

- **Project management plan updates** You might have updates for the project's communications management plan and the stakeholder engagement plan. These updates will follow your organization's change control approach and the project's integrated change control process.

- **Project document updates** You may need to update the issue log to document any issues that have been identified or resolved by managing communications. The lessons learned register is also updated. Recall that when lessons learned sessions are completed, they're available to be used and applied. The project schedule, the risk register, and the stakeholder register may also be updated as a result of managing communications.

- **Organizational process assets** Project records and correspondence with the stakeholders will be part of organizational process assets. As the project rolls along, there undoubtedly will be notifications to the stakeholders about resolved issues, approved changes, and the overall health of the project. This information should be kept for future reference.

Monitoring Communications

Throughout the project, customers and other stakeholders are going to need updates on the project performance, work status, and project information. The work performance information—the status of what's been completed and what's left to do—is always at the heart of performance reporting. Stakeholders want to be kept abreast of how the project is performing, but also what issues, risks, and conditions in the project have evolved.

Monitoring communications is the process of following the communications management plan, distributing information, and sharing how the project is performing. Performance reporting is the process of collecting, organizing, and disseminating information on how project resources are being used to complete the project objectives. In other words, the people footing the bill and who are affected by the outcome of the project need some confirmation that things are going the way the project manager has promised. Adaptive projects aim to be open and transparent, so communications monitoring ensures that the project facilitator is not hoarding information, updating centralized information radiators, and communicating with the team and stakeholder as needed.

Based on changing conditions within the project, the project manager and team may need to go back to communications planning, update the communications management plan, and then manage communications accordingly. At the heart of monitoring communications is performance reporting. Performance reporting covers more than just cost and schedule, although these are the most common concerns. Another huge issue is the influence of risks on the project's success. The project manager and the project team must continue to monitor and evaluate risks, including pending risks and their impact on the project's success.

Another major concern, in predictive projects, is with performance reporting and the level of quality. Recall that quality is about meeting project scope requirements and ensuring that the deliverables are fit for us. Testing, inspection, and other actions in quality control are measuring how well the project has performed against the quality expectations. No one will praise the project manager and the project team for completing the project on time and on budget if the quality of the work is unacceptable. In fact, the project could be declared a failure and canceled as a result of poor quality, or the project team may be forced to redo the work, business could be lost, or individuals could even be harmed as a result of the poor quality of the project work.

Examining the Tools for Monitoring Communications

Stakeholders expect you to keep them abreast of the project's performance, issues, conditions, changes, risk, and other concerns about the project. You'll utilize the following tools to monitor communications, but understand that you, the project manager, being involved and available is the strongest asset for communications:

- **Expert judgment**   One of the best tools and techniques you can use is to rely on the expertise of others. Experts, such as members of the project team, stakeholders, and consultants, can help you identify shortcomings or problems in your communications. These experts can help you ensure that your message is timely, appropriate, and on target with the correct stakeholders. The team, in adaptive projects, are considered local domain experts and will be self-led and self-organizing, so they'll be making decisions about how best to get the work done during the project iteration.

- **Project management information system**   You'll use some tool, probably part of your project management information system, to collect, assemble, and generate information about the project. You could use a simple spreadsheet, but the collection of project information is going to be more cumbersome, while a large, complex project management information system (PMIS) requires the knowledge and skill of both the project manager and the project team to use it effectively.

- **Data representation**   You can create a chart, matrix, or other data representation tool to track the current level of stakeholder engagement and the desired level of stakeholder engagement. This tool is called a *stakeholder engagement assessment matrix*. It's basically a table of how engaged your stakeholders currently are and where you'd like their engagement to be in the future. Communications helps to achieve your stakeholder engagement goals. I'll discuss stakeholder engagement in more detail in Chapter 13.

- **Interpersonal and team skills**   To communicate effectively, you need some interpersonal and team skills. You have to be able to talk with people, observe team members, create dialogue, and respond to questions and requests. Basically, you need to be a good communicator, to be able to connect with people, and to be approachable.

- **Meetings**   Meetings enable the project manager, project team, stakeholders, and experts to have conversations about the project. Meetings can help you and the stakeholders determine whether the current communications approach is working or whether refinements regarding how you and the stakeholders communicate are necessary.

Reviewing Project Performance

The project manager will host performance review meetings to ascertain the progress and level of success the project team is having with the project work. Performance review meetings focus on the work that has been completed and how the work results are living up to the time and cost estimates. In addition, the project manager and the project team will evaluate the project scope to protect it from change and creep. The project manager and the project team will also examine quality and its effect on the project as a whole.

Finally, the project manager must lead a discussion on pending or past risks and then determine any new risks, as well as the overall risk likelihood and its potential impact on the project's success.

Analyzing Project Variances

Performance review meetings are not the only tools the project manager uses to assess project performance. Prior to the performance reviews, or spurred by a performance review, the project manager needs to examine the work performance information on time, scope, quality, and cost variances within the project. The project manager will examine the estimates supplied for the time and cost of activities and compare them with the time and cost actually experienced.

The goals of analyzing project variances include the following:

- Prevent future variances
- Determine the root cause of variances
- Determine whether the variances are an anomaly or if the estimates were flawed
- Determine whether the variances are within a predetermined acceptable range, such as −10 percent or +5 percent
- Determine whether the variances can be expected on future project work

In addition to examining the time and cost variances, which are the most common, the project manager must examine any scope, resource, and quality variances. A change in the scope can skew time and cost predictions. A variance in resources, such as the expected performance by a given resource, can alter the project schedule and even the predicted costs of a project. Quality variances may result in rework, lost time, lost monies, and even the rejection of the project product.

 EXAM TIP Performance reporting is often based on the results of earned value management (EVM). Adaptive projects can use EVM too, though it's a bit more rare than predictive projects. See Chapter 7 for detailed information on how to calculate EVM.

Examining the Results of Monitoring Communications

The goals of monitoring communications are to share information regarding the project's performance with the appropriate stakeholders and to improve upon the established communication process. Of course, performance reporting is not something done only at the end of the project or after a project phase; it is done according to a regular schedule, as detailed in the communications plan or as project conditions warrant.

There are five outputs of monitoring communications:

- **Work performance information**   Recall that work performance information is the analyzed work performance data and is usable information for project decisions. Communications management will create work performance information regarding how well the project's communications management plan is working.

- **Change requests**   Performance results may prompt change requests to some areas of the project. The change requests should flow into the change control system (CCS) for consideration and then be approved or denied.

- **Project management plan updates**   You may have to edit the project management plan based on the outcome of this process. Stakeholder communication preferences may change, interests on different project areas can change, and reactions to how the information is sent may also prompt updates to the project management plan. The communications management plan and the stakeholder engagement plan are the two likely components to be updated.

- **Project document updates**   Will the project end on schedule? Will the project be on budget? How much longer will it take to complete the project? How much more money will this project need to finish? Earned value management can answer many of these questions for the project management team. You'll update the appropriate project documents based on the conditions within the project. The issue log, lessons learned register, and stakeholder register are the documents likely to be updated.

Chapter Summary

Communication is arguably a project manager's most important skill. Project managers have to communicate with management, customers, project team members, and other stakeholders involved with the project. Communication is the project manager's foundation. Without effective communication, how will work get completed, progress reported, and information dispersed?

Communications planning centers on asking, "Who needs what information and when do they need it?" Consider all of the different channels for communication on any project. There are many different possibilities for information to be lost, messages to be skewed, and progress to be hindered. The formula for calculating the communication channels is $N(N - 1)/2$, where N represents the number of stakeholders. As a general rule, larger projects require more detail—and detail means more planning for communications.

Adaptive projects embrace communication by value interactions with individuals rather than processes and tools. This means face-to-face communication whenever possible, being honest, trusting people, and not hoarding information. In fact, information is transparently shared with stakeholders through information radiators that may include burndown charts, Kanban boards, and other project details. Adaptive projects are to be open, transparent, and collaborative.

The communications management plan organizes and documents the communication processes, acceptable modalities for types of communication, and the stakeholder expectations for communication. The plan should detail how information is gathered, organized, accessed, and dispersed. The plan should also provide a schedule of expected communication based on a calendar schedule, such as project status meetings. Some communications are prompted by conditions within the project, such as cost variances, schedule variances, or other performance-related issues.

Questions

1. You are the project manager of the BlueSky Network Upgrade Project. You have 15 project team members, and you're speaking with them about the importance of communication. You show them the communications model and give examples of each of the components of the model. One of the project team members asks for an example of noise. Of the following, which one is an example of noise?

   A. Fax machine

   B. Ad hoc conversations

   C. Contractual agreements

   D. Distance

2. You are the project manager for the JHG Project. Management has requested that you create a document detailing what information will be expected from stakeholders and to whom that information will be disseminated. Management is asking for which one of the following?

   A. The roles and responsibilities matrix

   B. The scope management plan

   C. The communications management plan

   D. The communications worksheet

3. Which of the following will help you, the project manager in an adaptive project, complete the needed communications management plan by identifying the stakeholders' communication needs?

   A. Identification of all communication channels

   B. Formal documentation of all communication channels

   C. Formal documentation of all stakeholders

   D. Lessons learned from previous similar projects

4. You are the project manager for the JGI Project. You have 32 stakeholders on this project. How many communication channels do you have?

   A. Depends on the number of project team members

   B. 496

   C. 32

   D. 1

5. You are the project manager for the KLN Project. You had 19 stakeholders on this project and have added three team members to the project. How many more communication channels do you have now compared with before?

A. 171

B. 231

C. 60

D. 1

6. Mary is the scrum master for a project in her organization. She has created an information radiator with burndown charts, a Kanban board, and information on error tracking and testing. Paul, her manager, wants to know why Mary isn't using Microsoft Project or other software to track and share her information. What's the best response Mary should offer Paul?

A. Agile projects should use low-tech, high-touch tools.

B. Agile projects change too quickly for project management software to be effective.

C. Agile projects don't allow technology tools to share information.

D. She doesn't know how to use Microsoft Project, so this way is faster for her.

7. Beth is a project manager for her organization, and she is working with the stakeholders to develop a communications management plan. She wants to acknowledge the assumptions and constraints in the project. Which one of the following is an example of a project communication constraint?

A. Ad hoc conversations

B. Demands for formal reports

C. Stakeholder management

D. Team members in different geographical locales

8. Project managers can present project information in many different ways. Which one of the following is not a method a project manager can use to present project performance?

A. Histograms

B. S-curves

C. Bar charts

D. Responsible, accountable, consulted, informed (RACI) charts

9. For your PMI examination, you'll need to know many terms that deal with project communications. Of the following, which term describes the pitch and tone of an individual's voice?

A. Paralingual

B. Feedback

C. Effective listening

D. Active listening

10. You are the project manager of the KMH Project. This project is slated to last eight years. You have just calculated EVM and have a cost variance (CV) of −$3,500, which is outside of the acceptable thresholds for your project. What type of report is needed for management?

    A. Progress report

    B. Forecast report

    C. Exception report

    D. Trends report

11. You are presenting your project performance to your key stakeholders. Several of the stakeholders are receiving phone calls during your presentation, and this is distracting people from your message. This is an example of what?

    A. Noise

    B. Negative feedback

    C. Outside communications

    D. Message distracter

12. You are the project manager for the OOK Project. You will be hosting the daily scrum meetings for the project. Of the following, which one is not a valid rule for project the daily scrum?

    A. Schedule recurring meetings as soon as possible.

    B. Allow project meetings to last as long as needed.

    C. Distribute meeting agendas prior to the meeting start.

    D. Allow the project team to contribute information in the meeting .

13. In a Scrum project, what role is most likely to communicate directly with the project customers?

    A. Product owner

    B. Scrum master

    C. Project sponsor

    D. Development team

14. Gary is the project manager of the HBA Update Project, and his company has hired you as a project management consultant. Gary is confused about the timing of some of the project management processes. In particular, Gary doesn't understand the concept, purpose, and timing of the lessons learned documentation. He asks for your help. When does lessons learned identification take place?

    A. At the end of the project

    B. At the end of each project phase

    C. Throughout the project life cycle

    D. Whenever a lesson has been learned

15. Gary is the project manager of the HBA Update Project, and his company has hired you as a project management consultant. Gary is confused about the timing of some of the project management processes. He now has a good understanding of the lessons learned purpose, but he's still confused about why you've recommended that the project team participate in the lessons learned documentation, too. Why should a project team complete lessons learned documentation?

   A. To ensure project closure

   B. To show management what they've accomplished on the project

   C. To show the project stakeholders what they've accomplished on the project

   D. To help future project teams complete their projects more accurately

16. You are the project manager for the PMU Project. Your project has 13 members. You have been informed that next week your project will receive the 7 additional members you requested. How many channels of communication will you have next week?

   A. 1

   B. 78

   C. 190

   D. 201

17. Performance reporting should generally provide information on all of the following except for which one?

   A. Scope

   B. Schedule

   C. Labor issues

   D. Quality

18. You are the project manager of a project that will last 18 months and includes three different countries. As part of your communications management plan you've scheduled face-to-face meetings with the project team, and you're utilizing web conferencing software for the virtual team. Based on this information, the process of sending information from the project manager to the project team is called what?

   A. Functioning

   B. Matrixing

   C. Blended communications

   D. Transmitting

19. George is the product owner of the 7YH Project. In this project, George considers the relationship between himself and the customer to be of utmost importance. Which one of the following is a valid reason for George's belief in the importance of this relationship?

    A. The customer will complete George's performance evaluation. A poor communications model between George and the customer will affect his project bonus.

    B. The customer is not familiar with project management. George must educate the customer about the process.

    C. The customer is always right.

    D. The communications between the customer and George can convey the project objectives more clearly than can the language in the project contract.

20. You are the project manager for your company, and you're working with the project team to develop the project's communications management plan. The project team is confused about some of the communications terms. Basically, they want to know how communication actually happens and how you can prove the communication was effective. Which one of the following means that communication has occurred?

    A. The transfer of knowledge

    B. The outputting of knowledge

    C. The presence of knowledge

    D. The transmission of knowledge

Answers

1. **D.** Noise is anything that interferes with the transmission and understanding of the message. Distance is an example of noise. A, a fax machine, is an example of a decoder. B is incorrect because ad hoc conversations are informal conversations. C, contractual agreements, are a type of formal communication.

2. **C.** Management is requesting a communications management plan, which details the requirements and expectations for communicating information among the project stakeholders. A is incorrect because a roles and responsibilities matrix depicts who does what and who makes which decisions. B, the scope management plan, is also incorrect because this plan explains how changes to the scope may be allowed, depending on the circumstances. D is not a valid choice for the question.

3. **D.** Lessons learned and historical information from a previous project are ideal inputs to communications planning even for adaptive projects. While it's true adaptive projects don't plan heavily, they'll still need to identify the stakeholders and plan, to some extent for communications. A, B, and C are incorrect because these choices do not fully answer the question. Lessons learned from previous, similar projects are the best tool to identify stakeholders' requirements for communication.

4. **B.** Using the formula $N(N - 1)/2$, where N represents the number of stakeholders, gives us 496 communication channels. A, C, and D are incorrect. These values do not reflect the number of communication channels on the project.

5. **C.** This is a tough question, but typical of the PMP exam. The question asks how many more communication channels exist. You'll have to calculate the new value, which is 231, and then subtract the original value, which is 171, for a total of 60 new channels. A is incorrect because 171 is the original number of communication channels. B is incorrect because this value reflects the new number of communication channels. D is not a valid choice.

6. **A.** Agile projects use low-tech, high-touch tools to simply communication so that everyone can communicate easier and without the overhead technical tools may require. B is incorrect as it's possible to use a project management software in an agile project even if the project changes quickly. C is incorrect because agile projects do allow technology tools, but it's not the best practice. D is incorrect; Mary may not know how to use Microsoft Project, but that's not the best reason for using this approach in the project.

7. **D.** Team members who are not located physically close together can be a communications constraint, since it can be tougher to communicate when distance between team members exists. A, B, and C are all incorrect because these are not project communications constraints.

8. **D.** RACI charts do not show project performance, but instead show accountability of the resources involved in the project. A, B, and C are incorrect because these choices do present project performance.

9. **A.** Paralingual describes nonverbal elements such as the pitch and tone of a voice. B, feedback, is a request to confirm the information sent in the conversation. C, effective listening, is the ability to understand the message through what is said, through facial expressions, gestures, tone, pitch, and so on. D, active listening, is the process of confirming what is understood and asking for clarification when needed.

10. **C.** An exception report is typically completed when variances exceed a given limit. A is incorrect. Progress reports describe the progress of the project or phase. B is incorrect because this is not a valid answer. D, a trends report, is an analysis of project trends over time.

11. **A.** Noise is the correct answer, because their phone calls are distracting from your message. B, C, and D are incorrect because they do not answer the question. Negative feedback can mean the recipient didn't respond well to the message you've sent. Outside communications isn't a valid term. And a message distracter can be the pitch, inflection, and body language that sends a message that conflicts with what you're saying to your audience.

12. **B.** Project meetings should have a set time limit. A, C, and D are incorrect answers because these are good attributes of the daily scrum. Note that the agenda for the daily scrum is predetermined with information on what the team has done since the last meeting, what will the team do today, and what impediments may stand in the way of the project team members.

13. A. The product owner is seen as the liaison between the development team and the project customers. The product owner represents the businesspeople who are driving the requirements of the project, so the product owner will communicate directly with the project customers. B, C, and D are incorrect.

14. C. Lessons learned takes place throughout the project life cycle, not just at the end of the project or its phases. A, B, and D are incorrect choices.

15. D. Lessons learned documentation helps future project teams complete their projects with more efficiency and effectiveness. A, B, and C are incorrect because each statement does not reflect the intent of lessons learned documentation: to help future project teams.

16. C. The project currently has 13 team members, and next week, 7 additional team members will come aboard, thus making a total of 20 team members. Using the formula $N(N - 1)/2$, where N is the number of identified stakeholders, the communication channels equal 190. A, B, and D are all incorrect.

17. C. Labor issues are not part of performance reporting. A, B, and D are all part of performance reporting.

18. D. When information is sent, it is considered to be transmitted regardless of the technology involved. A, B, and C are all incorrect.

19. D. George and the customer's relationship can allow clearer communication on the project objectives than what may be expressed in the project contract. The contract should take precedence on any issues, but direct contact is often the best way to achieve clear and concise communication. Agile projects value collaboration over contracts. A is an incorrect choice because the focus is on personal gain rather than the good of the project. B is incorrect because the customer does not necessarily need to be educated about the project management process. C is incorrect because the customer is not always right—the contract will take precedence in any disagreements.

20. A. The transfer of knowledge is evidence that communication has occurred. B and C do not necessarily mean the knowledge has originated from the source and been transferred to the recipient. D is also incorrect because messages are transmitted, but knowledge is transferred.

Managing Project Risks

In this chapter, you will

- Plan for risk management
- Identify project risks
- Complete qualitative risk analysis
- Complete quantitative risk analysis
- Plan the risk responses
- Implement risk responses
- Monitor project risks

A *project risk* is an uncertain event or condition that can have a positive or negative impact on the project. That's correct—it's possible for a risk to have a positive impact. Risks that have a positive impact are also known as *opportunities*. Technically, risk isn't a bad thing. It's the impact that can be painful, costly, or delay the project work. Most project managers look at risk the same way they'd look at leftover shrimp cocktail. Yuck. Some risks, though, are good for the project, and the project manager wants to accept them; other risks aren't so welcome.

Let's look at this from another point of view. Imagine a golfer teeing up. To the right of the tee box is a water hazard, and just beyond the water is the green. The golfer can either avoid the water and take longer to get to the green or try to shoot over the water and get to the green in fewer strokes. Driving up the fairway is the safer play, but cutting over the water will improve the golfer's score. The risk with the water hazard is that if he can't make the shot, then he's down a penalty stroke.

 VIDEO For a more detailed explanation, watch the *Risk Contingency Reserve* video now.

Risk, as in the golfing scenario, must be in proportion to the reward the risk-taker can realize as a result of taking the chance. The willingness to accept the risk is called the *utility function*. Some call the utility function your *risk tolerance*—the amount of risk you'll take on in relation to the impact the risk event may bring. Your risk appetite (think yummy!) is how much risk you'll accept in relation to the reward the risk may bring. An experienced golfer may have a high-risk appetite, so he's willing to accept the water hazard. A golf hack like me would likely have a low risk tolerance and drive up the fairway away from the water. Someone with a high tolerance for risk is called a *risk-seeker*, while someone with a low tolerance for risk is called *risk-averse*.

Risk works this way in project management, too. With some projects, you and your organization are willing to accept risks to realize rewards such as cost savings, time savings, or on-the-job training opportunities. On other projects—typically, those projects with high-impact and high-profile characteristics—you're not so willing to accept the risks. In this chapter, we'll look at the six processes that dictate project risk management, and you'll have plenty of risk management questions on your Project Management Institute (PMI) exam.

Projects that are predictive have definable work and the risk is usually well-known, experienced in previous projects, or can be manageable through up-front planning. For example, construction projects have some readily identifiable risks: safety, permitting, vendor delivery, and cash flow. These risks are well-known, and likely plentiful, in the definable work of construction. Agile projects, however, have high uncertainty in their work. Knowledge work doesn't take place in a defined space and with clear objectives, so this introduces risk to the success of the project. High-uncertainty projects change often and are complicated, but measures are taken to deliver value early, to minimize adverse risks, and to take on defects before problems escape to production.

Risks that exist within your project are individual risk events that can affect, for better or worse, the project objectives. The overall project risk, however, is the cloud of risk surrounding even doing the project. The overall project risk describes the risk of project success or failure, the risk of not meeting the project objectives, and the risk of other factors that expose the organization to positive or negative outcomes. For the most part, I'll be addressing individual risk events in this chapter, but know that risks can exist in the organization, in a program, in a portfolio, and in a project. Integrated risk management is an organizational approach to managing the overall risk distribution and risk exposure through all of the organization's activities.

Let me be clear: the risks you can readily identify are the *known risks*. The risks that are more ambiguous, such as weather or vendor delays, are called *known unknowns*. You can anticipate and plan for the known unknowns, but the planning is about the probability of the event and the impact the risk might have on the project objectives. Project risk describes the likelihood of the overall project being successful for the organization. Individual project risks are the risks within the project. When a risk event actually happens, it can shift from being just a risk to being an issue in the project.

The project management processes described here are presented in the most logical order. They are iterative processes that occur throughout the project life cycle. Pay special attention to monitoring risks, because new risks can creep into the project or be discovered as the project moves toward closure.

Planning for Risk Management

Risk management planning is not the identification of risks or even the response to known risks within a project. Risk management planning refers to how the project management team will complete the risk management activities within the project.

These activities really set up the project to manage the six other risk management activities effectively. Risk management planning creates the risk management plan.

At the onset of the project is an acknowledgment of the risks that exist in the project, based on the type of work the project is undertaking. These uncertain risk events that you're quick to identify (and even the risks that aren't so quickly identified) are event-based risks. Event-based risks happen when, for example, equipment is late from the vendor or materials are installed incorrectly. Nonevent risks are risks within the project that aren't necessarily tied to an event. For example, there may be reasonable doubt surrounding the project cost estimate because this type of work has never been attempted by the organization before. Another nonevent risk could be issues that result from new laws or regulations that are introduced during the project's life cycle. You should be familiar with two types of nonevent risks:

- **Variability risks** Expectations in the project will vary. For example, production of the project team could go up or down, quality errors could fluctuate from high to low, or weather can be unusual and affect the project. Variability risks are addressed through a special analysis called *Monte Carlo analysis*. This approach examines the possible swings of high and low risks and helps the project manager ask "what-if" questions to identify and create responses for the risks.

- **Ambiguity risks** The future is uncertain, so events in the future are ambiguous. It's tough to predict what will happen in the marketplace, what new laws or regulations may be enacted, or what complexity issues an IT project may encounter. Ambiguity risks are managed by identifying the knowledge gap, hiring experts to help with the risks, and benchmarking against best practices in the discipline. Ambiguity risks can also be managed through incremental development life cycles, prototyping the project or portions of the project, and creating simulations to create expected outcomes.

Some risks are nearly impossible to plan for, because you won't know about the risk event until it actually happens. These risk events, sometimes called *unknowable-unknowns*, can wreck a project. Imagine a construction project that unearths a bunch of dinosaur bones. The discovery is a great find for archeologists, but it stops the construction project, delays progress, and can have huge financial impact for the company paying for the project. To combat these unknowable-unknowns, the project needs resilience. Project *resilience* means the organization and the project have several characteristics:

- Budget and schedule contingency
- Flexibility in the project management approach
- Defined change management processes
- Empowered project team
- Frequent risk review for warning signs of emergent risk events
- Communication with stakeholders for adjusting the project scope or project strategy to address emergent risk events

By deciding the approach to each of the risk management activities before moving into them, the project management team can more effectively identify risks, complete risk analysis, and then plan risk responses. In addition, planning for risk management also enables the project management team to create a strategy for the ongoing identification and monitoring of existing risks within the project.

Of course, adaptive projects are uncertain by design: the scope of the work can change at any time. This uncertainty is risk. When projects can change at any time, there is a risk that the change may cause previous work to be discarded, adjusted, or reworked to accommodate the new change in the project. Agile attempts to combat this risk in its approach, through small iterations of project work that are demonstrated frequently to the customer. This approach helps the team get an ongoing understanding of what the customer values in the project. If a team waits for long periods to show progress, the risk of large changes by the customer are more probable and more difficult to incorporate than smaller changes introduced during these frequent reviews. The more uncertain the project requirements are coupled with technical uncertainty of the project, the more complex and riskier the project becomes.

VIDEO For a more detailed explanation, watch the *Agile Risk Management* video now.

Preparing for Risk Management Planning

There are five inputs to risk management planning. Some are more important than others. It's essential for the project management team to understand the priority of the project, which shouldn't be too tough to do. As with all project management processes, you have decisions to make about tailoring. The size of the project, its complexity, and its importance or priority in the organization will directly affect your risk management planning and other risk management processes. In an adaptive environment, there's more uncertainty accepted as part of the adaptive framework, as opposed to a predictive life cycle, where the project is more risk averse.

You'll need the following to prepare for risk management:

- **Project charter** The project charter defines the high-level objectives for the project and also identifies the initial known risks.

- **Project management plan** Risk management planning considers all of the project's subsidiary plans, baselines, project documentation, and supporting detail. The project manager will pay special attention to the project scope, project communications, cost, and schedule because these knowledge areas can be most widely affected by risk.

- **Project documents** The stakeholder register is referenced for stakeholder concerns, threats, perceived threats, contact information, and roles involved in the project.

- **Enterprise environmental factors** An organization's attitude toward risk may vary (as I mentioned) based on the type, size, and profile of the project.

- **Organizational process assets**   An organization may have a predefined approach to risk management. If that's the case, the project management team uses the organization's approach and follows its established procedures. For example, an organization could define risk tolerance levels, risk categories, templates, roles and responsibilities, and more. A project team may also use other similar projects to guide the current risk management planning activities.

Completing Risk Management Planning

Planning for risk happens in—surprise, surprise!—planning meetings, where the project team develops the risk management plan and analyzes the inputs previously mentioned to make the best decisions for the current project. It's possible that the risk management plan is developed, or at least started to be developed, in the project's kickoff meeting. More likely, you'll host risk planning meetings to dig into the risk management. Though the project team comprises the primary participants at the risk management planning meeting, attendees may include the project manager, stakeholders, and other subject matter experts within an organization who influence the risk management processes.

The point of the risk management planning meetings is to plan an approach for how risks will be managed in the project. This is not the same as risk identification; in risk management planning, the focus is on how to manage, monitor, and track risks. You'll also likely do some stakeholder analysis to get a sense of the stakeholder concerns, threats, and perceived threats for the project objectives. You'll want to define the stakeholder appetite for risk and how that'll affect the depth of risk management.

EXAM TIP   Risk management planning in adaptive projects isn't as formal as in predictive projects. During the sprint planning sessions, for example, the team examines the work and the complexity of the work and then decides what needs to happen next in the project and who'll take on what work. This is an example of the development team being local domain experts, self-organizing, and self-led. The project facilitator needs to trust the development team to make good decisions.

The purpose of these risk management planning meetings is to create the risk management plan and to define the cost and schedule for risk management activities. Let's face facts: it'll take time and monies for most projects to identify, test, and challenge the risks that may exist within the project. The decisions made in these initial meetings enable monies and time to be incorporated within the project. Risk responsibilities are also assigned in these meetings, as are the risk terminologies the project will use. Risk management planning also defines and tailors the following for the project:

- Risk templates the project should use
- Definitions and terms for risk levels
- Probability according to risk type
- Impact of the risks
- Guidelines for the probability and impact matrix to be used during risk analysis

Creating the Risk Management Plan

The whole point of risk management meetings and analysis is to create the risk management plan. This plan does not detail the planned responses to individual risks within the project—this is the purpose of the risk response plan. The risk management plan is responsible for the overall risk management strategy and for determining the following:

- The project's risk management methodology
- Roles and responsibilities for risk management
- Funding for risk management activities and how the contingency reserve and management reserve will be created
- Timing of risk management processes within the project
- Risk categories within the project
- Ongoing risk management activities that will happen throughout the project's life cycle

Defining the Risk Management Methodology

The methodology is concerned with how the risk management processes will take place. It asks the following:

- What life cycle approach is being utilized?
- What tools are available to use for risk management?
- What approaches are acceptable within the performing organization?
- What data sources can be accessed and used for risk management?
- What approach is best for the project type and the phase of the project?
- Which approach is most appropriate given the conditions of the project?
- How much flexibility is available for the project given the conditions, time frame, and project budget?

Identifying Risk Roles and Responsibilities

The roles and responsibilities identify the groups and individuals who will participate in the leadership and support of each of the risk management activities within the project plan. In some instances, risk management teams outside of the project team may have a more realistic, unbiased approach to risk identification, impact, and overall risk management needs than the actual project team does.

Creating a Risk Management Budget

Based on the size, impact, and priority of the project, you may need to establish a budget for the project's risk management activities. This section of the risk management plan defines a cost estimate for the resources needed to complete risk management. These costs are rolled into the project's cost baseline. A project with high priority and no budget allotment for risk management activities may face uncertain times ahead.

PART II

Identifying the Risk Management Schedule

The risk management process needs a schedule to determine how often, and when, risk management activities should happen throughout the project. If risk management happens too late in the project, the project could be delayed because of the time needed to identify, assess, and respond to the risks. A realistic schedule should be developed early in the project to accommodate risks, risk analysis, and risk reaction.

Defining a Project's Risk Categories

Based on the nature of the work, there should be identified categories of risks within the project. Figure 11-1 depicts one approach to identifying risk categories by using a risk breakdown structure (RBS). Throughout the project, the risk categories should be revisited to update and reflect the current status of the project. If a similar risk management plan is available from a previous project, the project team may elect to use this plan as a template and tailor the risk categories accordingly. There are four general categories of risks:

- **Technical, quality, or performance risks**   Technical risks are associated with new, unproven, or complex technologies being used on the project. Changes to the technology during the project implementation can also be a risk. Quality risks are the levels set for expectations of impractical quality and performance. Changes to industry standards during the project can also be lumped into this category of risks. Knowledge work projects typically have technical, quality, or performance risks.

- **Project management risks**   These risks deal with faults in the management of the project: the unsuccessful allocation of time, resources, and scheduling; unacceptable work results (low-quality work); and poor project management as a whole. For organizations new to agile, the roles and responsibilities of the agile approach may introduce risks as people may feel uncertain about who does what.

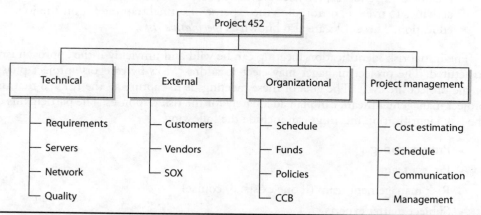

Figure 11-1   An RBS can organize risks by categories.

- **Organizational risks**   The performing organization can contribute to the project's risks through unreasonable cost, time, and scope expectations; poor project prioritization; inadequate funding or the disruption of funding; and competition with other projects for internal resources.

- **External risks**   These risks are outside of the project, but directly affect it—for example, legal issues, labor issues, a shift in project priorities, or weather. "Force majeure" risks can be scary and usually call for disaster recovery rather than project management. These are risks caused by earthquakes, tornadoes, floods, civil unrest, and other disasters.

Depending on the discipline that you work in, you may identify and categorize risk beyond these generic categories I've listed here. The idea is to create risk themes so you can group associated risks by topic. This enables you to identify trends in the risks and look for root causes to attack many risks at once. An RBS is an ideal way to visualize where project risks are lurking in each phase or within the project as a whole.

Identifying the Project Risks

Risk identification is the systematic process of combing through the project, the project plan, the work breakdown structure (WBS), and all supporting documentation to identify as many of the risks that may affect the project as possible. Remember, a risk is an uncertain event or condition that may affect the project outcome. Risks can be positive or negative. In the big picture of risk identification, there are two categories of risks:

- **Pure risks**   These risks have only a negative outcome. Examples include loss of life or limb, fire, theft, natural disasters, and the like. These risks are often referred to as *insurable risks*.

- **Business risks**   These risks may have negative or positive outcomes. Examples include using a less experienced worker to complete a task, allowing phases or activities to overlap, or forgoing the expense of formal training for on-the-job education. These risks are also known as *speculative risks*.

The initial risk identification meeting can be wild and unwieldy if the approach isn't structured. The project manager may elect to address risks by category, project phase, or the project life cycle. The goal of these meetings is to capture all the risks so that the project management team can plan adequately for the risk responses. The participants of the risk identification meetings can include the following:

- Project manager
- Project team
- Risk management team (if one exists, of course)
- Subject matter experts
- Customers

- End users
- Other project managers
- Stakeholders
- Risk management experts

Risk identification is not a one-time event. The project manager should encourage the project team and these participants to be continually on the lookout for risk events as the project moves toward closure. The risk management plan also includes timings for iterations of risk identification and management. Risk identification is an iterative process because new risks can creep into the project or existing risks may be identified later as more detail becomes available. You'll need several inputs to complete risk identification:

- **Requirements management plan**   The requirements management plan will help you identify the project requirements that may be risk-laden or especially sensitive to risk events.

- **Schedule management plan**   How the project is structured can actually create risks or avoid risks. Generally, the faster the pace of the project, the more risks the project will experience.

- **Cost management plan**   You'll likely need funds for risk identification and for risk responses. Your cost management plan should address the organization's approach to requesting funds for contingency reserves and risk responses.

- **Quality management plan**   The quality management plan and the organization's approach to quality management may create risks or, more likely, help the project avoid risks.

- **Resource management plan**   This plan helps the project manager anticipate how the project will be staffed and the roles that can contribute to risk identification and management. The plan also identifies the physical resources the project needs and may help to identify associated risks with these items.

- **Risk management plan**   This lone output of risk management planning is needed during risk identification because the plan will identify the organization's and the project's proper approach for identifying risks within the project.

- **Scope baseline**   The project scope statement includes the assumptions that the project is based on. These assumptions are often sources of risk within the project. You'll use the WBS and the WBS dictionary to examine the work packages and deliverables for risk events.

- **Schedule baseline**   Examine the schedule baseline to see deadlines, milestones, and expectations of delivery that may not be realistic, that are based on assumptions, or that are ambiguous.

- **Cost baseline**   Examine the cost baseline to see what risks may be lurking with financing, expenditures, timing of funding needs, and other variables that may be subject to false assumptions or may be ambiguous.

- **Project documents**   The project manager will need several project documents to identify project risks: assumptions log, cost estimates, duration estimates, issue log, lessons learned register, resource requirements, requirements documentation, and the stakeholder register. Examine all of these documents for risk events, ambiguity, risk sensitivity, and insight to positive or negative risks for the project objectives.

- **Procurement documents**   There is always risk associated with hiring a third party to complete a portion of the project work. An analysis of the agreements is needed to identify the risks associated with the vendor completion of the project work, the reliability of the vendor, and the ramifications of vendor-based work on the project schedule, costs, quality, and scope.

- **Enterprise environmental factors**   When it comes to risk identification, having commercial databases, academic studies, benchmarking results, white papers, and other statistics and information related to your discipline is ideal.

- **Organizational process assets**   If an organization has completed projects similar to the current project, using the historical information such as checklists, actual data, and risk statement formats can help with the risk identification.

 EXAM TIP   Risk planning in adaptive projects is not as in-depth as in predictive projects. Agile projects don't value the upfront, involved processes that predictive projects embrace. This doesn't mean you won't plan or discuss risks; it's just not as formal as in a predictive project management approach.

Finding Project Risks

Now the fun part of risk identification: anything goes, as long as it can be perceived as a risk. All of the risk identification participants should identify as many risks as possible, regardless of their perceived initial threat. I'm not really talking about sunspots and asteroid crashes here, but relevant risks should be recorded, regardless of their size and impact on the project. What begins as a small risk can bloom into something much larger as the project progresses.

Reviewing the Project Documentation

One of the first steps the risk identification participants can take is to review the project documentation, including the project plan, scope, and other project files. Constraints and assumptions should be reviewed, considered, and analyzed for risks. This structure review takes a broad look at the project plan, the scope, and the activities defined within the project.

Relying on Risk Identification Methods

You can use five methods to gather project information regarding risks. You'll likely see these on your exam:

- **Brainstorming**   Good, old-fashioned brainstorming is the most common approach to risk identification. It's usually completed by a project team with subject matter experts to identify the risks within the project. You might do brainstorming activities in a longer meeting called a *risk workshop*. The risks are identified in broad terms and posted, and then the risks' characteristics are detailed. Your pal, the RBS, can help facilitate the brainstorming process. The identified risks are categorized and will pass through the qualitative and quantitative risk analyses later. I'll discuss those in just a few pages—no peeking!

- **The Delphi Technique**   The Delphi Technique, shown in Figure 11-2, is an anonymous method used to query experts about foreseeable risks within a project, phase, or component of a project. The results of the survey are analyzed by a third party, organized, and then circulated to the experts. There can be several rounds of anonymous discussion with the Delphi Technique without fear of backlash or offending other participants in the process. The Delphi Technique is completely anonymous, and the goal is to gain consensus on project risks within the project. The anonymous nature of the process ensures that no single expert's advice overtly influences the opinion of another participant.

  I'm often asked why this approach is called the Delphi Technique. It was developed during the Cold War as a forecasting and consensus-building device and was named after the Oracle at Delphi. Delphi is a Greek archeological site that, according to legend, is the center of the universe; the Oracle of Delphi was a high priestess said to predict the future. As fascinating as Greek mythology is, there won't be any legends on your PMI examination. Sorry.

- **Interview sessions**   Interviewing subject matter experts and project stakeholders is an excellent approach to identifying risks on the current project based on the interviewees' experiences. The people responsible for risk identification share the overall purpose of the project, the project's WBS, and, likely, the same assumptions as the interviewee. The subject matter expert, through questions and discussion, shares his insight on what risks he perceives within the project. The goal of the

Figure 11-2
The Delphi Technique uses rounds of anonymous surveys to gain consensus.

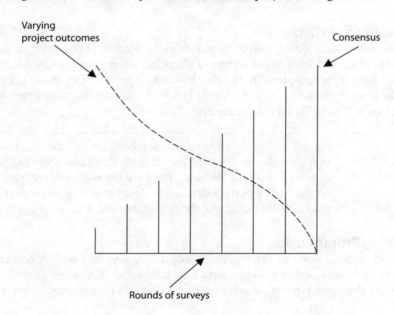

Varying project outcomes

Consensus

Rounds of surveys

process is to learn from the expert what risks may be hidden within the project, what risks this person has encountered in similar work, and what insight the person has into the project work.

- **Root-cause analysis** Project managers and the project team often see the impact of a risk, but not always its cause. Root-cause analysis aims to find out why a risk event may be occurring, the causal factors creating the risk events, and then, eventually, how the events can be mitigated or eliminated.

- **SWOT analysis** *SWOT* stands for strengths, weaknesses, opportunities, and threats. SWOT analysis is the process of examining the project from the perspective of each characteristic. For example, a technology project may identify SWOT as follows:

  - **Strengths** The technology to be installed in the project has been installed by other large companies in our industry.

  - **Weaknesses** We have never installed this technology before.

  - **Opportunities** The new technology will enable us to reduce our cycle time for time to market on new products. *Opportunities* are things, conditions, or events that enable an organization to differentiate itself from competitors and improve its standing in the marketplace.

  - **Threats** The time to complete the training and simulation may overlap with product updates, new versions, and external changes to our technology portfolio.

 EXAM COACH You can use SWOT as you prepare to pass your PMI exam. Look at your scores for the end-of-chapter exams. In which chapters are you strong or weak? Which chapters are threatening your exam? And which exam objectives can you ace on the actual test? Continue to work smart—your goal is to pass the exam.

Using Checklists

Checklists are a quick approach to risk identification. The lowest of the RBSs, such as those rated very low, might serve as a checklist, for example. More likely, similar projects that have been completed in the past have risk registers from which the current risk identification process can benefit. Although checklists can be created quickly and easily, it's impossible to build an exhaustive risk checklist.

 EXAM TIP The danger in using or relying on risk identification checklists is that the risk identification participants don't consider risks that aren't on the checklists. Even for projects that have been completed over and over, based on the nature of the work, the project team must actively seek to identify risks that are outside of the organizational process assets checklists.

Using Prompt Lists

Most organizations do the same type of projects over and over. A construction company manages construction projects. An IT department will manage IT projects. When you're doing the same type of projects over and over, it's easy to rely on your tacit knowledge about the risks that are inherent to the type of projects you're managing. A prompt list, however, can cause you and the project team to pause and really consider what risks may be present in the activities and the project. You can also use a prompt list to identify risks that surround the project. PESTLE is a prompt list that asks questions about project risks using the prompts of Political, Economic, Social, Technological, Legal, and Environmental. Two other prompt lists are TECOP (Technical, Environmental, Commercial, Operational, and Political) and VUCA (Volatility, Uncertainty, Complexity, and Ambiguity).

Examining the Assumptions

All projects have assumptions. Assumption analysis is the process of examining the assumptions to see what risks may stem from false assumptions. Examining assumptions is about gauging the validity of the assumptions. For example, consider a project to install a new piece of software on every computer within an organization. The project team has made the assumption that all the computers within the organization meet the minimum requirements for installing the software. If this assumption is wrong, cost increases and schedule delays will occur.

Examining the assumptions also requires a review of assumptions across the whole project for consistency. For example, consider a project with an assumption that a senior employee will be needed throughout the entire project work; the cost estimate, however, has been billed at the rate of a junior employee.

 EXAM TIP   Software development projects need to pay down technical debt. Technical debt, sometimes called *code debt*, is the refactoring and cleanup of code that's designed for a short-term win versus a more robust design that's long-lasting but takes longer to create. Ideally, it's best to avoid this risk by avoiding technical debt as the work is created, though in software development, it's not always easy to do this while a programmer is coding. Another option is to make architectural adjustments to code debt early in the project.

Utilizing Diagramming Techniques

The project team can utilize several diagramming techniques to identify risks:

- **Ishikawa**   These cause-and-effect diagrams are also called *fishbone diagrams*, as shown in Figure 11-3. They are great for analyzing the root causes of risk factors within the project. The goal is to identify and treat the root of the problem, not the symptom.

- **Flowchart**   System or process flowcharts show the relationships between components and how the overall process works. These are useful for identifying risks between system components.

- **Influence**   An influence diagram charts out a decision problem. It identifies all the elements, variables, decisions, and objectives, and also how each factor may influence another.

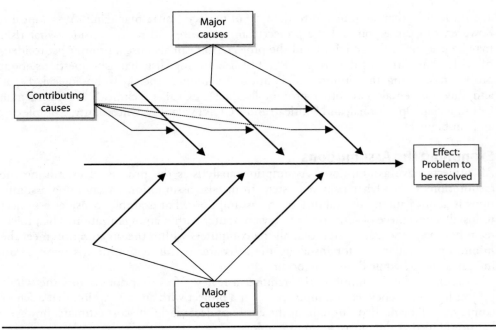

Figure 11-3   Ishikawa diagrams are also known as fishbone diagrams.

Creating a Risk Register

The only output of risk identification is the project's risk register. The risk register is a component of the project management plan that contains all the information related to the risk management activities. It's updated as risk management activities are conducted to reflect the status, progress, and nature of the project risks. The risk register includes the following:

- **Risks**   Of course, the most obvious output of risk identification is the risk that has been successfully identified. Recall that a risk is an uncertain event or condition that could potentially have a positive or negative effect on project success.

- **Risk owners**   Risk owners, or potential risk owners, are identified in the risk register. The risk owner is the person who will be accountable for the risk and for tracking the risk and who typically has authority to respond to the risk event should the risk be moving from uncertainty to certainty within the project.

- **Potential responses**   The initial risk identification process may yield solutions and responses to identified risks. This is fine, as long as the responses are documented here. Along with the risk responses, the identification of risk triggers may also occur. *Triggers* are warning signs or symptoms that a risk has occurred or is about to occur. For example, should a vendor fail to complete her portion of the project as scheduled, the project completion may be delayed.

- **Root causes of risk**   Risk identification can identify why risk conditions exist. Project managers can also use *if-then* statements based on the *cause* of the risk event to predict the *effect* of the risk event.

- **Updated risk categories**   Risk identification may prompt the project team to identify new categories of risks. These new categories should be documented in the risk register, and if an RBS is utilized, it will need to be updated as well.

Creating a Risk Report

Another output of risk identification is a risk report. The risk report explains the overall project risks and provides summaries about the individual project risks. You'll update the risk report through the project as more information becomes available through analysis and experience in the project. The report will be updated with risk responses and the response outcomes, plus any additional details as a result of monitoring risks in the project. Your risk report, depending on what's required in the organization, may include sources of overall project risk exposure, trends among the individual risks, number of threats and opportunities, and other related information.

Using Qualitative Risk Analysis

The first, and somewhat shallow, risk analysis is qualitative analysis. Qualitative risk analysis "qualifies" the risks that have been identified in the project. Specifically, qualitative risk analysis examines and prioritizes the risks based on their probability of occurring and the impact on the project if the risks do occur. Qualitative risk analysis is a broad approach to ranking risks by priority, which then guides the risk reaction process. The end result of qualitative risk analysis (once risks have been identified and prioritized) can either lead to more in-depth quantitative risk analysis or move directly into risk response planning.

The status of the project will also affect the process of qualitative risk analysis. Early in the project, there may be several risks that have not yet surfaced. Later in the project, new risks may become evident and need to pass through qualitative analysis. The status of the project is linked to the available time needed to analyze and study the risks. There may be more time early in the project, while a looming deadline near the project's end may create a sense of urgency to find a solution for the newly identified risks.

 EXAM TIP   When you think of "qualitative," think of qualifying. You are qualifying, or justifying, the seriousness of the risk for further analysis. Some certified Project Management Professional (PMP) candidates like to remember that qualitative is a list. The two L's in *qualitative* and *list* tie the two together.

Preparing for Qualitative Analysis

As with most of the project planning processes, the project management team is included in the rapid analysis of the project risks. There are four inputs to qualitative analysis:

- **Project management plan**   Within the project management plan is the risk management plan, the key input to qualitative risk analysis. The plan will dictate the process, the methodologies to be used, and the scoring model for identified risks. In addition to the risk management plan, the identified risks from the risk register will obviously be needed to perform an analysis. The roles and responsibilities will be a vital input for qualitative risk analysis.

- **Project documents**   While the project manager can use any of the project documents that are relevant to risk, you'll likely reference the assumptions log, the risk register, and the stakeholder register.

- **Enterprise environmental factors**   Risk databases, industry studies, internal risk management policies, and program governance can all be considered as part of the risk analysis.

- **Organizational process assets**   Past projects and lessons learned—the organization's historical information—are ideal resources for the qualitative risk analysis process. There's no need to reinvent the wheel.

 EXAM TIP   You'll always update the risk register when any new information about a risk is discovered.

Completing Qualitative Analysis

During the risk identification process, all possible risks are identified. Of course, not all risks are worth responding to, while others demand attention. Qualitative analysis is a subjective approach to organizing and prioritizing risks. Through a methodical and logical approach, often performed with subject matter experts and historical information, the identified risks are rated according to probability and potential impact.

Data gathering is another tool and technique you can rely on during qualitative risk analysis. Interviews are used to gather data, but the project manager has to use caution and establish trust with the interview subjects. Confidentiality is key to gathering data from stakeholders; you don't want a stakeholder to keep a risk impact a secret because she fears backlash for sharing the risk information.

Once you have gathered data, you'll need to do a quality assessment of the data to determine its accuracy and reliability. You'll examine the risks for their impact on project objectives, such as scope, time, and cost. Sometimes the risk data you've gathered is, well, weak, and you'll have to go back and gather more data to analyze the risks sufficiently to determine their full impacts on project objectives.

Applying Probability and Impact

The project risks are rated according to their probability and impact. Risk *probability* is the likelihood that a risk event may happen, while risk *impact* is the consequence that the result of the risk event will have on the project objectives. Two approaches exist to ranking risks:

- **Cardinal scales**   Identify the probability and impact on a numerical value, from .01 (very low) to 1.0 (certain).
- **Ordinal scales**   Identify and rank the risks from very high to very unlikely.

Creating a Probability-Impact Matrix

Each identified risk is fed into a probability-impact matrix, as shown in Figure 11-4. The matrix maps out the risk, its probability, its possible impact, and a risk score. The risks with higher probability and impact are a more serious threat to the project objectives than risks with lower impact and consequences. The risks that are threats to the project require quantitative analysis to determine the root causes, the methods to control the risks, and effective risk management. We'll discuss quantitative risk management later in this chapter in the section "Preparing for Quantitative Risk Analysis."

The project is best served when the probability scale and the impact scale are predefined prior to qualitative analysis. For example, the probability scale rates the likelihood of an individual risk happening and can be on a cardinal scale (.1, .3, .5, .7, .9) or on an ordinal scale (very high, high, medium, low, and very low). The scale, however, should be defined and agreed upon in the risk management plan. The impact scale, which measures the severity of the risk on the project's objectives, can also be ordinal or cardinal.

Figure 11-4
A probability-impact matrix measures the identified risks within the project.

Risk	Probability	Impact	Risk Score
Data loss	Low	High	Moderate
Network speed	Moderate	Moderate	Moderate
Server downtime	High	Low	Moderate
E-mail service down	Low	Low	Low

Odds and impact

Each identified risk

Subjective score

Figure 11-5
The results of a probability-impact matrix create the risk score.

Probability	Risk Scores				
0.9	0.05	0.09	0.18	0.36	0.72
0.7	0.04	0.07	0.14	0.28	0.56
0.5	0.03	0.05	0.10	0.20	0.40
0.3	0.02	0.03	0.06	0.12	0.24
0.1	0.01	0.01	0.02	0.04	0.08
	0.05	0.10	0.20	0.40	0.80
	Impact				

Legend ☐ Low
☐ Moderate
☐ High

By identifying and assigning the scales to use prior to the process of qualitative analysis, all risks can be ranked by the system, including future identified risks. A shift in risk-rating methodologies midproject can cause disagreements with regard to how the project risks should be handled.

A probability-impact matrix multiplies the value for the risk probability by the risk impact, giving a total risk score, as shown in Figure 11-5. The risk's scores can be cardinal, and then preset values can qualify the risk for a risk response. For example, an identified risk in a project is the possibility that the vendor may be late in delivering the hardware. The probability is rated at .9, but the impact of the risk on the project is rated at .1. The risk score is calculated by multiplying the probability times the impact—in this case, resulting in a score of .09.

The scores within the probability-impact matrix can be referenced against the performing organization's policies for risk reaction. Based on the risk score, the performing organization can place the risk in differing categories to guide risk reaction. There are three common categories, based on a Red-Amber-Green (RAG) rating risk score:

- **Red condition**   High risk. These risk scores are high in impact and probability.

- **Amber condition (also called yellow condition)**   These risks are somewhat high in impact and probability.

- **Green condition**   Risks with a green label are generally fairly low in impact, probability, or both.

Relying on Data Precision

Here's the truth about qualitative risk analysis: it's easy, fast, cheap, and not very reliable. One of the toughest parts of qualitative risk analysis is the biased, subjective nature of the process. A project manager and the project team must question the reliability and reality of the data that leads to the ranking of the risks. For example, Susan may have great confidence in herself when it comes to working with new, unproven technologies. Based on this opinion, she determines the probability of the work risk to be a very low score.

However, because she has no experience with the technology because of its newness, the probability of the risk of failure is actually very high. The biased opinion that Susan can complete the work with zero defects and problems is slightly skewed because she has never worked with the technology before. Obviously, a low-ranked score on a risk that should be ranked high can result in detrimental effects on the project's success.

Data precision ranking takes into consideration the biased nature of the ranking, the accuracy of the data submitted, and the reliability of the data submitted to examine the risk scores. Data precision ranking is concerned with the following:

- The level of understanding of the project risk
- The available data and information about the identified risk
- The quality of the data and information about the identified risk
- The reliability of the data about the identified risk

The assessment of the risks will help you determine nine things about the risk events:

- **Urgency**   Does the risk response need to happen immediately to address the risk properly?
- **Proximity**   How soon will the risk event happen?
- **Dormancy**   How long after the risk occurs will it take to realize that the risk event has occurred?
- **Manageability**   How easy will it be to manage the risk event?
- **Controllability**   How easy will it be to control the risk outcome?
- **Detectability**   How easy will it be to realize that the risk event is likely to occur?
- **Connectivity**   What's the relationship between a single risk event and other risks within the project?
- **Strategic impact**   Will the risk affect the organizational goals?
- **Propinquity**   How important is the risk event and its outcomes perceived by the stakeholders?

Building a Hierarchical Chart

It's tempting, and often convenient, to rate risks based only on probability and impact. However, you can rate risks based on several factors, such urgency, proximity, and impact, to create a more robust chart. By scoring any number of factors, you can create histograms, pie charts, or bubble charts. In a bubble chart, shown in Figure 11-6, you'll plot out the factors from low to high and add the variable of the size of the bubble to show the bubble impact value. The larger the bubble, the larger the impact of the risk. Where the bubbles land in the chart, based on the factors selected, will help determine which risks need additional analysis, aren't acceptable, or have low factors and might be acceptable in the project.

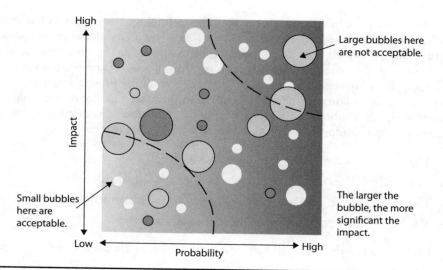

High

Impact

Low

Probability

High

Large bubbles here are not acceptable.

The larger the bubble, the more significant the impact.

Small bubbles here are acceptable.

Figure 11-6 A bubble chart enables you to plot two risk factors as well as the impact of the risk (bubble size).

Assessing the Risk Score

Once the qualitative risk assessment has been completed, you can step back, heave a sigh of relief, and then acknowledge that this process will need to be repeated throughout the project as new risks come into play. Risk assessment is an ongoing, iterative process that lasts throughout the project. Want some more sad news? The risk ratings in the qualitative risk matrix can change based on conditions in the project or as more information about the risks becomes available.

One nice thing about the qualitative risk analysis process is the ability to categorize risks. Remember the RBS? The qualitative risk analysis process may give you an opportunity to create new risk categories that you've identified or to reorganize the RBS. The goal of updating the RBS is to group risks by common categories to create better risk responses later in the risk management processes.

Finally, assessing the risk score gives the project manager an opportunity to address near-term risks. Imminent risks are usually considered of higher urgency than future risks. Consider the risk ranking, the time needed for the risk response, and the conditions that indicate the risk is coming to fruition.

Examining the Results of Qualitative Risk Analysis

Qualitative risk analysis happens throughout the project. As new risks become evident and are identified, the project manager should route the risks through the qualitative risk analysis process. The end results of qualitative risk analysis include the following:

- **Assumptions log** Assumptions can be updated, and new assumptions are added to the log.

- **Issue log**   Any new issues discovered are added to the log, and issues that have changed are updated to reflect their new status.

- **Risk register**   New risks that have been identified are added to the register, while existing risks will have their attributes updated to reflect the qualitative risk analysis findings.

- **Risk report**   The risk report is updated with any changes to the summary on the individual risks and the overall risk ranking of the project. This enables the project manager, management, customers, and other interested stakeholders to comprehend the risk, the nature of the risk, and the condition between the risk score and the likelihood of success for a project. The risk score can be compared to that of other projects to determine project selection, the placement of talent in a project, prioritization, the creation of a benefit/cost ratio, or even the cancellation of a project because it is deemed too risky.

- **Risk categories**   Within the risk register, categories of risks should be created. The idea is that not only will related risks be lumped together, but some trend identification and root-cause analysis of identified risks may be possible as well. Having risks categorized should also make it easier to create risk responses.

- **Near-term risks**   Qualitative analysis should also help the project team identify which risks require immediate or near-term risk responses. Risks that are likely to happen later in the project can be acknowledged, enabling imminent risks to be managed first. Urgent risks can go right to quantitative analysis and risk response planning.

- **Low-priority risk watch list**   Let's face it: not all risks need additional analysis. However, low-priority risks should be identified and assigned to a watch list for periodic monitoring.

- **Trends in qualitative analysis**   As the project progresses and risk analysis is repeated, trends in the ranking and analysis of the risk may become apparent. These trends can enable the project manager and other risk experts to respond to the root cause, predict trends to eliminate, or respond to the risks within the project.

Preparing for Quantitative Risk Analysis

Quantitative risk analysis involves numerically assessing the probability and impact of the identified risks. It also creates an overall risk score for the project. This method provides a more in-depth analysis than qualitative risk analysis and relies on several different tools to accomplish its goal. The development team can help the project facilitator or risk expert better understand the risks and the effect the risks may have on the project's value.

Qualitative risk analysis typically precedes quantitative risk analysis. I like to say that qualitative analysis qualifies risks, while quantitative analysis quantifies risks. All or a portion of the identified risks in qualitative risk analysis can be examined in the quantitative analysis. The performing organization may have policies on the risk scores in qualitative analysis that require the risks to advance to the quantitative analysis. The availability of time and budget may also be a factor in determining which risks should pass through quantitative analysis. Quantitative analysis is a more time-consuming process and is, therefore, also more expensive than qualitative analysis.

Quantitative risk analysis goals include these:

- Quantify the cost and impact of the risk exposure.
- Ascertain the likelihood of reaching project success.
- Ascertain the likelihood of reaching a particular project objective.
- Determine the risk exposure for the project.
- Determine the likely amount of the contingency reserve needed for the project.
- Determine the risks with the largest impact on the project.
- Determine realistic time, cost, and scope targets.

Interviewing Stakeholders and Experts

Interviews with stakeholders and subject matter experts can be one of the first tools used to quantify the identified risks. These interviews can focus on worst-case, best-case, and most-likely scenarios if the goal of the quantitative analysis is to create a triangular distribution. Most quantitative analysis, however, uses continuous probability distributions. Figure 11-7 shows five sample distributions.

Continuous probability distribution examines the probability of all possibilities within a given range. For each variable, the probability of a risk event and the corresponding consequence of the event may vary. In other words, depending on whether the risk event occurs and how it happens, a reaction to the event may also occur. The distribution of the probabilities and impact includes the following:

- Normal
- Lognormal
- Beta
- Triangular
- Uniform

 EXAM TIP It's doubtful you'll be tested on these risk distributions for the exam. The *PMBOK Guide* mentions them only briefly, so you just need to be topically aware of them. Don't invest hours memorizing the subject.

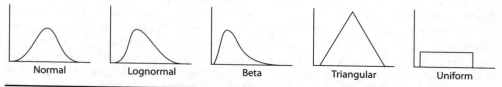

Figure 11-7 Risk distributions illustrate the likelihood and impact of an event within a project.

Figure 11-8
Tornado diagrams show the top risks to the smallest risks to a project in descending order.

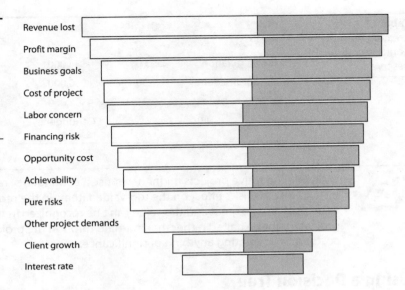

Applying Sensitivity Analysis

Sensitivity analysis, part of data analysis, examines each risk to determine which one has the largest impact on the project's success. All other risks in the project are set at a baseline value and then compared against the rest of the risks individually. The individual risk is then examined to see how it may affect the success of the project. The goal of sensitivity analysis is to determine which individual risks have the greatest impact on the project's success and then to escalate the risk management processes based on these risk events.

The tornado diagram is best used when completing sensitivity analysis. The tornado diagram maps out all the variables in a situation from largest to smallest impact on the project or situation. If you've ever seen a tornado, you know it's really big on top and small at the bottom—and that's what the tornado diagram looks like, too, as shown in Figure 11-8. The closer the bar is to the top of the diagram, the more impact it has on the situation, project, or investment. The closer the bar is to the bottom of the chart, the less impact it has on the situation. Tornado diagrams are also sometimes called *tornado plots* or *tornado charts*.

Finding the Expected Monetary Value

The expected monetary value (EMV) of a project or event is based on the probability of outcomes that are uncertain. For example, one risk may cost the project an additional $10,000 if it occurs, but there's only a 20 percent chance of the event occurring. In its simplest form, the EMV of this individual risk impact is, thus, $2,000. Project managers can also find the expected monetary value of a decision by creating a decision tree.

Table 11-1 is an example of a simple risk matrix that determines the expected monetary value for some sample risks. Note that the sum of the EMV reveals what the contingency reserve for these risks should be.

Table 11-1	Risk	Probability	Impact	EMV
Creating the Contingency Reserve	Data loss	.40	–$12,000	–$4,800
	New regulation	.80	–$34,000	–$27,200
	Vendor discount	.30	+$10,000	+$3,000
	Hardware issue	.45	–$65,000	–$29,250
			Contingency reserve =	$58,250

EXAM TIP Adaptive projects might never use a contingency reserve, but instead test the risk's effect on the top-valued items in the product backlog. If the risks are too great and the value can't be recognized in the project, the project might be halted rather than burning through the project's time and costs without creating anything of significance.

Using a Decision Tree

A decision tree is a method used to determine which one of two or more decisions is the best. For example, it can be used to determine buy-versus-build scenarios, lease-or-purchase equations, or whether to use in-house resources rather than outsourcing project work. The decision tree model examines the cost and benefits of each decision's outcome and weighs the probability of success for each of the decisions.

The purpose of the decision tree is to make a decision, calculate the value of that decision, or determine which decision costs the least. Follow Figure 11-9 through the various steps of the decision tree process.

Completing a Decision Tree

Let's look at an example. As the project manager of the new GFB Project, you have to decide whether to create a new web application in-house or send the project out to a developer. The developer you would use (if you were to outsource the work) quotes the project cost at $175,000. Based on previous work with this company, you are 85 percent certain the developer will finish the work on time.

Figure 11-9
Decision trees analyze the probability of events and calculate decision values.

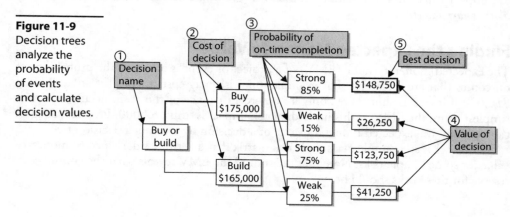

Your in-house development team quotes the cost of the work as $165,000. Again, based on previous experience with your in-house developers, you feel 75 percent certain they can complete the work on time. Now let's apply what we know to a decision tree:

1. "Buy or build" is simply the decision name.

2. The cost of the decision if you "buy" the work outside of your company is $175,000. If you build the software in-house, the cost is $165,000.

3. Based on your probability of completion by a given date, you apply the 85 percent certainty to the "strong" finish for the Buy branch of the tree. Because you're 85 percent certain, you're also 15 percent uncertain; this value is assigned to the "weak" value on the Buy branch. You complete the same process for the Build branch of the tree.

4. The value of the decision is the percentage of strong and weak applied to each branch of the tree.

5. The best decision is based solely on the largest value of all possible decisions.

Using a Project Simulation

Project simulations enable the project team to play "what-if" games without affecting any areas of production. The Monte Carlo analysis (sometimes called the Monte Carlo technique) is the most common simulation. This technique got its name from Monte Carlo, Monaco (world-renowned for its slot machines, roulette wheels, and other games of pure chance). The Monte Carlo technique, typically completed using a computer software program, completely simulates a project by using values for all possible variables to predict the most likely model.

Examining the Results of Quantitative Risk Analysis

Quantitative risk analysis is completed throughout the project as risks are identified and passed through qualitative analysis, as project conditions change, or on a preset schedule. The end result of quantitative risk analysis should be reflected in a risk report and includes the following:

- **Overall project risk exposure**   The overall project risk exposure is documented in the project's chances of success, which indicates how likely the project is to reach its key objectives. The degree of inherent remaining variability in the project is assessed. This means how much risk the project is carrying based on the variations of possible project outcomes.

- **Probabilistic analysis**   The risks within the project enable the project manager or other experts to predict the likelihood of the project's success. The project may be altered by the response to certain risks; this response can increase cost and push back the project's completion date. The results of quantitative analysis can be shown through tornado diagrams and S-curves to plot out the project's risks. The analysis also can identify the major risk events, contingency reserve needed, and which risks have the most uncertainty and most probability of happening.

- **Prioritized list of individual project risks**   The risk events are prioritized by their likelihood of occurring and the impact on the project if the risk events do occur.

- **Trends in quantitative analysis**   As the project moves toward completion, quantitative risk analysis may be repeated. In each round of analysis, trends in the identified risks may become visible. The trends in the risk can help the project team eliminate the root causes of the risk, reduce their probability, or address their impact.

- **Recommended risk responses**   Risk response planning is covered in detail in the next section, but the risk report may also include the recommended risk responses. These recommendations will serve as an input to planning the risk responses formally.

Planning for Risk Responses

Risk response planning is all about options and actions. It focuses on how to decrease the possibility of risks adversely affecting the project's objectives and how to increase the likelihood of positive risks that can aid the project. Risk response planning assigns responsibilities to people and groups close to the risk event. Risks will increase or decrease based on the effectiveness of risk response planning.

The responses to identified risks must be in balance with the risks themselves. The cost and time invested in responding to a risk must be met with the gains from reducing the risk's impact and probability. In other words, a million-dollar solution for a hundred-dollar problem is unacceptable. The individuals who are assigned to the risk must have the authority to react to the project risk as planned. In most cases, several risk responses may be viable for the risk—the best choice for the identified risk must be documented, agreed upon, and then followed through should the risk come to fruition.

Preparing for Risk Responses

To prepare successfully for risk response, the project manager, project team, and appropriate stakeholders rely on just two inputs: the risk management plan and the risk register. The inputs for planning the risk responses include the following:

- **Project management plan**   Resource management plan, risk management plan, and cost baseline

- **Project documents**   Lessons learned register, schedule, team assignments, resource calendars, risk register, risk report, and stakeholder register

- **Enterprise environmental factors**   Risk appetite and risk thresholds of the key stakeholders

- **Organizational process assets**   Templates for the risk management plan, risk register, risk report, any historical databases, and lessons learned from similar projects

Creating Risk Responses

The project team can employ several tools and techniques to respond to risks. Each risk should be evaluated to determine which category of risk response is most appropriate. When a category has been selected, the response must then be developed, refined, documented, and readied for use if needed. In addition, secondary responses may be selected for each risk. The purpose of risk response planning is to bring down the overall risk of the project to an acceptable level. In addition, risk response planning must address any risks that have unacceptably high scores.

Escalating the Risk Event

Not all risks should be managed at the project level. Some risks that are outside of the boundary of the project should be escalated when the project team, project sponsor, or project manager believes the risk management would exceed the authority the project manager has over the risk event. In these instances, the risk is escalated to management, a program manager, or the portfolio manager in the organization. The escalated threat should be communicated to the new owner of the risk event to explain why it's beyond the project boundaries, and the new owner must also agree to accept the risk as part of her responsibility. Like negative risk events, threats and opportunities can be escalated.

Avoiding Negative Risks

Avoidance is simply avoiding the risk. This can be accomplished in many different ways and generally happens early in the project, when any change will result in fewer consequences than it would if implemented later in the project plan. Examples of avoidance include the following:

- Changing the project plan to eliminate the risk
- Clarifying project requirements to avoid discrepancies
- Reducing the project scope to avoid the risk
- Using a proven methodology rather than a new approach

 EXAM TIP   One avoidance risk strategy is to shut down the entire project to avoid the risk entirely.

Transferring Negative Risks

Transference is the process of transferring the risk (and the ownership of the risk) to a third party. The risk doesn't disappear—it just becomes someone else's problem. Transference of a risk usually costs a premium for the third party to own and manage. Here are some common examples of risk transference:

- Insurance
- Performance bonds

- Warranties
- Guarantees
- Fixed-priced contracts

Mitigating Negative Risks

Mitigating risks is an effort to reduce the probability and/or impact of an identified risk in the project. Mitigation is done based on the logic before the risk happens. It is more cost-effective to reduce or eliminate a risk than repair the damage caused by the risk. The risk event may still happen, but, ideally, both the cost and impact of the risk will be very low.

Mitigation plans can be created to be implemented should an identified risk cross a given threshold. For example, a manufacturing project may have a mitigation plan to reduce the number of units created per hour should the equipment's temperature reach a given threshold. The reduction is the number of units per hour that it may cost the project in time. In addition, the cost of extra labor to run the equipment longer because the machine is now operating at a slower pace may be attributed to the project. However, should the equipment fail, the project would have to replace the equipment and would be delayed for weeks while awaiting repairs.

Here are some examples of mitigation:

- Adding activities to the project to reduce the risk probability or impact
- Simplifying the processes within the project
- Completing more tests on the project work before implementation
- Developing prototypes, simulations, and limited releases

Managing the Positive Risk and Opportunities

Although most risks have a negative connotation, not all risks are bad. There are instances when a risk may create an opportunity that can help the project, other projects, or the organization as a whole. The type of risk and the organization's willingness to accept risks will dictate the appropriate response.

Escalating a Positive Risk

When a risk, even a positive risk, is outside of the project manager's authority or outside the scope of the project, the risk is escalated. Once an opportunity is escalated, it's no longer monitored by the project manager or team; it's owned by some other entity in the organization, and the project manager and team return to focus on the project scope.

Exploiting Positive Risks or Opportunities

When an organization would like to take advantage of a positive risk that will likely happen, it can exploit the risk. Positive risk exploitation can be realized by adding resources to finish the project faster than was originally planned, increasing quality to recognize sales and customer satisfaction, utilizing a better way of completing the project work, or using any other method that creates the positive outcomes of the identified risk.

Sharing Positive Risks

The idea of sharing a positive risk really means sharing a mutually beneficial opportunity between two organizations or projects, or creating a risk-sharing partnership. When a project team can share the positive risk, ownership of the risk is given to the organization that can best capture its benefits.

Enhancing Positive Risks

This risk response seeks to modify the size of the identified opportunity. The goal is to strengthen the cause of the opportunity to ensure that the risk event does happen. Enhancing a project risk looks for solutions, triggers, or other drivers to ensure that the risk does come to fruition so that the rewards of the risk can be realized by the performing organization.

Accepting the Risks

Risk acceptance is the process of simply accepting the risks because no other action is feasible, or because the risks are deemed to be of small probability, impact, or both, and a formal response is not warranted. *Passive* acceptance requires no action; the project team deals with the risks as they happen. *Active* acceptance entails developing a contingency plan should the risk occur. Acceptance may be used for both positive and negative risks.

A *contingency plan* is a predefined set of actions the project team will take should certain events occur. Events that trigger the contingency plan should be tracked. A *fallback plan* is a reaction to a risk that has occurred when the primary response proves to be inadequate.

Updating the Risk Register

Are you noticing a theme here? Every time new information about the project's risks is learned, the risk register has to be updated. Updates to the risk register with regard to risk responses include the following:

- Identified risks and how each one can threaten the project
- Risk owners and their responsibilities for the risk events
- Risk response strategies and the responses to risk events
- Symptoms and warning signs of risk
- Budget and schedule impacts of the risk response activities
- Contingency reserves for time and costs
- Contingency plans and triggers to implement the plan
- Fallback plans
- Residual risks (risks that are expected to remain after a risk response)
- Secondary risks (new risks created as a result of a risk response)

Creating Contracts for Risk Response

When multiple entities are involved in a project, contractual agreements may be necessary to identify the responsible parties for identified risks. The contract may be needed for insurance purposes, customer acceptance, or the acknowledgment of responsibilities between the entities completing the project. Transference is an example of contractual agreements for the responsibility of risks within a project. Adaptive projects might transfer the risk that the development team does not have the required skills or enough project team members to create all of the requirements in the product backlog. This procurement decision, which I'll discuss in the next chapter, will increase costs for the project.

Justifying Risk Reduction

To reduce risk, additional time or monies are typically needed. The process and logic behind the strategies to reduce the risk should be evaluated to determine whether the solution is worth the tradeoffs. For example, a risk may be eliminated by adding $7,500 to a project's budget. However, the likelihood of the risk occurring is relatively low. Should the risk happen, it would cost, at a minimum, $8,000 to correct, and the project would be delayed by at least two weeks.

The cost of preventing the risk versus the cost of responding to it must be weighed and justified. If the project manager gambles that the risk won't happen and doesn't spend the $7,500 cost for the risk response and then the project moves forward as planned without the risk happening, it has theoretically saved $15,500 because the risk did not happen and the response to the risk did not need to happen.

However, if the risk does happen without the $7,500 preventive risk response, the project will lose at least $8,000 and will be delayed at least two weeks. The cost inherent in the project delay may be more expensive than the solution to the risk. Choosing to solve the risk to reduce the likelihood of delaying the project may be wiser than ignoring the risk.

Creating a Project Contingency Response

A contingency response is a predefined set of actions the project team will take should certain events occur. Contingency plans are sometimes called *worst-case scenario plans* or *fallback plans*. Events that trigger the contingency plan should be tracked. A fallback plan is a reaction to a risk that has occurred when the primary response proves to be inadequate. Most risk acceptance policies rely on a contingency allowance for the project. A project contingency allowance is the amount of money the project will likely need in the contingency reserve based on the impact, probability, and expected monetary value of a risk event.

Updating the Project Plan

The risk reactions, contingency plans, and fallback plans should all be documented and incorporated into the project plan—for example, updating the schedule, budget, and WBS to accommodate additional time, money, and activities for risk responses. The responses to the risks may change the original implementation of the project and should be updated to reflect the project plan and intent of the project team, management, and other stakeholders. A failure to update the project plan and the risk register may cause risk reactions to be missed—and skew performance measurements.

There's a chance you'll also need to update the scope, cost, and schedule baselines to reflect the changes to these components of the project. For example, you may edit the project scope as part of risk response. This change in the project scope may in fact affect the costs and schedule of the project, so you'd need to reflect these baselines, too. This is a great example of the integrated nature of project management. Any decision you make here in risk management, particularly in risk responses, can affect the entire project and will cause a need to update the project management plan accordingly.

You'll also need to update the assumptions log if you've identified risks that change the project assumptions. It's also possible that during the management of the risk, you had to generate new assumptions about how the project would behave if you were to enact certain risk responses. The technical documentation that supports the project management plan may also need to be updated if you've added risk responses that affect the project deliverables.

Implementing Risk Responses

After you and the team have created the risk responses and resources have been assigned to the risk events, you'll go on with the project and never look at this again. Kidding! You'll actually monitor the risk events and implement your risk responses. You need to have confidence in the responses you've created and have good communication with the risk owners to implement the responses. Of course, you'll also need to document the outcome of implementing responses. Let's take a look at this process in more detail.

Preparing to Implement Risk Responses

To implement risk responses, you'll need three inputs:

- **Risk management plan** The roles and responsibilities of the risk management plan are needed to make certain the right people are carrying out the right responses. You'll also need the risk management plan to identify and communicate the risk thresholds, which will signal when the risk response is needed.

- **Project documents** The lessons learned register, risk register, and risk report are inputs to this process.

- **Organizational process assets** Historical information from similar projects can help the project manager and the project team implement the risk responses.

Reviewing the Tools and Techniques for Implementing Risk Responses

You should be familiar with three tools and techniques for implementing risk responses:

- **Expert judgment**   This common tool and technique is also used in implementing risk responses. Experts can help to implement the risk response or even modify the risk response based on conditions within the project. The development team should feel safe enough to communicate impending risks and empowered enough to take action on the risks.

- **Interpersonal and team skills**   The project manager may need to influence the risk owner to act on the risk that needs the response. The risk owner could be outside of the project team, so influencing is the interpersonal skill that's needed: influence that person to act to keep the project moving.

- **Project management information system**   The PMIS can help ensure that the risk response activities are integrated into the schedule, resource planning, and cost of the project.

Examining the Results of Implementing Risk Responses

There are just two results of implementing risk responses:

- **Change requests**   As you might expect, change requests could be generated, because the risk response may cause a change to the project's cost or schedule baseline. The change request must be documented and must flow through the integrated change control process.

- **Project document updates**   Lots of project documents could be updated because of the risk response. Documents that might need updating include the issue log, lessons learned register, project team assignments, risk register, and the risk report.

Monitoring Project Risks

Risks must be actively monitored, and new risks must be responded to as they are discovered. Risk monitoring and control is the process of monitoring identified risks for signs that they may be occurring, controlling identified risks with the agreed-upon responses, and looking for new risks that may creep into the project. Risk monitoring also is concerned with the documentation of the success or failure of risk response plans and keeping records of metrics that signal risks are occurring or disappearing from the project.

Risk monitoring is an active process that requires participation from the project manager, the project team, key stakeholders, and, in particular, risk owners within the project.

As the project progresses, risk conditions may change and require new responses, additional planning, or the implementation of a contingency plan.

There are several goals to risk monitoring:

- Confirm that risk responses are implemented as planned.
- Determine whether risk responses are effective or whether new responses are needed.
- Confirm that project assumptions are still valid.
- Determine the validity of the project assumptions.
- Determine whether the risk exposure has changed, evolved, or declined due to trends in the project progression.
- Track the risk contingency reserve for costs and schedule.
- Confirm that policies and procedures happen as planned.
- Monitor the project for new risks.

Preparing for Risk Monitoring and Control

A project manager's work is never done—at least not until the project is closed. Risk monitoring and controlling is an active process. There are several inputs the project team and the project manager must rely on to monitor and control risks effectively:

- **Project management plan**   Specifically, you're after the risk management plan. This plan defines the organization's approach to risk management. It is not the strategy for specific risks within a project, but the overall strategy for risk analysis and planning.

- **Issue log**   You'll reference the issue log to track open issues and to determine whether you'll also need to update the risk register.

- **Lessons learned register**   Document the lessons learned from the risk management processes and use these lessons in the current and future projects.

- **Risk register**   The risk register is the central repository for all project risk information. It includes the identified risks, the potential responses, the root causes of risks, and any identified categories of risk.

- **Risk report**   Update the risk report with status, overall project risk exposure, and the risk response strategy.

- **Work performance data**   The results of project work can provide data about the number of risk events, their statuses, and other facts about the risks within the project.

- **Work performance reports**   Work performance reports can help the project manager see if new risks are entering the project based on performance and status of the project.

Monitoring and Controlling Risks

Risk monitoring and control happens throughout the project. These are not solitary activities that are completed once and never revisited. The project manager and the project team must actively monitor risks, respond with the agreed-upon actions, and scan the horizon for risks that have not been addressed. Risk monitoring and control is a recurring activity that requires input from all project participants.

Project risk should be on the agenda at every project team meeting. The periodic risk review is a regularly scheduled discussion throughout the project to ascertain the level of foreseeable risks, the success of risk responses in the project to date, and a review of pending risks. Based on circumstances within the project, risk rankings and prioritization may fluctuate. Changes to the project scope, team, or conditions may require qualitative and quantitative analyses.

 EXAM TIP   The velocity of the development team can signal a risk for the project. If the team has predicted that it can complete 35 user story points in the sprint but its progress to done has been limited, it's a sign that the team's estimated velocity is faulty. However, the team's velocity early in the project is expected to be unstable, and within a few iterations the velocity and expected number of user stories completed per iteration will normalize.

Completing Risk Response Audits

You don't just assume your risk responses work—you have to test them. A risk response audit examines the planned risk responses, how well the planned actions work, and the effectiveness of the risk owners in implementing the risk responses. The audits happen throughout the project to measure the effectiveness of mitigating, transferring, and avoiding risks. The risk response audit should measure the effectiveness of the decision and its impact on time and cost. Of course, you'll update the risk register once the audit has been completed.

Analyzing Project Variances

A *variance* is the difference between what was planned and what was experienced. No one likes to hear that variances are in the project, but ignoring variances can only lead to more risks, more troubles, and more headaches. Cost variances can eat into the project budget, which in turn creates new risks, such as running out of cash, having to choose a lower grade of materials, or even removing deliverables from the scope. Cost variances can also force the project manager to have to ask for more funds, which is not a pleasant experience.

Schedule variances are just as deadly. Delays in the project work, vendor deliveries, and time estimates that were too optimistic can eat into the management reserve and consume the project's float. These risks can create new risks. Consider the risks inherent to the schedule variance responses:

- Crashing the project
- Fast-tracking the project

- Overworking the project team
- Rushing the project work
- Rushing through quality control and quality audits to regain time

Remember earned value analysis? Earned value analysis measures project performance. When project performance is waning, the project is likely missing targeted costs and schedule goals. The results of earned value analysis can signal that risks are happening within the project or that new risks may be developing.

For example, a schedule performance index (SPI) of .93 means the project is off schedule by 7 percent. A risk based on this value could mean that the project team is having difficulty completing the project work as planned. Additional work will continue to be late, the project will finish late, and quality may suffer as the team attempts to rush to complete assigned tasks.

Measuring Technical Performance

Throughout the project, the project team's technical competence with the technology being used in the project should increase. The level of technical achievement should be in proportion to the expected level of technical performance within the project. If the project team is not performing at a level of expected technical expertise, the project may suffer additional risks because of the discrepancy. Technical performance can be measured by the successful completion of activities throughout the project or project phases.

Monitoring Contingency Reserve

As risk events happen, you'll need to keep an eye on the risk reserves and how this budget for risk events is being depleted. Let's say you have a risk reserve of $250,000 based on your quantitative analysis. At the beginning of a risk event, you'll use some of the reserve to offset the impact of the event or to pay for the risk response. The cost of the actual risk event is subtracted from the $250,000—let's pretend in this instance it's $90,000. Now the reserve has only $160,000 to cover the remaining risk events in the project. To monitor the contingency reserve, you'll need to see what risk events still remain in the project, determine their probabilities and impacts, and compare the remaining risk exposure to what's left in the reserve.

Examining the Results of Risk Monitoring and Control

Risk monitoring and control helps the project become more successful. Risk monitoring and control measures the planned responses to risks and creates reactions to unplanned risks. The outputs of risk monitoring and control also aim to help the project reach its objectives. Consider these outputs:

- **Work performance information** What happens in the project as a result of monitoring risks and risk responses will create work performance information. This information affects what needs to be communicated and what actions the project manager and team may take next, and it helps with project decisions.

- **Change requests**   Risk monitoring may require updates to the project's cost or schedule baseline. The update of a baseline will need a change request that follows the integrated change control process. Project management plan updates could also be an output of this process, and these updates will also require a change request. Corrective actions are taken to bring the project back into compliance with the project plan. Preventive actions are taken to bring the project back into alignment with the project management plan.

- **Project document updates**   As the project moves along and the project manager and the project team complete the risk assessments, audits, and risk reviews, they'll need to record their findings in the risk register, risk report, or both. This update may include the reevaluation of the risk's impact, probability, and expected monetary value. For all risks in the project, the risk register should record what happened with the risk event and its impact on the project. The project's assumptions log, issue log, lessons learned register, risk register, and risk report can all be updated because of this process.

- **Organizational process assets updates**   The risks from the current project can help other project managers in the future. Therefore, the project manager must work to ensure that the current risks, their anticipated impact, and their actual impact are recorded. The current risk matrix, for example, can become a risk template for other projects in the future. This is true for just about any risk document—from risk responses to the risk breakdown structure, lessons learned, and checklists.

- **Project management plan updates**   All component plans are potentially updated because some risk responses will require change requests that in turn require updates to the project management plan. As risks occur, the responses to those risks should be documented and updated in the risk response plan. Should risk rankings change during the project, the change in ranking, the logic behind the change, and the results of the risk rank change should be documented in the individual risk response plans. Risks that do not occur should be documented and considered closed in the risk response plan. Issue and assumptions logs as well as the lessons learned may also need to be updated.

Chapter Summary

All projects include some level of risk—just how much the project stakeholders are willing to accept varies by project and organization. The quantification of the stakeholders' tolerance for risk is called the utility function: the higher the project's importance, the lower the utility function. Low-priority projects are generally more likely to accept risks than those projects that have a big impact on your organization. Some organizations may define their utility function as a risk-reward ratio, where a project with a large amount of risk must equate to a large amount of reward for doing the project.

Adaptive projects embrace uncertainty, as the project requirements are likely to change throughout the project. This uncertainty, however, is risk. Agile projects try to overcome this risk challenge by taking on the product requirements that first have the most value for the project customer. Changes to the product backlog can introduce rework, scrap, and wasted efforts as these changes can interfere with project completed work. By delivering value early in the project, having a stable architecture, and paying down technical debt on a continual basis, the risk of significant interruption in the deliverables and value is diminished, but rarely eliminated.

Recall that at the launch of the risk planning process, the risk management plan is created. This plan addresses how the project's risk management approach will be directed. This plan is not specific to the risks within the project, but it creates the boundaries, expectations, and general rules for the risk management process. Once this plan is in place and everyone is in agreement to abide by it, the project-specific risk management activities can commence.

The first stop is all about risk identification. This isn't a private meeting—the project team, project manager, project sponsor, vendors, stakeholders, end users, and even customers can participate as necessary. Any project-relevant risks are documented. It's good to have a variety of participants, because their points of view can help identify risks that may have been overlooked otherwise.

As risks are identified, the project manager can use the Delphi Technique to build a consensus on which risks have the highest impact on the project. This anonymous approach enables participants to speak freely about the risks, unhindered by the opinions of other stakeholders. The comments on the identified risks are distributed to all the participants, who can comment, concur, or dismiss opinions on the identified risks. Through rounds of discussion, participants reach a consensus on the risks.

Quick, subjective, qualitative risk analysis almost always happens before quantitative analysis. Qualitative analysis qualifies the risk for more analysis or identifies the risk as a low-level risk event and adds it to the low-level risk watch list. More serious risk events and the prioritized risk events of qualitative analysis go onto quantitative analysis. Quantitative analysis provides an in-depth look at the risk events and aims to quantify the risks.

Implementing the risk responses happens as planned in the project. When a risk response happens, the response will likely take time and money from the reserves in the project for risk events. Specifically, the risk exposure for the project is tied to a dollar amount. The risk exposure is offset by a contingency reserve. Should risk events happen, monies from the contingency reserve are used to counteract the events. Ongoing monitoring of the risk events and their impact is essential to effective risk management.

Involved with all of these processes is the risk register. It's the project's journal and database of risks, their status, their impact, and any supporting detail about the risk events. As more information is gathered about the risks, the project management team updates the risk register. As the project moves past risk events, their statuses and outcomes are updated in the risk register. The risk register is part of the project management plan and becomes, once the project closes, part of organizational process assets for future projects.

Questions

1. Mary and Thomas are project managers for their organization, and they're discussing risk management and risk responses. Thomas insists that an organization should never accept a project risk, and Mary says that sometimes it's okay. They've called on you, a project management expert, to help with this decision. When is it appropriate to accept a project risk?

   A. It is never appropriate to accept a project risk.

   B. All risks must be mitigated or transferred.

   C. It is appropriate to accept a risk if the project team has never completed this type of project work before.

   D. It is appropriate if the risk is in balance with the reward.

2. Frances is the project manager of the LKJ Project. Which of the following techniques will she use to create the risk management plan?

   A. Risk tolerance

   B. Status meetings

   C. Planning meetings

   D. Variance meetings

3. You are the project manager of the GHK Project. You and the manufacturer have agreed to substitute the type of plastic used in the product to a slightly thicker grade should there be more than 7 percent error in production. The thicker plastic will cost more and will require the production to slow down, but the errors should diminish. This is an example of which of the following?

   A. Threshold

   B. Tracking

   C. Budgeting

   D. JIT manufacturing

4. You are a project manager consultant for the Allen T1 Company, and you're helping them create a risk management plan for their project management office. You're explaining the concept of risk tolerance and how it affects the risk management policies. An organization's risk tolerance is also known as what?

   A. The utility function

   B. Herzberg's Theory of Motivation

   C. Risk acceptance

   D. The risk-reward ratio

5. The customers of the project have requested additions to the project scope. The project manager notifies you that additional risk planning will need to be added to the project schedule in this predictive project. Why?

A. The risk planning should always be the same amount of time as the activities required by the scope change.

B. Risk planning should occur whenever the scope is adjusted.

C. Risk planning should occur only at the project manager's discretion.

D. The project manager is incorrect. Risk planning does not need to happen at every change in the project.

6. Jason is the project manager for his organization, and he's working with his project team to identify and analyze project risks. Jason begins to create a risk register as part of this process, but his team doesn't understand what a risk register is or its purpose. Which one of the following best describes the risk register?

A. It documents all of the outcomes of the other risk management processes.

B. It's a document that contains the initial risk identification entries.

C. It's a system that tracks all negative risks within a project.

D. It's part of the project's project management information system (PMIS) for integrated change control.

7. You are a project management consultant for the Steinberg Organization, and you're helping them categorize risks they may encounter in their projects. For starters, you identify some basic risk categories, but your client wants to see some examples of these categories. You tell them, for example, that _____ include(s) fire, theft, or injury, and offer(s) no chance for gain.

A. Business risks

B. Pure risks

C. Risk acceptance

D. Life risks

8. Complete this sentence: A project risk is a(n) _____ occurrence that can affect the project for good or bad.

A. Known

B. Potential

C. Uncertain

D. Known unknown

9. Bradley is the scrum master for his organization, and he's working with his project team to identify risks. Some of the project team members are confused as to when risk identification should happen in the project. When should risk identification happen?

    A. As early as possible in the initiation process

    B. As early as possible in the planning process

    C. Throughout the product management life cycle

    D. Throughout the project life cycle

10. You are the project manager of the KLJH Project. This project will last two years and has 30 stakeholders. How often should risk identification take place?

    A. Once at the beginning of the project

    B. Throughout the execution processes

    C. Throughout the project

    D. Once per project phase

11. Ruth is a project management expert and consultant for businesses creating project management offices. Ruth's current client wants help to improve risk identification. Which one of the following is an acceptable tool for risk identification?

    A. Decision tree analysis

    B. Decomposition of the project scope

    C. The Delphi Technique

    D. Pareto charting

12. You are the project manager for a hybrid project that will create a new and improved web site for your company. Currently, your company has more than 8 million users around the globe. You would like to poll experts within your organization with a simple, anonymous form asking about any foreseeable risks in the design, structure, and intent of the web site. With the collected information, subsequent anonymous polls are submitted to the group of experts. This is an example of _____.

    A. Risk identification

    B. A trigger

    C. An anonymous trigger

    D. The Delphi Technique

13. Alice is a project manager for her organization, and she's working with the project team to identify project risks and rank them by impact and probability. Which risk analysis technique provides the project manager with a risk ranking?

    A. Quantifiable

    B. Qualitative

C. The utility function

D. SWOT analysis

14. A table of risks, their probabilities, impacts, and numbers representing the overall risk scores is called a _____.

    A. Risk table

    B. Probability-impact matrix

    C. Quantitative matrix

    D. Qualitative matrix

15. You are presented with the following table:

Risk Event	Probability	Impact Cost/Benefit	EMV
1	.20	−4,000	
2	.50	5,000	
3	.45	−300	
4	.22	500	
5	.35	−4,500	

What is the EMV for Risk Event 3?

    A. $135

    B. −$300

    C. $45

    D. −$135

16. You are presented with the following table:

Risk Event	Probability	Impact Cost/Benefit	Ex$V
1	.35	−4,000	
2	.40	50,000	
3	.45	−300,000	
4	.30	50,000	
5	.35	−45,000	

Based on the preceding numbers, what is the amount needed for the contingency fund?

    A. Unknown with this information

    B. $249,000

    C. $117,150

    D. $15,750

17. The water sanitation project manager has determined that the risks associated with handling certain chemicals are too high. He has decided to allow someone else to complete this portion of the project. So he has outsourced the handling and installation of the chemicals and filter equipment to an experienced contractor. This is an example of which of the following?

A. Avoidance

B. Acceptance

C. Mitigation

D. Transference

18. A project manager and the project team are actively monitoring the pressure gauge on a piece of equipment. Sarah, the engineer, recommends a series of steps to be implemented should the pressure rise above 80 percent. The 80 percent mark represents what?

A. An upper control limit

B. The threshold

C. Mitigation

D. A workaround

19. You are presented with the following table:

Risk Event	Probability	Impact Cost/Benefit	Ex$V
1	.20	−4,000	
2	.50	5,000	
3	.45	−300	
4	.22	500	
5	.35	−4,500	
6			

What would Risk Event 6 be, based on the following information: Marty is 60 percent certain that he can get the facility needed for $45,000, which is $7,000 less than what was planned for.

A. .60, $45,000, $27,000

B. .60, $52,000, $31,200

C. .60, $7,000, $4,200

D. .60, −$7,000, −$4,200

20. You are the project manager for your organization, and you're working with the project team to identify the project risks, rank the risks on probability and impact, and then create a risk contingency reserve. As part of these processes, you want to explore multiple scenarios of risk events in the project, so you're utilizing different tools to analyze the project risks. Based on this information, which of the following can determine multiple scenarios, given various risks and the probability of their impact?

    A. A decision tree

    B. The Monte Carlo technique

    C. A Pareto chart

    D. A Gantt chart

Answers

   1. D. Risks that are in balance with the reward are appropriate for acceptance. Risk acceptance as a response planning technique to an identified risk is appropriate when the cost of a mitigation strategy is equal to or greater than the cost of the risk event to the project should the risk event occur. A, B, and C are all incorrect because these solutions are all false responses to risk management.

   2. C. Planning meetings are used to create the risk management plan. The project manager, project team leaders, key stakeholders, and other individuals with the power to make decisions regarding risk management attend the meetings. A, B, and D are incorrect because these choices do not fully answer the question.

   3. A. An error value of 7 percent represents the threshold the project is allowed to operate under. Should the number of errors increase beyond 7 percent, the current plastic will be substituted. B is incorrect because tracking is the documentation of a process through a system or workflow, or the documentation of events through the process. C, budgeting, is also incorrect. D is incorrect because JIT manufacturing is a scheduling approach to ordering the materials only when they are needed to keep inventory costs down.

   4. A. The utility function describes an organization's willingness to tolerate risk. B is incorrect. Herzberg's Theory of Motivation is a human resource theory that describes motivating agents for workers. C is also incorrect. Risk acceptance describes the action of allowing a risk to exist because it is deemed low in impact, low in probability, or both. D, the risk-reward ratio, is incorrect. This describes the potential reward for taking on a risk in the project.

5. **B.** When the scope has been changed, the project manager should require risk planning to analyze the changes for risks to the project's success. Predictive projects can't absorb changes as easily as adaptive projects, so additional planning is required. A is incorrect. The scope changes may not require the same amount of time as the activities needed to complete the risk planning. C is incorrect because risk planning should not occur at the project manager's discretion. Instead, it should be based on evidence within the project and the policies adopted in the risk management plan. D is also incorrect. When changes are added to the project scope, risk planning should occur.

6. **A.** The risk register documents all the outcomes of the other risk management processes. B, C, and D are all incorrect definitions of the risk register.

7. **B.** Pure risks are the risks that could threaten the safety of the individuals on the project. A is incorrect because business risks affect the financial gains or losses of a project. C and D are incorrect because these terms are not relevant.

8. **C.** Risks are not planned; they are left to chance. The accommodation and the reaction to a risk can be planned, but the event itself is not planned. If risks could be planned, Las Vegas would be out of business. A, B, and D are all incorrect because these terms do not accurately complete the sentence.

9. **D.** Risk identification is an iterative process that happens throughout the project's life cycle. Adaptive projects also participate in risk identification. A and B are both incorrect because risk identification is not limited to any one process group. C is incorrect because risk identification happens, technically, throughout the project management life cycle, which is unique to each project, and not through the product management life cycle.

10. **C.** Risk identification happens throughout the project. Recall that planning is iterative: as the project moves toward completion, new risks may surface that call for identification and planned responses. A is incorrect. Risk identification should happen throughout the project, not just at the beginning. B is incorrect because risk identification is part of planning, not execution. D is incorrect because the nature of the project phase may require and reveal more than one opportunity for risk identification.

11. **C.** The Delphi Technique, an anonymous risk identification method, is the correct answer. A is incorrect. Decision tree analysis is appropriate for calculating the expected monetary value of a decision, but not risk identification. B is incorrect because the decomposition of the project scope will result in the WBS. D is incorrect. Creating a Pareto chart is part of quality control, not risk identification.

12. **D.** An anonymous poll that enables experts to submit their opinions freely without fear of backlash is an example of the Delphi Technique. A, B, and C are incorrect. These choices do not accurately answer the question.

13. **B.** The risk ranking is based on the very high, high, medium, low, and very low attributes of the identified risks. A is incorrect because it is not relevant to the question. This answer is quantifiable, not quantitative. C is incorrect. The utility function is an organization's tolerance for risk. D, SWOT analysis, is part of risk identification.

14. **B.** A table of risks, their probabilities, and their impacts equate to risk scores and is included in a risk probability-impact matrix. A is incorrect because it does not fully answer the question. C and D are incorrect because a risk matrix can be used in both quantitative and qualitative risk analyses.

15. **D.** Risk Event 3 has a probability of 45 percent and an impact cost of –$300, which equates to –$135. A, B, and C are incorrect answers for the formula.

16. **C.** The calculated amount for each of the risk events is shown in the following table:

Risk Event	Probability	Impact Cost/Benefit	Ex$V
1	.35	–4,000	–1,400
2	.40	50,000	20,000
3	.45	–300,000	–135,000
4	.30	50,000	15,000
5	.35	–45,000	–15,750
			–117,150

A, B, and D are incorrect answers because they do not reflect the contingency amount needed for the project based on the preceding table.

17. **D.** Because the risk is not eliminated but transferred to someone else or another entity, it is considered transference. A is incorrect because the risk is not being avoided—it is just being handled by another entity. B is incorrect because the project manager has not accepted the risk, deciding instead to allow another entity to deal with it. C is incorrect. The risk has not been mitigated in the project.

18. **B.** The 80 percent mark is a threshold. A is incorrect. An upper control limit is a boundary for quality in a control chart. C is incorrect. Mitigation is a planned response should a risk event happen. D is also incorrect. A workaround is an action to bypass the risk event.

19. **C.** Marty is 60 percent certain that he can save the project $7,000. The $4,200 represents the 60 percent certainty of the savings. A, B, and D are all incorrect since these values do not reflect the potential savings of the project.

20. **B.** The Monte Carlo technique can reveal multiple scenarios and examine the risks and probability of impact. A, a decision tree, helps guide the decision-making process. C, a Pareto chart, helps identify the leading problems in a situation. D, a Gantt chart, compares the lengths of activities against a calendar in a bar chart format.

CHAPTER 12

Managing Project Procurement

In this chapter, you will

- Plan for project procurement
- Select the project vendors
- Create contracts for the project work
- Control and administer the contractual relationships
- Close out the contract with the project vendors

Projects routinely require procurements. Projects need materials, equipment, consultants, training, books, software, hardware, and lots of other stuff to help make them successful. Project procurement management is the process of purchasing the resources necessary to meet the needs of the project scope. It's also about the control and delivery of the promises made between the buyer and the seller. Adaptive projects have to consider the uncertainty of the project scope and how that may affect their procurement processes.

Procurement management also involves planning, requesting seller information, choosing a source, administering the contract, and closing out the contract. Procurement management, as far as your Project Management Professional (PMP) exams are concerned, focuses on the practices from the buyer's point of view, not the seller's. Usually. Sometimes, you may be presented as the vendor that is completing a project for your customer, the buyer. You should also recognize that the seller can be seen as a contractor, subcontractor, vendor, or supplier. In whatever situation you encounter on your exam, always do what's "fair" for both parties and what's in the best interest of the project scope.

When you're buying anything from a vendor, the buyer needs a contract. A contract becomes a key input to many of the processes within the project. The contract, above anything else, specifies the rules and agreements for the project.

Here's a neat twist: when the seller is completing obligations to supply a product, the Project Management Institute (PMI) treats those obligations as a project. In other words, if ABC Electricians is wiring a building for your company, ABC Electricians is the performing organization completing its own project. Your company becomes the customer of its project—and is, of course, a stakeholder in its project.

In the scenarios described in this chapter, the seller will be outside of the performing organization. The buyer will be managing a project and procuring resources from a vendor. However, all of the details in this chapter can be applied to internal work orders, formal agreements, and contracts between organizational units within a single entity.

Planning for Procurement

Procurement planning is the process of identifying which parts of the project should be procured from resources outside of the organization. Generally, procurement decisions are made early on in the planning processes. Think about a large multibillion-dollar project, sometimes called a *megaproject*. This type of endeavor can span countries and introduce threats and opportunities for buyers and sellers, and lots of planning and procurement experts will be needed to create contracts for such a project. Contracts can be written to address the span of the project, currency exchange rates, and pricing for bulk purchasing. If the project does span multiple countries, however, the complexity of the contracting increases, to include international legalities, management of work in different countries, regulations, and even holidays, language, and culture.

Large construction projects also address logistics and supply chain management through contracting. Procurement lead times, lead time to produce the materials needed, and then delivery of materials to job sites can become complex and will likely require expert judgment to help guide through the process, planning, and execution of the contracted work. Logistics can even include one- or two-year lead times for materials; the procurement processes could start even before the entire design of the product is complete based entirely on the early requirements in the project. Delays in delivery of materials can cost the project millions, so backup vendors and suppliers are often located to help alleviate the risk of missed opportunities. In addition, countries may require an organization to purchase materials from suppliers within the country where the project work is occurring, rather than importing all good from suppliers outside of the country.

A popular trend in public projects is transparency—not just of the cost of the project, but also of the actual project work. Right now, you could search the Web and find live webcam footage of construction projects, access job reports, and web sites dedicated to information about public projects. Webcams serve not only as good public relations by the seller for the communities and taxpayers, but can also affect claims, because the video evidence supports or denies claims of what happened on the job site.

Organizations are also contracting with sellers on a trial basis, rather than committing to a long contract on their first engagement. The trial period enables both parties to see how the other works. Sellers would contribute to a portion of the project and, based on their performance, could then go on to be awarded additional project work if their work is acceptable to the buyer.

Agile projects have considerations for procurement, too. Often in agile projects, the project team consists of both internal and contract-based developers. All members of the project team should be treated as part of the team, and the team should not succumb to an "us-against-them" mentality. Agile projects might also be treated as a part of a master service agreement, where the agile project is an addendum or supplement to the contract; this enables the change-driven approach to agile to be effective and to abide by the terms of the contract.

The Agile Manifesto clearly tells us that we value "customer collaboration over contract negotiation." The keyword here is *collaboration*; agile practitioners need to shift from the mindset of winners and losers to partnership. The partnership aspect means that we're sharing the risk and the reward of the adaptive project approach. Project managers may not be involved directly with the negotiation of the contract details, but should be involved in the give-and-take that's needed when scope obligations shift and causes a disruption in the contract agreement. Vendors need to be educated, in some instances, on the agile approach and how change is likely to occur in the project and how this change might affect their mindset and approach to the project work.

Procurement follows a logical approach, but you'll still need to plan for each step:

1. Create a statement of work or terms of reference to describe what's going to be procured.

2. Determine a high-level budget of what the procured items or services should cost.

3. In some cases, you'll advertise the procurement opportunity.

4. Determine the qualified sellers for the procurement opportunity.

5. Give the sellers the statement of work and invitation to bid documents.

6. Receive and review the sellers' proposals for technical aspects, quality, and cost.

7. Determine which seller you'll purchase from.

8. Negotiate the terms with the seller and finalize the contract.

The project schedule is also important to consider when procurement decisions are made. Consider the time between when the purchase decision is made and when the purchase actually happens. Then consider the time between when the purchase happens and when the vendor actually delivers the goods or services. In light of the schedule, it's often more practical to hire an expert to complete the work than to do the work in-house because of limited resources, the expertise of the internal resources, and the promised (or demanded) project completion date.

There are six inputs to the plan purchases and acquisitions processes:

- **Project charter** The charter defines the high-level objectives—what the project aims to accomplish, milestones, and the summary budget.

- **Business documents** A business case is often needed to ensure that what you're purchasing is in line with the project's objectives and purpose. The benefits management plan is also needed to reference when the project benefits are needed, which will determine due dates and obligations for the seller in the contract.

- **Project management plan** The project management plan is needed because the decisions made in the project may affect the procurement process, and the procurement process can alter previous plans and decisions in the project. From the project management plan, you'll pay special attention to the scope baseline as part of your procurement planning. Because the project scope statement defines the project work—and only the required work—to complete the project, it also defines the limitations of the project. You'll also reference the quality management plan and the resource management plan.

- **Project documents** Within the big category of project documents, you'll include seven documents for procurement planning:
  - **Milestone list** The project's milestone list will contribute to scheduling requirements for the seller.
  - **Project team assignments** Project team assignments are referenced as an input to determine whether the project team has the needed skills or whether a vendor should perform the activities.
  - **Requirements documentation** The requirements documentation defines the requirements for project acceptance. These documents may also contain information about the contractual and legal obligations the project must adhere to. Consider technical requirements, safety, licenses and permits, insurance, environmental, and industry-specific requirements.
  - **Requirements traceability matrix** You'll need to continue to trace the requirements to the actual deliverables, even if the deliverables are from a seller.
  - **Resource requirements** Resources include people and things. A project manager may need to hire a consultant, a contractor, or a new employee to complete the project work. Resource requirements may also include tools, equipment, and materials. All of this costs—cha-ching!—money.
  - **Risk register** In Chapter 11, I discussed the risk register: the centralized database of all project risks and their impact. The risk exposure, risk owners, and risk responses may all need to be considered for possible procurement decisions.
  - **Stakeholder register** The project manager and team will need the contact information for the stakeholders interested in the procurement decisions. Some decisions in procurement may affect the interests of stakeholders—consider costs, materials, schedules, and contractual obligations.
- **Enterprise environmental factors** These are the conditions of the marketplace—the available products, services, and results; the availability of the things you'd like to purchase; and the terms and conditions of the purchase agreement. Enterprise environmental factors also include the seller's past experience, regulatory requirements, legal advice for the purchasing, and any contract management systems your organization uses.
- **Organizational process assets** When it comes to purchases, you likely have rules and procedures unique to your organization regarding how you can purchase resources for your project. The internal rules in your organization police how the project manager may purchase, negotiate, agree to contractual obligations, and pay the vendor. (If you don't have these rules and policies in your organization, allow me to offer my services directly to you. Sign on the dotted line.)

Considering Agile Agreements

Just because we value collaboration over contract negotiation in adaptive projects doesn't mean we don't negotiate. We negotiate with both parties in mind, not just what's good for the performing organization and certainly not with the winner-loser mindset. There are a few considerations for this approach you should know for your PMP exam:

- **Multitiered structures in agreements**   Allow things such as warranties, arbitration, and claim resolution to be put into a master agreement for the project. Items that may change due to the changing project, such as service rates and resources needed, can be detailed in a schedule of services. Finally, the agile components, such as the project scope of work, schedule, and budget, can be entered into a statement of work. This approach gives flexibility for both parties and sets some boundaries for the project.

- **Emphasize value delivered**   Rather than structuring contracts on specific milestones and deliverables that could change in the project, the negotiation can center on value-driven items in the spirit of agile.

- **Fixed-price increments**   By assigning value to user stories, the contract can be priced by user story points completed. This allows the customer more control over where the procurement funds are spent and allows the vendor flexibility to avoid the risk of quoting a fixed fee for the entire project, which is likely to change.

- **Not-to-exceed limitations**   With this approach, a maximum amount of funds could be set aside for procured work with the understanding the product backlog may change, but the vendor is selling hours of work up to a predefined limited amount. Both parties share the risk in this equitable approach.

- **Graduated time and materials**   This approach offers the vendor an incentive for delivering the product earlier than what was anticipated and offers a penalty fee, in the form of a lower cost per hour rate, when the project is completed later than what was anticipated.

- **Early cancellation option**   If the vendor reaches 50 percent completion, for example, and the customer determines the balance of the project is no longer needed, the organization can pay a settlement fee for less than the balance due on the project. The organization shares the risk of paying for more than the work delivered, but the vendor shares the risk of earning income for work it didn't have to do.

- **Dynamic scope option**   For fixed-fee contracts, the vendor will allow the organization to enter additional work items at predefined points in the project. This allows the customer to change the project scope in an agile format but limits the vendor from doing more work than what it has agreed to do for the fixed fee.

- **Team augmentation**   The vendor places its employees in the organization as part of the agile project team and sells the time utilized by the organization for the labor on the team. This gives the organization the flexibility to lead agile projects, and it ensures the vendor profitability for its employees placed as contractors on the project team.

PART II

- **Full-service suppliers**   It's often tempting for an organization to hire multiple vendors to contribute to a project, but this leads to silos and walls within the project. Vendors will only want to contribute to the project for what they've been hired to do rather than serve as generalizing specialists and take on different roles. Caution must be used when bringing multiple vendors into an agile project to ensure that everyone involved is working together for the business value of the project.

 VIDEO   For a more detailed explanation, watch the *Agile Procurement Decisions* video now.

Determining the Contract Type

There are multiple types of contracts when it comes to procurement. The project work, the market, and the nature of the purchase determine the contract type. Here are some general rules that PMP exam candidates, and project managers, should know:

- A *contract* is a formal agreement between the buyer and the seller. Contracts can be oral or written—although written is preferred.
- The United States backs all contracts through the court system.
- Contracts should clearly state all requirements for product acceptance.
- Any changes to the contract must be formally approved, controlled, and documented.
- A contract is not fulfilled until all of its requirements are met.
- Contracts can be used as a risk mitigation tool, as in transferring the risk. All contracts have some level of risk; depending on the contract type, the risk can be transferred to the seller. If a risk response strategy is to transfer, risks associated with procurement are considered secondary risks and must go through the risk management process.
- There are legal requirements governing contracts. For a contract to be valid, it must meet the following requirements:
  - Contain an offer
  - Be accepted
  - Provide for a consideration (payment)
  - Be for a legal purpose
  - Be executed by someone with the capacity and authority
- The terms and conditions of the contract should define breaches, copyrights, intellectual rights, and force majeure.

 EXAM TIP   *Force majeure* is a powerful and unexpected event, such as a hurricane or other natural disaster.

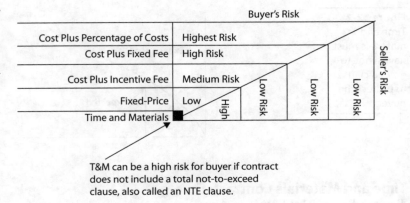

Figure 12-1
Fixed-price
contracts transfer
risk to the seller.

T&M can be a high risk for buyer if contract
does not include a total not-to-exceed
clause, also called an NTE clause.

Fixed-Price Contracts

These contracts must clearly define the requirements the vendor is to provide. They may also provide incentives for meeting or exceeding contract requirements—such as meeting deadlines—and require the seller to assume the risk of cost overruns, as Figure 12-1 demonstrates.

Cost-Reimbursable Contracts

These contract types pay the seller for the product. The payment to the seller includes a profit margin—the difference between the actual costs of the product and the sales amount. The actual costs of the product fall into two categories:

- **Direct costs**   Costs incurred by the project for the project to exist. Examples include the equipment needed to complete the project work, the salaries of the project team, and other expenses tied directly to the project's existence.

- **Indirect costs**   Costs attributed to the cost of doing business. Examples include utilities, office space, and other overhead costs.

Cost-reimbursable contracts require the buyer to assume the risk of cost overruns. There are three types of cost-reimbursable contracts:

- Cost plus fixed fee
- Cost plus percentage of costs
- Cost plus incentive fee

EXAM TIP   Cost plus percentage of costs is not used often—and isn't allowed in many organizations. Don't plan on seeing this contract type on your exam.

Figure 12-2
Time and
materials must
have a not-to-
exceed clause
to protect the
buyer.

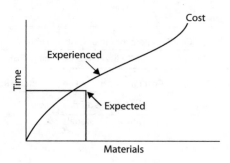

Time and Materials Contracts

Time and materials (T&M) contracts are sometimes called *unit price contracts*. They are ideal when an organization contracts out a small project or when smaller amounts of work within a larger project are to be completed by a vendor. T&M contracts, however, can grow dangerously out of control as more work is assigned to the seller. Although a T&M contract is easy to create and administer, it can pose a threat to the buyer if a "not-to-exceed" clause is not included in the contract. A not-to-exceed clause states the maximum amount of monies the vendor can bill for the contracted work. Figure 12-2 is an example of how T&M contracts can pose a risk for the buyer.

Understanding Contract Types

On the PMP examination, you can anticipate a few questions on contract types. Familiarize yourself with Table 12-1.

Contract Type	Acronym	Attribute	Risk Issues
Cost plus fixed fee	CPFF	Actual costs plus profit margin for the seller.	Cost overruns represent risk to the buyer.
Cost plus percentage of cost	CPPC	Actual costs plus profit margin for the seller.	Cost overruns represent risk to the buyer. This is the most dangerous contract type for the buyer.
Cost plus incentive fee	CPIF	Actual costs plus profit margin for the seller.	Cost overruns represent risk to the buyer.
Cost plus award fee	CPAF	Actual costs plus a buyer-determined award for completing the project.	Award is at the discretion of the buyer, and the seller may be disappointed in the award fee.
Fixed-price	FP	Agreed price for a contracted product. Can include incentives for the seller.	Seller assumes risk.
Lump-sum	LS	Agreed price for a contracted product. Can include incentives for the seller.	Seller assumes risk.

Table 12-1 Common Contract Types

Contract Type	Acronym	Attribute	Risk Issues
Firm fixed-price	FFP	Agreed price for a contracted product.	Seller assumes risk.
Fixed-price incentive fee	FPIF	Agreed price for a contracted product. Can include incentives for the seller.	Seller assumes risk.
Fixed-price with economic price adjustments	FP-EPA	Mostly used for long-term contracts. This fixed-price contract has provisions for economic adjustments, such as inflation, cost increases, or regulatory cost increases. These typically refer to a financial index as a guide for approved cost increases.	Changes in agreed-upon provisions, such as the cost of materials or inflation, can drive up the overall costs of the project. There is uncertainty in this longer-term contractual agreement, and uncertainty brings risk.
Time and materials	T&M	Price assigned for the time and materials provided by the seller.	Contracts without not-to-exceed clauses can lead to cost overruns.
Unit price	UP	Price assigned for a measurable unit of product or time. (For example, $130 for an engineer's time on the project.)	Risk varies with the product. Time represents the biggest risk if the amount needed is not specified in the contract.

Table 12-1   Common Contract Types (*Continued*)

EXAM TIP   The contractual relationship between the buyer and the seller is often considered confidential. The terms, conditions, and private nature of a contractual relationship are known as *privity*.

Using the Procurement Planning Tools

Procurement planning should be done early in the planning processes, with certain exceptions. As needs arise, as project conditions change, or as other circumstances demand, procurement planning may be required throughout the project. Whenever procurement planning happens early in the project, as preferred, or later in the project, as needed, a logical approach to securing the proper resources is necessitated.

Determining to Make or Buy

The decision to make or buy a product is a fundamental aspect of project management and is a data analysis tool and technique. In some conditions, it is more cost-effective to buy; in others, it makes more sense to create an in-house solution. The make-or-buy analysis should be made in the initial scope definition to determine whether the entire project should be completed in-house or procured. As the project evolves, additional make-or-buy decisions are often needed.

Figure 12-3
Project managers need to know the make-or-buy process.

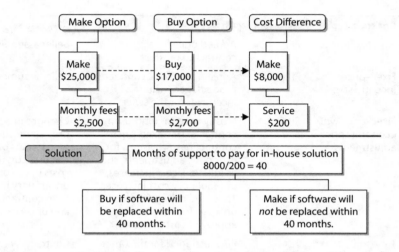

 VIDEO For a more detailed explanation, watch the *Make or Buy Decisions* video now.

The initial costs of the solution for the in-house or procured product must be considered, but so, too, must the ongoing expenses of the solutions. For example, a company may elect to lease a piece of equipment. The ongoing expense of leasing the piece of equipment should be weighed against the expected ongoing expense of purchasing the equipment and the monthly costs to maintain, insure, and manage the equipment.

For example, Figure 12-3 shows the mathematical approach to determining whether it is better to create a software program in-house or to buy one from a software company. The in-house solution will cost your company $25,000 to create your own software package and, based on historical information, another $2,500 per month to maintain it.

The development company has a solution that will cost your company $17,000 to purchase, but the development company requires a maintenance plan for each software program installed, which will cost your company $2,700 per month. The difference between making the software and buying it is $8,000. The difference between supporting the software the organization has made and allowing the external company to support their software is only $200 per month.

The $200 per month is divided into the difference between creating the software internally and buying it—which is $8,000 divided by $200, or 40 months. If the software is to be replaced within 40 months, the company should buy the software. If the software will not be replaced within 40 months, it should build the software.

There are multiple reasons why an organization may choose to make or buy. Table 12-2 provides some common reasons for making and buying.

Reasons to Make	Reasons to Buy
Less costly	Less costly
Can use in-house skills	In-house skills are not available or don't exist
Can control the work	Small volume of work
Can control intellectual property	More efficient
Learn new skills	Transfer risks
Available staff	Available vendor
Can focus on core project work	Project team can focus on other work items

Table 12-2   Common Reasons to Make or Buy Software

EXAM TIP   You may be presented with one or two questions on make-or-buy analysis. In the preceding example, and on the exam, you won't be confronted with the tax benefits of make or buy—although in your job as a project manager, you may be. For the exam, focus on determining which is the most cost-effective, fair solution. Note that hiring vendors to complete the project work in agile projects means the knowledge gained by doing the work leaves with the vendor.

Examining the Results of Procurement Planning

The procurement planning process should happen early in the planning processes. The outputs of procurement planning enable the project manager and the project team to proceed with confidence in the procuring of products and services needed to complete the project successfully. If the project team determines early in the project that there's no need for procurements, then, obviously, the remaining procurement processes are unnecessary for the project.

The Procurement Management Plan

This subsidiary project plan documents the decisions made in the procurement planning processes and specifies how the remaining procurement activities will be managed. The plan details the following:

- Timeline for procurement activities, including time for procurement and vendor delivery
- Contract management metrics and strategy
- Roles and responsibilities for the parties involved in the procurement processes, including stakeholders, the vendors, the project team, procurement officers, and the project manager
- Requirements for performance bonds, vendor insurance, legal jurisdiction, payment terms, and agreed currency
- How vendors will be selected
- The type of contracts to be used

- The process of independent estimating
- The risk management approach for contracted work
- Identification of an approved vendors list (if appropriate according to organizational requirements)
- The procurement forms, such as contracts, the project team is required to use
- How multiple vendors will be managed to supply their contracted products

Using the Procurement Statement of Work

In the procurement statement of work (SOW), the seller fully describes the work to be completed and/or the product to be supplied. The SOW becomes part of the contract between the buyer and the seller. It is typically created as part of the procurement planning process, and it enables the seller to determine whether they can meet the written requirements of the SOW.

Particular industries have different assumptions about what constitutes an SOW. What one industry calls an SOW may be called a statement of objectives (SOO) in another. An SOO is a document describing a problem to be solved by the seller. In procurement management, you may see terms of reference to identify the procured tasks for the seller, the standards, approval requirements, schedule for the seller, and what the seller must submit to the buyer. The terms of reference statement is similar to the SOW but includes more about both parties agreeing to the particulars of the contracted work.

 EXAM TIP The SOW can be updated as the project moves through negotiations with the vendor or as more details about the purchase become available.

Creating the Procurement Documents

The primary outputs of the plan-contracting process are the procurement documents. These documents guide the relationship between the buyer and the seller. Communication between the buyer and the seller should always be specific as to the requirements and expectations of the seller. In initial communications, especially when requesting a price or proposal, the buyer should include the contract statement of work, relevant specifications, and, if necessary, any nondisclosure agreements (NDAs). Requests from buyers to sellers should be specific enough to give the seller a clear idea of what the buyer is requesting, but general enough to enable the seller to provide viable alternatives.

Here are some specific documents the project manager—and the PMP candidate—should be familiar with:

- **Invitation for bid (IFB)**   From buyer to seller. Requests that the seller provide an estimate for the procured product or service.

- **Request for quote (RFQ)**   From buyer to seller. Requests that the seller provide a price for the procured product or service.

- **Request for proposal (RFP)**   From buyer to seller. Requests that the seller provide a proposal to complete the procured work or to provide the procured product.

- **Purchase order (PO)**   From buyer to seller. A form of unilateral contract that the buyer provides to the vendor that shows that the purchase has been approved by the buyer's organization.

- **Request for information (RFI)**   From buyer to seller. Requests that the seller provide more information about the seller's products and/or services.

- **Bid**   From seller to buyer. Price is the determining factor in the decision-making process.

- **Quotation**   From seller to buyer. Statement of price for the procured product or service. Price is the determining factor in the decision-making process.

- **Proposal**   From seller to buyer. Other factors, such as skill sets, reputation, or ideas for the project solution, may be included and used in the decision-making process.

 EXAM COACH   Obviously, you've made a financial commitment to pass the PMP, but have you made a contract with yourself? Have you set the terms of your study efforts, your positive outlook for passing the exam, and the reward you'll receive for a passing score? Make a deal with yourself for passing your PMI exam—you deserve it!

Creating Source Selection Criteria

Another output of the plan-contracting process is the evaluation criteria. This is used to rate and score proposals from the sellers. In some instances, such as with a bid or quote, the evaluation criteria are focused just on the price the seller offers. In other instances, such as a proposal, the evaluation criteria can be multiple values: experience, references, certifications, and more. The project management team can use any combination of the following questions to help determine which vendor should be selected to supply the project's procurement needs:

- Does the vendor understand the project needs?

- What's the vendor's experience with adaptive project management?

- What's the overall cost of the project?

- What's the life-cycle cost of the deliverable?

- Does the seller have the technical capability to complete the deliverable?

- What's the vendor's technical approach to the project's needs?

- What's the vendor's management approach to creating the deliverable?

- Does the seller have the financial backing to deliver as promised?

- Will the vendor have sustained capacity and interest in the project's deliverable for future assignments?

- What is the vendor's business model? Is it a small business, woman-owned, or small disadvantaged business that may qualify for the contract as defined in some governmental agencies?

- Can the vendor provide references?
- Who retains the intellectual and proprietary property rights?

These questions—and others—can help the project management team make the best decision when it comes to choosing which vendor should support the project. For your PMP exam, always choose the vendor that offers the best solution for the project.

Conducting Procurements

Once the plan-contracting process has been completed, you can begin the actual process of asking the sellers to participate. Fortunately, the sellers, not the buyers, perform most of the activity in this process—usually at no additional cost to the project. The sellers are busy trying to win the business. Both parties should work together to share the risk and reward of the project. There are six inputs to the conduct procurement process:

- **Project management plan**   From the project management plan, you'll reference the scope management plan, requirements management plan, communications management plan, risk management plan, procurement management plan, configuration management plan, and the cost baseline. All of the project management plan components will affect procurement.

- **Project documents**   The lessons learned register, project schedule, requirements documentation, risk register, and stakeholder register are all inputs for conducting procurements.

- **Procurement documents**   These are created in plan-contracting processes. These are the invitation for bid (IFB), request for proposal (RFP), and request for quote (RFQ) documents. You can also include any independent cost estimates and the source selection criteria.

- **Seller proposals**   Vendors will provide the project manager a response to an IFB, RFP, or RFQ. Proposals will undergo an evaluation to determine how well the proposals satisfy the procurement needs of the organization.

- **Enterprise environmental factors**   Laws and regulations are enterprise environmental factors that can affect the procurement processes. Other enterprise environmental factors to consider are the economic conditions, the marketplace conditions, past experiences with the seller, other agreements in place, and any contract management systems.

- **Organizational process assets**   Yes, you've seen organizational process assets throughout the project, but the specific asset you're considering is a history of qualified sellers. A list of qualified sellers (also preferred sellers or approved sellers) generally includes contact information, history of past experience with the seller, and other pertinent information. In addition to the internal qualified seller list, other resources can help you determine which sellers may qualify for the proposed work, including Internet resources, industry directories, trade associations, and so on.

Hosting a Bidder Conference

Buy some donuts and make the coffee—all your bidders are coming over! A bidder conference, also called a *contractor conference* or *vendor conference*, is a meeting with prospective sellers to ensure that all sellers have a clear understanding of the product or service to be procured and are all on equal footing. Bidder conferences enable sellers to query the buyer on the details of the project statement of work to help ensure that their proposals are adequate and appropriate for the proposed agreement. At this point in the process, all sellers are considered equal.

Advertising for Sellers

Have you ever opened your Sunday newspaper and checked out the classifieds? Chances are, you've seen classified ads announcing opportunities for organizations to bid on upcoming projects. That's the idea behind this tool and technique. These advertisements usually run in newspapers or trade journals specific to the industry of the organization. Some government agencies require advertisements inviting sellers to solicit the project work, attend a bidder conference, or present a proposal for the described work.

Creating a Qualified Sellers List

One of the inputs to this process is to rely on your organizational process assets' qualified sellers list. If the organization doesn't have such a list, the project management team can start creating one. The qualified sellers list can be created through trade magazines, interviews, the Internet, interviews with past customers, and even site visits. It's a bunch of fun!

Selecting a Seller

Once the sellers have presented their proposals, bids, or quotes (depending on what the buyer requested), you can examine their documents to determine which sellers are the best choices for the project work. In many instances, price may be the predominant factor for choosing a particular seller—but not always. Other factors besides price may also be taken into consideration:

- *The cost of an item may not reflect the true cost to the performing organization if the item cannot be delivered in a timely manner.* If a seller promises to have a product on site by a specific date and fails to do so, the project can be delayed, costing the organization thousands—or more—in losses.

- *Proposals can be separated into two categories: technical and commercial.* The technical category describes the approach and methodology to complete the project work. The commercial category delves into the price to complete the project work. An evaluation takes into consideration both categories to determine the best choice for the project.

- *Critical, high-priority projects may rely on multiple sellers to complete the project work.* This redundancy can balance risk, cost, and opportunity among multiple vendors.

- *Adaptive projects are likely to change in scope, and the vendor must understand the agile approach.* Vendors may not be aware of the project management approach, and that can disrupt the contracted services and expectations of both parties.

Examining Vendor Responses

The *procurement document package* is a collection of documents prepared by the buyer and sent to each of the vendors that may participate in the procurement process. The procurement document package defines the requirements of the purchase, specifies the needs, and describes how the vendor should respond.

The end result of requesting a seller response is, as expected, a collection of proposals, bids, or quotes, depending on what the buyer asked for. These documents indicate the sellers' abilities and preparedness to complete the project work. The proposals should be in alignment with the stated expectations of the buyer, and they may be presented orally, electronically, or in hard-copy format. Of course, the relationship between the buyer and seller—and the type of information being shared—will determine which modality is the best choice of communication.

Choosing the Seller

For the performing organization to finalize the process of selecting a vendor, there must first be eligible sellers. Assuming more than one seller can satisfy the demands of the project, the project manager can rely on eight tools and techniques:

- **Weighting system** A weighting system takes out the personal preferences of the decision-maker in the organization to ensure that the best seller is awarded the contract. A weighting system creates a matrix, as shown in Figure 12-4. Weights are assigned to the values of the proposals, and each proposal is scored. Because the weights are determined before reviewing the proposals, the process is guaranteed to be free of personal preferences and bias. The seller with the highest score is awarded the contract.

| Possible Score | 20 | 20 | 15 | 10 | 10 | 5 | 20 | 100 |
Value	Experience	Certifications	Level IV Engineers	Security Clearance	Start Date	Waste Removal	Price	Total Score
ABC Constructions	15	20	7	10	10	5	12	79
Allen Builders	12	20	12	10	10	0	10	74
FRJ Construction	18	20	11	0	10	5	18	82
Howe & Who Construction	18	15	5	0	5	5	15	73
Martin & Martin	9	20	13	10	5	0	18	65
Ralph Engineers	15	8	8	0	10	5	17	73

Figure 12-4 A weighting system scores values to the seller's ability to deliver goods or services.

- **Independent estimates**   These estimates are often referred to as *should/cost* estimates. These estimates are created by either the performing organization or outside experts to predict what the cost of the procured product should be. If there is a significant difference between what the organization has predicted and what the sellers have proposed, either the statement of work was inadequate or the sellers have misunderstood the requirements.

- **Screening system**   A screening system is a tool that filters or screens out vendors that don't qualify for the contract. For example, the project manager could say that only vendors that have built eight bridges in Utah can qualify for the contract. Sellers that don't meet the requirements are removed from the selection process, and their proposals are not considered.

- **Contract negotiation**   The performing organization creates an offer, and the seller considers the offer. The contract negotiation process is an activity to create a fair price for the work the seller is to complete. The performing organization and the seller must agree on the expectations, requirements, authorities, terms, technical and business management approaches, price, and any other pertinent factors covered within and by the contract prior to signing the contract.

- **Seller rating systems**   Seller rating systems are used by organizations to rate prior experience with each vendor that it has worked with in the past. The seller rating system can track performance, quality ratings, delivery, and even contract compliance. The project manager of the current project can reference this internal seller rating system to determine the expectations of working with a vendor based on the vendor's past performance.

- **Expert judgment**   Sometimes, the project manager isn't the best person to make a decision as to which vendor should be selected. Consider very large projects, such as building a new skyscraper. The project manager likely wouldn't be the only person involved in making the procurement decision, but rather a team comprising different experts would contribute to the decision.

- **Proposal evaluation techniques**   This big bucket of tools and techniques can include objective and subjective considerations from experts within the organization, weighting systems, multiple reviewers, scoring systems, screening systems—just about any source-selection technique that the project management team feels like using. The point is that there are many different approaches to compare and contrast proposals, so the project management team should use all of the appropriate techniques available to make the best decision for the good of the project.

- **Internet search**   No doubt the Internet has changed the way companies buy and sell goods and services. Many commercially available goods can be located online at a guaranteed fixed price for organizations. However, complex goods and services often can't use the Internet for cost estimating, budgeting, and exact pricing. The Internet can be used as a tool for procurement, but it's often just the start of the buyer–seller communication process.

Examining the Results of Seller Selection

The primary output, other than the selected seller, of the selecting seller process is a contract between the buyer and the seller. A contract is a legally binding agreement between the buyer and seller in which the seller provides the described product and the buyer agrees to pay for the product. Contracts are known by many names:

- Agreement
- Subcontract
- Purchase order
- Memorandum of understanding

 EXAM TIP A *letter of intent* is not a contract, but a letter stating that the buyer is intending to create a contractual relationship with the seller. A *letter contract* is a contract that may be used when the work needs to start immediately. A letter contract is often considered a "stopgap" solution in procurement.

Contracts have to be signed by a person with the power to authorize the requirements and payment specified in the contract. This role is called the *delegation of procurement authority*. Whether this person is the project manager depends on the procurement policies of the performing organization.

In some organizations, all contracts flow through centralized contracting. Centralized contracting requires all contracts for all projects to be approved through a central unit within the performing organization. Other organizations use a decentralized contracting approach, which assigns a contract administrator or contract officer to the project.

PMP candidates should also be familiar with several other outputs of the conduct procurement process:

- **Project management plan updates**   When dealing with large, unwieldy contracts, you may need to create a new subsidiary management plan. This subsidiary plan, the contract management plan, defines how the contract will be administered through the duration of the project. The contract may cause integration management to kick in. Changes to the procurement process, or changes to the procured item itself, may cause ripples in the procurement management plan, which also means updates to the project management plan.

- **Project document updates**   The procurement process can create a need for the project documents to be updated. You may need to update the requirements documentation and the associated requirement traceability matrix. Based on the details of the contract type selected, new risks may be introduced into the project, so the risk register and risk response plans may also need to be updated.

- **Requirements traceability matrix**   Procurement can cause the RTM to be updated to reflect the procurement deliverables.

- **Resource calendars**   The demand and availability of resources related to the contracted decision should be documented. This documentation includes when resources are active in the project and when they're not needed and can be utilized elsewhere.

- **Contract award**   The vendor that is selected for the project work is awarded the project contract. The contract includes the statement of work, schedule, performance requirements of the vendor, seller requirements, pricing, payment obligations, warranty of the work, and any terms for penalties. Some contracts define termination and alternative dispute resolution should there be claims or should the need diminish for the goods and services the contract provides.

- **Stakeholder register**   Sellers become stakeholders of the project, so it stands to reason that the stakeholder register should also be updated.

Controlling Project Procurements

Controlling procurements is the process of ensuring that both the buyer and the seller live up to the agreements in the contract. The project manager and the contract administrator must work together to make certain the seller meets their obligations, just as the vendor will ensure that the buyer lives up to their agreements as well. If either party does not fulfill its contractual requirements, legal remedies may ultimately be pursued.

 EXAM TIP   Because of the legalities associated with the contract, contract administration is often handled as an operation of the organization rather than as part of project management.

Another aspect of contract administration, especially on larger projects with multiple sellers providing various products, is the coordination between the contractors. The project manager or contract officer schedules and confirms the performance of the sellers so that the deliverables, schedule, and performance of a contractor do not infringe or adversely affect the performance of another contractor.

Within the contract must be the terms for payment. Typically, the performance and progress of the contractor is directly linked to payments it receives. The project manager must track performance and quality to approve or decline payment as needed. The contract should define the metrics for acceptance to avoid disagreements on performance.

This process is integrated into the project's control as a whole. You will likely perform procurement control along with other project management control processes to ensure that what happens in procurement doesn't adversely affect the remainder of the project. You'll direct and manage the procurement work and do quality control on what the vendor provides. You'll also need to perform integrated change control on any of the changes the procurement may bring about—or that get introduced to the project that could affect the contracted work. Finally, you will always be looking to control the risks associated with the procured work.

Completing the Procurement Control Process

The actual process of completing procurement control relies heavily on communication between the project manager, the contract officer, and the seller. You'll likely utilize expert judgment to help with laws and regulations and sometimes for insight to the application area the contract is addressing. The communications plan may have considerations for how and when the communication between the buyer and seller should take place and what the purpose of the communication should be. Several tools and techniques can assist the project management team with the contract administration process:

- **Claims administration** Uh-oh! Claims are disagreements between the buyer and the seller, usually centering on a change, who made the change, and even whether a change has occurred. Claims, also called disputes and appeals, are monitored and controlled through the project in accordance with the contract terms. The contract can, and usually does, determine the path to resolution, which may include arbitration or litigation to resolve the claims between the buyer and seller. No fun. Alternative dispute resolution is an agreed-upon approach to work out the claim without, usually, involving the expense of lawyers and court cases.

- **Procurement performance reviews** The buyer has to confirm that the seller is living up to the terms of the contract. Specifically, the buyer reviews the quality of what the vendor has created, the cost of what's been created, and whether the vendor is on schedule and in alignment with the agreement and the project scope. All of these items are documented in the terms of the contract—no fudging from the vendors is allowed.

- **Performance reporting** Performance reporting is the communication between the project manager and management on how the seller is performing under the guidelines in the contract. This is part of communications and should be documented within the communications management plan. The buyer has to confirm that the vendor is living up to the terms of the contract.

- **Contract change control system** The contract change control system defines the procedures for how the contract may be changed. The process for changing the contract includes the forms, documented communications, dispute resolution procedures, tracking methods, the procedures for getting the changes approved within the performing organization, and the conditions within the project, business, or marketplace that justify the need for the change. The system is part of integrated change control.

- **Inspections and audits** If you hired an architect to build your dream home, would you wait until the house is completely built before inspecting the work? Of course not. You'd have to, and likely want to, perform periodic inspections, audits, and walkthroughs of the home as it's under construction. The same is true in project management: the buyer completes inspections and audits to confirm that the seller is abiding by the contracted requirements for the project.

PART II

 EXAM TIP Who's administering a contract manually? Information technology (IT) can help the project manager, the project management team, and the vendor efficiently abide by the terms of the contract and keep the project moving forward.

Reviewing the Results of Procurement Control

Procurement control calls for communication between the seller and buyer, the project manager and the vendor, and the stakeholders. There must be significant documentation of the agreement between the buyer and the seller before the procured work begins. Once the procured work, service, or product has been delivered from the seller to the buyer, there must be agreement that the delivery is in alignment with the original agreement. The procurement control process has five outputs:

- **Work performance information** Performance reporting is the communication between the project manager and management on how the seller is performing under the guidelines in the contract. This is part of communications and should be documented within the communications management plan. The buyer has to confirm that the vendor is living up to the terms of the contract. Specifically, the buyer reviews the quality of what the vendor has created, the cost of what's been created, and whether the vendor is on schedule. All of these items are documented in the terms of the contract—no fudging from the vendors is allowed. Performance reviews can be an input to future procurement decisions.

- **Change requests** Changes to the project's scope, costs, or schedule can directly influence the contracted work between the buyer and the seller. Changes that affect the project contracts must flow through the contract change control system. Recall that the contract change control system defines the procedures for how the contract may be changed. The process for changing the contract includes the forms, documented communications, tracking methods, dispute resolution procedures, the procedures for getting the changes approved within the performing organization, and the conditions within the project, business, or marketplace that justify the need for the change. The system is part of integrated change control. The vendor may not be obligated to accept the changes to the contract, and this can create claims and disputes between the vendor and the buyer.

- **Project management plan updates** You may need to update the project management plan based on the outcomes of controlling procurement. For example, the project's procurement management plan could be updated based on procurement decisions. You may also need to update the schedule baseline based on the abilities of vendors to deliver the goods and services requested.

- **Project document updates** Any procurement documentation should be included as part of the project's supporting detail and will become part of organizational process assets. Change requests related to the procured goods and services, technical specifications from the vendor, performance reports, and other communications are all included as part of project documentation.

- **Organizational process assets updates** All procurement communications, outcomes of performance reporting, outcomes of inspections and audits, vendor invoices, and any documentation created and submitted by the vendor will become part of the project's archive and is technically an update to the organizational process assets.

Performing Contract Closure

Contract closure is analogous to administrative closure. Its purpose is to confirm that the obligations of the contract were met as expected. The project manager, the customer, key stakeholders, and, in some instances, the seller, may finalize product verification together to confirm that the contract has been completed.

Contract closure can also be linked to administrative closure, because it is the process of confirming that the work was finished. If the contract was terminated, contract closure is reviewed, and the contract is considered closed because of the termination. The project records should be updated to reflect the contract closure and the acceptance of the work or product.

Auditing the Procurement Process

The successes and failures within the procurement process of the project are reviewed from the procurement planning stage through to contract closure. The intent of the audit is to learn what worked and what didn't during the procurement processes. This knowledge can then be applied to other areas within the current project and to other projects within the performing organization.

Negotiating Settlements

Before the contract can be officially closed, all issues, disputes, claims, and disagreements must be settled between the buyer and the seller. The terms of the contract override all other agreements, so this is one of the first things the two parties must agree upon (again!). The goal is to settle the disagreement in a fair manner, usually through alternative dispute resolution, which can include mediation and arbitration. If the buyer and seller cannot agree upon a settlement to an issue, then the claim is escalated to litigation and the court system. Almost all contracts define the court where the claim and associated lawsuit will be filed.

Completing Contract Closure

Once the deliverables have been accepted and the contract has been closed, it's essential that you collect all of the contract information and record it in the contract file. A *contract file* is a complete indexed set of records of the procurement process and is incorporated into the administrative closure process. These records include financial information as well as information on the performance and acceptance of the procured work.

Assuming the procured work is acceptable and meets the requirements of the contract, the contract can be closed. The formal closure of a project comes in a written notice from the contract officer to the seller. The notice informs the seller that the work is acceptable and that the contract is considered closed. The formal closure process may vary according to the size of the project. The requirements for contract closure should be documented within the contract.

Chapter Summary

Projects can buy or build as much as they need in order to be successful. Part of the procurement process is deciding what needs to be procured. The WBS and the project scope can help the project management team determine what things or services need to be procured in order for the project to be completed. Once the decision of what needs to be procured is made, the project manager can, often with the help of expert judgment, ask the vendors for bids, quotes, or proposals based on the details of the project manager's SOW.

Vendors may need to attend a bidder conference to get clarification on the SOW—plus, it helps to chat with the project manager to get a clear understanding of what the project calls for. Vendors will then provide their quotes, bids, or proposals, according to what the project manager has requested. Then they'll hope they win the gig.

Adaptive projects and procurement can be tricky as the project's product is likely to change and evolve as the project moves forward. The organization and the vendor need to work together to identify the approach, the terms of the contract, and what changes to the product will do to the cost and expectations of both parties. Collaboration is crucial for vendors and organization to work together and share the risk and reward of the project.

Once the project manager's organization has made the decision as to what vendor will be providing the service, the contract is issued. Now both parties have to live up to the terms and conditions of the contract. Of course, if there are issues that escalate during contract administration, there can be—gulp!—claims between the buyer and seller.

The project manager and the vendor should work together for the best interest of the project. During contract closure, the buyer inspects the project work and confirms that the vendor delivered and performed according to the contract terms. Then everyone lives happily ever after.

Case Study: Litke Greenhouse and Nursery Procurement Processes

Litke Greenhouse and Nursery is an agricultural supplier in Knoxville, Tennessee. The firm specializes in commercial and home-based plants, ranging from orchids and roses, to dogwood and jasmine trees. Ros Litke, owner, sponsored a project to create a year-round garden and showcase that would offer several features:

- A greenhouse that could hold plants
- An educational facility for classes and seminars
- A marketing piece that could gain national attention
- A tourist destination for gardeners, photographers, and local residents

The project scope called for the design and installation of a large greenhouse like no other facility in the Southeast. The greenhouse simulates a lush Smoky Mountain cove with adult trees, younger saplings, indigenous plants, a water feature with rainbow trout, and a limited number of birds. The project was dubbed "Snapshot of East Tennessee" because it reflected the ideal East Tennessee environment.

Planning for Procurement

Ros Litke, the project sponsor, named Jen Stein as the project manager and Ty Koenig as the project manager assistant. When Jen, Ty, and the project team planned this project, they identified which deliverables in the WBS they would be able to create in-house and which items needed to be procured. The internal team was qualified to complete the placement of the plants, the design of the garden environment, and the installation of the water feature. The deliverables in the WBS that required procurement included the following:

- The architectural design and construction of the greenhouse
- The fish and wildlife for the greenhouse
- The marketing process to inform the public of the final product

The project team, Jen, and Ty determined that Litke Greenhouse and Nursery would need to procure these resources because the internal talent did not have the skillsets to complete the required work. In addition, the fish and birds required for the project would need to come from a supplier. Although Litke Greenhouse and Nursery does have a full-time marketing manager, it was determined that this individual, Jeff Honeycutt, did not have the time to dedicate to the complete campaign. In addition, Jeff did not have the skills needed to create the desired web site to promote the new space. Jeff was, however, involved with selecting the vendor for the marketing campaign.

As there were multiple items to procure, different procurement documents were created.

Procuring the Architectural Design

The vision of the finished project was discussed in detail with Ros, Jen, and Ty. The details of the facility were documented and mapped to a statement of work. The SOW defined the design of the architectural plans according to the specifications of Litke Greenhouse and Nursery.

With the SOW created, Jen created a request for proposal that she submitted to five selected architectural and construction organizations.

Procuring the Wildlife

Based on the planned space of the facility, it was determined that 8 birds and 144 rainbow trout would need to be procured. Jen created a request for quote for this procurement, because price was the only determining factor in the selection. The RFQ was sent to five suppliers of the birds and fish.

Procuring the Marketing

Jeff, the full-time marketing pro at Litke Greenhouse and Nursery, worked with Jen and Ty to define the SOW for the marketing. Because of the nature of the work to be procured, a request for proposal was created. Jeff wanted a marketing company to see the whole vision of the project and then share that vision with the public.

Hosting a Bidder Conference

Jen and Ty agreed to meet with each of the proposed bidders to discuss the RFP and the project and to answer any questions the bidders might have. The conferences were held on a preset date, as detailed in the RFP, and each bidder had the opportunity to schedule a 40-minute session with Jen and Ty. This enabled all the vendors to clarify any issues and to gather as much detail as possible to create the proposal that they believed would be most valuable to the buyer.

A bidder conference was allowed for both the architectural and the marketing procurement processes. During the marketing bidder conferences, Jen and Ty relied on Jeff's marketing experience to help lead the conversation and to answer vendor questions.

A bidder conference was not needed for the procurement of the fish and birds. Jen and Ty did allow the bidders to contact them to clarify any questions on the procured items. Only one bidder for the wildlife called with a question: "How many female rainbow trout would the project require?"

Selecting a Vendor

Jen and Ty read each of the proposals and bids supplied by the sellers. The bid for the wildlife was the easiest decision to make because it was driven solely by price. Although all of the bids supplied for the wildlife were close, Jen and Ty selected the vendor with the lowest price. All of the vendors guaranteed their fish and fowl to be healthy and disease-free.

The architectural selection process was not as clear, because of the proposals involved. Ty assisted Jen in creating evaluation criteria to compare and contrast each proposal. Proposals were ranked according to the following specifications:

- Qualifications and experience of each firm
- Ability to address all issues in the provided SOW
- Ability to fulfill the design and construction based on the determined timeline
- New ideas presented within the proposal
- Price

Based on this ranking of information, Jen selected an architectural firm to design and build the facility. Jen and Ty followed a similar approach in selecting the marketing vendor, but also involved Jeff to make the best decision.

Negotiating the Contract

After selecting the vendors for each of the items that needed procurement, Jen worked with the vendors to negotiate the contract. Each contract was relative to the type of work or item to be procured. For example, the architectural firm initially wanted a cost plus percentage of costs contract. This would have caused the final price for the project to fluctuate based on the costs of the materials throughout the project.

Jen negotiated with the seller to use a fixed-price and incentive fee contract for the project. This contract ensured that the vendor would receive a guaranteed fee for the project work, but it also created an opportunity for the vendor to gain a bonus if the contracted work was completed ahead of schedule.

The contracted work for the marketing was assigned to a time and materials contract. This contract type allowed the selected marketing firm to bill for time invested in the project's marketing creation, the web site, and on marketing literature. The contract did, however, include a not-to-exceed fee for the entire project work. Jen and the seller agreed that reports on the expense of the work would be provided every two weeks. This would enable Jen to track the marketing expenses against the deliverables the seller was creating.

Questions

1. You are the project manager of the Adams Construction Project. Some of the work in the project contains pure risk that you're not willing to accept. You decide to mitigate the pure risks in this project. Which of the following may be used as a risk mitigation tool?

   A. The vendor proposal

   B. The contract

   C. The quotation

   D. Project requirements

2. You are the project manager for the 89A Project, and you'd like to procure a portion of the project to a vendor. You'd like to create a contract with your vendor that would provide an incentive for the vendor if they complete user stories faster than expected, but also include a penalty fee if the vendor is running late. What type of contract would be best for this project?

   A. Graduated time and materials

   B. Cost plus incentive fee

   C. Not-to-exceed time and materials

   D. Fixed fee with bonus

3. Britney is the project manager of the FTG Software Project. She's relying on the project scope to help her analyze the procurement needs of the project. The project scope statement can help a project manager create procurement details. Which one of the following best describes this process?

   A. The project scope statement defines the contracted work.

   B. The project scope statement defines the requirements for the contract work.

C. The project scope statement defines the contracted work, which must support the requirements of the project customer.

D. Both parties must have and retain their own copy of the product description.

4. Yolanda has outsourced a portion of a project to a vendor. The vendor has discovered some issues that will influence the cost and schedule of its portion of the project. How must the agreement be updated?

A. As a new contract signed by Yolanda and the vendor.

B. As directed by the contract change control system.

C. As a memo and SOW signed by Yolanda and the vendor.

D. Project management contracts have clauses that allow vendors to adjust their work according to unknowns.

5. You are creating a new contract for some procured work in the project. Your manager wants you to define how issues and claims will be resolved, including the possibility of any lawsuits related to the procured work. In this adaptive project you've selected a multitiered structure for the project contract. Where would issues and claims be documented in the contract?

A. Lightweight statement of work

B. Schedule of services

C. Master agreement

D. Contract addendum

6. Terry is the project manager of the MVB Project. She needs to purchase a piece of equipment for her project. The accounting department has informed Terry that she needs a unilateral form of contract. Accounting is referring to which of the following?

A. The statement of work (SOW)

B. A legally binding contract

C. A purchase order

D. An invoice from the vendor

7. You are a project management consultant for the Hopson Company and you're working with them to determine the best vendor and contract choice for a portion of their agile project. The purpose of a contract is to distribute between the buyer and seller a reasonable amount of what?

A. Responsibility

B. Risk and reward

C. Reward

D. Accountability

8. You are the project manager of the Communications Projects for your organization. Management has stressed that you use privity throughout this project. Privity is what?

   A. The relationship between the project manager and a known vendor

   B. The relationship between the project manager and an unknown vendor

   C. The contractual, confidential information between customer and vendor

   D. The professional information regarding the sale between customer and vendor

9. Sammy is the project manager of the DSA Project. He is considering proposals and contracts presented by vendors for a portion of the project work. Of the following, which contract is least risky to the DSA Project from Sammy's perspective?

   A. Cost plus fixed fee

   B. Cost plus percentage of cost

   C. Cost plus incentive fee

   D. Fixed-price

10. Bradley is the project manager of the Warehouse Remodeling Project for his company. He is in the process of determining which contracts to use in this project. His company is risk-averse, so the correct choice of contract is important to Bradley. Of the following contract types, which one requires the seller to assume the risk of cost overruns?

   A. Cost plus fixed fee

   B. Cost plus incentive fee

   C. Lump-sum

   D. Time and materials

11. Benji is the project manager of the PLP Project. He has hired an independent contractor for a portion of the project work. The contractor is billing the project $120 per hour plus materials. This is an example of what?

   A. Cost plus fixed fee

   B. Time and materials

   C. Unit price

   D. Lump-sum

12. Mary is the project manager of the JHG Project. She has created a procurement statement of work (SOW) for a vendor. What project component is the procurement SOW based on?

   A. The project scope statement

   B. The work breakdown structure (WBS)

   C. The scope baseline

   D. The WBS dictionary

13. You are the project manager for a software development project for an accounting system that will operate over the Internet. Based on your research, you have discovered that it will cost you $25,000 to write your own code. Once the code is written, you estimate you'll spend $3,000 per month updating the software with client information, government regulations, and maintenance. A vendor has proposed to write the code for your company and charge a fee based on the number of clients using the program every month. The vendor will charge you $5 per month per user of the web-based accounting system. You will have roughly 1,200 clients using the system per month. However, you'll need an in-house accountant to manage the time and billing of the system, so this will cost you an extra $1,200 per month. How many months will you have to use the system before it is better to write your own code than to hire the vendor?

   A. 3 months

   B. 4 months

   C. 6 months

   D. 15 months

14. Henry has been negotiating with the ABN Contracting Company for two weeks regarding some procured work on the project. Henry has sent the ABN Contracting Company a letter of intent. This means what?

   A. Henry intends to sue the ABN Contracting Company.

   B. Henry intends to buy from the ABN Contracting Company.

   C. Henry intends to bid on a job from the ABN Contracting Company.

   D. Henry intends to fire the ABN Contracting Company.

15. Martha is the project manager of the MNB Project. She wants a vendor to offer her one price to do all of the detailed work. Martha will issue which type of document?

   A. A request for proposal (RFP)

   B. A request for information (RFI)

   C. A proposal

   D. An invitation for bid (IFB)

16. You are the project manager for your company, and you have six vendors on your project. You've worked with the vendors collectively to organize and schedule their overlapping work, scope control, and changes within their contract requirements. You have created many procurement documents in this project. Which one of the following is true about procurement documents?

   A. They offer no room for bidders to suggest changes.

   B. They ensure receipt of complete proposals.

   C. They inform the performing organization why the bid is being created.

   D. The project manager creates and selects the bid.

17. You are the project manager of the SRQ City Network Project for your company. You will be managing the selection of several vendors to participate in this process, and your project team wants to know when seller selection actually happens. In what process group does the select seller event happen?

   A. Initiating

   B. Planning

   C. Executing

   D. Closing

18. You have an emergency on your project. You have hired a vendor who is to start work immediately. What contract is needed now?

   A. T&M

   B. Fixed-price

   C. Letter contract

   D. Incentive contract

19. You are the project manager for a seller and are managing another company's project. Things have gone well on the project, and the work is nearly complete. There is still a significant amount of funds in the project budget. The buyer's representative approaches you and asks that you complete some optional requirements to use up the remaining budget. You should do what?

   A. Negotiate a change in the contract to take on the additional work.

   B. Complete a contract change for the additional work.

   C. Gain the approval of the project stakeholder for the requested work.

   D. Deny the change because it was not in the original contract.

20. There are some risks that you can do little about. In your most recent project, for example, a tornado has wrecked your construction project. The tornado is known as what?

   A. A force majeure

   B. A risk transference

   C. Direct costs

   D. An unknown unknown

Answers

1. **B.** Contracts can be used as a risk mitigation tool. Procurement of risky activities is known as transference; the risk does not disappear, but the responsibility for the risk is transferred to the vendor. A, C, and D are all incorrect. A vendor proposal, a quotation, and project requirements do nothing to serve as a risk mitigation tool.

2. **A.** Of all the choices presented, A is the best choice. A graduated time and materials contract offers vendor a higher hourly rate for completing work ahead of schedule, but lowers their hourly rate when they fall behind schedule. B is incorrect because costs plus incentive fee is more for predictive project work where materials, not just labor, are being utilized. In addition, cost plus contracts are risky for the buyer. C is incorrect because not-to-exceed time and materials contracts don't offer an incentive fee. D is incorrect because fixed fee with a bonus isn't a valid contract type.

3. **C.** The project scope statement defines the details and requirements for acceptance of the project, serves as a valuable input to the process of determining what needs to be procured, and defines what the end result will be. When dealing with vendors to procure a portion of the project, the procured work must support the requirements of the project's customer. A is incorrect because the project scope statement defines the project as a whole, not just the contracted work, which may be just a portion of the project. B is incorrect because the project scope statement does not define the requirements for the contract work. D is also incorrect because the vendor likely will not have a copy of the product description.

4. **B.** This is the best answer of all the choices presented. The contract change control system will determine the best route to incorporate the change. A, while feasible, is not the best answer to the question. A new contract does not update the original agreement and may cause delays because the contract may have to be resubmitted, reapproved, and so on. C and D are not viable answers.

5. **C.** A master agreement for the multitiered structure is where items such as issues, resolution, and warranties can be documented for the entire project. A is incorrect because the lightweight statement of work is reserved for the dynamic items such as scope, schedule, and budget. B is incorrect because the schedule of services is used for items such as the service rate and product descriptions. D is incorrect because a contract addendum is for additions to existing contracts, not issues and resolutions.

6. **C.** A purchase order is an example of a unilateral contract. A, B, and D are all incorrect answers. An SOW is a statement of work, and a legally binding contract does not fully answer the question. D, an invoice from the vendor, is not what the purchasing department is requesting.

7. **B.** A fair contract shares a reasonable amount of risk and reward between the buyer and the seller. A is incorrect because a contract may transfer the majority of the responsibility to the vendor. C is incorrect because the reward is not an appropriate answer to the question. D is also incorrect because the accountability of the services contracted to the vendor is not shared between the buyer and the seller.

8. **C.** Privity ensures the confidentiality in the agreement between the buyer and seller. A, B, and D are incorrect choices because these do not fully answer the question.

9. **D.** A fixed-price contract contains the least amount of risk for a buyer. The seller assumes all of the risk. A, B, and C are incorrect because these contract types carry the risk of cost overruns being assumed by the buyer.

10. C. A lump-sum contract provides a fixed fee to complete the contract; the seller absorbs any cost overruns. A and B are incorrect because these contracts do not require the seller to carry the risk of cost overruns. D is incorrect because a time and materials contract requires the buyer to pay for cost overruns on the materials and the time invested in the project work.

11. B. The contractor's rate of $120 per hour plus the cost of the materials is an example of a time and materials contract. A is incorrect because a cost plus fixed fee contract charges the cost of the materials, plus a fixed fee, for the installation or work to complete the contract. C is incorrect because a unit price contract has a set price for each unit installed on the project. D is also incorrect because a lump-sum contract does not break down the time and materials.

12. C. The SOW is developed from the scope baseline. A, B, and D are all incorrect because these are the three components of the scope baseline.

13. C. The monies invested in the vendor's solution would have paid for your own code in six months. This is calculated by finding your cash outlay for the two solutions: $25,000 for your own code creation; zero cash outlay for the vendor's solution. The monthly cost to maintain your own code is $3,000. The monthly cost of the vendor's solution is $7,200. Subtract your cost of $3,000 from the vendor's cost of $7,200, and this equals $4,200. Divide this number into the cash outlay of $25,000 to create your own code, and you'll come up with 5.95 months. Of all the choices presented, C, 6 months, is the best answer. A, B, and D are all incorrect because they do not answer the question.

14. B. Henry intends to buy from the ABN Contracting Company. A, C, and D are all incorrect because these choices do not adequately describe the purpose of the letter of intent.

15. D. An invitation for bid (IFB) is a request for a sealed document that lists the seller's firm price to complete the detailed work. A and B, request for proposal (RFP) and request for information (RFI), are documents from the buyer to the seller requesting information on completing the work. C, a proposal, does not list the price to complete the work, but instead offers solutions to the buyer for completing the project needs.

16. B. Procurement documents detail the requirements for the work to ensure complete proposals from sellers. A is incorrect because procurement documents allow input from the seller to suggest alternative ways to complete the project work. C is incorrect because informing the performing organization as to why the bid is being created is not the purpose of the procurement documents. D is not realistic.

17. C. The select seller event happens during the execution process group. The process is the conduct procurement process and is based primarily on the outcomes of the procurement planning process. A, B, and D are all incorrect because these process groups do not include source selection.

18. C. For immediate work, a letter contract may suffice. The intent of the letter contract is to allow the vendor to get to work immediately to solve the project problem. A, B, and D are all incorrect because these contracts may require additional time to create and approve. When time is of the essence, a letter contract is acceptable.

19. C. Any additional work is a change in the project scope. Changes to the project scope should be approved by the mechanisms in the contract change control system. The stakeholder needs to approve the changes to the project scope. A, B, and D are not realistic expectations of the project. This question borders on the PMP Code of Professional Conduct. Typically, when a project scope has been fulfilled, the project work is done. The difference in this situation is that the additional tasks are optional requirements for the project scope.

20. A. Force majeure, sometimes called "an act of God," is a natural disaster that can wreck a project. B, risk transference, is incorrect because this describes the response to the risk, not the tornado itself. C, direct cost, describes costs that cannot be shared with other organizations but that are attributed directly to your project. D, an unknown unknown, does not fully describe the tornado as well as A does, so this choice is also incorrect.

CHAPTER 13

Managing Project Stakeholders

In this chapter, you will

- Identify the project stakeholders
- Plan for stakeholder management
- Manage stakeholder engagement
- Monitor stakeholder engagement

I've always said that the hardest part of the project isn't execution, following processes or regulations, or even planning complex work. The hardest part of the project is dealing with people. People can be demanding, unreasonable, and rude; they can shift their priorities; and they can exhibit many other bad behaviors you've probably already experienced as a project manager. People can also be wonderful, kind, caring, and genuinely interested in the project. They can be reasonable, can understand how their demands don't mesh with what they've already asked you for in the project, and can be your biggest allies in getting the project done. Working with people can be challenging in predictive or adaptive; people are people regardless of the project approach.

These people are the project stakeholders, and they are looking to you to complete the project work, to keep project spending at or below budget, and to meet or beat project deadlines. Stakeholders are the people who are affected by your project and those who can affect your project—for better or worse. Stakeholder management is about identifying the stakeholders, but it's so much more. It's also about creating a plan for engaging with stakeholders, keeping stakeholders involved in the project, and keeping the project team involved in the process, too.

 VIDEO For a more detailed explanation, watch the *Engaging Project Stakeholder Management* video now.

Agile projects promote team, project manager, and stakeholder interactions. Often the developers and the stakeholders can communicate directly about the project requirements, issues, and goals of the current iteration. Transparency is important in agile, and that requires open communication and trust among all the stakeholders.

Change is expected, so access to the project team isn't as guarded as you might find in a project with a predictive life cycle, though there are rules about interrupting the project team and the roles and responsibilities in agile projects. Stakeholders can attend project meetings, review project artifacts, and participate in reviews in agile projects.

There are just four processes in this knowledge area: identifying stakeholders, planning stakeholder management, managing stakeholder engagement, and monitoring stakeholder engagement. The basic theme of these four processes is this: you need to identify, engage, mentor, and manage how you interact with the project stakeholders. If you master this knowledge area, you'll be on your way to becoming a fantastic project manager—and a certified one.

Identifying Project Stakeholders

Just to be clear, stakeholders are the people who can affect your project and who can also be affected by your project. Stakeholders can positively or negatively affect a project. Your project can do the same to stakeholders' lives. For instance, imagine a construction project to replace an existing bridge and all the people who could be involved in that project. You'll work with architects, engineers, construction gurus, and the day-to-day workers on the project. There will be city planners, government inspectors, and other bureaucrats involved in the project. You'll also have all of the people who live near the bridge eagerly awaiting its completion and possibly aggravated by the inconvenience your project causes them.

All of these people are stakeholders who can affect your project, and all of their lives will be affected by your project. Now imagine what would happen if you didn't take the time to identify the correct stakeholders for the project. What would happen if you fail to identify the government agencies for the bridge project? Or you forget to identify the people who use the bridge every day as part of their commutes? Or you don't identify the architect for the bridge? Stakeholder identification is vital to project success. You and the project team must pause and really think about the stakeholders and how your project affects them, and also how the stakeholders can affect your project.

Stakeholder identification should happen as early as possible in the project. If you wait too long to identify the stakeholders properly, you may end up missing decisions and requirements that will cause the project to stall; you could also possibly create bad relationships with the stakeholders and perhaps cause turmoil within the project. Stakeholder identification is a project initiating activity and requires the project manager, the project team, and other stakeholders to help identify who should be involved in the project. As you identify stakeholders, you'll classify them according to their power, influence, interests, and other characteristics to help you better manage the project and monitor stakeholder engagement.

Preparing for Stakeholder Identification

Let's go back to that bridge construction project. How do you know who should be included as a stakeholder? You could rely on your experience as a project manager and the experience of colleagues you know who are part of the project, but what other things would help you really capture all of the stakeholders in the project? When it comes to stakeholder identification, you have to consider how many stakeholders are in the project. You'll consider the complexity of the stakeholder relationships: the more connected the stakeholders are to one another, the greater the risk of miscommunication among the stakeholders. And you'll also consider your communication technology that will help you better communicate with the stakeholders.

You should always consult the following seven items as you begin stakeholder identification:

- **Project charter**   The project charter should identify some of the parties involved in the project. The charter can identify the project sponsor, of course; the project manager; and other parties affected by the project, including all the people who are working with the project manager to plan and complete the project. For example, in the bridge construction project, your project charter may include any vendors that your company has partnered with to complete the work.

- **Business documents**   The business case defines the project objectives and will identify some of the key stakeholders. The benefits management plan is also needed, because this defines the expectations of the stakeholders and can help identify the recipients of the benefits, who are stakeholders in your project. Adaptive projects might refer to "businesspeople" to represent the customers or operational stakeholders of the project, rather than business documents.

- **Project management plan**   Initially you won't have much of a project management plan, but as the plan is developed, you'll reference the communications management plan and the stakeholder engagement plan to help direct your engagement with, interaction with, and identification of stakeholders.

- **Project documents**   The project documents probably won't be a help in the initial round of stakeholder identification, but the change log, issue log, and requirements documentation can help you identify stakeholders later in the project.

- **Agreements**   When you have a contract between two or more parties, you've identified some stakeholders. In the bridge construction project, you'll procure materials and probably hire resources from different companies. These companies are stakeholders in your project—they can affect your project in a positive or negative way depending on how they live up to the terms of the contract. You'll also have internal stakeholders who are identified through procurement documents—consider the employees you work with to complete procurement. Your company may have a central contracting office, an accounts payable office, and a procurement office. These are all stakeholders now because they, too, can affect your project positively or negatively. In this instance, procurement documents will help you identify project stakeholders.

- **Enterprise environmental factors**   You can identify stakeholders through the enterprise environmental factors you're working with in your project. The culture of your company, how your organization is identified, and the departments and offices you're obliged to work with can all reveal project stakeholders.

Your industry regulations, government agencies, and industry standards are also part of enterprise environmental factors, and these elements can help you identify stakeholders, too. Depending on where the project is taking place in the world, you may also have local influences that should be considered as stakeholders.

- **Organizational process assets** Don't forget to look at past projects to identify current stakeholders. If you've done similar work in the past, your current project will probably include some of the same or similar stakeholders. Your organizational process assets can also include stakeholder identification approaches, a stakeholder register template, and lessons learned. Use what already exists so you can work smarter and not harder.

These seven elements are the inputs to stakeholder identification. You'll want to gather these elements as early as possible in the project to begin identifying the stakeholders. Don't wait too long into the project to identify stakeholders, or you could find that you haven't considered all of the stakeholders and their concerns for the project. Of course, in agile projects you likely won't have these documents, so you'll rely more on the product owner or the individual who represents the customers to help identify stakeholders. Typically, the stakeholders in an agile project are defined as customers, users, or sponsors.

Launching Project Stakeholder Identification

After you've gathered the needed inputs to stakeholder analysis, you can officially launch stakeholder identification. Stakeholder identification aims to identify the stakeholders, document who the stakeholders are, and record their interests, contributions, and expectations for the project. There are five tools and techniques for stakeholder identification, but they are exhaustive and broad reaching. You should know these tools not just for your examination but also for your role as a project manager: expert judgment, data gathering, data analysis, data representation, and meetings.

You can host a brainstorming meeting, where participants can brainstorm all the possible stakeholders that project includes—this is a fine approach to stakeholder identification. A similar approach, called *brain writing*, enables the brainstorming participants to review the brainstorming questions and topics before the meeting and prepare their response before the session begins. Both approaches are examples of data gathering.

Stakeholder identification is also linked closely with project communications. Recall that you'll plan for project communication and identify who needs what information, when the information is needed, and how the information is to be delivered. Stakeholder identification and communication planning can go hand in hand because you'll need to identify the stakeholders before you can determine what communication demands they may have. Interactive communication is typical among stakeholders as stakeholders will actively communicate with one another, not just to you and the project team. Consider meetings, forums, videoconferences, phone calls, and ad hoc conversations where stakeholders will discuss the project, but you won't be involved in that conversation.

When you go about identifying stakeholders you'll likely need to provide communication to the stakeholders about your project. Recall that you sending information to stakeholders is a push communication, as opposed to already identified stakeholders pulling information from you, such as a project website or electronic forum. Communication and stakeholder engagement work closely together.

Performing Stakeholder Analysis

Some stakeholders are more important than others. Yeah, I said that. Some stakeholders (such as the CEO of your company, who's counting on your team to implement a new piece of software) are probably more important than others (such as the new receptionist who doesn't like the new software). The receptionist may be a stakeholder, but the CEO of the company has far more power and influence than the receptionist does. Stakeholder analysis is the process of analyzing and classifying the stakeholders and interests in the project. It helps you determine and prioritize the needs and requirements of the stakeholders.

Stakeholder analysis follows three steps:

1. Identify and document the stakeholders' contact information, knowledge, expectations of the project, and their level of influence over project decisions.

2. Prioritize and classify stakeholders based on their power, influence, expectations, and concerns for the project.

3. Plan for managing the stakeholders based on possible negative or positive scenarios in the project that may affect the stakeholders.

Stakeholder analysis aims to identify stakeholders and their stakes in the project. Stakes in the project can include the following:

- **Interest** The stakeholder is affected by the project.
- **Rights (legal or moral rights)** The stakeholder may have legal rights, such as physical safety, or moral rights, such as environmental concerns, regarding where the project work is taking place.
- **Ownership** The stakeholder has ownership of an asset.
- **Knowledge** The stakeholder has knowledge that can help the project.
- **Contribution** The stakeholder is contributing to the project through funds, resources, or other types of support.

 EXAM TIP To help you identify stakeholders, you may find it useful to ask known stakeholders who else should be involved in the project.

Classifying Stakeholders

One of the best tools in stakeholder analysis is a classification model. A classification model is a way to group and prioritize stakeholders. There are six models (three of which are similar) you should know for your PMP:

Figure 13-1
A power/influence grid helps prioritize stakeholders.

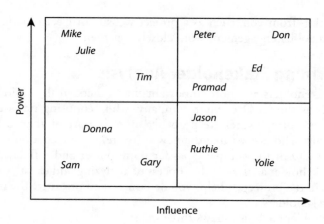

- **Power/influence grid** This grid, as shown in Figure 13-1, plots out the amount of power and influence each stakeholder has over the project. You'll position each stakeholder on this grid based on the amount of power and influence the stakeholder has. Stakeholders with high power and high influence are top priority. Stakeholders with little power and influence are still considered, but they have less priority than other stakeholders in the project.

- **Power/interest grid** This grid also maps out stakeholders' power over the project, but it considers their interest in the project as a consideration for prioritization of their project needs, expectations, and contributions.

- **Impact/influence grid** This classification model considers the influence the stakeholder may have over the project, but it also considers the impact the stakeholder can bring to the project. Consider stakeholders who may have little influence but whose presence or absence from the project could have great impact—such as a key project team member.

- **Salience model** This model, shown in Figure 13-2, maps out stakeholders' power, urgency, and legitimacy in the project. Power means that the stakeholders can enforce their will on the project's success. Urgency describes the stakeholders' need for attention. Legitimacy describes if the person's involvement in the project is even warranted.

- **Stakeholder cube** This model is a three-dimensional cube that combines the power, influence, and impact grids.

- **Direction of influence** This illustrates stakeholders' influence on the project in one of five ways:

  - **Upward** Senior management, customer, or steering committee

  - **Downward** Project team, subject matter expert, or consultant

  - **Outward** Suppliers, vendors, government agencies, or the public

Figure 13-2
A salience
model tracks
stakeholders'
power, urgency,
and legitimacy.

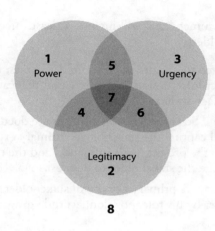

1. Dormant
2. Discretionary
3. Demanding
4. Dominant
5. Dangerous
6. Dependent
7. Definitive
8. Nonstakeholders

- **Sideward**   Peers of the project manager or middle management who may need the same resources the project manager needs in the project
- **Prioritization**   Priority levels of stakeholders in a large project; some stakeholders are of greater priority than others

Finalizing Stakeholder Identification

The final two tools and techniques for stakeholder identification are meetings and expert judgment. First, let's talk about meetings. Stakeholder identification meetings, sometimes called *profile analysis meetings*, help the project manager and the management team realize the expectations and interests of the key project stakeholders. These meetings are useful to identify and document the different roles in the project, the types of stakeholders you'll work with, and all the differing objectives, interests, and inputs for the project.

As you meet with your project team and your key stakeholders, you may also rely on expert judgment to help identify and analyze stakeholders. Expert judgment simply means you're working with someone who has more insight on the stakeholders, or the type of work being done, or she can identify stakeholders you may have overlooked. Experts can be individuals from the project team, business leaders in your company, clients, vendors, consultants, government agencies, focus groups, and more. You're working with these people and groups to ensure that you've identified all of the stakeholders in the project.

Creating the Stakeholder Register

Stakeholder identification is only as good as the documentation that comes out of the process. The stakeholder register is the only output of stakeholder identification. It's a log of all the stakeholder information you've gathered in the project. It will help you communicate with project stakeholders; help ensure that you understand the stakeholders' needs, wants, and expectations; and help you classify stakeholder objectives and priorities. Adaptive projects don't formally have a stakeholder register, though it's not uncommon to have some listing or document of the people involved and affected by the project.

The stakeholder register is a document that will include at least three types of information about your project stakeholders:

- **Identification**   You'll need to capture the stakeholder names, project role, company position, contact information, and where they're located should you need to meet with them face-to-face.

- **Assessment information**   Stakeholders' expectations are documented in the stakeholder register. You'll capture the stakeholders' primary expectations, their expected contributions to the project, their influence, and the periods during the project when you anticipate the stakeholder to be most involved and interested.

- **Stakeholder classification**   A primary activity of stakeholder identification is to classify each stakeholder by his role, position, attitude toward the project, and other factors.

The creation of the stakeholder register isn't a one-time event. You'll refer to the stakeholder register throughout the project and update it as new information becomes available. For example, stakeholders may leave the project, new stakeholders could be identified in the project, and stakeholder attitudes and influences can evolve as the project is in motion. Change requests might be generated as a result of stakeholder identification, though not in the initial round of identification. As you identify more and more stakeholders and they learn about the project, they may want additions or modifications to the project requirements.

Planning Stakeholder Management

After you've identified the stakeholders, how will you manage them? Planning stakeholder management creates the stakeholder engagement plan and helps you and the project team create a strategy for stakeholder management and engagement. Agile projects welcome stakeholder engagement and involvement as we need the stakeholders' ongoing support, vision, and direction of what constitutes success in the project.

Imagine, for example, that you're the project manager of a large project to install new software throughout your company. Some of your stakeholders are excited for the new software—these are positive stakeholders. Other stakeholders hate the idea of changing software and learning something new—these are negative stakeholders. Finally, some of the stakeholders don't care either way—these are neutral stakeholders. Each of these stakeholder types needs to be considered by you and the project team as you develop your stakeholder engagement plan. If this imaginary project is an agile project, we'll need to understand why a stakeholder may want changes, why their vision for the product changes, and have ongoing determinations about our assumptions and understandings of what the project is to create.

Planning stakeholder management is the process of determining how stakeholders will be affected and how you'll manage the project in consideration of the stakeholders. This means you'll be working to engage the stakeholders—to get them involved in the project, to maintain their interest, to calm their fears and allay any threats the project may be causing—and working with the stakeholders to create relationships with the project team, customers, vendors, and other stakeholders in the project. You, the project manager, are at the center of stakeholder management, but you also want your project team to work proactively to engage stakeholders in support of the project's objectives.

This planning process, like almost all the planning processes, creates a plan. The stakeholder engagement plan defines your approach for stakeholder engagement. As the project moves through its life cycle, the stakeholder concerns, interests, support, and interactions may fluctuate. It's because of this fluctuation in stakeholder involvement that you'll likely revisit stakeholder engagement planning many times throughout the project. Don't worry—this is expected, because stakeholder engagement planning is an iterative activity that occurs throughout the entire project.

Preparing to Plan for Stakeholder Management

You won't just rush into stakeholder engagement planning—surely by this point in the book you know that you'll always arm yourself with some inputs to start off these processes effectively. This planning process is no different. Although you may have a good idea what stakeholders expect from the project, you also need to consider what stakeholders expect from you as the project manager. This includes the key stakeholders, such as your project sponsor and the project customer, but you must also consider your most trusted stakeholders: the project team.

To plan for stakeholder management, you'll need six inputs:

- **Project charter** The charter defines the key performance indicators, the project purpose, and other factors that will influence your stakeholder engagement planning.
- **Project management plan** Yes, yes, the stakeholder engagement plan is part of the project management plan, but you're going to need a bunch of other stuff from the project management plan to help you create the stakeholder engagement plan. You'll need the following:
  - **Resource management plan** Identifies the physical and human resources
  - **Communications management plan** Defines who needs what information and when
  - **Risk management plan** Identifies the roles and responsibilities associated with risks
- **Project documents** You'll need several project documents to help you plan your stakeholder management approach in a predictive or hybrid project:
  - **Assumptions log** Identifies assumptions and constraints associated with stakeholders
  - **Change log** Addresses changes that affect the stakeholders, who can request changes, can make decisions about changes, can be affected by approved and proposed changes
  - **Issue log** Enables you to communicate with stakeholders to assign and manage issues in the project
  - **Project schedule** Identifies people who will be responsible and affected by scheduled activities in the project

- **Risk register** Identifies the people who are risk owners and identifies stakeholders who will be affected by risks within the project
- **Stakeholder register** Identifies all of the project stakeholders
- **Agreements** If you're procuring goods and services you'll have stakeholders from the vendor and stakeholders from your purchasing or contracting department.
- **Enterprise environmental factors** Recall that organizational structure, the culture of the organization, and even the politics can all affect how you plan for stakeholder management.
- **Organizational process assets** Of course, you'll rely on organizational process assets to help with the current project's stakeholder engagement planning. Consider elements such as historical files, templates, lessons learned, and other data from past projects as part of your organizational process assets items.

If you're working through project planning, you'll probably already have these inputs readily available. These are similar inputs you'll use in planning the project communications. Stakeholder management and communications work together, but there is a difference between the two. Project communications is about getting the right stakeholder the right information at the right time. Stakeholder engagement is about getting stakeholders involved and acting on the communications you provide. Adaptive projects don't have beefy plans like predictive projects often do, but it's still a good idea to understand who'll be involved with the project and who the project affects.

Creating the Stakeholder Engagement Plan

Now that you've gathered the necessary inputs to planning stakeholder engagement, you'll need to gather the correct experts to help. Stakeholder engagement planning isn't a solo activity—you'll need experts from within your organizations and possibly outside consultants to help with the planning. Subject matter experts for creating the stakeholder engagement plan include senior management, consultants, the project team, leaders within the organization, other project managers with similar project experience, and other needed and identified experts within your organization. The goal is to include as many readily available experts to help you accurately plan an approach to engage your stakeholders.

After you have decided which experts to include, you'll gather these experts together, either one-on-one or through a group format, by hosting meetings. Meetings are one of the tools and techniques for creating the stakeholder engagement plan. Stakeholder meetings can be traditional conference room events, focus groups, or even panels. The goal isn't to get fancy, but to define the needed engagement level for the stakeholders. Engagement levels define the amount of interest each stakeholder has in the project, but also the stakeholder's level of engagement for the project. There are five engagement levels:

- **Unaware** The stakeholder doesn't know about the project and the effect the project may have on him.

- **Resistant**   The stakeholder knows about the project and doesn't want the change the project may bring.

- **Neutral**   The stakeholder knows about the project, but neither supports nor resists the project.

- **Supportive**   The stakeholder knows about the project and is supportive of the change the project will bring about.

- **Leading**   The stakeholder knows about the project, is supportive of the change the project may bring about, and is working to make the project successful.

In larger projects with lots of different stakeholders, you may find it beneficial to create a stakeholder engagement assessment matrix. This is a table that defines all of the stakeholders and their engagement levels in the project. This can help you identify stakeholder trends, commonalities, and group stakeholders by their levels of support for the project. Stakeholders are tagged in the matrix, with *C* for current engagement level and *D* for their desired engagement level. Not all stakeholders need to be in the leading category, but your strategy may work to get most stakeholders to at least the supportive level for the project.

EXAM TIP   The product owner is closely associated with the customers of the project. The product owner will communicate with and represent the project customers, who are key stakeholders, in an agile project.

Examining the Stakeholder Engagement Plan

There's only one result of planning for stakeholder management: the stakeholder engagement plan. The stakeholder engagement plan aims to engage stakeholders and keep stakeholders engaged throughout the entire project. The plan may contain sensitive information that shouldn't necessarily be shared with everyone; in fact, you may need to protect the contents of the stakeholder engagement plan from the project team and other stakeholders. The stakeholder engagement plan defines several things:

- Changes the project will bring to stakeholders

- Current and desired levels of stakeholder engagement

- Interrelationships among stakeholders

- Communication requirements throughout the project

- Information to be distributed to stakeholders and why the information is needed by the stakeholders

- Timing of communications

- Conditions and methods for updating the stakeholder engagement plan

Managing Stakeholder Engagement

As a project manager, you'll constantly work to engage the project stakeholders. This means communicating, fostering relationships, facilitating meetings, negotiating, settling disputes, and managing all of the questions, demands, and inputs from the stakeholders. Managing stakeholder engagement is a constant, ongoing activity—it's what's expected of you as the project manager. You'll be available to the project stakeholders, and this also means you must seek out stakeholders when conditions and situations call for you to get stakeholders more (or less) involved in the project.

Managing stakeholder engagement works right along with the project communications, but it involves more than just communicating. Think of all the different types of stakeholders who could be affected by any of your projects. Surely some of these stakeholders require a bit more attention than others. And some of your stakeholders may offer minimal input, stay out of the way, or dodge the project as much as possible. Other stakeholders may be in your office once, twice, or several times every day with a new emergency. That's stakeholder engagement: giving your time and attention to what's most important in the project while maintaining stakeholder interest, commitment, and buy-in of the project objectives. Agile projects rely on face-to-face conversations to communicate project information, and video technologies and online meetings can facilitate these face-to-face conversations.

 EXAM TIP The Agile Manifesto is really about stakeholder engagement: making certain we understand what is value for the project customers and creating a collaboration between the team and the stakeholders. We all want a win.

Stakeholder influence on the project objectives is usually highest in the early parts of the project. Once you've garnered commitment from the stakeholders, identified and agreed upon the project scope, and set the project team to work executing the plans, stakeholder influence should wane. As the project moves forward, some stakeholders may still try to influence the project regarding their particular objectives and goals, and you may have to get the project sponsor involved to squelch some of the more overbearing stakeholders. You'll also manage, track, and report on issues that happen in the project that may affect stakeholders. It's an ongoing process.

Preparing to Manage Stakeholder Engagement

Although one of the official inputs to this process is the project management plan, the stakeholder engagement plan is the part of this overall plan that's most helpful at this stage. Recall that the stakeholder engagement plan describes the approach you'll use to get the stakeholder involved in the project and to communicate with the stakeholders, along with the desired level of stakeholder engagement. You'll rely on this plan, along with other parts of the project management plan (such as the communications management plan) to work with the stakeholders to create synergy, promote buy-in, and interact with the stakeholders.

As I mentioned, much of stakeholder engagement is related to the communications management plan. It is the second plan referenced for managing stakeholder engagement. This plan will help you review the communication requirements of the project stakeholders. You'll need to know what information should be communicated and when and how the stakeholders are expecting the communication. Of course, not all information is to be distributed to all the stakeholders—some people just don't need (or want) to know everything. The communications management plan defines who needs what information—this is important so you don't send confidential information to the wrong people.

The risk management plan, also part of the overall project management plan, is an input to the manage stakeholder engagement process. You'll need the risk management plan to review the risk categories in your project, to outline the stakeholder tolerance and appetite for risk, and to reference the reporting formats for risk events. Most project managers, when thinking of risk events, think of the impact to the project in the form of time and money, but it's also important to consider how the risk events will affect your project stakeholders.

Recall that change is inevitable in most projects, especially adaptive projects. You'll need to consider the project approach, the change management plan, and the change log as part of stakeholder engagement. The approach, predictive or adaptive, will determine how change is managed and communicated. The change log documents the changes that have occurred in the project and the changes that have been proposed in the project. The change log will help you manage stakeholder engagement because you'll need to relay information about changes to the appropriate parties. Change can be a sensitive issue in some instances, so always examine the change and think through all the possible scenarios and reactions the stakeholders may have to the change. Cost and schedule are the two largest concerns most stakeholders have with changes, but you may also need to consider the effect a change has on the project scope. In addition, changes to one part of the project scope may mean changes in other parts of the scope. It's also possible that you'll be forced to remove things from scope because of time, costs, risks, or other concerns. This is another item that needs to be communicated delicately to stakeholders.

The issue log, lessons learned register, and the stakeholder register are also part of the project documents you'll reference during stakeholder engagement. The issue log addresses how issues may affect stakeholder engagement. The lessons learned register documents lessons from the current project so you can better manage the remainder of the project in regard to stakeholder engagement. And you'll reference the stakeholder register because this document identifies all of the stakeholders you're trying to engage in the project.

Enterprise environmental factors are also an input to the manage stakeholder engagement process. The culture of your organization, the political climate, and the governance of the organization all affect stakeholder engagement. You'll also need to be familiar with personnel policies, communication channels, approaches for working in international environments, and the geographic locale of project resources.

Finally, you'll also rely on organizational process assets to help you prepare in managing stakeholder engagement. Your organization may have forms, templates, and requirements for communications. You may have issue management policies to follow that may alter your approach to stakeholder engagement. Whatever the organizational process assets that can affect your stakeholder engagement, it's a good idea to think through what's being communicated, how you're communicating the information, and what is the anticipated reaction from the stakeholder.

Managing Stakeholder Relationships

Managing the stakeholder engagement is really about creating and fostering relationships with the people in your project. You want the project to be successful, and you need the buy-in and synergy from your project stakeholders. Sure, some low-influence, low-power stakeholders can refuse to support the project, may object to the project goals throughout the entire project life cycle, and may hate your guts, but you can still be successful. The relationships created in stakeholder engagement can develop into a lovely rhythm or a dreadful rut. Projects are not as enjoyable when you're fighting challenging stakeholders the entire time. No one wants to do that.

 EXAM TIP Collaboration, partnerships, and synergy are all words to describe the nature of stakeholder engagement in adaptive projects. Keep stakeholders excited and involved in the project. The highest priority in the Agile Manifesto is to satisfy the customer through early delivery of value.

For your PMI exams, remember that you want stakeholders to be supportive of the project. This means you'll use communication methods and interpersonal skills as your stakeholder engagement tools and techniques. You know about communication already—it's how you spend the bulk of your time as a project manager. You have planned the communication, identified who needs what information, and documented when the information will be needed, and you know the modality of the information. Good communicators generally make good project managers. Interpersonal skills are the characteristics that make people like you, or at least work with you, as a project manager. Interpersonal skills involve the following:

- **Trustworthiness** People need to be able to trust the project manager.
- **Conflict management** Stakeholders will look to the project manager to resolve conflicts.
- **Cultural awareness** Cultural differences among the project team and stakeholders can affect the stakeholder engagement and project management approach. Organizations new to agile may face challenges with the culture of the organization and the launch of a new project management approach.
- **Observation and conversation** The project manager needs to observe the interactions among the project team, must be available to help, and must be able to converse with people.

- **Active listening**   As project manager, you need to ensure that you understand the message and its underlying meaning. It requires the listener to completely understand, respond, and remember what is said. Active listening requires concentration on the other person in the conversation resulting in improved understanding of another person.

- **Overcoming resistance to change**   As project manager, you need to help stakeholders see why the project is important and how it affects their lives.

Of course, project management isn't all about getting people to like you and trust you. Project management is really about getting things done. Management skills, such as the following, are the tools you'll need as part of stakeholder engagement to move the project toward its completion:

- **Negotiation**   You'll have to lead negotiations regarding give and take on project objectives.

- **Influence**   You'll need to persuade people to buy in and support the project.

- **Facilitation**   Through meetings and messages, you'll build consensus on project goals.

- **Political awareness**   Politics happen. The project manager must be aware of the politics and power that surround and affect the project.

- **Behavior management**   You'll have to modify stakeholder behavior to lead them to accepting the project and its objectives.

Managing stakeholder engagement takes practice and time. The longer you work as a project manager, the better you'll become at engaging stakeholders. Treat people with respect, don't make promises you cannot keep, and always do what's in the best interest of the project, and you'll be well on your way not only to engaging stakeholders, but to becoming a leader in your project environment.

 EXAM TIP   Agile projects practice stakeholder engagement throughout the project by keeping stakeholders informed through transparent communication, welcoming changes, demonstrations, and delivering value throughout the project.

Reviewing Stakeholder Engagement Results

Because stakeholder engagement is a process—and something you'll do throughout the project—you can expect some outputs of the process. Although it may be important for you to know the results of stakeholder engagement for your PMI exam, it's also important that you know what all the actions in this process are creating for your project. Of course, you don't want to do a process just because it's handy and makes sense; you want to do it because you're creating things that can help your project become more successful—and this will make you more successful in your career, too.

Managing stakeholder engagement creates three outputs:

- **Change requests**   Change requests can come as a result of stakeholder engagement. Changes to the project scope or schedule, corrective actions, and preventive actions are all changes that can stem from stakeholder engagement. Changes can also happen with the communication approach and interaction with the project stakeholders.

- **Project management plan updates**   Based on what you learn in stakeholder engagement, you may need to update the project management plan. Updates are likely in the stakeholder engagement plan and in the project communications management plan. Stakeholders may change the way they want you to communicate with them, the information they want about the project, or even how they want the information delivered. If there are changes, defects, issues, and even conflict resolution, you may need to update the project management plan to reflect these concerns.

- **Project documents updates**   You may need to update the stakeholder register if new stakeholders are identified in the project, stakeholder information changes, or stakeholders leave the project. Changes can result from stakeholder engagement, so the change log may need to be updated. You may also have new issues or issue resolutions, so you'll update the issue log. And you may make updates to the lessons learned register.

Monitoring Stakeholder Engagement

Monitoring stakeholder engagement doesn't mean you're monitoring what stakeholders do; instead, you're monitoring the overall effectiveness of the stakeholder engagement process. Think of it as a checkup for the project management team and key stakeholders to ensure that all of the stakeholder management work is being done properly, effectively, and according to the stakeholder engagement plan. As the project moves deeper into its life cycle, you and the project team will work through stakeholder engagement. This process ensures that you're following the stakeholder engagement plan and meeting stakeholder expectations. The sprint review meeting, or demo meeting, held throughout the project is a great example of monitoring stakeholder engagement—and it keeps stakeholders excited and involved in the project.

Monitoring stakeholder engagements also occurs when conditions in the project change. For example, let's revisit the bridge construction project. If the bridge construction project is expected to last six months, that's six months of some unhappy residents who are delayed or detoured because of your bridge project. The residents may be happy for the new bridge, but the pain of the delays and detours is still aggravating. Now imagine there's been rough weather, delays resulting from delivery of poor materials, or other issues that have crept into the project, forcing your timeline to be expanded to ten months. Conditions within the project have changed, and you'll need to communicate with the stakeholders about the delay, but you'll also need to continue to engage the stakeholders in the project. You'll have to remind them about the new bridge, emphasize how much safer it will be for them, and communicate other upbeat information to keep the stakeholders engaged.

 EXAM TIP Don't engage the stakeholders only when there is good news or bad news. Monitoring stakeholder engagement is a continuous process throughout the project.

Preparing to Monitor Stakeholder Engagement

To control stakeholder engagement, you'll need some inputs to the project. Specifically, you'll need five things to get this process moving:

- **Project management plan**   The project management plan will define the life cycle of the project, the execution of the project work, human resource requirements, roles and responsibilities, staffing management, change management, and communication requirements for stakeholders. Specifically, you'll need the resource management plan, communications management plan, and stakeholder engagement plan.

- **Project documents**   All of the supporting details for the project and the corresponding documentation can contribute to monitoring stakeholder engagement. Consider the issue log, lessons learned register, project communications, risk register, and stakeholder register.

- **Work performance data**   You'll need insight into how well the project is performing in order to communicate with and engage the stakeholder appropriately. Remember, data is raw data, just the facts and info without any processing.

- **Enterprise environmental factors**   The cultural and political climates, governance framework, and personnel policies are all enterprise environmental factors to consider as inputs for monitoring stakeholder engagement. You might also need risk thresholds, communication channels, international trends, and knowledge about the locale of project resources.

- **Organizational process assets**   You'll need to consider policies for social media, ethics, security, and risk management. Organizational process assets also include communication requirements in the organization, standards for information management, and historical information from similar projects.

Components of Monitoring Stakeholder Engagement

Monitoring stakeholder engagement means that you, the project team, and the key stakeholders are communicating with one another on a consistent basis. If, for example, your project team is conveying information to stakeholders that differs from what you're telling stakeholders, trouble will abound. When stakeholders hear conflicting information about the project, they'll be confused and concerned, and often they may choose to listen only to the message that suits them best. The foundation for stakeholder engagement, and controlling stakeholder engagement, begins with a solid foundation of communications.

To monitor stakeholder engagement in a predictive project, you'll need several components to help with the process:

- **Project management plan** The project management plan helps you monitor stakeholder engagement because it establishes the project governance and project framework. You'll utilize the resource management plan, communications management plan, and stakeholder engagement plan.

- **Project documents** Specifically, you'll need the issue log, lessons learned register, project communications, risk register, and stakeholder register.

- **Work performance data** Key performance metrics are measured, analyzed, and reported. This includes such objectives as time, cost, percentage of work completed, quality control measurements, and any other factors that need to be measured in your project. These elements will help you communicate the project's health and manage the stakeholder expectations of the project's success. You'll typically measure work performance at predesignated points in the project, such as at milestones or key project deliverables.

- **Enterprise environmental factors** The usual business in the enterprise environmental factors will help you monitor stakeholder engagement. This usual business includes the culture, politics, personnel administration, risk thresholds, communication channels, global aspects of the project, and the geographical location of resources.

- **Organizational process assets** Organizational process assets are also used to monitor stakeholder engagements. The policies and procedures for social media, ethics, security, and risk, change, and data management are included in organizational process assets. You might also reference guidelines on information management and historical information from past, similar projects.

Reviewing the Outputs of Stakeholder Engagement

So, you're working at monitoring stakeholder engagement. Guess when this process ends? When execution is done and the project moves into closing, that's when. It's a long, iterative controlling process that you'll do throughout the entire project. As you monitor stakeholder engagements, you'll be creating four things for your project and organization:

- **Work performance information** You'll collect and organize performance data from across the project into comprehensive work performance information. This is needed for project communications with the stakeholders. You'll share project status, project performance reports, forecasts for costs and schedule, and other information with the stakeholders.

- **Change requests** Yes, change requests can be a result of monitoring stakeholder engagement. Corrective actions and preventive actions are the most likely changes you'll have as a result of monitoring stakeholder engagement. Adaptive projects can have change requests for the product backlog at any time.

- **Project management plan updates** You may need to update the project plan as a result of monitoring stakeholder engagement. Although all areas of the project management plan may need to be updated, the most likely components to be updated are the resource management plan, communications management plan, and stakeholder engagement plan.

- **Project document updates** Just as you may need to update the project management plan, you may also need to update the project documents. Specifically, the stakeholder register will likely be updated as a result of controlling the stakeholder engagement, as will the issue log to reflect any issue changes or new issues in the project.

Chapter Summary

Project stakeholder management is an ongoing activity that ensures that the stakeholders are identified, analyzed, and engaged throughout the project life cycle. It's no secret that in many projects, people are excited about the new endeavor, but as the project moves into its planning and execution, their excitement and interest can wane. It's up to the project manager to ensure consistent communication with stakeholders and actively engage them in an ongoing effort during the project.

Adaptive projects aim for stakeholder engagement throughout the project with sprint reviews, openness to change requests, and facilitation done by the product owner or customer representative. Adaptive projects aim to keep stakeholders excited and involved in the project by first delivering high-level business value for the project customers. Face-to-face conversation is always best regardless of the news, but transparency in project information is paramount. Transparency builds trust, stakeholder buy-in, and keeps everyone informed of the project progress.

This knowledge area has just four processes. The first process is to identify the project stakeholders. Recall that this activity should occur as early as possible in the project to ensure that the correct stakeholders are identified and classified for proper planning and engagement. If you fail to identify a stakeholder, the stakeholder could, based on their power and influence in the organization, cause your project to be delayed, create additional costs, or even have it canceled. That's why it's imperative to find and classify the project stakeholders.

The second process in this knowledge area is to plan stakeholder engagement. This process creates the stakeholder engagement plan to ensure that the stakeholders have been identified and that their needs are met during the project. Through the analysis and classification of the stakeholders, you'll identify their levels of engagement. Recall that there are five levels of stakeholder engagement: unaware, resistant, neutral, supportive, and leading. Determining these classifications can help you set goals in a stakeholders' engagement assessment matrix to move stakeholders to new levels of engagement.

The third process, management of engaging the project stakeholder, really comes down to interpersonal skills and management skills. Interpersonal skills are such characteristics as trustworthiness, the ability to resolve conflicts, and the ability to overcome resistance to change. These are more of the soft skills of project management that foster a good working relationship between the project manager and the stakeholders. The second set of skills is lumped into management skills. These are activities such as facilitating consensus, influencing people for project support, negotiating agreements, and changing organizational behavior for the betterment of the project.

The final process in project stakeholder management is the monitoring of stakeholder engagement. This process ensures that the project manager, the project team, and other stakeholders are all being engaged and contributing to the project as needed. Through information management systems, the project manager can collect performance data, create reports and communications, and track events in the project for the stakeholders. Expert judgment and meetings can also help the project manager ensure that the stakeholders are being engaged and are informed as directed in the stakeholder engagement plan.

Questions

1. You are the project manager of the GUY Project for your organization. This project has recently been chartered, and you're starting the process of stakeholder identification. In this process, you're working with your project team, some of the known stakeholders, and your project sponsor. Which one of the following inputs will you not need for the stakeholder identification process?

   A. Organizational process assets

   B. Risk management plan

   C. Agreements

   D. Project charter

2. Beth is the project manager for a large healthcare project. She is working with the project sponsor to define the steps she'll use to perform stakeholder analysis. Which of the following correctly defines the steps for stakeholder analysis?

   A. Identify and document the stakeholder information, create a communications management plan, plan for stakeholder management.

   B. Identify and document the stakeholder information, prioritize and classify the stakeholders, create the communications management plan for stakeholder management.

   C. Identify and document the stakeholder information, prioritize and classify the stakeholders, plan for stakeholder management.

   D. Create a focus group for known stakeholders, identify and document the stakeholder information, prioritize and classify the stakeholders, plan for stakeholder management.

3. You are the project manager for your organization. Management has asked you to create a stakeholder classification model to show the amount of authority stakeholders have over project decisions in relation to how much their political capital and position in the company could affect the project. What type of stakeholder classification model should you create?

    A. A power/influence grid

    B. A responsibility assignment matrix (RAM) matrix

    C. An impact/influence grid

    D. A responsible, accountable, consulted, informed (RACI) chart

4. Henry has been tasked to create a salience model for his project. This model defines three characteristics for project stakeholders. Which one of the following is not one of the three characteristics of the stakeholders mapped in the salience model?

    A. Power

    B. Urgency

    C. Legitimacy

    D. Influence

5. You are the project manager of a large technology project for your company. This project will span the United States and parts of Europe. There are key stakeholders in all countries represented. As part of your stakeholder analysis, you'd like to create a document that captures all of the stakeholders' contact information, assessment information, and classification in the project. What type of document are you creating?

    A. Stakeholder directory

    B. Stakeholder engagement plan

    C. Stakeholder register

    D. Stakeholder communications matrix

6. Terry is the project manager of the ARB project for his company. Terry approaches Scott for his insight about the schedule for releasing the product the project will create. Scott doesn't know anything about the project Terry is working on and is surprised to learn about the product. What type of stakeholder is Scott?

    A. Unaware

    B. Uninformed

    C. Neutral

    D. Sensitive

7. You are a project management consultant for your company, and you're meeting the stakeholders for the first time. This project is the first adaptive project in your organization, and some of the stakeholders are wary of the approach. Mary, a stakeholder, tells you that she hates the project and hopes that it fails miserably. What type of stakeholder is Mary?

A. Resistant

B. Unhappy

C. Honest

D. Defiant

8. You are the project manager of the HQL Project for your company. Henry, a stakeholder, is in favor of your project, and he's working with you to express the importance of the project. Henry has offered to help with the project, communicate with other stakeholders, and host status meetings. What type of stakeholder is Henry?

A. Supportive

B. Cheerleader

C. Contractual

D. Leading

9. Sammy is the project manager of the KHG Project. Some of the stakeholders in this project are opposed to the project, some are in favor of the project, and some are neutral. Management has asked Sammy to create a chart that shows the current status of engagement for each stakeholder and the desired level of engagement for each stakeholder. What type of chart is management asking for?

A. Stakeholder engagement mapping

B. Stakeholder engagement control chart

C. Stakeholder histogram

D. Stakeholder engagement assessment matrix

10. You are the project manager of the GUY Project for your company, and you're working with your project team on some stakeholder issues. You want to examine the interrelationships among the project stakeholders for better communications. What project management plan will you refer to?

A. Project communications management plan

B. Project stakeholder engagement plan

C. Project stakeholder register

D. Project staffing management plan

11. Holly is a new project manager, and she's confused about the need for the change log and how it relates to the stakeholder engagement. Why is the change log an input to the management stakeholder engagement process?

   A. Because it documents any changes to the stakeholder contact information

   B. Because it documents any changes to the stakeholder register

   C. Because it communicates changes to the stakeholders

   D. Because it communicates changes about the stakeholders to management

12. Part of stakeholder management is the reliance on interpersonal skills. Which one of the following is an interpersonal skill?

   A. Facilitation

   B. Analysis of product scope

   C. Conflict resolution

   D. Influence

13. Just as you need interpersonal skills, you'll also need management skills to engage the stakeholders effectively in the project. Which one is a management skill?

   A. Trustworthiness

   B. Active listening

   C. Influence

   D. Conflict resolution

14. As a PMP candidate, you should be familiar with the inputs, tools and techniques, and outputs of the project management processes. The management of stakeholder engagement creates three outputs. Which one of the following is not an output of the process?

   A. Issue log updates

   B. Change requests

   C. Project management plan updates

   D. Project schedule for stakeholder communications

15. You are coaching several new project managers on effective control of stakeholder engagement. The project managers are confused as to why change requests come from this process. What is the most likely type of change that will come from monitoring stakeholder engagements?

   A. Technology change

   B. Errors or omissions in requirements

   C. External changes

   D. Corrective actions

16. Ned is the project manager of the NHQ Project, and he's meeting with a few key stakeholders to determine their roles, interests, concerns, influence, and attitudes about the project. What type of meeting is Ned hosting?

    A. Kickoff meeting

    B. Stakeholder classification meeting

    C. Profile analysis meeting

    D. Stakeholder status meeting

17. You are the scrum master for a project in your organization. The development team, the product owner, and the project customers are experiencing a demo of what's been created in the sprint. What type of communication is happening in this meeting?

    A. Interactive

    B. Push-pull

    C. Conferring

    D. Cooperative

18. You are the project manager of a large construction project. You have created a web site that enables the different functional managers to log in to a secured area, run queries, and generate reports on the time, cost, scope, changes, risks, and human resources aspects of your project. What type of communication is this?

    A. Pull

    B. Push

    C. Conferring

    D. Static

19. Which one of the following examples best describes a push communication?

    A. A blog about the project

    B. A secured blog for functional managers

    C. A project newsletter sent to the stakeholders from the project manager

    D. The project management plan

20. Your project has 45 stakeholders as of today. You've just learned that next week, 29 new stakeholders will be joining the project. How many more communication channels will you have next week?

    A. 406

    B. 990

    C. 1711

    D. 2701

Answers

1. **B.** The risk management plan is not an input to the stakeholder identification process. A, C, and D are incorrect because these answers are inputs to the stakeholder identification process.

2. **C.** Of all the choices presented, C is the best answer. Stakeholder identification starts with the project manager identifying and documenting the stakeholders' contact information, knowledge, expectations of the project, and their level of influence over project decisions. Then the project manager must prioritize and classify stakeholders based on their power, influence, expectations, and concerns for the project. Finally, Beth should plan for managing the stakeholders based on possible negative or positive scenarios in the project that may affect the stakeholders. A, B, and D are incorrect because these answers do not reflect the correct ordering of steps for stakeholder analysis.

3. **A.** Management is asking you to create a power/influence grid. Evaluating the amount of power and influence a stakeholder has over the project will determine where the stakeholder is placed on the grid. Stakeholders with high power and high influence are top priority. Stakeholders with little power and influence are still considered, but they have less priority than other stakeholders in the project. B is incorrect because a RAM is a responsibility assignment matrix. C is incorrect because this classification model focuses on the influence of the stakeholders and their impact, not their power. D is incorrect because a RACI is a responsibility matrix that tracks a person's responsibility, accountability, consulted, or informed status for each assignment in the project.

4. **D.** A salience model plots out a person's power, urgency, and legitimacy in the project. It does not include their influence. A, B, and C are incorrect because these answers are part of the salience model.

5. **C.** You are creating a stakeholder register. The stakeholder register is the only output of stakeholder identification. It's a log of all the stakeholder information you've gathered in the project. It will help you communicate with project stakeholders; ensure that you understand the stakeholders needs, wants, and expectations; and help you classify stakeholder objectives and priorities. A and D are incorrect because there are no project management documents called the stakeholder directory or the stakeholder communications matrix. B is incorrect because the stakeholder engagement plan defines how the stakeholders will be identified and engaged and how stakeholder engagement will be controlled.

6. **A.** Scott is an unaware stakeholder. Scott doesn't know about the project and the effect the project may have on him. B and D are incorrect choices because there is no stakeholder classification known as uninformed or sensitive. C is also incorrect because neutral describes a stakeholder who is neither opposed nor in favor of the project.

7. **A.** Mary is a resistant stakeholder. Mary knows about the project and doesn't want the change the project will bring. Although Mary may be unhappy, honest, and defiant, these answers are not stakeholder classification types, so choices B, C, and D are incorrect. For organizations that are new to adaptive project management, there will likely be some resistance as stakeholders learn about the benefits of the project and how it can bring value.

8. **D.** Henry is considered to be a leading stakeholder. Henry knows about the project, is supportive of the change the project may bring about, and is working to make the project successful. A, supportive, isn't the best choice because Henry is doing more than just supporting the project—he's helping the project be successful. B, cheerleader, and C, contractual, are not valid stakeholder classification types.

9. **D.** Management is asking Sammy to create a stakeholder engagement assessment matrix to see where stakeholder engagement is now and where it should be in the future. A, B, and C are incorrect because these are not valid charts for stakeholder engagement assessments.

10. **B.** The stakeholder engagement plan defines several things to the project manager about the stakeholders, including information about the interrelationships among the project stakeholders. A, C, and D are incorrect. The project communications management plan does not define the interrelationships among stakeholders. C, the stakeholder register, defines contact information about each stakeholder. D, the project staffing management plan, addresses human resource needs, not communications and stakeholder management.

11. **C.** The change log will help Holly manage stakeholder engagement because she will need to relay information about changes to the appropriate parties. Change can be a sensitive issue in some instances, so always examine the change and think through all of the possible scenarios and reactions the stakeholders may have to the change. Changes to the stakeholder information are reflected in the stakeholder register, not the change log, so A and B are incorrect. D is also incorrect because the change log isn't needed to update and communicate changes about the stakeholders.

12. **C.** Conflict resolution is an interpersonal skill a project manager will need to engage and manage stakeholders' interests in the project. A is incorrect because facilitation is a management skill. B is incorrect because analysis of the product scope is not an interpersonal skill. D is also incorrect because influence is one of the managerial skills.

13. **C.** Influence is considered a management skill because you'll need to persuade people to buy in and support the project. A, B, and D are all incorrect because these answers are part of the interpersonal skill set for project managers.

14. **D.** The schedule for stakeholder communications is more likely a part of the project communications management plan. A, B, and C are incorrect because these answers are outputs of the manage stakeholder engagement process. The process creates three outputs: issue log updates that are part of the project document updates, change requests, and project management plan updates.

15. **D.** Defects are changes that have already happened. A defect is a change that differs from what was planned in the project. A defect to be solved requires a change through a corrective action to get the results back in alignment with the project scope. A, B, and C are all examples of common change requests, but the most likely change from monitoring stakeholder engagements will be from corrective actions.

16. **C.** This is an example of a profile analysis meeting. Ned is learning and documenting as much as he can about the stakeholders to better engage them in the project. A is incorrect because the kickoff meeting launches the project. B and D are incorrect because the stakeholder classification meeting and the stakeholder status meeting are not valid meeting types.

17. **A.** This is an example of interactive communications, in which information is being communicated among stakeholders, such as in a forum or meeting. B, C, and D are incorrect because push-pull, conferring, and cooperative are not valid communication types.

18. **A.** This is an example of pull communication because the functional managers are retrieving information from your web server. B is incorrect because push communications require the project manager to push information out to the stakeholders through e-mail or other media. C and D are incorrect because conferring and static are not valid communication types.

19. **C.** Push communication means that one person is sending out the information to other people. Of all the choices, the newsletter sent from the project manager to the project stakeholders is the best example of a push communication. A and B are incorrect because the blog, secured or not, represents pull communication. D is incorrect because although the project management plan provides information, it's not a definitive communication method.

20. **C.** To solve this problem, you'll need to use the communications channel formula of $N(N - 1)/2$, where N represents the number of stakeholders. You'll first have to find the current number of communication channels, which is 990. Then, you'll find the channels with added stakeholders, which is 2701. Finally, you'll find the difference between 2701 and 990, which is 1711 more communication channels. A is incorrect because 406 represents the communication channels among just the 29 additional stakeholders. B is incorrect because 990 represents the current number of communication channels. D is incorrect because 2701 is the total number of communication channels, not the difference in the number communication channels between this week and next.

PART III

PMP Agile Exam Testing Areas

Leading an Agile Project

In this chapter, you will

- Build a solid foundation for agile project management
- Explore agile project management approaches
- Plan increments and iterations

The most recent Project Management Professional (PMP) Exam Content Outline, which you should review on the Project Management Institute (PMI) web site, covers much more of agile project management than previous PMP exams. You'll need a solid understanding of agile and predictive/agile blends, called *hybrid* project management, for your PMP exam even if you don't manage agile projects. Throughout this book I've introduced agile concepts for each of the major exam components, but now I'll dive into agile project management.

 VIDEO For a more detailed explanation, watch the *Agile Overview* video now.

Agile project management is a broad topic—and it's evolving daily in the project management space. It's difficult to describe a definitive approach to agile project management, because there are many different approaches to agile project management. Approaches splinter into new approaches all the time. Unlike waterfall project management, where it's easy to see the project from initiating to closing, some agile projects flow through repetitive cycles, called *iterations*, and other approaches, while following repetitions of work, create increments of deliverables. While it all sounds tricky—and it can be—you'll be happy to know the PMP exam will be much more direct and question you about the mainstream concepts of agile project management.

Hybrid projects are a combination of predictive and agile—where you might do a bit more planning up front than a typical agile project, but you'll shift into agile principles thereafter. Or you might start with agile prioritization of requirements and then plan and become adverse to change. Who knows? Hybrid approaches are custom approaches to specific projects—and there are no steadfast rules in hybrid, other than the focus is on delivering value to stakeholders. This chapter will help you create a strong foundation of agile project management for the PMP exam.

Defining Agile Project Management

Agile project management is all about value realization and welcoming change and is not as document heavy as predictive project management. In predictive project management, such as building a new house, you'll plan everything up front, in detail, down to the cabinets in the kitchen. Once you have a solid set of plans, stakeholder approval, a budget, and a schedule, the predictive project manager becomes averse to change. Agile projects, which typically have been in the software development arena, don't do as much up-front planning as predictive projects. Certainly, there's a sense of where the project is going, but agile projects begin by prioritizing stakeholder requirements from most important to least important, build out the deliverables based on priorities, and welcome change throughout the project. Obviously, there are some project types for which agile is inappropriate.

You're familiar with my classic example of building a house. Building something physical is easy to assess; you can drive by the job site, take a quick peek on the construction project, and determine whether the crew has made progress. These physical projects describe industrial work. Industrial work is typically centered on physical labor, and it's easy to see results and predict time and cost, and everyone has a good sense of where the project is going.

With other projects, such as software development, creative work, and writing, it isn't always easy to see progress. You can see someone staring off into space in front of her computer, and you really don't know if she is working out a solution or daydreaming about sugary beaches in Florida. This type of work is knowledge work and is sometimes called *invisible work*. With knowledge work, you cannot always see what people are about to create. Therefore, knowledge work expects changes, has agility to move directions quickly, and is easier to adapt, change, and do rework than changing the floorplan for a new home construction project.

An industrial project, such as building a house or a skyscraper, is very visible. It is stable. You are talking about running things, about getting things done. It has structure. There are definite yes and no answers, and there are codes for compliance that you must follow. It is task-driven because you install the foundation and build the framework. You have one person in charge, command, and control. You have industry standards and easy-to-measure performance because you can look at it and see how far along you are. For this task, you can say how much it will cost to install these light fixtures because we have an hourly rate for our workers.

Knowledge work is more invisible. When I am coding, you do not see anything. There are a lot of changes. Agile expects change, which includes the environment. There is less structure. There are lots of questions in knowledge work. Agile encourages empirical processes, which are decisions and action based on observation and experience. Agile project management drives team autonomy, meaning the team is self-led and self-organizing, rather than led by a command-and-control approach. Agile leaders want the team to experiment and to use innovation. The agile team is seen as an asset, not a cost.

Reviewing the Agile Manifesto

In 2001, 17 software developers went on a ski trip to Utah. During their time together they discussed software project management and its challenges utilizing the waterfall approach. From their conversation over the three-day trip, they developed a charter and simple approach for successful software development projects: the Agile Manifesto. The Agile Manifesto is universal to all agile projects, regardless of the agile approach the organization may adapt. While I don't expect your PMP exam to ask specific questions on this document, understand the document will help you have an agile mindset and apply the principles to tricky exam questions. Each of the following items begin with the thought of "we have come to value," where "we" represents the group of agile leaders and agile organizations.

- **Individuals and interactions over processes and tools** Individuals and interactions are valued over processes and tools because we want to focus on the people. Things get done by people—not processes, not organizations, not software or tools, but by people. Processes and tools are still going to be utilized, but the focus begins with people. Embrace the concept that people do the work and successful projects are more than just having a framework, processes, and fancy tools. Agile projects are people driven.

- **Working software over comprehensive documentation** The value in an agile project doesn't have to be software, but remember this is where agile began. The idea is the value exists in a working product for the project customer. There is no value, or little value, in documentation in most agile projects. Value is about satisfying the business need and rarely does documentation satisfy a business need. Documentation, if we are required to do it, should be barely sufficient and just in time. Documentation might have to be there because you have an industry or organizational requirement and you may be required to have it for compliance, but documentation is less valuable than working software or the project deliverables.

- **Customer collaboration over contract negotiation** Contracts are unusual in agile because contracts want to know specific things. In agile projects, you cannot always be specific, so agile project management favors customer collaboration over contract negotiation. Agile must be flexible, accommodating, and willing to change, while contracts are just the opposite. They are rigid, uncooperative, specific. Agile is uncertain, and contracts are legal documents. Legal documents want things that are certain and often want to define everything in the project.

- **Responding to change over following a plan** Agile projects welcome change; predictive projects are averse to change. There is not much up-front planning in agile, and agile projects are commonly called *change driven*. Within agile projects, we have uncertainty up front, so change is expected and welcome in an agile environment.

PART III

Building the Agile Mindset

What does it mean to be agile? Being agile does not mean you are just using the approach of Scrum, Lean, or Kanban. It is about following a methodology and having an agile mindset. It is more than just the methodology, as agile isn't really a cookbook for success. Agile really wants you, the team, and the organization as a whole to have an agile mindset, which is a way of being adaptable. Agile wants all the stakeholders to collaborate and get people involved to accomplish business value. Of course, all agile project managers first have to learn the foundations of agile—and that's largely what your exam will test you on. All agile project managers really begin by doing agile, understanding the mechanics of agile and the iterations, and following the agile rules.

Being agile is really what you want to focus on for the tougher exam questions. First, you, as the project manager or the scrum master or whatever title you have in your agile environment, must embrace this idea of the agile mindset. You must understand and coach others on agile principles, and by coaching, you are really selling the ideas and principles of agile. You will have to educate others, such as your project sponsor, your project team, and key stakeholders. Agile is still relatively new, and no doubt you are going to have some skeptical people. Expect skeptics and coach them and sell them on the idea of agile—show them the value by delivering value early, rather than make promises and getting bogged down in the rules and procedures of agile.

As the agile leader with the agile mindset, you'll also need to coach the team, the developers, and the people getting stuff done in the project. When agile is first implemented, the team is going to want to know why you are doing this. Why is the agile approach better, and why are we changing from what we've been using forever? Too many project managers, in my opinion, treat the project team like children. The best way to show the team why agile is valuable is to experience the benefits. You experience the benefits by coaching the team to quick victories, quick wins. Initially, you'll do lots of handholding, coaching, and listening to the team grumble and ask questions. They may be hesitant to change, but soon they'll see the value in agile and the new freedom agile offers that predictive projects cannot. Your team needs to experience this idea of a safe environment so they can try new things. A saying in agile is that you are going to fail early, fail fast. The idea, though, is that you want the team and the organization to feel safe to experiment and to be innovative in the project so that you get out of the team's way.

It's often tough, as a project manager, to let the developers work the way they feel is best. Project managers with an agile mindset coach more and command-and-control less. This means let the team decide on new approaches and let the team try new things and share the outcomes. In predictive project management, the project manager is seen as the leader, but that's not the case in agile. Agile projects encourage emergent leadership, where anyone on the team can become a leader. Anyone can be a leader, and leadership roles can change in different portions of the project.

As an agile project manager, with whatever title your approach names you, always aim to practice servant leadership. Servant leadership means that you carry food and water for the team. You aren't literally carrying food and water for the team, but rather you get the team the things they need to get the work done. You serve as a shield against distractions and interruptions for the team. You get rid of impediments. You get the team the things that they need to move forward.

While all of this sounds fantastic, there is still a formal approach to agile project management. All stakeholders must know the rules, the processes, how to interact with team members, and how to get to the end. You need some formality in agile; it cannot be too loose, but you also can't be too structured either. It'll take time, experimentation, and flexibility to find the right balance control and achievement. You know that agile is a change-driven approach, and when starting agile, you are going to implement changes, not only to the scope but with how people work.

Leading an Agile Project

The role of the agile project manager is largely about coordination, coaching, and communicating. You'll serve as coach to make certain everyone is following the rules of agile and to protect the developers from interruption. Interruptions often come from stakeholders, sometimes called the *businesspeople*. Businesspeople and developers will need to work together throughout the project, but there must be a balance so that there's not too many meetings, but also not a gap in needed communications. When launching an agile project, we set expectations, make the rules, and get commitments from the people involved.

This is a key part of agile: agile projects do not act as a wall between businesspeople and the people doing the work. These two roles are going to work together daily throughout the project. We want to build projects around motivated individuals, around people who are excited, and around people who are motivated to do the work. How do we get them motivated? One way to get people motivated is to provide them the environment and the support that they need. Then, you must trust them. You trust people to do the work, to get the work done. Agile project stakeholders need transparency, so agile project managers must be transparent and simply state facts about the project, good, bad, or indifferent. One the most efficient and effective methods of transparency to convey information is a face-to-face conversation. You want to talk to people and look people in the eye. I know this is a challenge when we have noncolocated teams or virtual teams, but you want to have face-to-face conversations. I am not talking about just you, the project manager, but all members and stakeholders of an agile project.

 EXAM TIP Face-to-face conversations are the best method for transparent communication.

Technically, you are not leading an agile project, but rather you're leading people to a result. When you are marching toward a result, how do you know you are making progress? Working software is how we know we are making progress. Of course, working software does not have to mean coding if your agile project centers on a different domain, but progress is shown in things that are done. If there is a lot of busywork, a lot of fury, tons of meetings, chatter, and a big cloud of dust, then that does not equate to progress.

Agile processes promote a sustainable workload, where people can get things done, at a reasonable pace, indefinitely. Agile project managers must not overwork the team. Good agile project management calls for uniform, reasonable, practical efforts to create the product. In that constant, sustainable effort you and the team have continuous attention to technical excellence and good design. You want the approach of the solution to be simple—and that doesn't mean easy.

Simplicity, in agile project management, is the art of maximizing the amount of work not done. The product that is created is all about value and is sometimes called the *minimal viable product* (MVP). The work not done, what you elect not to do, doesn't add value for the customer. The team needs to discover what is the least amount of effort they could do and still keep customers happy. The best architectures, requirements, and designs emerge not from you, not the businesspeople, but from the self-organizing team. At regular intervals, the team reflects on how to become more effective, and then they will tune and adjust and adapt their behavior.

Exploring Agile Approaches

Agile project management is not just one approach to getting things done, but rather many different approaches and different philosophies to project completion. Your PMP exam will test you on the common principles of agile project management, but you may have a few specific questions from the different methodologies of agile. All agile approaches are largely based on the Agile Manifesto, and they share three common actions:

- Transparency requires trust, agreement, and open communication throughout the project. One of the first examples of transparency begins with project's Definition of Done (DoD). The DoD defines how we know when the project is done.

- Inspection is the review of the artifacts, the progress, and the quality of the work, and then you do not hide discoveries. Our findings are out there for everyone to see. Inspection should not get in the way of the work, but inspection is most beneficial when you have skilled inspectors inspecting the work.

- Adaptation is needed when issues arise. In other words, if the solution is not going to be acceptable, fix the problem. Adjustments are made as soon as possible to minimize additional deviation. You fix the problem right now. Do not keep moving forward in the project with this problem because you will have more and more work based on the current faulty product. You don't want a future deliverable based on a past problem. Fix this problem as soon as possible to minimize additional deviations from what the customer expects.

You can remember these three principles of agile project management by thinking TIA: transparency, inspection, and adaptation. All approaches to agile project management have these three principles. On your exam, when you're faced with a tough agile or hybrid question, think of TIA. You'll want to determine what the project manager can do to be transparent, what the team can do to inspect the work results and the approach, and what inspections are needed to reach value within the project.

Diving into Scrum

The most common agile approach is Scrum. Scrum is a rugby term, and it's where the players huddle around the football, heads down, and the ball gets back in play. Scrum, in agile, is not necessarily something new. It really started in 1995 by its founders Jeff Sutherland and Ken Schwaber. Scrum is not just a framework for processes, but rather a characteristic of product management, not just project management. It is an agile approach that follows repeatable activities to move the project toward the Definition of Done. The project moves through iterations, called *sprints*, to work on the most important to least important requirements of the stakeholders.

While there are many different approaches to agile, all agile projects work in sprints, iterations, or increments. An increment is a chunk of usable product developed in each sprint. An increment is a potentially releasable part of the final product. Each increment is appended to the prior increments. Think of a choo-choo train; each increment is just another boxcar in the train. In most incremental projects, the product owner doesn't release an increment every four weeks; several increments will create key, usable benefits that will then be released. The product owner will determine what qualifications have to be in place before a release may occur. An increment is the sum of all the sprints that you have completed.

 VIDEO   For more details on Scrum, see the *Introduction to Scrum* video now.

Iterations are also sprints, and they build on what's been completed in the past, but they refine and improve on the product as a whole. Imagine sketching out a painting and then refining the sketch, painting over the sketch, repainting the sketch, and so on, until the painting is perfected. That's the idea behind iterations—you iterate on what you've completed. Creating a web site is a good example of an iterative project, as the team and product owner can quickly see a mockup and then a functional prototype, then the text is added, then more functionality is added, and so on. This is, unfortunately, where things get blurry in agile: iterations may, or may not, qualify for incremental releases to the customer. The product owner may determine some iterations create an increment and should be released. Other products may not be released until the entire product is created. Every project is different.

Before the team gets to the requirements in a sprint, the team needs a vision statement. The vision statement describes the goals and why the project exists. It's a simple document that keeps the purpose of the project and the value the project brings in the forefront. A vision statement is a short document that must have five elements to be considered good:

- Unambiguous definition of the project
- Clear and simple language

- Alignment with the organization's value
- Realistic expectations of the project
- Short and direct

Next, at the launch of the project's first sprint, there should be a product roadmap. The product owner is likely to work with you, the scrum master, and the team to develop a product roadmap. This is one area where agile projects shine over predictive. If you're building a house, there is no benefit to the homeowner until the house is completely done. The homeowner can't move into a portion of the house until the entire house is ready. In agile projects, the customer could begin using a portion of the software, such as version 1, while your team continues to build and create version 2. Each release of the software builds on what's already been created.

The product roadmap is a map of how the project should move from start to finish with intermittent deliverables to the stakeholders. It's an ideal document of how the team will get from the start to the end. It answers what conditions must be met to allow the product owner to do a release, what the components of a release are, and the result of the project.

Figure 14-1 is the big picture of scrum, and it begins with the product backlog, which is all known requirements. The product backlog is owned and maintained by the product owner, a businessperson who knows what the business values and knows how a Scrum project works. The product owner keeps the product backlog prioritized based

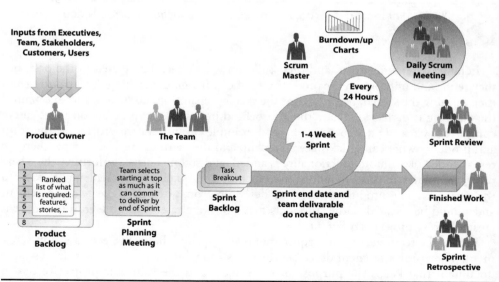

Figure 14-1 Scrum follows a logical and iterative approach throughout the project.

on the business value and the expected monetary value of the item. When changes are requested, the product owner evaluates the change, puts it into the product backlog, and reprioritizes the list of requirements with the new addition. Adding a requirement does not mean it goes to the bottom of the product backlog; it could be an important change and be pushed to the top of the backlog, plopped in the middle, or appear somewhere near the bottom—it's all based on value.

 EXAM TIP User stories are predominantly prioritized based on the value to the customer, but some user stories carry significant risks and should be moved to earlier in the project. The product owner and team can calculate the expected monetary value of the risk for the user story just as we discussed in Chapter 11: Probability X Impact = Expected Monetary Value.

In Scrum, when the actual work of creating the deliverable is performed, is called a *sprint*. Sprints can last from two to four weeks, though four weeks is the most common approach. At the start of each sprint, the product owner, the developers, and the scrum master all meet to plan out the work for the sprint. This meeting, called *sprint planning*, focuses on the product backlog and how much work the developers believe they can accomplish. The team reviews the items in the prioritized sprint backlog, which are called *user stories*. The items are called user stories because they tell a little story about the user, how'd they'd use the action, and the value they'd receive from the action.

Creating the Sprint Backlog

The team, working with the product owner, will review the most valuable user stories from the product backlog and determine how many of the user stories they can complete during the sprint. This first meeting of each sprint is the sprint planning meeting. The team all agrees on the chunk of work that they feel they can accomplish during the next sprint. This chunk of selected user stories always starts with the most important items in the backlog first. Sometimes you'll see this concept as "eating your dessert first" as we get to the good stuff that creates the most value for the customers. The user stories that are selected for the sprint are now referred to as the *sprint backlog*. The sprint backlog does not change once it is created. The sprint backlog helps the team create a sprint goal: what the team will accomplish during the next sprint. Each sprint repeats this process of sprint planning, and this meeting typically lasts eight hours for a four-week sprint.

 EXAM TIP User stories should not be so big that they can't be completed during one sprint of the project. You do not want stories so big that they span several sprints. You want the story to be sized appropriately so that it can be done in one four-week iteration or however long the sprint is in your project.

Completing the Daily Work

Next, we get into our daily work. This is the heart of the project where the team is focused on getting the work done. In this portion of the project, it's the team, not a project manager, that determines who'll do what in the project and what's important to get done next. This is why scrum teams are considered to be self-organizing and self-led. They don't look to a project manager to tell them what to do. However, early in a scrum project, the role of the scrum master, which is similar to a project manager, is to coach the team. The scrum master may help the team determine who'll do what task, coordinate events, and provide some control over the work. As the project moves along, the scrum master will control activities less, and the team will become more self-led.

Sometimes I am asked, "What if somebody wants to do a six- to eight-week sprint or even a ten-week sprint? What's the problem with that?" Longer sprints introduce risk, because it's long time to work on a product without review and interaction from the customer. Longer sprints might also affect the ability to go to market because I have a deliverable that could be a released increment at a two-to-four-week sprint, but the product owner must wait for the end of the ten-week sprint. Remember, the product owner and customer don't see or receive any value until the end of the sprint.

Another consideration for the sprint duration is that the team is likely going to change. People will quit, win the lottery, get hit by a bus, or go to different projects. Your team is going to change. Changing team members during a sprint is not recommended; people leaving or joining a team during the middle of a long sprint creates new risks and problems: learning curve, team formation phases, communication challenges, and work assignments. It's a mess—four-week sprints are ideal.

Hosting the Daily Scrum

Every 24 hours in a scrum project there is an event called the daily scrum. This is a meeting where the team can assess how they are doing for their sprint goal. The team can do some forecasting, discuss the likelihood of completing all items in the sprint, and discuss any roadblocks in the project. The daily scrum happens every day at the same time and at same place throughout the sprint. In the daily scrum, the team answers three questions:

- What have you accomplished since we last met?
- What will you accomplish since our last daily scrum?
- Are there impediments to your progress?

Extremely large projects, or even programs, could have multiple teams contributing to the customer's goal. In that case, you would have daily scrums happening in each project. To help coordinate all of the different projects, a representative from each project will also meet for a scrum of scrums. Each representative will discuss their project's accomplishments, next plans, and impediments, and they'll discuss if their project work could interfere with other project work. While it's unusual, a massive project could duplicate this effort and call for a scrum of scrum of scrums where multiple projects are grouped and have one representative to speak for all projects in their group to other representatives of grouped projects.

Leading the Sprint Review Meeting

At the end of the sprint, you have the sprint review, a four-hour meeting for a four-week sprint, where the developers review what's been completed in the sprint. Only completed items are demonstrated in the sprint review; if the item doesn't meet the Definition of Done, the item is returned to the product owner for prioritization in the product backlog. It's common for the project customers to request changes during the sprint review. The customer will see the demo, see what's possible, and have ideas for improvement to their value. This is fine because in agile we welcome and expect changes.

Performing the Sprint Retrospective

The final ceremony of the sprint is a three-hour meeting called the *sprint retrospective*. The sprint retrospective is a type of lessons learned meeting on what went well, or not so well, during the past sprint. The goal of the meeting is to look for opportunities to improve the product and the project. The product owner, the developers, and the scrum master attend this meeting to transparently inspect and review the communication, successes, and failures of the project. This is not an opportunity to place blame, but to honestly discuss the wins and losses of the sprint. The retrospective helps the team improve upon the project work for the next sprint. For your exam, retrospectives are required, but there are times when the product owner, the scrum master, and the development team agree that a retrospective isn't needed, so it can be skipped. Skipping a retrospective is a rare event.

 EXAM TIP Only the product owner can cancel the sprint. You do not see this often unless there is a drastic reason, such as the project goal has become obsolete. If the customers changed their mind about the project or a technology has changed, or some other significant event, that could warrant the product owner to cancel the sprint. Anything that is done when the sprint is canceled should still go through the sprint review, and then the items that are not done should go back to the product backlog so that the product owner can reprioritize. It is unusual to cancel a sprint.

Working with User Stories

A user story, like its name implies, is a story of a role utilizing some functionality to get value from the functionality. For example, as a salesperson, I want to place orders via an app, so I can make more sales. User stories follow a formula of role, function, and value. For example, "As a <role>, I want <function>, so I can realize <value.>" User stories are the items in the product backlog, they are a small chunk of functionality, and they generally take up to 40 hours to create. User stories are written on sticky notes or index cards and are sometimes called *story cards*. You can even purchase preprinted sticky notes that guide you through the user story requirements.

A user story is just a small chunk of functionality that equates to about one to three days of work. You might also see it defined as that it equates to 40 hours of work. This is depending on what resource you are looking at. The idea is that it is less than 40 hours to create, typically about one to three days. A user story, which we will look at an example of in just a moment, is generally written on an index card or a sticky note that will go up on a big whiteboard where everybody can see it. This helps us interact with the user story, prioritize items, and move things around.

Creating User Stories

User stories should be easy to understand by everyone on the team. Strictly speaking, user stories are created by the product owner, and they go into the product backlog. Realistically speaking, user stories are written by everyone on the team, though it's the product owner who'll be responsible for the user stories and the prioritization of the user stories in the product backlog. Each user story should aim to create value. When a person proposes a user story and the value is being considered for project inclusion, it's called a *candidate story*—it is worth considering but hasn't yet been fully included in the project requirements.

In user story formats, you give the scenario of what the role is doing and the action that is happening, such as purchasing things from your web site. And you provide the result, which is the realized value of the action. One of my favorite approaches to writing user stories is called the three Cs:

- **Card**   User story can fit on one card
- **Conversational**   Quick details that are easy to understand
- **Confirmation**   Customer confirms the user story has been completed

During the sprint review, the development team demonstrates the completed user story functionality. For example, say a company is selling car parts, and the user story reads: "As a customer, I want to search for a car part, so I can order it online." In the sprint review, the team could read the card and then show the action and the completed result. This is quick and easy to understand and simple to demonstrate as a user story that has met the Definition of Done. Of course, not all user stories are so simple, but your exam will test you on the concept.

Another common approach that you will see is to utilize the user story acronym of INVEST:

- **Independent**   This can be prioritized in any order in the product backlog.
- **Negotiable**   The team and product owner can make tradeoffs for cost and function.
- **Value**   The value of the user story action is apparent.
- **Estimable**   The required effort to create the function can be estimated.
- **Small**   It should be able to be completed in one iteration.
- **Testable**   The results can be tested for completion and accuracy.

Estimating User Stories

The developers can do only so much work in a four-week time period, and we need a way to predict how much work the developers can take on. The developers need to look at the user stories in the prioritized product backlog and determine how big, or how small, the user stories are and assign points to stories based on the size of the user story. The bigger the story, the more story points it receives. A story point is just a way to size the stories we are about to take on, from large to small. This does not mean assigned story points reflect prioritization, but only reflects how big the user stories are. User story sizing is all relative—this story point is really tricky, so we'll give it ten points, and this story point is tiny, so we'll give it two points.

Story point sizing helps the team predict how much work, or more precisely, how many story points, they can complete in an iteration. When a scrum project launches, the team can look at a chunk of the project work in the prioritized backlog and determine if they can complete it over the next four weeks. Each user story in the chunk is sized based on effort, complexity, and duration to do the work, though it's not really a precise duration estimation, but a rough estimate of the amount of work the developers can realistically complete within the sprint.

It's tricky to do user story sizing, so a good approach is to think in terms of T-shirts. This story is a small; this story is an extra-large. User stories are relative to one another—the small and extra-large story can help you triangulate other stories for their size too. You want to make certain that sizing is correct, but also uniform. This approach helps the team avoid incorrect sizing when dreading certain parts of the project: I hate this activity, so this is a "jumbo awning size" doesn't fit in proportion to the other user stories. T-shirt sizing for estimating is an example of affinity estimating, where all stories are estimated by the same types of rules.

In affinity estimating, the product owner, the development team, and the scrum master participates. The estimates are created from the top of the product backlog, and the process begins with some proven reference points, such as past projects or similar work, like analogous estimating. It is difficult to say this estimate is a definitive estimate. In the early sprints, it'll be tricky to predict how much work the developers can complete, but over time, this prediction will normalize. Stories are sized using story points. The team predicts how many story points they can complete in a sprint. The selected stories from the product backlog become the sprint backlog. Now in the next sprint planning meeting the team has a good sense of how many user story points they can complete. With each new sprint the team can be more accurate in predicting how many points they're able to complete. The number of story points a team completed in a sprint is called *velocity*. Velocity can be unpredictable to start, but over time, the velocity of the team will become stable.

Another approach to user story sizing is the Fibonacci sequence. The Fibonacci sequence can be seen by examining the top of a seashell, the branching of a tree, and other places in nature. You take two consecutive numbers, starting with zero and one, and add them together to predict the next number in the sequence. For example, one and two is three. Then you'll add two and three for five. Then three and five for eight. This pattern forms a spiral, like the top shown in Figure 14-2. How this relates to affinity estimating is each number in the pattern is relative to the other numbers—it's not random. When estimating user stories with the Fibonacci sequence, you'll generally use numbers 1, 2, 3, 5, 8, and 13, though some organizations take sizing out to 21 points. The bigger the user story, the bigger the number it receives in the sequence.

Figure 14-2
The Fibonacci
sequence creates
a spiraled pattern
as the numbers
grow in size.

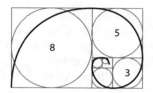

EXAM TIP   The number of user story points doesn't have to equal the expected velocity of the team. For example, if the team's velocity is 30, the selection of user stories should fit within the 30-story point velocity, not exactly 30, but approximately 30. That could be 28, could be 31, or might even be 33. It's approximate.

Introducing Extreme Programming

Other than Scrum, Extreme Programming (XP) is where you will probably have the next largest number of agile questions on your exam. XP began in 1996 on the now famous (in agile nerd circles) Chrysler Comprehensive Compensation System, a project to replace multiple payroll systems with one uniform system for the organization. The core value of XP is simplicity first. XP teams want to get rid of extra features, get rid of waste, keep things simple, and find the simplest thing that could possibly work to satisfy customer requirements. Like Scrum, XP expects changes to happen throughout the project, and the XP team welcomes change. A difference, however, is that XP acknowledges the risk that a deadline-driven project introduces. Projects that have deadlines are not realistic with the time it will take to create the deliverable, and there's added stress of the deadline for the project team. The deadline can also create the XP team to feel overworked, under pressure, and afraid to innovate. Know that concept for your exam.

XP uses a weekly and quarterly cycle to describe its timeboxed approach. A weekly cycle, like a scrum sprint, is an iteration. On the first day of each week, the team meets to discuss what's been accomplished, choose the prioritized user stories to create during the week, and decide how the team will go about creating the selected user stories. This concept is similar to sprint planning, but it's shorter than a typical sprint. The quarterly cycle is a release, and it is planned and updated each week in the weekly cycle based on what the customer prioritization of requirements are. Basically, the accomplishments of each week help determine what will be released each quarter.

Slack in XP is created by adding in some low-level requirements that can be dropped from the weekly cycle if the schedule gets tight. If things are going smoothly, the low-level requirements can be added into the weekly cycle without creating a burden for the project team. Another concept that works to address time management in XP is the Ten-Minute Build. This means the system that compiles all the code and to run all the tests can complete the compilation and testing within a ten-minute timeframe.

A ten-minute build encourages the team to create an automated build approach, test frequently, and follow continuous integration. Continuous integration happens when the code is developed or changed, and then the code is tested immediately to find and fix integration errors.

XP follows the test-first programming approach. This approach may seem backward, as you must have code to test before testing it, the policy means the tests are written first, the test will fail because there's no code to pass the test, and then the developer can write the code to pass the test. By writing the test first, the paired programmers know what the code must be to pass the required test.

XP, as in Figure 14-3, follows a logical approach to getting work done. There are loops built into the approach that make everything iterative as you move through the project. Your exam may lightly touch on the approach, so you should be familiar with the approach.

Planning the XP Project

User stories are written.

A release schedule is created.

Plans for frequent, small releases are developed.

A project is segmented into iterations.

Each iteration begins with an iteration planning session.

Figure 14-3
XP incorporates planning and feedback loops through its life cycle.

Managing the XP Project

Colocated teams work in an open workspace.

Establish a sustainable pace of work.

Each day begins with a 15-minute standup meeting (all participants stand).

Project velocity is frequently measured.

Team members are trained in other roles.

Retrospectives help fix problems in XP.

Designing

Keep things simple.

Create a system metaphor to quickly explain the project.

Class, responsibilities, and collaboration (CRC) cards help design the system.

Spike iterations are used to address risks.

Don't add features and functions until they are requested.

Refactor, which means cleaning up the code, happens throughout the project.

Coding

A customer role should be available for input.

Establish standards for all coding.

Unit tests are written first.

Programmers utilize paired programming.

Code is frequently integrated, but by only one programming pair at a time.

An integration server is required for project.

All code is collectively owned, and any programmer can review or edit code.

Testing

Unit tests are required for all code.

All code must pass the unit test before release.

Bugs in the code require new tests to be created.

Acceptance testing is required, and results are tracked and shared.

Communicating in XP

XP has five central values, the first being communication. XP, like Scrum, relies heavily on face-to-face communication, even if it's over a web conferencing software, like Zoom or Microsoft Teams. You know that when effective communication happens, you receive feedback. This is a core attribute of XP: get feedback early and often. This is part of XP's fail early, fail fast approach. When people fail fast, fail early, they get feedback as to what's working or isn't working so they can make adjustments and move forward in the project. XP also calls for a safe environment for people to experiment and to fail in. There's no negative feedback—if the experiment didn't work, the team knows what didn't work and they can move on without fear of retribution.

Keeping Things Simple

Simple does not mean easy. Simple means not overengineering the solution, not creating complex code, and designing a solution that's direct and easy to implement. In XP, you'll ask for the simplest thing that will work to satisfy the customer requirements. A temptation I often see among developers is to assume requirements will be coming in the project, so they'll go ahead and address their assumptions. This is scope creep and is project poison. XP teams should only address requirements they know with certainty, not requirements they think may be coming later in the project.

Working with Feedback

Recall that in Scrum there is a sprint retrospective to give teams an opportunity to improve and work better in the next sprint. XP has a similar, though less formal, concept through immediate feedback. Feedback shouldn't be judgmental, but constructive, and it should guide the team to make better decisions. When giving feedback, team members should be respectful, honest, and focus on what's worked or didn't work—it's not all negative. This is not an opportunity to place blame, but an opportunity to move forward in the project.

Working with Courage

To fail early, fail fast, fail often, we need courage. When developers experiment, their work is visible to everyone on the team. That takes courage. The team openly shares code, collectively owns the code, and has the authority to correct each other's code. One approach in this concept is called *pair programming*. One person works as a developer, and a person next to them that is watching that person develop the code. Actually, it is more than just watching. The second programmer helps catch mistakes, offers improvements, and helps the programmer however is needed. The person programming is called the *driver*, and the person helping is called the *navigator*. The driver and navigator switch roles every 1.5 to 3 hours.

Respecting the Team

To communicate effectively, work together through paired programming, and try new approaches, the team members must respect one another. XP embraces the concept that everyone is responsible, not any one individual, for the success or failure of the project. Everyone works differently, but you the team must work together.

Reviewing the XP Roles and Responsibilities

There are eight roles in an XP project that you must know for your exam. You won't need to know these in-depth, but you should be familiar with their responsibilities and be able to recognize what each role does in the project.

- **Customer or product owner**   This role, like the product owner in scrum, represents the business values and is responsible for writing user stories, prioritizing the requirements, and helping programmers understand the value of user stories. While this role may not be the actual customer or businessperson, they serve as a representative for the business or customer, so they need good insight to what the customer values and what's expected as an end result of the project.

- **Coach**   The XP coach coaches the team members on the XP approach, keeps things moving along, oversees the work of the project, and helps implement process improvements as a result of team feedback. The coach isn't the same as a project manager, but does help coordinate activities among the project and ensures everyone is following the rules and contributing.

- **Programmer**   Not too hard figure out what this role does, right? The programmer programs the code to satisfy the requirements of the customer. Programmers also derive the tasks needed to complete user stories and works on unit testing in the project.

- **Tester**   The tester runs functional tests on the code the programmers have created. Functional tests are also called *integration tests* and are more robust than the unit tests the programmers do. The tester role will also document the test results.

- **Tracker**   This role has some project management duties as the person will track the work assignments to confirm things are "on track" in the project. If things aren't going as expected, the person will work to make certain assignments are going to plan. The tracker also meets with programmers, the coach, and the customer to report on project progress.

- **Doomsayer**   The cheeriest role in XP projects, the doomsayer monitors risk, poor results, and issues with the project. The doomsayer communicates frequently about the conditions of events that could threaten the project's success. The role's objective is to be honest and transparent about the health of the project.

- **Manager**   The XP manager is responsible for delivering the project as promised. The manager is responsible for communicating status to the project customer, schedules meetings for release planning, and often serves as the doomsayer and tracker roles.

- **Gold owner**   The gold owner pays for the project and is often the project sponsor in an organization.

Traditionally, XP teams are colocated for face-to-face communication and osmotic communications. Of course, with more and more people working remotely, this is fading as an XP rule. You'll also see that XP roles are sometimes called *generalizing specialists*, meaning a role can do more than one thing, rather than serving as a silo and doing only one thing.

One of the key things for your exam is a sustainable pace. Know this concept of sustainable pace. When the team examines the product backlog they'll start with the items at the top, which are the most important, and the team will determine how many story points they can complete in the iteration. When they go into that iteration, we do not want to encourage them, "Well, how about you take on 30 or 35?" Well, that is going to lead to overtime and long hours, and that is not sustainable. What we aim for is what will lead us to a sustainable velocity. Remember, velocity is how much a team can get done in an iteration, so we want something that is uniform and sustainable.

Working with Other Agile Approaches

All of the agile project management approaches are typically built around the concepts in the Agile Manifesto. You'll also see that these methodologies usually come from software development projects. This is important to remember, as agile project management most often centers on knowledge work projects. It's easier to change software code than it is to change a concrete wall. On your exam, scenario questions may describe the project work, and that'll give you some mental insight to agile or predictive based on the type of work the project is completing.

For your PMP exam you should be familiar with a few other agile approaches. While Scrum and XP have the most prominence, you might see a question or three on other agile methodologies. All of the agile project management concepts have similarities:

- Communication must be transparent and honest.
- Change is welcome and expected.
- Project requirements are prioritized.
- Team and businesspeople collaborate.
- Documentation should be minimally sufficient.

Lean Product Development

Lean product development originated in Toyota's manufacturing in the 1940s but has evolved into an agile approach for software development and hybrid project management. It has been said that Lean means less: less resources in the project, less work in progress, less money, and less time. While that concept is nice, it's not always realistic—the bigger the project scope, typically the bigger the schedule, budget, and resources needed. The real principle of Lean wanting to use less means less than what you might typically utilize without using the Lean approach in project management.

Product development relies on feedback from the customer to improve the product. For example, you purchase a new car, and while it's nice, there are little quirks that you don't like: the buttons on the radio, the way the seat feels when you turn a corner, and the noise from the turn signal. These little quirks can be reported to the manufacturer, but it's too late, because the product has already been created. With Lean product development, the goal is to get the product right the first time through smaller iterations, prototypes, and open communication with the customers.

PART III

There are five principles of Lean product development that you should know:

1. *Define what value means to the customer.* This is sometimes called the voice of the customer, and it is about understanding what the customer values and what quality means to the customer. In the early design of a solution, there is an identification of costs to quality ratio. The design must balance what the customer values in relation to how much the customer is willing to pay for the solution. In other words, the customer may want a deluxe interior, but their budget typically won't allow them to pay for deluxe interior. By reducing waste, prototyping features, alternative identification, and increasing efficiency, the solution can achieve customer satisfaction.

2. *Reduce waste and identify the value stream.* A value stream is the shortest path between what the customer wants, what the business creates to satisfy that desire, and how much the customer is willing to pay for the solution. Value stream mapping aims to get rid of the bureaucracy, red tape, and unnecessary processes that clog the value steam and get in the way of the customer getting the solution as efficiently as possible.

3. *Create flow in the process.* The goal is to make the flow of the work as smooth as possible, eliminate bottlenecks, and limit the work in progress (WIP). By utilizing a pull system, such as Kanban, resources are utilized when they are available, and this helps to reduce waiting time for assignments and helps to balance the work in the pipeline. In this step, teams and managers also aim to defer commitment until the last responsible moment to avoid making premature decisions that can affect the work, schedule, and scope.

4. *Empower the team.* Team members have the authority to be self-organizing and self-led and to make decisions on what work needs to be done and who'll do the work on the project. To do this, however, you need team members who are willing to learn more than one role and be cross-functional on the team. You'll also need the right resources to complete the work. You can't expect someone who has never written a line of code to hop in and start developing a new app.

5. *Learn and improve during the project.* Like all the agile project management approaches, Lean also utilizes learning sessions to explore what has, or has not, worked. Open communication, opportunities to share team feedback, and learning by experimentation is encouraged. Learning is also needed for team members to learn new skills and move into new roles in the project.

Recall from Chapter 8 the idea of Plan-Do-Check-Act (PDCA) and how the cycle is used to improve upon the quality of the project. Lean utilizes that strategy to remove waste. Within Lean there are seven wastes that you should aim to remove. These originated in the Toyota Production System and were morphed from a manufacturing environment to the software development environment by Mary and Tom Poppendieck. The following are the seven wastes of Lean for software projects:

- **Partially done work**   Guess how much value there is in unfinished work. Zero. When customers put a hold on features or requirements, the time already spent on creating some portion of the requirement is wasted. Sometimes this can create problems in the integration of the code and often creates a rushed atmosphere when the requirement is given approval to move forward.

- **Extra processes**   When there are added processes such as extra steps for approval, requirements for documentation that no one reads, or other organizational bureaucracy, it's waste for the project effort and schedule.

- **Extra features**   It's not unusual for developers to do a little scope creep to add a cool, little feature that often goes unused. These extra features take time and can bloat the final product. It's wasteful and should not happen.

- **Task switching**   I get people mad at me for this one: multitasking is a myth. You can do only one task at a time. When a developer hops between tasks, it's wasteful due to the context switch between the two tasks—it takes time to recall what you were doing and then ramping up on the newly switched to task. Do one thing at a time to completion.

- **Waiting**   One of the easiest wastes to attack is waiting time. If you're waiting on customers to give approval to completed work, it's a waste. Waiting time, from customers, other teams, or silos in the project, is a bottleneck of productivity and should be removed. Waiting time for a simple go/no-go decision on a feature can stall the entire project. Communicate the urgency to keep things moving in the project.

- **Motion**   Moving around chunks of data, being disorganized when naming and saving files, and then having to search for files creates waste. I personally know I've spent hours looking for files that should have been called *project management quality*, but in my wisdom I named the file PMQ instead. That's not a helpful naming structure when I need the file months later.

- **Defects**   Escaped defects are errors in the software that have made it all the way into the customers' hands. These defects have escaped through the testing and quality control activities and are now the most expensive defects to repair because it'll take money to correct the error and time to regain the reputation and trust the project team has created with the customer. The escaped defect can also have ramifications for the customer; consider a defect in a software used in healthcare and how the defect could directly affect the lives of the patients.

Feature-Driven Development

Created specifically for software development projects, feature-driven development (FDD) is an agile approach that doesn't get much attention. While FDD does use short iterations and welcomes change, it can be a bit more rigid than Scrum or XP. FDD's rigidity is ideal for complex, long-term software development projects. FDD, unlike any other agile approach, skips meetings and utilizes documentation for communication.

While this can appear challenging for communication, it's actually ideal when the project team is large, there are multiple developers that aren't colocated, and you need a history of documented communication.

FDD has six roles you should recognize for your exam:

- **Project manager**   Oversees the project as a typical project manager.
- **Chief architect**   Designs and models the system and leads planning with other developers.
- **Development manager**   Oversees the daily activity and coaches the development team.
- **Chief programmer**   Assists the chief architect and development manager and may lead smaller development teams within the project.
- **Class owner**   Works with the chief programmer and designs, codes, and tests the features of the system.
- **Domain expert**   This is a businessperson, like the product owner role in Scrum. This person understands the customers' needs and what they value.

FDD follows a strict, five-step approach to project management, unlike what you have seen in other agile approaches. FDD is ideal for large organizations and projects that are extensive, may seem to be ongoing, and developers are not colocated. The five steps of FDD are as follows:

1. Develop the overall model. Based on the customers' problem that the project should solve, the model is a big outline of what the solution should include. This is led by the chief architect.

2. Build a features list. Like the product backlog in Scrum, the features list is a prioritized list of project requirements that the client wants in the solution. Features in the list should take no longer than two weeks to create. If the feature is estimated to take longer than two weeks, the feature is too big and needs to be decomposed into smaller features.

3. Plan by feature. The team will work with the domain expert to prioritize the features, but also with the chief architect to consider all the technical requirements needed to deliver the features. This step also considers the risks, technical dependencies, team bandwidth, and impediments that could threaten the feature's success.

4. Design by feature. This activity is led by the chief programmer, but the entire team is involved in the design review. The goal is to first determine which features the team can accomplish in a two-week iteration and then determine which developers will work together, or alone, to tackle the feature in the iteration.

5. Build by feature. Now the developers get to work creating the solution. A test for the feature is written, the code is written, and when the feature passes the test, the feature can be added to the build.

Dynamic Systems Development Method

The Dynamic Systems Development Method (DSDM) evolved in 1994 from developers using the Rapid Application Development (RAD) project management approach. DSDM provides more structure than RAD, utilizes iterations, and is a great approach when working with vendors as part of your agile project. DSDM also offers a unique approach as it can be blended with Scrum, PRINCE2, and other project management approaches. There are eight principles of DSDM that are similar to all agile project management approaches:

- Focus on the business need.
- Deliver the work on time.
- Collaborate.
- Quality cannot be compromised.
- Build incrementally.
- Develop iteratively.
- Communicate continuously, directly, and clearly.
- Demonstrate control.

I doubt you will see many questions on DSDM on your exam, but it's worthwhile to note this approach can be used for large, complex projects and smaller, quick projects. DSDM also leverages some of the tools and techniques of Scrum, XP, and hybrid project management such as timeboxing for iterations and the MoSCoW prioritization approach for requirements. DSDM has an overall goal of ensuring that every requirement and deliverable meet the organization's strategic goals. This helps prevent scope creep and ensures value for the customer. Finally, like other project management approaches, DSDM prioritizes requirements and delivers the most important features to the customer as soon as possible.

Crystal Agile Methodologies

Crystal approaches to agile project management are a family of practices that are color coded to reflect their risk to human life, size of the project team, and risk within the project. For example, a large healthcare software project that directly affects a patient could be coded as Crystal Sapphire or Crystal Diamond, while a software project to find restaurants in your neighborhood could be coded as Crystal Clear. In addition, the size of the project team helps determine which color you'd use if the project doesn't directly affect human life. As a general rule, the Crystal color and approach you'd use based on team size are as follows:

- **Crystal Clear**   Eight or fewer team members
- **Crystal Yellow**   10 to 20 team members
- **Crystal Orange**   20 to 50 team members
- **Crystal Red**   50 to 100 team members

Crystal approaches all follow the same three rules: deliver results frequently, look for opportunities to improve, be colocated for osmotic communication. Then, depending on the complexity and risk within the project, the following rules can be tailored and adapted to the project size:

- Create a safe space to discuss ideas and experiment.

- Keep the team focused on the work and free from distractions.

- Have subject matter experts available for quick feedback.

- Provide tooling for the team, such as automated testing and configuration management.

Crystal does provide autonomy to the development teams, like other agile approaches. Crystal also encourages face-to-face communication. However, with more and more people working remotely, communication within the model can be cumbersome. Crystal has lots of freedom and doesn't follow the same structured approach that Scrum and XP do, so teams can struggle with direction and focus on what's important to the customer. A strong project manager or coach needs to be trained on Crystal to help the team choose what's important and keep working toward value-based priorities first.

Utilizing a Kanban Approach

While not a robust approach like the other agile project management methodologies, Kanban is a framework for organizing work, being transparent, and showing the flow of the work. Kanban means signboard and is pronounced "con-bon." You can technically use Kanban in any agile and predictive project management methodology, but it's most popular in XP. A Kanban board, as in Figure 14-4, shows all stages of the work and where the work items are located in the workflow.

Work begins on the left side of the Kanban board and flows from left to right. The goal is to limit the work in progress and allow anyone on the team who has the right skillset and capacity to take a card from the left and begin the workflow. When a person chooses a card and moves it into the workflow, this is known as the *commitment point*. Visual signals are the sticky notes that flow through the columns. Each column represents a phase of the project work, such as Backlog, In Progress, and Testing. The columns can be given

Figure 14-4
A Kanban board shows all the stages of the work.

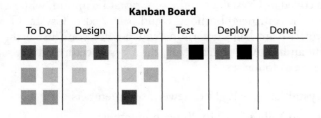

any logical name that works for your project's workflow. Each card must flow through each column—no skipping over segments. When the card has passed through all of the columns and it is completed, it's known as the *delivery point*.

Chapter Summary

Agile project management is about getting value to the customers as quickly as possible. Through increments, which are small releases, and iterations, which are repetitive cycles, agile teams create value for the customer. Most agile approaches follow an approach that's been dubbed as eating your dessert first (something I'm a fan of). Eating your dessert first means you get the most desirable things to the customer as quickly as possible. Working from a big list of prioritized items, the team works from the top to the bottom of the list. If changes happen to the list, which is expected and is totally fine in agile, the changes are prioritized in the list, and the team takes on the work in the next iteration. All agile approaches also embrace the Agile Manifesto, a document that sets the values of agile in four key concepts:

- Individuals and interactions over processes and tools
- Working software over comprehensive documentation
- Customer collaboration over contract negotiation
- Responding to change over following a plan

Scrum is the most popular approach to agile project management, and you're sure to see the approach on your exam. Scrum has just three roles: the product owner, the scrum master, and the developers. The product owner prioritizes the product backlog and writes the user stories. The scrum master coaches stakeholders and keeps things moving along. The developers develop the code to create the features of the solution for the customer. Meetings within scrum are called ceremonies; the daily scrum, the sprint planning meeting, the sprint review, and the sprint retrospective are all events in each sprint, or iteration, in a scrum project.

Extreme Programming has some of the same characteristics of scrum, such as user stories and a prioritized backlog. XP is the only approach that utilizes pair programming to create the code. XP utilizes one-week iterations, as opposed to scrum's two- to four-week sprints, and a quarterly timeboxed period to release items to the customer. XP also calls for a test-first development approach. The developers write the test, which will fail because there is no code, and then they'll write the code to pass the test; if it passes, they'll move on. If the code fails, they'll fix the problem before performing an integration. The XP project follows five steps for the entire project in each iteration: planning, managing, designing, coding, and testing.

In this chapter, we also explored some less common agile approaches you might see on your exam. Lean is lean because it aims to accomplish the project with less work, resources, money, and time than traditional project management. Lean begins with understanding value, reducing waste, creating flow, empowering the team, and persistent learning throughout the project. Another agile approach that doesn't have the popularity as Scrum is feature-driven development (FDD). This approach also uses short iterations and welcomes change but differs in that it skips meetings and focuses more on written communication among the team. We finished the chapter with a quick look at the Dynamic Systems Development Method (DSDM) that follows iterations, welcomes change, and works great with large, complex projects. The Crystal family of agile project management has different colors to signify the threat to human life, such as Crystal Diamond and Sapphire, and the size of the project team, such as Crystal Clear for a small team or Crystal Red with a team larger than 50 members.

You know that roughly half of your exam will focus on agile and hybrid methodologies, so it will behoove you to spend some time on these approaches and their characteristics for your exam. Of all the agile approaches, I recommend you really know Scrum before all the others. There are many attributes of Scrum that are universal to all projects and the concepts of scrum project management will help you answer these other questions too. This chapter provided a big picture of agile project management and will help you have a good foundation for the PMP exam.

Questions

1. Sarah is a scrum master assigned to an information technology–based company in California. She is responsible for delivering a significant software application that will enhance the user experience in grocery shopping. In a recent customer survey, 76 percent of clients expressed concern that the application had too many features and was difficult to use. What likely occurred because of this concern?

   A. Did not effectively use scrum sprints.

   B. Failed to produce a minimum viable product (MVP) for her clients in sprints.

   C. Did not create an effective stakeholder engagement plan.

   D. The participating grocery stores did not make their requirements for the application clear.

2. Sally is the project manager for a mechanical engineering consulting firm. The organization has had several major projects that were completed months behind schedule. To rectify this issue, the organization wants to adopt more agile methodologies. However, before these methods can be implemented into the project, what should Sally do first?

   A. Place current projects on hold and adjust them to the new agile changes.

   B. Assess organizational culture and readiness for the proposed agile shift in culture.

   C. Provide agile training for employees who are willing to participate in the first project team.

   D. Ask workers to vote on whether they want to participate in the new projects.

3. Mike has recently taken over as a project manager at a horticultural organization. He is assigned to a project that has been ongoing for more than four years. Within two weeks, Mike notices that there has been a high turnover rate for team members during the project. To accommodate these changes, Mike decides on adopting agile methodologies. What action should Mike take to shift to a hybrid approach?

A. Evaluate the benefits of incorporating agile practices.

B. Review a historically similar project to determine the current project's feasibility.

C. Ensure the organization can continue funding the project.

D. Downsize the number of team members to nine individuals, plus or minus two.

4. Peter is starting a large and long-term technology project that will last seven years. The project includes an operating system that is near the end of its life cycle. It also includes a requirement to process cards. The debit and credit card system includes cards with only a magnetic stripe, while some have a security chip. Eventually, the magnetic stripe–only cards will be phased out, but both card types must be supported for the time being. The operating system in question will be supported for another two to three years, with an unknown new operating system arriving next year. Those are the challenges that Peter is aware of, but there will be other technological changes, updates, and challenges during the next seven years. Generally speaking, what mindset should Peter have in managing this project?

A. An eye on the future because he knows change is coming.

B. A fixed mindset because Peter can work only with the technology he has.

C. An agile mindset because he should focus on the present with an eye to change.

D. A waterfall mindset. One thing after another, in its order. He should plan for the next seven years.

5. Leah is an agile coach for an organization that is seeking to adopt agile project management methodologies into its daily processes. Leah is assigned to a research & development (R&D) team that has historically had issues relating to a lack of good leadership and guidance. Upon further investigation, Leah determines why this R&D team has had these issues. Previous team leaders have made all the decisions for the team. These actions lead to the team members never being completely satisfied with the team leader's decisions. What Agile Manifesto principle should Leah work to embrace on projects with this group?

A. Working software over documentation

B. Individuals and interactions over processes and tools

C. Responding to change over following a plan

D. Customer collaboration over contracts

6. Matthew is a project manager within an organization that has traditionally used a command-and-control style of project management. However, business analysts have recommended that their competitors have seen a lot more success by adopting agile project management methodologies. The management team has tasked Matthew with conducting a pilot project using the agile methods. Which of the following characteristics should Matthew *not* consider when selecting a pilot project?

A. Three- to six-month schedule

B. Real business need

C. High visibility

D. A detailed project management plan

7. Preston is working on an initiative to introduce agile concepts into the organization. Preston selects a small ongoing project to write a hypothetical situation for. After three weeks of reviewing case studies through similar organizations, Preston presents a change proposal to the management team. However, the team rejects this proposal as it does not accurately reflect their own organization's processes. What did Preston likely forget to address when developing the change proposal?

A. Making sure to address the personal side of the change initiative

B. Not considering other approaches to project management

C. Choosing an appropriately sized project to try the new approach on

D. Presenting the wrong type of agile approach to the team

8. You are the project manager for an agile team developing a food blender designed to be quieter than the average blender on the market. The Research & Development (R&D) department currently requires extensive documentation before they will accept any changes to the blender's original design. As a servant leader, which action would *not* be an action you should take to create a shared understanding between the R&D department and the agile team?

A. Working with the R & D department to review the required documentation

B. Assisting with creating a shared understanding of how agile deliverables meet those requirements

C. Evaluating the amount of documentation required, so teams are spending more time delivering a valuable product instead of producing exhaustive documentation

D. Compromising with all parties so that everyone receives a feature they want

9. Leonardo is an agile coach for a pilot project team that is looking to adopt agile methodologies. Most team members have little technical domain knowledge and are unfamiliar with how to employ agile methods effectively. Leonardo recognizes this and does not want to have the team fail on their first agile project. What can Leonardo do to help adjust the team to agile methodologies?

   A. Let the team members figure everything out as agile teams should be empowered and self-directing.

   B. Recommend terminating the project until the team members learn agile methodologies.

   C. Perform a retrospective to address the project team's deficiencies in agile methodologies.

   D. Assign and direct the team members until they gain the necessary skills to become self-directing.

10. Kevin is the business analyst for a team that has been assigned to develop a new software program for an agricultural organization, and he will work with the customer to build out the product requirements. The organization is proficient in using traditional means of project management but will incorporate scrum techniques into the new program. Kevin is not familiar with these techniques. Which of the following actions should Kevin request to serve his role best?

    A. Request for the most proficient software development test to approve or reject the minimum viable product (MVP) during each sprint review as he is most familiar with the software.

    B. Request mentorship from an agile coach as his role closely aligns with that of a product owner.

    C. Request to be assigned to another project as he is only familiar with traditional project management.

    D. Request for one of the testers to take the role of the end-user and prioritize the user stories in the product backlog.

11. Peter has joined an organization and has been assigned to replace a scrum master midway in a long-term project that is using a hybrid of agile methods. The team is using a product backlog, and they are efficient at their work. They are releasing working software in increments, but Peter notices a disparity between the project's original vision and what is being produced. The project team does not seem to notice this. They view the fact that they are moving through the backlog quickly as a huge success. Peter needs to bring back the project's original mission and vision to the team quickly as it is getting away from him. What can Peter show the project team to reestablish the original vision?

    A. Product backlog

    B. Quality management plan

    C. Project charter

    D. Schedule baseline

12. You are a project manager who also happens to be a scrum master for a small agile team. Naturally, the team is self-organizing, and there are no specified titles or roles on the team. A couple of the team members are getting frustrated and come to you. They want you, as a project manager, to tell people what to do a little more. How should you handle this dynamic?

    A. Assign roles and tasks

    B. Work to remove impediments

    C. Stop using scrum

    D. Make a WBS

13. Lindsay is a project manager for a complex software development project. Her project follows the best agile practices. Lindsay is looking to ensure that knowledge transfer is happening within her project team. How can Lindsay encourage knowledge transfer engagingly?

    A. Ask each developer to write documentation on each process they complete.

    B. Encourage developers to pair together and program together.

    C. Make two developers on the team responsible for each process.

    D. Ensure that the functional manager knows how to complete each process.

14. In agile working environments, which of the following practices would be most effective for osmotic communication to work?

    A. Colocated teams

    B. Distributed teams

    C. Team members understanding each other's culture

    D. A team in the norming stage

15. Adam has joined an agile team. He approaches the agile coach to understand how stories and features are prioritized in the risk-adjusted backlog. Which one of the following would be the best answer?

    A. Risk impact or risk probability

    B. Expected monetary value or business value

    C. Cost-benefit ratio or customer value

    D. Risk mitigation impact or user impact

16. Near the completion of the first iteration, the agile project team must demonstrate the potentially shippable product increment to the project stakeholders. What scrum ceremony would be appropriate to conduct this demo?

    A. Sprint review

    B. Daily standup

    C. Sprint retrospective

    D. Deliverables meeting

17. Skylark Inc. is transitioning to an agile development approach. They have selected Project RTM to develop a breakthrough water purifying device and have tasked your team with the development of an app to measure the water purity. The development team consists of cross-functional skilled resources. The team approaches you and states that they do not know what the final product will look like and are unsure how to proceed without a fully defined scope. What would you advise them?

    A. Follow the project charter.

    B. Start with short iterations following the most promising approach and learn as you go.

    C. Ask the customer for more detailed information about the device.

    D. Perform a research-spike.

18. An organization is about to begin a series of similar projects. The projects will be managed consecutively; some will be using a traditional waterfall development approach, while others will be using an adaptive approach. For one of the projects, where the focus is more on the work stream's improvement and efficiency, the organization wants to adapt a lean approach to the project. Which of the following would not be considered an example of a form of waste?

    A. Code testing

    B. Task switching

    C. Code waiting for test results

    D. Assigning a developer to multiple projects at the same time

19. Your development team has been working through the first four sprints of the project and has been able to release product increments after each sprint. During the fifth sprint review meeting, one of the stakeholders is unsatisfied with the progress and advises the product owner that their most recent business requirement is missing from the product increment. What likely happened during the sprint planning meeting?

    A. The product backlog was not up-to-date.

    B. The sprint backlog was not prioritized.

    C. The stakeholder register was not up-to-date.

    D. The scrum master failed to identify priority.

20. Max is a developer on a team that is developing software for lawyers. There is no set scope for this software, but the team does have a budget and deadline. The team meets daily for 15 minutes to discuss what they have accomplished, what they hope to accomplish, and anything that may be standing in their way. A person who facilitates the daily meetings removes any blockers a teammate may have and encourages the team to keep making progress. What kind of project methodology approach does Max's team have?

   A. Scrum

   B. Plan-driven

   C. Kanban

   D. Predictive

21. Brittany's IT project is going well. She meets with her team about once a week to review a board containing tickets that represent work items. There are columns that a card can fall under Backlog, In Progress, Testing, and Done. When a developer is ready to start work, they pull a ticket into their workflow from the Backlog pipeline into the In Progress pipeline. When a developer has coded the ticket, a QA analyst pulls the ticket into the Testing column. After testing, the ticket is closed and goes into the Done column. What kind of project management approach does Brittany's project have?

   A. Scrum

   B. Kanban

   C. Hybrid

   D. Predictive

Answers

1. **B.** In this scenario, Sarah likely did not produce an MVP for her clients in regular sprints. As a result, she failed to capture the requirements of the most important stakeholder: the customer. A is incorrect because the sprints may or may not have been effective, the issue is in creating the product that is just enough for what the customer needs. C is incorrect because a comprehensive stakeholder engagement plan may have prevented the situation; it is more suited for more traditional project management than agile methods. D is incorrect because as the customer primarily measures value, they are ultimately the ones who decide how the application should be developed, not the grocery stores.

2. **B.** Sally should determine whether the organization is ready for the agile shift in culture. Choices A, C, and D are viable solutions after assessing the organizational culture. When an organization shifts to agile, there can be a disruption along with the learning curve agile approaches require.

3. **A.** Mike should review the benefits of incorporating agile practices. This action will ensure the requirements are defined and that the team can adjust to changing requirements through continuous feedback and delivery. B is incorrect because no two projects are exactly alike, and many external factors will need to be considered. C is incorrect; while continuing to fund the project is important, it does not directly answer a hybrid approach. D is incorrect. It's true that the ideal team size for an agile project management team is between five and nine people, but simply reducing the team size won't address the root causes of the issues the project is facing.

4. **C.** Having an agile mindset means working on the most important items first and understanding and accepting that change is likely to happen in project. B is incorrect because a fixed mindset is unlikely to help Peter in an agile or hybrid project. Not only are there known technological changes, but there are also known unknowns as well. D is incorrect; elements of the waterfall approach are likely to help Peter organize the project, but it would be unwise to create fixed plans years ahead. Peter should not ignore the current technology that he has to work with and focus on the immediate work through agile approaches. Peter should employ an agile mindset with an eye on current challenges and a willingness to adapt to the coming changes.

5. **B.** In this scenario, the team is needing more focus on the individuals and their interactions than any other element. Agile encourages the team members to be self-led, rather than the project manager or scrum master making the project decisions for the team. A is incorrect because working software isn't the focus on the problem in the scenario. C is incorrect because the question centers on not valuing or respecting the people in the project team. D is also incorrect as there is no mention of contracts in the scenario. It's tempting to choose this answer because of collaboration, but this point in the manifesto is about working with vendors, not internal project teams.

6. **D.** Matthew should not create a detailed project management plan associated with a traditional waterfall methodology. A is incorrect because the project should be big enough to be deemed a real project but short enough to use the benefits quickly. B is incorrect because a real business need should not be a toy project, but a real one people know needs to be done and is likely to be troubled by the same issues as other projects. C is incorrect because the project should be one that people will see and notice, be easy to publicize its success, and have a good business spokesperson to spread the word.

7. **A.** A key component for change acceptance is the human side of introducing the change. The best changes in the world will meet resistance and take longer to accomplish if implemented without regard to the human side of change. B is incorrect because there is not enough information to determine whether considering other approaches to project management are valid. C is incorrect as choosing an appropriately sized project is not valid as Preston did select a small project in this scenario. D is also incorrect as presenting the wrong type of agile approach to the team does not best answer the question.

8. **D.** The servant leader aims to make certain the team has what they need, but also keeps everyone focused on the primary goals of the project, which is to create a quiet blender for customers. Compromising usually involves parties agreeing to give up a feature they want, which results in a "lose-lose" situation. Choices A, B, and C describe how you, as the project manager, can remove organizational impediments that are activities that a servant leader does want to do in an agile project.

9. **D.** While assigning and directing team members may seem backward, Leonardo can more seamlessly transition from a traditional to an adaptive approach if he leads them at the start. When an organization or team first moves into agile, the servant leader should coach and direct the team initially. Over time and with experience the team will become more self-led and self-organizing. Choices A, C, and B are incorrect options that are not ideal as they are forcing agile concepts onto the team without them being ready to adopt those methodologies themselves. The servant leader should not threaten the team or take a totally hands-off approach to the project.

10. **B.** For this scenario, Kevin should receive training and coaching from an agile coach, product owner, or scrum master. Kevin needs to learn how agile projects operate, and a coach can help him with the mechanics of agile and serving as a product owner or working along with a product owner in the project. A is incorrect because testing the product is needed, but at the right level of testing. In addition, testing the product doesn't help Kevin navigate the scrum approach in the scenario. C is incorrect as Kevin is needed on the current project and should work to learn and embrace agile in the organization. D is also incorrect as the test has a different skillset than that of a product owner.

11. **C.** The project charter is a good reminder of the original vision for the project and will help the team, and ideally a product owner, to prioritize the product backlog. What the team is creating must be valuable to the customer or the product is considered a failure. A is incorrect because showing the team the product backlog would not be efficient as they would view it as evidence that they are on the right track. B is not the best choice as there likely is not a quality management plan in this agile approach. Recall that the quality management plan defines how quality assurance, quality control, and process improvements can take place in a project. D is incorrect as the schedule baseline does not seem to be an issue in this project. Peter needs to get this project team back to basics, and the best start is to review the project charter. The project charter will give the team a high-level overview of the project and allow Peter to make the case that the team needs to refocus on the original vision.

12. **B.** Having both of these roles can be problematic, especially if team members are not embracing agile. You'll likely need to remove the impediments by coaching the team on their responsibilities and tracking the velocity for the team members. The key is to find out what the team's obstacles are and work to remove them. In doing this, you'll be a helpful project manager and scrum master. A is incorrect because Scrum doesn't have roles and tasks like traditional project management.

C is incorrect because, while you could stop using scrum, it's not a valid reaction to a few typical complaints. D is incorrect because a WBS doesn't fit into the changing priorities and requirements of Scrum.

13. **B.** Of all the choices presented, pair programming ensures knowledge transfer between the two programmers. While none of the answers fully satisfies the question, this is the best of all choices presented. Remember, on your actual exam you will have to choose the best answer presented, not the best answer you have in your mind. Paired programming will ensure that multiple people understand and have experience completing the work. A is incorrect written documentation, which is helpful to some extent, but comprehensive documentation is not valued in agile practices. C is incorrect as having two people responsible for a process isn't a valid agile approach. D is incorrect as the functional manager does not need to know how to complete each process in the agile environment.

14. **A.** Osmotic communication is the useful sharing of information that flows between team members working near each other as they can overhear each other's conversations. B is incorrect as it is impossible for distributed or virtual teams to experience osmotic communication because not all team members are in the same physical environment. C is incorrect as understanding other teams' culture is valuable, but it does not ensure osmotic communication in a project. D is also incorrect as even noncolocated teams move through the norming stage of team development.

15. **B.** Stories are prioritized in agile projects based on their expected monetary value and their business value. A is partially correct because the impact and probability does forecast the expected monetary value, but this is not done for all user stories. C and D are incorrect choices as the cost-benefit ratio, risk mitigation impact, and user impact are not valid assessments of value in the product backlog prioritization.

16. **A.** At the completion of each sprint, the developers will demonstrate a potentially shippable product increment to the project stakeholders. This occurs during a sprint review. During the review, the agile project team and stakeholders collaborate about what was done in the concluded iteration. Feedback from the product owner and customers are documented and prioritized into the product backlog after the sprint review. B is incorrect, as the daily standup meeting is a short (usually 15-minute) timeboxed event for the development team to inspect progress toward the iteration goal and plan work for the next 24 hours. C is incorrect as a retrospective is an opportunity for the project team to inspect itself and create a plan for improvements to be enacted during the next iteration. D, a deliverables meeting, is not a valid agile project management meeting.

17. **B.** In agile, the best way to proceed in cases where there are many unknowns is to identify and follow the most promising approach and work in short iterations so you can learn and adapt as more is discovered. A is incorrect as the project charter may provide a high-level overview of the project, but it won't provide the in-depth scope statement the team is asking for. C is a tempting choice, but this is the role of the product owner, not the development team. D is incorrect; a research-spike might be a good option but is not the best choice presented.

18. A. Out of all the listed options, testing the code would be the only necessary activity that would not be considered waste in Lean. Options B, C, and D are all wastes in Lean. Task switching, waiting time, and having a developer move between projects are all waste in Lean projects.

19. A. The development team sets sprint goals based on the product backlog, and it is up to the product owner to ensure it is prioritized. Given that the first four sprints were successful in delivering product increments, it is most likely that the product owner did not reprioritize the backlog with the stakeholders' changing requirements. B is incorrect as the sprint backlog is based on the selected user stories from the product backlog. C is incorrect. Updating the stakeholder register would not affect the creation of the items in the product backlog. D is incorrect as the scrum master does not set priority in the product backlog; that's the responsibility of the product owner.

20. A. This is an example of a scrum project. In a scrum project, the team meets daily for a scrum meeting to discuss what work everyone is doing and work through any blockers. There is a scrum master who is responsible for facilitating this meeting and motivating the team. B and D are incorrect choices as these would not be plan-driven nor predictive because there is no set scope for this project. C is also incorrect as Kanban is not evident in this example because there is no evidence of how project work is accomplished.

21. B. This is a clear example of a Kanban project. The workflow presented describes a Kanban board in which work items are pulled into various statuses by the people doing the work. Choices A, C, and D are incorrect as there is no evidence to suggest that this project is a scrum, hybrid, nor predictive project.

CHAPTER 15

Engaging Agile Stakeholders

In this chapter, you will

- Incorporate stakeholder value into agile projects
- Build momentum and stakeholder synergy
- Explore agile team engagement
- Practice servant leadership

It's been said many times that you don't manage stakeholders, you engage them. The idea of engaging stakeholders is more than just an e-mail or quick meeting at the launch of the project. Stakeholder engagement means you consistently work to keep stakeholders involved in the project, excited for the value the project brings them, and you communicate the importance and urgency needed for their involvement in the project. Stakeholder engagement is more than just a connection to the individuals; it's keeping the stakeholder involved in the project from launch to completion. In any project, predictive or agile, it's not unusual for stakeholders' interest and investment in the project to wane as the project moves forward.

 VIDEO For a more detailed explanation, watch the *Agile Stakeholders Engagement* video now.

Stakeholder engagement is already a big topic I've discussed in this book, so you might be wondering why there is another chapter on stakeholder engagement. Stakeholder engagement in agile project management is a bit different than predictive projects, and for your exam you'll need to answer questions on stakeholder engagement in predictive, agile, and hybrid projects. In agile projects, especially if an organization is new to agile practices, there are different types of rules and expectations for stakeholders. In a predictive project, you've likely seen stakeholders hop into the project kickoff meeting to confirm the charter and overall plan, and then you'll never hear from them again. In agile, stakeholders are expected to be involved. The product owner and team will communicate and ask questions with the stakeholders—something that's not as common as in a predictive project.

Agile projects, and sometimes hybrid projects, don't utilize a stakeholder engagement plan or a communications management plan like predictive projects do. There's no plan for who needs what information, when is it needed, the modality it is expected in, or a fixed schedule of communication events. In agile projects, the iterative flow of work triggers communication and the information radiator, Kanban boards, and osmotic communications promote transparency of the project information. Atop all of the mechanics of agile project management and stakeholder engagement, there's the practice of servant leadership. Servant leadership coaches and consults with the project team members and project stakeholders.

Stakeholder Engagement in Agile Projects

All projects have stakeholders, regardless of the predictive, agile, or hybrid approach your organization takes. Stakeholders are people who can affect the project or are affected by the project. Typical stakeholders are customers, the project sponsor, the development team, vendors, end users, functional managers, project management office (PMO) officers, and you, the project manager. In each agile approach, whether it's Scrum, XP, Crystal, or hybrid, the official title of the person does influence how you, the project manager, and the individual interact and are engaged in the project. These individuals also are going to engage with other stakeholders in their capacity. It's crucial at the launch of the project for everyone to understand how the agile approach will work and the expectations of each person to interact with one another. There are no islands in agile project management.

In a predictive environment, the project manager is seen as the communication contact point for all stakeholders. Management and customers may have expectations for communication and engagement from you: weekly reports, presentations, risk assessments, and lots more. The project manager is seen as the hub for communication and engagement. In an agile project, all that is just not the same. Agile projects take less of a command-and-control position for the project management role and distribute the project management responsibilities among different roles. For example, in a Scrum approach, the product owner communicates with the businesspeople about requirements. The scrum master coaches stakeholders on involvement and the approach. The developers can ask the project customers for clarity on user stories and features.

This can be a big switch for people when an organization first introduces agile. There is a learning curve from how the project communication and engagement used to work and how this all works now in an agile environment. The project manager role in an agile project will need to serve as a coach, mentor, and educator in the team, the stakeholders, and management. The agile project manager must understand how agile works as people will look to her for advice, direction, and help to learn the process. A switch to agile can be frustrating to people who are used to getting reports and weekly updates sent to them. Patience, edification, and communication are three principles you'll need to bring the organization to understand, accept, and eventually embrace agile.

Here's some good news for you: short iterations, such as the four-week scrum, keeps stakeholders involved. The product backlog is prioritized from most important to least important according to the product owner and stakeholders. The developers choose the user stories from the top of the product backlog, and that's what they create first. Now, at the end of the sprint, there is the sprint review, a demo of what the developers have created for the project customers. In the sprint review, the key customers are shown the immediate value of agile: the team has created the most important items first for the customers. That's exciting and creates immediate engagement and buy-in to the project approach. The iterative approach in agile project management keeps stakeholders involved throughout the project.

Incorporating Stakeholder Values

Stakeholder engagement is all about getting, and keeping, stakeholder buy-in, for the project. You need stakeholders to maintain their excitement and agreement for the project to continue. There are few things worse than a project where the stakeholders fade away, push your project to the bottom of their to-do list, and ignore your questions, e-mails, and phone calls. That's one of the dangers of a predictive project: stakeholders' excitement for the project wanes because there isn't enough interaction—or return on investment—while the project is in motion. Agile, by design, keeps people involved.

The key word that you see over and over in agile projects is *value*. Value is in finished work. The work is based on what the project customers and end users value. Recall the product backlog; the backlog is prioritized based on value. What's most important is at the top, and the least important is way down at the bottom. Agile calls for the product owner and the stakeholders to commit to the project by persistently prioritizing the backlog. While it's true that the product owner is the individual responsible for prioritizing the backlog, they are acting with the customers to understand what the customer most values and wants from the project. The person who represents the business, regardless of the agile approach, must communicate and engage the organization to truly understand the order of value in the product backlog.

You can continue to see the value prioritization for stakeholders in the sprint planning meeting. The developers examine the list prioritized product backlog, and they'll choose their next chunk of work from the top. The team gets to work creating the most valuable items first. At the end of the sprint, customers are invited to the sprint review to see what the team has created. During the sprint review, the team shows the customers and product owner what they've created. In the first few sprint reviews, the team, by working on the prioritized items, is engaging the stakeholders and building trust and excitement.

In a predictive environment, the project manager had to create a schedule for communicating a plan for stakeholder engagement. In agile project management, the schedule is already created as part of the approach. At regular intervals, which all key stakeholders know about, the project ceremonies are predetermined. There's no surprise or overlooked meeting notices. From the start of the project, all participation events for stakeholders are defined and scheduled. Everyone knows when they'll need to be involved in the project and what the flow of the project work will be. It's not a mystery.

A truth that many project managers miss is that to maintain stakeholder engagement, you need the right stakeholders. In any project, you'll have a big mess if you've failed to properly identify all the stakeholders. It's frustrating and embarrassing when you over-look a stakeholder from the start. Take time to ask stakeholders who else needs to be involved and aware of your project. Make certain you've created a stakeholder register for the entire project. It's easy to assume that you've identified all the stakeholders in an agile project; after all, agile is fast and simple. It's often the people aspect of agile that can wreck your project.

All stakeholders want you to create value. Value is spoken about in terms of deliverables, product, and releases. Value is the results, action, and benefit realization of the deliverables you create. Just as joining a gym won't make you healthy, it's the utilization of the gym that gets you toned. Agile deliverables have to be able to be used by the stakeholder—there's no value in work in progress, only value in reaching the Definition of Done (DoD). You want to frequently talk about the DoD. What does DoD look like? What's the definition of DoD? That is what you will use to show progress to the organization, customers, and stakeholders.

Synergy and stakeholder engagement, the value of the project community, are fostered in the agile approach. The idea of community value stems from the Agile Manifesto: we focus on individuals and interactions. The team and the stakeholders develop a sense of community, a sense of belonging, to the project purpose. When people feel part of the project, they feel valued, and they are going to have respect for one another. Respect is important not just for the people involved, but it's also needed considering the short duration of each iteration. Respect is needed for the end user, the people who will use the product. Respect is needed for the code that is being developed and the rules of the approach. Stakeholder engagement is not cheerleading and charisma. It's being honest and transparent on all fronts of the project. Agile teams must be truthful in communication, transparent in our data, and fair in our actions and decisions. Agile teams do not hide results or the work.

Conflict may happen in the flow of the agile project. Conflict is to be expected, but being rude, vindictive, and unprofessional is not. Positive conflict creates solutions and allows us to work together to figure things out. During the daily standup meeting, for example, the discussion of impediments to progress can sometimes bring out conflict. I've seen the impediment to progress be the completion of another team member's work. Sally can't move forward with her assignments until Mark has completed his work. And now Mark is late, and Sally is afraid her work will be late, too. This is a conflict, and an honest and transparent conversation needs to happen. Without acknowledging the conflict, you have little hope to resolve it.

During the sprint retrospective is another time when conflicts can boil up. The sprint retrospective is an opportunity to discuss what worked and didn't work and to implement Lean principles of removing waste. The goal in a retrospective isn't to place blame, but to honestly discuss the success and failures of the last iteration. The project manager and the team must go into the meeting with an understanding of the meeting's purpose and a hopeful outcome. The hopeful outcome is that the next iteration is better than the one just completed. The stakeholder engagement here is among the team, not the customers. The engagement is for the team to discuss how they can improve their approach in the next iteration, rather than letting the conflict and issues fester for months; the problem can be discussed, and a resolution sought. Remember, the team members are stakeholders, perhaps the most important stakeholders, in a project. You need them positively engaged and working toward the Definition of Done to achieve the value the customer expects in the project.

Building Stakeholder Synergy

What does it mean to be agile? Being agile does not mean you are just using the approach of Scrum or Lean or Kanban. It is about following a methodology and having an agile mindset. It is more than just the methodology, as agile isn't really a cookbook for success. Agile means that you, the team, and the organization have an agile mindset, a way of being adaptable. Agile wants all the stakeholders to collaborate and get people involved to accomplish business value. Of course, all agile project managers first have to learn the foundations of agile—and that's largely what your exam will test you on. All agile project managers really begin by doing agile, understanding the mechanics of agile, using iterations, and following the agile rules.

Being agile is really what you want to focus on for the tougher exam questions. First, you, the project manager or the scrum master or whatever title you have in your agile environment, must embrace this idea of the agile mindset. You must understand and coach others on agile principles, and by coaching, you are really selling the ideas and principles of agile. You will have to educate others, such as your project sponsor, your project team, and key stakeholders. Agile is still relatively new, and no doubt you are going to have some skeptical people. Expect skeptics and coach them and sell them on the idea of agile—show them the value by delivering value early, rather than make promises and getting bogged down in the rules and procedures of agile.

 EXAM TIP Stakeholders who have low influence and low power over the project shouldn't be ignored. Keep them informed, monitor their status, and try to share the value the project can bring them. Not every stakeholder will have a high interest in the project.

As the agile leader with the agile mindset, you'll also need to coach the team, the developers, and the other people getting stuff done in the project. When agile is first implemented, the team is going to want to know why you are doing this. Why is the agile approach better, and why are we changing from what we've been using forever? Too many project managers, in my opinion, treat the project team like children. The best way to show the team why agile is valuable is to experience the benefits. You experience the benefits by coaching the team to quick victories, quick wins. Initially, you'll do lots of handholding, coaching, and listening to the team grumble and ask questions—they may be hesitant to change, but soon they'll see the value in agile and the new freedom agile offers that predictive projects cannot. Your team needs to experience this idea of a safe environment so they can try new things. There is a saying in agile that you are going to fail early, fail fast. The idea, though, is that you want the team and the organization to feel safe to experiment and to be innovative in the project and that you get out of the team's way.

PART III

It's often tough, as a project manager, to let the developers work the way they feel is best. Project managers must do more coaching and less command and control. This means let the team decide on new approaches, and let the team try new things and share the outcomes. In predictive project management, the project manager is seen as the leader, but that's not the case in agile. Agile projects encourage emergent leadership, where anyone on the team can become a leader. Anyone can be a leader, and leadership roles can change in different portions of the project.

As an agile project manager, with whatever title your approach names you, always aim to practice servant leadership. Servant leadership means that you carry food and water for the team. You aren't literally carrying food and water for the team, but rather you get the team the things they need to get the work done. You serve as a shield against distractions and interruptions for the team. You get rid of impediments. You get the team the things that they need to move forward.

While all of this sounds fantastic, there is still a formal approach to agile project management. All stakeholders must know the rules, the processes, how to interact with team members, and how to get to the end. You need some formality in agile; it cannot be too loose, but you also can't be too structured either. It'll take time, experimentation, and flexibility to find the right balance control and achievement. You know that agile is a change-driven approach, and when starting agile, you are going to implement changes, not only to the scope but for how people work.

Leading Stakeholder Conversations

In all flavors of agile, for your exam, you will need to lead stakeholder conversations. This means you will be taking charge, finding out information for the team, and facilitating meetings such as the daily standup, reviews, and retrospectives. The team will look to you, especially early in the project, to help them communicate with one another and figure out who'll do what on the project. Recall from Chapter 9 that early in the team development process, when the team is norming and then storming, it's the project manager's role to help people figure things out without being too much in control. In agile, that's true too. You'll help the team members determine their roles, help them break up the tasks for the iterations, and coach them along in the process. You don't, however, want to take away from the self-led and self-organizing approach that agile calls for. As the project moves onward, you'll take less and less control and let the team determine things for themselves.

Stakeholder conversations also means you've got information available for stakeholders. Being transparent is a key attribute of a good agile project manager. One approach to transparency is an information radiator: a big board with all the facts about the project work, a burndown chart, and the velocity of the team, for example. The information radiator is a form of pull communication as any stakeholder can view the board and get updates on the project. Some organizations I've consulted in have huge electronic boards that are updated daily with new stats. Other organizations, and what I actually prefer, is a low-tech, high-touch approach to sharing information. Low-tech, high-touch means that there's little technology to use or learn. High touch means that the information radiator can be updated by hand—markers and sticky notes that anyone can use.

Another pull communication technique is a project web site or web service to publish project information.

Push communication in agile is anytime you or a stakeholder is sending information, such as an e-mail or report. Push communication isn't used quite as much as in predictive projects. Information isn't hoarded, but it's publicly available for anyone to pull from. You'll have push information in sprint reviews, and retrospectives, but these are interactive communications, more than just a one-way message, like an e-mail. Push communications can be effective when you have a large number of stakeholders to communicate with and manage. One approach to engage large groups of stakeholders is to group stakeholders by affinity, such as sales, finance, engineering, and manufacturing. Now you can communicate specific messages to the groups instead of managing long messages or overlooking specific content for groups.

 EXAM TIP The scrum master or project manager role in an agile project is not the center of communication. The project manager role facilitates conversations rather serving as an intermediary between developers and the businesspeople. Don't be tricked by thinking the team, the product owner, and the customers cannot speak with one another—they should.

Face-to-face communication is the most effective method to communicate in an agile project. Certainly in today's world that face-to-face communication may be through web conferencing software. With face-to-face communication we have the advantage of nonverbal clues, feedback, and clarity, and we lose the time-gap you can have in e-mail approaches. Everyone has experienced the delay of waiting for a response to an e-mail. In agile, it's best to get a face-to-face conversation going to get the information quickly and without ambiguity. We already have seen the value in face-to-face conversations through the different ceremonies in agile, such as sprint planning, the daily standup, reviews, and retrospectives.

Meetings in predictive environments, such as weekly status meetings, can become ineffective with time, drone on for too long, and not always have a clear agenda and structure. Effective meetings can be a great way to build consensus among the stakeholders, such as a requirements workshop to identify requirements and build collaboration. Agile aims to combat the meeting madness by first timeboxing meetings. Scrum has prebuilt timeboxes into the approach:

- Sprint planning—up to eight hours for a four-week sprint
- Daily scrum—15 minutes maximum
- Sprint review—up to four hours for a four-week sprint
- Sprint retrospective—up to three hours for a four-week sprint

For projects with shorter iterations, the meeting time can be adjusted in proportion to the iteration duration. All participants go into each ceremony with an idea of why the meeting is happening, the expected duration, and what they need to bring to contribute to the meeting. There's not a lengthy agenda to review and prep for; just be prepared to contribute in alignment with the meeting purpose. A question I get often, especially with people coming from a predictive environment, is who should keep minutes in these meetings. Formal minutes aren't really applicable in agile. Sure, you might keep meeting notes, but there's not Robert's Rules of Order for agile meetings. Remember, agile doesn't value unnecessary documentation.

Knowledge sharing is critical in agile projects. We want to share information with everyone who needs the information; this is our transparency. This includes, in software development, collective code ownership. Often developers want to claim the code as their own and that other developers should not touch it. That's just not the case in agile approaches like XP. In XP everyone owns the code and is everyone is responsible for the code. Any developer can edit any code at any time. This requires trust and transparency, and people have to let go of the ego when they develop features.

Planning for Effective Engagement

In-depth planning is not something you do much of in an agile environment when it comes to the product the project is creating. Sure, there is some up-front planning, but much of the product is expected to change from day 1, so there's little value in creating the plan. Where there is value in planning is to plan on how best to engage the stakeholders. Stakeholder engagement, really people engagement, is vital to the success of the agile project. All of stakeholder engagement begins with the identification of project stakeholders. Stakeholders need to feel welcome and safe, but they also need clear directions on what is expected of them in the project. They need to know who will be communicating with them, who they need to give information to, and when they need to attend events in the project.

A big concept that you'll probably see in your exam is green zones versus red zones. Green zones represent the good stuff, and red zones are the bad stuff. In the green zone you have stakeholders who take responsibility, aren't defensive when mistakes are pointed out, but also not feeling threatened. People operating in the green zones are working to build mutual success and find solutions. Stakeholders, especially team members, persuade rather than direct. Stakeholders can be firm but not rigid. As a project manager in the green zone, you are looking for both short-term and long-term solutions, but also considering other people's points of view and avoiding the command and control that's more likely in a predictive environment. Team members and customers also welcome feedback and understand that conflict is natural. Conflicts among stakeholders in the green zone mean that people don't get angry but speak calmly and directly about issues.

The red zone has all the opposite attributes of the green zone. A red zone person blames others and acts defensively rather than owning mistakes. People feel threatened, hold grudges, and resort to blame, shame, and accusations. Red zone stakeholders often have binary thinking, meaning it's X or Y or it's right or wrong, rather than utilizing critical thinking and seeing the problem and solution from a different perspective. Red zone stakeholders do not want feedback and feel that they have to win at any cost, rather than collaborate and look for a win-win solution. Red zone people make the mistake of seeing other stakeholders as the enemy, rather than teammates.

The red zone and green zone concept is really addressing emotional intelligence. Emotional intelligence is defined as the ability to understand the root causes of your emotions. Emotional intelligence includes the skills to better manage your own emotions, while developing an understanding of the influence emotions have on others. As a project manager, emotional intelligence helps you identify who you are and how you can better interact with others. In the PMP People exam domain, you'll likely encounter at least a few questions about emotional intelligence, so it's good to have a high-level understanding. There are four quadrants that define emotional intelligence, as shown in Figure 15-1. The four quadrants of emotional intelligence are as follows:

- **Self-management**   Individuals have self-control, are conscientious of others, can adapt their behavior to the situation, and have some level of drive, ambition, and motivation to accomplish tasks. This is an inward-facing component of emotional intelligence.

- **Self-awareness**   Individuals have an understanding of how their behavior affects others. Self-awareness requires an honest assessment of one's emotions and an understanding of how emotions affect others. This is an inward-facing component of emotional intelligence.

- **Relationship management**   Individuals have the ability to influence people, develop people, and inspire others through leadership. The agile concept of collaboration is an emotional intelligence factor in the social skills quadrant. This is an outward-facing component of emotional intelligence, meaning it is how one interacts with other people and their emotions.

- **Social awareness**   Another outward-facing quadrant, social awareness is the empathy one feels toward other people. Understanding the organizational context, the situation, and the protocol to behave in a working environment is social awareness.

Figure 15-1
Know the four quadrants of emotional intelligence for your PMP exam.

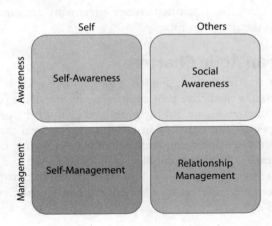

Structuring Team Stakeholder Engagement

The agile project team, regardless of the agile approach your project is taking, can be the most influential set of stakeholders. These are the people doing the work and creating the value, not the product owner, coach, scrum master, or other role. Value, we know from the Agile Manifesto, is in the results of the work, so it stands to reason that the project team can influence the value of the project more than any other stakeholder. Considering this, it's important to know some key aspects of the agile team in an agile environment.

Agile doesn't have the top-down, command-and-control concept of a predictive project. The project manager isn't the hub of communication, direction, and leadership in an agile environment. The project management activities are distributed among the different roles in agile projects. The project team takes on the task assignment through the concept of being self-led and self-organizing. This is a cornerstone of agile project management that can be a stumbling block for many people coming from a predictive environment. It's the team that decides who'll do what in the project. If there is, let's say, a strong personality on the project team, this person can influence who does what for the team. That may get things done, and more passive personalities may just roll with the decisions, but that isn't the agile approach. The team, not one person, should decide, with respect and trust, who does what on the project.

Stakeholder engagement among the team also means that the team is operating in a safe environment where they can experiment with different approaches to the work and be innovative. A safe environment and permission to experiment means that they don't fear what management or other roles will say if their experiments fail. The team needs to feel that's it proper to try new things to get results, and when trying new things, it's expected that there will be failures. Fear of retribution for innovations that didn't work out stifles creativity, keeps the team in the preapproved boxes, and can prevent time and cost savings discovered through innovation. Knowledge work requires experimenting and learning from results. If you've ever programmed, you know that trial and error isn't uncommon when it comes to developing new products. Agile environments should encourage innovation but shouldn't punish team members when innovations don't always work. Success often comes after many attempts at trying something new and rarely on the first attempt.

Creating an Agile Charter

One concept you see in both predictive and agile projects is the idea of an agile charter. Agile charters, like predictive project charters, authorize the project to exist in the organization. Agile charters frame out the high-level goals of the project and acknowledge that change is expected and welcome in the project. The real value in the agile charter is in the creation, not in using a standardized template. Creating the charter from scratch with the project team and key stakeholders builds ownership and buy-in. Ideally, the charter is short, even one page if possible. You can also use the charter to periodically check that the items the project is creating are in alignment with the vision that charter identifies.

There's little value in heavy documentation. Agile project charters have eight components you should recognize for your exam:

- **Who will be engaged?** Stakeholder identification happens with the agile project creation and aims to identify all the stakeholders in the project as quickly and early as possible.

- **What is the project about?** An overview of the technology, type of work, and expectations of the project is needed in the charter. The charter should address what the team will be working with, identify some key roles and responsibilities, and determine the value that customers want from the project at completion.

- **Where will the project take place?** The project location is identified and clearly communicated. While remote projects are becoming more and more common, especially in the IT space, there are still physical projects, such as installing equipment or renovating a home, that are site specific, and workers will have to be physically on-site. For site-specific projects, the charter should also define working hours and access to the site.

- **When will the project start and end?** A timeframe for the project's estimated duration is included in the charter. The high-level timeframe gives everyone an idea of how much work is reasonable to accomplish within the window of project duration. While the customers may have a long list of requirements, the list may not fit into the available time for the project. This is okay, as the project aims to accomplish the most important items in the product backlog first, so items that don't fit into the project duration might be important, but just not as important for items higher up in the backlog.

- **Why does the project exist?** The charter frames the business value for the project and defines why the organization is doing the project. This project identification communicates the purpose for the project and key items the customers expect as a result of the project. This is often tied to the project's Definition of Done and success criteria.

- **How are the goals of the project to be achieved?** Without going into giving directions, the charter should define how the work will get done. This can be the type of software utilized, standards and code, and requirements for compliance in the project. This portion of the charter can also map out the agile approach the team will utilize, such as Scrum or XP.

- **What is the vision statement for the project?** This is a summary of what the project will accomplish. This is the quick elevator talk about what the project will create for the organization or the end users of the product. Some organizations use the idea of the project tweet for the vision statement, and others write a loftier mission statement without getting into the particulars of the project work.

- What are the rules of the project defined in the agile charter? Sometimes called the *constitution*, team rules define how the team will work together, the collaboration needed in the project, and the expectations of the team members' behavior. Some charters may include a code of conduct for the project team or just a general guide of treating each other with respect. Communication rules define the requirements of agile meetings, who attends the meetings and when, and how communications are to happen for colocated teams and remote teams. The norms for the group, such as working hours and best practices, might also be included with the rules of the project.

Exploring the Project Team

To effectively engage the project team, you'll need to really understand the characteristics of a successful agile team. Agile teams, specifically the developers or people creating the value, begin with the idea of a generalizing specialist. Generalizing specialists are team members who have more than one technical skill, and they can contribute in different areas of the project. In a predictive project, people tend to "stay in their swim lane" and focus on only their predefined assignments and responsibilities. In agile, we want team members to contribute to many areas of the project. This means that effective team members have knowledge of the core work, such as developing code, in the project, but also an understanding of the business domain, testing, or other complementary domains that the project encounters. No one knows everything, but there are opportunities for people to shift roles, learn new skills, and help the project be a success in many areas.

You might have heard of high-performing teams to describe a good project team. High-performing teams in agile projects begin with a shared vision for the project team. All team members must have a clear understanding of what creates value for the customer, understanding where the project is going, and be able to share the definition of done. When I consult on projects, I always begin by asking the client how they know the project is done. A vision for done is usually a vision for project success and value for the customer. If you don't have that among the project team, people may not be working for the value the customer expects.

 EXAM TIP In hybrid and longer agile projects, you might want to create a resource calendar just as you do in a predictive project. The resource calendar shows you when resources are available and when you'll be utilizing particular resources in the project.

It's a good idea, in agile projects, to keep the team size small. Bigger teams create complexity. Smaller teams, such as fewer than 12 people, keep things as a shallow structure, make communication and management of tasks easier, and help the team organize the work they are doing in each iteration. Big, massive teams are harder to organize, and they create bottlenecks where some team members are overloaded with work and others don't have much to do because there isn't enough work to go around, or the team members aren't qualified to do the work such as having a bunch of testers with not much code to test. This again is a good example of why teams need generalizing specialists. There are eight characteristics to identify a high-performing team in agile projects:

- The team is self-organizing. This means the team can decide who will work on what tasks.

- The team is empowered. The team has the freedom to experiment and tackle the work as they see fit to do so.

- The team believes they can solve any problem. The team members have a positive, can-do attitude.

- The team believes success is the only option. Everyone on the team believes that they can successfully complete the iteration, the task, and the project.

- The team is responsible. In agile, the team must be self-led and then own its decisions and commitments; this becomes evident when team members demonstrate the results of the iteration in the sprint review.

- The team trusts one another. The idea of collective code ownership, relying on one another and being transparent, calls for the team to trust each other throughout the project.

- The team is consensus driven. The team is not overpowered by any one individual; everyone's opinion and vote carries the same weight.

- The team can agree to disagree with respect. Respect each other and working through constructive disagreement are facets of effective team collaboration.

These eight characteristics can be seen in the agile concept of self-directing teams. Agile teams are empowered to make decisions, work collectively on tasks, and make local decisions. This sometimes can be seen in that the role of the project manager, or scrum master, is hands-off when it comes to decision-making in the project. This is true, to an extent, because the project manager role is more of a facilitator and coach than in a predictive project. Local decision-making calls for the team to decide how long user stories will take to complete, which can be up to three days in duration, who'll do what task, and how best to tackle the iteration or sprint backlog.

With projects that are not performing well, you will find five dysfunctions of a team:

- **Absence of trust among the project team members** When people don't trust one another in a team, they'll horde information, avoid responsibility, and be more combative when it comes time to make decisions.

- **Fear of conflict among some team members** Some people are less likely to argue or constructively disagree and will take a passive approach to conflict management. This is evident in the withdraw resolution approach to disagreement: one person simply gives up and yields to the other person.

- **Lack of commitment**   If the project team doesn't believe in the value of the project or they feel their work isn't important, they may be uncommitted to the project success.

- **Accountability avoidance**   People will try to shift blame, not take responsibility or be accountable for failures in the project, or not communicate their mistakes. This is often seen in the retrospective of the iteration.

- **Inattention to quality**   Quality is built into the project work, and sloppy work will create bugs and defects that testers may discover, or the defects can escape the project and make their way into production. Paying attention to quality and the expectations of the work is crucial as each team member can directly affect the quality of the project and its deliverables.

 EXAM TIP   When presented with questions where team members and other stakeholders are in a disagreement, aim for collaboration and a resolution that protects the value of the project and the organization. Follow the rules, be in compliance with government regulations, keep people safe, and protect the value.

Creating a Team Space

As more and more people work from home rather than in an office, the notion of the team space will likely fade away. For your exam, however, it'd be good to be familiar with the concept. A team space is an open office space environment dedicated to the colocated project team. Everyone on the team operates in the team space, can see one another, and can communicate quickly. No other work is allowed in the team space, only project work by the project team. This creates a sense of community and ownership by the team for the project work. Communication is quick and easy, and osmotic communication is encouraged.

 EXAM TIP   Osmotic communication is the communication that happens just by being present or near the conversation. Some might say it's when you overhear conversations, but you're not really part of the conversation. This isn't eavesdropping or spying; it's just picking up information by being in the space where the communication is happening.

The team space keeps everyone within 33 feet of each other, removes obstruction from lines of site, and gets rid of the cubicle farm. You might hear some people call this a *war room*, but that name is also fading away from the agile vernacular. The main part of the team space, where everyone works and operates is called the *commons*, because it's the common area for all of the team members. Team spaces typically have alcoves, tiny offices, or even old phone booths for private conversations, quick meetings, quiet work, or phone calls. These little nooks are called *caves* and are ideal for quiet concentration and one-on-one conversations.

Coaching the Team

Team members don't know everything and will often look to you to help them make the best decision in the project. Even though you are operating in an agile or hybrid project, it's still expected that you'll call on expert judgment for advice and direction. The team shouldn't only look to the project manager in the agile project, but also the business-people, the product owner role, and others who can offer insight. If your organization is shifting into agile, the project manager role may be more involved in the first few iterations to help the team and stakeholders follow the rules and procedures. Over time, the team will pass through the learning curve and become more independent and self-led.

Whenever people try a new skill, be it golf, programming, or working in an agile project, it takes practice, time, and experience to perfect the skill. The Dreyfus Model of Adult Skill Acquisition describes the five stages people move through as they perfect a skill. While you may not have several questions on this topic, it's important and relative to new agile teams and organizations. Here are the five components of the model:

- **Novice**   The first stage is simply following the rules and making basic analytical decisions.
- **Advanced beginner**   At this stage, the person still follows the rules, but now has a better understanding of the rules.
- **Competent**   Armed with experience, the person understands the rules and which rules are best applied for different scenarios.
- **Proficient**   Now the person can analyze the scenario and create a strategy rather than just relying on the rules and best practices.
- **Expert**   The individual knows how to act in the scenario and relies on intuition based on experience and mastery of the practice.

With experience and good coaching, the project team moves through these stages and successfully gets things done in the project. Of course, not everyone will want to achieve the expert level if they don't see the value in the skill acquisition. Some people will just want to know enough to get the work done and move on, and that's often fine if there's no long-term value in the skill for the individual. Another approach to describe skill mastery is Shu-Ha-Ri that has a similar evolution of skill acquisition. Shu means the person starts by following the rules and best practices. Ha means the guidelines are mastered, and there's more flexibility surrounding the rules. Ri means the person has mastered the practice and can transcend the rules and best practice.

Each style of agile has a slightly different approach for how you'll coach or lead the team. All of the approaches, agile, Kanban, Lean, and Crystal, have a consistent principle: communicate how the team will work together to identify problems and issues with honesty and transparency. The project management role is each approach should work with the team to identify triggers and signals of an upcoming problem. In the daily standup meeting, for example, you should ask the team if there are any impediments, roadblocks, or other issue that can prevent them from moving forward. Persistently asking for the team to look for issues and risks to progress is a core part of all agile project management approaches.

Resolving Differences in an Agile Project

People are going to have conflict; it's natural. When people work together on a project, big or small, chances are there are going to be differences of opinion on the best way to get the work done. A rule in agile is that while conflict is natural, we want to collaborate, work together, and respect one another. We don't plow over other people's opinions and force decisions, even if we know we're right. We need to listen, consider perspectives, and look at the whole scenario to choose the most effective solution for the value in the project.

When conflicts happen, the team members should work together to resolve the issue, rather than the project manager role stepping in and making decisions. When the team shifts into the storming phase, conflicts can blow up, and that does call for the project manager to step in and help cool things off, offer some coaching, and direct the team to treat each other with respect and fairness. There are five levels of conflict among stakeholders you may have to facilitate, but rarely force decisions:

- **Problem solve** This is the most common level where the discussion is cool, respectful, and fact-based. Both parties aren't emotionally attached to a solution and just want the best for the project.

- **Disagreement** This is when egos begin to emerge in an argument and people are more interested in saving their reputation than finding a solution. No one likes to be wrong or appear foolish.

- **Contest** The parties in the disagreement are focused on winning the debate rather than working together to find a solution. The conflict can escalate to personal attacks and demeaning comments.

- **Crusade** The stakeholders are focused on protecting the group they represent and crushing the perceived opposition. This level can create riffs of conflict among segments of the team.

- **World war** The people in the conflict now have a vendetta against each other and are focused on destroying or sabotaging. While rare, this level can create massive disruption in the project and in the organization. Often there is a history of unresolved conflict between the two antagonists in the disagreement.

Collaboration isn't just for project team members who are in disagreement, but for everyone in the project. Collaboration is for the entire agile team, but also for the customers who are influencing the product and deciding what the end result of the project will be. There are five approaches to collaboration in agile projects:

- **Accept the scenario** The easiest thing to do is to just accept the scenario and live with it. This can be a software bug, a change that wasn't really requested, or a decision that's been made outside of the project.

- **Avoid the scenario**   Avoidance, like the risk response, aims to create a workaround to the issue or problem. Imagine a software glitch that happens every time a user copies text in a program. The glitch isn't a big problem, but a warning dialog box opens. Workaround code is some code to automatically shut the dialog box so the user can continue working. It's not great, but it works for now.

- **Ameliorate the scenario**   Ameliorate means to reduce the effect of the problem. The teams wants a new server for integration and one for testing—something that's just outside the budget for the project. You and the team collaborate and decide that an older server could be reused in the project for the integration and testing. While not super-fast, it's better than the current server the team is using.

- **Cover up the problem**   This solution hides the problem altogether from the customer, which isn't being transparent in agile. Imagine an app that is supposed to find restaurants within a few miles of where the customer is located. For the demo, the team preloads the surrounding ZIP codes and restaurants into the app, so it appears things are working fine, when in reality the geographical mapping isn't working at all.

- **Resolve the problem**   The best solution is to get rid of the problem for the customer. Rather than hide the problem or create a workaround, fix the issue so the product is working the way it is supposed to. While this is ideal and noble, it's not always the most practical solution when you consider the return on the investment for the time and costs to fix the problem, especially if it's a small issue and a small impact. We all know that sometimes little glitches can be time-consuming and costly to fix.

Chapter Summary

Stakeholder engagement in agile projects, as in predictive projects, begins with stakeholder identification. You must know who the stakeholders are before you can effectively engage the stakeholders. Unlike predictive projects, however, the agile framework begins with predefined roles, such as the scrum master, product owner, facilitator, or coach. The trickier part of the engagement equation is fully identified people and groups that are outside of the project, the customers and end users. You don't want to get deep into a project and suddenly realize your inventory app will affect the manufacturing group, the sales group, and overseas customers. A robust stakeholder identification is needed to avoid issues with stakeholders who are identified late in the project.

The agile team must have a clear understanding of what the stakeholders want from the project—the value they see in the project completion. The business representative, such as the product owner, needs to understand the problem the project aims to solve or the opportunity the project aims to achieve. The vision of the value must be clearly explained to the project team and is often included in the project charter. Some agile projects utilize a vision statement to quickly communicate what the project is to do, the project's Definition of Done, and the value the project will create for the customers. The agile project charter also defines the goals and rules for the project team. The charter should have consensus among the team members and key stakeholders before the actual work begins.

Throughout the project there are opportunities to keep stakeholders engaged with the project work. Recall that in scrum you have the sprint planning meetings, the daily scrum, sprint reviews, and the sprint retrospective. These ceremonies are key points to help the team and stakeholder see the value the project is working toward, show results for the daily work, and build momentum, excitement, and synergy for the stakeholders. These meetings are a form of knowledge sharing; the team and the businesspeople transparently share knowledge of what is wanted in the project, clarity on the deliverables, and honest updates on the project progress.

Communication and stakeholder engagement are closely related. Communication in the team space relies on face-to-face communication, whenever possible, and keeping the project team in a colocated locale. Of course, this hasn't been possible in recent years as more and more people are working from home. Web conferencing software, such as Zoom and Microsoft Teams, help with face-to-face communication, but we lose the osmotic communication and sometimes subtle, instant feedback from body language. The team space is called the commons, and it's the open floor plan where everyone can see one another. The private areas for phone calls, private conversations, or deep thinking in the knowledge work are called caves. Caves and commons are terms you'll likely see on the exam.

When people work together, you can expect some degree of conflict. Conflicts are natural and can help the team create new ideas, become more cohesive, and find the best solution for the project value. Sometimes, however, conflicts can fester and blow into major disagreements among stakeholders and groups of stakeholders. As a general rule, we expect the stakeholders to treat each other with respect, work toward the common goal of value in the project, and resolve differences. The role of the project manager should not interject with solutions and conflict resolution immediately but should facilitate the disagreement when needed, remind stakeholders of the rules of agile, and work to keep stakeholders respecting each other through the disagreement.

Questions

1. John is the project manager of a software development project. He has chosen to use the Scrum framework. His team does not have any agile experience. John has established that each sprint will have seven phases: Planning, Design (create mockups of user stories), Comprehension Testing (conduct comprehensive testing using mockups), Analysis (report testing results and reiterate design), Build (build functioning feature and test quality), Demo/Launch/Release, and Retrospective. Each sprint will be conducted in a four-week intervals. What else should John include in the sprint?

   A. Product backlog

   B. Time for coaching

   C. Burndown chart

   D. Kanban board

2. You are in the planning phase of a two-year bridge construction project. You know you will need at least ten construction workers at any given point every month to complete the project within the two-year deadline. What tool should you use to ensure you can maintain the minimum number of workers during the entire construction process?

   A. Kanban board

   B. Gantt chart

   C. Work breakdown structure

   D. Resource calendar

3. Sally is a scrum master working at the Acme Corporation, which recently switched to using agile methodology. Sally has just begun working with a team of software developers on a new web site when a stakeholder pulls her aside and asks for a detailed project plan. What should Sally do next?

   A. E-mail a copy of the project plan to the stakeholder.

   B. Tell the stakeholder; agile does not use project plans.

   C. Meet with the stakeholder and give them an introductory walk-through of the agile methodology.

   D. Ask a team member to update the stakeholder every Friday.

4. Mikayla is a project manager with many years of experience in the construction industry. After moving into the software development industry, she manages her first lean, agile project. What might she want to ensure her project team understands in a lean, agile project more so than in a traditional waterfall project when planning for potential problems?

   A. The definition of the problem

   B. The triggers and signals of an upcoming problem

   C. The roles of those involved in the problem

   D. The strategy for addressing the problem

5. Another scrum master in your organization has come to you for advice. The scrum team needs an effective way to keep the product owner and other stakeholders informed about how the project progresses. What tools would you advise him to use?

   A. Project roadmaps and story maps

   B. Prototypes and wireframes

   C. Team task board with WIP limits

   D. Velocity and risk burndown charts

6. Sherry works for a company that designs and delivers custom workflow solutions for its customers. Sherry is a scrum master for the Harding Project, one of many active projects in this business. Sherry's project has just concluded a sprint and has held the sprint review with the product owner and other stakeholders. Sherry schedules and holds a sprint retrospective that identifies changes to several development tasks that will increase her business unit's efficiency. What is this an example of?

   A. Business value assessment

   B. Task decomposition

   C. Waste reduction

   D. Rolling wave planning

7. Jonathon is a scrum master for Project W, which is two iterations into its deployment. Jonathon has identified several stakeholders who are not interested in how Project W is progressing and do not seem to have much influence on the project itself. How should Jonathon manage these stakeholders?

   A. Invite them to daily standups.

   B. Ignore them. Given their low power and influence, they cannot impact Project W.

   C. Ensure they receive regular project updates.

   D. Regularly check in to see how they are doing.

8. Thelma is the scrum master for Project E, which is in its ninth iteration, has a velocity of 63 story points, and is on budget. After a recent sprint review, a stakeholder approached her and asked that a few features be added and prioritized. Thelma asked them to speak with the product manager about their request. What is the best reason Thelma did this?

   A. Thelma does not like this stakeholder.

   B. The product owner is the only one who can add features to Project E.

   C. The stakeholder is not following agile procedure by speaking to Thelma.

   D. The product owner will be able to determine the features' value to Project E.

9. Hank is the scrum master for Project W, which is in its third iteration and one week behind schedule. After a recent sprint review, a stakeholder approached him and complained about not getting project updates. What should Hank do next?

   A. Refer the stakeholder to information radiators.

   B. Invite the stakeholder to daily standups.

   C. Speak with the stakeholder and get more information.

   D. Assign a team member to send that stakeholder updates.

10. Richard is the scrum master for Project W, which is nine iterations into deployment and has a velocity of 38 story points. Recently Richard discovered that a stakeholder was circumventing established processes and escalating complaints to Richard's manager instead of bringing them up at the sprint review. How should Richard handle this scenario?

    A. Confront the stakeholder directly.

    B. E-mail all the stakeholders, reminding them how to report issues.

    C. Hold a special meeting to surface complaints.

    D. Align with his manager on the best approach.

11. Quincy is the scrum master for Project W, which is nine iterations into deployment and has a velocity of 38 story points. At a recent sprint review, Quincy asked the stakeholders if they were receiving his weekly project updates. What is the most likely reason for this question?

    A. Quincy does not believe anyone reads his updates.

    B. This question is common in agile projects.

    C. There were several questions in the meeting that were answered in his e-mails.

    D. Quincy wants to ensure his e-mails are being received and are useful.

12. Xavier is the scrum master for Project Q, which is in its ninth iteration and has a velocity of 76 story points. After a recent meeting, one stakeholder became agitated at the progress Project Q is making. After reviewing prior experiences with the project, Xavier determines that the stakeholder consistently attends meetings but has been unable to convince the steering committee to change several items. What should Xavier do next?

    A. Keep this stakeholder informed on progress.

    B. Invite the stakeholder to all project meetings.

    C. Do nothing. The product owner will help them.

    D. Assign a team member to update the stakeholder.

13. Marlene is the scrum master for Project E, which is in its eighth iteration and has a velocity of fifty-eight story points. Recently Marlene realized she has an extremely high number of stakeholders, and it is becoming hard to manage. What should Marlene do to make this task easier?

    A. Group stakeholders by need and manage the groups.

    B. Hire a project coordinator to assist.

    C. Assign a developer to help manage the stakeholders.

    D. Only manage high power stakeholders.

14. John is an agile project manager, and his team utilizes Kanban as its primary system to manage projects. John loves the fast changes that come with his assigned projects, but sometimes he struggles with one aspect. A few core personalities dominate his organization; one is named Linda. Linda can approve a charter and get a project going based on her word, which is a blessing and a curse for John. Linda is an ally, so she can sometimes get a project moving that might otherwise not go anywhere. On the other hand, Linda sometimes asks the team to initiate projects based on her preference and instinct. John is getting heat from people inside the organization who sometimes have trouble seeing every project's value. How can John show the benefits of some of these controversial projects?

   A. Do a cost-benefit analysis on each project.

   B. Direct complaints to Linda.

   C. Ignore complaints.

   D. Compare the projects to company stock price.

15. Paul manages an agile software development project that has changed significantly throughout several agile sprints. When originally conceived, the project had numerous potential benefits identified in its charter and other founding documents. Paul is worried that while the team is releasing its increments quickly and functionally, it may not provide the benefits that were initially promised. Everyone is excited about the functionality of the software and the speed at which it is being built. Paul does not want to be seen as negative and wants to ensure the software is meeting the original vision and creating value. How should Paul address the situation?

   A. Keep quiet because it is agile and is supposed to change.

   B. Create a new charter.

   C. Review the charter and other founding documents with key stakeholders.

   D. Change the project backlog to fix the issue.

16. Sean is the scrum master for Project E, which is beginning its first iteration. After the kickoff meeting, a stakeholder approaches Sean and tells him he is concerned his team will not benefit from Project E until the project is done. How is Sean most likely to respond?

   A. Agile projects deploy incremental benefits over each iteration.

   B. The stakeholder is correct. His team will benefit only once the project is complete.

   C. Refer the stakeholder to the product owner.

   D. Re-prioritize tasks so this stakeholder benefits sooner.

17. Neal is the scrum master for Project K, which is two iterations into deployment. A stakeholder approaches Neal with an idea for a new feature and asks how to submit the change request. How should Neal respond?

    A. Direct the stakeholder to enter their idea into the product backlog.

    B. Direct the stakeholder to the project team.

    C. Refer to project documentation on the change control board.

    D. Enter the task on behalf of the stakeholder into the backlog.

18. You are incorporating the requirements management plan for an organization that is incorporating agile methodologies to improve productivity. The management team has tasked you to determine cross-functional requirements and smooth out relations between all key stakeholders. What would your recommendation to the management team be in this scenario?

    A. Facilitate a requirements workshop with key stakeholders to formulate user stories.

    B. Develop a survey and distribute it to all key stakeholders to ascertain the product requirements.

    C. Conduct interviews with each stakeholder to determine each of their requirements.

    D. Perform a job shadowing exercise with the intended end users of the existing software.

19. Laurie is a project manager who is versed in agile methodologies. Laurie was recently hired by a small firm who wants to shake up their project management department and move to agile practice. Senior management believes in Laurie and her experience, but they also do not understand the agile approach and benefits. They want her to be a change agent, but her project team and colleagues have only experienced waterfall projects. How can Laurie create the change that her senior management has mandated?

    A. Wait a year or two until she is part of the group.

    B. Mentor key team members in agile.

    C. Start scrum sprints and let them learn as they go.

    D. Conform to the rest of the team.

20. You are the scrum master for your organization, and the team has just completed a four-week sprint. What is the next event that should happen, and what's the expected duration of the ceremony?

    A. Sprint retrospective—up to three hours

    B. Sprint review—up to four hours

    C. Sprint review—up to three hours

    D. Sprint retrospective—up to four hours

Answers

1. **B.** John should include several hours each sprint for mentoring as the team is new to the agile approach. The product owner maintains the product backlog. Burndown charts and Kanban boards are tools.

2. **D.** For this scenario, you should use a resource calendar. A resource calendar is used to plan, manage, and monitor resources, including both employees and equipment. A Kanban board is an agile project management tool designed to help visualize work, limit work-in-progress, and maximize efficiency. A Gantt chart is a visual view of tasks scheduled overtime. A work breakdown structure is a deliverable-oriented hierarchical decomposition of the work to be executed by the project team to accomplish the project objectives and create the required deliverables.

3. **C.** This stakeholder is likely used to a predictive life cycle and is not used to agile concepts of backlogs, iterations, etc. Educating the stakeholder on these differences will help them understand agile flexibility. Agile does not have a project plan in the way predictive projects do, so there may be nothing to e-mail. Telling the stakeholder there is no project plan that is as accurate as the project roadmap could be considered a high-level strategy. Having a team member update the stakeholder weekly pulls that team member away from work and does not provide the stakeholder with the information they need.

4. **B.** Because agile projects are adaptive, it is critical to be aware of triggers and signals of an upcoming problem. In agile projects, the scope is not defined for the entire project up front, meaning the team will need to have a shared understanding of what potential problems may arise and how to get ahead of them. While understanding the definition of the problem, the roles of those involved in the problem, and the strategy for addressing the problem are all critical in any project, these are done similarly across agile projects and waterfall projects. Because waterfall projects involve more scope definition up front, the triggers and signals of an upcoming project can be better anticipated in a waterfall project than in an agile project. Therefore, in an agile project, the team should have a greater shared understanding of what they may look for to catch an upcoming problem.

5. **D.** Although all the tools listed can be used to communicate project information to stakeholders, only the velocity and risk burndown charts track progress over time. Velocity charts show how much work the team has completed in each iteration, and risk burndown graphs show how well the team is managing the project risks. Story maps are essentially a high-level planning tool that agile stakeholders can use to map out the project priorities. The team's task board helps gain insight into the current iteration and identify bottlenecks to improve lead times.

6. **C.** Business value assessment and task decomposition are incorrect because the development process changes are about Sherry's internal business processes, not about her project's scope (which is her customer's business processes). Rolling wave planning is incorrect because this situation is not at the level of project planning. Waste reduction is correct because the sprint retrospective has identified unnecessary activities (waste) in Sherry's project.

7. **D.** Low-power and low-influence stakeholders should be monitored, but unless they express additional interest do not need to be closely tied to the project. Stakeholders should not be included in regular standups. They are for the project team to share statuses with each other. Stakeholders should never be ignored. Doing so invites risk that they will impact the project. Since these stakeholders have little interest in the project, regular updates will likely be ignored.

8. **D.** The product owner is best able to determine which features will provide value to Project E. So, while anyone can add tasks to a backlog, only the product owner can prioritize them. Thelma not liking the stakeholder is not the best answer. The product owner is the person who can help Thelma the best and prioritize the features for the project.

9. **C.** Before taking action, Hank should understand more about the stakeholder's complaint. For example, they do not know there are information radiators or may not be on the correct e-mail list. Referring the stakeholder to information radiators or assigning a team member to help is not ideal as Hank does not understand where the problem is. Daily standups are intended for the project team to share updates on their work.

10. **D.** Of all the choices presented, the best is to collaborate with the manager on the issue. Given that the stakeholder approached his manager, Richard should align with his manager on the complaint's nature and the best path forward. This will help show a united front and help ensure the stakeholder is appropriately managed. Confronting the stakeholder directly is not ideal as they may have had valid reasons for going around Richard. E-mailing all the stakeholders is an indirect answer that does not directly address the one stakeholder who went around Richard. A special meeting to surface complaints is not ideal. Issues should be brought up during the standup meeting, reviews, and retrospective.

11. **D.** Quincy is asking to ensure his method of communication is effective and is working. Doing so allows him to tailor his communications to fit stakeholder needs. Not believing anyone reads his updates is not the best answer to this question. This question is not necessarily common in agile projects. Having the same question pop up is not the best answer.

12. **A.** Given the stakeholder's low power and high influence Xavier should keep this stakeholder informed on the project. Inviting the stakeholder to more meetings or assigning a team member to update them is not ideal given their power and influence. Doing nothing risks further agitating this stakeholder.

PART III

13. A. Marlene should group stakeholders by like needs and then manage those groups. This will allow her to communicate with everyone more easily. Hiring a coordinator or working longer hours is not the best option in this scenario. Assigning a developer to help manage stakeholders will reduce productivity. Only managing high-power stakeholders risks negatively impacting the other stakeholders.

14. A. A cost-benefit analysis or any benefit analysis is for new projects, and this is a form of transparency. This will give John the reasoning he needs to justify his projects. If a project has a low cost-to-benefit ratio, he can present that to someone like Linda. Linda now has a chance to see the results of her instinctual choices in black and white. If she chooses to proceed with a seemingly ill-advised project, then the onus is on her. While powerful stakeholders can often drive a project, a benefits analysis should be employed even if an individual or group drives the project with significant power.

15. C. Paul may be managing an agile project, but in this case, the project has a charter. The project's key benefits should match the charter, even if many of the details have changed. In taking the charter and any other founding project documents to his sponsor and other key stakeholders, it is a chance to make sure that the vision is realized. In doing so, Paul can help prevent scope creep and ensure that key benefits can be instituted in upcoming releases if that is not being done already. Paul should not adjust the project backlog. Agile projects naturally create change, but that should not be done at the cost of the original vision and associated benefits.

16. A. Agile projects deliver the most valuable items first and in increments, so this stakeholder will begin seeing small, incremental benefits as the project progresses. The stakeholder is incorrect as agile provides deployments continually. Referring the stakeholder to the product owner is not the best answer. Re-prioritizing tasks is not ideal as this may not align with Project E's objectives.

17. A. Agile projects allow anyone to propose an idea for a feature into the backlog. Neal should direct the stakeholder to the product owner to enter the feature into the backlog. Sending the stakeholder to the project team is not the best response as the team does not control or prioritize the items in the product backlog. Agile projects do not have a change control board. Adding the task story on behalf of the stakeholder is not ideal as the product owner is responsible for managing the product backlog.

18. A. You should facilitate a requirements workshop for the key stakeholders. Workshops can be used to determine functional requirements and allow key stakeholders to formulate user stories. Requirements workshops is a great method build collaboration among the stakeholders. While the other options can be used to obtain provisions, the workshop is the most collaborative way of doing so as stakeholders can talk to each other in real time.

19. **B.** Laurie has a mandate from her senior management team to change her department. She was recently hired. If she waits a year or two to be accepted by the group, change gets harder. Conformity serves no one in this situation, and forcing an agile methodology without context can create resentment and problems. Laurie should immediately begin mentoring key stakeholders in agile concepts. By teaching them and getting them on board, they can teach others, and in time she can have the department running in an agile or a hybrid fashion. Doing so will bring the requested change and make the department more dynamic.

20. **B.** A sprint review follows the iteration completion and precedes the sprint retrospective. A sprint review for a four-week sprint should last up to four hours. The other choices are incorrect as the sprint retrospective happens after the sprint review and it should last up to three hours for a four-week sprint.

16

Measuring Agile Project Performance

In this chapter, you will
- Define agile metrics
- Measure agile performance
- Chart agile performance

Agile projects can crash and burn just as easily as predictive projects. There is no guarantee of project success just because your organization is taking a different approach. The success, just as in predictive projects, comes only through hard work, diligence, assuring quality throughout the project, and reasonable expectations. No matter what the approach, if you don't have enough money or enough time to deliver everything the customer expects, the project won't be a success from the customer's perspective. You cannot, regardless of opinion, fit five pounds of dirt in a three-pound bag. Agile does take steps to balance time, cost, and scope, but if customers and management don't buy into setting realistic expectations and the prioritization of features, your project is doomed from the start.

Now pretend you work at an organization that buys into the agile approach. They're excited, understand the roles and responsibilities, and follow the Agile Manifesto and its protocols. The organization will, regardless of its adherence to the rules, still want to know how the project is performing. You can't be, as my poker friends say, all loosey-goosey, having a sandwich, and not pay attention to what's happening. Just because you're working in an agile or hybrid project doesn't mean you won't need to track performance.

 VIDEO For a more detailed explanation, watch the *Measuring Agile Project Performance* video now.

Tracking performance means measuring and communicating how well the project is doing on time, cost, scope, but also in the process itself. You'll have opportunities to review how the project team feels about the work, about one another, and about what's worked or hasn't worked. Most of the performance reporting, however, is based on the quality of the product, rather than the adherence to processes. For your

Project Management Professional (PMP) exam, you'll need to recognize the inspection of the deliverables and a little on software testing. You won't need to be a software tester, but you will need to be topically familiar with some testing approaches. Many project managers, in my experience, fluff over the testing component in their projects—a big mistake. It's always better to keep mistakes out of the customers' hands than to fix defects and unhappy customers later.

Defining Agile Metrics

There's an old adage with some mystery as to who said it first, but the line is: what gets measured gets done. Regardless of who coined the phrase, it's pretty much true when it comes to key deliverables in project management. In a predictive environment, there are all kinds of ways to track project performance, from earned value management to statistical sampling. In an agile project, there aren't the same concrete deliverables to measure and see progress. In fact, there can be several iterations before there's anything to release to the organization at all.

Just because there aren't physical things doesn't mean you can't measure progress in an agile project. Knowledge work is still work, and there is a result of effort that can be forecasted, baselined, and measured against expectations. This doesn't mean you want to look for metrics such as lines per code written, total hours worked, or tests run against the system. You want metrics that are measuring actual results of the project, the value that customers are looking for in the product.

The primary measurement of progress, in pure agile projects, is in working software. Agile projects aim to achieve customer satisfaction by delivering valuable software early and often. Working software, in a broader sense, is in results that the customer can actually use. Regardless of what the agile or hybrid project is creating, there is no value in unfinished work. Until the work creates a deliverable that can actually be used, there is no value. Usually in agile projects the measurement is simply put against created software that can be released, even in little portions, to the customer. However, you also need methods to measure the progress of the team to how close they are to completing chunks of the project.

 EXAM TIP Velocity is an empirical measurement of the team's progress. It's factual evidence of how the team is working, not a goal.

A few years ago, I was consulting for a government project that was shifting from an old COBOL accounting system to a newer, modern solution. With the sensitive nature of the system and organizational processes already in place, it was impossible to implement intermittent releases. This was a massive software development project that affected thousands of people who aimed to seamlessly switch overnight from the old solution to the new solution. There was no value in all of the work and millions of dollars invested in the project until actual cutover happened. Measuring progress in this project was tedious, but the measurement was against the quality of deliverables, system and code tests successfully passed, and hours consumed against hours allotted for the project. My point is that the value of working software isn't realized, regardless of what's measured, until the software or solution is being utilized by the customers. There is no value in the organization by just creating; the value for the organization is actual implementation of the product, not the creation of the product.

 EXAM TIP Transparency is key to communicating project status. It's not good to hide project information; always share good and bad news factually and openly. The communication formula of N(N-1)/2, where N represents the number of stakeholders, is a good example of how larger projects need to communicate clearly, openly, and frequently.

Earned Value Management

I covered earned value management earlier in this book, so I'm certain you recall that earned value management is a suite of formulas to show project performance. Earned value management is based upon the project's budget and how much work the team has completed in proportion to how much money the project has spent. Earned value is the percentage of work performed times the project budget; for example, you're 10 percent done, and the budget is $500,000. The earned value is $50,000. While that's great for some projects, it gets a bit messy in agile projects because of the changing requirements and uncertainty of what you'll be creating throughout the project.

In addition, recall that while predictive projects use the Triple Constraints of Project Management, agile projects use an inverted triangle to represent the constraints, as in Figure 16-1. In agile projects, the time and costs for the project are fixed, and the scope can vary. As the team creates the prioritized items in the product backlog, the time and costs are eaten up—until all of the time and costs are gone, and then the project is done. Calculating earned value management in agile can be futile as the expected changes and inability to predict what'll actually be created in the project. Unlike predictive projects, agile projects don't usually have milestones as the milestones will likely change anyway.

Figure 16-1
Agile uses an inverted triangle to represent the flexible and fixed constraints.

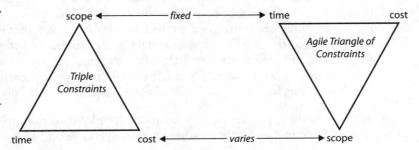

Some in the agile community push back on the Agile earned value management (EVM), as there is zero value created until there is a product release to the customers. That is a fine philosophical argument, but when management, or your PMP exam, requires you to do some number crunching, you have to do what's required. To complete Agile EVM, you'll need four things:

- **Actual cost of the release** The costs are needed to calculate the suite of formulas. You'll need the anticipated cost per release, not just the cost for the entire project. You can predict this by the cost of each story point in an iteration and the velocity of the team.

- **Estimated product backlog** The product backlog represents the remaining project scope.

- **Product release plan** This is when the increments will be released and the expected number of iterations.

- **Assumed velocity** This is the number of user story points the team can complete per iteration.

The base formulas for agile EVM are like traditional earned value management:

- **Planned value** This is the value of the planned work to be completed in the iteration. For example, if the cost per user story point is $1,600 and there are 35 user story points, the planned value for iteration is $56,000.

- **Earned value** This is the value of the work actually completed in the iteration. If the team completes only 30 user story points, the earned value would be 30 times $1,600, for an earned value of $48,000.

- **Actual cost** This is the cost of the work actually completed in the iteration. This is the actual money spent in the project. If the team had to work overtime or hire a resource to help with the project and they spent $55,000, that would be the actual cost for the iteration.

- **Budget at completion** This is the anticipated cost for the product release; there may be several iterations to get to a release. The product release plan will predict, though not always reliably, how many iterations will be needed. For example, if there are three iterations to get to the first release, you can predict the budget at completion (BAC) for the release by taking the number of iterations times the velocity and then times the cost per user story point. Here's the formula: 3 iterations with a velocity of 35 equates to 105 story points. Each story point, in this example, is $1,600, so the BAC for the release is $168,000.

With these metrics you can quickly calculate the EVM for the project. Table 16-1 shows a breakdown of earned value management for an agile project.

What is the expected velocity?	40
What is the cost per story point?	$1000
How many iterations per release?	4
How complete is the project?	50%
How complete should the project be?	55%
How much has the project spent?	$83,000
Budget at completion (for the product release)	160,000
Actual costs	$83,000
Earned value	$80,000
Planned value	$88,000
Cost variance	–$3,000
Schedule variance	–$8,000
Cost performance index	0.96
Schedule performance index	0.91
Estimate at completion	$166,000
Estimate to complete	$83,000
To-complete performance index (BAC)	1.04
To-complete performance index (EAC)	0.96
Variance at completion	–6,000

Table 16-1   Earned Value Management Applied to Agile

Personally, I'm not a fan of earned value management in agile projects. You can get a sense of how well the project is performing by using product and sprint burndown charts, looking at completed items in a Kanban chart, or just being involved in the project. You shouldn't have to run the numbers to see whether the project is going well. However, I'll concede that some managers may be resistant to agile approaches and want to cling to their older, predictable ways, so you just might have to create some formulas to show how well the project is doing. In addition, I'd expect a question or two on earned value management in agile or hybrid projects on your exam.

 DIGITAL CONTENT   In the *EVM Worksheet file*, I've included a separate page for calculating EVM in agile projects.

Return on Investment

If you were running a business to sell an application, you'd have to calculate your return on investment (ROI). ROI is calculated by taking the income generated by the product, the application you've created in this scenario, minus all the costs to create and market

PART III

the application. For example, if your app brought in $754,000 and you spent $285,000 to create and market the application, you'd subtract the costs of $285,000 from $754,000 for a return, or net profit, of $469,000. That's simple business math that any organization will do to show their profit from a project or ongoing operation. All businesses exist for one common reason: to make money.

Projects, whether they're agile, predictive, or hybrid, exist for one of two reasons in an organization: to cut costs or to generate revenue. Consider a project that will cut down on the time to manage insurance; this project will effectively be cutting costs by saving time and effort for the staff. A savings in costs can directly affect the organization's profitability. Projects that create a product or solution to sell to customers is all about increasing revenue for the organization. This logic also applies to not-for-profit organizations. Consider the esteemed Project Management Institute, a not-for-profit organization. Its projects, such as its long-PMBOK 7 project, is a product it sells to the public. That's creating revenue. Another project Project Management Institute (PMI) took on, was its continuing education registration project, to streamline how PMP and other credentialed members report their professional development unit. The project made the process easier and faster than in the past—more efficiency for all involved. A better usage of the organization's funds means it can invest more monies elsewhere in the organization and work toward its mission of promoting and supporting the project management profession.

In agile projects, the focus of this chapter, a return on investment, means how long it will take the organization to recoup the costs of the project for the product or the in-house cost-cutting solution that is being created. Intermittent releases throughout the project get the most-valuable features out to the organization so there is some quick return on investment for the project work. Agile is designed to create and release the prioritized items first to the customers, which means there's a faster ROI on the deliverables the team has created. The longer it takes to create a usable increment, as defined in the release plan, the longer it will take for the organization to recoup the costs and realize the ROI. Management horizon is the break-even point of when the solution created by the project equates to the cost of the project. Once you are past the management horizon, a positive ROI is created.

Measuring Agile Performance

While earned value management and return on investment are nice ideas, they aren't always practical to agile projects. They can be time-consuming to create and may not always reflect situations within the project that are affecting performance. Consider a project that has features dependent on architecture and structure in the software. The architecture and structure have to be created behind the scenes before the more glamorous, prioritized features of the product can be released or brought into a work in progress (WIP). You won't always get to create the most-prized features immediately due to other requirements that are needed in order to allow other features to work properly. Software development takes time.

Fortunately, agile has performance reviews built into the approach. In this section, I'll dive into the performance-review components of agile that you must know for your exam—and to really implement agile in an organization. All of these components of agile performance must be communicated and explained to stakeholders if they're new to agile, another nod to the communication and stakeholder engagement requirements of an agile project. If stakeholders don't know what to expect or how to tell if a project is performing well, or not so well, they'll get frustrated and almost always assume the worst. It's up to the coach, facilitator, scrum master, or the project manager role in an agile project to educate others on how things work.

Reviews and Retrospective

In agile, especially in scrum projects, you'll have opportunities to review the work completed and discuss how well the project has performed. The sprint or iteration review is performed by the project team, and it's a demonstration of what they've completed and why. This meeting comes at the end of a sprint, and the entire team and key stakeholders attend. The demo is led by the developers, not the project manager, and they'll discuss what they've created and how it contributes to the value of the project. This is especially important for those features that are behind the scenes, such as the architecture and setup of the programming environment. The team needs to show everyone what they have completed in the sprint. Work that hasn't been completed isn't demonstrated. There is no value in work that's incomplete. Incomplete user stories aren't demonstrated, and they're returned to the product owner for prioritization in the product backlog. Often, these unfinished user stories go back to the top of the product backlog, and the team attacks them again in the next iteration, though it is possible that other features have been added and are now more important than previously identified features.

 EXAM TIP Face-to-face communication is the best and preferred way to communicate in agile projects. With many teams now working remotely, it's a good idea to schedule some initial face-to-face meetings to help the team meet one another.

The retrospective is an opportunity for the team to discuss what worked and what hasn't worked in the project. It's the entire team's responsibility to share what has and hasn't worked in the project, not just the project manager's role. A retrospective is not an opportunity to point fingers and place blame, but rather a time to focus on how the team can improve upon the project. The point of the retrospective is to learn from mistakes in the past iteration, allowing the team to better improve upon our performance in the next iteration. In predictive projects, we often do a lessons learned meeting at the end of the project or the end of the phase. While this is a good practice, it does have a deficiency; the lessons we've learned can't be implemented in the current project because we're done with the project or phase. In agile we can take time to learn from each other and look for opportunities for project performance improvement in the next iteration of the project.

For your exam, you'll need to understand the difference between a review and a retrospective. Reviews always follow the daily work at the end of a sprint or iteration. Reviews are a demonstration of the work the developers have just created. Businesspeople, which are your key stakeholders, will attend along with the product owner, the scrum master, and all the developers. The point of a review is to show completed work. From this review will get feedback and likely changes from the businesspeople. A retrospective comes after the review, and the point of this meeting is to improve upon project performance. A retrospective always comes after the sprint review and before the sprint planning meeting for the next iteration.

Understanding Velocity

Velocity is calculated by simply identifying the number of user story points completed in an iteration. Recall that user story points are assigned to user stories in relation to the size of the user stories. Consider a project team that is reviewing the user stories in a sprint planning session. The team will evaluate each user story from the top down in the product backlog and then size the user stories in relation to other user stories. So, for example, a user story could be identified as large, medium, or small. More likely, user stories are given points where the more points assigned means the larger the user story is in relation to the other user stories in the product backlog.

The team will then select the number of user stories they think they can complete in an iteration. For example, the team believes it can achieve 40 user story points per iteration. The 40 user story points is the goal of the sprint; the user stories selected from the prioritized product backlog cannot exceed 40 user story points. The team has already said they can do 40 story points in the next iteration, so the sizing of the user story points helps the team and really all stakeholders understand how much work the team can get done in the next iteration.

When the team completes an iteration and it has completed all of the features for that iteration, the total number story points completed represents the team's velocity for the iteration. In this example, if the team did complete 40 user story points, its velocity would be 40. In the next iteration, if the team completed only 35 user story points, its velocity would be 35. It's common in the first few iterations for the velocity to fluctuate, but over time and with experience velocity will stabilize. Velocity helps the product owner, the developers, and the project management role understand how well the project is performing and do some forecasting of how long the project will last.

 EXAM TIP I'll discuss risk management in the next chapter, but for now, know that items in the product backlog are bumped to the top based on their risk score. The risk score is the same expected monetary value calculation of impact times probability. The risk adjusted backlog doesn't affect the velocity of the team—velocity is simply the completion of user story points.

How velocity affects project duration is a simple calculation. The total number of user story points in the product backlog is divided by velocity. For example, consider a project that has 945 user story points and the team's velocity is 45. Now you'll divide 945, which is the total number of user story points in the product backlog, by 45, which is the team's velocity. The result is 21, which represents the number of iterations it will take to complete all of the features in the product backlog. On your exam, you may be asked to predict how long a project will take given a scenario like this example. To predict project duration, you would need to know how long each iteration lasts. In this example, each iteration is four weeks. Therefore, 21 iterations, at a four-week duration each, would equate to 84 weeks. That is a rough estimate of how long this project would take to complete.

One final consideration for velocity is any disruption of the planned iteration duration. For example, a company holiday can affect the total number of working days in the iteration. A four-week sprint has 20 working days, but a four-day weekend knocks the sprint down to just 18 working days. The project manager and the team should consider the reduction in available days when selecting the total number of user stories to complete in the next iteration.

Lead Time and Cycle Time

Lead time and cycle time are two metrics you need to know for your PMP exam, and you'll need to measure in your agile projects to show performance. First up is lead time. Lead time measures the duration between when a customer makes a request all the way to the time they receive the results. Lead time and cycle time track the tasks to create the features within a sprint, not the items waiting in the prioritized product backlog. If a team isn't using Scrum but is simply utilizing a Kanban board, lead time starts as soon as the feature is placed on the Kanban board.

Imagine a customer asked for a feature that's a form on a web site to enter shipping information. They make this request in October. The form is created and finally delivered to the customer in February. The lead time, in this extreme example, is five months, because it took five months from when the customer first requested the form until the form was delivered to the customer.

Cycle time describes the duration of how long it took the team to complete the work on a feature. The cycle time is the actual work time to create the feature the customer has requested. In the scenario of the web form, the lead time was five months. The actual working time, which is the cycle time, took the team only one week to complete the work. Lead time shows how long the feature was in waiting to be delivered; cycle time represents the actual effort to create the feature. The longer the lead time, the longer it took to deliver value to the customer. To be fair, the feature request could be low in the list of priorities in the Kanban board, so the lead time could be large and not really represent a problem, though in my example, this is really an extreme situation. Figure 16-2 shows the relationship of lead time in cycle time.

Figure 16-2
Lead time is
whole duration
from request
to completion.
Cycle time is
the duration of
actual work on a
feature.

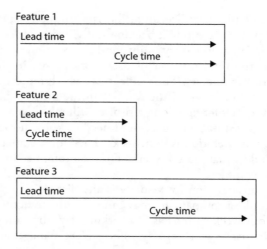

Cycle time helps the team, the project manager, or the coach understand how effective they are at creating features. You do want to measure cycle time because it helps the team understand the needed limitation on work in progress. As a general rule, switching between tasks is a waste. If a feature is a simple piece of work to create, such as a web form for a shipping address, and it has a long cycle time, the team has likely switched or started new work before finishing the web form. It's better to start and finish one feature at a time, rather than put too many items in the WIP or hop from task to task.

Lead time and cycle time really give you valuable information about the effectiveness of the team's workflow. This information can help you identify bottlenecks, features that the team deems unimportant, and even issues the team may have with stakeholders. Lead time and cycle time can also help you predict and really understand the capacity your team has for work. This is one approach to tracking work performance so the team can understand their effectiveness in delivering value to the customer.

Charting Performance

While agile projects don't place value on unneeded documentation, there's often a need to document how well the project is performing. Your supervisor, customer, or key stakeholder may be asking for status reports and other documents to show project performance. You might also want to document project performance for transparency in the project—something all agile project managers should aspire to do. One of the best ways to document and share project performance, such as on your information radiator, is through charts.

Charting project performance is a quick way to show stakeholders, rather than just tell stakeholders, how things are going in the project. Charts can tell a story, and if you share the story in a public place, you're making the information transparent, showing honesty on the project performance, and building trust with the project team and the project stakeholders. Besides improving communication, charts are a great way for the agile team to analyze what's working in the project, opportunities for improvements, and areas of the project where performance may be threatened.

On your PMP exam, you'll likely see questions about agile charting. You should recognize the charts I'll explain in this section. You'll need to understand why a project manager would use a chart, what the chart aims to communicate, and the story that the chart is telling. On the PMP exam, PMI has added some hotspot-type questions, where you'll need to click an area in the graphic that answers the question. I imagine that you'll see questions asking you to click the area in the chart that show a performance issue or click the area in the graphic that shows velocity for the second sprint. Let's hop in now and exam the typical agile project charts.

Burndown and Burnup Charts

You probably already know burndown and burnup charts, as I've mentioned them occasionally throughout this book. These are so important for agile projects and your exam that it warrants a quick conversation here. A burndown chart is used when you have a long list of items, such as features in the product backlog, and by completing each item, the list is burned down. As you complete more and more items in the list, the list sizzles down and down until you're done. In agile, a burndown chart can be used for the product backlog and the sprint backlog. In predictive projects, you can use a burndown chart to illustrate how much money is left in the budget.

 NOTE Incremental and iterative describe the work approach in the process. Recall that increments append to what's already been created. Iterative describes the iteration, or repetition, in the work to refine what's already been created. Increments chop up the work into working increments. Iterations build upon and refine previous features on the way to the final release of the project.

Figure 16-3 is a burndown chart for a sprint backlog. The y-axis represents the total number of tasks in the sprint backlog, and the x-axis represents the timeline for the sprint, 28 days in this scenario. The solid line in the chart is the ideal flow of work over the sprint—steady work each day to reach the iteration's end with all the tasks completed. The ideal line is just that: ideal. It is based on estimates and is not always accurate. The dashed line in the chart shows the actual work performed and correlates to the x-axis to show how much work is remaining and correlates to the y-axis to show how many days are left in the sprint to do the work. Every day in the sprint a point will be added to the actual line to show progress against the ideal line. If the dashed line, the actual work, is above the ideal line, then there is more work to do, and the team is running late on planned work for the sprint. If the dashed line is below the ideal line, then the team is ahead of schedule on the project tasks. You don't want the actual work to be too far above or below the ideal line. A big fluctuation between the two can mean that the estimated work for the sprint wasn't accurate.

Figure 16-3
Burndown charts show the remaining items left to do in a backlog.

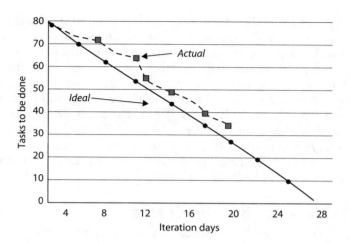

Figure 16-4 is a burnup chart. Similar to the burndown chart, this chart shows the accumulation of completed features, completed tasks, or work hours completed. It's ideal for any time you want to show the accumulation of something rather than the completion of an item. You can use a burnup chart for the sprint backlog, product backlog, or tracking the total accumulation of work hours or workdays in an iteration or project. In this burnup chart, the total number of user stories completed for the product backlog is shown on the y-axis, and each iteration is plotted across the x-axis. The solid line represents the number of user stories in the product backlog, and the dashed line represents the user stories completed in each iteration.

Notice how the solid line in Figure 16-4 moves upward from 130 to 170. This shows the addition of features needed during the project. Because agile expects and welcomes changes, the total number of user stories can increase, or decrease, during the project.

Figure 16-4
Burnup charts show the accumulation of items completed.

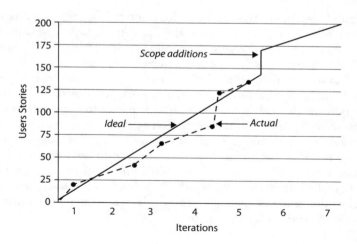

The burnup chart can track the total number of user stories in the product backlog, and when new stories, due to change requests, are added to the product backlog, the y-axis reflects this in the chart. A good exam question would be to define why the solid line changed during the project. And, of course, the answer is because there were additional features added to the product backlog.

Release Burndown

Similar to the burndown chart used in a sprint, another type of burndown chart is the release burndown, as in Figure 16-5. This chart is used to illustrate the timing of the product releases and the likelihood of meeting promised dates in the release plan. Recall that a release, in Scrum, is determined by the product owner, and it's the accumulation of iterations' deliverables that shift from project development to the organization or customer. The end of an iteration doesn't always equate to a release as a release. The product owner, customer, or businesspeople in the project determine what features and functionality should be completed by the developers to equate to a release of the product.

The release burndown chart maps out the total story points, expected work hours, or effort on the y-axis. The number of expected sprints in the project is on the x-axis. This is an important concept for your exam: the number of expected sprints is based on the velocity of the project team. Once the velocity has stabilized, then the forecasting of the project duration can be created. As a reminder, if the team is completing 40 user story points per iteration and there are 600 story points in the backlog, the project can be expected to take 15 iterations. Based on this calculation, the y-axis is the total number of story points in the product backlog, and the x-axis is the number of sprints in the project.

Figure 16-5
A release burndown chart shows the timing of product releases.

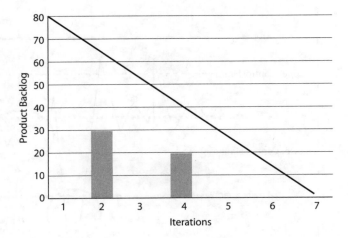

Using a Control Chart in Agile Projects

The control chart in predictive projects is typically associated with quality control. Recall that the control chart plots out the mean and control limits of a process. A control chart is used to show the stability of a repeatable process and the variations of the process. The farther away a result of measurement is from the mean, the more significance there is in the variance. Within the upper and lower control limits there are variances that are of normal variation. When variances drift beyond the upper or lower control limits, then there is a special cause of the variance, and some root-cause analysis should be plead for.

You can use a control chart to establish the expected mean, or normality, for the cycle time of the team. Recall that a cycle time is the actual time the team actually works on the feature. Lead time is how long the feature waits for development to begin, the cycle time, and then the delivery to the customer. You can create control charts for features completed in an iteration, items in the Kanban backlog, or issue resolution for customers. Many project management software tools, such as Jira, have control chart reporting to automate the chart creation. Figure 16-6 is a control chart for issue resolution in software development.

In Figure 16-6 the points in the line represent the issues in the project. The y-axis represents the total number of days an issue took to resolve, the cycle time. The dashed line represents the mean for issue resolution for the period of the project or iteration. When the solid line trends upward or downward, it's moving away from the expected mean, and issues are taking longer to resolve than what's been expected.

Some issues, or features, will take longer to complete than others and can skew the deviation of the project. You know that something can be resolved quickly, and other items will require deep thinking, trial and error, or asking for expert judgment to help.

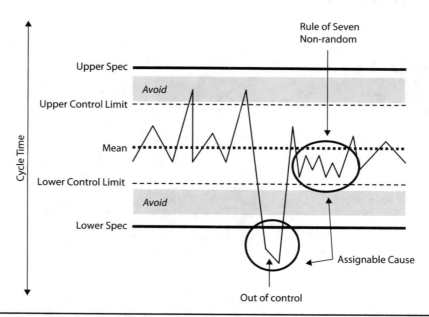

Figure 16-6   Control charts show the stability of a process over time.

All these trickier issues or features that take more time will bump up the resolution or completion date and are considered special causes. Recall that a special cause needs an explanation and is considered out of control. Just as in quality control, when there are six measurements in a row, all on one side of the mean, it's called the Rule of Seven. The Rule of Seven shows a trend in the project, and this too is a special cause.

Exploring Cumulative Flow Diagram

You're most likely to use a cumulative flow diagram with tasks in a Kanban board. Recall that in Kanban tasks are pulled from the queue into the WIP, moving from left to right through each phase of the project work. A cumulative flow diagram can seem overwhelming at first glance, but it's actually a simple stack diagram showing the number of tasks in each Kanban column. For example, a software development project can have a Kanban board with four columns: Backlog, Development, Testing, and Deployed. The chart will show how many items are in each column of the Kanban board.

In Figure 16-7, the cumulative flow diagram shows the total number of items on the y-axis and the total number of days on the x-axis. When you look at the cumulative flow diagram, each shaded shape in the chart is stacked according to the columns of Backlog, Development, Testing, and Deployed. The shaded areas within the chart show how many items are in each phase of the project work. For example, the product backlog has 200 items total, while there are a total of 85 items deployed from the project. The cumulative flow diagram can also show when there are significant changes to the product backlog. When the customer adds items to the project, this increases the number of user stories or features to be created. In a cumulative flow diagram, this displays as a stair step in the product backlog portion of the chart.

The WIP is represented by items in the chart that are between the product backlog and the deployment. At a glance, the number of items in the WIP should be uniform

Figure 16-7
Cumulative flow diagrams show the number of items in each phase of a project.

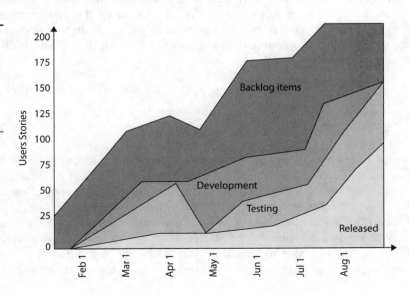

along the chart. Ideally, the shaded areas of the chart trend upward from left to right with the number of items deployed increasing, the number of items to do in the product backlog decreasing, and the phases representing the WIP staying uniform throughout the project. When there's a change between the items in WIP and deployment, there's likely a bottleneck or blocker in the project, and the issue should be addressed during your daily standup meeting.

Testing in Agile Projects

Another facet of project performance is to test what the developers have created before the feature is demonstrated and released to the organization. Testing is a form a quality control, and the plan to test, where quality is baked into the process, is a form of quality assurance. Like all projects, quality assurance aims to prevent mistakes from entering the project, while quality control aims to prevent mistakes from getting into the customers' hands. Testing in agile projects is to verify the code created works to satisfy the expectations of the user story and that the code created does not break anything else in the system.

There are countless web sites, books, training, and even certifications on software development testing. The concept of testing is philosophical and complex. What one organization does for testing, a competing organization would do differently. You can argue that there is, or is not, a proper approach to testing for any project, but the truth is, you and your organization have to decide what works best in your environment, for the type of project your creating, and for the results your customer expects. For projects with high criticality, such as a healthcare project where your solution can directly affect human lives, the testing may be much more robust than a project to create a fun little app that simulates a gumball machine.

For your exam, you should recognize the widely accepted approaches to testing I'll share in this section. You don't need to be a master at any of these to answer a few exam questions. You'll want to work with the team to ensure they're not overestimating what they can create in a duration, and you want to make certain they're planning adequately for quality assurance and quality control in their work. Keep three ideas in mind when it comes to testing:

- Quality is planned into the project, not inspected into the project.
- Deliver what the customer has requested.
- Don't break things when you create things.

Agile creates features for customers quickly, and that means testing also needs to happen early and often. Testing in agile projects is described as continuous testing. When features are created, the features are testing. Automated software testing can help the team and testers plow through rapid development and get the features into the increment for eventual release to the organization. You don't want testing to be a bottleneck in the flow of production, but you also don't want to rush testing and miss quality concerns that customers are sure to find. Bugs and issues that pass all the way through to the end user (customer in some cases) is poor quality, and these defects are called *escaped defects*.

Employing Acceptance Test–Driven Development

Acceptance test-driven development means that the acceptance tests are written first, and then the code is developed to pass the test. Tests are written with multiple roles to ensure that different perspectives are involved to create robust code, accurate results, and precise tests. For example, the developers, the customers, and the testers meet to discuss the acceptance test for a feature. The portion of the program that is collaborated on and tested is called a *unit*, and you'll often see testing refer to *unit testing*.

When deploying acceptance test-driven development, you're implementing the Three Amigos approach. Yes, the Three Amigos is a real term to describe the perspective of the project customers, the developers, and the testers:

- **Customers**   What's the problem to be solved?
- **Developers**   How can the problem be solved?
- **Testers**   What about other aspects of the solution?

Acceptance test-driven development is first about collaboration among the development team, testers, and customers to create a robust approach to the solution and to ensure that the developers' time is invested creating exactly what the customers want. This approach also ensures that the developers know what the conditions to pass the test will be, so they develop to pass the test, rather than the develop what they believe to be true only to discover that what they have created isn't exactly what the customers wanted and the tests fails and time has been wasted.

Acceptance test-driven development follows a five-step approach:

1. Collaborate to write a single unit test.
2. Run the test, which will fail.
3. Write the simplest code to pass the test.
4. Refactor, which is to clean up the code, and continue to pass the test.
5. Run accumulating unit tests as the project moves forward.

Working with Behavior-Driven Development

Behavior-driven development has evolved from the acceptance test-driven development. The same approach is used with writing the tests by collaborating with the customer, refactoring, and accumulating tests over time. The addition with behavior-driven development goes back in time and starts with the user story rather than the code the developers create. By starting with the user story and questioning all facets of the story, the value of the user story is clearly known to the developers, testers, and customers.

Behavior-driven development uses the Five Whys approach for each user story. Five Whys, like a three-year old, asks "why?" five times for each answer given. You don't always have to ask "why?" five times in a row, but rather embrace the concept of asking "why?" to fully understand the value for the project customer and what they really want out of the user story. It helps everyone to fully understand what the project customer is expecting as a result of the user story.

For example, consider this user story: "As a salesperson, I want my customers to place orders online so sales can come in faster." Now let's ask "why?" five times.

Why? So customers can place orders whenever they want.

Why? So we can generate more sales.

Why? So we can increase revenue and market share.

Why? So I don't have to be with the customer to place an order.

Why? So I replicate my efforts for better sales.

This approach would then use the principles of test-driven development to build upon the perspective of the salesperson, one of the Three Amigos in this scenario, to create the tests to pass these solutions. Behavior-driven development isn't a real technical concept, but it's used to facilitate the conversation between the developers and the businesspeople. The process shouldn't be rushed, but each answer can be expounded upon, especially for the highly prioritized items in the product backlog, to ensure that all roles in the project know exactly what they are asking for and what the team will be creating and testing.

Exploratory Testing in Agile

Rather than taking an in-depth structured approach to testing the software, exploratory testing explores the software created and looks for defects by actually using the system. Exploratory testing is a thinking activity where the tester has to think like the user, experiment with different parts of the system, and play a "what-if" role when testing the solution. Exploratory testing relies on the tester to investigate the solution and discover problems—like a real user would do—with the software. Testers aren't directed or given test scripts, but have freedom and independence in their approach to testing the software.

Often in agile, software development tests are completed through testing software to speed up the testing process. Tests are written to pass the testing software, but the problem is that testing software can't think or explore, but people can with exploratory testing. Automated testing, while fantastic to save time and keep the project moving, is controlled and predictable. The problem is that users aren't predictable, and they'll tinker and explore and find errors and problems in the software. That's what exploratory testing tries to prevent. Rather than always automate the process with testing software, exploratory testing thinks like a user and works spontaneously through the testing process.

Exploratory testing is also known as *session-based testing* because it's a session of testing. There are five components of session-based testing:

- Establish classification of software bugs. This helps the tester categorize the issues found, performs root-cause analysis, and documents risks the bug may create.

- Write a test charter. The test charter is the umbrella of what needs tested, how the feature should work, and the areas the test should explore.

- Define the timebox. The session for testing usually begins with a 90-minute session and can be extended or reduced by up to 50 percent. Testers aren't interrupted during the testing session.

- Review the results. At the end of the session, the tester creates an evaluation of what they've discovered.

- Debrief the team. Finally, the testers share their findings with the team. The team and the testers collaborate on next steps and next items to test.

Chapter Summary

One of the fundamental rules of agile project management is that you must be transparent—both with good news and with bad news. Showing how well the project is performing is being transparent; things like honest conversations with stakeholders, information radiators, and charting out the project performance will garner trust with stakeholders and keep them supportive of the project. Early in the project the team will work on the most valuable items first. While it's ideal that the team will have some early wins in the project, the team members may also go through some initial fluctuations in their productivity as they get to know each other, get into the project work, and explore the best way to tackle the assignments.

The primary measurement of progress, in agile projects, is in working software. Regardless of the charts and conversations, if the team isn't making progress on the product, the project isn't performing well. There's no value in half-finished work. This is evident during scrum's sprint review where the developers demonstrate what they've completed in the project. Work that remains unfinished is given back to the product owner for a return trip to the product backlog for prioritization and selection for the sprint backlog. The accumulation of increments leads the product owner to release the product to customers, not simply the completion of an iteration. There may be several iterations before a product is suitable for use by the customers.

One approach you can use in agile is earned value management. EVM is a suite of formulas to show project performance. Earned value management is based on the project budget and the percentage of work completed. A value is attached to the work performed, which is earned value, and from that you can extrapolate all of the EVM values, such as cost performance index and schedule performance index. There is some hesitancy to embrace EVM in agile projects because of the uncertainty of the project scope, but agile uses a fixed cost and a fixed schedule and a prioritization of features to contain an unwieldy project scope. You may have a few questions on EVM on your PMP exam.

Organizations want to predict a return on investment, which is the total amount spent on the project in ratio to what the project earns for the organization. The earnings can come from money saved to new revenue the product brings back to the organization. Throughout the agile process there are performance reviews built into the approach. Consider the sprint reviews and the sprint retrospectives in addition to the daily scrum or the daily standup meeting. These are opportunities to review the work completed, to review the performance of the team, and to discuss any roadblocks that are keeping the team from moving forward.

Throughout the project you'll keep an eye on the velocity of the project team. Velocity directly shows the ability of the project to get things done and is usually expressed by the number of user story points the team completes per iteration. Early in the project, the velocity may be unstable, but over time the velocity normalizes, and then you can predict how long the project is likely to take to complete. In each iteration, you'll also look at the lead time and the cycle time of features and requests from customers. Lead time measures the duration of when a customer makes a request and when the request is fulfilled. Cycle time shows the duration of how long the team actually worked on the request to complete the feature for the customer. You'll often see lead time and cycle time associated with Kanban.

In addition to just monitoring the team's performance, you'll likely need to chart out some factors of team performance. Charting the project performance is shared with stakeholders through information radiators and in other communications. Two of the best charts you can create in agile project management are burnup and burndown charts. A burnup chart shows the accumulation of user stories or iteration tasks and shows the relationship between what's done and what's left to do. A burndown chart is similar, though it shows the list of tasks or requirements burning down in the project, such as the total number of features left to develop in the product backlog. A product owner may create a release burndown where she's mapped out the planned releases for the project and showing the burndown of the releases still to happen. Cumulative flow charts and control charts can also show performance and issues in the project.

In this chapter, I also discussed testing in agile. Testing is a type of quality control, and it confirms that what the team has created is of quality and meets the expectations of the customer. One of the most common approaches to testing is acceptance test-driven development. This approach writes the test the unit must pass, and then the developers create the code to pass the test. The end result, the green light, is to pass the test. Exploratory testing is much more independent and allows testers to explore the software and experiment with the software the team has created. Exploratory testing examines the software from the end user's perspective to find and report defects before they escape to the customer.

Questions

1. Over lunch with your colleague, Bruce, the topic of iterative development arises. Bruce says that iterative development is better than incremental development when a usable delivery is needed early on for a project. Which of the following is true?

   A. Incremental development and iterative development mean the same thing and can be used interchangeably.

   B. Iterative development is planned in complete detail in the planning stage, while incremental development plans at a high level and develops the scope more and more over time.

   C. Incremental delivery yields a usable piece of the project in each iteration.

   D. Iterative delivery yields a usable piece of the project in each iteration.

2. Jane has joined an agile team as a replacement for Marcus. As an agile coach, what would you teach Jane to focus on as the highest priority?

   A. Customer satisfaction by delivering valuable software early and often.

   B. Welcome change to requirements, even late in the development.

C. Maximize the work done and complete as many requirements as is possible.

D. Use iteration to plan the work effectively.

3. Jane has been assigned to lead a distributed agile team. Being an experienced agile project manager, Jane knows that agile project management approaches value face-to-face communication as the best way to convey information. However, it can be challenging for distributed teams since not all team members are in the same physical space. To help them communicate, the best option for Jane would be:

A. Ask the team to follow a common language for all project communications.

B. Inform the team members to share photos of themselves.

C. Set up a few initial face-to-face meetings for everyone to meet and get introduced.

D. Define common working hours so everyone in the team can better communicate.

4. Adam has joined an agile team. He approaches the agile coach to understand how stories and features are prioritized in the risk-adjusted backlog. Which one of the following would be the best answer?

A. Risk impact or risk probability

B. Expected monetary value or business value

C. Cost-benefit ratio or customer value

D. Risk mitigation impact or user impact

5. Etka is the scrum master for a project that is just starting its fifth iteration and has a velocity of 52 story points. While planning for the next iteration with the product owner, Etka notices a major company holiday that will span three working days. How should Etka adjust her plan for the next iteration?

A. The project is more important. Tell the project team to work through the holiday.

B. Ask for volunteers from the project team to continue working.

C. Find a team that does not celebrate that holiday to pick up the slack.

D. Reduce the planned number of story points to account for the holiday.

6. Johann is the scrum master for Project C, which is intended to update Speaker Corporation's web site. During a planning session for Project C, Johann is asked to put together a rough budget for the project. What is the best place for information to help Johann with this task?

A. Examine documentation about prior web site updates at Speaker Corporation.

B. Ask his project team members about other projects they have worked on.

C. Consult with other scrum masters he knows.

D. He cannot, because as an agile project, the budget and scope frequently change.

7. Ben is the scrum master for a project that just had its kickoff. During a recent team meeting, Ben and his team discussed how the team would know when any given piece of work is completed. What is the best term to describe this?

   A. Definition of Done

   B. Definition of ready

   C. Acceptance criteria

   D. Retrospective

8. Your scrum team is composed of three developers, one product owner, two vendors responsible for testing and acceptance, and three key end users. What is the maximum number of communication channels for your scrum team?

   A. 45

   B. 36

   C. 15

   D. 14

9. You are working on a banking application for mobile users. Your development team is looking for information on their performance to see if their efficiency is on the right track after their third sprint release. Which statement is true about a team's velocity in an agile environment?

   A. Velocity is an empirical measure of a team's progress, used for estimation, not a goal or metric by which team performance is measured.

   B. Teams with no slack time focus on individual objectives, increasing their velocity in the long term.

   C. Features are loosely estimated to make planning simpler, thus increasing velocity.

   D. Scrum teams perform at full potential early on and reduce velocity as complexity decreases.

10. Leah is working on a project in SpaceTek International, Ltd., as an agile practitioner. The agile team has just finished the first iteration, and during the retrospective meeting, the lessons learned documentation is being created with recommendations to improve future iterations' performance. Which of the following should the team not include in the lessons learned documentation?

   A. Only successes to identify best practices to apply to future iterations

   B. The rationale behind choosing a corrective action

   C. Cause of variances

   D. Improvements to be enacted during the next iteration

11. You are a scrum master for a marketing development firm, and you are working closely with your team to bring incremental value to your client by using an agile mindset. Your team has gone through several sprints and is about to start planning for their next sprint. You have collected relevant information about the team's velocity. Based on the following graph, what would you recommend to the team to help increase the accuracy of the team's velocity?

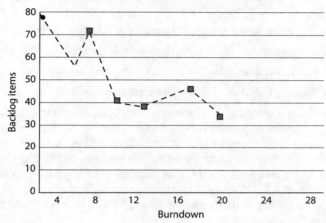

A. Increase the quality of work in each sprint.

B. Work only up to the sprint goal and not any further.

C. Increase the quality of estimates for story points.

D. Ask the product owner to provide more accurate story points.

12. You have been working closely with your scrum team's product owner to understand the various business requirements. The product owner has prioritized these requirements according to the user's urgency and the business value gained through its fulfillment. Upon meeting with the entire scrum team, the developers have also spent time prioritizing their sprint requirements. Which artifact can the product owner refer to when looking for the features released in the current sprint?

A. Sprint backlog

B. Product backlog

C. Release planning document

D. Project management plan

13. Ali has been hired by an organization to teach agile methodologies to a team of developers and plans to use a web site development project in doing so. As an agile coach, Ali's primary goal is to highlight value delivery to the team while reinforcing agile pillars and values throughout the process. Feedback loops are often inserted into sprints to ensure continuous learning throughout the development lifecycle. Whose role is it to ensure lessons learned are shared among the team, and during which ceremony?

   A. The entire team, and during the sprint retrospective meeting

   B. The entire team, and during the daily standup meeting

   C. The scrum master, and during project retrospective meeting

   D. The entire team, and during project retrospective meeting

14. Patricia works at a software development company. They work in two-week sprints to complete features requested by stakeholders during road mapping sessions. All the features receive estimates for their effort level and are subsequently prioritized by order of importance in an easily accessible Kanban board. Developers draw from the features and work on them as they have time available. A scrum master hosts daily meetings to discuss blockers or anything else that requires attention from the stakeholders or the project sponsor. Which chart can best show the work in process in this scenario?

   A. Flowchart

   B. Cumulative flow diagram

   C. Burndown chart

   D. Control chart

15. Tom is the scrum master for Project V, which is now in its third iteration. The team has a velocity of 56 story points. A stakeholder approaches Tom and asks to see Project V's work breakdown structure. How should Tom respond?

   A. Refer the stakeholder to information radiators.

   B. Agile projects do not have a work breakdown structure.

   C. Escalate this issue to the product owner.

   D. Invite the stakeholder to the daily standups.

16. Geraldine is the scrum master for Project L, which is 9 iterations into deployment and has a velocity of 40 story points. There are 383 user story points remaining in the product backlog. If each iteration lasts for three weeks, how long will it take the team to complete all of the items in the product backlog?

   A. Impossible to know

   B. Nine iterations

   C. 30 weeks

   D. 33 weeks

17. Penny is the scrum master for Project S, which is six iterations into deployment and on schedule. Recently Penny added a task to the backlog to double-check several deliverables against their quality checklists. The product owner pushes back and asks why Penny wants to take project time to do this. What is Penny's most likely response?

    A. The project team needs to fill their schedules.

    B. Quality checks are an essential part of any project.

    C. Penny thinks the project may fail.

    D. Agree with the product owner and remove the checks.

18. Thelma is the scrum master for Project Q, which is six iterations into deployment, has a velocity of 52 story points and is on budget. At a recent retrospective, the team noted that several deliverables required rework due to poor quality. What should Thelma do next?

    A. Add those tasks back into the backlog.

    B. Reprimand the team for poor quality.

    C. Ensure future tasks have sufficient time for quality assurance.

    D. Escalate the issue to the product owner.

19. Consider a project with a budget of $987,500, where $601,000 has been spent, and the project is 60 percent complete. The current velocity for the team is 35, and the predicted cost per user story is $2,165. The product owner has created a release plan that has four iterations contributing to a release. The project is supposed to be 80 percent complete by this time, but due to some delays and rework they are slightly late. Based on this information, what is the project's cost performance index?

    A. .98

    B. $400,000

    C. 1.40

    D. $601,000

20. You have been assigned to be the product owner for an online board game designed to teach biology to users. Your team has decided on more than 230 user stories based on its perception of what the target demographic will want in the game. To prepare for testing, you implement the Three Amigos approach in acceptance test–driven development. Which one of the following is not one of Three Amigos you'd consider?

    A. Customers

    B. Developers

    C. Businesspeople

    D. Testers

Answers

1. **C.** Incremental delivery yields a usable piece of the project in each iteration. Incremental and iterative development have similar but not identical definitions and cannot be used interchangeably. Iterative development means that the project is built in successive levels, but it is not always usable in the first few iterations. Neither iterative nor incremental development involves detailed planning in the initial stages. Detailed planning is typical of waterfall development.

2. **A.** The question is asking where the highest focus should be. The foremost focus agile teams should have is delivering working software that brings value to the customer resulting in high customer satisfaction. This is based on the first agile principle. All the other principles, although valid and essential, support this key-value delivery objective.

3. **C.** For distributed teams, setting up some initial face-to-face meetings for everyone on the team to meet is proven to be the best and most effective strategy to improve virtual and remote communication later in the project. It is easier for a team to connect and follow up with an e-mail or phone call once they have met face-to-face. Defining common working hours or language might be helpful but can be viewed as rigid and disrespectful. Sending photos is unlikely to assist in this scenario and is certainly not the best option to follow.

4. **B.** Stories are prioritized on agile projects based on their expected monetary value (EMV) and features based on their business value. Option A is partially correct because that is how we calculate EMV; however, that does not account for feature stories, and the question does not specify only risk stories. Options C and D are not real terms.

5. **D.** Etka should reduce the planned number of story points to account for the missing days. This will allow her team to continue work while giving them the break they deserve. Etka could tell the team to work through the holiday, but this would negatively impact their relationship and may not be legal in some areas. Asking for volunteers could work, but she would likely get only a few, which would impair their relationship. Finding another team to pick up the slack is not optimal as that team is unfamiliar with this project.

6. **A.** Johann should consult prior projects at Speaker and look for those similar to Project C. This will give him a rough idea of what Project C will cost in terms of time and money. Asking the project team and consulting with other scrum masters is not ideal as the projects they have worked on may not be similar to Project C. While agile projects are intended to be flexible, it is still possible to put together a rough budget based on historical information.

7. **A.** The Definition of Done is an agreed-upon definition of when something is completed. This may include having gone through various checks, user acceptance, or other criteria. It is beneficial for quality as it ensures buy-in once something is marked as done. The definition of ready is an agreed-upon way to

tell when a task is ready to begin work. This may include having the business sign-off on requirements or other criteria. The customer uses acceptance criteria to define when something is formally accepted. A retrospective is conducted at the end of a sprint to review lessons learned.

8. **A.** There are 45 communication channels, including the scrum master, the team consisting of 10 members, and using formula N(N-1)/2 gives you 45 communication paths. The other answers are not correct.

9. **A.** As an agile manager, you aim to improve velocity by improving processes and removing obstacles by setting a quantitative velocity goal. Other options are anti-patterns that should be looked out for by agile project managers.

10. **A.** Note that the question asks which of the mentioned options will not be part of lessons learned documentation. Although it is equally important to capture the successes throughout a project as these can identify best practices to apply to future projects and processes, documenting only the success is not enough. One of the primary objectives of conducting a retrospective is to provide the agile team an opportunity to inspect itself and create a plan for improvements to be enacted during the next iteration. Therefore, the lessons learned document also includes documenting the causes of issues, reasoning behind the corrective action chosen, and other types of lessons learned about people, relationships, processes, and tools. Identifying a project issue isn't enough—understanding where the issue originated and its impact gives more context to the issue and helps set up recommendations for improvements moving forward. In short, the lessons learned document spells out both what worked well and what did not. It is focused on what the team would do if they had the project to do over again, knowing what they know now.

11. **C.** As the scrum team matures, the accuracy of their work should increase with each sprint. Focusing their efforts to systematically right-size the user stories will allow the team to better plan their work in each sprint and increase the accuracy of the velocity by delivering a consistent number of story points per iteration.

12. **A.** The scrum team will meet at the beginning of the sprint to prioritize the backlog in which they choose and plan what work they intend to include in their next sprint. This information is prioritized in the sprint backlog. The product backlog is the backlog of features for the project. C, the release planning document, isn't a valid document for this question. D, the project management plan, isn't an actual document utilized in agile projects.

13. **A.** It is up to the entire team to ensure lessons learned are shared and incorporated throughout the project. The feedback mechanism is built into each sprint through the sprint retrospective meeting to improve on future sprints.

14. **B.** The cumulative flow chart shows the number of items in each phase of the project, which would include the WIP. A flowchart shows the flow of information through a system. A burndown chart shows the total number of tasks or features remaining in the backlog. A control chart shows the stability of a process over time.

15. **B.** Agile projects do not use a work breakdown structure, instead of the plan tasks by iteration or release. Information radiators display information about project health. The product owner is not likely able to help. Daily standups are for the team to update each other.

16. **C.** To find this answer you'll determine how many iterations left in the project by dividing the total number of story points, 383, by the current velocity, 40. This is ten iterations total to complete all of the items in the product backlog. As each iteration is 10 weeks, the answer is 10 times 3, for 30 weeks total. Choices A, B, and D are incorrect calculations of the remaining duration.

17. **B.** Quality checks should be continually conducted during a project. This helps ensure the final product meets specifications. Filling up someone's schedule is not a good reason to add work. Thinking the project may fail is not a good answer. Agreeing with the product owner robs the project the chance of catching poor-quality deliverables.

18. **C.** Thelma should ensure that future tasks have sufficient time for quality assurance testing. This will help avoid escaped defects. Returning those tasks to the backlog is not a good answer as they have already been delivered. Reprimanding the team is not the best option as it will not help mitigate future defects. The product owner is unlikely able to assist in this scenario.

19. **A.** To find this answer, you'll use the formula of earned value divided by actual costs. Earned value is 60 percent of the project's budget, which is $592,500. The actual costs of the project is $601,000. The formula would be $592,500/$601,000 for a cost performance index of .98. Choices B, C, and D are not valid calculations for the cost performance index.

20. **C.** The Three Amigos approach used in acceptance test-driven development considers the perspective of the customers, developers, and testers. Businesspeople may be part of the customers, though customers can include people outside of the organization, such as school teachers, in this scenario. A, B, and D are incorrect choices as customers, developers, and testers are the Three Amigos.

CHAPTER 17

Managing Risks in Agile Projects

In this chapter, you will

- Manage risk and issues
- Detect and resolve problems
- Solve problems in agile projects

In predictive project management, risk management is an ongoing activity, but there's a lot of up-front planning, estimating, and predicting. In agile projects, there is still an ongoing approach to manage the risk events, but there is less up-front planning and anticipation of risks for the entire project. Agile projects have risk management cooked into the process—though it's something many agile teams overlook. I've often seen agile teams skip over the whole idea of risk management and rush right into the good stuff by creating deliverables for the clients. Skipping risk identification and management is a risk. In agile projects, risks are often lurking just beneath the surface: not having an understanding of the agile approach, technical assumptions that can quickly become risks, and user stories that are poorly written for the project team.

 VIDEO For a more detailed explanation, watch the *Managing Risks in Agile Projects* video now.

Risk management follows a logical approach: risk identification, risk analysis, risk response planning, and then monitoring of the risk events. Risk identification, the first step in any risk management practice, is often the step agile projects often struggle with. Risk identification is arguably the most important risk management activity; if you don't identify the risks, you certainly can't manage them. Risk management, in agile, focuses more on the negative risk events, the results that can threaten the project objectives, rather than the positive risk events, such as time and cost savings, that we always consider in predictive projects. Agile risk management has a focus on the negative events that will disrupt the project and skew the good results.

The idea of continuous improvement is included in agile projects and risk management. Continuous improvement and risk management fit together because you're attacking the risk of a project not performing at its best when performing continuous improvement.

You, in the role of the project manager, need to see how well the project is performing on velocity, lead time, and cycle time, and how stakeholders are responding during the reviews of the iteration. Wild velocity numbers, too many items at the work-in-progress (WIP) stage, and stakeholders who reject the results of an iteration are all signs that risks exist in the project, and any of these examples could be a sign that the risk has come to fruition. If that's the case, you'll need to manage the issue.

On your PMP exam, you'll have plenty of questions dealing with risk—it's a big concept I've already covered in this book. For the agile approach to risk, however, you'll need to consider the rules and best practices of agile to determine what is the best thing to do next in the project. All risk events in agile threaten the value of the project, so always consider the value the project is creating and how the risk threatens the project. The goal is to balance some risk exposure in proportion to the reward the exposure may bring. In other words, it's often not cost effective, or possible, to eliminate all risk events in the project. Trying to completely safeguard the project from every conceivable risk event may drastically reduce the value the project is aiming to create.

Managing Risks and Issues

A risk is an event or condition that can threaten the goals of the project. In agile projects, the goal of the project is to create value, so risks threaten the value. When you consider risks in an agile project, you're looking at uncertain events that could happen, not events that definitely will happen. For example, if your team members are on multiple projects at once, there's a risk they won't be able to work on your project when needed. There's no real evidence of them not being available, but it's uncertain that they'll be time-committed to your project. If you're working with a vendor, it's uncertain the vendor will deliver on time in the project.

Issues are risk events that have happened in the project; issues may stem from identified or unidentified risk events. Things will happen in the project that you never anticipated: new technologies emerge, your organization is sold, customers decide the project is no longer needed. In my experience, issues often emerge because of poor emotional intelligence, poor communication, or poor requirements to start with. Issues, regardless of where they originate from, can drain the morale of the project team and cause finger pointing and politics to flare up in the project.

In predictive projects, risk management is ongoing, but mostly completed during the up-front planning stages of the project. In traditional project management, you, the team, key stakeholders, and subject matter experts work together to do risk identification. You will collaborate in activities such as brainstorming, mind mapping, and maybe executing a few rounds of surveys using the Delphi Technique. These risk identification activities are effective, but agile works with quick bursts of iterations, shorter planning sessions, and no intensive, up-front planning. There's no need for in-depth risk planning sessions in agile projects, because the scope of the project is likely to change many times during the project. As the scope changes, so do the identified risk events.

Agile teams often focus on the technical risk events within the project scope. The team will often serve as the subject matter experts, so their focus on risk is a focus on the work they'll be doing in the project. It's easiest, and most logical, to think about risks that are in your area of expertise. Developers can easily identify risks with the coding approach. Testers can quickly talk about risks in the tests and methodology they'll be using. Where agile projects often miss the mark, and where the project management role must step up, is to identify and discuss risks with stakeholder interest, the risk appetite of the organization, and the shifting landscape of the organization. Risk is, as you know, anything that threatens the value the project will create. For your exam, the entire team, not just the project management role, is responsible for risk management.

Risk management is somewhat built into the agile approach, but, in reality, it's not always effective. A sprint planning meeting focuses on what work the team can complete in the next iteration. Ideally, the team considers the risk within the selected features and how they'll do the work. However, there's not a real prompt in the process to consider the risk associated with the activities. I find that the can-do mentality, while good, can cause the team to ignore the threats of the project and only later deal with the issues the overlooked risks have created. While the team doesn't want to get bogged down with time-consuming risk identification and analysis, there must be a balance to consider the risk that can prevent the team from reaching their sprint goals and creating value.

Problem Detection and Resolution

In an agile project, like all projects, there is risk. Risks are uncertain events that haven't happened yet. Issues are risk events that have occurred. One of the events where you can consistently address risk is in the daily standup. Remember one of the questions you ask in each standup: are there any problems or impediments or blockers or roadblocks that are preventing us from moving forward? This is one of the first steps to risk identification in agile projects.

Consider that agile projects are typically software development projects. There are unique risks in software development, which introduces the term *technical debt*. Technical debt is when you have a backlog of work because the team hasn't had regular cleanup, maintenance, and standardization. In software development, you'll find developers write quick code, take shortcuts, and sometimes write code to fix a previous error without actually correcting the original error. Refactoring is a way to address technical debt.

Many software projects use the phrase *red-green-refactor* to describe the approach to software development. Red means that the code has failed the test. Green means the code has been adjusted to pass the test. Refactoring means that developers clean up the code to make it tight, comprehensive, and compliant with standards. This all takes time, of course, so a risk consideration when doing story point sizing is to also include some time, a buffer, to allow time to refactor and clean up the technical debt.

Technical debt is like borrowed money. It adds up over time and accumulates interest. Technical debt, when it accumulates, will take additional time to address. All the shortcuts and little workarounds that the developers have made is paid back with interest, but in this instance, the interest is added time. I've had long conversations with developers when it comes to technical debt. A common theme on why technical debt exists begins with poor up-front definition, because developers are sometimes pressured to get the sprint done to get to the value the product owner and customers are waiting for.

This is tricky, as up-front definition often means documentation of the requirements, but in agile, you want documentation to be barely sufficient; you do not want too much. The documentation of the value, the result of the project, can be documented prior to the project launch by a business analyst or the product owner, but there's no agile requirement for a business case or feasibility study—and that's a risk many projects face. The requirements can, and will, change in agile, but the more up-front planning and certainty in the prioritized items, the less technical debt, rework, and time wasted there'll be in the project. Of course, you want a balance of what the customers want and the heavy documentation we often see in predictive projects.

Another risk that's common in large software projects is when multiple teams are working on different parts of the same code. This is parallel development; you have two different teams working in unison to develop the code. If the teams aren't working in synchronization and setting clear boundaries, sometimes called *swim lanes*, redundancy of effort creeps in, and developers begin writing code that conflicts with what other teams are doing. Transparency, collective code ownership, and good communication are needed to avert this risk.

Earlier in this book I addressed lead time and cycle time. Lead time is how long a user story, for example, takes to go through all the different stages of the project to get to the Definition of Done. Risks can be lurking in lead time. Cycle time is really a subset of lead time. Cycle time is how long it takes to go through part of the process. Cycle time describes the individual chunks of the process: how long does it take to go through the development? How long does it take to go through the testing? A control chart, which can show the mean duration for cycle time, can be used to identify risks with pieces of the project and the overall duration for developing features.

Project cycle time is the cycle time for the whole project. It's the total amount of time the team requires to get to the Definition of Done. Productivity is the rate of efficiency and describes how quickly the team can get the project done. You can also track, if you really needed to, the productivity of each team member. While the whole team is responsible for getting the project work done, you might want to track how productive an individual team member is on the project.

Risk identification should always include an examination of defect cycle time. Defect cycle time is the amount of time between when a defect was discovered and when it was fixed. The longer the defect time, typically the more expensive the defect. The reason why is that when you have an exceptionally long defect time, your team is continuing to develop code. If you discover the defect right away but the team continues to develop, the defect may affect other code that's been developed. The team has been building on faulty code that could affect downstream code.

The defect rate is how many escaped defects make it all the way to production. Escaped defects make it all the way to the customer. These are the most expensive issues because it also affects your reputation. The defect rate is the frequency of defects. An increase in defects means we have a problem with testing, and ultimately there is a problem with the code. If, over time, your defect rate is climbing rather than decreasing or even stabilizing, this is a big problem, and it'll take time and an in-depth look at the entire process from coding to testing.

Completing Variance Analysis

A variance is the difference between what was planned and what actually happened in the project. Most of the time, when you're examining variances, you're looking at cost and schedule variances; however, there might be other key performance indicators that you want to track. It's not unusual to track scope, quality, particular features, and specific customer-requested functions. Cost and schedule variants, in a predictive project, as in Figure 17-1, is where you can pinpoint the amount of time and monies to reach a specific deliverable or milestone. This is where the concept of the performance measurement baseline comes into play. The performance measurement baseline is the analysis of schedule, cost, and scope, which are three defined factors in a predictive project.

In Figure 17-1 you'll see the ideal S-curve, which demonstrates how time and costs are consumed in a project to create deliverables. The solid S-curve is the ideal progression of the progress, but the dashed line represents the actual time and cost to reach Milestone A. The difference between the dashed line and the solid line represents a variance. The greater the distance between the two lines, the greater the variance and issue or issues in the project.

While that's great in a predictive project, in agile it's tricky to do the same approach because you don't know everything that's going to be in the project scope. Certainly, the project manager and the product owner role have some idea of deliverables based on the release plan, product roadmap, and velocity, but there's no certainty in the agile scope. Lack of certainty, which is uncertainty, equates to risk in the project success. Risk is, after all, uncertain.

In agile, variances center on performance. Performance variances are seen in the completion of the sprint backlog, which is the amount of work the team believes they can accomplish in an iteration. There is first the average day-to-day variances. People doing

Figure 17-1
The S-curve shows the cost and schedule variance to reach a milestone.

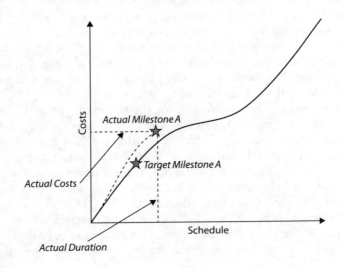

the work are going to have good days and bad days and ups and downs with their performance. Special causes of variance are anything unusual that causes a problem. For example, the power went out for an afternoon, and the business had to close. A team member caught the flu, and they've been out of work for three days. An emergency pulled the team off the project. These variances are called *special causes* of variance and are exceptions to the project.

When examining the team's performance for variances, you'll use trend analysis. Trend analysis allows you to identify a repetition of performance, which is a trend, that you can predict. Trend analysis is based on time-series data, and you'll compare and contrast the same data in each time period. Typical things you can use trend analysis for in agile and hybrid projects are time, budget consumption, number of user stories completed, overall team velocity, and user story points selected in ratio to user story points completed. Based on the trend, you'll look for relationships among the data points and team. Relationships mean particular types of work, a particular technology, a feature or function, or a team member and how they're performing when they work with a particular area of the project. Trend analysis provides insight into current issues and risks and helps you and the team improve future performance.

Trend analysis is based on things that have already happened, not what is currently in motion or what we think will happen. Measurements on things that have already happened are called *lagging metrics*. Based on lagging metrics, we can explore leading metrics, where we are trying to predict what will happen. From lagging metrics we can play what-if games to try to predict performance, problems, or risk.

Working with the Risk-Adjusted Backlog

In a predictive project, risks can be either positive or negative. In an agile project, however, risks are only considered to be negative. Risks are seen as anti-value as they threaten the goals of the project. In a predictive project, you might identify a risk that could happen toward the tail end of the project, such as cutting over from one operating system to another. The risk is significant and might wreck the whole project, but there's much work to do before you even get to that risk in the project timeline. You and the team do all the work to churn along in the predictive project, and then you deal with the risk when it is more imminent than at the start of the project.

In agile projects, you won't wait for the risk event. Instead, the product owner and the team look for significant risks in the project, and these are brought upward in the prioritized product backlog. There's no waiting for the significant risk to come into play or to threaten the work that's already been done. Instead, the risk is tackled as soon as responsibly possible rather than way downstream in the project timeline. This is grooming the product backlog for risk, also called creating the *risk-adjusted backlog*. Risky items are bubbled to the top of the product backlog to take them on sooner rather than later. If the risk event happens late in the project, it can wreck much of the preceding work leading up to the risk event. By taking it on earlier in the project, the risk doesn't wreck much work, and the overall threat to the project success is lowered.

Agile risk analysis is qualitative and subjective, and its scoring is totally based on a gut feeling or preference, though it's often based on experience and subject matter experts. The product owner will look at the return on investment (ROI) for the feature and how the risk threatens the ROI for that particular feature. This also where business reps, such as a business analyst, will identify the ROI for each user story, each item, in the product backlog and then compare the probability and impact for a risk score. While this is often a qualitative score, it's also possible that the businessperson can use a financial score and create a somewhat fast expected monetary value (as I discussed earlier in this book).

Recall that the expected monetary value takes a risk with an impact of, for example, $45,000 and a 30 percent chance of happening. This risk's expected monetary value is –$13,500. This can be done for each risk event or just particular user stories that are most sensitive to risk, failure, or success for the customer. It's possible that you could have a contingency reserve for the risk events, which is even more likely in a hybrid project than a pure agile project. The risk-adjusted backlog would prioritize risk events with a greater negative expected monetary value.

While the idea of creating the expected monetary value and prioritizing based on the negativity and significance of risk events is ideal, it's not always practical. Agile wants to move quickly without deep thinking on what might happen, so often risk scoring is kept simple with a qualitative approach, with a Red-Amber-Green (RAG) rating, or just on a scale of 1–10 where 10 is the most serious probability and impact score.

Promoting Continuous Improvement

Problem solving happens throughout agile projects, and it's done by the entire team. Problem solving is a continuous improvement activity on agile projects. The primary goal of problem solving is prevention-driven: solve problems before the problem happens. Recall that agile is knowledge work, so problem solving in agile means you think through the problems, experiment, and innovate without the fear of failure and with the liberty to do so without retribution for trying new things. A team that gets reprimanded for trying new things to prevent risks isn't going to work independently and freely, and that in itself is a risk to the value of agile.

Using good problem-solving techniques removes the mindset of command and control and delegates the authority to the individuals on the team. The caveat to this, however, is that the team agrees to work on solving only real problems, not the perception of problems, and to steer clear of what-if scenarios. There must be a balance between actual problems that can threaten the project's value. Early in the project, during the norming phases of the project, the agile project manager may need to guide the team and reassure the team members that they have permission to try new things to address problems. Later, when the team has shifted into norming and performing, the team members become more independent and self-led to address problems as they see fit.

Agile projects welcome change, but change can create stress for the team, especially new teams in agile, and change can create new risk and issues. You, as the agile project manager role, need to check in with the team after major project changes. You'll also want to check in with the team after their solution to problems have been implemented to see how their change affected the project; we just don't assume that the change the team has made has solved the problem.

Here's the reality of all projects, and of life really: some problems can't be solved. Even with team engagement, agile best practices, and the smartest, experienced people on the project, there are some problems where you won't find a solution. For problems that don't have an efficient, apparent, or affordable solution, you want to work around these problems. You'll want to track and monitor the problems for shifts in probability and impact.

A common problem that can't be easily solved is a stakeholder who is on a mission to destroy your project. That is not going to be much fun. There's not a whole lot you can do about it if that individual is not happy. In this common scenario, you'll have to deal with it, work around it, and keep moving forward. Unless the stakeholder has a lot of power and a high amount of influence, then you'll just need to monitor the person and keep her informed. You need to realize that you can't please everyone all the time. The person's attitude isn't a concern for the value of the project.

Problem Solving in Agile Projects

Recall Parkinson's law, where work expands to fill the time allotted to it. If you give 40 hours to complete a task, it'll take 40 hours to do. Another law, from Parkinson, is his law of triviality: time spent on any item of the agenda will be in inverse proportion to the sum of money involved. In other words, team and management spend too much time on things that don't matter and too little time on the big, serious items the project demands. You might also see this called *bike shedding*, from the concept of Parkinson's criticism of management, where management will ignore the complexities of building a nuclear powerplant and instead choose to argue over the materials needed to build a shed for employees' bicycles.

The point of Parkinson's law of triviality is an easy one to grasp: don't get trapped in the argument of building bike sheds. Focus on the major points of the project that need to be solved. Little items might be important to some, but if the little items don't contribute the prioritized value and really don't matter much in the big picture of the project, squash the argument. If you're like me, you've seen management and teams argue over trivial things in the project that suck time from value creation and from focusing on the big goals of the project. I once left a meeting, in disgust, because the folks in the room argued for 30 minutes over capital letters or lowercase letters for the project name. Once the project was done, the name of the project had no lingering effect on the organization. Focus on getting things done and creating value, and remember, fast and good are often better than slow and perfect.

Solving Scrum Problems

Some product owners and customers feel the need to insert a change during the sprint review. Without a change they may feel they're not participating in the work. Jeff Atwood, a blogger on software development, documented the idea of a programming duck. The story goes that an artist working on chess software knew that in the review the manager would consistently request a change in the work. The artist anticipated the change so when he created the animation for the queen in the software, he added a duck for the queen to carry around. Sure enough, upon review of the chess animation, the manager liked everything, but asked the artist to remove the duck.

The idea of Atwood's duck is that teams purposely create something in the software that's easy to remove and obvious enough that the reviewer will ask for the removal. While I doubt you'll see Atwood's duck on your exam, the concept is simple: know your audience and anticipate their concerns and movements in the project.

Problem solving in Scrum projects has three levels, as shown in Figure 17-2. Problem solving begins with the process-level activities. Process-level activities are the predefined activities in Scrum that people new to agile may wrestle with: sprint planning, the daily scrum, sprint reviews, and sprint retrospectives. When you're working with people who are new to the scrum approach, they may be resistant to the new rules, roles, and expectations that happen in agile. The understanding of process-level activities and buy-in from the people involved require the scrum master to be more involved in ensuring that everyone is following the Scrum approach, following the rules of Scrum, and coaching people on their roles and responsibilities.

In Scrum, the next tier of problem solving is the quality and performance level of the team. You know that sometimes teams are cobbled together by whoever is available in the organization, rather than by who's the best person for the team. The quality of the work can be constrained by the person's ability to do the work in the project. It's a simple fact: if the person doesn't know how to do the work, the quality of the work product will suffer in quality and in time, and value is threatened. Training, coaching, and even asking to replace the individual can all be methods to solve this awkward problem.

The final tier of problem solving in Scrum is team dynamics. If the team doesn't work cohesively, the product they create likely won't be cohesive either. The forming and storming stages of team development are crucial to the team coming together to work toward a common goal rather than just remaining a collection of individuals. This is one reason why colocation, though not always practical, is preferred for team development. Forming and storming phases are not easy to do over in a web meeting. The team needs to be unified and agree to work together, collectively, to the defined goal and value of the project.

Figure 17-2
There are three levels of Scrum problem solving.

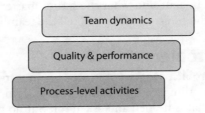

Team dynamics

Quality & performance

Process-level activities

In addition to these three tiers of problem solving in Scrum, there are six concepts the scrum master does to help the team become more cohesive and focus on the value the project creates:

- **Devil's advocate**   The devil's advocate is a skeptic, but the role isn't to be antagonistic, but to help the team think through issues and possible outcomes their decisions may have on the project.

- **Query and motivate**   Ask lots of questions to get the team thinking, but questions can sometimes throw doubt and take away the freedom to innovate in the project. Be sure to follow up the challenges with motivation; it's good to experiment and innovate in the project.

- **Forget the small stuff**   Don't let the team get bogged down in the small stuff, the bike sheds, of the project. These meta problems can suck the time, and energy, from the bigger goals of the project.

- **Reflective listening**   Reflective listening, an agile term, is traditionally known as *active listening*, where the receiver of the message paraphrases what's been said to make certain she understands the message.

- **Avoid command and control**   Listen to your team's ideas, offer feedback, but don't tell the team what to do. Scrum teams are self-led and self-organizing; a scrum master that tells the team what to do isn't a good scrum master.

- **Lead teams to solutions**   A continuation of avoiding command and control is to ask questions of the team members to lead them to the best solution to the problem. Even if you know the answer or best approach, lead the team to the solution through questions and conversation, rather than simply telling the team what to do.

Problem solving in Scrum projects is based on collaboration—a cornerstone of any agile project. On your exam, look for opportunities to collaborate with others rather than telling others what to do. The scrum master isn't the same as a predictive project manager. You want to coach and facilitate rather than laying out directions for the team to follow. Collaboration means you work with the team, rather than working over the team. Avoid the command-and-control mentality at all costs. A trick question could ask about a new team in agile and what the scrum master should do. You'll coach the team on what to do in the project rather than tell the team what to do.

Solving XP Problems

XP aims to solve problems as part of its strategy in software development. XP begins with the idea of keeping things simple in the project. Simplicity in agile is the fundamental rule "we will do what is needed and asked for, but no more." The idea of only delivering what was requested removes scope creep, a typical problem in software development, and removes assumptions the team may have about the deliverable for the client. This rule makes the requirements for the project very specific, because if it's not requested, not documented, the team simply isn't going to create it.

A term you'll see associated with XP is the planning game technique. The planning game treats the work as a game to avoid an emotional attachment to decisions and work in the project. The game now has a goal, rules, and playing pieces. Playing pieces are the user stories and the goal of the game is to put as many user stories into production within the life of the game. The players in the game are the developers and the customers, which work together to define the user stories and then get the most important user stories out to production. Within the game, the players work at a sustainable pace, rather than long hours, to get the game pieces to production.

Another theme of XP that contributes to problem solving is *continuous integration*. Continuous integration means that each developer refactors their contribution to the code and openly shares their improvement with others. Design improvement doesn't mean just refactoring, but collaborating to remove elements of the code that aren't needed in the deliverable to the customer. The team works together to ensure that they are delivering only what was requested, so design improvement can strip out elements that weren't requested or are no longer needed in the final deliverable.

XP also uses a theme called *shared understanding*. Shared understanding describes the rules of the XP approach for the organization and what the team will create. Shared understanding has four concepts you should know for your exam:

- **Simple design** Don't overcomplicate the solution and create things that aren't needed.

- **System metaphor** The metaphor is a simple story to describe how the solution will work. The metaphor provides an understanding for the solution architecture and naming conventions of the project work.

- **Collective code ownership** No one person owns their code, but all developers can edit the code at any time. The entire team is responsible for the success or failure of the code.

- **Coding standard** The team collectively agrees on standards for the code, naming conventions, and other nomenclature for components of the code. By agreeing up-front and establishing rules for the project, issues are prevented by eliminating conflicts and different terminology within the code.

Solving Problems in Lean Projects

Recall that Lean projects want to avoid waste. By removing waste and identifying bottlenecks, the project can move with more ease and more precision. Waste is anti-value, just as risk is anti-value, and the more waste a project has, the less value is created. Problem solving in Lean involves all parties affected by the problem. It's always a good idea to get the people who will be affected by the problem, such as managers or end users, in the discussion to explain the problem and how the issue will affect them. A developer, for example, may not see the problem at the same magnitude as an end user of the software.

For your exam, you might have questions specific to Lean problem solving, but truthfully, these eight problem-solving steps can be applied to any agile project. The eight steps of Lean problem solving are as follows:

1. *Identify the problem.* You need to identify the problem before you can effectively solve the problem. This step requires a detailed description of the problem and its impact.

2. *Break down the problem.* Decomposing the problem into separate sections can help address different solutions and responses to the problem. Breaking down the problem makes the problem more manageable.

3. *Establish targets.* Define what the desired outcome should be, what's acceptable, and what's unacceptable. Define a range of variance for the problem, such as measurements and performance for the solution. For example, the printer must printer within a 16th of an inch from the edge of the paper. That's something you can measure and a goal you can work toward.

4. *Perform root-cause analysis.* You don't want to address the symptoms of the problem, but attack the root cause of the problem. Root-cause analysis, as I discussed in Chapter 8, looks for causal factors of the effect you're trying to eliminate.

5. *Define responses.* Responses are the countermeasures your team can apply to the root cause to eliminate or reduce the effect of the issue. When defining countermeasures, you're looking for consensus for which response is the most appropriate in the project.

6. *Implement countermeasures.* Once the team is in agreement on the best approach for the issue, the countermeasure can be implemented. Ideally, this happens in a test environment to see the results of the solution before it is implemented into productivity. You don't want the solution to create new problems in the project.

7. *Confirm and test.* Once the solution has been implemented, you'll need to test the results to confirm that the solution hasn't created new problems in the test environment. If the solution created new problems, you'll often roll back the solution and try again. Sometimes the new problem is minor and is addressed through these same issue resolution techniques.

8. *Standardize the solution.* Once the solution is working in the test environment, then it can be implemented in production as part of the overall project solution. This is standardization, meaning that the solution is standard in the product the project is creating. Just to be clear, this step happens only once the solution has been thoroughly tested in the test environment.

Chapter Summary

Risks, in agile projects, are uncertain events that can threaten the project value. Risks in agile are seen only as negative, and the team works collectively to manage the risk events. Agile risk management can use some of the same processes as in a predictive project, but not nearly to the same depth. Agile risk management identifies risks, works quickly through qualitative analysis, finds appropriate responses, and then monitors the risk and the risk response result. The primary difference, other than speed, of the agile risk management approach is the lack of in-depth, up-front risk planning we see in predictive projects. Agile risk management examines risk that attacks the prioritized product backlog, rather than the entire project, because the requirements of the agile project are likely to change.

Issues are risk events that have occurred. Issues in agile must be identified, discussed, and then a resolution implemented. Issue management in agile projects can happen daily in the standup meeting. The goal of issue resolution is to identify the issue, the root cause of the issue, and a solution. The solution should be agreed upon, tested, reviewed, and then implemented. You don't want a solution to the issue to cause new risks and issues for the customer. In this chapter, we discussed risks and issues and common themes you should know for your PMP exam. Much of risk and issue management are similar to what you've already seen in the predictive risk management approach, but rather than heavy, up-front planning, issues and risks are managed in each iteration of the project.

For your exam, know the concept of the risk-adjusted product backlog. Recall that the risk-adjusted product backlog examines the significant risk events in the project and prioritizes the features that have significant risk associated. By moving the features laden with risks higher in the product backlog, the team can address the risks early in the project rather than waiting for the risk events to happen later in the project and wreck the preceding work. This approach can be a go/no-go decision point for the project based on the outcome of the risk event. This saves time and money for the organization by seeing the risk results early, rather than later in the project.

Risk is anti-value in agile projects and must be monitored and controlled. Risk management is built into agile projects by utilizing communications in the iteration planning, daily standup, demonstrations, and retrospectives. These ceremonies offer discussion, reviews of the work, and opportunities to address risks and issues. In this chapter, I discussed the nuances of solving problems and addressing risk in Scrum, Lean, and XP projects. Recall that scrum masters coach and guide the team to decisions, rather than the command-and-control mentality associated with predictive projects. Lean projects aim to eliminate waste and get stakeholders involved in the risk and issue conversation. XP projects try to keep things simple by delivering only exactly what was requested of the team.

Questions

1. You're working with an agile team, and they are having trouble understanding risk events rather than issues. Which one of the following statements best describes the difference of risk and issues in an agile project?

   A. Risk are negative events that have been identified. Issues are negative events that you didn't identify.

   B. Risks and issues are the same thing as they both can threaten the project's value.

   C. Risk events are anything that threatens the project's scope. Issues are events that threaten anything other than project scope.

   D. Risks threaten the projects' value. Issues are risk events that have happened.

2. A Scrum team is in the middle of sprint execution. During the daily standup meeting, one of the development team members raises the concern that an end user keeps calling him to include more work items in the current sprint and seek help from the scrum master. What is the best thing the scrum master should do?

   A. Inform the end user to join the team so the team can understand his needs better.

   B. Ask the team to talk to the end user and inform him not to disturb them during the sprint.

   C. The scrum master should talk to the end user and explain how sprint planning is performed.

   D. Involve senior management in solving the problem.

3. You are the scrum master for your organization. The chief information officer (CIO), who is the project sponsor, has approached you about a new requirement for the agile project the organization has recently launched. The CIO insists that this new requirement be moved to the top of the product backlog and asks you to do so. Who is responsible for accepting or rejecting a change request to keep the priorities in the backlog up-to-date?

   A. Development team

   B. Product owner

   C. Scrum master

   D. Project sponsor

4. The scrum team is working in iterations to develop an online catalog for your organization. The product will have three beta releases before launch. During the middle of the third sprint, the product owner revises the sprint backlog by adding a new feature to save additional clicks and improve the user experience. He ensures that the sprint goal is unchanged though this addition may add risks to the sprint. Which entity is permitted to add work to the sprint backlog during the sprint?

   A. Scrum team

   B. Development team

   C. Product owner

   D. Scrum master

5. You are part of the development team on a project that has just concluded the current sprint. At the sprint review, the scrum team and the stakeholders collaborated on what was done in the sprint. The stakeholders reject one of the product features that the development team has demonstrated in the sprint review. The scrum team is unsure what happens next to the rejected user story and how they'll move forward with correcting the problem. Which is the best next step for this issue?

   A. Automatically place the user story into the sprint backlog of the next sprint.

   B. Delete the user story from the product backlog and drop it from the project.

C. Work with the product owner to rewrite the user story to address the rejection reasons.

D. Place the user story in the product backlog to be re-prioritized.

6. You are the scrum master for your organization, and you're coaching the team and key stakeholders on the best practices for Scrum. Your organization has worked in a waterfall environment for many years, and the idea of agile project management is new to everyone at the organization. There is a risk that the new approach to getting work done will be disruptive and may not flow well in the organization. You tell stakeholders that an essential recommendation for effective governance and better productivity above all other recommendation is which one of the following?

A. Colocation

B. Information radiators

C. Kanban boards

D. Caves and common rooms

7. Charles has been assigned as a full-time scrum master on an agile team. The team is at the end of the second week of a three-week sprint when a team member becomes ill and cannot continue to work any longer. The team is committed to delivering 45 story points in this sprint. What is the most appropriate action for Charles to take with this issue?

A. Ask the remaining team to work longer hours to finish the committed stories.

B. Jump in to start development to assist the team.

C. Ask the team to deliver what they can in the sprint.

D. Extend the sprint timebox so the committed stories can be completed.

8. Margret is on a scrum team working on a telecommunications project. The scrum master encourages the team to be self-led and self-organizing. Halfway through the current sprint, one of the development team members encounters a tricky problem. What would be the most helpful action the team member could take to improve the team's problem-solving proficiency?

A. Immediately inform the scrum master since it is their job to remove impediments to progress.

B. Bring the problem to other team members and ask for help.

C. Move ahead to work on the next item, so velocity is not disrupted.

D. Keep moving forward and make a note of it to discuss during the retrospective meeting.

9. Keith is the scrum master for an automotive industry software team working on improvements for the anti-lock brake system. It is a yearlong hybrid project with a quarterly release cycle, each comprising three sprints of a month timebox. Halfway through the current sprint, a key stakeholder calls Keith into a meeting and explains that the competitive market has shifted and the product that the team is building is no longer viable. What is the best thing for Keith to do next in this serious issue?

    A. Work with the team to re-prioritize the backlog.

    B. Prepare the team to be assigned to a new project.

    C. Cancel the sprint.

    D. Check with the product owner to see if the viability of the project has changed.

10. Jeffrey is the scrum master for a project that is just finishing its second iteration. During the first iteration, the project team noted that several deliverables required rework after they were deployed. This has cost the project team time to investigate the root cause of the rework, though the issue may not yet be solved. What should Jeffrey do next?

    A. Cancel the next iteration and have the team focus on finding the problem.

    B. Consult with the project's product owner about solutions.

    C. Do nothing. The project team will figure it out as they go.

    D. Allot time within the next iteration to identify the root cause of the quality issue.

11. As a scrum master, you have been working closely with your development team and product owner on a recent iteration, and it is time to initiate the implementation phase. However, before you move forward, you will evaluate the risks that may impact your sprint goals. What is the most powerful aspect of risk management when using an agile mindset?

    A. Repeating your risk management plan within each sprint.

    B. Using Monte Carlo simulation since you are managing a software development project.

    C. Critical-to-Quality (CTQ) flow-down and flow-up analysis.

    D. Agile projects do not require risk management, as it requires up-front planning.

12. You are part of a development team and working with your scrum master on risk assessment and identification. The risks associated with product features are determined during your sprint planning meeting and identified on the product backlog. Who is responsible for re-prioritizing the product backlog to reflect the risk?

    A. Product owner

    B. Scrum master

    C. Development team

    D. End user

13. William has been colocated with his team for 18 months and serves his team as a scrum master. Because of a pandemic, the team has moved out of the project office and now works remotely with the goal of maintaining the same level of collaboration as before. The risk is that the team will lose momentum and collaboration will break down. The situation is challenging and will take some time for the team to adjust. What would be the most important thing for William to address with his remote team?

   A. A new communication plan along with gaining the team's commitment to the plan

   B. Setting a firm schedule for everyone to be always online

   C. Asking everyone to have their camera on to create an office atmosphere

   D. Asking team members to find another way to colocate

14. Timothy is the scrum master for Project E, which is in its sixth iteration; the team has a velocity of 45 story points and is over budget by $12,500. During the retrospective for the fifth iteration, the team communicated that several tasks they had worked on did not seem to provide any value for Project E. They feel there's a risk for more nonvalue tasks in the project. What should Timothy do with this information?

   A. Do nothing. The product owner prioritized them.

   B. Raise the issue at the next sprint review.

   C. Speak with the product owner about the issue.

   D. Have the project team ignore similar features going forward.

15. Catherine is the scrum master for Project RQW, which is in its early planning stages. During a recent meeting, one stakeholder was incredibly worried about an electrical outage possibility during the project work. In the risk matrix, all the risks' probability and impact have been scored in the following table. What should Catherine do with the stakeholders' risk concern for the electrical outage in the project?

Risk	Probability	Impact
Vendor delay	1	4
Electrical outage	5	1
Hardware configuration	3	2
Coding synch	1	2
Network latency	4	5
Data storage capacity	2	4

   A. Exploit

   B. Mitigate

   C. Accept

   D. Transfer

16. Jess is the scrum master for Project M, which is nine iterations into deployment, has a velocity of 42 story points, and is on budget. Recently Project M experienced a major risk, which was promptly dealt with. This event has triggered another, separate risk to occur. What is the name for this event?

   A. Residual risk

   B. Aftershock risk

   C. Related risk

   D. Secondary risk

17. Jerry is the scrum master for Project XBN, which is nine iterations into its deployment and is on budget. The product owner recently raised a concern that Project XBN may not meet a specific deadline for the next iteration. How is Jerry most likely to respond?

   A. Work with the team to prioritize items in the next iteration's backlog.

   B. Escalate the issue to the steering committee.

   C. Work with the team to crash the schedule.

   D. Stay out of the team's way and let them figure things out.

18. Mikayla is a project manager with many years of experience in the construction industry. After moving into the software development industry, she manages her first Lean project. What might she want to ensure her project team understands in a Lean project more so than in a traditional waterfall project when planning for potential problems because of risk?

   A. The definition of the problem

   B. The triggers and signals of an upcoming problem

   C. The roles of those involved in the problem

   D. The strategy for addressing the problem

19. Gary is the scrum master for a local software development project. A minimum viable product (MVP) is required to be delivered to the client at the end of every sprint (approximately every two weeks). Gary oversees a scrum team consisting of 19 individuals. The deadline for the release of the next deliverable to the client is in three days, but the scrum team feels it will not be ready to produce an MVP in time. Before any further developments can be made, Gary decides to determine the source of the conflict and prevent it from happening again. What was the most likely reason why the scrum team experienced the risk of delay?

   A. The sprint duration was too short.

   B. There were too many individuals assigned to the scrum team.

   C. The scope of the project was beyond the team's capabilities.

   D. There was a lack of user stories for the team to clarify the client's requirements.

20. Victor is the scrum master for Project BDS, which has a budget of $125,000. During planning, he noticed several risk events that had a high chance of occurring and would severely impact Project BDS. All of the risk events deal with the networking requirements of the project. He and the team acknowledge they are not skilled in the physical requirements of the network and would like additional help to satisfy these requirements in the project. What risk response should Victor and the team choose for these risks?

A. Transfer

B. Mitigate

C. Accept

D. Cancel Project S

Answers

1. **D.** In agile, risks are negative events that threaten the project's value. Issues are risk events, identified or not, that have occurred in the project. The other choices are not valid explanations of risk and issues.

2. **C.** The scrum master is responsible for promoting and supporting scrum by helping everyone understand scrum theory, practices, rules, and values. The scrum master is designed to assist anyone outside the scrum team to understand which of their interactions with the scrum team are of help and which are not. The product owner is the primary person responsible for overseeing the product backlog and maximizing the product's value resulting from the development team's work. The members do not add or remove items arbitrarily during the sprint. All requests must be addressed to the product owner for value-based prioritization for the upcoming sprints.

3. **B.** A product backlog is a meticulously compiled list of everything that is known to be fundamental in the product. It is the single source of requirements for any changes to be made to the product. The product owner is the primary individual responsible for the product backlog, including its content, availability, and ordering. That is because the product owner represents the business's desires and therefore understands the value the product is expected to deliver better than other team members. All requests wanting to change a product backlog item's priority must address the product owner.

4. **B.** The sprint backlog is a gauge for the development team to show what the functionality will be in the next increment. It also discloses the work that will be necessary to deliver that functionality into a "done" increment. The development team is the only entity that can alter its sprint backlog during a sprint. The sprint backlog is a highly transparent and very real-time picture of what the development team plans to accomplish during the sprint, and it belongs solely to the development team. If the product owner wants to change the work planned during the sprint, they should do this in accordance with the development team.

5. C. When the stakeholder rejects a user story during the sprint review, it doesn't mean the feature is removed from the project, but rather needs to be corrected and reviewed again. A is incorrect, because the story is not automatically moved to the next sprint backlog, but returns to the product owner for clarity, prioritized in the product backlog, and follows the regular rules of scrum. B is incorrect; rejected features aren't necessarily deleted from the project but return to the regular rules of scrum. If the customer requests for the feature to be removed altogether from the product, then there is work to remove the user story and completed work in the increment. D is tempting, but the user story must first be rewritten to address why the work wasn't satisfactory to the customer, and then it's added to the product backlog for prioritization. Determining why the work was rejected would be the proper next step in making the necessary corrections. If the team has a gap in understanding the business or the customer's expectations, a feature can be rejected. Misunderstandings arise because of missed acceptance criteria or due to poorly written user stories. The first steps are correcting or rewriting the user story. Then it can be placed into the backlog and re-prioritized. Placing the user story back in the backlog to be re-prioritized without addressing why the feature was rejected will not resolve it.

6. A. Colocation is highly recommended, if possible, for new agile teams. Even if the team is virtual, it would be best that they be colocated for planning and at least one to two iterations. While it is possible to be distributed and still be productive, collaborating and sharing views among members is easy when a team shares the same workspace. Colocations help teams discuss and iron out their differences at each stage of the project and work productively and efficiently. The delays arising from time zones and unreliable communication tools can be minimized when teams are sitting together and discussing the problem face-to-face. For example, testers can work closely with development teams, understand their requirements, and develop effective test plans. This continuous communication helps teams to arrive at better decision-making and problem-solving techniques. B and C are incorrect choices; information radiators and Kanban boards are fine tools for sharing information, but colocation is a cornerstone of agile projects. D, caves and commons, describes the little nooks, the caves, for private conversations, phone calls, and quiet work, and the open office approach, the commons, for all developers.

7. C. The team should deliver what they can within the sprint and explain the variance. All incomplete product backlog items are re-estimated and put back on the product backlog. The unfinished features can be addressed in the subsequent sprint based on (re)prioritization. A is incorrect; asking the team to work longer hours will make them counterproductive in the long term, and this action will not align with the agile principle of maintaining a sustainable pace. B is incorrect; while the scrum master could assist the development team with outstanding work, this would likely create a gap with his role and responsibilities. D is incorrect as extending the sprint timebox would lead to a loss of accountability and opportunity for improvement. If the sprint length is consistently modified, the scrum team loses the ability to write stories effectively, manage the backlog, estimate effort, and lose personal accountability. The timebox exists for accountability and to help each role learn and develop.

8. **B.** Agile teams rely on collaborative problem solving rather than individual ingenuity. This allows problems to be solved more quickly; it also generates better solutions by drawing upon a broader range of viewpoints. This collaborative way of working encourages project team members to openly share their problems and help sustain knowledge for the future, improving the team's problem-solving proficiency. A is incorrect; although it is the scrum master's role to remove impediments, that primarily refers to external roadblocks. C is incorrect as this answer assumes the problem can be put aside for later resolution. In addition, of all the choices presented, it's better to collaborate with the team for a solution to maintain the current velocity in the project. D is incorrect as not completing the work will be evident in the sprint backlog, during the sprint review, rather than bringing up the unfinished work during the retrospective.

9. **D.** In this question, it is vital to understand the agile roles and their responsibilities. The only person who has the information needed to assess the project's viability is the product owner. Therefore, the scrum master should connect with the product owner and ask if the project is still viable to continue. A is incorrect as the product owner is also the sole person responsible for managing the product backlog and maximizing the product's value resulting from the development team's work. B is incorrect as the team may not be moving onto a different project just yet. C is incorrect as the scrum master cannot cancel the sprint.

10. **D.** Jeffrey should schedule within the next iteration to coach the team to determine why the deliverables' quality is low. It is better to address the quality issues early in the project than to allow the issues to grow and create new risks in the project. A is incorrect as canceling the iteration will prevent any progress on the project. B is not the best choice as the product owner is not likely to know the source of poor quality. C is incorrect as doing nothing runs the risk of continuing poor quality and damage to the team's reputation. Doing nothing is almost always the worst choice in a project.

11. **A.** The most powerful aspect of risk management is repetition. Going through the assessment multiple times generates an in-depth understanding of the product and may enable your risk control to be more robust. B and C, Monte Carlo and CTQ, are not the best choices for this question as the question doesn't identify the size of the project and other factors for choosing these risk management approaches. D is incorrect; agile projects do incorporate risk planning and management as appropriate to the project's complexity and size as determined by the agile team.

12. A. The product owner's responsibility is to update the product backlog, even when speaking of the risk-adjusted prioritized product backlog document. Even though the team and the scrum master have worked together to identify the risks, the product backlog is always maintained by the product owners. Choices, B, C, and D are incorrect choices for this question.

13. A. It is critical to a team's success with the changing working environment to agree on a new way of working and collaborating. This will be a team decision. William's role will facilitate the conversation and ensure the team develops a new communication plan that works for everyone to complete the project successfully. Choices B and C are not valid answers as requirements for persistent presence online isn't realistic. While some web collaboration software can show presence, it's likely not realistic for web cameras to be streaming all the time. D isn't the best choice as a pandemic can prevent the team from colocating at all.

14. C. Timothy should share these concerns with the product owner so they may prioritize tasks appropriately. The product owner should communicate with the team why features are valuable and work toward a shared vision for each user story. A is incorrect as doing nothing creates or allows the additional tasks with low value to continue being prioritized. B is not the best choice as sprint reviews are intended to demonstrate what the team has completed in the iteration. D is not a valid choice as the team cannot continue ignoring prioritized features from the product backlog.

15. C. Given the low impact, Catherine may recommend acknowledging this risk is there but accepting its occurrence if it pops up. A is incorrect as exploiting is a positive risk response. B is incorrect as mitigation attempts to reduce the likelihood or impact of a risk. D is incorrect as transferring a risk involves a third party accepting the risk (e.g., insurance).

16. D. A risk that occurs as the result of responding to another risk is called a secondary risk. A is incorrect as a residual risk is risk left over after a primary risk is responded to. B and C are not valid as aftershock and related risks are fictional types of risks.

17. A. Jerry can collaborate with the team to help ensure specific tasks are completed in a particular sprint by re-prioritizing them in the backlog. B is incorrect; the steering committee is unlikely to be able to assist. C is not a valid answer as crashing the schedule means putting additional resources on the task. D is incorrect; while the team is self-led and self-organizing, the best choice is to collaborate with the team to help them meet project goals.

18. B. Because agile projects are adaptive, it is critical to be aware of triggers and signals of an upcoming problem that a risk event could create. In agile projects, the scope is not defined for the entire project up front, meaning the team will need to have a shared understanding of what potential problems may arise and how to get ahead of them. A is incorrect; while understanding the definition of the problem, the roles of those involved in the problem, and the strategy for addressing the problem are all critical in any project, these are done similarly across agile projects and waterfall projects. Because waterfall projects involve more scope definition up front, the triggers and signals of an upcoming project can be better anticipated in a waterfall project than in an agile project. In an agile project, the team should have a greater shared understanding of what they may look for as risk events may happen. C and D are incorrect choices as the roles and risk response strategy are good to know, but these choices don't best answer the question to anticipate the problem rather than respond to the issue created.

19. **B.** A development team's ideal size is between three and nine people, not including the scrum master and product owner. In this scenario, there are 19 people on the scrum team. When too many people are on a scrum team, communication failure, coordination, and task assignments are issues. Of all the choices presented, this answer has the most certainty. A is incorrect as a sprint duration of two weeks is acceptable for the Scrum methodology. C is not a valid answer because scope of the project may have been a factor in this conflict, and there was not enough information to suggest that this was the source of the risk. D is an incorrect choice as a lack of user stories could be an issue, but the team and scrum master should have identified this problem, if it were the case, during the sprint planning session rather than move forward with the work. Of all the choices presented, the size of the project team is too large.

20. **A.** Transferring risk moves the risk to a third party. This is a good option for high impact and probability risks but generally costs more than other responses. In addition, if the team doesn't have the needed skills to address the risks and requirements and there's not enough time or reason to train the team, transferring the risk is a valid option. B is incorrect as mitigation would attempt to reduce the impact or likelihood of the risk but keep the risk responsibility on the team. C is not valid as accepting the risk isn't the best choice presented, especially considering the high likelihood and impact of the networking risks. While always tempting, canceling the project, D, is not the best option as these risks could be transferred.

PART IV

PMP Exam Considerations

Understanding the Code of Ethics and Professional Conduct

In this chapter, you will

- Explore the PMI Code of Ethics and Professional Conduct
- Learn the structure of the code
- Learn about the code's stance on fairness and honesty
- Adhere to the code's mandatory standards

In 1981, back when Jordache jeans and the song "Bette Davis Eyes" were all the rage, some folks at the Project Management Institute (PMI) were more concerned with ethics than parachute pants. The PMI created the Ethics, Standards, and Accreditation Group to generate a code of ethics for the project management profession. Sounds like a bunch of fun, doesn't it? By the end of the '80s, the group's discussions and reports evolved into the "Ethics Standard for the Project Management Professional." In 1998, this document became the early version of a new Code of Ethics. The Code of Ethics was a code that all PMI members, whether certified as a project manager or not, agreed to abide by in their professional practices. Consequently, in January 1999, the Ethics, Standards, and Accreditation Group approved a process for ethics complaints to be filed, reviewed, and then acted on if a complaint proved valid.

Since the late '90s, the global economy has changed. The business world has been shaken by billion-dollar companies going bankrupt, we've all witnessed how the Internet has changed how we do business, and we've experienced the rise of worldwide competition for jobs. Part of all this chaos is the realization that ethics and moral standards vary among countries, companies, and cultures. The PMI Code of Ethics and Professional Conduct, once just a one-page document, has now become a robust document covering the breadth of project management ethics for today's project environments.

PMI also has considered the boom in its membership population. The PMI has grown from just a few hundred U.S.-based members to several hundred thousand members worldwide. From its inception, the goal of the Code of Ethics and Professional

Conduct was to create a moral guideline for project managers of all industries to subscribe to a common concept of fairness and honesty and to be held to a higher level of expectations than project managers who were not members of the PMI. At least that was the theory. I'm sure most of us know project managers who are PMI members but who certainly don't subscribe to the PMI Code of Ethics. Shame on them.

Because the PMI Code of Ethics and Professional Conduct was outdated, the PMI created a new governing body, the Ethics Standard Review Committee, to examine the project management Code of Ethics in regard to this new world that project managers operate within. Part of this committee's work was to include a global approach to the review of the now-defunct Code of Ethics and Professional Conduct, the ethical considerations of the global market, and a desire to create a more exact and detailed description of what the ethics and character of a PMI member should be. The result was the current PMI Code of Ethics and Professional Conduct.

Although the concepts in the PMI Code of Ethics and Professional Conduct are applicable to all project managers regardless of certification status, you will be tested on these principles. Your PMI examination will include these ethical concepts throughout the exam. You'll be tested on ethics as part of your overall project management knowledge, not just on a separate section on the code. After all, ethics are interspersed in your duties as a project manager, so it is appropriate that they be included in your examination as well.

The PMI Code of Ethics and Professional Conduct is arranged by chapters and sections. And, as is the case with most documents from the PMI, you'd think a bunch of attorneys wrote the thing. No offense to my pals at the PMI—it's a great document. Really. However, in this chapter, I'll break down the document into a slightly less formal, and much less official, approach. I hope you like it.

 VIDEO   For a more detailed explanation, watch the *PMI Code of Ethics and Professional Conduct* video now.

Learning the Code of Ethics

The first chapter of the PMI Code of Ethics and Professional Conduct paints the big picture of what the code is intended for. The vision of the code is, no doubt, that the project management community will adopt the code in their day-to-day operations and lives as representatives of the PMI. The code is needed because project managers are often in situations where their ethics could be jeopardized. When you consider issues with project labor, unscrupulous vendors, and the temptation of personal gain for project managers, it's a great idea to have a Code of Ethics and Professional Conduct. Let's take a detailed look at this first chapter.

Exploring the Code's Vision and Purpose

The project management community should do what's "right and honorable." I'm sure we all want to reflect those values in our conduct and see them in the conduct of other project managers. The PMI Code of Ethics and Professional Conduct goes beyond our role as project manager. The code wants adherence in all areas of our lives: "at work, at home, and in service to our profession." Don't most of us live, eat, and sleep project management, anyway?

The real purpose of the code is reputation. From the PMI's point of view, the code and our agreement to adhere to the code will raise the perception of the ethical values project managers agree to—and are expected to abide by—as members and participants in PMI programs. The code is also a motivation to become a better project management practitioner. In theory, establishing a globally accepted code for our ethics and behavior should raise our credibility, reputation, and collective behavior to new standards.

Participating in the Code

In the past, Project Management Professionals (PMPs) were expected to adhere to the PMP Code of Conduct. Certified Associates in Project Management (CAPMs) were expected to adhere to the CAPM Code of Conduct. And members of the PMI who were credentialed as PMPs or CAPMs were also held to a separate ethical standard. It made more sense, of course, to create a blanket code of ethics for all members and certified candidates. Now, basically, everyone who's a PMI member, a CAPM, a PMP, Program Manager Professional (PgMP), or any other PMI designation must agree to participate in this PMI Code of Ethics and Professional Conduct.

NOTE Kudos to the PMI on this decision! A simple solution is usually the best solution. I'm thrilled with this new code, its detailed descriptions, and its application to all PMI participants.

Learning the Code Details

The code includes four values that are core to the ethics and standards for project managers:

- Responsibility
- Respect
- Fairness
- Honesty

These four values are the focus of the final four chapters of the Code of Ethics and Professional Conduct. Within each of these values are aspirational standards and mandatory standards. Basically, as project managers, we should aspire to some characteristics of these standards, and we must adhere to other facets of these standards.

The code contains some comments for examples and clarification. You'll also find a glossary of terms in the code—something our pals at the PMI haven't provided before. I'll list those terms at the end of this chapter. No peeking!

Serving Responsibly as a Project Manager

The second chapter of the PMI Code of Ethics and Professional Conduct centers on responsibility. We project managers already have a level of responsibility based on the organizational structure in which we operate (from functional to projectized).

Defining Responsibility

According to the Code of Ethics and Professional Conduct, it is our responsibility, or duty, to take ownership for the decisions we make—or fail to make. It's also our duty to take ownership of our actions—or lack of actions. Finally, it's our duty to take ownership of the results of those decisions and actions.

 NOTE To be a great project manager, you must take responsibility. For example, if you plagiarize someone else's work and get caught, you don't shift the blame. You act responsibly and own up to your actions. We all know there are some sleazy, crooked people out there who'd much rather cheat their way to success and steal from others than put in the time and do what's right. Don't be one of those people.

Aspiring to Responsibility Expectations

Project managers need to aspire to responsibility. Here are the details of the responsibility aspirations for this section of the Code of Ethics and Professional Conduct:

- Project managers need to make decisions that don't adversely affect the best interests of society, public safety, and the environment.
- Project managers should accept only assignments that mesh with their background, experience, skills, and qualifications.
- Project managers keep their promises.
- Project managers take ownership of and accountability for their errors and omissions and make quick and accurate corrections. When errors are discovered, project managers communicate them to the proper parties and act to repair those errors immediately.
- Project managers protect proprietary and confidential information. No gossiping or blabbing.
- Project managers uphold the Code of Ethics and Professional Conduct and hold others accountable to it as well.

Remember that these are aspirations of the responsibility portion of the Code of Ethics and Professional Conduct. There will be tough instances, mutually exclusive decisions, and scenarios that will call these aspirations into question.

Adhering to the Mandatory Standards of Responsibility

Project managers have to deal with regulations, laws, contracts, and other mandatory requirements in their projects. This section acknowledges those requirements. Let's take a look at what the Code of Ethics and Professional Conduct calls for:

- Project managers have a mandatory responsibility to adhere to regulatory requirements and laws.
- Project managers adhering to this code have a mandatory responsibility to report unethical or illegal conduct to management and those affected by the conduct.
- Project managers are required to bring valid, fact-driven violations of the Code of Ethics and Professional Conduct to the PMI for resolution.
- Disciplinary action should commence for project managers who seek to retaliate against a person raising ethics violations or concerns.

Project managers must adhere to these points and agree to participate in them in their roles in the project management community.

Adhering to the Respect Value

Rodney Dangerfield always quipped, "I don't get no respect." And Aretha Franklin sang "R-E-S-P-E-C-T" in *Blues Brothers 2000*. Okay, I may be reaching here when it comes to a topic intro, but how many times in a project management book are you going to see Aretha Franklin *and* Rodney Dangerfield mentioned, and in the same paragraph no less?

My point is that both of these performers were talking about the same thing: the admiration and reverence they believed they deserved from their peers. Respect in the PMI Code of Ethics and Professional Conduct centers not only on the respect we may deserve as project managers, but also on the respect that others are due through their work and contributions to our projects. Respect in project management also is aimed toward our respect for the environment we operate within.

Aspiring to Respect

Respect among individuals and toward the environment promotes trust, confidence, and shared ownership of the project work and deliverables. PMI lists four standards for respect:

- Learn about the norms and customs of others, and avoid behavior that others may find disrespectful.
- Listen to others and seek to understand their points of view and opinions.
- Don't avoid people whom you have conflicts or disagreement with. Approach them in an attempt to resolve your differences.
- Conduct yourself professionally, even when those you deal with don't act professionally.

PART IV

Adhering to the Mandatory Values of Respect

Project managers are to "take the high road" in their dealings with clients and stakeholders. We demand of ourselves and of fellow project managers four things regarding respect. Here's what the Code of Ethics and Professional Conduct details:

- Project managers negotiate in good faith.
- Project managers don't influence decisions for personal gain at the expense of others.
- Project managers are not abusive toward others.
- Project managers respect the property rights of others.

Being a Fair Project Manager

Ever hear the phrase, "All's fair in love and war"? Or how about, "Life just isn't fair"? Sure you have. So, what is fairness? Do we need the wisdom of King Solomon to know what's fair? Is fairness different from justice? These are the types of questions the PMI Code of Ethics and Professional Conduct hopes we will ask ourselves and others.

Fairness is our duty to make decisions and act impartially and objectively. Our behavior, as project managers, is to be void of competing self-interests, prejudice, and favoritism. Sounds wonderfully complex, doesn't it?

Aspiring to Fairness

Project managers are to aspire to four things in the realm of fairness:

- Project managers should demonstrate transparency in decision-making.
- Project managers must constantly be impartial and objective and take corrective actions when appropriate.
- Project managers provide equal access to information to those who are authorized to have that information.
- Project managers make opportunities equally available to all qualified candidates.

These are some of the lofty aspirations we must have as project managers. They are also characteristics we should strive toward in our day-to-day lives.

Adhering to the Mandatory Standards on Fairness

PMI participants must adhere to five values regarding fairness. Two of the standards apply to conflict-of-interest scenarios, while the remaining three requirements center on favoritism and discrimination. Project managers are to do the following:

- Fully disclose any real or potential conflict of interest.
- Refrain from participating in any decision where a real or potential conflict of interest exists until we, the project managers, have disclosed the situation, have an approved mitigation plan, and have the consent of the project stakeholders to proceed.

- Refrain from hiring or firing, rewarding or punishing, or awarding or denying contracts based on personal considerations such as favoritism, nepotism, or bribery.

- Refrain from discriminating against others on the basis of race, gender, age, religion, disability, nationality, or sexual orientation.

- Always apply the rules of the organization (the organization being your employer, the PMI, or other performing organization) without favoritism or prejudice.

I think it's safe to say, with regard to these requirements, that if we follow the rules of our employers, the laws of our country, and the calling voice of our conscience, we'll be all right.

Being an Honest Project Manager

Honesty is being truthful in our conversations and in our actions. This means that we, as project managers, don't overpromise, don't agree to deadline dates that we know we can't meet, and don't sandbag our budgets and deliverables. We do what we say we'll do, and we say what's truthful. Like the other values in the Code of Ethics and Professional Conduct, honesty has both aspiring and mandatory standards.

Aspiring to Honesty

According to the Code of Ethics and Professional Conduct, project managers should aspire to five traits of honesty:

- Seek the truth.
- Be truthful in communications and conduct.
- Provide accurate and timely information.
- Provide commitments and promises in good faith.
- Strive to create an environment where others feel safe to tell the truth.

These five aspirations are noble. As project managers, we are often rushed by stakeholders to get the work done. These five aspirations cause us to pause and reflect on what's honest and truthful in our communications to project team members, stakeholders, *and ourselves*.

 EXAM TIP To answer project management ethics questions, you should first abide by the laws of the country in which you're doing business. Second, follow your company's policies. Third, follow the cultural standards of the location where the project is being managed. Fourth, follow your own ethics. Fifth, as a last resort, if you don't know what to do, imagine what an angel would do and answer the question accordingly.

Living the Honesty Requirements

There are just two mandatory standards for honesty in the Code of Ethics and Professional Conduct:

- We do not engage in or condone behavior that is designed to mislead others. This includes, but isn't limited to, the following:
  - Creating misleading statements
  - Creating false statements
  - Stating half-truths
  - Providing information out of context
  - Withholding information that, if known, would render our statements as false
- We do not engage in dishonest behavior with the intention of personal gain at the expense of others.

Basically, as project managers, we don't lie. We are required, according to the code, to tell the truth regardless of the impact it may have on us, our project team, or our projects. How many project managers do you know who are living by this requirement?

Chapter Summary

PMPs agree to abide by the PMI Code of Ethics and Professional Conduct—it's part of the exam application process. Although no document can force anyone to behave ethically and professionally, this document encourages all PMI members to adhere to a standard of ethics, morals, and professionalism. The goal of the PMI Code of Ethics and Professional Conduct is to promote ethics in project management as a profession, and you'll be tested on these concepts on the PMP exam. It will behoove you to read over the actual PMI document from the PMI web site and familiarize yourself with the associated concepts, sections, and key terms.

The code includes four values for all PMI members: responsibility, respect, fairness, and honesty. You can apply these four values to all areas of a project—from initiation all the way through closing. As a project manager, you'll likely face some ethical choices, but these four values can help guide you through the correct decisions. These four values also make up the major sections of the Code of Ethics and Professional Conduct. For each of these values, you'll find mandatory standards and aspirational standards: things we're required to do and things we should do.

As a project manager, you may find yourself working with people from different cultures and countries than your own. You should treat other cultures with respect; just because your culture may differ from that of others doesn't mean your culture is better or worse. When you're working in a country other than your home, you should first educate yourself regarding how to behave in this new environment. You'll want to understand the politics, the culture, and the work ethic to operate better in the environment. Finally, just because you take the initiative to learn about and respect other cultures doesn't mean they'll do the same for you. Regardless of how you are treated, treat others with respect; you'll win their respect in return.

Questions

1. You are the project manager of the JKN Project. The project customer has requested that you inflate your cost estimates by 25 percent. He reports that his management always reduces the cost of the estimates, so this is the only method to get the monies needed to complete the project. Which of the following is the best response to this situation?

   A. Do as the customer asked to ensure that the project requirements can be met by adding the increase as a contingency reserve.

   B. Do as the customer asked to ensure that the project requirements can be met by adding the increase across each task.

   C. Do as the customer asked by creating an estimate for the customer's management and another for the actual project implementation.

   D. Complete an accurate estimate of the project. In addition, create a risk assessment on why the project budget would be inadequate.

2. You are the project manager for the BNH Project. This project takes place in a different country than where you are from. The project leader from this country presents a team of workers who are all from his family. What should you do?

   A. Reject the team leader's recommendations, and assemble your own project team.

   B. Review the résumés and qualifications of the proposed project team before approving the team.

   C. Determine whether the country's traditions include hiring from the immediate family before hiring from outside the family.

   D. Replace the project leader with an impartial project leader.

3. You are about to begin negotiations on a new project that is to take place in another country. Which of the following should be your guide on what business practices are allowed and discouraged?

   A. The project charter

   B. The project plan

   C. Company policies and procedures

   D. The Code of Ethics and Professional Conduct

4. One of your project team members reports that he sold pieces of equipment because he needed to pay for his daughter's school tuition. He says that he has paid back the money by working overtime without reporting the hours worked so that his theft remains private. What should you do?

   A. Fire the project team member.

   B. Report the team member to his manager.

   C. Suggest that the team member report his action to human resources.

   D. Tell the team member you're disappointed in what he did, and advise him not to do something like this again.

5. You are the project manager of the SUN Project. Your organization is a functional environment, and you do not get along well with the functional manager leading the project. You disagree with the manager on how the project should proceed, the timings of the activities, the suggested schedule, and the expected quality of the work. The manager has requested that you get to work on several of the activities on the critical path even though you and she have not solved the issues concerning the project. What should you do?

A. Go to senior management and voice your concerns.

B. Complete the activities as requested.

C. Ask to be taken off the project.

D. Refuse to begin activities on the project until the issues are resolved.

6. The PMI has contacted you regarding an ethics violation of a PMP candidate. The question is in regard to a friend who said he worked as a project manager under your guidance. You know this is not true, but to save a friendship, you avoid talking with the PMI. This is a violation of what?

A. The Code of Ethics and Professional Conduct to cooperate on ethics violations investigations

B. The Code of Ethics and Professional Conduct to report accurate information

C. The Code of Ethics and Professional Conduct to report any PMP violations

D. The law concerning ethical practices

7. You are the project manager for the Log Cabin Project. One of your vendors is completing a large portion of the project. You have heard a rumor that the vendor is losing many of its workers due to labor issues. In light of this information, what should you do?

A. Stop work with the vendor until the labor issues are resolved.

B. Communicate with the vendor about the rumor.

C. Look to secure another vendor to replace the current one.

D. Negotiate with the labor union to secure the workers on your project.

8. You are the project manager for the PMH Project. Three vendors have submitted cost estimates for the project. One of the estimates is significantly higher than the others. In this scenario, you should do what?

A. Ask the other vendors about the higher estimate from the third vendor.

B. Use the cost estimates from the historical information.

C. Take the high cost to the vendor to discuss the discrepancy before reviewing the issue with the other vendors.

D. Ask the vendor that supplied the high estimate for information on how the estimate was prepared.

9. You are the project manager of the LKH Project. This project must be completed within six months. The project is two months into the schedule and is starting to slip. As of now, the project is one week behind schedule. Based on your findings, you believe that you can make some corrective actions and recover the lost time over the next month to get the project back on schedule. Management, however, requires weekly status reports on cost and schedule. What should you do?

A. Report that the project is one week behind schedule but will finish on schedule based on cited corrective actions.

B. Report that the project is on schedule and will finish on schedule.

C. Report that the project is off schedule by a few days but will finish on schedule.

D. Report that the project is running late.

10. As a contracted project manager, you have been assigned a project with a budget of $1.5 million. The project is scheduled to last seven months, but your most recent earned value management (EVM) report shows that the project will finish ahead of schedule by nearly six weeks. If this happens, you will lose $175,000 in billable time. What should you do?

A. Bill for the entire $1.5 million, since this was the approved budget.

B. Bill for the $1.5 million by adding work at the end of the project.

C. Report to the customer the project status and completion date.

D. Report to the customer the project status and completion date, and ask if the customer would like to add any features to account for the monies not spent.

11. You are the project manager of the PMH Project. You have been contracted to design the placement of several pieces of manufacturing equipment. You have completed the project scope and are ready to pass the work to the installer. The installer begins to schedule you to help with the installation of the manufacturing equipment. You should do what?

A. Help the installer place the equipment according to the design documents.

B. Help the installer place the equipment as the customer sees fit.

C. Refuse to help the installer, since the project scope has been completed.

D. Help the installer place the equipment, but insist that the quality control be governed by your design specifications.

12. You are the project manager of the 12BA Project. You have completed the project according to the design documents and have met the project scope. The customer agrees that the design document requirements have been met; however, the customer is not pleased with the project deliverables and is demanding additional adjustments be made to complete the project. What is the best way to continue?

A. Complete the work as the customer has requested.

B. Complete the work at 1.5 times the billable rate.

C. Do nothing. The project scope is completed.

D. Do nothing. Management from the performing organization and the customer's organization will need to determine why the project failed before adding work.

13. You are the project manager of the AAA Project. Because of the nature of the project, much of the work will require overtime between Christmas and New Year's Day. Many of the project team members, however, have requested vacations during that week. What is the best way to continue?

A. Refuse all vacation requests, and require all team members to work.

B. Allow vacation requests only for those team members who are not needed during that week.

C. Divide tasks equally among the team members so each works the same amount of time.

D. Allow team members to volunteer for the overtime work.

14. You are a project manager for your organization. Your project is to install several devices for one of your company's clients. The client has requested that you complete a few small tasks that are not in the project scope. To maintain the relationship with the client, you oblige her request and complete the work without informing your company. This is an example of what?

A. Effective expert judgment

B. Failure to satisfy the scope of professional services

C. Contract change control

D. Integrated change control

15. You are completing a project for a customer in another country. One of the customs in this country is to honor the project manager of a successful project with a gift. Your company, however, does not allow project managers to accept gifts worth more than $50 from any entity. At the completion of the project, the customer presents you with a new car in a public ceremony. What should you do?

A. Accept the car, since it is a custom of the country. To refuse it would be an insult to your hosts.

B. Refuse to accept the car, since it would result in a conflict with your organization's policy on gifts.

C. Accept the car and then return it, in private, to the customer.

D. Accept the car and then donate the car to a charity in the customer's name.

16. A project team member is sabotaging your project because he does not agree with it. What should you do?

    A. Fire the project team member.

    B. Present the problem to management.

    C. Present the problem to management with a solution to remove the team member from the project.

    D. Present the problem to management with a demand to fire the project team member.

17. You are the project manager of a project in Asia. You discover that the project leader has hired family members for several lucrative contracts on the project. What should you consider?

    A. Cultural issues

    B. Ethical issues

    C. Organizational issues

    D. Political issues

18. Of the following, which one achieves customer satisfaction?

    A. Completing the project requirements

    B. Maintaining the project cost

    C. Maintaining the project schedule

    D. Completing the project with the defined quality metrics

19. A PMP has been assigned to manage a project in a foreign country. The disorientation the PMP will likely experience as he gets acclimated to the country is known as what?

    A. Sapir-Whorf hypothesis

    B. Time dimension

    C. Ethnocentrism

    D. Culture shock

20. You are the project manager for an information technology project. It has come to your attention that a technical problem has stopped the project work. How should you proceed?

    A. Measure the project performance to date, and account for the cost of the technical problem.

    B. Rebaseline the project performance to account for the technical problem.

    C. Work with the project team to develop alternative solutions to the technical problem.

    D. Outsource the technical problem to a vendor.

PART IV

Answers

1. **D.** It would be inappropriate to bloat the project costs by 25 percent. A risk assessment describing how the project may fail if the budget is not accurate is most appropriate. A, B, and C are all incorrect, since these choices are ethically wrong. The PMP should always provide honest estimates of the project work.

2. **C.** You should first confirm what the local practices and customs call for in regard to hiring family members before others. A and D are incorrect, since they do not consider the qualifications of the project team leader and the project team. In addition, they do not take into account local customs. B is incorrect as well. Although it does ponder the qualifications of the project team, it does not consider the local customs.

3. **C.** The company policies and procedures should guide the project manager and the decision he makes in the foreign country. A and B are incorrect because these documents are essential, but they usually do not reference allowed business practices. D is incorrect because, although the PMI Code of Ethics and Professional Conduct does possess crucial information, the company's policies and procedures are most specific to the project work and requirements.

4. **B.** This situation calls for the project team member to be reported to his manager for disciplinary action. A is inappropriate because the project manager may not have the authority to fire the project team member. C is inappropriate because the project manager must take action to bring the situation to management's attention. D is also inappropriate because no formal disciplinary actions are taken to address the problem.

5. **B.** The project manager must respect the delegation of the functional manager. A, C, and D are all inappropriate actions because they do not complete the assigned work the functional manager has delegated to the project manager.

6. **A.** By avoiding the conversation with PMI in regard to your friend's ethics violation, you are, yourself, violating the Code of Ethics and Professional Conduct to cooperate with the PMI. B, C, and D are incorrect answers because they do not fully answer the question.

7. **B.** The project manager should confront the problem by talking with the vendor about the rumor. A is incorrect and would delay the project and possibly cause future problems. C is incorrect and may violate the contract between the buyer and seller. D is also incorrect—the agreement is between the performing organization and the vendor, not the labor union.

8. **D.** Most likely, the vendor did not understand the project work to be procured, so the estimate is skewed. A clear statement of work is needed for the vendors to provide accurate estimates. A and C are inappropriate actions because they discuss another vendor's estimate with the competing vendors. Choice B, historical information, isn't a viable solution because costs may have changed since the historical information was created. In addition, there's no evidence in

the question that historical information even exists. This information should be kept confidential between the buyer and seller. In some government projects, you may be required to announce the winning bid.

9. **A.** The project manager should report an honest assessment of the project, with actions on how he plans to correct the problem. B and C are incorrect because they do not provide honest answers to management. D is incorrect because it does not provide a solution to the problem.

10. **C.** An honest and accurate assessment of the project work is always required. A and B are incorrect because these actions do not reflect an honest assessment of the work. D is incorrect because it offers gold plating and recommends additional changes that were not part of the original project scope. In addition, because this is a contracted relationship, the additional work may not be covered within the original project contract and may result in legal issues.

11. **C.** When the project scope is completed, the contract is fulfilled, and the project is done. Any new work items should not be sent through. In this instance, the contract change control system should be invoked, or a new contract should be created. A, B, and D are incorrect because these choices are outside of the scope and have not been covered in the contract.

12. **C.** When the project scope has been completed, the project is completed. Any additional work, without a contract change or new contract, would be dishonest and would betray the customer or the project manager's company. This is a good example of a question where none of the choices is a good one, but you must choose the best answer available. Of course, in a real project, you'd have many other choices and options to achieve customer satisfaction. A and B are both incorrect because additional work is not covered in the current contract. D is incorrect because the project did not fail—the deliverables met the requirements of the project scope and the design document.

13. **D.** This is the best choice for this scenario, because it allows the project team to be self-led and is sensitive to the needs of the project team. A, B, and C are all autocratic responses to the problem, and while the results may seem fair, D is the best choice.

14. **B.** When the project manager completes activities outside of the contract and does not inform the performing organization, it is essentially the same as stealing. The PMP must be held accountable for all the time invested in a project. A is incorrect because this is not expert judgment. C is incorrect because the contract has not been changed or attempted to be changed. D is also incorrect because the changes the project manager completed for the customer were not sent through any change control system. Instead, they were completed without documentation or reporting.

15. **B.** This is the best answer. Although this solution may seem extreme, accepting the car in public would give the impression that the project manager has defied company policy. In addition, accepting the car would appear to be a conflict of interest for the project manager. A, C, and D are all incorrect. Accepting the car, even with the intention of returning it or donating it to charity, would conflict with the company's policies regarding the acceptance of gifts.

PART IV

16. **C.** The problem should be presented to management, with a solution to remove the project team member from the project. Remember that whenever the project manager must present a problem to management, she should also present a solution to the problem. A is incorrect because it likely is not the project manager's role to fire the project team member. B is incorrect because it does not address a solution for the problem. D is incorrect because the project manager's focus should be on the success of the project. By recommending that the project team member be removed from the project, the problem is solved from the project manager's point of view. Management, however, may come to the decision on their own accord to dismiss the individual from the company altogether. In addition, a recommendation from the project manager to fire someone may be outside the boundary of human resources' procedure for employee termination.

17. **A.** The project manager should first determine what the country's customs and culture call for when hiring relatives. It may be a preferred practice in the country to work with qualified relatives first before hiring other individuals to complete the project work. B, C, and D are not the best choices in this scenario. They may be used to follow up after first examining the cultural issues within the country.

18. **A.** The largest factor when it comes to customer satisfaction is the ability to complete the project requirements. B, C, and D are incorrect because achieving these factors, while good, is not as complete as achieving the project requirements, which may include the cost, schedule, and quality expectations.

19. **D.** Culture shock is the typical disorientation a person feels when visiting a foreign country. A is incorrect. The Sapir-Whorf hypothesis is a theory that posits an individual can understand a culture by understanding its language. B is incorrect because time dimension is the local culture's general practice for respecting time and punctuality. C is incorrect because ethnocentrism is a person's belief that her own culture is the best and that all other cultures should be measured against it.

20. **C.** When problems arise that stop project tasks, the project manager should work with the team to uncover viable alternative solutions. A and B do nothing to find a solution to the problem, so they are incorrect. D is incorrect because the solution for the problem has not necessarily been addressed. The end result of C, to find an alternative solution, may result in outsourcing the problem to a vendor, D, but should not be the first choice in this scenario.

Passing the PMP Exam

In this chapter, you will

- Learn solid tips to help you pass the PMP exam
- Walk through the project management processes
- Review the key principles of agile project management

Obviously, you want to pass your Project Management Professional (PMP) exam on the first attempt. Why bother sitting for an exam if you know you're not prepared? In this chapter, you'll find the details you must know to pass the exam. These facts won't be everything you need to know to pass the PMP exam, but you can bet you won't pass the exam if you don't know the critical information contained in this chapter.

Tips to Pass the Exam

For starters, don't think of this process as "preparing to take an exam"—think of it as "preparing to pass an exam." Anyone can prepare to take an exam: just show up. Preparing to pass the PMP exam requires project management experience, diligence, and a commitment to study.

Prepare Before the Exam

In the days leading up to your scheduled exam, follow these tips to prepare yourself for success:

- *Get some moderate exercise.* Find time to go for a jog, lift weights, take a swim, or do whatever workout routine works best for you.

- *Eat smart and healthy.* If you eat healthy food, you'll feel good and feel better about yourself. Be certain to drink plenty of water, and don't overdo the caffeine.

- *Get your sleep.* A well-rested brain is a sharp brain. You don't want to sit for your exam feeling tired, sluggish, and worn out.

- *Time your study sessions.* Don't overdo your study sessions—long, crash-study sessions aren't that profitable. In addition, try to study at the same time every day, at the time your exam is scheduled.

Create Your Own Answer Key

If you could take one page of notes into the exam, what information would you like to include on this one-page document? Of course, you absolutely cannot take any notes or reference materials into the exam area. However, if you can create and memorize one sheet of notes, you absolutely may re-create this once you're seated in the exam area.

Practice creating a reference sheet so you can immediately, and legally, re-create this document once your exam has begun. You'll be supplied with several sheets of blank paper and a couple of pencils. Once your exam process begins, re-create your reference sheet. The following are key pieces of information you'd be wise to include on your reference sheet (you'll find all of this key information in this chapter):

- Activities within each process group
- Estimating formulas
- Communication formula
- Normal distribution values
- Agile project life cycles
- Earned value management formulas
- Project management theories

As more and more people are opting to take the exam online with a proctor, you aren't allowed any paper or pens during the test. In fact, your entire desk must be cleared, and you'll have to use your webcam to show your desk and work area to confirm no notes are in sight for the exam. With the online exam, you do get to use an electronic whiteboard, but you're limited on how you can draw on the whiteboard. It's more convenient to do the online testing, but certainly not as robust as a testing center environment.

Also note that when taking the exam online there are two 10-minute breaks during the test at scheduled intervals, not when you feel the urge to take a break. Once the break begins, you cannot go back to previously answered questions in the exam. Breaks aren't scheduled in the testing center, so any breaks you take will require you to pass through the security procedures again—all while your exam clock keeps ticking.

Testing Tips

The questions on the PMP exam aren't always direct and easy; they may offer a few red herrings, and some people have reported that they found taking the exam as challenging as reading *War and Peace*. But there are some practical, exam-passing tips. For starters, you may face questions that state, "All of the following are correct options, except for which one?" The question wants you to find the incorrect option or the option that would not be appropriate for the scenario described. You're looking for the answer that doesn't fit with the others listed. Be sure to understand what the question is asking for. It's easy to focus on the scenario presented in a question and then see a suitable option for that scenario in the answer. However, if the question is asking you to identify an option that is not suitable, then you just missed the question. Carefully read the question to understand what is expected for an answer.

Here's a tip that can work with many of the questions: identify what the question wants for an answer, and then look for an option that doesn't belong with the other possible answers. In other words, find the answer that doesn't fit with the other three options. Find the "odd man out." Here's an example:

EVM is used during the _____.

  A. Controlling activities of the project

  B. Executing activities of the project

  C. Closing activities of the project

  D. Entire project

Notice how options A, B, and C are exclusive? If you choose A, the controlling phase, it implies that earned value management (EVM) is not used anywhere else in the project. The odd man out here is D, the entire project; it's considered the "odd" choice because, by itself, it is not an actual process group. Of course, this tip won't work with every question—but it's handy to keep in mind.

For some answer choices, it may seem like two of the four options are both possible correct answers. However, because you may choose only one answer, you must discern which one is the best choice. Within the question, there will usually be some hint describing the progress of the project, the requirements of the stakeholders, or some other clue that can help you determine which answer is the best one for the question. Questions on the PMP exam include the following:

- **Multiple choice**   Only one answer is correct.
- **Multiple response**   More than one answer can be selected.
- **Matching**   You'll have to match up items between two lists.
- **Hotspot**   You'll click an area of a graphic to answer the question.
- **Limited fill in the blank**   You'll have to type in the correct answer.

Answer Every Question—Once

The PMP exam has 180 questions. You need to answer every question. Do not leave any question blank, even if you don't know the answer to the question. A blank answer is a wrong answer. As you move through the exam and you find questions that stump you, use the "mark question" option in the exam software, choose an answer you suspect may be correct, and then move on. When you have answered all of the questions, you are given the option to review your marked answers.

Some questions in the exam may prompt your memory to come up with answers to questions you have marked for review. However, resist the temptation to review those questions you've already answered with confidence and haven't marked. More often than not, your first instinct is the correct choice. When you completed the exams at the end of each chapter, did you change correct answers to wrong answers? If you did it in practice, you'll likely do it on the actual exam.

Use the Process of Elimination

When you're stumped on a question, use the process of elimination. For each question, there'll be four choices. On your scratch paper, write down "ABCD." If you can safely rule out A, cross it off your paper. Now focus on which of the other answers won't work. If you determine that C won't work, cross it off your list. Now you have a 50–50 chance of finding the correct choice. In recent years, PMI has added the option to "strike out" answers in the exam testing software, so use that tool as well.

If you cannot determine which answer is best, B or D in this instance, here's the best approach:

1. Choose an answer in the exam (no blank answers, remember).

2. Mark the question in the exam software for later review.

3. Circle the "ABCD" on your scratch paper, jot any relevant notes, and then write the question number next to the notes.

4. During the review or from a later question, you may realize which choice is the better of the two answers. Return to the question and confirm that the best answer is selected.

Everything You Must Know

As promised, this section covers all the information you must know going into the exam. It's highly recommended that you create a method to recall this information. Here goes.

The 49 Project Management Processes

You'll need to know the 49 project management processes and what each process accomplishes in the project. Note that as of this writing, the PMP exam continues to list *PMBOK Guide* (*A Guide to the Project* Management *Body of Knowledge*), Sixth Edition, as a reference for the exam. These processes are part of the *PMBOK Guide*. Here's a quick rundown of each process group and their processes.

Initiating the Project
There are just two processes to know for project initiation:

- Develop the project charter
- Identify the project stakeholders

Planning the Project
There are 24 processes to know for project planning:

- Develop project management plan
- Plan scope management
- Collect requirements

- Define scope
- Create WBS
- Plan schedule management
- Define activities
- Sequence activities
- Estimate activity durations
- Develop schedule
- Plan cost management
- Estimate costs
- Determine budget
- Plan quality management
- Plan resource management
- Estimate activity resources
- Plan communications management
- Plan risk management
- Identify risks
- Perform qualitative risk analysis
- Perform a quantitative risk analysis
- Plan risk responses
- Plan procurement management
- Plan stakeholder engagement

Executing the Project

There are ten executing processes:

- Direct and manage project work
- Manage project knowledge
- Manage quality
- Acquire resources
- Develop the project team
- Manage the project team
- Manage communications
- Implement risk responses
- Conduct procurements
- Manage stakeholder engagement

PART IV

Monitoring and Controlling the Project

There are 12 monitoring and controlling processes:

- Monitor and control the project work
- Perform integrated change control
- Validate scope
- Control scope
- Control schedule
- Control costs
- Control quality
- Control resources
- Monitor communications
- Monitor risks
- Control procurements
- Monitor stakeholder engagement

Closing the Project

There is only one closing process:

- Close project or phase

Earned Value Management Formulas

For EVM formulas, remember the following five rules:

- Always start with *EV*.
- *Variance* means subtraction.
- *Index* means division.
- Less than 1 is bad in an index, and greater than 1 is good, with the exception of the to-complete performance index (TCPI).
- Negative is bad in a variance; positive is good.

The formulas for earned value analysis can be calculated manually or through project management software during your projects. For the exam, you'll want to memorize these formulas. Table 19-1 summarizes all the formulas, as well as a sample, albeit goofy, mnemonic device.

Quick Project Management Facts

This section has some quick facts you should know at a glance. Hold on—this moves pretty fast.

Name	Formula	Sample Mnemonic Device
Planned value	PV = percent complete of where the project should be	Please
Earned value	EV = percent complete × budget at completion	Eat
Cost variance	CV = EV – AC	Carl's
Schedule variance	SV = EV – PV	Sugar
Cost performance index	CPI = EV/AC	Candy
Schedule performance index	SPI = EV/PV	S (this and the following two spell "SEE")
Estimate at completion	EAC = BAC/CPI	E
Estimate to complete	ETC = EAC – AC	E
To-complete performance index (BAC)	(BAC – EV)/(BAC – AC)	The
To-complete performance index (EAC)	(BAC – EV)/(EAC – AC)	Taffy
Variance at completion	VAC = BAC – EAC	Violin

Table 19-1   A Summary of the Most Common EVM Formulas

Organizational Structures

Organizational structures are relevant to the project manager's authority. A project manager's authority over project decisions varies according to the organizational structure:

- **Organic or simple**   The project manager has little to no authority.
- **Functional**   The project manager has little to no authority.
- **Multidivisional**   The project manager has little to no authority.
- **Weak matrix**   The project manager has little authority.
- **Balanced matrix**   The project manager has low authority.
- **Strong matrix**   The project manager has high to almost total authority.
- **Project-oriented**   The project manager has high to almost total authority.
- **Virtual**   The project manager has low to moderate authority.
- **Hybrid**   This may be a blend of multiple organizational types; the authority level depends on the organization.
- **Project management office**   The project manager has high to almost total authority.

Work Breakdown Structure (WBS) Facts

The WBS is the big picture of the project deliverables in a predictive project. It is not the activities that will create the project, but the components that the project will create. The WBS helps the project team and the project manager create accurate cost and time estimates.

PART IV

It also helps the project team and the project manager create an accurate activity list. Agile projects don't have a WBS.

Project Scope Facts

Projects are temporary endeavors to create a unique product or service. They are selected by one of two methods:

- **Benefit measurement methods**   These include scoring models, benefit-cost ratios, and economic models.
- **Constrained optimization models**   These include mathematical models based on linear, integer, and dynamic programming.

The project scope defines all the required work, and only the required work, to complete the project. Scope management is the process of ensuring that the project work is within scope and protecting the project from scope creep. The scope baseline, which includes the WBS and the WBS dictionary, is the baseline for all future project decisions because it justifies the business need of the project. There are two types of scope:

- **Product scope**   Defines the attributes of the product or service the project is creating
- **Project scope**   Defines the required work of the project to create the product

Scope validation is the process completed at the end of each phase and of each project to confirm that the project has met the requirements. It leads to formal acceptance of the project deliverable.

The project scope in an agile project is the product backlog. The product backlog is maintained, or groomed, by the product owner. The product owner is responsible for the user stories in the product backlog and will prioritize the user stories from top to bottom. The developers choose the amount of work they believe they can complete in the next iteration starting at the top of the product backlog. The items selected by the developers become the sprint backlog in agile project management. The product backlog and requirements will likely change as the project moves forward.

Project Time Facts

Time can be a project constraint. Effective time management is the scheduling and sequencing of activities in the best order to ensure that the project completes successfully and in a reasonable amount of time. These are some key terms related to time management:

- **Lag**   The amount of time waiting between activities.
- **Lead**   Activities come closer together and even overlap.
- **Free float**   The amount of time an activity can be delayed without delaying the next scheduled activity's early start date.
- **Total float**   The amount of time an activity can be delayed without delaying the project's finish date.

- **Float**   Sometimes called *slack*—a perfectly acceptable synonym.
- **Duration**   The amount of work periods required to complete an estimated activity. This may be abbreviated as "du." For example, du=8d means the duration is eight days.

There are three types of dependencies between activities:

- **Mandatory**   This hard logic requires a specific sequence between activities.
- **Discretionary**   This soft logic prefers a sequence between activities.
- **External**   Due to conditions outside of the project, such as those created by vendors, the sequence must happen in a given order.

There are three types of precedence between activities that you should know for the exam:

- **Finish to start (FS)**   The predecessor activity must finish before the successor activity can start.
- **Finish to finish (FF)**   The predecessor activity must finish before the successor activity can finish.
- **Start to start (SS)**   The predecessor activity must start before the successor activity can start.

Agile projects have predetermined time boxes for the events in a project. Each iteration is predetermined by a time box, typically ranging from two to four weeks. The items selected by the developers, called the *sprint backlog*, are the items completed in one iteration. In XP, the iteration is typically two weeks in duration. The iteration length isn't the duration of the entire project, but a smaller portion of the project in which the sprint backlog will be completed.

Project Cost Facts

There are several methods of providing project estimates:

- **Bottom-up**   Project costs start at zero, each component in the WBS is estimated for costs, and then the "grand total" is calculated. This method takes the longest to complete, but it provides the most accurate estimate.
- **Analogous**   Project costs are based on a similar project. This is a form of expert judgment, but it is also a top-down estimating approach, so it is less accurate than a bottom-up estimate.
- **Parametric modeling**   Price is based on cost per unit. Examples include cost per metric ton, cost per yard, and cost per hour.

There are four types of costs attributed to a project:

- **Variable cost**   The cost is dependent on other variables. For example, the cost of a food-catered event depends on how many people register to attend the event.

- **Fixed cost**   The cost remains constant throughout the project. For example, a rented piece of equipment has the same fee each month even if it is used more in some months than in others.

- **Direct cost**   The cost is directly attributed to an individual project and cannot be shared with other projects. Examples include airfare to attend project meetings, hotel expenses, and leased equipment that is used only on the current project.

- **Indirect cost**   The cost of doing business. Examples include rent, phone, and utilities.

Quality Management Facts

The *cost of quality* is the money spent investing in training, in meeting requirements for safety and other laws and regulations, and in taking steps to ensure quality acceptance. The cost of quality is also known as the cost of conformance. The *cost of nonconformance*, sometimes called the *cost of poor quality*, is the cost associated with rework, downtime, lost sales, and waste of materials.

Common quality management charts and methods include the following:

- **Ishikawa diagrams**   Find causes and effects that contribute to a problem. These are also called fishbone or cause-and-effect diagrams.

- **Flowcharts**   Show the relationship between components and the flow of a process through a system.

- **Pareto diagrams**   Identify project problems and their frequencies. These are based on the 80/20 rule: 80 percent of project problems stem from 20 percent of the work.

- **Control charts**   Plot out the result of samplings to determine whether projects are "in control" or "out of control." Agile projects can use a control chart to track cycle time and defect repair to see if the process is out of control.

- **Just-in-time ordering**   Reduces the cost of inventory, but requires additional quality because materials would not be readily available if mistakes occurred.

Human Resource Facts

PMP candidates should be familiar with several human resource theories for the exams:

- **Maslow's Hierarchy of Needs**   There are five layers of needs for all humans: physiological, safety, social (such as love and friendship), esteem, and the crowning jewel of self-actualization.

- **Herzberg's Theory of Motivation**   There are two catalysts for workers: hygiene agents and motivating agents.

  - **Hygiene agents**   These do nothing to motivate, but their absence demotivates workers. Hygiene agents are the expectations all workers have: job security, a paycheck, clean and safe working conditions, a sense of belonging, civil working relationships, and other basic attributes associated with employment.

  - **Motivating agents**   These are the elements that motivate people to excel. They include responsibility, appreciation of work, recognition, opportunity to excel, education, and other opportunities associated with work besides financial rewards.

- **McGregor's Theory of X and Y**   This theory states that "X" people are lazy, don't want to work, and need to be micromanaged. "Y" people are self-led, motivated, and can accomplish things on their own.

- **Ouchi's Theory Z**   This theory holds that workers are motivated by a sense of commitment, opportunity, and advancement. People will work if they are challenged and motivated. Think participative management.

- **McClelland's Theory of Needs**   This is also known as the Three Needs Theory, because there are just three needs for each individual: need for achievement, need for affiliation, or need for power.

- **Vroom's Expectancy Theory**   People will behave based on what they expect as a result of their behavior. In other words, people will work in relation to the expected reward.

Communication Facts

Communicating is the most important skill for the project manager. With that in mind, here are some key facts you should remember about communications:

- The communication channels formula is $N(N - 1)/2$. N represents the number of stakeholders. For example, if you have 10 stakeholders, the formula would read $10(10 - 1)/2$, or 45 communication channels. Pay special attention to questions wanting to know how many additional communication channels you have based on added stakeholders. For example, if you have 25 stakeholders on your project and have recently added 5 team members, how many additional communication channels do you now have? You'll have to calculate the original number of communication channels, $25(25 - 1)/2 = 300$, and then calculate the new number with the added team members, $30(30 - 1)/2 = 435$, and, finally, subtract the difference between the two: $435 - 300 = 135$, which is the number of additional communication channels.

- Fifty-five percent of communication is nonverbal; an additional 30 percent is paralingual.

- Effective listening is the ability to watch the speaker's body language, interpret paralingual clues, and decipher facial expressions. Following the message, effective listening has the listener asking questions to achieve clarity and offering feedback.

PART IV

- Active listening requires receivers of the message to offer cues, such as nodding the head to indicate that they are listening. It also requires receivers to repeat the message, ask questions, and continue the discussion if clarification is needed.

- Communication can be hindered by trendy phrases, jargon, and extremely pessimistic comments. In addition, other communication barriers include noise, hostility, cultural differences, and technical interruptions. Noise is defined as anything that interferes with the transmission and/or the receipt of communication.

- Agile embraces face-to-face communication, transparency, and osmotic communication by keeping the team co-located whenever possible. Data about project performance is openly shared through information radiators and events within the project such as the sprint review, demonstrations, and the daily standup meeting.

Risk Management Facts

Risks are unplanned events that can have positive or negative effects on the projects. Most risks are seen as threats to the project's success—but not all risks are bad. For example, let's say there is a 20 percent probability that a project will realize a discount in shipping, which will save the project $15,000. If this risk happens, the project will save money; if the risk doesn't happen, the project will have to spend $15,000. Risks should be identified as early as possible in the planning process. A person's or an organization's willingness to accept risk is the utility function (also called the *utility theory* or *risk tolerance level*). The Delphi Technique can be used to build consensus on project risks.

Agile projects don't do as much up-front planning for risk events as predictive projects do. Agile projects take more of a qualitative approach to finding a risk score, which can be done for user stories. The product backlog can also be prioritized for risk events to bring larger risk events to the top of the product backlog so that larger risk events can be taken on earlier in the project. Risk events in agile are seen only as negative; anything that threatens the project's value is a risk. Issues are risk events that have occurred.

The only output of the risk planning process is the risk management plan. There are two broad types of risks:

- **Business risks** The loss of time and finances (where a downside and upside exist). Business risk is often referred to as speculative risk.

- **Pure risks** The loss of life, injury, and theft (where only a downside exists). Pure risk is often referred to as insurable risk.

Negative risks can be responded to using one of four methods:

- **Avoidance** Avoid the risk by planning a different technique to remove the risk from the project.

- **Mitigation** Reduce the probability or impact of the risk.

- **Transference** The risk is not eliminated, but the responsibility and ownership of the risk are transferred to another party (for example, through insurance).

- **Acceptance** The risk's probability or impact may be small enough that the risk can be accepted, or the project team is not capable of mitigating the probability of a risk, such as a hurricane.

Positive risks can also be responded to using one of four methods:

- **Exploiting** The organization can take advantage of the benefits a positive risk will create.

- **Sharing** A project or organization can partner with another entity through joint ventures or teaming agreements to share a positive risk event.

- **Enhancing** The project manager tries to make the positive risk event happen in the project by enhancing the conditions for the positive risk event to be realized and increasing the positive impact should the risk event be realized.

- **Acceptance** The project manager can also accept positive risks.

Risks are ranked and scored to assess their probability and impact on the project:

- **Qualitative analysis** This approach qualifies the risks for further analysis.

- **Quantitative analysis** This method assigns numeric values to probability and impact. This approach calculates a risk factor (or exposure) in dollars or time.

- **Cardinal scale** This is a numeric ranking (such as from .01, very low, to 1.0, certain).

- **Ordinal scale** This is a word ranking (such as high, medium, low).

Procurement Facts

A statement of work (SOW) is provided to the potential sellers so they can create accurate bids, quotes, and proposals for the buyer. A bidder conference may be held so sellers can query the buyer on the product or service to be procured.

A contract is a formal agreement, preferably written, between a buyer and seller. To be valid, a contract must have the following:

- An offer
- Acceptance
- Consideration
- A legal purpose
- Capacity to enter into a contract

On the exam, procurement questions are usually from the buyer's point of view. All requirements the seller is to complete should be clearly written in the contract.

Requirements of both parties must be met, or legal proceedings may follow. In the Agile Manifesto, the topic of procurement is directly addressed by stressing collaboration is valued over contract negotiation. Because agile projects change so often, it can be challenging for vendors working in an agile project because they can't know exactly what the final product the project creates will be.

Contract types include the following:

- **Cost-reimbursable contract** Requires the buyer to assume the risk of cost overruns.
- **Fixed-price contract** Requires the seller to assume the risk of cost overruns.
- **Time and materials contract** Good for smaller assignments, but can impose cost overrun risks to the buyer if the contract between the buyer and seller does not include a not-to-exceed clause. This clause, commonly called an NTE clause, puts a cap on the maximum amount for the contract time and materials.
- **Purchase order** A unilateral form of contract. It is an example of a fixed-price contract.
- **Letter of intent** Not a contract, but shows the intent of the buyer to purchase from a specific seller.

Stakeholder Management Facts

Stakeholder management used to be tucked into project communications, but it's so important that it's now its own knowledge area in the *PMBOK Guide*. Stakeholder management is still closely related to communications management, but it's more than just communicating with stakeholders. You'll complete four processes as part of stakeholder management:

- **Identify stakeholders** This is part of project initiation.
- **Plan stakeholder management** This is part of the planning process group (obviously).
- **Manage stakeholder engagement** This is part of the executing process group.
- **Control stakeholder engagement** This is part of the monitoring and controlling process group.

Stakeholder identification is one of the first processes you'll undertake in a project. You need to identify the stakeholders to ensure that you're including all of the right people in the project planning. Once you've identified a stakeholder, you'll record the person's information in the stakeholder register.

There's a three-step approach to stakeholder management:

1. Identify stakeholders as early as possible in the project.
2. Identify the project impact and support of each stakeholder.
3. Plan how to influence each stakeholder.

You'll need to know about the stakeholder classification models for your PMI examination. These are grids to plot out stakeholder power, influence, and interest in the project. Here are four common models:

- **Power/interest grid**   How much power/interest do the stakeholders have?
- **Power/influence grid**   How much power/influence do the stakeholders have?
- **Influence/impact grid**   How much influence (involvement of decisions) and impact on project change do the stakeholders have?
- **Salience model**   This model classifies stakeholders based on power, urgency, and legitimacy for the project.

Agile Project Management Facts

On your PMP exam, about half of the exam will focus on agile and hybrid projects. You'll need to know agile even if you don't work in an agile environment. Agile projects are typically knowledge-work projects, such as developing software or designing a web site. Predictive projects are industrial projects, where labor is completing a task such as painting the wall, installing fixtures, or constructing a building. Hybrid projects are custom to an organization and use components of both knowledge work projects and industrial projects that suit the organization's needs.

There are several agile approaches you should recognize for the exam, but the most popular is Scrum. Scrum begins with a prioritized product backlog, which is a long list of all the features, called *product backlog items* (user stories is another term often used), that the project should complete. In the sprint planning meeting, the team sizes the user stories and selects the amount of work they can complete within the sprint. Every day in the sprint the team meets for 15 minutes in the daily scrum to discuss what was completed yesterday, what is planned for today's work, and impediments to progress. At the end of the sprint there are two ceremonies: the sprint review and the sprint retrospective. The sprint review is a demo of the completed work the team has completed. The sprint retrospective is a lessons learned meeting to improve project performance in the next sprint. The cycle then repeats with a new sprint planning meeting.

Extreme Programming (XP) uses weekly cycles to review the work to do, the completed work, and the task assignment for the team. Each quarter a release is planned for the work completed during the weekly iterations. XP uses slack by buffering in low-level requirements that can be dropped if not completed by the quarterly deadline. Test-first is an XP concept that requires the programmer to run a test on code before the code is completed. The test will fail, but now the programmer knows what the code must do to pass the test. Once the code passes the test, the code is continuously integrated and checked for any new errors.

Other agile approaches you may see on the exam include the following:

- Lean product development aims to eliminate waste, define value from the customers' perspective, empower the team, provide constant learning, and improve as the project progresses.

PART IV

- Feature-driven development has strict rules, relies on documentation for communication, and is ideal for large and long-term software development projects with large teams of programmers.

- The Dynamic Systems Development Method (DSDM) has a rigid structure and is often used when vendors are involved in the project work. DSDM allows the approach to be blended with other project management approaches, such as Scrum or even predictive projects.

- Crystal agile methodologies use color coding to symbolize the project's team size and effect on human life. Crystal tries to deliver results frequently, improve processes, and colocate teams whenever possible for improved communications.

- Kanban is not as robust as other agile methodologies, and you'll likely just see Kanban boards on your exam. In Kanban, work begins on the left side of the Kanban board and flows from left to right. The goal is to limit the work in progress and allow anyone on the team who has the right skillset and capacity to take a card from the left and begin the workflow.

A Letter to You

My goal for you is to pass your exam. As I teach my PMP Exam Prep Seminars for different organizations around the globe and online, I'm struck by one similarity among the most excited course participants: these people want to pass their exam. Sure, project management is not the most exciting topic, but these individuals are excited about passing their exam. I hope you feel the same way. I believe that your odds of passing the PMP are like most things in life; you're going to get out of it only what you put into it. I challenge you to become excited, happy, and eager to pass the exam.

Here are ten final tips for passing your PMP examination:

- Prepare to pass the exam, not just take it.

- If you haven't done so already, schedule your exam. Having a deadline makes that exam even more of a reality.

- If you haven't done so already, create a clutter-free area for studying.

- Study in regular intervals right up to the day before your examination.

- Repetition is the mother of learning. If you don't know a formula, repeat it and repeat it. Then repeat it again.

- Create your own flashcards from the terms and glossary in this book.

- Always answer the exam questions according to how the Project Management Institute (PMI) expects something done, not how you'd do it at your organization.

- Practice creating one page of notes that you'll re-create at the start of your exam.

- Create a significant reward for yourself as an incentive to pass the exam.

- Make a commitment to pass.

If you're stumped on something I've written about in this book or if you'd like to share your PMP success story, drop me a line at cs@instructing.com. Finally, I won't wish you good luck on your PMP exam—luck is for the ill prepared. If you follow the strategies I've outlined in this book and apply yourself, I am certain you'll pass the exam.

All my best,

Joseph Phillips, PMP, PMI-ACP, PSM, ITIL, Project+, CTT+

www.instructing.com

PART V

Appendixes and Glossary

- **Appendix A**   Project Management Documents
- **Appendix B**   About the Online Content
- **Glossary**

Project Management Documents

Projects are full of plans, reports, and other documents. Having a clear understanding of each document type and why they may or may not be needed in a project can help you, the Project Management Professional (PMP) candidate, to answer exam questions correctly. The following are the project management elements.

activity attributes   The activity characteristics such as the activity codes, predecessor and successor activities, leads and lags, resource requirements, dates, constraints, and assumptions.

activity cost estimate supporting detail   The collection of documents that detail how the project's cost estimate was created, which includes the following information:

- The scope of the work that the estimate is based on
- The basis for the estimate
- Documentation of the assumptions used in the estimate creation
- Documentation of the constraints used in the estimate creation
- The range of possible estimates, such as the +/– percentage or dollar amount

activity duration estimate   An estimate of the likely time it will take to complete the project, a phase, or individual activities within the project.

activity list   The collection of schedule activities.

affinity diagram   A tool that helps the project team sort ideas and data. This simple tool clusters similar ideas and is useful after a brainstorming session.

agile charter   A document that authorizes the project to exist in the organization. Agile charters frame out the high-level goals of the project and acknowledge that change is expected and welcome in the project. Agile charts are typically one-page documents.

agreement   A document that defines what the project aims to accomplish for a person, customer, stakeholder, business, or organization. An agreement can be a verbal agreement, but it is more likely documented in a contract, memorandum of understanding, memo, or e-mail.

analogous estimate   An estimate based on a previous similar project to predict the current project's time or cost expectations.

assumptions log   A document in which all assumptions identified in the project are documented and the status of each as an assumption is monitored. Assumptions need to be tested to determine risk likelihood.

backlog   Narratives about the product requirements that need to be completed. These are often prioritized, numbered, and scheduled for creation based on time, budget, and stakeholder demand.

bar chart   A histogram that typically depicts the project activities and their associated start and end dates. This is also known as a Gantt chart.

benefits management plan   A project management plan that defines how the project will create and deliver the benefits for the organization.

bill of materials (BOM)   Defines the materials and products needed to create the items defined in the corresponding work breakdown structure. The BOM is arranged in sync with the hierarchy of the deliverables in the WBS.

burndown chart   A chart that shows the remaining tasks or user stories to create in ratio to the total number of tasks or user stories completed. As the team completes more tasks or user stories, the balance of task or user stories goes down and the accumulation of items completed goes up.

burnup chart   A chart that shows the accumulation of tasks or user stories completed by the project team.

business case   Documents the financial reasoning for the project and the end result of a feasibility study. A business case is often needed for the project charter to justify the project's existence.

cause-and-effect diagram   A diagram that illustrates how potential problems within a project may contribute to failure or errors within the project. This is also known as Ishikawa diagram, fishbone diagram, or why-why diagram.

change log   A document that records all changes that happen during the project. It's useful for scope verification, quality control, and tracking changes.

change management plan   A project management plan that defines how the project will manage changes.

change request   A documented request to change the project's scope, which is managed through the project's integrated change control process.

checksheet A checklist that is used as part of requirements gathering, task execution, quality control, and other aspects of the project to ensure that a task or process is completed accurately. This is also known as a tally sheet.

claim A documented disagreement between the buyer and the seller. Claims are often settled through negotiations, with mediation, or in the courts, depending on the terms of the contract.

communications management plan A subsidiary plan to the project management plan that defines who needs what information, when the information is needed, the frequency of the communication, and the accepted modalities for the communication needs.

configuration management plan A project management plan that defines the configurable items and the formal process for how these items are allowed to be changed during the project.

contingency plan Part of the monitor and control risk process includes the option of executing a contingency plan to respond to worst-case scenarios with risk impact.

contract A legal relationship between the buyer and the seller that describes the work to be completed, the fee for performing the work, a schedule for completing the work, and acceptance criteria to deem the contract complete. If a project is being completed by one organization for another organization, there is typically a contractual relationship between the seller and the customer. Contracts may be inputs for the project charter.

contract management plan A plan that is used for significant purchases. This plan directs the acquisition and adherence of both the buyer and the seller to the terms of the contract.

contract statement of work A document that defines the products and services that are being procured to satisfy portions of the project scope statement.

control chart A quality control tool that illustrates the stability of a process and enables the project management team to determine whether the process may have trends and predictability.

cost baseline A time-phased budget that tracks the planned project expenses against the actual project expenses. This document is used to measure, monitor, and control project costs in conjunction with the cost management plan.

cost management plan A project management subsidiary plan that defines the structure for estimating, budgeting, and controlling project costs.

cost plus fee or cost plus percentage of costs A contract in which the buyer pays the seller a fee for the contract work or deliverable plus an additional fee based on the percentage of the total costs for the goods or services provided.

cost plus fixed fee A contract in which the buyer pays the seller the costs of the materials and/or labor to complete the contract work or deliverable, plus a predetermined fee.

cost plus incentive fee A contract in which the buyer pays the seller the costs of the materials and labor plus an incentive bonus for reaching objectives set by the buyer. Incentives are typically based on reaching schedule objectives.

cumulative flow diagram A stacked chart that shows the total number of items in each phase of the project, such as the backlog, development, testing, and released. This chart can be used to identify too many items in WIP and bottlenecks in the project.

decision tree A diagram that identifies and evaluates each available outcome of a decision and the decision's implication, consideration of each choice, and value of each decision.

defect repair request A change request to repair defects within the project deliverables.

fallback plan A worst-case scenario plan to enable the organization to "fall back" if a project plan needs to be scrapped because of risks or issues.

fishbone diagram A diagram that illustrates how potential problems within a project may contribute to failure or errors within the project. This is also known as cause-and-effect diagram and Ishikawa diagram.

fixed-price or lump-sum contract A contract that defines the total price for the work or product the organization agrees to purchase.

flowchart A visual representation of a process through a system.

force-field analysis diagram A diagram that plots the strengths and weaknesses of the forces (stakeholders) that have influence over project decisions.

formal acceptance documentation A document that formally records that the project customer and/or sponsor has accepted the project deliverables.

Gantt chart A bar chart that shows scheduling information and relationships among tasks. Tasks are represented by nodes. The length of the node combined with the calendar shows the duration of the activity.

histogram A bar chart that shows the distribution of values.

historical information Past project documentation and lessons learned documents are often used as inputs and references for current projects. Current project documentation and lessons learned documentation become historical information for future projects within an organization.

independent estimate A document that serves as a means for evaluating estimates provided by potential vendors to complete the work the contract calls for. An independent estimate is often created by a third party for the performing organization for a fee. This is also known as a third-party estimate and a should-cost estimate.

influence diagram A decision chart that shows the relationships between and among causal factors, events, situations, and other project conditions.

invitation for bid   A document inviting a prospective vendor to bid on the contents of the contract statement of work. This is a price-based decision model.

Ishikawa diagram   A diagram that illustrates how potential problems within a project may contribute to failure or errors within the project. This is also known as a cause-and-effect diagram or fishbone diagram.

issue log   A document that records all issues, their statuses, and resolutions.

Kanban chart   Kanban is a framework to show the work in the project on a chart or sign board. The chart shows all phases of development the team is using in columns, such as To Do, Development, Testing, and Production. Each feature is written on a sticky note, and the note is pulled from left to right in columns of the Kanban chart. This chart shows work items waiting to start, items in the different phases of the project, and completed items.

lessons learned register   A document listing the results of quality control and other types of lessons learned, which becomes part of organizational process assets. Lessons learned documentation is created throughout the project's life cycle.

milestone chart   A chart that depicts the promised milestone completion and the actual milestone completion dates. This is sometimes called a milestone schedule.

milestone list   The documented collection of the project milestones and their attributes, deadlines, and requirements. The milestone list is part of the overall project management plan.

nondisclosure agreement (NDA)   A procurement document that requires the vendor not disclose information about the contract to anyone within or outside of the performing organization.

organizational breakdown structure   A document showing the decomposition of the project's hierarchy of organizations, departments, and disciplines related to the work packages in the work breakdown structure. This document helps the project management team determine which disciplines or departments are responsible for which work packages as identified in the work breakdown structure. Or, this is a document that depicts the organization's departments, teams, functional departments, and business units.

organizational chart   A visual representation of the hierarchy of an organization depicting all the positions and reporting structures of the organization's members.

parametric estimate   An estimate based on a parameter, such as a cost per metric ton or number of hours to complete a repetitive activity.

Pareto chart   A histogram that shows the categories of failure within a project. A Pareto chart ranks the failures from largest to smallest, which then enables the project management team to attack the largest problems within the project. Pareto charts are based on Pareto's law, which states that 80 percent of the problems are related to 20 percent of the causes.

performance reports   The project's communications management plan defines the expectations and frequency of the project performance reports. Performance reports update the necessary stakeholders on the status and progress information and may include bar charts, S-curves, histograms, and tables. These reports provide documentation about the project and project team's overall performance during the project execution. Performance can measure work results, time, cost, scope, quality, and other specifics within the project.

PMBOK Guide   A book published by the Project Management Institute (PMI) that serves as a guide to the project management body of knowledge. It is generally accepted in the project management discipline as providing good practices for most projects, most of the time.

probability and impact matrix   Demonstrates through either a cardinal or an ordinal scale the probability, impact, and risk score of each identified risk event. The process is a result of risk analysis.

procurement management plan   A subsidiary plan of the overall project management plan that defines the processes and policies for choosing, selecting, and working with a vendor on the project. The plan defines the contracts that should be used, the standard procurement documents, and the conditions to work with (and sometimes manage) the client–vendor relationship.

procurement statement of work   A document from the buyer to the seller describing exactly what the seller wants to purchase. This document is part of the procurement package.

product backlog   A list of all items, features, and user stories the customer wants delivered in the project. The product owner prioritizes the backlog with the most important items at the top, and the developers choose items they can complete in the iteration from the top of the product backlog.

product roadmap   A product roadmap outlines the vision, direction, priorities, and progress of a product over time. It's a plan of how the project will move from start to finish with intermittent deliverables to the stakeholders. It answers what the conditions must be met to allow the product owner to do a release, what the components of a release are, and the result of the project. It's a plan of action that aligns the organization around short- and long-term goals for the product or project and how they will be achieved.

product scope   The features and functions of the product, service, or result that a project may bring about.

product scope description   Defines the product, service, or condition that the project promises to create. As the project moves through planning, the product scope description becomes more detailed.

project calendar   The time when project work is allowed to happen within the project.

project charter   The document that authorizes the project or project phase. It identifies the business needs and the new product, service, or result the project will bring about in the organization.

project closure documents   The documentation of the project's completion, closure, and transfer of the project deliverables to other parties within the organization or to the project customers. If the project has been canceled, the project closure documents detail why the project has been canceled and what has happened to the project deliverables that may have been created during the limited project execution.

project management plan   A document that defines all of the accepted project management processes for the current project, including how the project will be initiated, planned, executed, monitored, controlled, and closed. Predictive projects utilize a project management plan; some hybrid projects may also use a project management plan. The project management plan comprises the following:

- Project scope management plan
- Change management plan
- Configuration management plan
- Requirements management plan
- Schedule management plan
- Cost management plan
- Quality management plan
- Resource management plan
- Communications management plan
- Risk management plan
- Procurement management plan
- Stakeholder engagement plan
- Schedule baseline
- Cost baseline
- Scope baseline
- Performance measurement baseline
- Project life-cycle descriptions
- Development approach

project notebook   A notebook that contains the project team's individual project records. The project notebooks become part of the organizational process assets.

project organization chart   A chart that shows the interrelationships among the project manager, the project sponsor, the project team, and possibly stakeholders.

project presentation   Formal project communication that often happens in the form of a presentation. These presentations become part of the organizational process assets.

project records   All of the project documentation and communication that should be kept and managed by the project management team. These project records become part of the organizational process assets.

project reports   Project reports vary by organization, but generally include information on the project's status, lessons learned, issue logs, and project closure. Project reports become part of the organizational process assets.

project schedule network diagram   A visual representation of the sequence of project activities. The most common project schedule network diagram is the precedence diagramming method, which uses predecessors and successors to illustrate the flow of the project work.

project scope management plan   A subsidiary plan of the overall project plan. It defines how the project scope will be defined, documented, verified, managed, and controlled. This plan also defines how the project's work breakdown structure will be defined, maintained, and approved. The scope validation process is also documented within the project scope management plan. Finally, this plan defines the scope change control process the project will adhere to.

project scope statement   A document that defines the scope of the project and the work required to deliver the project scope. The project scope statement provides several pieces of project information:

- Project objectives
- Product scope description
- Project requirements
- Project boundaries
- Project deliverables
- Product acceptance criteria
- Project constraints
- Project assumptions
- Initial project organization
- Initial defined risks
- Schedule milestone
- Fund limitations
- Cost estimates
- Project configuration management requirements
- Project specifications
- Approval requirements

project statement of work (project SOW)   Defines the products or processes that the project will provide. This document is an input to the project charter.

proposal   A response to a request for proposal (RFP), which often includes project approaches, ideas, and suggestions to complete the procured work, in addition to a price.

published estimating data   A collection of production rates, material costs, labor trades, and industry-specific price guidelines.

qualified seller lists   A list of vendors that are qualified to do business with the performing organization.

quality baseline   A document that defines the quality objectives for the project. Results of project performance measurement are compared against the quality baseline so that improvements may be made. If the work is acceptable, the project may continue.

quality checklist   A project management tool used to ensure that a series of steps have been performed as planned and required by the project management team.

quality management plan   A subsidiary project management plan that defines how the project management team will adhere to and implement the requirements of the performing organization's quality policy.

RACI chart   A responsibility assignment matrix that documents the project roles and the responsibilities for each within the project. In a RACI chart, the activities of *responsible, accountable, consult,* and *inform* are used (hence, the acronym RACI).

request for information (RFI)   A request from the buyer to the seller asking for more details about the goods or services the seller sells.

request for proposal (RFP)   A request from the buyer to potential vendors to provide a price, approaches, and ideas on how to complete the proposed work to be procured.

request for quote (RFQ)   A document inviting a prospective vendor to bid on the contents of the contract statement of work. This is a price-based decision model.

requirements management plan   A project management plan that defines how requirements will be identified, documented, and managed during the project.

requirements traceability matrix   A table that identifies each requirement at its origin and traces the requirement throughout the project.

resource breakdown structure (RBS)   A hierarchical decomposition of the resources required to complete the deliverables within the project.

resource calendar   A calendar that defines when people and equipment are available for the project's use. The resource calendar identifies whether a resource is idle, on vacation, or being utilized on the current project or another one within the organization.

resource management plan   A project management plan that defines how the project is staffed and how the project team will be defined, managed, and controlled. This plan also addresses physical resources that are needed for the project.

responsibility assignment matrix (RAM)   Illustrates the connection between the project work and the project team members who will complete the project work.

risk-adjusted backlog   The product backlog prioritizes user stories based on their risk score or expected monetary value. Typically, the items that are riskiest are placed at the top of the backlog so that the team can tackle the riskiest items first.

risk breakdown structure (RBS)   The project risks are depicted in a hierarchy of risk categories.

risk management plan   Defines how the risk management activities within the project will occur. A risk management plan is a subsidiary plan of the overall project management plan. The risk management plan includes the following:

- Methodology
- Roles and responsibilities
- Budgeting
- Timing
- Risk categories
- Definitions of risk probability and impact
- Updated risk categories

risk register   A component of project management planning that documents the outcome of all risk management activities. The risk register includes the following:

- List of identified risks
- List of potential responses
- Root causes of risk
- Risk prioritization
- Probabilistic analysis
- Risk trends

risk-related contractual agreement   An agreement often needed should the planned response to a risk event use transference.

risk report   Communicates and summarizes the status of individual project risks and the overall project risks.

run chart   Similar to a control chart, shows measured trends over time.

scatter diagram   A quality control diagram that shows the relationship between two variables within a project.

schedule activities   A collection of activities. The work package is decomposed into the tasks needed to create the work package deliverable. This is also called the activity list.

schedule baseline   A baseline depicting the expected start and completion dates of project activities, dates for the milestones, and finish dates for the entire project or project phase.

schedule comparison bar chart   A bar chart that depicts the discrepancies between the current activity status and the estimated activity status. This is often referred to as a tracking Gantt chart.

schedule network templates   An organization that repeats the same type of projects may elect to use schedule network templates. These templates are prepopulated with activities and their preferred sequence. Often, schedule network templates are based on previous similar projects and are adapted for the current project.

scope baseline   Comprises the project's scope statement, the work breakdown structure, and the work breakdown structure dictionary.

sprint backlog   The list of tasks from the sprint planning meeting and the expectations of what they team will complete during the sprint.

stakeholder register   A directory of the project stakeholders and their characteristics.

strategic plan   An organizational plan that is considered when a project is being chartered. All projects within an organization should support the organization's strategic plan.

subnetwork template   Illustrates repetitive work in a project, such as the creation of identical floors within a skyscraper. This is part of the network diagram.

summary budget   Addresses the predetermined budget allotted for a project or a rough order of magnitude estimate based on the preliminary project scope statement. This is often included in the project charter.

summary milestone schedule   A schedule of when the project management team can expect the milestones within the project to be reached. This schedule is part of the project charter.

team charter   Documents team values and ground rules; defines expectations between the project team members and the project manager.

team management plan   Part of the resource management plan that defines when project members are needed, how the project team will be acquired, and when the project team members can be released from the project.

teaming agreement   A contract that defines the limited relationship between two or more organizations in their attempt to seize an opportunity. When the opportunity is done, the contractual relationship defines how the teaming agreement may end.

text-oriented responsibility format   When roles and responsibilities need more documentation than a responsible, accountable, consulted, informed (RACI) chart or a responsibility assignment matrix (RAM) can provide, a text-oriented version is used. This is also known as position description or role-responsibility-authority form.

PART V

three-point estimate   An estimate based on the average of the optimistic, most likely, and pessimistic time estimates.

time and materials contract   A simple contract type in which the buyer pays the seller for the time and materials to deliver the product or service the contract calls for. This contract type should have a not-to-exceed clause to cap the contract's total costs.

tree diagram   A hierarchical chart that shows the relationship of parent–child objects. Technically, the work breakdown structure can be a tree diagram.

user story   A story of a role utilizing some functionality to get value from the functionality. User stories follow a formula of "As a <role>, I want <function>, so I can realize <value>." User stories are the items in the product backlog, are a small chunk of functionality, and generally take up to 40 hours to create.

vision statement   A summary of what the project will accomplish. It is a quick definition about what the project will create for the organization or the end users of the product.

WBS dictionary   A companion document to the work breakdown structure (WBS) that details each item in the WBS. Every entry in the WBS dictionary includes its related code of account identifier, responsible organization, schedule, quality requirements, and technical references, and may include charge numbers, related activities, and a cost estimate.

WBS template   A WBS from a previous similar project or the organization's methodology that has been adapted and modified to map to the current project's deliverables.

work breakdown structure (WBS)   A document that visualizes the deliverables that make up the project scope. The WBS uses a code of accounts to number and identify the elements within the decomposition. The smallest item within the WBS is called the work package.

work package   The smallest item in the WBS that cannot, or should not, be decomposed any further as a project deliverable.

work performance data   Raw data from observations, outcome of activities, and measurements from the project work.

work performance information   Refers to the work on the project, and when analyzed, the information is usable to make decisions in the project.

work performance reports   Work performance information that is formatted, packaged, and presented in a report for management and stakeholders. This is often used for decision-making purposes.

About the Online Content

This book comes complete with TotalTester Online customizable practice exam software with 360 practice exam questions, as well as other book resources including video training from the author; worksheets for time value of money, earned value, and a float exercise; a printable copy of the trifold memory card included in the print book; and an Exam Scores spreadsheet for the end-of-chapter quizzes.

System Requirements

The current and previous major versions of the following desktop browsers are recommended and supported: Chrome, Microsoft Edge, Firefox, and Safari. These browsers update frequently, and sometimes an update may cause compatibility issues with the TotalTester Online or other content hosted on the Training Hub. If you run into a problem using one of these browsers, please try using another until the problem is resolved.

Your Total Seminars Training Hub Account

To get access to the online content you will need to create an account on the Total Seminars Training Hub. Registration is free, and you will be able to track all your online content using your account. You may also opt in if you wish to receive marketing information from McGraw Hill or Total Seminars, but this is not required for you to gain access to the online content.

Privacy Notice

McGraw Hill values your privacy. Please be sure to read the Privacy Notice available during registration to see how the information you have provided will be used. You may view our Corporate Customer Privacy Policy by visiting the McGraw Hill Privacy Center. Visit the **mheducation.com** site and click **Privacy** at the bottom of the page.

Single User License Terms and Conditions

Online access to the digital content included with this book is governed by the McGraw Hill License Agreement outlined next. By using this digital content you agree to the terms of that license.

Access   To register and activate your Total Seminars Training Hub account, simply follow these easy steps:

1. Go to this URL: **hub.totalsem.com/mheclaim**

2. To register and create a new Training Hub account, enter your e-mail address, name, and password on the **Register** tab. No further personal information (such as credit card number) is required to create an account.

   If you already have a Total Seminars Training Hub account, enter your e-mail address and password on the **Log in** tab.

3. Enter your Product Key: `jknd-3tgz-gfr9`

4. Click to accept the user license terms.

5. For new users, click the **Register and Claim** button to create your account. For existing users, click the **Log in and Claim** button.

   You will be taken to the Training Hub and have access to the content for this book.

Duration of License   Access to your online content through the Total Seminars Training Hub will expire one year from the date the publisher declares the book out of print.

Your purchase of this McGraw Hill product, including its access code, through a retail store is subject to the refund policy of that store.

The Content is a copyrighted work of McGraw Hill, and McGraw Hill reserves all rights in and to the Content. The Work is © 2022 by McGraw Hill.

Restrictions on Transfer   The user is receiving only a limited right to use the Content for the user's own internal and personal use, dependent on purchase and continued ownership of this book. The user may not reproduce, forward, modify, create derivative works based upon, transmit, distribute, disseminate, sell, publish, or sublicense the Content or in any way commingle the Content with other third-party content without McGraw Hill's consent.

Limited Warranty   The McGraw Hill Content is provided on an "as is" basis. Neither McGraw Hill nor its licensors make any guarantees or warranties of any kind, either express or implied, including, but not limited to, implied warranties of merchantability or fitness for a particular purpose or use as to any McGraw Hill Content or the information therein or any warranties as to the accuracy, completeness, correctness, or results to be obtained from, accessing or using the McGraw Hill Content, or any material referenced in such Content or any information entered into licensee's product by users or other persons and/or any material available on or that can be accessed through the licensee's product (including via any hyperlink or otherwise) or as to non-infringement of third-party rights.

Any warranties of any kind, whether express or implied, are disclaimed. Any material or data obtained through use of the McGraw Hill Content is at your own discretion and risk and user understands that it will be solely responsible for any resulting damage to its computer system or loss of data.

Neither McGraw Hill nor its licensors shall be liable to any subscriber or to any user or anyone else for any inaccuracy, delay, interruption in service, error or omission, regardless of cause, or for any damage resulting therefrom.

In no event will McGraw Hill or its licensors be liable for any indirect, special or consequential damages, including but not limited to, lost time, lost money, lost profits or good will, whether in contract, tort, strict liability or otherwise, and whether or not such damages are foreseen or unforeseen with respect to any use of the McGraw Hill Content.

TotalTester Online

TotalTester Online provides you with a simulation of the PMP exam. Exams can be taken in Practice Mode or Exam Mode. Practice Mode provides an assistance window with hints, references to the book, explanations of the correct and incorrect answers, and the option to check your answer as you take the test. Exam Mode provides a simulation of the actual exam. The number of questions, the types of questions, and the time allowed are intended to be an accurate representation of the exam environment. The option to customize your quiz allows you to create custom exams from selected domains or chapters, and you can further customize the number of questions and time allowed.

To take a test, follow the instructions provided in the previous section to register and activate your Total Seminars Training Hub account. When you register, you will be taken to the Total Seminars Training Hub. From the Training Hub Home page, select **PMP All-in-One Exam Guide** from the Study drop-down menu at the top of the page, or from the list of Your Topics on the Home page, and then click the Total Tester link to launch the Total Tester. You can then select the option to customize your quiz and begin testing yourself in Practice Mode or Exam Mode. All exams provide an overall grade and a grade broken down by domain.

Other Book Resources

The following sections detail the other resources available with your book. You can access these items by selecting the Resources tab or by selecting **PMP All-in-One Exam Guide** from the Study drop-down menu at the top of the page or from the list of Your Topics on the Home page. The menu on the right side of the screen outlines all of the available resources.

Video Training from the Author

Video MP4 clips from the author of this book provide detailed examples of key certification topics in audio/video format. You can access these videos by navigating to the Resources tab and selecting **Videos for PMP All-in-One Exam Guide**.

Downloadable Content

The Resources tab also includes links to download additional content that accompanies this book. The downloadable content for this book includes worksheets for time value of money, earned value, and a float exercise; a printable copy of the trifold memory card included in the print book; and an Exam Scores spreadsheet for the end-of-chapter quizzes.

Technical Support

For questions regarding the TotalTester or operation of the Training Hub, visit **www.totalsem.com** or e-mail **support@totalsem.com**.

For questions regarding book content, visit **www.mheducation.com/customerservice**.

8/80 Rule   A planning heuristic for creating the WBS. This rule states that the work package in a WBS must take no more than 80 hours of labor and no fewer than 8 hours of labor to create.

A Guide to the Project Management Body of Knowledge (PMBOK Guide)   The PMI publication that defines widely accepted project management practices. The PMP exam is largely based upon this book.

abusive manner   Treating others with conduct that may result in harm, fear, humiliation, manipulation, or exploitation. For example, berating a project team member in front of the team because she has taken longer than expected to complete a project assignment may be considered humiliation.

acceptance   A risk response appropriate for both positive and negative risks, but often used for smaller risks within a project.

acceptance test-driven development   Testing approach that considers the perspective of the customers, developers, and testers. The test is written before the coding, and then the developers create code to pass the known test.

acknowledgment   The receiver signals that the message has been received. An acknowledgment shows receipt of the message, but not necessarily agreement with the message.

active listening   A communication method in which the message receiver restates what's been said, asks questions, and prompts for clarity to fully understand and confirm the message; this provides an opportunity for the sender to clarify the message if needed.

active observation   The project manager observes and interacts with the worker to ask questions and understand each step of the work being completed. In some instances, the observer could serve as an assistant in doing the work.

active problem-solving   A form of problem-solving that begins with problem definition. Problem definition is the ability to discern between the cause and effect of the problem. Root-cause analysis looks beyond the immediate symptoms to the cause of the symptoms, which then affords opportunities for solutions.

activity list   The primary output of breaking down the WBS work packages.

activity network diagram   Diagrams, such as the project network diagram, that show the flow of the project work.

actual cost (AC)   The actual amount of monies the project has spent to date.

adaptive life cycle   The adaptive life cycle first creates a project scope for the project, and then the project may utilize an iterative or incremental approach to create deliverables. Adaptive life cycles are commonly called change-driven life cycles as the project scope, though approved, is likely to change as the development team creates deliverables.

adjourning   The last of the five stages of the Tuckman ladder. Once the project is done, either the team moves on to other assignments as a unit or the project team is disbanded and individual team members go on to other work.

affinity diagram   A diagram that breaks down ideas, solutions, causes, and project components and groups them with other similar ideas and components for further analysis.

affinity estimating   When user stories are sized in relation to the size of other user stories in the product backlog.

agile charter   Agile charters authorize the project to exist in the organization. Agile charters frame out the high-level goals of the project and acknowledge that change is expected and welcome in the project.

Agile Manifesto   Created in 2001, this document describes the aspirations of agile project management. The Agile Manifesto describes the value of individuals and interactions over processes and tools, working software over comprehensive documentation, customer collaboration over negotiation, and responding to change over following a plan.

agile project management   A flexible approach to project management that relies on iterations of project work to create value in product deliverables for the project customers. Agile is change-driven, and work is based on a prioritized product backlog. Agile projects are knowledge work projects, such as software development.

agile risk   A negative event or condition that can affect the project's value.

alternative analysis   The identification of more than one solution. Consider roles, materials, tools, and approaches to the project work.

alternative dispute resolution   When an issue or claim must be settled before the contract can be closed, the parties involved in the issue or claim will try to reach a settlement through mediation or arbitration.

alternatives generation   A scope definition process of finding alternative solutions for the project customer while considering the customer's satisfaction, the cost of the solution, and how the customer may use the product in operations.

ambiguity risks   Risks that have an uncertain, unclear nature, such as new laws or regulations, marketplace conditions, and other risks that are nearly impossible to predict.

analogous estimating   A somewhat unreliable estimating approach that relies on historical information to predict what current activity durations should be. Analogous estimating is more reliable, however, than team-member recollections. Analogous estimating is also known as top-down estimating and is a form of expert judgment.

application areas The areas of expertise, industry, or function in which a project is centered. Examples of application areas include architecture, IT, healthcare, and manufacturing.

assumptions log An assumption is something that is believed to be true or false, but it has not yet been proven to be true or false. Assumptions that prove wrong can become risks for the project. All identified project assumptions are recorded in the assumptions log for testing and analysis, and the outcomes are recorded.

Atwood's duck Purposefully creating something customers will want removed, called the duck, to satisfy the customers' desire to persistently change a feature during the product review.

autocratic A decision method in which only one individual makes decisions for the group.

avoidance A risk response to avoid the risk.

avoiding power The project manager refuses to act, get involved, or make decisions.

balanced matrix structure An organizational structure in which organizational resources are pooled into one project team, but the functional managers and the project managers share the project power.

behavior-driven development Based on acceptance test–driven development but uses the Five Whys approach to really understand why a feature is to be included in the product.

benchmarking The process of comparing two similar entities to measure their relative performance.

benefit/cost ratio (BCR) models An example of a benefits comparison model that examines the benefit-to-cost ratio.

bicycle shedding Focusing on the bicycle shed materials rather than the construction of the nuclear power plant. The idea is from the law of triviality, where too much time is spent on the trivial, rather than focusing on what's important.

bid A document the seller provides to the buyer. Price is the determining factor in the decision-making process.

bidder conference A meeting of all the project's potential vendors to clarify the contract statement of work and the details of the contracted work.

bottom-up estimating The most accurate time-and-cost estimating approach a project manager can use. This estimating approach starts at "the bottom" of the project and considers every activity, its predecessor and successor activities, and the exact amount of resources needed to complete each activity. Bottom-up estimating accounts for each component of the WBS and arrives at a sum for the project. It is completed with the project team and can be one of the most time-consuming and reliable methods used to predict project costs.

brain writing   A brainstorming approach in which the topic is introduced and then everyone writes down their ideas. After a time period, the ideas are openly shared with the other participants. This approach can be used with collecting requirements, stakeholder identification, and other project activities.

brain-netting   A brainstorming approach that utilizes web tools to enable virtual teams to brainstorm and collaborate on ideas.

brainstorming   An approach that encourages participants to generate as many ideas as possible about the project requirements. It is also a common approach used to identify risks and is usually completed by a project team with subject matter experts. No idea is judged or dismissed during the brainstorming session.

budget estimate   An estimate that is somewhat broad and is used early in the planning processes as well as in top-down estimates. The range of variance for the estimate can be from –10 percent to +25 percent.

burndown chart   A chart that shows the number of user story points in the product backlog in relation to how many user stories the team is able to create in each iteration. As more iterations happen and the team completes the user stories, a downward trending line shows fewer and fewer user stories remaining in the backlog, and this reveals a trend for velocity and expectations about when the project can realistically complete all of the user stories.

burnup chart   Similar to a burndown chart, a burnup chart also shows the amount of user story points in the product backlog in relation to how many user stories the team is able to create in each iteration. As more iterations happen and the team completes the user stories, an upward trending line shows the accumulation of user stories accomplished and the remaining story points in the backlog. This chart also reveals a trend for velocity and expectations about when the project can realistically complete all of the user stories.

business risks   Risks that may have negative or positive outcomes. Examples include using a less experienced worker to complete a task, allowing phases or activities to overlap, or forgoing the expense of formal training for on-the-job education.

business value   A quantifiable return on investment. The return can be tangible, such as equipment, money, or market share. The return can also be intangible, such as brand recognition, trademarks, and reputation.

cardinal scales   A ranking approach to identify the probability and impact by using a numerical value, from .01 (very low) to 1.0 (certain).

cause-and-effect diagrams   Diagrams that show the relationship between variables within a process and how those relationships may contribute to inadequate quality. The diagrams can help organize both the process and the team opinions, as well as generate discussion on finding a solution to ensure quality.

caves and commons Caves are small nooks used for quiet, focused work by the project team members such as private conversations, phone calls, and deep thinking. Commons are the open workspaces for face-to-face communication and transparency among the project team.

change control board (CCB) A committee that evaluates the worthiness of a proposed change and either approves or rejects the change.

change control system (CCS) A system that communicates the process for controlling changes to the project deliverables. This system works with the configuration management system and seeks to control and document proposals to change the project's product. The CCS is documented in the scope management plan.

change log A log in which all changes that enter into a project are recorded. The characteristics of the change, such as the schedule, cost, risk, and scope details, are also recorded.

change management plan A subsidiary plan that details the project procedures for entertaining change requests: how change requests are managed, documented, approved, or declined.

charismatic leadership The leader is motivating, has high energy, and inspires the team through strong convictions about what's possible and what the team can achieve. Positive thinking and a can-do mentality are characteristics of a charismatic leader.

checklist A list of items to complete in a particular order. This tool can be utilized in quality management, risk identification, and project execution.

choice of media The best modality to use when communicating that is relevant to the information being communicated.

claims Disagreements between the buyer and the seller, usually centering on a change, who did the change, and even whether a change has occurred. Claims are also called disputes and appeals and are monitored and controlled through the project in accordance with the contract terms.

closure processes The final group of processes in the project management life cycle in which the project phase or project is closed. This is where project documentation is archived and project contracts are also closed.

code of accounts A numbering system for each item in the WBS. The PMBOK Guide is a good example of a code of accounts, as each chapter and its subheadings follow a logical numbering scheme. For example, PMBOK 5.3.3.2 identifies an exact paragraph in the PMBOK Guide.

coding standards An agreed-upon approach to how the code will be built, the naming system for the coding, and other standards for the code. This is always used in an XP project.

collaborate/problem-solving   This approach confronts the problem head-on and is the preferred method of conflict resolution. Multiple viewpoints and perspectives contribute to the solution.

collective bargaining agreement constraints   Contracts and agreements with unions or other employee groups may serve as constraints on the project.

collective code ownership   An XP principle that everyone owns and is responsible for the code the developers are creating. Anyone can edit the code in the project at any given time in the project.

commercial database   A cost-estimating approach that uses a database, typically software-driven, to create the cost estimate for a project.

commitment point   When a worker selects a card in Kanban and moves it into the workflow, they are committed to finishing the work.

communication assumptions   Any communication issue that the project management team believes to be true but hasn't proven to be true. For example, the project management team may assume that all of the project team members can be reached via cell phone, but actually some parts of the world, as of this writing, don't have cell signals.

communication barrier   Anything that prohibits communication from occurring.

communication channels formula   A formula that reveals the total number of communication channels within a project: $N(N - 1)/2$, where N represents the number of identified stakeholders.

communication constraints   Anything that limits the project management team's options when it comes to communication. Communication constraints such as geographical locales, incompatible communications software, and even limited communications technology can affect the project team.

communications management plan   A project management subsidiary plan that defines the stakeholders who need specific information, the person who will supply the information, the schedule for the information to be supplied, and the approved modality to provide the information.

competency   This attribute defines what talents, skills, and capabilities are needed to complete the project work.

compromising   This approach requires that both parties give up something; it is considered a lose–lose approach.

configuration identification   This includes the labeling of the components, how changes are made to the product, and the accountability of the changes.

configuration management plan   A subsidiary plan that is an input to the control scope process. It defines how changes to the features and functions of the project deliverable—the product scope—may enter the project.

configuration management system A system that defines how stakeholders are allowed to submit change requests, the conditions for approving a change request, and how approved change requests are validated in the project scope. Configuration management also documents the characteristics and functions of the project's products and any changes to a product's characteristics.

configuration status accounting The organization of the product materials, details, and prior product documentation.

configuration verification and auditing The scope verification and completeness auditing of project or phase deliverables to ensure that they are in alignment with the project plan.

conflict of interest A situation in which a project manager may have two competing duties of loyalty. For example, purchasing software from a relative may benefit the relative, but it may do harm to the performing organization.

context diagram A diagram that shows the relationship between elements in an environment. For example, a context diagram would illustrate the networks, servers, workstations, and people that interact with these elements of the environment.

contingency reserve A contingency allowance to account for overruns in costs. Contingency reserves are used at the project manager's discretion and with management's approval to counteract cost overruns for scheduled activities and risk events.

contract A formal agreement between the buyer and the seller. Contracts can be oral or written—though written is preferred.

contract change control system Defines the procedures for how a contract may be changed. The process for changing the contract includes the forms; documented communications; tracking; conditions within the project, business, or marketplace that justify the needed change; dispute resolution procedures; and the procedures for getting the changes approved within the performing organization.

contract closure The formal verification of the contract completeness by the vendor and the performing organization.

contract statement of work (SOW also CSOW) A document that requires that the seller fully describe the work to be completed and/or the product to be supplied. The SOW becomes part of the contract between the buyer and the seller.

control account A WBS entry that considers the time, cost, and scope measurements for that deliverable within the WBS. The estimated performance is compared against the actual performance to measure overall performance for the deliverables within that control account. The specifics of a control account are documented in a control account plan.

control chart A chart used to show the stability of a process, such as lead time or cycle time, in the project. It can be used in agile projects to show instability of resolving customer requests and variations from the mean and control limits.

control quality   An inspection-driven process that measures work results to confirm that the project is meeting the relevant quality standards.

control threshold   A predetermined range of acceptable variances, such as +/−10 percent off schedule. Should the variance exceed the threshold, project control processes and corrected actions will be enacted.

cost aggregation   Costs are parallel to each WBS work package. The costs of each work package are aggregated to their corresponding control accounts. Each control account is then aggregated to the sum of the project costs.

cost baseline   A time-lapse exposure of when the project monies are to be spent in relation to cumulative values of the work completed in the project. The cost baseline shows the aggregated costs of all the work packages within the work breakdown structure (WBS).

cost budgeting   The cost aggregation achieved by assigning specific dollar amounts for each of the scheduled activities or, more likely, for each of the work packages in the WBS. Cost budgeting applies the cost estimates over time.

cost change control system   A system that examines any changes associated with scope changes, the cost of materials, and the cost of any other resources, and the associated impact on the overall project cost.

cost management plan   A plan that details how the project costs will be planned for, estimated, budgeted, and then monitored and controlled.

cost of conformance to quality   The cost associated with the monies spent to attain the expected level of quality. It is also known as the cost of quality.

cost of nonconformance to quality   The cost associated with not satisfying quality expectations. This is also known as the cost of poor quality.

cost of poor quality   The monies spent to recover from not adhering to the expected level of quality. Examples may include rework, defect repair, loss of life or limb because safety precautions were not taken, loss of sales, and loss of customers. This is also known as the cost of nonconformance to quality.

cost of quality   The monies spent to attain the expected level of quality within a project. Examples include training, testing, and safety precautions.

cost performance index (CPI)   A measure of the project based on its financial performance. The formula is CPI = EV/AC.

cost plus award fee contract   A contract that pays the vendor all costs for the project, but also includes a buyer-determined award fee for the project work.

cost plus fixed fee contract   A contract that requires the buyer to pay for the cost of the goods and services procured plus a fixed fee for the contracted work. The buyer assumes the risk of a cost overrun.

cost plus incentive fee   A contract type that requires the buyer to pay a cost for the procured work, plus an incentive fee, or a bonus, for the work if terms and conditions are met.

cost plus percentage of costs   A contract that requires the buyer to pay for the costs of the goods and services procured plus a percentage of the costs. The buyer assumes all of the risks for cost overruns.

cost variance (CV)   The difference of the earned value amount and the cumulative actual costs of the project. The formula is $CV = EV - AC$.

cost-benefits analysis   A process to study the trade-offs between costs and the benefits realized from those costs.

crashing   A schedule compression approach that adds more resources to activities on the critical path to complete the project earlier. When crashing a project, costs are added because the associated labor and sometimes resources (such as faster equipment) cause costs to increase.

critical path   The path in the project network diagram that cannot be delayed, or the project completion date will be late. There can be more than one critical path. Activities in the critical path have no float.

cross-functional teams   The team includes generalizing specialists—designers, developers, testers, and other roles—that are getting the work done and serving in more than one role that contributes to the final product of the project. The goal is to remove the silo mentality where each person does one task only.

Crystal   Agile project management family of practices that are color coded to reflect their risk to human life, size of the project team, and risk within the project.

Crystal clear   From the Crystal project management approach and used with eight or fewer team members.

Crystal orange   From the Crystal project management approach and used with 20 to 50 team members.

Crystal red   From the Crystal project management approach and used with 50 to 100 team members.

Crystal yellow   From the Crystal project management approach and used with 10 to 20 team members.

cultural and social environment   Defines how a project affects people and how those people may affect the project. Cultural and social environments include the economic, educational, ethical, religious, demographic, and ethnic composition of the people affected by the project.

cultural norms   Describe the culture and the styles of an organization, such as work ethics, hours, view of authority, and shared values; these can affect how the project is managed.

cumulative flow diagram   A stacked chart that shows the total number of items in each phase of the project, such as the backlog, development, testing, and release. This chart can be used to identify too many items in WIP and bottlenecks in the project.

cycle time   The total duration of time the developers worked on a feature for the project customer.

daily scrum   Daily 15-minute meeting where each team member explains what they've accomplished since the last meeting, what they're accomplishing today, and if there are any impediments for the scrum master to resolve. The participants typically stand in the meeting, and this meeting is sometimes called a daily stand-up.

daily scrum duration   The daily scrum meeting should last up to 15 minutes.

data precision   The consideration of the risk ranking scores that takes into account any bias, the accuracy of the data submitted, and the reliability of the nature of the data submitted.

decision tree   A method to determine which of two or more decisions is the best one. The model examines the costs and benefits of each decision's outcome and weighs the probability of success for each of the decisions.

decoder   The device, such as a fax machine, that decodes a message as it is being received.

defect cycle time   The amount of time between when a defect was discovered and when it was fixed. The longer the defect time, typically the more expensive the defect will be.

defect rate   The total number of escaped defects that make it all the way to the customer.

Definition of Done (DoD)   The qualifications that are required and defined for a product, user story, or increment of a product to be considered done. It's important to define what constitutes "done" for each item in the product backlog, such as passing a specific test.

definitive estimate   One of the most accurate estimate types, this is used late in the planning processes and is associated with bottom-up estimating. You need the WBS to create the definitive estimate. The range of variance for the estimate can be from –5 percent to +10 percent.

deliverable   A product, service, or result created by a project. Projects can have multiple deliverables.

delivery point   The final column in a Kanban board that represents the completion of a work item through the workflow.

Delphi Technique   An anonymous method of querying experts about foreseeable risks within a project, phase, or component of a project. The results of the survey are analyzed by a third party, organized, and then circulated to the experts. There can be several rounds of anonymous discussion with the Delphi Technique, without fear of backlash or offending other participants in the process. The goal is to gain consensus on project risks within the project.

design of experiments   An approach that relies on statistical scenarios to determine what variables within a project will result in the best outcome.

development team   Small, cross-functional group in a Scrum project that is responsible for selecting the amount of prioritized user stories from the product backlog to take into a sprint. The development team is responsible for building, testing, and creating the potentially shippable product.

direct costs   Costs incurred by the project in order for the project to exist and cannot be shared among projects. Examples include the equipment needed to complete the project work, salaries of the project team, and other expenses tied directly to the project's existence.

discretionary dependencies   These dependencies are the preferred order of activities. Project managers should use these relationships at their discretion and document the logic behind the decision. Discretionary dependencies enable activities to happen in a preferred order because of best practices, conditions unique to the project work, or external events. Also known as preferential or soft logic.

Dreyfus Model of Adult Skill Acquisition   Describes the five stages people move through as they perfect the skill. The five components are novice, advanced beginner, competent, proficient, and expert.

duty of loyalty   A project manager's responsibility to be loyal to another person, organization, or vendor. For example, a project manager has a duty of loyalty to promote the best interests of their employer.

Dynamic Systems Development Method (DSDM)   Evolved in 1994 from developers using the Rapid Application Development (RAD) project management approach. DSDM provide more structure than RAD, utilizes iterations, and is a great approach when working with vendors as part of your agile project. DSDM also offers a unique approach as it can be blended with scrum, PRINCE2, and other project management approaches.

early finish   The earliest a project activity can finish. Used in the forward pass procedure to discover the critical path and the project float.

early start   The earliest a project activity can begin. Used in the forward pass procedure to discover the critical path and the project float.

earned value (EV)   The physical work completed to date and the authorized budget for that work. It is the percentage of the BAC that represents the actual work completed in the project.

effective listening   The receiver is involved in the listening experience by paying attention to visual cues from the speaker and paralingual characteristics and by asking relevant questions.

emergent leadership   Leadership doesn't have to come from the top down, but anyone on the agile team can emerge as a leader.

encoder   The device, such as a fax machine, that encodes the message being sent.

enhancing   A risk response that attempts to enhance the conditions to ensure that a positive risk event will likely happen.

enterprise environmental factors (EEFs)   Conditions that affect how the project manager may manage the project. Enterprise environmental factors come from within the project, such as a policy, or they may be external to the organization, such as a law or regulation.

escalating   A risk response that is appropriate for both positive and negative risk events that may be outside of the project manager's authority to act upon.

estimate at completion (EAC)   Forecasting formulas that predict the likely completed costs of the project based on current scenarios within the project.

estimate to complete (ETC)   An earned value management formula that predicts how much funding the project will require to be completed. Three variations of this formula are based on conditions the project may be experiencing.

expected monetary value (EMV)   The monetary value of a risk exposure based on the risk's probability and impact in the risk matrix. This approach is typically used in quantitative risk analysis because it quantifies the risk exposure.

expert power   The project manager has deep skills and experience in a discipline (for example, years of working in IT helps an IT project manager better manage IT projects).

explicit knowledge   Easily communicated knowledge that can be quickly and easily expressed through conversations, documentation, figures, or numbers.

exploit   A risk response that takes advantage of the positive risks within a project.

exploratory testing   An unstructured approach that requires the thinker to think and explore the software independently of a script or automated testing software. Exploratory testing is also known as session-based testing, and each session lasts for 90 minutes and can be increased or reduced by 50 percent in duration.

external dependencies   Dependencies outside of the project's control. Examples include the delivery of equipment from a vendor, the deliverable of another project, or the decision of a committee, a lawsuit, or an expected new law.

external QA   Quality assurance provided to the external customers of the project.

external risks   Risks that are outside of the project, but directly affect it—for example, legal issues, labor issues, a shift in project priorities, or weather. "Force majeure" risks call for disaster recovery rather than project management. These are risks caused by earthquakes, tornadoes, floods, civil unrest, and other disasters.

Extreme Programming (XP)   Agile project management approach that uses iterations, pair programming, collective code ownership, and an XP coach to complete the user stories of the product backlog. XP also utilizes test-first programming, where tests are created and then the code is written to pass the recently created test.

fast tracking   A schedule compression method that changes the relationship of activities. With fast tracking, activities that would normally be done in sequence are allowed to be done in parallel or with some overlap. Fast tracking can be accomplished by changing the relation of activities from FS to SS or even FF or by adding lead time to downstream activities. However, fast tracking does add risk to the project.

FDD chief architect   Designs and models the system and leads planning with other developers.

FDD chief programmer   Assists the chief architect and development manager and may lead smaller development teams within the project.

FDD class owner   Works with the chief programmer and designs, codes, and tests the features of the system.

FDD development manager   Oversees the daily activity and coaches the development team.

FDD domain expert   A businessperson, like the product owner role in Scrum. This person understands the customers' needs and what they value.

FDD project manager   Oversees the project as a typical project manager.

Feature-Driven Development (FDD)   Agile approach that utilizes a product backlog to complete the project work but follows a more rigid approach to agile project management than other approaches.

feedback   The sender confirms that the receiver understands the message by directly asking for a response, questions for clarification, or other confirmation.

Fibonacci sequence   A sequence of numbers used for user story sizing estimation in agile estimating. The Fibonacci sequences consists of the numbers 1, 2, 3, 5, 8, 13, 21, …, where each number in the sequence is defined by adding the two numbers that precede it. For example, 1+2=3, and 2+3=5. To estimate story size, the team gives each user story up to 21 points—with 21 points being the largest story and 1 point being the smallest story.

finish-to-finish   An activity relationship type that requires the current activity to be finished before its successor can finish.

finish-to-start   An activity relationship type that requires the current activity to be finished before its successor can start.

fishbowl windows   The virtual team uses videoconferencing to ensure that all team members can view other team members and can communicate quickly, no matter where the other workers are located among all the virtual team members. Each team member has a "window" into the other team members as they work.

five levels of conflict   There are five levels of conflict that may increasingly call on the project management role to get involved in reminding the team to be respectful and to work together for the value in the project. The five levels are problem solving, disagreement, contest, crusade, and world war.

Five Whys   A root-cause analysis technique that asks why five times to fully understand the reason for including a feature in the product.

fixed costs   Costs that remain constant throughout the life of the project (such as the cost of rented equipment for the project, the cost of a consultant brought on to the project, and so on).

fixed-price contracts   Also known as firm fixed-price and lump-sum contracts, these agreements define a total price for the product the seller is to provide.

fixed-price incentive fee   A fixed-price contract with opportunities for bonuses for meeting goals on costs, schedule, and other objectives. These contracts usually have a price ceiling for costs and associated bonuses.

fixed-price with economic price adjustments   A fixed-price contract with a special allowance for price increases based on economic reasons such as inflation or the cost of raw materials.

flowchart   A diagram illustrating how components within a system are related. Flowcharts show the relationship between components and help the project team determine where quality issues or risks may be present so that the team can plan appropriate remedies.

focus groups   A moderator-led requirements collection method that elicits requirements from stakeholders.

follow-the-sun approach   For large projects with multiple teams working together in locations spread across multiple time zones, this approach enables the work to be passed on to the next team in workday increments from east to west.

force majeure   An "act of God" that may have a negative impact on the project. Examples include fire, hurricanes, tornadoes, and earthquakes.

forming   The first of the five stages of the Tuckman ladder, in which the project team meets and learns about their roles and responsibilities on the project. Little interaction among the project team happens in this stage as the team is learning about the project and project manager.

fragnet A representation of a project network diagram that is often used for outsourced portions of a project, repetitive work within a project, or a subproject. Also called a subnet.

free float The total time a single activity can be delayed without affecting the early start of its immediately following successor activities.

functional analysis The study of the functions within a system, project, or, what's more likely in the project scope statement, the product the project will be creating. Functional analysis studies the goals of the product, how the product will be used, and the expectations the customer has of the product once it leaves the project and moves into operations. Functional analysis may also consider the cost of the product in operations, which is known as life-cycle costing.

functional structure An organization that is divided into functions, where each employee has one clear functional manager. Each department acts independently of the other departments. A project manager in this structure has little to no power and may be called a project coordinator.

funding limit A feature of most projects, in which a budget is determined in relation to the project scope. The budget may include a qualifier, such as plus or minus 10 percent based on the type of cost estimate created.

funding limit reconciliation An organization's approach to managing cash flow against the project deliverables based on a schedule, milestone accomplishment, or data constraints.

future value A benefit comparison model used to determine a future value of money. The formula to calculate future value is $FV = PV(1 + I)n$, where PV is present value, I is the given interest rate, and n is the number of periods.

general management skills Include the application of accounting, procurement, sales and marketing, contracting, manufacturing, logistics, strategic planning, human resource management, standards and regulations, and information technology.

governance framework Describes the rules, policies, and procedures that people within an organization abide by. This framework addresses the organization, but it also addresses portfolios, programs, and projects. Regarding portfolios, programs, and projects, the governance framework addresses alignment with organizational vision, risk management, performance factors, and communications.

green zones and red zones Green zones are the favorable attributes of a high-performing team, such as welcoming feedback, being respectful, considering other people's opinions and perspective, and working together to get to the definition of done. Red zones are the negative aspects of a performing team, such as being secretive, having an all-or-nothing mindset, not being respectful, and not trusting teammates.

guilt-based power   The project manager can make the team and stakeholders feel guilty to gain compliance in the project.

halo effect   The tendency to judge a person based on seemingly related characteristics, though the characteristics are not, in fact, related.

hard logic   Logic that describes activities that must happen in a particular order. For example, the site must be excavated before the foundation can be built. The foundation must be in place before the framing can begin. Also known as a mandatory dependency.

Herzberg's Theory of Motivation   Frederick Herzberg's theory discusses the motivating agents and hygiene agents that affect a person's willingness to excel in his career.

hierarchical organizational chart   A chart showing the relationship between superior and subordinate employees, groups, disciplines, and even departments.

hybrid life cycle   A combination of predictive and adaptive life cycles. Depending on the organization and the discipline, the components of the project that are established will follow a predictive life cycle, while the project components that are not fully defined may follow the adaptive life-cycle approach.

hybrid projects   A project that combines aspects of predictive project management, such as detailed project management planning, and agile practices, such as the product backlog. Hybrid projects utilize strategies from predictive and agile project management.

hybrid structure   An organization that creates a blend of the functional, matrix, and project-oriented structures.

increment   A completed and functional portion of the product backlog that may, or may not be, released to the customers. Increments can be released at the end of iteration, after several iterations, or at the end of the project.

incremental life cycle   An adaptive approach where the processes and approaches to accomplish project work are repeated in each cycle to create continued increments of a product.

independent estimates   Estimates, often referred to as "should cost" estimates, that are created by the performing organization or outside experts to predict what the cost of the procured product should be.

indirect costs   Costs that are representative of more than one project (for example, utilities for the performing organization, access to a training room, project management software license, and so on). Indirect costs are expenses attributed to the cost of doing business such as utilizes, office space, and other overhead costs.

industrial work   Industrial work is typically centered on physical labor, and it's easy to see results and predict time and cost.

influence diagram   A diagram that charts out a decision problem. It identifies all the elements, variables, decisions, and objectives and also how each factor may influence another.

influence/impact grid Stakeholders are mapped on a grid based on their influence over the project in relation to their influence over the project execution.

information presentation tools A software package that enables the project management team to present the project's health through graphics, spreadsheets, and text. (Think of Microsoft Project.)

information radiator Typically a centralized, high-touch, low-tech tool to provide agile project transparency on the project work, burndown chart, WIP, defects, and other pertinent project information. The information radiator is often displayed on a wall for anyone to review at any time.

information retrieval system A system to store, archive, and access project information quickly and effectively.

informational power The project manager has power and control of the data gathering and distribution of information.

ingratiating power The project manager aims to gain favor with the project team and stakeholders through flattery.

integrated change control A process to consider and control the impact of a proposed change of the project's knowledge areas.

interactional leadership The leader is a hybrid of transactional, transformational, and charismatic leader characteristics. The interactional leader wants the team to act, is excited and inspired about the project work, yet still holds the team accountable for their results.

interactive communication The most common and most effective approach to communication, when two or more people exchange information actively. Examples are status meetings, ad hoc meetings, phone calls, and videoconferences.

internal dependencies Internal relationships to the project or the organization. For example, the project team must create the software as part of the project's deliverable before the software can be tested for quality control.

internal QA Quality assurance provided to management and the project team.

international and political environment The consideration of the local and international laws, languages, communication challenges, time zone differences, and other non-collocated issues that affect a project's ability to progress.

interpersonal skills The ability to interact, lead, motivate, and manage people.

interviews A requirements collection method used to elicit requirements from stakeholders in a one-on-one conversation.

inverted Iron Triangle of Project Management Predictive projects ideally have a fixed scope, while the cost and schedule for a project can be expanded. Agile projects invert this model and have fixed cost and schedule and allow the scope to be expanded. Lower priority items can be pushed out of the triangle because of lack of funds and/or time.

INVEST   An approach to write user stories using the acronym of INVEST. INVEST means the user story should be independent, negotiable, valuable, estimable, small, and testable.

invitation for bid (IFB)   From buyer to seller. Requests the seller to provide a price for the procured product or service.

Iron Triangle of Project Management   A theoretical model based on the characteristics of time, cost, and scope, which each constitute one side of the triangle. If any side of the Iron Triangle is not in balance with the other sides, the project will suffer. The Iron Triangle of Project Management is also known as the Triple Constraints of Project Management, as all projects are constrained by time, cost, and scope.

I-shaped and T-shaped people   I-shaped people have depth in a specific subject matter, but not much cross-functionality. T-shaped people are cross-functional roles; they have depth but can also collaborate and contribute in more than one area.

Ishikawa diagrams   Cause-and-effect diagrams, also called fishbone diagrams, that are used to find the root cause of factors that are causing risks within the project.

ISO   The International Organization for Standardization is an independent, nongovernmental international organization that sets standards and specifications for products, services, and systems to ensure quality, safety, and efficiency. The ISO is instrumental in facilitating international trade.

issue   A risk event that has occurred in the project.

issue log   A logbook of the issues the project team has identified and dates by which the issues must be resolved. Issues are points of contention, where some question of the project's direction needs to be resolved. All identified issues are documented in the issue log, along with an issue owner, a deadline to resolve the issue, and the outcome of the issue.

iteration   A timeboxed period of work. Scrum utilizes a two- to four-week iteration called a sprint. XP utilizes a one-week iteration.

iterative life cycle   An adaptive approach where the processes and approaches to accomplish project work are repeated in each cycle.

Kaizen   A component of Lean that asserts that small changes over time add up to big results. It focuses on small, incremental changes to improve the product, the workflow, and how the team operates.

Kanban   A framework to show the backlog of work items and the flow of the items through columns to the delivery point. Kanban aims to be transparent and to limit the WIP and is a pull system as work is pulled from the left into the workflow on the right.

Kanban Method   The Kanban Method visualizes project work on a Kanban board, which enables the team to see the progress of the work and pull the work through the flow. As new work items are needed, they are added to the "to-do" column in the board. Any team member who is available and competent can start a work task, and the task flows through the system and is documented on the Kanban board.

key stakeholder   Stakeholders who have the authority to make decisions regarding the project, such as managers, the project manager, program manager, and customers.

knowledge work   Sometimes called invisible work. This describes the work that is tough to see physical progress as the work takes place predominantly in the worker's brain.

known unknown   An event that will likely happen within the project, but when it will happen and to what degree is unknown. These events, such as delays, are usually risk-related.

lag time   Positive time that moves two or more activities further apart.

lagging metrics   Metrics based on things that have already happened in the project, such as the defect rate or team velocity.

laissez-faire leadership   The leader takes a hands-off approach to the project. This means the project team makes decisions, takes initiative in the actions, and creates goals. While this approach can provide autonomy, it can make the leader appear absent when it comes to project decisions.

late finish   The latest a project activity can finish. Used in the backward pass procedure to discover the critical path and the project float.

late start   The latest a project activity can begin. Used in the backward pass procedure to discover the critical path and the project float.

law of triviality   From Parkinson's spoof on management, the time spent on any item of the agenda will be in inverse proportion to the sum of money involved.

lead time   In a predictive project, lead time is used when scheduling activities. Lead time is negative time that allows two or more activities to overlap where ordinarily these activities would be sequential. In an agile project, lead time describes the total duration a feature took from the moment it was requested by the customer until the developers created the feature for the customer.

leadership   Aligning, motivating, and inspiring the project team members to do the right thing, build trust, think creatively, and challenge the status quo.

leading metrics   Metrics used to predict future trends in the project.

leading stakeholder status   Part of stakeholder analysis classification. A leading stakeholder is aware of your project, wants your project to be successful, and is working to make certain the project is a success.

Lean   Originally used in manufacturing environments, Lean has been adapted to IT environments. Lean teams work through three phases—building, measuring, and learning—to keep work results aligned with customer expectations. Lean aims to reduce waste and boost productivity.

Lean product development   Agile approach based on Toyota's manufacturing approach in the 1940s. Lean aims to utilize fewer resources, less cost, reduce work in progress, and finish faster than traditional project management approaches.

learning curve   An approach that assumes the cost per unit decreases the more units workers complete, because workers learn as they complete the required work.

lessons learned   Documentation of what did and did not work in the project implementation. Lessons learned documentation is created throughout the project by the entire project team. When lessons learned sessions are completed, they're available to be used and applied by the entire organization. They become part of the organizational process assets.

letter contract   A stopgap contract that enables the vendor to begin working on the project immediately. It is often used as a stopgap solution.

letter of intent   Not a contract, but a letter stating that the buyer is intending to create a contractual relationship with the seller.

low-priority risk watch list   A list of low-priority risks that are identified for periodic monitoring.

low-tech and high-touch   Solutions that are easy to use and don't rely on complex technology or require special skills; examples include whiteboards, sticky notes, and posters. Low-tech, high-touch solutions eliminate the learning curve from the more technical solutions for an agile team.

majority   A group decision method in which more than 50 percent of the group must be in agreement.

make-or-buy decision   A process in which the project management team determines the cost effectiveness, benefits, and feasibility of making a product or buying it from a vendor.

management   Utilizing positional power to maintain, administrate, control, and focus on getting things done without challenging the status quo of the project and organization.

management reserve   A percentage of the project duration to combat Parkinson's Law. When project activities become late, their lateness is subtracted from the management reserve.

mandatory dependencies   Relationships that establish the natural order of activities. For example, you can't begin building your house until your foundation is in place. These relationships are called hard logic.

Maslow's Hierarchy of Needs   Abraham Maslow's theory posits the five needs all humans have and work toward: physiological, safety, love, esteem, and self-actualization.

mathematical model   A project selection method to determine the likelihood of success. These models include linear programming, nonlinear programming, dynamic programming, integer programming, and multiobjective programming.

matrix diagram   A data analysis table that shows the strengths between variables and relationships in a matrix.

McClelland's Theory of Needs   A theory developed by David McClelland that states that our needs are acquired and developed by our experiences over time. All people are, according to this theory, driven by one of three needs: achievement, affiliation, or power.

McGregor's Theory of X and Y   Douglas McGregor's theory states that management views workers in the Y category as competent and self-led and workers in the X category as incompetent and needing to be micromanaged.

media selection   Based on the audience and the message being sent, the media should be in alignment with the message.

medium   The device or technology that transports a message.

meeting management   A form of communication that involves how the meeting is led, managed, and controlled to influence the message being delivered. Agendas, minutes, and order are mandatory for effective communications within a meeting.

milestone   A significant point or event in the project's progress that represents the completion of certain aspects of the project. Projects usually create milestones as the result of completing phases within the project.

milestone list   A list that details the project milestones and their attributes. It is used for several areas of project planning but also helps determine how quickly the project may be achieving its objectives.

mind mapping   An approach that maps ideas to show the relationship among requirements and the differences between requirements. The map can be reviewed to identify new solutions or to rank the identified requirements.

mitigation   A risk response effort to reduce the probability and/or impact of an identified risk in the project.

Monte Carlo analysis   A project simulation approach named after the world-famous gambling district in Monaco. The simulation, performed with a computer software program, predicts how scenarios may work out, given any number of variables. The process doesn't actually churn out a specific answer, but a range of possible answers. When Monte Carlo analysis is applied to a schedule, it can examine, for example, the optimistic completion date, the pessimistic completion date, and the most likely completion date for each activity in the project and then predict a mean for the project schedule.

multicriteria decision analysis   A method to rate potential project team members based on criteria such as education, experience, skills, knowledge, and more.

multidivisional structure   An organizational structure that includes duplication of efforts within the organization, but not within each department or division of the organization. The project manager has little authority in this structure, and the functional manager controls the project budget.

murder board A committee that asks every conceivable negative question about a proposed project to expose the project's strengths and weaknesses and to kill the project if it's deemed unworthy of the organization's commitment. Also known as a project steering committee or project selection committee.

negative stakeholder status Part of stakeholder analysis classification. A negative stakeholder does not want the project to exist and is opposed to the project.

net present value Evaluates the monies returned on a project for each period the project lasts.

neutral stakeholder status Part of stakeholder analysis classification. A neutral stakeholder is aware of your project and is not concerned about whether the project succeeds or fails.

noise Anything that interferes with or disrupts a message.

nominal group technique A technique similar to brainstorming, in which participants are encouraged to generate as many ideas as possible, but the suggested ideas are ranked by a voting process.

nonverbal communication Facial expressions, hand gestures, and body language that serve as nonverbal cues that contribute to a message. Approximately 55 percent of communication is nonverbal.

norming One of the five stages of the Tuckman ladder, in which project team members go about getting the project work, begin to rely on one another, and generally complete their project assignments.

oligopoly A market condition in which the market is so tight that the actions of one vendor affect the actions of all the others.

opportunity cost The total cost of the opportunity that is refused to realize an opposing opportunity.

ordinal scales A ranking approach that identifies and ranks the risks from very high to very unlikely or to some other value.

organic or simple structure Describes a loosely organized business or organization, likely with no formal departments, where people work alongside one another regardless of their roles and titles. The project manager probably has little control over the project resources and may not be called a project manager.

organization chart A traditional chart that depicts how the organization is structured by department and disciplines. This chart is sometimes called the organizational breakdown structure (OBS) and is arranged by departments, units, or teams.

organizational knowledge repositories The databases, files, and historical information that you can use to help you plan and manage your projects better. This organizational process asset is created internally to your organization through the ongoing work of operations and other projects.

organizational process assets (OPAs)   Organizational processes, policies, procedures, and items from a corporate knowledge base. Organizational process assets are grouped into two categories to consider: processes, policies, and procedures; and organizational knowledge bases.

organizational risks   The performing organization can contribute to the project's risks through unreasonable cost, time, and scope expectations; poor project prioritization; inadequate funding or the disruption of funding; and competition with other projects for internal resources.

organizational system   A system in which multiple components are used to create things that the individual components could not create if they worked alone. The structure of the organization and the governance framework create constraints that affect how the project manager makes decisions within the project. The organizational system directly affects how the project manager utilizes her power, influence, leadership, and even political capital, to get things done in the environment.

osmotic communication   The communication that happens just by being present or near the conversation.

Ouchi's Theory Z   William Ouchi's theory is based on the Japanese participative management style. His theory states that workers are motivated by a sense of commitment, opportunity, and advancement.

paralingual communication   The pitch, tone, and inflections in the sender's voice that affects the message being sent.

parallel development   Two or more teams working in unison to develop the code; this can create risks in agile projects.

parametric estimate   A quantitatively based duration estimate that uses mathematical formulas to predict how long an activity will take based on the quantities of work to be completed or to predict what costs will be needed for a project (for example, cost per hour and cost per unit). It can include variables and points based on conditions.

Pareto diagram   A histogram that illustrates and ranks categories of failure within a project.

Parkinson's Law   A theory that work expands so as to fill the time available for its completion. It is considered with time estimating, because bloated or padded activity estimates will fill the amount of time allotted to the activity.

passive observation   The project manager observes a worker and records information about the work being completed without interrupting the process; sometimes called the invisible observer.

payback period   An estimate to predict how long it will take a project to pay back an organization for the project's investment of capital.

performance report   A report that depicts how well a project is performing. Often, the performance report is based on earned value management and may include cost or schedule variance reports.

performing   One of the five stages of the Tuckman ladder. If a project team can reach the performing stage of team development, they trust one another and work well together, and issues and problems are resolved quickly and effectively.

personal or charismatic power   The project manager has a warm personality that others like.

PESTLE   A prompt list used for risk identification. PESTLE examines risks in the political, economic, social, technological, legal, and environmental domains.

physical environment   The physical structure and surroundings that affect a project's work.

planned value (PV)   The work scheduled and the budget authorized to accomplish that work. It is the percentage of the BAC that reflects where the project should be at a particular point in time.

planning game   An XP approach to treat the work as a game to avoid an emotional attachment to decisions and work in the project.

planning package   A WBS entry located below a control account and above the work packages. A planning package signifies that more planning needs to be completed for this specific deliverable.

planning poker   A story-sizing method in which each person decides on the size of the user story and then everyone reveals their sizing in unison. This encourages the team to converse to reach a consensus on the user story sizing for each item in the product backlog.

plurality   A group-decision method in which the largest block of voters makes the decision, even if they don't represent more than 50 percent of the group. (Consider three or four factions of stakeholders for three or more different choices, none of which receives more than 50 percent of the vote.)

PMI member   Anyone, whether certified as a project manager or not, who has joined the Project Management Institute.

PMI Talent Triangle   Defines three areas of PDUs for PMI-certified professionals to maintain their certification: technical project management, leadership, and strategic and business management.

positional power   The project manager's power is a result of the position she has as the project manager. This is also known as formal, authoritative, and legitimate power.

positive stakeholder status   Part of stakeholder analysis classification. This stakeholder sees the benefits of the project and is in favor of the change the project is to bring about.

potentially shippable product   The work product that has met the definition of "done" and could be shippable. The potentially shippable product doesn't have to be released, but it could be if the product owner determines to do so.

practitioner   A person who is serving in the capacity of a project manager or contributing to the management of a project, portfolio of projects, or program. For example, a program manager is considered to be a project practitioner under this definition.

precedence diagramming method   A network diagram that shows activities in nodes and the relationship between each activity. Predecessors come before the current activity, and successors come after the current activity.

predictive project management   A traditional project management approach that plans and predicts everything that is to occur within the project. Predictive project management is based upon a clearly defined project scope and project plan. Predictive is sometimes called plan-driven or described as a waterfall approach, and it is resistant to change.

present value   A benefit comparison model to determine the present value of a future amount of money. The formula to calculate present value is $PV = FV \div (1 + I)n$, where FV is future value, I is the given interest rate, and n is the number of periods.

presentation   In formal presentations, the presenter's oral and body language, visual aids, and handouts all influence the message being delivered.

pressure-based power   The project manager can restrict choices to get the project team to perform the project work.

privity   The confidential and secret nature of the contractual relationship between the buyer and the seller.

probability and impact matrix   A matrix that ranks the probability of a risk event occurring and its impact on the project if the event does happen; used in qualitative and quantitative risk analyses.

process groups   A collection of related processes in project management. There are five process groups and 49 project management processes. The five process groups are initiating, planning, executing, monitoring and controlling, and closing.

procurement management plan   A project management subsidiary plan that documents the decisions made in the procurement planning processes. The procurement plan defines how the project will acquire goods and services.

procurement planning   A process to identify which parts of the project warrant procurement from a vendor by the buyer.

product acceptance criteria   A project scope statement component that works with the project requirements, but focuses specifically on the product and what the conditions and processes are for formal acceptance of the product.

product backlog   An agile document, typically used in Scrum, that lists all of the known requirements for the project, often called user stories. These requirements are maintained and prioritized by the product owner. The product backlog prioritizes requirements from most important to least important. The development team pulls the prioritized items from the backlog into their sprint, which is a work iteration. The product backlog is maintained by the product owner.

product breakdown   A scope definition technique that breaks down a product into a hierarchical structure, much like a WBS breaks down a project scope.

product owner   Scrum role that is responsible for building, prioritizing, and maintaining the features of the product backlog; writing the user stories; and being the liaison between the developers and the project customers.

product roadmap   A map of how the project will move from start to finish with intermittent deliverables to the stakeholders. It answers what conditions must be met to allow the product owner to do a release, what the components of a release are, and the result of the project. The roadmap helps predict when potentially shippable products can be released.

product scope   The attributes and characteristics of the deliverables the project is creating. It defines the features and functions that characterize the product.

product scope description   A narrative description of what the project is creating as a deliverable for the project customer.

product vision   Defines exactly what the end result of the project should create in terms of functionality and value for the customers.

professional development units (PDUs)   Credit for education and project management–based experiences that are earned after the PMP to maintain the PMP certification. PMPs are required to earn 60 PDUs per three-year certification cycle. Of the 60 PDUs, a minimum of 35 hours must come from educational opportunities.

profile analysis meeting   An analysis meeting to examine and document the roles in the project. The role's interests, concerns, influence, project knowledge, and attitude are documented.

program   A collection of related projects working in unison toward a common deliverable.

progressive elaboration   The process of gathering project details. This process uses deductive reasoning, logic, and a series of information-gathering techniques to identify details about a project, product, or solution.

project   A temporary endeavor to create a unique product, service, or result. The end result of a project is called a deliverable.

project assumptions   A factor in the project planning process that is held to be true but not proven to be true.

project benefits management plan   A document created and maintained by the project sponsor and the project manager. The plan defines what benefits the project will create, when the benefits will be realized, how the benefits will be measured, and how the benefits will be sustained.

project boundary   States what is included in the project and what's excluded from the project. This helps to eliminate assumptions between the project management team and the project customer.

project business case   A document or presentation created and maintained by the project sponsor that shows the financial validity of why a project is chartered and launched within the organization. Typically, the project business case is created before the launch of the project and may be used as a go/no-go decision point.

project calendars   Calendars that identify when the project work will occur.

project charter   A document that authorizes the project. It defines the initial requirements of the project stakeholders. The project charter is endorsed by an entity outside of the project boundaries.

project constraint   Anything that limits the project manager's options. Consider a predetermined budget, deadline, resources, or materials the project manager must use within the project—these are all examples of project constraints.

project cycle time   The cycle time for the whole project to reach the Definition of Done.

project environment   The location and culture of the environment in which the project work will reside. The project environment includes the social, economic, and environmental variables the project must work with or around.

project float   The total time the project can be delayed without passing the customer-expected completion date.

project life cycle   The group of phases that make up the project. Project life cycles are unique to the type of work being performed and are not universal to all projects.

Project Management Institute (PMI)   An organization of project management professionals from around the world, supporting and promoting the careers, values, and concerns of project managers.

project management office (PMO)   A central office that oversees all projects within an organization or within a functional department. A PMO supports the project manager through software, training, templates, policies, communications, dispute resolution, and other services. Sometimes called a project office or program office. The PMO can be supportive, controlling, or directive.

project management plan   The documented approach of how a predictive project will be planned, executed, monitored and controlled, and then closed. This document is a collection of subsidiary management plans and related documents.

Project Management Professional (PMP)   A person who has proven project management experience and has qualified for and then passed the PMP examination.

project management risks   Risks that deal with faults in the management of the project: the unsuccessful allocation of time, resources, and scheduling; unacceptable work results; and poor project management.

project manager   The role of leading the project team and managing the project resources to achieve the objectives of the project effectively.

project network diagram   A diagram that visualizes the flow of the project activities and their relationships to other project activities.

project objectives   The measurable goals that determine a project's acceptability to the project customer and the overall success of the project. Objectives often include the cost, schedule, technical requirements, and quality demands.

project portfolio management   The management and selection of projects that support an organization's vision and mission. It is the balance of project priority, risk, reward, and return on investment. This is a senior management process.

project presentations   A useful technique to provide information to customers, management, the project team, and other stakeholders.

project records   All project communications are part of the organizational process assets. This includes e-mails, memos, letters, and faxes.

project reports   Formal communications on project activities, their statuses, and conditions.

project requirements   The demands set by the customer, regulations, or the performing organization that must exist for the project deliverables to be acceptable. Requirements are often prioritized in a number of ways, from "must have," to "should have," to "would like to have."

project scope   Defines all of the work, and only the required work, to complete the project objectives.

project scope management plan   A project management subsidiary plan that controls how the scope will be defined, how the project scope statement will be created, how the WBS will be created, how scope validation will proceed, and how the project scope will be controlled throughout the project.

project variance   The final variance, which is discovered only at the project's completion. The formula is VAR = BAC – AC.

project-oriented structure   An organizational structure that assigns a project team to one project for the duration of the project life cycle. The project manager has high to almost complete project power in this structure.

proposal A document the seller provides to the buyer. The proposal includes more than just a fee for the proposed work. It also includes information on the vendor's skills, the vendor's reputation, and ideas on how the vendor can complete the contracted work for the buyer.

pull communication A communication approach that pulls the information from a central repository, such as a database of information. Pull communications work well for large groups of stakeholders who want to access project information at their discretion. Consider a project web site, where stakeholders can periodically visit for a quick update on the project status.

punitive or coercive power The project manager can punish the project team.

purchase order (PO) A form of unilateral contract that the buyer provides to the vendor showing that the purchase has been approved by the buyer's organization.

pure risks Risks that have only negative outcomes. Examples include loss of life or limb, fire, theft, natural disasters, and the like.

push communication A communication approach that pushes information from the sender to the receiver without any real acknowledgment that the information was actually received or understood. Examples include e-mails, letters, faxes, voicemail messages, and other communication modalities that the sender packages and sends to receivers through some intermediary network.

qualitative risk analysis An approach that "qualifies" the risks that have been identified in the project. Specifically, qualitative risk analysis examines and prioritizes risks based on their probability of occurring and their impact on the project should they occur.

quality According to the American Society for Quality, the degree to which a set of inherent characteristics fulfills quality requirements.

quality assurance A management process that defines the quality system or quality policy that a project must adhere to. QA aims to plan quality into the project rather than inspect quality into a deliverable.

quality baseline Documents the quality objectives for the project, including the metrics for stakeholder acceptance of the project deliverable.

quality control An inspection-driven activity, often performed by the project team or professional inspectors and testers, to verify that quality exists within the project deliverables and to keep mistakes from being released to the customers.

quality management plan A plan that defines what quality means for the project, how the project will achieve quality, and how the project will map to organizational procedures pertaining to quality.

quality metrics The operational definitions that specify the measurements within a project and the expected targets for quality and performance.

quality planning   The process of first determining which quality standards are relevant to your project and then determining the best methods of adhering to those quality standards.

quantitative risk analysis   An approach that attempts to numerically assess the probability and impact of the identified risks. It also creates an overall risk score for the project. This method is more in-depth than qualitative risk analysis and relies on several different tools to accomplish its goal.

quarterly cycle   A timed release in an XP project.

quotation   A document the seller provides to the buyer. Quoted price is the determining factor in the decision-making process.

RACI chart   A matrix chart that shows the relationships among activities and project team members; it stands for responsible, accountable, consulted, and informed.

RAG rating   An ordinal scale that uses red, amber, and green (RAG) to capture the probability, impact, and risk score.

receiver   The person who receives the message.

red-green-refactor   The approach to writing and cleaning up software development. Red means that the code has failed the test. Green means the code has been adjusted to pass the test. Refactoring means that developers clean up the code to make it tight, comprehensive, and compliant with standards.

refactoring   A process by which the development team cleans up its code throughout the project. Refactoring clarifies the code and cleans up the shortcuts and quick fixes that can pile up throughout the project. Continuous refactoring is paramount when it comes to creating quality software in agile.

referent power   The project manager is respected or admired because of the team's past experiences with her. This is about the project manager's credibility in the organization.

refinement   An update to the work breakdown structure.

regression analysis   A statistical approach to predicting what future values may be, based on historical values. Regression analysis creates quantitative predictions based on variables within one value to predict variables in another. This form of estimating relies solely on pure statistical math to reveal relationships between variables and to predict future values. It is used in projects to examine the relationship among project variables such as cost, time, labor, and other project metrics.

release burndown   A burndown chart that shows the total number of remaining releases to do in the project and the accumulation of releases the project has completed.

request for proposal (RFP)   A document the buyer provides to the seller. Requests the seller to provide a proposal to complete the procured work or to provide the procured product.

request for quote (RFQ)   A document the buyer provides to the seller. Requests the seller to provide a price for the procured product or service.

requirements documentation   Documentation of what the stakeholders expect in the project that defines all of the requirements that must be present for the work to be accepted by the stakeholders.

requirements management plan   A subsidiary plan that defines how changes to the project requirements will be permitted, how requirements will be tracked, and how changes to the requirements will be approved.

requirements traceability matrix (RTM)   A table that maps the requirements throughout the project all the way to their completion.

reserve analysis   Cost reserves are for unknown unknowns within a project. The management reserve is not part of the project cost baseline, but it is included as part of the project budget.

residual risks   Risks that are expected to remain after a risk response.

resistant stakeholder status   Part of stakeholder analysis classification. A resistant stakeholder is aware of your project, but doesn't support the changes your project will create.

resource breakdown structure (RBS)   A hierarchical breakdown of the project resources by category and resource type. For example, you could have a category of equipment, a category of human resources, and a category of materials. Within each category, you could identify the types of equipment your project will use, the types of human resources, and the types of materials.

resource calendars   Calendars that identify when project resources are available for the project work.

resource management plan   A plan that defines staff acquisition, the timetable for staff acquisition, the staff release plan, training needs for the project team, any organizational compliance issues, rewards and recognitions, and safety concerns for the project team doing the project work.

resource-leveling heuristic   A method to flatten the schedule when resources are overallocated. Resource leveling can be applied using different methods to accomplish different goals. One of the most common methods is to ensure that workers are not overextended on activities.

responsibility   The work that a role performs.

responsibility assignment matrix (RAM)   A chart that shows the correlation between project team members and the work they've been assigned to complete.

return on investment   The difference between the total costs of the project and the returns the product brings to the organization. Return on investment can be through cost-saving features or through increased revenue in the organization.

reward power   The project manager can reward the project team.

rewards and recognition system   A part of team development in which the project manager has the authority to reward the project team for work performed.

risk   An uncertain event or condition that can have a positive or negative impact on the project.

risk identification   The systematic process of combing through the project, the project plan, the work breakdown structure, and all supporting documentation to identify as many risks that may affect the project as possible.

risk management plan   A project management subsidiary plan that defines how risks will be identified, analyzed, responded to, and monitored within the project. The plan also defines the iterative risk management process that the project is expected to adhere to.

risk owners   The individuals or entities that are responsible for monitoring and responding to an identified risk within the project.

risk register   A project plan component, usually a centralized database, that contains all of the information related to the risk management activities. It's updated as risk management activities are conducted to reflect the status, progress, and nature of the project risks, as well as their outcome.

risk report   A report that explains the overall project risks and provides summaries about the individual project risks.

risk response audit   An audit to test the validity of the established risk responses.

risk response plan   A subsidiary plan that defines the risk responses that are to be used in the project for both positive and negative risks.

risk responsibilities   The level of ownership an individual or entity has over a project risk.

risk score   The calculated score based on each risk's probability and impact. The approach can be used in both qualitative and quantitative risk analysis.

risk-adjusted backlog   The product backlog prioritizes user stories based on their risk score or expected monetary value.

risk-related contractual agreements   When the project management team decides to use transference to respond to a risk, a risk-related contractual agreement is created between the buyer and the seller.

role   Denotes what a person is specifically responsible for in a project. Roles are usually tied to job titles, such as network engineer, mechanical engineer, and electrician.

rolling wave planning   The imminent work is planned in detail, while the work in the future is planned at a high level. This is a form of progressive elaboration.

root cause identification   A process that aims to find out why a risk event may be occurring, the causal factors for the risk events, and then, eventually, how the events can be mitigated or eliminated.

rough order of magnitude   A rough estimate used during the initiating processes and in top-down estimates. The range of variance for the estimate can be from –25 percent to +75 percent.

round robin   A brainstorming approach in which the team forms a circle and each person shares one idea, in order, around the circle. This helps ensure that everyone can contribute and gives everyone a chance to speak and to listen to other ideas.

Rule of Seven   A component of a control chart that illustrates the results of seven measurements on one side of the mean, which is considered "out of control" in the project.

rules of the project   Defined in the agile charter and sometimes called the constitution, team rules define how the team will work together, the collaboration needed in the project, and the expectations of the team members' behavior.

run chart   A QC tool that shows the results of inspection in the order in which they've occurred. The goal of a run chart is first to demonstrate the results of a process over time and then to use trend analysis to predict when certain trends may reemerge.

scatter diagram   A QC tool that tracks the relationship between two variables over time. The two variables are considered related the closer they track against a diagonal line.

schedule baseline   The planned start and finish dates of the project.

schedule management plan   A subsidiary plan in the project management plan. It defines how the project schedule will be created, estimated, controlled, and managed.

schedule milestones   Specific dates established by the customer that define when phases of the project should be completed. Milestones are often treated as project constraints.

schedule performance index (SPI)   A measure of the project based on its schedule performance. The formula is $SPI = EV/PV$.

schedule variance (SV)   In schedule network analysis, a schedule variance is a comparison of what was planned and what was experienced with regard to a project's schedule. In earned value management, a schedule variance is the difference between the earned value and the planned value. The formula is $SV = EV – PV$.

scope baseline   A combination of three project documents: the project scope statement, the work breakdown structure, and the WBS dictionary. The creation of the project deliverable will be measured against the scope baseline to show any variances from what was expected and what the project team has created.

scope creep   Undocumented, unapproved changes to the project scope.

scope validation   The formal inspection of the project deliverables, which leads to project acceptance.

scoring models   Models that use a common set of values for all of the projects up for selection. For example, values can be profitability, complexity, customer demand, and so on.

screening system   A tool that filters or screens out vendors that don't qualify for the contract.

Scrum   An Agile approach to project management where the development team accomplishes prioritized work in defined iterations, called sprints, and then the work is reviewed and demonstrated before moving on to the next sprint. Its goal is to deliver value as quickly as possible to the project customers.

scrum master   An individual who serves the team by removing roadblocks, protecting the development team from distractions, ensuring that all members are following the scrum rules, and coaching and educating stakeholders on scrum practices. The scrum master acts as a servant leader to the team by getting the team what they need to be successful.

scrum of scrums   When a large project is tackled by several scrum teams, a representative from each team meets to discuss the project's progress, impediments, and if any work may affect other scrum teams.

scrum team   A work team that includes the product owner, the scrum master, and the development team. The typical project management activities are divided among these three roles in a Scrum project.

secondary risks   New risks that are created as a result of a risk response.

self-awareness   This quadrant of emotional intelligence includes self-confidence and honest emotional assessment of how their behavior may affect others. This is an inward-facing component of emotional intelligence.

self-management   Individuals have self-control, are conscientious of others, can adapt their behavior to the situation, and have some level of drive, ambition, and motivation to accomplish. This is an inward-facing component of emotional intelligence.

seller rating systems   Systems used by organizations to rate prior experience with each vendor that they have worked with in the past. The seller rating system can track performance, quality ratings, delivery, and even contract compliance.

sender   The person who is sending the message.

sender-receiver models   Communication requires a sender and a receiver. Within this model may be multiple avenues to complete the flow of communication as well as feedback loops, but barriers to effective communication may be present as well.

sensitivity analysis   A quantitative risk analysis tool that examines each risk to determine which one has the largest impact on the project's success.

servant leadership   The leader puts others first and focuses on the needs of the people she serves. Servant leaders provide opportunity for growth, education, autonomy within the project, and the well-being of others. The primary focus of servant leadership is service to others. The servant leader has the mindset of carrying food and water for the team, which means she will get the team information, resources, and whatever the team may need to get their work done.

seven basic quality tools   Seven tools that are used in quality planning and in quality control: cause-and-effect diagrams, flowcharts, check sheets, Pareto diagrams, histograms, control charts, and scatter diagrams.

shared understanding   The rules of the XP approach for the organization and what the team will create. Shared understanding has four concepts you should know for your exam: simple design, system metaphor, collective code ownership, coding standard.

sharing   A risk response that shares the advantages of a positive risk within a project.

Shu-Ha-Ri   Shu-Ha-Ri is an evolution of skill acquisition and mastery. Shu means following the rules and best practices. Ha means the guidelines are mastered, and now there's flexibility surrounding the rules. Ri means the person has mastered the practice and can transcend the rules and best practice.

single source   Many vendors can provide what your project needs to purchase, but you prefer to work with a specific vendor.

situational power   The project manager has power because of certain situations in the organization.

smoothing   A conflict resolution approach that smooths out the conflict by minimizing the perceived size of the problem. It is a temporary solution, but it can calm team relations and boisterous discussions.

social awareness   The social awareness quadrant is empathy and understanding the root cause of others' emotional behavior. This is also where your organizational awareness and environmental understanding stems from. Understanding the organization, the situation, and the protocol to behave in that environment is about your social awareness. This is an outward-facing component of emotional intelligence.

social skills   This emotional intelligence quadrant includes the ability to influence people, develop others, inspirational leadership, and teamwork. This is an outward-facing component of emotional intelligence, meaning it is how you interact with other people and their emotions.

soft logic   The activities don't necessarily have to happen in a specific order. For example, you could install the light fixtures first, then install the carpet, and then paint the room. The project manager could use soft logic to change the order of the activities if desired.

sole source   Only one vendor can provide what your project needs to purchase. Examples include a specific consultant, specialized service, or unique type of material.

sprint   A predefined time period for the product owner, scrum master, and development team to complete a cycle of Scrum activities, including planning, execution, reviewing, and improvement. The sprint duration is usually two to four weeks, though it can be as little as one week.

sprint backlog   The selected items from the sprint planning meeting are decomposed into tasks for the team. These tasks are the sprint backlog and are the expectations of what they team will complete during the sprint.

sprint planning duration   The sprint planning meeting, at the start of each sprint, should last up to eight hours for a four-week sprint. Shorter sprints will have shorter planning sessions.

sprint planning meeting   A scrum meeting attended by the product owner, development team, and the scrum master to determine the amount of work that can be accomplished in the sprint based on the prioritized items in the backlog, the duration of the sprint, the complexity of the work, and the size of prioritized requirements.

sprint retrospective   The final ceremony of the sprint is a three-hour meeting called the sprint retrospective. The sprint retrospective is a lessons learned meeting on what went well or not well, during the past sprint. The goal of the meeting is to look for opportunities to improve the product and the project.

sprint retrospective duration   The sprint retrospective, held at the end of each sprint, should last up to three hours for a four-week sprint. Shorter sprints will have shorter retrospectives.

sprint review   A Scrum ceremony at the end of the sprint. This is a four-hour meeting for a four-week sprint, where the development team demonstrates what has been completed in the sprint. Only completed items are demonstrated in the sprint review.

sprint review duration   The sprint review, which is a product demo of what's been completed in the iteration, should last up to four hours for a four-week sprint. Shorter sprints will have shorter sprint review sessions.

stakeholder   Anyone who is affected by the existence of the project or who can affect the project's existence. Stakeholders can enter and exit the project as conditions change within the project.

stakeholder analysis   A scope definition process in which the project management team identifies and interviews the stakeholders and categorizes, prioritizes, and documents their wants and needs. Stakeholder analysis demands quantification of stakeholder objectives; goals such as "good," "satisfactory," and "speedy" aren't quantifiable.

stakeholder classification models   Charts and diagrams that help the project manager determine the influence of stakeholders in relation to their interest in the project. Common classification models include the power/interest grid, the power/influence grid, the impact/influence grid, and the salience model.

stakeholder engagement   Through communication, management skills, and interpersonal skills, the project manager works to keep the project stakeholders interested, involved, and supportive of the project.

stakeholder engagement plan   A plan that documents a strategy for managing the engagement of project stakeholders. The stakeholder engagement plan establishes stakeholder engagement and defines how the project manager can increase and improve stakeholder engagement. The project manager works with the project team and subject matter experts to create the plan.

stakeholder identification   A project initiation activity to identify, document, and classify the project stakeholders as early as possible in the project.

stakeholder management   The project management knowledge area that focuses on the management and engagement of the project stakeholders. There are four processes in this knowledge area: identify stakeholders, plan stakeholder management, manage stakeholder engagement, and monitor stakeholder engagement.

stakeholder notifications   Notices to the stakeholders about resolved issues, approved changes, and the overall health of the project.

stakeholder register   A documentation of each stakeholder's contact information, position, concerns, interests, and attitude toward the project. The project manager updates the register as new stakeholders are identified and when stakeholders leave the project.

start-to-finish   An activity relationship that requires an activity to start so that its successor can finish. This is the most unusual of all the activity relationship types.

start-to-start   An activity relationship type that requires the current activity to start before its successor can start.

statistical sampling   A process of choosing a percentage of results at random. For example, a project creating a medical device may have 20 percent of all units randomly selected to check for quality.

status review meeting   A regularly scheduled meeting to discuss the status of the project and its progress toward completing the project scope statement.

storming   One of the five stages of the Tuckman ladder, in which the project team struggles for project positions, leadership, and project direction. The project team members may become hostile toward the project leader, challenge ideas, and try to establish and claim positions about the project work. The amount of debate and fury can vary depending on whether the project team is willing to work together, the nature of the project, and the control of the project manager.

story point sizing   A relative approach to sizing user stories based on the complexity of the user story in relation to other user stories in the product backlog.

strong matrix structure   An organizational structure in which organizational resources are pooled into one project team, but the functional managers have less project power than the project manager.

style   The tone, structure, and formality of the message being sent should be in alignment with the audience and the content of the message.

subnet   A representation of a project network diagram that is often used for outsourced portions of projects, repetitive work within a project, or a subproject. Also called a fragnet.

subprojects   A smaller project managed within a larger, parent project. Subprojects are often contracted work with a deliverable that enables the larger project to progress.

sunk costs   Monies that have already been invested in a project.

supportive stakeholder status   This is part of stakeholder analysis classification. A supportive stakeholder is aware of the project and is supportive and hopeful that the project will be successful.

SWOT analysis   The process of examining the project from the perspective of each characteristic: strengths, weaknesses, opportunities, and threats.

system metaphor   Used in XP, it describes how the solution will work, the solution architecture, and the naming conventions of the project work.

system or process flowcharts   Flowcharts that illustrate the flow of a process through a system, such as a project change request through the change control system or work authorization through a QC process.

systems analysis   A scope definition approach that studies and analyzes a system, its components, and the relationship of the components within the system.

systems engineering   A project scope statement creation process that studies how a system should work, designs and creates a system model, and then enacts the working system based on the project's goals and the customer's expectations. Systems engineering aims to balance the time and cost of the project in relation to the scope of the project.

tacit knowledge   Knowledge that's more difficult to express because it's about personal beliefs, values, knowledge gain from experience, and "know-how" when doing a task.

team facilitator   The scrum master, coach, team lead, facilitator, or other title that acts as a servant leader to the team, ensures that everyone is following the rules, and teaches others about the agile approach.

team space   The dedicated room with an open office space for the project team members to be colocated, communicate face-to-face, and share transparent information.

technical debt   The backlog of work because the team hasn't had regular cleanup, maintenance, and standardization. Technical debt includes the cost of rework paid by implementing a short-term solution as opposed to creating a more stable solution that takes longer to create. Technical debt is paid through the time to refactor and clean up the code in a software development project.

technical, quality, or performance risks   Risks associated with new, unproven, or complex technologies being used on the project. Changes to the technology during the project implementation can also be a risk. Quality risks are the levels set for expectations of impractical quality and performance.

TECOP   A prompt list used in risk identification to examine the technical, environmental, commercial, operational, and political factors of the project.

template   A previous project that can be adapted for the current project, or a form that is prepopulated with organizational-specific information.

terms of reference (TOR)   Defines the obligations for the seller, what the seller will provide, and all of the particulars of the contracted work. Similar to the statement of work.

three amigos   Describes the three roles that contribute to acceptance test-driven development. The three roles are the customers, developers, and testers.

three Cs of user stories   A convention to write user stories using the three Cs of card, conversational, and confirmation to describe the user story.

three-point estimate   An estimating technique for each activity that requires optimistic, most likely, and pessimistic estimates to be created. Based on these three estimates, an average can be created to predict how long the activity should take.

time and materials contract   A contract type in which the buyer pays for the time and materials for the procured work. This is a simple contract, usually for smaller procurement conditions. These contract types require a not-to-exceed clause, or the buyer assumes the risk for cost overruns.

time reporting system   A system to record the actual time to complete project activities.

to-complete performance index (TCPI)   A formula to forecast the likelihood of a project to achieve its goals based on what's happening in the project currently. There are two different flavors for the TCPI, depending on what you want to accomplish. If you want to see whether your project can meet the budget at completion, you'll use this formula: TCPI = (BAC – EV)/(BAC – AC). If you want to see whether your project can meet the newly created estimate at completion, you'll use this version of the formula: TCPI = (BAC – EV)/(EAC – AC).

total float   The total time an activity can be delayed without delaying project completion.

transactional leadership   The leader emphasizes the goals of the project and offers rewards and disincentives to the project team. This is sometimes called management by exception, because it's the exception that is rewarded or punished.

transference   A risk response that transfers the ownership of the risk to another party. Insurance, licensed contractors, or other project teams are good examples of transference. A fee and contractual relationships are typically involved with the transference of a risk.

transformational leadership   The leader inspires and motivates the project team to achieve the project goals. Transformational leaders aim to empower the project team to act, be innovative in the project work, and accomplish through ambition.

tree diagram   A diagram that shows the hierarchies and decomposition of a solution, an organization, or a project team. The WBS and an organizational chart are examples of tree diagrams.

trend analysis   The science of using past results to predict future performance.

Triple Constraints of Project Management   Also known as the Iron Triangle of Project Management. This theory posits that time, cost, and scope are three constraints that affect every project.

T-shirt sizing   A user story sizing method where user stories are sized like T-shirts, meaning extra small, small, medium, large, and extra-large. This is a type of affinity estimating. Each story is sized after comparing it to other stories, not according to a predefined scale.

unanimity   A group decision method in which everyone must be in agreement.

unaware stakeholder status   Part of stakeholder analysis classification. An unaware status means the stakeholder doesn't know about the project and the effect the project may create on the stakeholder.

user story   Used in Scrum, a story of a role utilizing some functionality to get value from the functionality. User stories follow a formula: "As a <role>, I want <function>, so I can realize <value.>" User stories are the items kept in the product backlog, are a small chunk of functionality, and generally take up to 40 hours to create. User stories are prioritized by the product owner.

value analysis   Similar to value engineering, this approach examines the functions of the project's product in relation to the cost of the features and functions. This is where, to some extent, the grade of the product is in relationship to the cost of the product.

value engineering   An approach to project scope statement creation that attempts to find the correct level of quality in relation to a reasonable budget for the project deliverable while still achieving an acceptable level of performance of the product.

value stream   A Lean principle that includes all of the actions needed to create value for the project customer from the very start. It's about maximizing value and eliminating waste in the project.

variability risks   A type of risk based on the variations that may occur in the project, such as production, number of quality errors, or even the weather.

variable costs   Costs that change based on the conditions applied in the project (such as the number of meeting participants, the supply of and demand for materials, and so on).

variance   The difference between what was expected and what was experienced.

variance at completion (VAC)   A forecasting formula that predicts how much of a variance the project will likely have based on current conditions within the project. The formula is $VAC = BAC - EAC$.

velocity   The number of user story points a development team can complete during a sprint. Velocity helps predict the duration of the project. Velocity may be wild at first but normalizes after several sprints.

virtual structure   A structure that uses a network to communicate and interact with other groups and departments. A point of contact exists for each department, and these people receive and send all messages for the department.

vision statement   Describes the goals and why the project exists. The vision statement is a simple document that keeps the purpose of the project and the value the project brings in the forefront. It is a quick definition about what the project will create for the organization or the end users of the product.

visual signal   In Kanban, each work item is written on a card or sticky note, and it visually signals where that work item is in the workflow.

Vroom's Expectancy Theory   A theory that states that people will behave based on what they expect as a result of their behavior. In other words, people will work in relation to the expected reward.

VUCA   A prompt list used in risk identification that examines the volatility, uncertainty, complexity, and ambiguity of risk factors within the project.

WBS dictionary   A WBS companion document that defines all of the characteristics of each element within the WBS.

WBS template   A prepopulated WBS for repetitive projects. Previous projects' WBSs are often used as templates for current similar projects.

weak matrix structure   An organizational structure in which organizational resources are pooled into one project team, but the functional managers have more project power than the project manager.

weekly cycle   An iteration in an XP project to complete the selected items from the product backlog.

weighting system   A system that removes the personal preferences of the decision-maker in the organization to ensure that the best seller is awarded the contract. Weights are assigned to the values of the proposals, and each proposal is scored.

withdrawal   This conflict resolution method sees one side of the argument walking away from the problem, usually in disgust.

work breakdown structure (WBS)   A deliverables-oriented breakdown of the project scope.

work package   The smallest item in the work breakdown structure.

work performance data   Raw data, observations, and measurements about project components. Work performance data is gathered and stored in the project management information system (PMIS).

work performance information   The processed and analyzed data that will help the project manager make project decisions. Work performance information includes the technical performance measures, project status, information on what the project has created to date, corrective actions, and performance reports.

work performance reports   The formatted communications of work performance information. Work performance reports communicate what's happening in the project through status reports, memos, dashboards, or other modalities.

work-in-progress (WIP)   The allowed amount of work items that may enter a workflow. Often used in Kanban environments to restrict how many work items can reasonably enter a system to avoid overloading the team or creating bottlenecks.

XP coach   Coaches the team members on the XP approach, keeps things moving, oversees the work of the project, and helps implement process improvements because of team feedback.

XP customer or product owner   Represents the business values and is responsible for writing user stories, prioritizing the requirements, and helping programmers understand the value of user stories.

XP Doomsayer   Monitors risk, poor results, and issues with the project. The doomsayer communicates frequently about the conditions of events that could threaten the project's success. The role's objective is to be honest and transparent about the health of the project.

XP Gold Owner   The person who pays for the project and is often the project sponsor in an organization.

XP Manager   Responsible for delivering the project as promised, communicating status to the project customer, scheduling meetings for release planning, and often serving as the doomsayer and tracker roles.

XP Programmer Programs the code to satisfy the requirements of the customer. Programmers also derive the tasks needed to complete user stories and works on unit testing in the project.

XP Tester Runs functional tests on the code the programmers have created. The tester role will also document the test results.

XP Tracker Has some project management duties to track the work assignments to confirm things are "on track" in the project. The tracker also meets with programmers, the coach, and the customer to report on project progress.

INDEX